HUMAN SOCIETIES

THIRD EDITION
HUMAN SOCIETIES
AN INTRODUCTION TO MACROSOCIOLOGY

GERHARD LENSKI

JEAN LENSKI

McGRAW-HILL BOOK COMPANY

NEW YORK   ST. LOUIS   SAN FRANCISCO   AUCKLAND   BOGOTÁ   DÜSSELDORF
JOHANNESBURG   LONDON   MADRID   MEXICO   MONTREAL   NEW DELHI
PANAMA   PARIS   SÃO PAULO   SINGAPORE   SYDNEY   TOKYO   TORONTO

This book was set in Helvetica by Black Dot, Inc.
The editors were Lyle Linder, Janis M. Yates, and David Dunham;
the designer was Joan E. O'Connor;
the production supervisor was Dennis J. Conroy.
New drawings were done by J & R Services, Inc.
The cover photograph was taken by John Mahtesian.
R. R. Donnelley & Sons Company was printer and binder.

See Picture Credits on pages 489–492.
Copyrights included on this page by reference.

HUMAN SOCIETIES AN INTRODUCTION TO MACROSOCIOLOGY

1234567890DODO783210987

Library of Congress Cataloging in Publication Data

Lenski, Gerhard Emmanuel, date
   Human societies.

   Includes bibliographical references and indexes.
   1. Sociology. 2. Social evolution.
I. Lenski, Jean, joint author. II. Title.
HM51.L357 1978   301   77-2902
ISBN 0-07-037174-1

CONTENTS

PREFACE

This volume is an introduction to macrosociology, the study of the largest, most inclusive, and most complex of all social systems: human societies themselves. Interest in macrosociology has increased considerably in recent years as it has become apparent that the most critical problems of the contemporary world are essentially problems of malfunctioning societies.

Macrosociology is the only branch of science that specializes in the study of human societies per se (*Micro*sociology studies the social systems within societies, and other social sciences study such varied aspects of them as their economies, their political processes, their histories, and the psychic processes of their members.) But it falls to macrosociology to integrate the great mass of relevant material and to provide theories capable of illuminating these most complex and vital of social entities.

As interest in macrosociology has grown, so has appreciation of its value in teaching. Because it is concerned with the largest and most inclusive social systems, a macrosociological perspective can accommodate and integrate many of the more detailed materials of microsociology and social psychology. In fact, when entities such as labor unions, churches, communities, families, and individuals are studied within the context of the society of

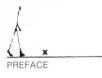

which they are a part, their own structure and functioning become clearer and more meaningful.

The theoretical perspective that shapes our analysis is best described as *structural-functional-ecological-evolutionary*. Although we usually, for the sake of convenience, refer to it as *ecological-evolutionary*, or simply as *evolutionary*, the perspectives of functionalism and structuralism are present and important. The great virtue of evolutionary theory, in our judgment, is its remarkable capacity for incorporating the insights of the other three perspectives within a framework that makes a critical contribution of its own: insight into the most fundamental processes of societal change and development.

We have been extremely pleased with the reactions of students and instructors to the previous editions of *Human Societies*, most pleased of all, perhaps, that it has proved helpful in understanding the processes of change in the contemporary world. One of our basic assumptions is that macrosociology is an essential tool for today's citizens. They need not understand all of the discipline's research techniques, but they should be aware of the findings of that research and they should understand the theories that interpret and give meaning to those findings.

Since no single volume can cover fully every facet of a subject as comprehensive as macrosociology, most instructors will wish to supplement the text in one area of another. For this reason, we have tried to incorporate all the major topics into our analysis, thus providing points of departure for more extended discussions. The instructor who wants to develop *socialization* more fully, for example, will find opportunities in Chapters 1, 2, 3, 5, 7, 9, 10, and 12. Similarly, instructors can put more emphasis on such subjects as population control, the role of women, or social stratification at numerous points, and in the context of societies of the past, present, and future.

The book is organized into three sections. In the first, human societies are established as biosociocultural systems, part of the natural world, and units involved in a unique evolutionary process. In the second section, we survey the first 99.9 per cent of human experience and trace the successive transformations of human societies from the remote prehistoric era to the eve of the Industrial Revolution. In the final section, we examine industrial and industrializing societies of the modern era, analyze their more serious problems, and conclude with a look at the future and what it may hold in store.

In sections two and three, we focus primarily on five major types of societies—hunting and gathering, horticultural, agrarian, industrializing, and industrial—and analyze them in terms of their basic technology, demographic patterns, economy, polity, social stratification, religion and ideology, and kinship. We believe that this holistic approach—viewing societies as systems of interrelated elements—is far more productive than the approach which examines a succession of institutions more or less independently of one another and of the larger social system of which they are a part.

CHANGES SINCE THE LAST EDITION

Although we have revised this edition extensively, the basic theory and organization of materials remain the same. We made changes for three reasons. First, we worked to make the text as clear and as readable as possible, rearranging materials at several points to achieve a better flow of ideas, deleting unnecessary details, and inserting examples at a number of points where they were needed. Second, we worked to strengthen the theoretical framework of the book, especially in the first three chapters. Third, we updated factual materials on contemporary societies and introduced the contributions of a number of recent publications.

All the changes are detailed in the *Instructor's Manual*, which is available from McGraw-Hill. We will, however, give a brief resume here of the more notable changes, in part to reassure old friends that much of the change in early chapters results from relabeling and rearranging, rather than from dropping important materials from previous editions. For example, *The Universals, Semispecialties,* and *Specialties* have become *Characteristics Humans Share with All Other Species, Characteristics Shared with Some Other Species,* and *Characteristics Unique to Our Species.* Related to this, a new subsection on *Biological Evolution* is simply an expanded statement of the eight-point summary (on page 11 of the second edition) of attributes all living things share.

Materials that were in the first four chapters of the last edition are now in the first three, largely because much of Chapters 3 and 4 of the second edition was consolidated. In addition, the material on human nature, which was (we see with hindsight) poorly located before, is now incorporated into the unit on *Characteristics Unique to Our Species.* Both Chapters 2 and 3 have significant new opening sections—the one, a discussion of the concept of systems and its relevance to the study of human societies, the other, a new analysis of sociocultural evolution.

In the section on preindustrial societies, the most important changes are in the chapter on horticultural societies. By greatly abbreviating our discussion of these societies in the New World, we have eliminated what many felt to be an unnecessary repetitiveness. We have also condensed and simplified the review of hominid prehistory in the chapter on hunting and gathering societies, eliminating most of the technical terminology from physical anthropology and archaeology and concentrating instead on what was happening to our ancestors.

The principal changes in the chapters on industrial and industrializing societies involve a heightened emphasis on the differences between socialism and capitalism. The discussion of ideology now follows the discussion of technology, setting forth at the outset the basic sources of the similarities and the differences in industrial societies. In the section on ideology, we have also juxtaposed discussions of Adam Smith and Karl Marx. The analyses of politics and economics are now for the first time in a chapter together,

underlining the linkages between these critical institutional systems.

The analysis of the causes of the Industrial Revolution has been revised somewhat and the discussion of the newest technologies expanded. Other changes in the third section range from a new discussion of women's changing role to a brief summary of Robert Heilbroner's pessimistic prognosis for the future developed in his recent book, *An Inquiry into the Human Prospect*. And we have, of course, updated the statistical and other factual information in this section, as well as introduced data on a number of new subjects.

ACKNOWLEDGMENTS

It is not possible to acknowledge all our intellectual debts in the brief space available. Those who read this volume will almost certainly recognize the influence of Thomas Malthus, Charles Darwin, Herbert Spencer, Karl Marx, Max Weber, Thorstein Veblen, William Graham Sumner, Albert Keller, William Ogburn, V. Gordon Childe, George Peter Murdock, R. H. Tawney, Sir Julian Huxley, George Gaylord Simpson, Leslie White, Julian Steward, and C. Wright Mills, to name but a few. The note citations at the end of this volume should be regarded as further acknowledgments of indebtedness and appreciation.

Quite a number of scholars have been kind enough to provide us with critical comments and suggestions for one or more of the three editions of *Human Societies*. Those to whom we owe a real debt in this connection include E. Jackson Baur, William Catton, Jr., Ronald Cosper, Alfred E. Emerson, David Featherman, George Furniss, Walter Goldschmidt, Amos Hawley, Paul Heckert, Joan Huber, Donald Irish, Peter Kott, Philip Marcus, Ross Purdy, Leo Rigsby, Norman Storer, Edward O. Wilson, and Everett K. Wilson.

We also thank our editor at McGraw-Hill, Janis Yates, for all she has done to facilitate the publication of this edition. And we remember with affection and respect our former editor, the late Ron Kissack, who contributed so much to the previous editions.

Gerhard Lenski

Jean Lenski

Chapel Hill

PART ONE:
THEORETICAL
FOUNDATIONS

CHAPTER 1
STARTING
POINTS

The most striking feature of the world today is the unprecedented pace of change. Never before have the conditions of life altered so fast for so much of the human population. Every human society is involved, and every area of human experience.

This modern social revolution is clearly evident in our language. Words and phrases that only a short time ago did not exist or had very different meanings have become an integral part of our thought, our speech, and our experience:

> . . . the Pill . . . the Bomb . . . nuclear power . . . solar energy . . . strip-mining . . . environmental crisis . . . population explosion . . . Third World . . . Fourth World . . . germ warfare . . . genetic engineering . . . organ transplants . . . pacemakers . . . automation . . . the computer . . . data banks . . . electronic surveillance . . . instant replay . . . black power . . . sexism . . . gay liberation . . . transsexual . . . rock . . . grass . . . the generation gap . . .

What has caused this revolution? Where is it leading? And most important, how can we control it? How can we make sure it does not

culminate in a nuclear holocaust, an ecological disaster, or an Orwellian 1984?

Questions like these force us to face an unpleasant fact: the members of human societies are like people hurtling through space on a rocket ship, with too little information about either their vehicle or its trajectory. For our survival depends on our societies, and they are moving swiftly into an unknown future. Yet most of us know remarkably little about them, how they work, or how they can be controlled.

*Sociology is the branch of modern science that specializes in the study of human societies.** Its aims and its interests are broad. Sociologists are concerned with every aspect of societal life from the behavior of individuals to the problems of entire societies, and their research has produced a tremendous amount of information during the last hundred years. In addition, significant contributions have been made by scholars in other disciplines, especially the other social sciences.

The purpose of this volume is to present the basic findings that have emerged from the many studies of human societies. To do this requires more than a review of the facts, however. If the facts are to be meaningful, we need an integrative framework to organize them. More specifically, we need a *theoretical perspective.*

In any large and active discipline, different theoretical perspectives are almost inevitable. One important difference is in *the magnitude of the entities people focus on.* Thus, microbiologists focus on cells and molecules, while other biologists study populations, species, and even entire phyla of plants and animals; microeconomists study the economic activities of individuals and firms, while macroeconomists investigate the operation of national and international economic systems. Similarly, *microsociologists* study small social units, such as individuals, families, and schools, while *macro*sociologists study larger social systems, especially total societies. (Smaller social systems enter into macrosociological analysis, however, because they are integral parts of every human society.) This volume is an introduction to macrosociology.

Another important difference in perspective concerns *the kinds of questions people ask and the kinds of information they seek.* In biology, for example, anatomists and physiologists are looking for answers to questions about the *structure* of living things and the *functions* of the various parts. Ecologists and evolutionists, in contrast, are more interested in the relationships of organisms with one another and with the environment, and in the processes of change that alter the characteristics and interrelationships of organisms.

Similar differences exist in sociology. For many years, the majority of

*For the convenience of readers, a Glossary is provided on pages 482–488. Definitions of all the basic terms used in this volume are available there.

sociologists were committed to a theoretical perspective known as *structural-functionalism,* which seeks to understand societies by studying their internal structures and the functions of their various parts. For the last twenty years, however, a growing number of sociologists have argued that this is not enough. If we are to understand our societies we must bring two additional perspectives to bear. We must study the relationships among societies, and between them and the environment. And we must study their similarities and differences, and the processes of change in their characteristics and relationships.

This newer approach is often called the *ecological-evolutionary* perspective. It could as easily be called the *structural-functional-ecological-evolutionary* perspective, however, since it is also concerned with the internal structure and functioning of societies.

HUMAN SOCIETIES: THEIR PLACE IN NATURE

The first thing an ecological-evolutionary perspective requires is that we establish the relationship of our societies to the rest of the world. Although this relationship is an important one, it is often misunderstood. In particular, it is easy to exaggerate the uniqueness of human societies and to think of them as products of human ingenuity, separate from the world of nature. But this is a mistake: *societies are part of the natural order.*

As many scholars have observed, the world of nature is structured rather like a system of wheels within wheels, with all the parts ultimately related. Thus, when we examine an object carefully, we discover it is made up of various differentiated parts which are, in turn, composed of still smaller parts. Similarly, when we look in the other direction, we see that our original object is part of a larger, more inclusive system, which is, itself, part of an even larger, more inclusive one.

Figure 1.1 provides a necessarily oversimplified view of this complex hierarchy. Elementary particles, such as protons and electrons, form the lowest level. These are combined in various ways to form atoms, such as carbon and radium. Atoms, in turn, are organized into molecules, such as water, salt, amino acids, and proteins. Though Figure 1.1 does not show it, molecules constitute more than a single level in the hierarchy, because certain of the simpler molecules, the amino acids, for example, are the building blocks for more complex and more inclusive molecules, such as the proteins.

Once we go beyond the level of molecules, we encounter the important division between living and nonliving things. Since our concern is with human societies, there is no need to examine all the levels in the hierarchy of nonliving matter. Suffice it to note that this hierarchy leads by degrees to the

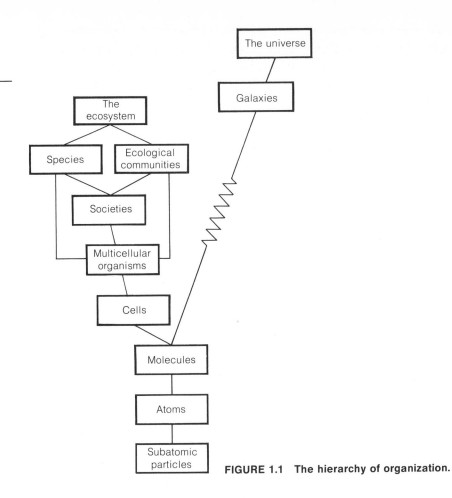

FIGURE 1.1 The hierarchy of organization.

level of the giant galaxies that wheel through space and ends with the universe itself.

Societies, however, are part of the biotic world: they are one of the ways in which living things (i.e., organisms) are organized. In the organizational hierarchy, societies are more inclusive than individual organisms, but less inclusive than an entire species. In other words, a social species is divided into a number of subunits called societies, and each society is comprised of numerous individuals. Not *every* species is social, however, as indicated by the line going directly from individual organisms to species in Figure 1.1. And this brings us to the question of why some species are organized this way while others are not.

◆ The Basic Function of Societies

The development of the societal mode of organization has been called "one of the great steps in evolution, as important as the emergence of the cell, the multicellular organism, and the vertebrate system."[1] Actually, societies evolved not once, but a number of times, independently and in widely scattered lines of the animal kingdom. They are concentrated in three areas: (1) many species of vertebrates, especially among mammals, birds, and fish; (2) the social insects (ants, termites, and many species of wasps and bees); and (3) the colonial invertebrates (such as corals, sponges, and Portuguese man-of-war).[2]

Why did so many and such diverse species develop this particular mode of organization? Quite simply, because being organized this way helped these species survive. In other words, the societal mode of life became common in the animal kingdom for the same reason characteristics like wings, lungs, and protective coloring became common: they are important *adaptive mechanisms.*

But societal organization is different from adaptive mechanisms that enable species to perform some particular activity—the way wings, for example, enable creatures to fly, or lungs enable them to exchange oxygen and other gases with the air. Rather, the thing that distinguishes social species from all the rest is a characteristic that has the potential for being used in a great variety of ways. For every social creature has *an enhanced capacity for cooperation.*

To those who study animal behavior, "cooperation" means simply that the individuals in a given species associate with and interact with one another for their mutual benefit. It does not mean they cooperate in every activity, nor does it imply that they are never competitive or antagonistic toward one another.

The types of cooperative activities in which the various social species engage include reproduction, nurture of young, securing food, and defense against predators and other dangers.* Some social species rely on cooperative behavior in virtually every facet of life. Others are less involved in, or dependent on, social activities. But every social species benefits substantially from the fact that its members are genetically programmed to try to solve at least some of their problems by acting together instead of individually.

Once we recognize that human societies are, first and foremost, adaptive mechanisms that are vital to the survival of our species, we see why we cannot divorce our study of them from the study of the rest of the biotic world.† We see, too, why it is imperative that students of human societies have a clear understanding of the biological foundations of the societal mode of organization in general and of human societies in particular.

*Even *non*social animals display cooperative activity in the area of reproduction (i.e., they reproduce sexually). But a species is not classified as "social" if its cooperative activity is limited to this single, though important, area.

†This is not to suggest that the study of human societies can be swallowed up by the biological sciences. It simply means it is necessary to study our societies from an ecological-evolutionary perspective, since it is in these terms that adaptive mechanisms can best be understood.

A Definition of Societies

Edward O. Wilson, a prominent zoologist and leader in the important new discipline of sociobiology, defines a society as "a group of individuals belonging to the same species and organized in a cooperative manner."[3] This has the virtue of simplicity and, at the same time, encompasses the most fundamental points.

Because we are concerned with human societies, however, we need to add something to his definition. Virtually every human society of which we have knowledge has had subgroups within it—families, communities, specialized organizations of various kinds—and Wilson's definition could apply equally well to them. By adding the word *autonomous* (i.e., free from outside political control), we exclude such subgroups. Thus, a society is *an autonomous group of individuals belonging to the same species and organized in a cooperative manner*. This clearly applies to American society, Soviet society, and Brazilian society, while it excludes America's AFL-CIO, Soviet Jewry, and

FIGURE 1.2 A society is an autonomous group of individuals belonging to the same species and organized in a cooperative manner: African elephants, Kenya. In times of danger, adults form a protective ring around their young.

the city of Rio de Janeiro. None of the latter is autonomous: all are politically subordinate to the societies of which they are part.

Sometimes it is not possible to say for certain whether a particular group of animals does or does not comprise a society. This is because social species, as we noted, rely on cooperative behavior in varying degrees. For example, apart from the nurture of their young, many mammals expend little time or energy on social activities, while some of the social insects are immersed in them. Thus, between completely solitary animals and the most social ones, there is a scale or continuum with infinitely fine gradations along which all the others are ranged.

In the case of human societies, there are gradations not only in terms of the cooperative behavior displayed by their members, but in terms of the autonomy of the groups as well. Consider, for example, a more or less typical American Indian society of the sixteenth or seventeenth century, an autonomous group whose members were caught up in a pervasive system of social activity. In time, the group established trade relations with Europeans or Americans and eventually came under their political control. This process often involved the gradual absorption of the Indian group by a larger, more powerful society. It would obviously be impossible, in such a case, to say at what point the Indian society ceased to exist (i.e., lost its autonomy) and became a subgroup within another society. Autonomy is clearly not an "all or nothing" quality. Rather, like cooperative behavior (and like many other phenomena, from weight to temperature), its existence is a matter of degree.

THE BIOLOGICAL FOUNDATION OF HUMAN SOCIETIES

The foundation of every society in the biotic world is the genetic heritage of the creatures who form it—which explains why both the structure of a termite society and the activities that go on within it are so different from those of a society of wolves or birds. If we want to understand the structure of human societies and what goes on in them, we obviously have to understand the genetic heritage of humans. Thus, we will spend the rest of this chapter examining this heritage. Our goal is not to understand how we differ from one another, but to understand those more fundamental and important characteristics that we all possess simply because we are members of Homo sapiens and not some other species.

During the last hundred years, there has been a lot of confusion and controversy on this subject of human nature. One view was popularized by some of Charles Darwin's more enthusiastic followers, who argued that science had proved Homo sapiens was not, after all, the exalted being humans so long imagined themselves to be, but only an animal that could be understood in purely biological terms.

Most scholars have since rejected this view on the grounds that it

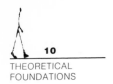

involves what a leading evolutionist, George Gaylord Simpson, once termed the "nothing but" fallacy. In his words:

> To say that man is nothing but an animal is to deny, by implication, that he has essential attributes other than those of all animals. This would be false as applied to any kind of an animal. As applied to man the "nothing but" fallacy is more serious than in application to any other sort of animal, because man is an entirely new kind of animal in ways altogether fundamental for understanding of his nature. It is important to realize that man is an animal, but it is even more important to realize that the essence of his unique nature lies precisely in those characteristics that are not shared with any other animal.[4]

In reacting against the "nothing but" fallacy, however, many social scientists backed into an equally unsatisfactory position. By ignoring or minimizing the biological foundations of human societies, they seemed almost to deny our animal heritage. Happily, however, there is a third view which recognizes that our species has some characteristics that are uniquely our own, some that we share with certain other species but not with all, and some that we share with all living things.

Characteristics Humans Share with All Other Species

When we first consider the world of living things in all its diversity and variety, it is hard to imagine that there are any characteristics which *all* plants and animals share. Yet beneath their obvious and immense differences, the human, the slime mold, the rose, and the amoeba are alike in some very important ways.

To begin with, all living things have *the same underlying structure.*[5] For every organism is composed of one or more cells, and all cells are composed of the same basic materials: water, mineral solids, and organic compounds such as carbohydrates, fats, proteins, nucleotides, and their derivatives. What is more, every cell contains everything that is necessary (genes, enzymes, etc.) for performing the most basic life functions. Therefore, *the same basic activities* go on in every organism, whether it is single-celled or highly complex. First, there is metabolism, a complex set of activities that might be said to "run the machinery of life."*[6] Second, every organism responds in a self-preserving way to internal and external stimuli. And third, every organism has a capacity for reproducing itself.

Why are the basic structure and functioning of such diverse forms of life fundamentally alike? Simpson answers that:

---

*Metabolism consists of three processes: *nutrition*, which provides the organism with the raw materials (nutrients) it requires; *respiration*, which uses the nutrients to produce energy; and *synthesis*, which uses them for tissue repair and growth.

. . . all living things are brothers in the very real, material sense that all have arisen from one source and been developed within the divergent intricacies of one process.[7]

In other words, the most basic things all forms of life share are these: (1) a *common heritage* (i.e., the first living things on earth passed on to all subsequent life the basic heritage of the living cell), and (2) *involvement in a common process* (i.e., all life emerged through the process of biological evolution).

It is now clear that we cannot fully appreciate our species' relationship to the rest of the biotic world, nor can we understand either our own innate nature or the origin of our societies, unless we have a grasp of the fundamentals of biological evolution. This subject is of particular interest to students of human societies for another reason as well: there is an important relationship between biological evolution and sociocultural evolution (i.e., the evolution of human societies), as we will see in Chapter 3.

Biological Evolution[8] Biological evolution is *the process of gradual change and development through which every species of plant or animal has developed out of a preexisting species.* This process has been going on for approximately 3.5 billion years, ever since life began on our planet. And every change in the characteristics of a species—whether it has involved appearance or behavior*—has been a manifestation of change in its genetic makeup. The complexity and diversity of plants and animals today testify to an incredible number of such changes.

Genes, the basic units of heredity, are complex chemicals that are present in every cell of every organism. Rather like sets of built-in commands, genes trigger a variety of chemical processes in various parts of a plant or animal and, in so doing, determine its structure, its functions, and how it differs from other organisms. When it reproduces, an organism passes on to its offspring precise copies of some or all of its own genes.† This is why the basic life processes are so orderly and predictable—why elephants do not give birth to butterflies, mushrooms do not grow as tall as oaks, and pigs do not produce chlorophyll.

To see how evolutionary change occurs, we must focus on a *population*. This term refers to an aggregation of organisms of the same species that tend to interbreed because of geographic proximity. A herd of bison, the sparrows of an offshore island, and the earthworms in a local patch of forest are all examples of a population. Although most reproductive activity takes place

---

*"Behavior" refers to *any response by an organism to internal or external stimuli.* Thus, behavior includes chemical processes like digestion and suntanning, and activities like hearing and thinking, as well as overt movements like crawling or biting.

†The copies are precise, that is, except in the event of mutation (see below).

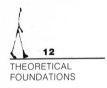

within a population, there is almost always occasional interbreeding with nearby populations of the same species.

The members of a population are fundamentally alike in both appearance and behavior, but they are not identical. This means that some genes in a population are found in every member, while the rest are found in varying proportions of them. Since the genetic heritage of a population consists of all these varied individual heritages, biologists have coined the term *gene pool* to refer to the genes of all the members considered collectively.

The ultimate origin of genetic variation, and of every gene in biotic history, is *mutation.* A mutation is essentially an accident: a slight alteration occurs in the chemical structure of a gene as it is being replicated, with the result that the "copy"—the gene that goes to the offspring—does not carry the same chemical message as the original—the gene of the parent.

Mutations occur continually in every population,* but they never happen for a "purpose" (such as to make a moth population a darker color so it will blend better against tree bark and therefore be safer from predators). Rather, mutations are *random*, or chance, occurrences. Most of them, in fact, are actually harmful to the genetic makeup of the offspring into which they are introduced—much the way a random bit of metal tossed into a smoothly running machine is far more likely to jam it than to improve its operation. But every now and then, a mutation *does* produce an "improved" gene, a gene that gives its bearer an advantage (usually a very slight one) in its efforts to survive and reproduce. In this way, some new genes eventually become numerous in a gene pool and may even become part of the genetic makeup of every individual in the population.

But mutations are only the beginning of genetic variation in species that reproduce sexually, as nearly all species do. Because this mode of reproduction involves the genes of two individuals, genes and sets of genes are, in effect, shuffled and reshuffled over the generations, creating ever new combinations, or *recombinations*, as they are called.

Just as important in the evolutionary process as a genetically varied population is the *environment.* This term refers to everything external to a population (or any other entity) that influences it or is influenced by it. Its environment includes inorganic matter, physical phenomena, other living things (among them, other populations of the same species), and everything the population requires to survive: food, moisture, air, light, and so on.

This relationship between population and environment is the most basic one in the biotic world. It is an intimate and dynamic relationship in which each contributes to, and is affected by, change in the other. And it is *this relationship that shapes evolution.*

We can understand how this happens if we focus on the gradual change

*The cause of most mutations is unknown, although some are known to result from exposure to such agents as x-rays and certain chemicals.

that takes place in a population's genetic attributes—or, more precisely, on the change in the composition of its gene pool. Over a period of time, some genes become more frequent, others become less so, and some become rare or even disappear. In short, some members of the population reproduce themselves (to be specific, they reproduce some of their genes) more frequently than others.

In order to determine who these successful reproducers in a population are, we must first identify the poorest reproducers. In most populations, the great majority of organisms do not reproduce at all. They die before reproductive age as a consequence of the universal tendency of living things to have more offspring than the environment can support. (An oyster, for example, lays more than a million eggs per season, a tapeworm 120,000 per day.[9]) Most mutants, as we have noted, are among these nonreproducers. The rest of the population, meanwhile, not only have different numbers of young, but young with different genetic potential for surviving and reproducing themselves.

Over the long run, the thing that determines this differential reproduction is the adaptive value of the various genes and sets of genes in the population. The genetic traits that "work best" for a particular species in a particular environment are "selected" for reproduction through a natural (i.e., not contrived by humans) process: hence the term *natural selection*. Each new generation of individuals in a population is essentially like the parental type, and it must cope with essentially the same environment. But each new generation also has a supply of genetic variations that will be put to the test, and discarded or used in the never-ending process of maintaining an adequate relationship with the environment or achieving a better one.

All the populations of a species normally change in unison—that is, the species *as a whole* evolves. This is what we would expect of reproductive units that share with one another, at least occasionally, their different genetic "solutions" to the challenges of similar environments. A population that is well adapted to its environment is more likely to reject genetic alterations than to accept them, and the same is true of the species as a whole: it tends to resist change. As a result, a species does not usually experience major structural change during its span on earth. Its change is gradual and not dramatic.

The story may be different, however, in *speciation*, the process by which a new species splits off from its parental line. Speciation takes place in a small population that has become reproductively isolated from others of its kind. This is typically a consequence of an increase in numbers that causes a particular kind of plant or animal to spread over such a wide area that some of its populations are struggling to survive on the outer fringe of the geographical area to which the species is adapted. Eventually, such a peripheral population may be completely cut off from the rest.

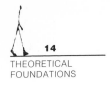

In a small, marginal population like this, one that barely manages to relate to its environment to obtain its basic needs, any useful new genetic trait (mutation or recombination) spreads rapidly. In effect, the rate of natural selection speeds up because of the peculiar circumstances. If such a population survives (and most do not), it will probably change more quickly than the other populations of its species, and not in unison with them. In a span of time that by evolutionary standards is very brief indeed (i.e., only hundreds or thousands of years), it may become so different genetically from the parental stock that effective interbreeding would no longer be possible if the separated populations were reunited. Two species would exist where there was one before.

Over the mind-boggling expanse of time since life first appeared on our planet, these same natural forces have been constantly at work, producing genetic variation purely at random, and then selecting from it through a process that is *not* random, but is guided by the relation of living things to their environments. The genetic heritage of every extant species, including our own, is thus quite literally the product of billions of years of biological experimentation.

Characteristics Humans Share Only with Some Other Species

We humans obviously have more in common with most living things than the heritage of living cells and the fact that we are all caught up in the process of biological evolution. In particular, we resemble other members of the mammalian class more than any other class of organisms. We share with them a strange assortment of traits that includes warmbloodedness; skin, usually covered with hair; teeth that come in only twice and are differentiated according to use (i.e., for tearing, grinding, etc.); external genitalia; internal fertilization; lungs; four limbs (or vestiges of them) with nails, claws, hoofs, or digits; a bony palate that enables us to breathe and chew at the same time; a relatively elaborate brain; a marked capacity for learning; and, in the female, mammary glands that secrete milk. And all mammals are also social animals: there is, at a minimum, the cooperative behavior displayed by mothers in the nurture of their young.

We have much more in common with some mammals than with others, of course. This was brought home in an entertaining way by author Clarence Day, who once speculated on the kind of civilization that might have developed if our species had evolved in the feline instead of the simian, or primate, line.

A race of civilized beings descended from the great cats would have been rich in hermits and solitary thinkers. The recluse would not have been stigmatized as peculiar, as he is by us simians. They would not have been a credulous people, or easily religious. False prophets and swindlers would have found few dupes. And what generals they would have made! What consummate politicians! . . .

They would never have become as poised or as placid as, say, super-cows. Yet they would have had less insanity, probably, than we. Monkeys' . . . minds seem precariously balanced, unstable. The great cats are saner. They are intense, they would have needed sanitariums; but fewer asylums. And their asylums would have been not for weakminded souls, but for furies.

They would have been strong at slander. They would have been far more violent than we in their hates, and they would have had fewer friendships. . . .

The super-cat-men would have rated cleanliness higher. Some of us primates have learned to keep ourselves clean, but it's no large proportion; and even the cleanest of us see no grandeur in soap-manufacturing, and we don't look to [manicurists] and plumbers for social prestige. A feline race would have honored such occupations; . . . the rich Vera Pantherbilt would have deigned to dine only with [manicurists].

None but the lowest dregs of such a race would have been lawyers spending their span of life on this mysterious earth studying the long dusty records of dead and gone quarrels. We simians naturally admire a profession full of wrangle and chatter, but that is a monkeyish way of deciding disputes, not a feline.

It is fair to judge peoples by the rights they will sacrifice most for. Super-cat-men would have been outraged had their right of personal combat been questioned. The simian submits with odd readiness to the loss of this privilege. What outrages him is to make him stop wagging his tongue. He becomes most excited and passionate about the right of free speech, even going so far in his emotion as to declare it is sacred. . . .

In a world of super-cat-men, I suppose there would have been few sailors; and people would have cared less for seaside resorts, or for swimming. . . .

Among them there would have been no antivivisection societies:

No Young Cats Christian Association or Red Cross work:

No vegetarians:

No early closing laws:

Much more hunting and trapping:

No riding to hounds; that's pure simian. . . .

They would have had few comedies on their stage; no farces. Cats care little for fun. In the circus, superlative acrobats. No clowns.

In drama and singing they would have surpassed us probably. Even in the stage of arrested development as mere animals, in which we see cats, they wail with a passionate intensity at night in our yards. Imagine how a Caruso descended from such beings would sing.[10]

Fanciful as this is, it points to a basic truth: our societies bear the special mark of our primate ancestry.

A lot has been written about the significance of our primate heritage for our physical development: our upright posture and flexible arms, our flexible hands with separated fingers and opposable thumbs, our year-round sexual readiness, our prolonged period of immaturity, our enlarged cerebrum, and

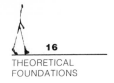

our complex nervous systems. Because of these and other physical features, we behave more like primates than like other animals, and the further removed those animals are from the primate line, the greater the difference. Thus, we have more in common with the primates (and especially with the suborder of anthropoids, which includes monkeys and apes as well as ourselves) than with other mammals; more with other mammals than with other vertebrates; and more with other vertebrates than with invertebrates.

The beautiful thing about Day's little fable, however, is that it draws attention to some of our less frequently noted anthropoid traits, and to their implications for our societies. For example, anthropoids are, on the whole, far more sociable than cats, which (except for the lion) are known for their solitary ways. And the thing that hits hardest as we read about those mythical cat people is what social creatures we humans really are.

This brings us back to the question of the function of our societies, the reason they exist—or, to be more specific, the reason humans have such a highly developed capacity for cooperative behavior. If we look back at our brief discussion of the functions of societies on page 7, we realize that we are one of the species that rely most heavily on social behavior. But that is not an exhaustive listing of societal functions. In fact, it does not include one that is extremely important in all species of mammals: to help them *learn*. As scholars in the important new subdiscipline of primatology have concluded, the principal reason apes and monkeys spend so much of their time in association with others of their species is because it enhances their opportunities for learning.[11]

Learning is *the process by which an organism acquires, through experience, information with behavior-modifying potential.* This means that when it comes to solving life's problems, an animal that can learn is not completely dependent on the behavioral repertoire that is part of its genetic makeup. Rather, *its own experiences* become a factor in shaping its behavior. The experiences of a social animal are less restricted than those of a solitary animal because it has more opportunity to observe, and communicate with, others of its species. In effect, a social animal stands to benefit from the experience of its fellows as well as from its own. Societal life thus multiplies the amount of information available to a population. In the words of two leading primatologists, "The group is the locus of knowledge and information far exceeding that of the individual member. It is in the group that experience is pooled."[12]

Like all capabilities in the biotic world, the ability to learn is genetically determined. So useful is this ability that it is even more widespread in the animal kingdom than is the societal mode of life. Some species, however, have very little capacity for learning, and what they have is restricted to responses to a narrow range of stimuli.[13] By contrast, humans and a few other primates have brains large and complex enough to store such a wide

FIGURE 1.3 All mammalian species have a marked capacity for learning: this is linked to the prolonged physical immaturity of mammalian young that requires them to remain in close contact with adults for a longer period than the young of most other species. Chimpanzee family, with sister nuzzling brother in mother's arms.

range of memories that they can learn by insight: they can see into a situation, as it were, and learn "directly" without having to go through a process of trial and error.[14]

All mammalian species have a marked capacity for learning. In part, this is linked to the advanced development of their brains and nervous systems. But there is another, equally important genetic attribute involved: the prolonged physical immaturity of mammalian young that requires them to remain in close contact with adults for a longer period of time than the young of most other species. Edward O. Wilson has called mother's milk the basis of mammalian society.[15] Because we are mammals, our survival depends on the societal mode of life, and on behaviors that we learn.

Characteristics Unique to Our Species

We do not need science to tell us our species is unique. People build skyscrapers, set off nuclear blasts, philosophize, compose symphonies, travel in space, and do thousands of other things no other animals can do.

This would seem to indicate that our genetic makeup is profoundly different from that of every other living creature.

We are not nearly as distinctive genetically, however, as our behavior suggests. The physical differences between us and the other anthropoids are, in fact, minor compared to the physical differences between them and most other animals.* Yet *behaviorally* the picture is reversed: apes and monkeys have far more in common with most other animals than they do with us.

The explanation of this seems to be that at some point in the course of evolution, our direct but distant ancestors crossed a critical threshold, after which a few relatively minor genetic changes opened the way to major changes in behavior. The breakthrough came when the process of natural selection produced one or more species of hominids† capable of creating symbols (e.g., words). The use of symbols meant a tremendous increase in the hominid capacity for learning, and this remarkable capacity for learning

*Recent studies have shown that, genetically, humans and chimpanzees are as close as sibling species of fruit flies.[16]

†This term refers to humanlike creatures, of which ours is the only surviving species.

FIGURE 1.4   The use of symbols meant a tremendous increase in the hominid capacity for learning, and this made possible a completely new way of adapting to the environment: the cultural mode of adaptation.

made possible a completely new way of adapting to the environment: *the cultural mode of adaptation.*[17]

Because culture is such a basic and crucial feature of human life, it is important that we understand precisely what it is. This term has been defined in a variety of ways over the years, but implicit in every definition has been the recognition that culture rests upon our species' great capacity for learning. Scientists, both social and biological, have increasingly come to speak of culture in terms of a *learned heritage* that is passed on from one generation of a society to the next. Moreover, they recognize that a society's cultural heritage is just as important to its survival as its genetic heritage. The essential distinction between them is in the way they are transmitted: one is passed on through genes, the other through symbols. Thus, we can most precisely define a society's culture by saying that it consists of its *symbol systems and the information they convey.**

What are symbols that they have made such a difference to our species? After all, the members of other species also communicate among themselves, using *signals* to convey information. In other words, both signals and symbols are *information conveyers*. But there is a vital difference: the meaning of a signal is wholly or largely determined by the genetic makeup of an animal; the meaning of a symbol is not.

The best way to understand this distinction is to look at examples of both kinds of information conveyers, beginning with signals.[19] Animals signal with movements, sounds, odors, color changes, and so on, and the signals they produce vary greatly in the amount of information they convey. The simplest type of signal is one that is used by an organism in only a single context and that has only one possible meaning—the sexually attractive scent released by the female moth, for example. In contrast, some species are able to transmit more complex information by varying the frequency or intensity of a signal or by combining different signals simultaneously or in sequence. Thus, a foraging honeybee returns to her hive and performs the "waggle dance" to direct her fellow workers to the food source she has located.[20] By varying the movements and vibrations that comprise the dance, she communicates enough information about direction and distance to enable her sisters to land remarkably near the target, and at the same time adds a comment on the quality of the food supply and the state of the weather.

In some species, especially birds and mammals, the use of, and the response to, signals is, to some extent, learned. For example, people communicate with such signals as yawns and laughter and blushes. But we

---

*A number of anthropologists and sociologists have included behavior and material artifacts in their definitions of culture, but it seems more appropriate to regard these as *products* of culture. This is in keeping with the recent trend described by Milton Singer in his article on culture in the *International Encyclopedia of the Social Sciences.* He reports that increasingly, in definitions and analyses of culture, "behavior, observed social relations, i.e., social structure, and material artifacts . . . are not themselves considered the constituents of culture."[18]

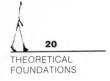

learn to modify these innate behaviors and to use them in new ways. Thus, we learn to smother a yawn as well as to yawn deliberately to indicate boredom. But whether it is simple or complex, and whether or not there is learning involved, a signal is essentially *an information conveyer whose meaning is determined genetically.*

Symbols, by contrast, do not depend on genetics. The ability to create and use symbols *is* genetically determined. But the form of a symbol and the meaning attached to it are *not.* Thus, a symbol is *an information conveyer whose meaning is determined by its users.*

Humans share this ability to create symbols with no other creature. Chimpanzees apparently are close to the neurological level that would make symbol creation possible for them.[21] But although some chimps have learned to *use* up to two hundred symbols that people have created especially for them, they themselves have not created any symbols. What is more, they do not exhibit any "prelanguage" features in the wild.[22] Yet human young exhibit such tendencies at a very early age, and before many years have passed, they are having a great time making up secret codes that adults cannot understand.

We can appreciate the significance of symbols only when we understand their "genetic independence." Take the sound of the third letter of our alphabet, for example. We use that sound to refer to the act of perceiving, to a bishop's jurisdiction, and to a large body of water, as well as to the letter itself. Spanish-speaking people, meanwhile, use it to say "yes," and French-speaking people to say "yes," "if," "whether," or "so." Obviously there is no connection between these various meanings, nor is there any genetically determined connection between the meanings and the sound. They are simply arbitrary usages adopted by the members of certain societies.

Further evidence that symbols are determined by their users and not by genes is the ease with which we alter them. When Chaucer wrote "Hir nose tretis, hir yen greye as glas . . . sikerly," he meant to say—in fact, he did say—"Her nose well-formed, her eyes gray as glass . . . certainly." English-speaking people have altered many of their symbols since his day. Slang is created by the reverse procedure: the symbol itself is unchanged, but it is assigned a new meaning. The words "bread" and "dough," for example, have both come to be used to refer to money.

Although linguistic symbols are the most basic and important, they are not the only kind we use. For not only sounds, but *any* thing that humans assign meaning to, is a symbol. Thus, the cross has become a symbol of Christianity, the hammer and sickle a symbol of Russian communism. Every nation in the world today has a flag to represent it, and standardized symbols communicate basic traffic directions on our highways.

Because they are not genetically determined, symbols can be combined and recombined indefinitely to form symbol systems of fantastic complexity, subtlety, and flexibility. There are no intrinsic limits to the amount and variety of information they can handle. The only limits are set by the physical characteristics of those who use them, that is, by the efficiency and capacity of the human brain and nervous system and the accuracy of our senses. And symbol systems help overcome even these limitations. For example, our species' memory (i.e., its capacity for storing information) has been greatly increased by the use of written symbols and written records.

In the final analysis, the importance of symbol systems lies not in what they are, but in what they have made it possible for our species to become. Although we are all born into the human family, we become truly human only through the use of symbols. Without them, we cannot develop the unique qualities we normally associate with humanness. For symbols are more than a means of communication: they are the basic tools with which we think and plan, dream and remember, create and build, calculate, speculate, and moralize.

The difference between a human mind without symbols and that same mind with them is eloquently described in accounts of Helen Keller's early life. Miss Keller became both deaf and blind before she learned to talk. By the age of seven, after years devoid of meaningful communication with other people, she had become very much like a wild animal. Then a gifted teacher, Anne Sullivan, began trying to communicate with Helen by spelling words into her hands. Helen learned several words, but she did not yet comprehend the real significance of symbols. Then, in a moment that both women later described in moving terms, Helen suddenly realized that *everything* had a name, that *everything* could be communicated with symbols! In her own words, she felt "a thrill of returning thought."[23] The world that exists only for symbol users began to open to Helen Keller.

Miss Keller's experience helps us understand why the ancients, in their accounts of creation, so often linked the beginning of language with the beginning of the world. One of the oldest written texts from Egypt, for example, tells how Ptah, the creator of the world and the greatest of the gods, "pronounced the names of all things" as a central part of his act of creation.[24] Language also figures prominently in Chinese and Hindu creation myths. The book of Genesis tells us that the first thing Adam did after he was created was to name all the beasts and birds; and the Gospel According to St. John opens with the lines, "In the beginning was the Word, and the Word was with God, and the Word was God." Significantly, the original Greek for "word" was *logos*, which meant not merely word, but meaning and reason. And *logos* is the root of our own word "*logic*," and of the suffix *-logy*, used to denote science, as in biology or sociology.

In more recent times, the great German pioneer scientist Alexander von Humboldt said, "No words, no world." And it is certainly true that the *human* world, the world of human societies, would not exist without words. Without

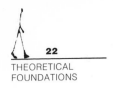

symbols, they would lack their most distinctive feature: *culture.* With symbols, however, each of them has developed a rich cultural heritage to supplement its genetic heritage.

Our Common Genetic Heritage

Attributes we share with the amoeba, attributes we share with the ape, attributes we share with no other living thing—these comprise our common genetic heritage. We have examined some facets of this heritage in detail, we have barely alluded to others. Now it is important to look at this heritage *as a whole* and consider its implications. For the complex cluster of traits that is part of every human is also *the biological foundation of every human society.*

Summarizing the traits that comprise our common heritage is not as easy as it might seem, however, for two reasons. First, there is no way to observe and study humans (except possibly newborn infants) *apart* from culture. After that, cultural influences become so pervasive that it is extremely difficult to distinguish between their effects and those of genetics.

The other reason it is so hard to identify our common traits is because of the *complexities* of human genetics. For example, an observable trait (i.e., a behavioral or physical characteristic) does not typically result from one particular gene, as we might suppose, but reflects the interaction of a number of different genes. Any given gene, meanwhile, usually affects not a single trait, but a number of different traits. What is more, most traits are not determined by heredity alone, but by both genetic endowment and environmental factors. Because of these complexities, many things are still poorly understood. Which genes or sets of genes are common to us all? Which are variable (i.e., either not present in everyone, or present in different forms)? And what is the relative contribution of inheritance and environment to the variance observed in a particular trait? Answers are beginning to emerge in all these areas, but they are still just that—a beginning.

Enough is now known, however, to put to rest some older views of our species' nature. One of these, the "tabula rasa" hypothesis, held that the newborn infant's mind is like a blank page and that the eventual content is supplied entirely by the environment.[25] This view was immensely popular among philosophers and social scientists in the eighteenth, nineteenth, and early twentieth centuries because it provided the basis for a highly optimistic view of the future. For if babies arrive in such malleable condition, it should be possible, with careful planning and proper education, to eliminate most of society's evils, such as war, crime, and economic exploitation. Events of the twentieth century, however, have raised grave doubts about human malleability and perfectibility.[26]

Meanwhile, the work of scientists and scholars in widely scattered disciplines has produced a clearer understanding not only of the human brain, but of many other components of our common genetic heritage. At the risk of oversimplifying an extremely complex and still controversial subject, we will try to identify those elements that are most relevant to the study of human societies.

First, all humans have *the same fundamental needs*. To begin with, there are those basic physical requirements (for food, water, sleep, oxygen, elimination, etc.) that must be satisfied at frequent intervals if we are to survive. We also have a variety of other physical needs in common, but needs whose satisfaction is not essential for individual survival or whose intensity varies greatly from one stage of life to another. These include sexual needs, the need for play,[27] the need for new experience, and the need for social experience. That these needs have as strong a genetic base as our "survival needs" has been well documented. The need for new experience, for example, is evident in the newborn infant, who exhibits a decided preference for visual variety and contrast and has "a bias to explore" that it begins to satisfy almost from the moment of birth.[28] The newborn also has such a fundamental need for social contact and stimulation that, if it is not satisfied, the child may not even survive.[29]

Second, we all develop *a variety of derivative needs*. Our common genetic makeup provides us with the potential for developing certain individual needs and desires in addition to those above, needs and desires that are largely the result of our social and cultural experiences. Because this experience varies from one society to another and among individuals in the same society, and also because genetic variations play a role in their development, the intensity of these needs varies greatly. But all of us have the potential for at least minimal development of any number of needs beyond those required for our mere survival. These include the need to control people and events, to possess things, to give and receive affection, to express one's self aesthetically and in other ways, to be respected and admired, to have emotional, aesthetic, or religious experiences, and to discern order and meaning in life.

Third, we all have *the same basic resources to use in satisfying our needs*. To begin with, we have such obvious physical equipment as legs, fingers, teeth, ears, bowels, heart, brain, and so on. Our brain is a particularly impressive resource: it provides us with the means of recording "memory traces" equivalent to the content of 1,000 twenty-four-volume sets of the *Encyclopaedia Britannica*.[30] Moreover, we are genetically programmed for the automatic performance of a variety of activities (e.g., digestion, growth, ovulation, circulation, etc.) and have many valuable response sets and reflex actions (e.g., we pull away when we touch something hot). Paradoxically, some of our resources are hard to distinguish from our needs. This is true, for

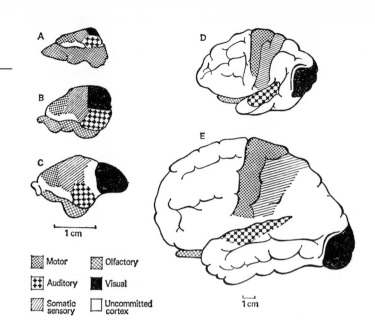

Motor

Auditory

Somatic
sensory

Olfactory

Visual

Uncommitted
cortex

Development of the cerebral cortex among the primates.
A = ground shrew; B = tree shrew; C = tarsius; D = chimpanzee;
E = Homo sapiens

FIGURE 1.5   The human brain is an impressive resource: note the size of the cerebral cortex of humans compared with other primates.

example, of the "exploring tendency" which is at one and the same time an expression of an innate need for new experience and a resource (i.e., an attribute that serves us in our efforts to satisfy other needs).

Because we all have essentially the same resources to use in satisfying the same basic needs, we behave in strikingly similar ways and develop strikingly similar social patterns. For example, because of the universal need for sleep, and because our eyes, unlike those of many species, are poorly designed for seeing in the dark, every human society has been geared to the same basic cycle of heightened daytime activity and reduced activity at night.

Fourth, we are all *dependent on the societal mode of life*, especially during our formative years. The human infant is born in a condition of extreme immaturity and helplessness. In fact, for its first year it experiences growth patterns (e.g., bone ossification, brain growth) that are part of *fetal* development in other primate species.*[31] Maturation proceeds at a slow pace: children require much longer to reach maturity than the young of most other species (e.g., even the anthropoid apes reach sexual maturity by about the

*The reason humans enter the world in an essentially embryonic state is apparently related to our brain. If the infant were to develop *in utero* an additional seven to twelve months, its increased head size would make birth impossible.

age of nine). And even as adults, most people cannot satisfy all their basic needs except through cooperative activities.

Fifth, as we have already observed, we all have *the capacity to create and use symbol systems*. This uniquely human ability, on which all culture rests, is compounded of a variety of genetic attributes, including such organs of speech as lips, tongue, palates, sinuses, and vocal cords. Far more important, however, are peculiarities of the human brain, specifically those unique areas of our cerebral cortex that control speech and abstract thought.[32] A growing number of linguists believe that despite the great variability of our 3,000 spoken languages—differences in vocabularies, in the sounds and combinations of sounds used, and in grammar, or the way words are "put together"—there is a "deep structure" common to them all.[33] In other words, our genetic heritage does not bestow on us a vague, generalized capacity for speech (i.e., for communicating with oral symbols) but appears actually to determine the basic structure this speech will assume.*

Sixth, related to our use of symbols, we all have *an immense capacity for learning, and for modifying our behavior in response to what we learn*. The result is a remarkable behavioral flexibility that frees us from the restrictions of a single, hereditary set of behaviors or response sets. We are able to devise alternate patterns of behaviors for virtually every circumstance of human life and develop new ways of satisfying our needs.

Seventh, we all have *a fully developed self-awareness*, an acute consciousness of ourselves and of our situation with respect to the rest of the world.† This aspect of human nature has been called both a blessing and a curse, and rightly so. Because of it, we are able to picture ourselves in situations we have never experienced, and thus we have the capacity to *plan*, individually and collectively, for the future, and to develop purposes and goals. Because of it, we are able to imagine things that have never been, and thus we have the capacity to *create*. But with our awareness and our foresight comes the realization that we are responsible for our actions, and thus we acquire the capacity for making moral judgments and *creating moral orders*, which all human societies are. Theodosius Dobzhansky, the late geneticist, once remarked that no other animal has to bear any thing comparable to the tragic discord that self-awareness has created in the human soul.[36]

Eighth, and finally, we all have *a genetically rooted motivation to satisfy our needs, and to put their satisfaction ahead of those of others*. The reason for this becomes evident when we consider the true social insects, whose societies are remarkably free from the discord so characteristic of our own.

---

*The deep-structure explanation also appears to be the only explanation for the amazing speed and ease with which all normal human young learn language.[34]

†Human consciousness and self-awareness evolved with the development of those lobes of our brain that control abstract thought. This permits us to think in a new time dimension: the future. Even the apes have only a rudimentary conception of that important dimension of existence.[35]

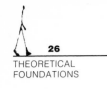

Their social relationships are harmonious because they are programmed genetically to respond to other members of the society in a wholly cooperative and altruistic manner. In other words, individuality is automatically suppressed with these creatures and cooperative behavior is unavoidable. The social behavior of mammals is not regulated to anything like this degree, however, and individuality is consequently far more pronounced. Thus, in mammalian societies, cooperative behavior is largely *learned* behavior, and self-assertive, self-seeking tendencies are never entirely suppressed.

In our own societies, the infant begins life exclusively concerned with the satisfaction of his or her own basic needs. Gradually, the child becomes aware of the needs of other people, and eventually grows more considerate of them. With even the best of us, however, our innate selfishness does not—indeed, it cannot—disappear. Rather, two things happen that dull its sharp edge.

First, we learn that cooperative behavior is essential if we are to attain the things we want, that in order to get, we must also give. Second, through social and cultural experience, the scope of our needs expands and some of our new needs cause us actually to *become* less self-centered, while others cause us to *behave as if we were* less self-centered. We really become less self-centered when we develop the desire to please people who love us or satisfy our needs, for example, or when we seek to protect our children or others with whom we identify very closely.* We may even develop a social conscience that compels us to attend to the needs of underprivileged or suffering people with whom we have no personal ties. On the other hand, we often simply give *the appearance* of being unselfishly motivated as a means to other ends, such as gaining popularity or respect, for example. Thus, most of our behavior continues to reflect self-seeking tendencies. And yet, because our needs have been modified, and because we have learned to satisfy our needs through cooperative means, human behavior is compatible with relatively harmonious social life.

One manifestation of our innate self-centeredness is the *expansive* quality of our socially derived needs and desires. When one of them is satisfied, another emerges to take its place. Thus, we are highly motivated to attain what we may think is all we really want out of life, but once we achieve it, we may become equally anxious for something more.[37]

Abraham Maslow, the psychologist, theorized that there is an inborn hierarchy of human needs in which our physiological needs are the most basic, followed by the need for safety, and then, in turn, by the need to belong and be loved, the need for esteem and respect, and the need for "self-actualization."[38] The more basic needs, according to Maslow, remain dominant in a person's life until they are satisfied, but the more fully they are

---

*Unfortunately, the development of a capacity to care for others carries with it the potential for an enhanced capacity to inflict harm on those *outside* the circle of one's loyalties.

satisfied the stronger the higher needs become. Thus, the most urgent need of one accustomed to having all of his or her physical and safety needs met will be the need to be loved and accepted by others. And the person whose needs are satisfied in every other respect may be driven by the need for "self-actualization"—the need for self-expression, perhaps, or for power, or for aesthetic experience. Although Maslow's theory is hardly definitive, it certainly appears consistent with what we can observe of human behavior.

By now it should be clear why we had to examine our biological heritage before we could examine our societies. When a single species combines such diverse and often contradictory attributes as ours does, we can expect its societies to be complex and difficult to understand, and what we have established in this chapter will illuminate what we encounter in those that follow.

As many of the great novelists and poets have recognized, a tremendous tension is built into the very fabric of human life: Homo sapiens is, at one and the same time, a social animal and an individualistic, self-seeking animal. It is this, more than anything else, which creates the drama in human life, and the uncertainties. And it is this which justifies one early sociologist's classic description of human societies as systems of "antagonistic cooperation."[39]

EXCURSUS: A BRIEF HISTORY OF SOCIOLOGY

Before going further in our analysis of human societies, it may be well to pause and take a look at sociology itself—its origins and history, its recent trends and current status. This brief excursus will also provide an opportunity to consider the relationship between sociology and the other social sciences.

Though sociology is a relatively recent addition to the scholarly world, its roots extend at least as far into the past as the writings of Plato and Aristotle. Philosophers then were already speculating about their own societies—comparing one with another and trying to understand the forces that shaped them.

The more immediate origins of modern sociology, however, lie in the sixteenth, seventeenth, and eighteenth centuries. This was a period during which the peoples of Western Europe, especially the educated minority, were confronted with a tremendous amount of information that could not be assimilated into their traditional belief systems. They learned that their earth was not, after all, the center of the universe. And they also learned, through the discovery of whole new continents populated by peoples with cultures radically different from their own, that Western Europe was not the center of the earth. At the same time, European societies were themselves changing. The Protestant Reformation had divided Western Europe, and the bitter religious wars that followed undermined much of the moral and intellectual authority of the clergy. Meanwhile, urban populations were growing in size and influence. All these factors contributed to the questioning of older theories and to renewed pondering about the nature of human life.

Among the consequences were two more or less independent developments, which laid the foundation for modern sociology. The first of these was the revival of interest in the systematic study of man and society, fostered by writers such as Thomas Hobbes, John Locke, Montesquieu, Jean Jacques Rousseau, John Millar, Adam Smith, and Thomas Malthus. Before the eighteenth century ended, these men had established the independence of social theory from theology and had laid the philosophical foundations of the modern social sciences. Some of them even went so far as to identify the phenomenon of sociocultural evolution—long before Darwin, or even Lamarck—and to formulate explanations for it.[40]

During this same period, others began making systematic, quantitative studies of various social phenomena. Birth and death rates were an early object of research; later there were studies of class, family income, jury verdicts, election results, and a variety of other phenomena. Sometimes those who were involved in developing theory were also involved in research, though this was usually not the case. By the end of the century, the quantitative tradition was firmly established; ties to theory were still imperfectly developed, but a basis had been established for the eventual integration of these two types of inquiry.[41]

The term "sociology" first appeared in the 1830s in the writings of a Frenchman, Auguste Comte. As a result, Comte is often referred to as the founder of modern sociology. This is an undeserved honor, however, since his writings were in an already established tradition and his own distinctive contribution was not that unique.

The most famous nineteenth-century sociologist, and the most influential in his own day, was an English scholar, Herbert Spencer. Through his writings, which were widely translated, he brought sociology to the attention of the educated classes throughout the world. Like others before him, Spencer was profoundly interested in sociocultural evolution, though he saw it as but one manifestation of a universal cosmic process linking the physical, biotic, and human worlds. Interest in evolution was further stimulated in that period by the writings of Charles Darwin, a contemporary of Spencer.

Another major contributor to the study of human societies in the nineteenth century was Karl Marx. Unlike Spencer, he stood apart from the emerging discipline of sociology, with the result that the relevance of his work to the discipline went unrecognized for many years. With the passage of time, however, this has changed. One reason has been the belated appreciation of the importance of the material base of human life—people's need for food, shelter, and the like, and the techniques for meeting these needs. Most of the other pioneer social scientists neglected or underestimated this.

Ironically, despite its European origins, sociology found more rapid acceptance in the United States. A number of leading American universities established professorships even before the turn of the century, and by the early decades of the present century, many institutions had established full-fledged departments of sociology. During the period between the two world wars, sociology continued to expand in the United States but failed to do so in Europe, partly because of attacks by totalitarian governments, especially in Germany and Russia, partly because of greater resistance to change and innovation by the faculties of European universities. As a result, sociology became primarily an American enterprise.

Following World War I, sociology underwent a number of important changes. Under American leadership the discipline became increasingly concerned with contemporary American society. Interest in other societies declined, as did interest in the historical dimension of human experience. To a large extent these changes reflected the desire of a new generation of sociologists to make the discipline more scientific. The result was a greatly heightened interest in field research, especially studies of local communities and their problems—crime, poverty, divorce, juvenile delinquency, illegitimacy, prostitution, the problems of immigrants, and so forth.

With this shift in the focus of interest, sociologists gradually abandoned the earlier evolutionary approach. In part, this was because of criticisms leveled against it, but primarily it was because the older approach seemed irrelevant to the concerns of the newer generation. Sociologists were forced to find a substitute for evolutionary theory—some new theoretical approach that could organize the growing but diffuse body of information on American society. By the late 1930s, the *structural-functional* approach emerged as the apparent successor to evolutionary theory.

The structural-functional approach to the study of human societies is, in effect, the sociological counterpart of the anatomical and physiological approaches in biology. Like anatomists, structural-functionalists are concerned with the identification and labeling of the many different parts of the things they study and with the structural relations among them (e.g., the structural patterns formed within business organizations, families, etc.). Like physiologists, they are interested in the functions each of the parts performs. Just as physiologists are concerned with the functions of organs, such as the liver, heart, and spleen, structural-functionalists are interested in the functions of institutions, such as the family, and of moral rules, such as the taboo against incest.

A professor at Harvard named Talcott Parsons was especially instrumental in establishing the structural-functional approach. Building on foundations laid around the turn of the century by Max Weber in Germany and Emile Durkheim in France, Parsons developed a theoretical system that was carried by his students into leading universities throughout the country.

Since World War II, sociology has grown substantially not only in the United States but in Europe, Japan, and Canada, and it has begun to take root in other areas as well. One significant development has been the changing attitude of Communist authorities in Eastern Europe. During the Stalin era and for some time thereafter, sociology was regarded as subversive and was illegal throughout the communist world. Today, however, restrictions are being removed and interest in the subject is growing, especially in Poland, Yugoslavia, and Hungary.[42] The development of sociology in other countries has reduced the un-

healthy concentration of the discipline in the United States that characterized the decades of the 1930s and 1940s.

Another notable development has been the movement of sociology beyond the confines of the academic community. Prior to the 1940s, sociologists were employed almost entirely by universities and colleges. Beginning during World War II and continuing to the present, there has been a growing demand for their services by government, industry, and other kinds of organizations.

Intellectually, too, sociology has made substantial progress. Two of the most important developments have been the increasing use of quantitative techniques and the emergence of *ecological-evolutionary* theory. The first of these was a natural outgrowth of sociologists' efforts to achieve greater precision in their descriptions of social phenomena and greater rigor in their analyses. This trend was given an enormous boost by the invention of computers, which enable researchers to handle large volumes of data and carry out complex statistical analyses that would otherwise be impossible.

The new ecological-evolutionary theory developed in response to the growing recognition that structural-functional theory alone cannot provide an adequate basis for understanding two crucial aspects of human life—*change* and *conflict*. Though these have been important throughout human history, they have never been more important than in our own century. A variety of events—such as the civil rights movement, the women's liberation movement, the Indochina War, the struggles in Lebanon and Northern Ireland, the population explosion, the environmental crisis, the impending energy crisis, and the continuing technological revolution—have contributed to the growing dissatisfaction with structural-functionalism.

Sociology and the Other Social Sciences

The study of human societies has never been exclusively a sociological concern. All the social sciences have been involved in one way or another. Most of the others, however, have focused on some particular aspect of the subject. Economics and political science limit themselves to a single institutional area. Human geography studies the impact of the physical and biotic environments on societies. Social psychology is concerned with the impact of social organization on the behavior and personality of individuals.

Only sociology and anthropology have been concerned with human societies per se. That is to say, only these two disciplines have interested themselves in the full range of social phenomena, from the family to the nation and from technology to religion. And only these two disciplines have sought to understand societies as entities in their own right.

In matters of research, there has been a fairly well established division of labor between the fields. Sociologists have, for the most part, studied modern industrial societies; anthropologists have concentrated on preliterate societies of both the past and present. This division of labor has made good sense, since the skills needed to study a remote tribe in the mountains of New Guinea are very different from those needed to study a modern industrial society such as our own.

From the standpoint of teaching and the development of theory, however, such a division is far less satisfactory. Many problems, especially those involving long-term evolutionary processes, require the contributions of both disciplines. Ignoring either may produce incomplete or biased interpretations and conclusions. As a consequence, there has been a long tradition of intellectual "borrowing" between sociology and anthropology, and this volume stands in that tradition.

With the revival of evolutionary theory,[43] scholars in these fields have come to recognize that both disciplines were neglecting agrarian societies—those societies which occupy the middle range in the evolutionary scale between primitive preliterate societies and modern industrial societies. In recent years, therefore, both sociologists and anthropologists have begun research in Southeast Asia, the Middle East, and Latin America.

The growing concern with agrarian societies has also led to increased contact between sociologists and historians. Since history is the study of written records of the past, historians have been the experts on agrarian societies of earlier centuries. Much of the older work by historians, with its heavy emphasis on the names and dates of famous men and events, is of limited value for the student of human societies. But that discipline has been changing too, and historians today are increasingly concerned with the basic social patterns and processes that underlie the more dramatic but usually less significant events on which their predecessors focused. As a result history and sociology are becoming more valuable to each other.

This trend toward interdisciplinary cooperation is evident today in all the social sciences, and even beyond. Scholars are coming to recognize that no discipline is sufficient unto itself. To the degree that any field cuts itself off from the others, it impoverishes itself intellectually. Conversely, to the degree that it communicates with other disciplines, it enriches itself and them.

CHAPTER 2 HUMAN SOCIETIES AS SOCIOCULTURAL SYSTEMS

One of the fascinations of human societies is their diversity. In any other social species, one society is remarkably like the next in size, complexity, and the activities of its members. This is hardly surprising, however, in view of the fact that one society is also remarkably like the next in its biological heritage and that this heritage determines the great majority of the species' characteristics.

Why, then, are human societies, which *also* have similar biological heritages, so different from one another in so many ways? Why are some huge and organizationally complex, while others are small and simple? And why are the activities of their members often so varied? Why, for example, are the members of some societies warlike, while the members of others are relatively peaceful? Why are some puritanical in relations between the sexes, while others are much more permissive?

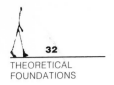

The explanation of the tremendous variations among human societies is that their similar biological heritages enable them to develop very *dis*similar cultural heritages. Without their cultures, human societies, too, would all be essentially alike. But with culture comes an extraordinary potential for creating diversity.

Because our societies, unlike those of other species, are both social *and* cultural units, sociologists and other social scientists often refer to them as *sociocultural* systems. This contraction of the two words is partly a convenience. But it is more than that: it is a reminder that the social and cultural aspects of human life are inextricably intertwined. In this chapter we will begin to explore the many implications of this fact.

HUMAN SOCIETIES AS SYSTEMS

The term *system*, which we have just linked with "sociocultural" and which appears frequently in sociological writing, is a simple word with a profound meaning. It can be applied to a wide range of phenomena, many of them in the world of nature. There are physical systems such as the solar system, star systems, weather systems, and systems of lakes and rivers. Every living organism is a system. And there are systems *within* organisms (digestive, reproductive, etc.), systems *among* organisms (colonies, societies), and systems that include organisms and their environments (ecological systems). Among the systems created by humans are a multitude of mechanical systems (cars, pianos) and a variety of such dissimilar ones as political, linguistic, mathematical, irrigation, and transportation systems. In every instance, the term is appropriate because *a system is an entity made up of interrelated parts.*

The key word in this definition is "interrelated." In the words of one expert, a system is a "bundle of relations."[1] For this reason, what happens to one of the component parts of a system has implications for other parts, and for the system as a whole. We are surrounded with instances of this: too much beer in the stomach has repercussions for the brain, for example, just as the alignment of an automotive system's wheels affects its steering. The nineteenth-century poet Francis Thompson captured the systemic qualities of the total universe in his line, "Thou canst not stir a flower without troubling of a star."[2]

The meaning of the concept *system* is best understood, however, if we focus on a smaller, more specific "bundle of relations," such as the mechanism of a clock. In working order, this entity is a mechanical system. Each of its components (gears, dial, hands, springs, etc.) is also an entity— and each remains an entity even if the mechanism is dismantled. But when the relations among the parts have been destroyed, the entity that is *the system* ceases to exist. A system, then, is clearly more than the sum of its parts: it is the sum of its parts *plus* the relations among them.

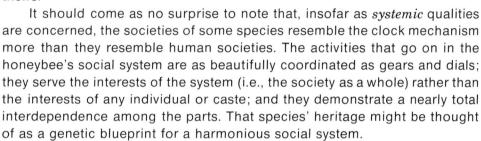

Systems vary a great deal in their internal coordination, that is, in the degree to which the functions of the parts are coordinated with one another and with the functioning of the system as a whole. Using this as a criterion, mechanical systems are the most nearly "perfect" systems there are. Consider the clock mechanism again. Each component exists, and each functions, for one purpose only: the purpose for which *the system* exists and functions (i.e., to mark the passage of time). Moreover, each component relates only to the other parts of its own system, and its operation is totally dependent upon theirs.

It should come as no surprise to note that, insofar as *systemic* qualities are concerned, the societies of some species resemble the clock mechanism more than they resemble human societies. The activities that go on in the honeybee's social system are as beautifully coordinated as gears and dials; they serve the interests of the system (i.e., the society as a whole) rather than the interests of any individual or caste; and they demonstrate a nearly total interdependence among the parts. That species' heritage might be thought of as a genetic blueprint for a harmonious social system.

The situation is quite different in sociocultural systems. For one thing, the coordination among their component parts is frequently poor. For another, their components do not always function in ways that are conducive to the well-being of the system (i.e., the society) as a whole. For example, their members are individualistic and independent, resist efforts to coordinate and control their behavior, and do not easily submit their wills to the system or group. In short, a genetic blueprint that is very different from the honeybee's, but just as compelling, *prevents* human societies from achieving the strict ordering of relations that characterizes some systems.

SYSTEM-NEEDS OF HUMAN SOCIETIES

Human societies exist for only one reason: to enable humans to satisfy their needs. But, being systems (however imperfect), societies have needs of their own. In short, certain conditions must exist if the particular "bundle of relations" that comprises a sociocultural system—or any other kind of system, for that matter—is not to disintegrate. The conditions necessary for societies to survive are sometimes called *functional requisites.*[3]

Although there is a great similarity between the needs of a society's members and those of the society, or system, itself, they are not precisely the same. For example, it is not fatal to an individual if he or she fails to have children. But the situation is different for a society, as we will see below.

The first of the system-needs is for *communication among the members.*

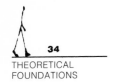

This is the sine qua non of every social organization, human or nonhuman, because if its members are unable to communicate (i.e., unable to exchange information among themselves) social behavior is impossible. Thus, every human society has, at a minimum, a spoken language.

Second, there must be *production of goods and services* to satisfy both the physical and psychic needs of the members. This requires a substantial store of information—not only on the subject of the production of material goods (i.e., about tools, techniques, location of resources), but also about the responsibilities that the members should assume and the contributions they should make toward the satisfaction of one another's needs. For in human societies, production, whether of food or of affection, is largely a cooperative effort.*

Third, there must be *distribution of the goods and services that are produced*. Producers and consumers are never precisely the same in any society: at a minimum, the essentials must be provided for the young. In human societies, the solutions to problems of distribution, like those of production, are essentially cultural answers and vary tremendously from one society to the next.†

Distribution poses an especially acute problem in societies where production is so highly specialized that there is little overlap between those who produce a given product or service and those who use it. This situation requires multiple and often highly complex cultural answers. A society must develop mechanisms that enable producers to exchange things with one another (e.g., systems of barter, monetary systems). It must also have mechanisms for moving goods and services from one place to another (i.e., transportation systems). And, perhaps most important, it must have mechanisms for determining who receives how much of those goods and services (i.e., stratification systems).

Fourth, there must be *protection of the members* from the dangers of their environment. These include physical hazards (storms, heat, cold, flood, etc.), other organisms (germs, wild animals, crop-destroying insects), and other human societies. To enable its members to protect themselves, individually and collectively, a society's culture may contain a diversity of techniques, ranging from techniques for building shelters and making clothing to techniques of healing and warfare.

No society can be entirely successful in defending its members against hostile forces, for every individual dies eventually. For the *society* to survive, however, it is only necessary that enough of its members live long enough

*Although hermits and other isolated individuals sometimes provide for their own basic material needs apart from society, they are nonetheless dependent on some society's accumulated store of information.

†This is not true in other animals' societies, where genetics provide solutions to the fundamental problems of production and distribution. The wild dogs of Africa, for example, on returning from a successful hunt, regurgitate some of the fresh meat they consumed to feed the mothers and pups that were unable to accompany them.[4]

and in good enough health to carry on its functions and to raise the next generation to adulthood.

Fifth, because death is the ultimate fate of every individual, *members must be replaced.* This need is partially satisfied by biological reproduction, which perpetuates the society's *genetic* heritage. But this is not enough. If the society is to survive, its *cultural* heritage must also be perpetuated. This is accomplished by means of the socialization process.

Socialization is the process through which individuals become functional members of their society. This complex process, which begins at birth and extends over many years, consists of social and cultural experiences and results in substantial modification of behavior. Through socialization, we develop in our earliest years those qualities we associate with "being human," but which are only potentialities in the newborn infant and emerge only through social experience. Later, we learn to assume responsibility for our own behavior and to satisfy many of our own needs through a variety of learned activities, both solitary and cooperative. Finally, as we reach adulthood, we take on a broad range of responsibilities, for ourselves and others, including the task of transmitting our society's culture to the next generation.

Finally, there must be *controls on the behavior of the members.* From a society's point of view, there are two reasons why the actions of its members and the relationships among them must be controlled and regulated: (1) to ensure that the vital work of the society gets done; and (2) to prevent intrasocietal conflict from disrupting societal life.

To some extent, these ends are achieved through biological mechanisms. Consider society's need for new members, for example. Physical attraction between the sexes helps ensure that mating will occur and infants be born. Then the infants must be cared for, and this need, too, is partially answered by our genetic makeup. The great majority of mothers of human infants, like those of all mammals, demonstrate an eagerness to be near and to nurture their babies (although prior social experiences also affect this relationship). Moreover, studies of nonhuman primate societies have shown that infants are very attractive not only to their mothers, but to other members of the society as well.[5] A similar innate appeal on the part of human infants probably helps ensure that they, too, are looked after and protected.

Biological mechanisms also help minimize disruption within human societies. Although people communicate primarily by means of symbols, we also use signals—genetically determined facial expressions, postures, noises, gestures, and so on—to let others know our moods and our intentions. We cannot always conceal our fear or anger, for example; these emotions may be "written all over us." Simply knowing what another person is prepared to do in a given situation (e.g., stand up and fight or back off) prevents much violence in human societies, just as similar mechanisms do for other species.

In human societies, however, the potential for neglect of socially neces-

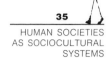

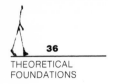

sary tasks and for socially disruptive behavior is so great that genetic mechanisms of control must be supplemented with cultural mechanisms. These mechanisms, usually called *social controls*, help order societal life by rewarding some types of behavior and penalizing others. The specific actions that are encouraged or suppressed, as well as the way this is done, vary from one society to the next. But every system of social control has two basic components. First, there is always a set of *norms* to define what kind of behavior is good or bad, better or worse, under various circumstances. Norms take the form of laws, rules, regulations, customs, guidelines, standards, and so forth. Second, there is always a set of *sanctions* to motivate and coerce people to behave in ways approved by their society. Sanctions are rewards and punishments, and they range all the way from a simple word of encouragement to a large monetary prize or appointment to an important office, from a fleeting frown on someone's face to punishments imposed by a court of law.

As sociologists have long noted, no system of social control can be effective if it depends exclusively on *external* rewards and punishments—that is, on sanctions that the members impose on each other. Rather, every person must assume a large degree of responsibility for his or her own conduct and therefore must be able to impose *internal* sanctions (e.g., guilt feelings or self-congratulation). This is why one of the major objectives of the socialization process is to internalize the standards and values of the group so that they are also the personal standards and values of the members. Although no society ever achieves this goal completely, it must at least approximate it. The alternative is anarchy, and the end of the society as an organization.

BASIC COMPONENTS OF SOCIOCULTURAL SYSTEMS

Every human society, because it is a system, is made up of various components and the relations among them. Even the simplest of these systems is so complex that it would be impossible to identify each of its component parts and detail all the relationships among them. Carried to its extreme, this would require, among other things, giving the life history of every member! Instead, our goal is to examine the most basic components that comprise every human society. These are (1) population, (2) culture, (3) material products, and (4) social structure.

Population

The first component of sociocultural systems is population, a term that refers to *the members of a human society considered collectively.* As this suggests, in studying human societies we are primarily concerned with the characteristics of the group, rather than with those of its individual members.* There are three aspects of a population that should be taken into account: (1) genetic constants, (2) genetic variables, and (3) demographic variables.

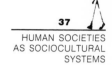

Genetic Constants   The genetic constants of a population are those of its attributes which are rooted in our common genetic heritage. They are the same for the population of every society and, for all practical purposes, the same from one generation to the next. Since we have already discussed this subject at length in Chapter 1, nothing need be added here beyond the observation that this heritage includes not only the ability to reason and to devise cultural solutions to problems, but also powerful emotions and appetites that evolved in our prehuman ancestors. Thus, the genetic constants are at one and the same time every society's most precious resource and the cause of many of its most serious problems.

Genetic Variables   In addition to that central core of traits that comprises the major portion of every individual's genetic heritage, each of us also has thousands of genes that are variable—that is, they are absent or occur in different forms in other individuals. Because these genes are not always distributed equally among societies, there is a *variable* genetic aspect to population as well as a constant one. Such variables range from traits like skin color, hair texture, and eye shape to characteristics of the blood, incidence of color blindness, and taste sensitivity.[6] From the standpoint of their impact on the life of human societies, genetic variables, relative to genetic constants, are of minor importance. And yet, because so much attention has been focused on certain of the external (i.e., racial) variables, it may be useful to examine this subject in some detail.

Although human populations have frequently been reproductively isolated, none has ever been cut off long enough to become a separate species—that is, so genetically different that its members could not subsequently mate with other human populations and produce fertile offspring. During those periods of isolation, however, as the processes of mutation and natural selection continued to fit each human group to its particular environment, populations developed gene pools (see page 12) in which the frequency of certain genes varied significantly. Among these genes were those responsible for the external characteristics on which the concept of *race* is built, such

---

*This concept of population is similar but not identical to the biological concept of population, which refers to "an interbreeding group" (see page 11). A human society is not necessarily an interbreeding group in this sense of a free flow of genes among its members. Cultural factors (e.g., religious beliefs, customs, laws) and geographical factors (e.g., the society's size, barriers such as mountains) may prevent or discourage marriage between some segments of the population.

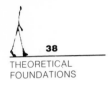

as the color of skin, hair, and eyes, hair type, body build, and shape of face and head.

A race, in other words, is simply a breeding population in which one or more of these traits occur with a frequency that is appreciably different from other breeding populations.[7] One anthropologist noted that this, the only scientifically valid definition of race, might permit us to continue subdividing our species into "breeding populations" until eventually every family or even every mated pair was identified as a distinct race.[8] This is not said here to suggest that the concept of race is arbitrary, or merely the invention of those who study race: racial traits are as valid a subject of research as any other human characteristics. It does help us see, however, that it is impossible to divide the human species into some specific number of clearly defined racial groupings.[9] It also makes it clear that the existence of racial divisions in no way diminishes the integrity or our species as an evolutionary unit.[10]

Members of modern societies often have difficulty appreciating the adaptive value of racial variables, because we no longer depend on them for our survival or well-being. When we encounter unpleasantly strong sunlight, for example, we adapt *culturally*: we create artificial shade, or we apply artificial "pigment" to our eyes (sunglasses) and, if we are lightly pigmented, to our skin (suntan oil). Until relatively recently, however, a population's *genetic* attributes were its primary means of adapting to the hazards of its environment, and even minor variations in certain characteristics, such as the ability to store body fat as an insulation against extreme cold, could determine which individuals survived and which did not.

This explains why many genetic variables, from skin color to body and facial form, are not randomly distributed across the globe, but occur in discernible geographical patterns.[11] For example, the pigment in our skin determines how dark it is and protects underlying cells from exposure to ultraviolet light. And darker skin is universal in hot, sunny regions,[12] with the heaviest pigmentation of all in the African Sudan, where solar radiation is the most intense and constant.[13]

The variety of skin that not only has little pigment to begin with, but will not produce more on exposure to the sun (i.e., the kind that will not tan, but only burn) is confined to a small minority of the populations of Northern Europe and their migrating descendants. Why did this characteristic develop? Not, apparently, because it had any adaptive value over the kind of skin that tans; it was not, in other words, "selected for." Probably it was simply a trait that persisted despite its disadvantage because, in that climate of long winters and heavily clouded skies, its disadvantage was not lethal as it would have been in so many areas before cultural modes of adaptation came to supplement genetic modes.[14]

The "sickling gene," found chiefly in populations of Africa, the Middle East, and India, in areas where a particularly deadly form of malaria occurs, provides a somewhat different illustration of the adaptive value of genetic variables. An individual who inherits this gene from both parents will develop sickle-cell anemia, a disease normally fatal before adolescence. But a far greater number of people in the population inherit the gene from only one parent, develop only mild symptoms of the anemia, and are also likely to be highly resistant to certain virulent forms of malaria. In areas with a high incidence of malaria, the sickling gene clearly has adaptive value: its benefits to a population outweigh its costs.[15]

Most variable traits are not as easy to identify as the ones we have discussed so far. As we saw in Chapter 1, this is because most of our characteristics result from the action of more than one gene and, in addition, are not determined by genes alone. Genes provide the *potential*, but the reality is determined by the interaction of genes and environment. And environment includes that of the prenatal period, even the preconception experience of sperm and egg. This dual determinancy of genetics and environment has been dramatically illustrated many times, as in the case of Jewish children born in Israeli kibbutzim and Japanese children born in America who tower over parents born, respectively, in the ghettos of Europe and in Japan. It is clear that most biological characteristics, from longevity to musical aptitude, are shaped by both genes and environment. But efforts to separate the two and measure their relative influence have generally proved frustrating and unprofitable.

One thing has been clarified, however: the relation between racial and nonracial genetic variables. Studies have been made, for example, of color blindness and blood characteristics, which are variables that can be precisely identified and are minimally affected by environmental factors, and whose gene frequency in a population can therefore be precisely calculated. When the distributions of these genes are plotted geographically, they ignore the lines of the geographic races.[16] For example, the genes that cause various types of color blindness have similar frequencies among such racially dissimilar groups as the Japanese and Africans, or the Hindus and North Europeans.[17] The frequency of the gene for type B blood, meanwhile, is essentially the same in the gene pools of the South Chinese, the Russians, and the West Africans; and essentially the same in those of the East Africans, New Guineans, and many East European populations (see Figure 2.1).[18] Studies like these make it clear that the traits used to define race are an extremely limited set of variables that are not correlated to any appreciable degree with other genetic variables that have been carefully analyzed.

One study has, in fact, spelled out in precise terms just how weak this relationship is. It was based on evidence gathered from around the world on fifteen different blood-type systems (the Rh positive and negative system, the ABO system, and thirteen others). An analysis of the frequency with which

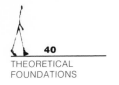

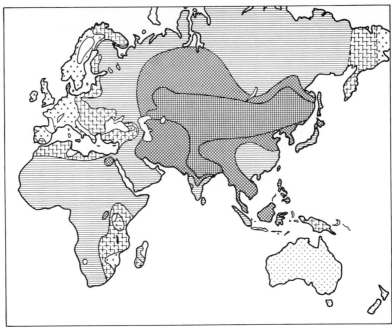

FIGURE 2.1   Distribution of type B blood: the gene responsible for this trait occurs with essentially the same frequency in populations in areas shown with the same pattern of markings.

these genes were distributed revealed that 84.4 per cent of the variance occurred within populations, 8.3 per cent between populations within the same race, and only 6.3 per cent between races.[19] With respect to these important characteristics, human populations differ very little from one another: far more variation exists *within* than between them. And as one prominent biologist recently remarked with respect to this study, there is no a priori reason to suppose that the distribution of genetic variables that are more difficult to study is very different.[20] In short, we apparently cannot look to genetic variables to explain most of the variations among human societies.

Demographic Variables   The demographic properties of a population include such things as its size; its overall density; how it is dispersed or concentrated (e.g., to what extent its members are concentrated in a few areas or spread out more evenly over its entire territory); the patterns of migration into and out of the society; its composition in terms of age and sex; and its birth and death rates. These characteristics, like certain clusters of genes, vary from one society to another. But these variations, unlike genetic variations, have clear, demonstrable, and far-reaching consequences for the lives of human societies.

Population size is by far the most variant demographic property: human societies range from twenty members or less (as in a number of societies of the recent past) to nearly a billion (as in China today). Variations in other demographic characteristics may appear insignificant in comparison. But appearances are sometimes deceptive. For example, two societies that have stable populations (i.e., neither growing in size nor declining) and annual death rates of 14 per 1,000 population and 40 per 1,000, respectively, may not seem so very far apart. But this seemingly modest variation means that the members of the first society have an average life span of seventy-one years, while the members of the second have an average of barely twenty-five!

In the chapters that lie ahead, we will have frequent occasion to consider the demographic variables indicated above. They have played an important part in the evolution of human societies. By contrast, we will have very little to say from here on about the genetic variables discussed in the previous section, since there is little to indicate that they have played a significant role in sociocultural evolution.

Culture

The second basic component of sociocultural systems is culture, *a society's symbol systems and the information they convey.* As we saw in Chapter 1,

FIGURE 2.2 Population pyramids of Mexico and the United States compared: the broad-based Mexican pyramid, reflecting the large proportion of young people, is typical of Third World nations today.

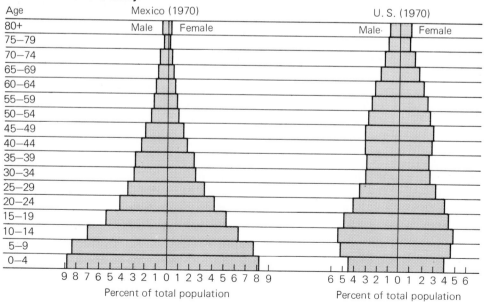

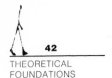
symbols are information conveyers that enable us to handle information in ways impossible for other creatures. We can *extract* more information from an experience (i.e., *learn* more), because symbols permit us thought processes denied other species. We can *share* more information, because symbols enable us to express so much of the subtlety, complexity, and diversity of our experiences. We can, in fact, do more with information *whatever* is involved: in recording it, accumulating it, storing it, combining it, or applying it, symbol users have a fantastic advantage over signal users.

The symbol systems and store of information that comprise a society's culture are like a foundation laid down by previous generations. Because each new generation has this base on which to build, it can avoid repeating some of the time consuming and less rewarding experiences of earlier generations. If the group has already learned the uses of fire, for example, or invented a plow, or devised a system of numbers, its members need not repeat the experiences by which the group acquired that particular element of culture. Rather, they can turn to new challenges and new experiences, which may result in further enrichment, or modification, of their culture.

We will examine both of the basic parts of culture in more detail, starting with symbol systems.

Symbol Systems   The most basic symbol system in any society is its *spoken language*. No matter how many other symbol systems a society may create, this remains the one with which its members develop their capacity for speech and are socialized, the one employed in their basic thought processes, and the one that bears the major burden of transmitting information among them.

At the heart of every spoken language is a mass of social conventions, or customary practices, that govern its vocabulary and its grammar. A vocabulary is a set of sounds with meanings attached to them, and the relationship between a sound and its meaning is embedded in the history of its use by those who share that language. To those who speak English, the word "bed" means a place to sleep, not because of any logical or necessary connection between the sound and the activity, but because this convention has been adopted by the members of English-speaking populations. Similarly, grammatical conventions tell us how words must be combined if they are to be meaningful and intelligible to those who use our vocabulary. It means one thing to say, "The bear ate Jack," something quite different to say, "Jack ate the bear," and nothing at all to say, "The ate bear Jack."

Unless we study a foreign language, most of us have the impression that there is something natural—even inevitable—about the way our own society and its language separate experience and thought into the bits of meaning we call words, and that learning another language is only a matter of learning the sounds another society applies to those same "units of experience." Yet as people conversant in two or more languages are well aware, words in one do not necessarily have an equivalent in the other. Americans and Russians were reminded of this some years ago during talks between President Kennedy and Chairman Khrushchev. Kennedy repeatedly said that the Russians should not miscalculate the will and intentions of the American people, and every time the word "miscalculate" was translated, Khrushchev flushed angrily. Kennedy later learned that the Russian language has no precise equivalent of this word, and the translator had seized on a Russian word, normally applied to a small child or uneducated person, meaning "unable to count." Khrushchev naturally assumed that Kennedy was implying he was not very bright![21]

One reason languages separate experience into different units is because the experiences of the people who *create and use* the languages are so different. For example, gauchos, the famous horsemen of the Argentine prairies, have 200 words to denote the different colors of horses, but only 4 for all the plants known to them: *pasto*, fodder; *paja*, bedding; *cardo*, wood; and *yuyos*, all others.[22] Meanwhile, the Eskimos have numerous terms to refer to the various phenomena that we call simply "snow." They have one word for dry-wind-driven snow, one for dry-packed-suitable-for-cutting-into-blocks-and-building-igloos snow, another for ice-crust-surface snow, and so on.[23] In yet another part of the world, the Dugum Dani, Stone Age horticulturists on the island of New Guinea, have seventy different words that refer to sweet potatoes, their staple crop;[24] and in the Middle East, Arabic is reputed to have a thousand words for sword, indicative of that culture's stress on poetry and emphasis on synonyms and figures of speech.[25] English is a language rich in numbers and units of measurement, perfect for describing and recording mathematical and scientific data. In short, language reflects the needs and concerns of those who use it.

Another reason languages differ in the way they categorize and classify experience is the haphazard and spontaneous manner in which they evolve. Consider the evolution of the word "bureau," for example. A bureau was originally something made of baize, a thick green cloth. Because these bureaus were usually put on writing tables and chests of drawers, the word was eventually extended to mean the furniture as well as the cloth. Later, because many government offices were equipped with bureaus, or writing tables, the offices themselves came to be known by that term (e.g., the Federal Bureau of Investigation).[26]

This process of change in language is so much a matter of chance that it is highly unlikely that the same pattern would occur in two societies. Even if two societies begin with the same language, as when a small group separates from the parent group to settle a new territory, linguistic differences are bound to develop unless there is a remarkably high level of communication between them. There is probably no better example of this in the modern era

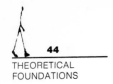
than in the differences between English as it is spoken in England, Australia, and America.*

So far we have talked about spoken language as if it were merely a neutral and passive vehicle for transmitting information. But as political leaders, propagandists, and advertisers have long recognized, individual words often acquire, through the process of association, powerful emotional connotations that enable them to convey a great deal of information beyond what is embodied in their formal definitions. A word like "communist," for example, has such strong negative associations for many Americans that they respond unthinkingly to the emotional content of the symbol. Words can also acquire strong positive associations, and these, too, may be used to manipulate emotions. For example, linking kinship terms with organizations or individuals, as in "Mother Russia," "Mother Church," or "Uncle Ho," can stimulate warm feelings of affection.

A leading linguist of the last generation, Edward Sapir, went so far as to claim that the way people perceive reality "is to a large extent unconsciously built upon the language habits of the group," and that as a result, different societies live in different worlds, "not merely the same world with different labels attached."[27] Though few scholars today would go this far, they recognize that language is more than a passive instrument of communication.[28] Language is, itself, part of our experience, and therefore it plays a part in determining what we feel, what we perceive, and what we do.

Supplementing the spoken language of every society is a repertoire of conventional gestures and facial expressions that are widely used and whose meanings are evident to members of the group. This "body language" should not be confused with the many facial expressions and body movements that are genetically determined, such as our involuntary reaction when we touch something hot, or the way we pucker up when we taste something bitter. True body language is symbolic, just as words are, for the form and meaning of the gestures and expressions are determined by those who use them. Consider, for example, the shrug of the shoulders. Americans, and a number of other peoples as well, use it to convey indifference, uncertainty, or a lack of information on the subject in question, with the specific meaning being indicated by the context in which it is used.

Body language may well be the oldest type of symbol used by our species, and it probably once played a relatively greater role in communication than it does today. Yet even now, it can be an invaluable means of transmitting information: people convey so much with a smile or frown, a tilt of the head, a movement of the hands. This is one reason many of us avoid

---

*Another interesting example is provided by the differences that are reported to be developing between East and West Germans. For an earlier period there are the differences that developed between the Saxons who settled in England and those who remained on the Continent. Because of the break in communication that developed, their speech is no longer mutually intelligible.

FIGURE 2.3   Two sides of a limestone tablet found in Mesopotamia, bearing some of the oldest known picture writing (about 3500 B.C.). Included are symbols for head, hand, foot, threshing sledge, and some numerals.

the telephone when we have an emotionally charged message to deliver. We know we can communicate our own feelings more effectively, and read those of others more clearly, when words, body language, and signals are all involved.

A third kind of symbol system in many societies is written language, a relatively recent development in human history. Archaeologists have determined that the first true written language was devised about five thousand years ago by temple authorities in Mesopotamia to enable them to keep a record of their business transactions.[29] These priests were stewards of their god's resources, and when they loaned out his animals or grain, it was imperative to get them back again. Even though the priest who made a loan might die, the god expected it to be recovered. To keep track of their god's property and thereby avoid incurring his wrath, the priestly community devised a primitive system of writing that involved a mixture of numerals, pictographs, and ideograms.

The arbitrary (i.e., symbolic) nature of this writing is clear. Even when a pictograph (essentially a picture) was used to represent a bull, it was a stylized representation that excluded many of the animal's features that might have been included. Moreover, the same features were used consistently, indicating that conventional forms of notation had already been established. Similarly, from a very early date, the pictograph of a jar came to represent a certain quantity of grain, rather than the jar itself. And finally, among these earliest examples of writing are a number of ideograms, which are "pure" symbols, in effect, for they are completely arbitrary and based solely on convention. They lack any visual similarity to the objects they represent (sheep, for example) just as our dollar sign bears no resemblance to the dollar.

As new uses for written records were discovered, new efforts were made to translate spoken language into this form. At an early date, kings and princes were recording their successes for posterity, priests their sacred rites

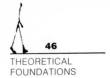

and traditions. At first, as the Mesopotamian priests' experience makes clear, a society's written symbols could express only a small part of what was possible with its verbal symbols. Gradually, however, written languages developed until they were capable of conveying the same information as spoken ones, and writing came into its own as a means of storing information, for communication across the barriers of space and time, and eventually as a medium of artistic expression, education, and entertainment.

As societies have acquired more information, it has frequently become necessary for them to expand their written languages beyond such basic symbols as alphabets and numerals. Thus, new symbol systems have evolved that greatly facilitate the handling of specialized kinds of information. For example, musicians devised musical notation so they could express the units of information that they create and use, and mathematicians and scientists developed a wide variety of symbol systems to use in studying or discussing abstract ideas, complex numbers, and so on. The specialized symbol systems now found in modern societies include languages for the deaf, the blind, engineers, stenographers, computer scientists, and others too numerous to mention.

Over the course of history, the relative importance of the three basic types of language—body, spoken, and written—has altered considerably. Body language, including symbolic gestures and facial expressions, may well have been dominant at a very early date, declining only when true speech evolved. Then, until quite recently, verbal symbols remained the primary means of transmitting information from one person to another and from one generation to the next. With the invention of the printing press and the subsequent spread of literacy, however, written language steadily increased in relative importance, largely because it could overcome space and time, the historic barriers to communication. During the last 100 years, thanks to such devices as the telephone, radio, motion pictures, and television, the spoken language, too, has overcome those barriers, altering the balance once again. And in the most recent, most dramatic development of all, a plethora of languages have been written for computers, enabling them to handle fantastic amounts of information of widely diverse kinds. More important than these vacillations in the relative importance of different types of language, however, is the fundamental trend that has persisted from early prehistoric times: *the human population has constantly expanded its capacity to handle information.*

Information Cultural information is *knowledge acquired through experience and conveyed through symbols.* A society's information is, in effect, a product of its experience: its experiences in the remote past, and in the recent past; its experiences with its environment, and with itself. Needless to say, no society's culture includes every thought of every member during its entire history. Rather, out of all the information that flows through its symbol systems, a society gleans what it considers valuable and attempts to preserve it.

Because every society has a unique past, every culture is unique. We can say this another way: out of diverse experience, diverse information emerges. What this means, of course, is that human societies not only have different amounts of information on a given subject; they frequently have different "facts" as well. Since we know that human senses and intellect are limited and fallible, this comes as no surprise. Even hard scientific "facts" established in modern societies must often be revised in the light of subsequent research.

Cultural information is not limited to the kind of ideas whose truth or accuracy is capable of being proved or disproved, however. Rather, it includes a group's total perception of reality: its ideas about what is real, what is true, what is good, what is beautiful, what is important, what is possible. When we discussed symbol systems, we saw that they, too, are so rooted in subjective experience that even individual symbols may be "units of experience"—which explains why a word like "mother" can be so emotionally charged. We also saw that the kind of information conveyed by symbol systems ranges from historical and statistical data to concepts of deity, attitudes toward horses (*and* plants), characteristics of snow, poetic inclinations, even music itself. Cultural information includes, quite literally, *everything humans are capable of experiencing and able to translate into symbolic form*.

Because all human societies have certain fundamental kinds of experiences in common, their cultures all include information on certain basic subjects:

1. Every culture has a substantial store of information about the biophysical environment to which the society must adapt, including its plant and animal life, soils and terrain, mineral resources and water supply, climate and weather conditions.
2. Every culture includes information about the social environment, the other human societies with which the group has contact.
3. Every culture contains information about the society itself: its origin, its people, its heroes, its history.
4. All cultures deal, however indirectly, with the basic philosophical question of the nature of reality—whether there is more to the world than is evident to human senses.
5. Every culture has a lot of what might best be called "coping" information: ideas and knowledge that help people solve their recurring problems, from feeding themselves to coping with intragroup conflict.

FIGURE 2.4 All cultures deal with the basic philosophical question of whether there is more to the world than is evident to human senses: dancers in Indonesia performing sacred dance drama of The Witch and The Dragon.

6.   Every culture contains information that enables individuals to make judgments about what is good and what is right and what is beautiful.

7.   All cultures have information created solely to satisfy culturally activated and intensified needs, such as the desire for artistic expression, for example, or for ritual.

Although this list is neither exhaustive nor detailed, it conveys something of the breadth of culture.

A great deal of the information in several of the categories above is ideological information. This includes ideas, thoughts, knowledge, and beliefs that keep individuals and society "on the track." For *ideology* is *information that is used to interpret experience and order social life.*

Ideology can be thought of as information that results from human efforts to make sense out of human experience.[30] Because we are users of symbols and creatures of culture, life can be overwhelming. We think, feel, hope, enjoy, and suffer as no other creatures can. We imagine what we cannot know and yearn for what may not exist. We live simultaneously in three worlds: the past, the present, and the future. We alone, apparently, live out our lives aware that death is inevitable. To complicate things further, we create for ourselves a profusion of cultural alternatives, in the face of which our genetic heritage is an inadequate guide. It is not surprising, therefore, that, as individuals, we need help in interpreting experience, finding meaning, and making choices. And, as we have seen, social systems require help in regulating and ordering our collective life.

Medieval Christianity is a good example of a highly developed and comprehensive ideology, the kind that satisfies virtually all these individual and societal needs.* At its center was a vision of a universe inhabited by various kinds of spiritual beings (seraphim, cherubim, humans, demons, devils, etc.) mostly under the dominion of God. God was perceived as the King above all earthly kings, but because His authority was challenged by Satan, the prince of darkness, people were confronted with a choice as to which to serve. Those who chose God (who would ultimately prevail) were obliged to subscribe to the Church's doctrines and conform to its code of morality. The latter enjoined Christians to be charitable to one another, honest, sober, hardworking, monogamous (better yet, celibate), obedient to all in authority, and regular in devotions and worship. Since no one could adhere perfectly to these requirements, the Church provided opportunities for people to confess their sins, do penance, and obtain absolution.

When we look closely at medieval Christianity, we find the three basic elements that comprise *every* ideology. First, there is a system of *beliefs* about the kind of world we inhabit. Second, there is a system of generalized *moral values* that emanate from, or are justified by, those beliefs. Finally, there is a system of *norms* that apply those general values to specific situations and spell out how the members of the group are to act in various circumstances, what they should and should not do.

There are two basic kinds of norms in every society. Some of them are part of official or legal codes of behavior that are systematically enforced by an authority, such as a government, a religious body, or other kind of organization. These norms are what we usually refer to as *laws*, *regulations*, or simply *rules*, and they are sometimes accompanied by more or less explicit statements of the sanctions that will be used to punish those who violate them. (A city ordinance, for example, may set a fine of $25 for littering streets or sidewalks.) In contrast, other norms are less formal, less official, and violations of them are less likely to be heavily or officially sanctioned. Thus, every society and every subgroup in a society, from the U.S. Senate to a family, has numerous informal rules, or customs, which are, in effect, the group's definition of desirable or acceptable behavior. They may apply to such diverse things as modes of dress, hairstyles, food preparation, the selection of marriage partners, the performance of various tasks, proper

*Marxism is an example of a well-developed and comprehensive *non*theistic ideology. Some ideologies, such as capitalism, do not attempt to address themselves to more than certain limited facets of human life.

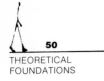
grammar, and attitudes toward children or older people—to name only a few. These nonlegal norms are as important in shaping behavior as legal norms.

As we saw on page 36, norms and their related sanctions (i.e., rewards and punishments) are the two components of every system of social control. This suggests why ideology can be such a danger politically. The leaders of a society already possess the powers of the machinery of state, thus enabling them to alter the legal norms, punish their enemies, and reward their friends. When *moral* authority is also conferred on them, the most powerful means of social control are all concentrated in the hands of only a few individuals.

Another fundamental body of information in every culture is *technology*. This is *information about the utilization of the material resources of the environment to satisfy human needs*. Compared to ideology, technology may seem to be a rather prosaic and uninteresting subject. Historians and social scientists have tended to ignore it,[31] and people have seldom come to blows over the relative merits of different technologies (though this is beginning to change). As we will see in the next chapter, however, the influence of technological information on the course of history and on the process of societal change and development has been all out of proportion to the recognition accorded it.

In every society, a large component of technological information concerns food: where and how to get it and how to process it for consumption or storage. There is also information about the other material resources available to the society and how they may be converted into useful forms—into fuel for heat, cooking, and other purposes; into clothing and shelter; into tools, weapons, ornaments, and other things the group needs or values.

Because a distinctive body of information tends to build up in response to each set of human needs, we sometimes speak of the subsistence technology of a society, or its military technology, or its communications technology. More often, however, we speak of a society's technology in the singular, because there is an underlying unity to this store of information. The principles of metallurgy, for example, are used in virtually every area of technological activity in a modern industrial society, and the same is true of other basic kinds of information.

3 • Material Products

The third component of sociocultural systems consists of material products, the result of the use of technological information to convert environmental resources into things societies' members need or want. These range from perishable items that are consumed within hours of production (such as certain foods) to things that may endure for centuries, such as pyramids, cathedrals, and plastic containers. They range, too, from purely utilitarian objects like hammers, bombs, and gasoline to nonessential or frivolous items like jewelry or Frisbees. And they include products, such as works of art, whose significance may persist beyond a single generation or extend beyond a single society.

A society's most important material products are its *capital goods*. This term refers to a society's accumulated goods that are devoted to the production of more goods. Thus, the more capital goods a society possesses, the more goods of various kinds it is able to produce, and the wealthier it tends to become (i.e., "the rich get richer").

The first capital goods were simple tools made of stone, wood, and bone, which enabled our ancestors to produce such essentials as fire, food, shelter, and more tools. Later, as the store of cultural information increased and as new environmental resources became available, the character of tools changed. Metals were especially important in this respect because they combined strength and durability with malleability. This culminated in the last 200 years in the production of the kinds of capital goods that are vital in modern industrial societies: machines and instruments of many kinds, railroads, motorized vehicles, electrical power systems, factory complexes, and so forth.

Early in human history another environmental resource was gradually transformed by human societies into what we might call *living* capital: domesticated animals. Their contribution to production has been crucial in every society which depended upon oxen or horses to pull plows and wagons, cattle or goats to provide milk and cheese, or sheep to provide wool. Domesticated animals have often been a society's primary capital investment and its medium of exchange as well. This was true, for example, in ancient Greece and Rome. Our word "pecuniary," which means "relating to money," derives from *pecus*, Latin for cattle.

As the mention of plows and wagons indicates, energy is a critical factor in production. In fact, energy production is the most fundamental activity in every human society. For in producing food, a society produces the energy that underlies every physical or mental activity of its members. No society can survive without a steady input of energy, and every social and cultural activity beyond mere survival requires an additional input. Thus, information about new sources of energy or new ways of increasing the flow of energy has always been of particular importance.

Social Structure

The fourth basic component of sociocultural systems is social structure. This refers to *the network of relationships among the members of a society*. These relationships make it possible for the members to satisfy their own individual needs as well as the system-needs of the society.

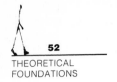

The kinds of relationships found in human societies are, to some extent, biologically determined. Social relationships in all mammalian societies, for example, are organized to take account of age and sex differences. Human societies, however, do not stop there. In most instances, they go much further, developing elaborate kinship networks and other complex social arrangements that reflect cultural influences. Thus, as we think about social structure in human societies, we should view it as an organizational and behavioral product of the interaction of culture and genetics.

Individuals　The two basic building blocks in every social structure are the individuals who make up the society and the roles they fill. Little need be added to what we have already said concerning the nature of individuals. Each person embodies a genetic heritage that is partly distinctive and partly shared, and each embodies a cultural heritage that is also partly distinctive and partly shared. From society's standpoint this is sometimes an asset and sometimes a liability. On the one hand, it ensures a high rate of individuality as a consequence of ever new recombinations of genetic and cultural elements in a single individual. This can have great adaptive value for a group, especially when it is confronted with new circumstances to which it must adjust. On the other hand, intragroup conflict results from this individuality, as we have seen. Whatever else we say about the members of human societies, however, we cannot say they are merely interchangeable cogs in a social machine.

Roles　The term *role* means in sociology the same thing it means in the theater—*a position that can be filled by an individual and that has certain distinctive behavioral requirements and expectations attached to it.*[32] Thus, just as a man may play the role of Macbeth on the stage, so he may "play" the roles of husband, father, and doctor in his home and community. In both instances, he finds that people expect him to act in certain ways, and not in others, simply because of the role he is occupying. If he fails to live up to their expectations—if he flubs his lines, for example, or neglects his family or patients—he will probably receive criticism, censure, or other penalties. The audience may boo him, his wife and patients leave him. On the other hand, if he fulfills the requirements of his roles and satisfies people's expectations of him, he will probably be applauded, loved, and well paid.

The behavioral requirements and expectations that are attached to "real life" roles are nothing other than the norms we discussed on pages 36 and 49. As we saw in our earlier discussion, norms may be extremely formal, as in the case of laws regarding murder or embezzlement, for example, or quite informal, as in the case of a neighborhood's expectations concerning property maintenance. Some norms involve fundamental moral issues; others deal with matters of mere etiquette. Some norms are so limited in scope that they apply only to the incumbents of a single, highly specialized role (e.g., only priests are expected to say the Mass), while others apply to a broad spectrum of roles (e.g., loyalty is expected of the incumbents of virtually every role).

Real life, unlike the stage, normally demands that an individual fill a number of roles simultaneously. This does not necessarily present a problem. A young woman, for example, may easily combine the roles of daughter, sister, niece, friend, college student, church member, and citizen. Later, however, when she tries to coordinate the requirements and expectations of new roles, such as wife, mother, and career woman, role conflict may well become a serious problem.

In a situation like this, an individual has several options. The first is to continue in the conflicting roles, disregarding or violating the norms of one or more of them and hoping that the penalties will not be too severe. A second option is to abandon one of the roles. The woman could give up her job, for example; or she might file for divorce, though that would probably do little to resolve her basic role conflict. A third possibility is to try to alter the norms attached to one of the roles so that it is more compatible with the others. Thus, the young woman might try to get some change made in her work assignment, or she might attempt to change her husband's and children's expectations of her, perhaps by altering their definition of the role of "mother" to mean a person who *shares* responsibilities for the care of children with a father. Her chances of success in changing her own family's definition of the role would obviously be influenced by developments in other families, since expectations for a role such as mother tend to develop on a societywide basis.

The options mentioned above are not available in every instance of role conflict. For example, it is sometimes virtually impossible to abandon a role. This is especially true in the case of *ascribed* roles, which are roles that are assigned us with little or no choice on our part. In every society, every individual has an age role and a sex role, and in many societies a racial or an ethnic role as well. (There are no racial or ethnic roles in societies where everyone is of the same racial or ethnic stock.) Thus, in American society, one is an adolescent white female, for example, or an elderly black male, or a middle-aged Chicano, whether one likes one's roles, and the expectations associated with them, or not. People sometimes try to change ascribed roles, as in the case of an older man who darkens his hair and understates his age, or a transvestite who misrepresents her sex. But deceptions involving ascribed roles are fraught with the risk of serious embarrassment, or worse, if they are discovered.

Redefining a role's requirements and expectations may also be impossible or, at best, extremely difficult. The reason is clear in the example we cited: changing the norms attached to the mother's role would simultaneously alter

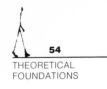
the norms attached to the father's. In short, every individual has a vested interest in minimizing the costs and maximizing the benefits of the roles he or she occupies, and any efforts to shift responsibilities (through redefining a role or simply through neglecting its obligations) naturally engender resistance. For roles are not isolated entities: they are elements in the complex web of social relationships that form the social structure of a society.

Roles serve many functions in societies, but four are of crucial importance. First, roles encourage specialization, which tends to increase the efficiency of human effort. Second, role specialization has an integrative effect: when people divide up the tasks necessary to their survival and well-being, they become more dependent on one another. Third, roles are a mechanism of social control: they harness people's energies to tasks that the group as a whole, or its more powerful members, regard as necessary and desirable. Fourth, roles are a mechanism for transmitting traditions from one generation to the next: individuals die, or leave the group for other reasons, but roles are not mortal. They can persist indefinitely. The role of rabbi, for example, has existed for over 2,500 years, contributing immeasurably to the survival of the Jewish group and to the preservation of its cultural heritage.

Groups In most societies, the members are divided into a variety of units we call groups. These range from small family groups and cliques to giant corporate entities of various kinds. In popular usage, the term "group" is sometimes applied indiscriminately to any aggregation of people, regardless of their other characteristics. Sociologists, however, limit the term to *an aggregation whose members (1) act together in a common effort to satisfy common, or complementary, needs, (2) have common norms, and (3) have a sense of common identity.**

As this definition suggests, human aggregations differ in their *degree* of "groupishness." Though some aggregations clearly qualify as groups (e.g., Jehovah's Witnesses) and others just as clearly do not (e.g., all the redheads in the United States), many are on the borderline (e.g., Americans of Irish descent). This last example reminds us that the degree of "groupishness" of an aggregation is not permanently fixed. Aggregations may take on more of the qualities of a group, or they may lose some. Their members may come to work together more closely; develop new, stronger, and more generally shared norms; and acquire a stronger sense of common identity; or just the opposite may occur, as happened with Irish-Americans during the last hundred years.

Despite the exclusion of aggregations such as redheads, the concept "group" still includes such a wide variety of organizations that it is necessary to differentiate among them. The most familiar way is by their basic functions.

*The term "group" may also be used to refer to a society, as the definition above indicates; in this section, however, we are concerned with the *internal* structure of societies.

Thus, we differentiate between families, churches, schools, political parties, and so forth.

Sociologists have also found it useful to differentiate among groups on the basis of their size and the intensity of the social ties among their members. Small groups in which there are face-to-face relations of a fairly intimate and personal nature are known as *primary groups*. Larger, more impersonal groups are known as *secondary groups*. Primary groups are of two basic types, *families* and *cliques*. In other words, they are organized around ties of either kinship or friendship. Secondary groups are also of two basic types, associations and communities. An *association* is a formally organized secondary group that performs some relatively specialized function or set of functions. Political parties, churches, labor unions, corporations, and governmental agencies are familiar examples. *Communities*, by contrast, are less formally organized and perform a wider range of functions.

Basically, there are two types of communities, geographical and cultural. *Geographical communities* are those whose members are united primarily by ties of spatial proximity, such as neighborhoods, villages, towns, and cities. *Cultural communities* are those whose members are united by ties of a common cultural tradition, such as racial and ethnic groups. A religious group may also be considered a cultural community if its members are closely integrated by ties of kinship and marriage and if the group has developed a distinctive subculture of its own.

As this last example indicates, associations may give rise to communities. The opposite can also happen: communities can give rise to associations. For example, in the 1960s, black militant associations emerged from black neighborhoods. When either of these possibilities is realized, the membership of the community and the membership of the association overlap to some extent. Usually, however, the community is larger because its membership requirements are less stringent (often membership is automatic by virtue of birth).

In addition to associations and communities, there are several other types of secondary groups, but the most important are *social and political*

FIGURE 2.5 Types of human groups.

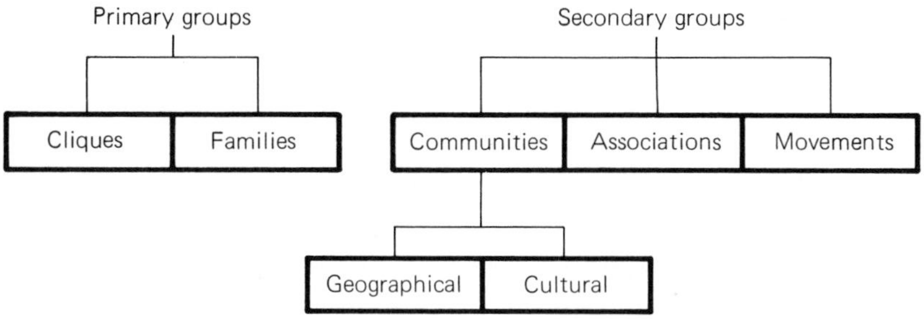

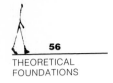

movements. These are loose-knit groups that hope to change the existing social order in some way. If such a group is successful in developing a following, a more tightly organized association is usually formed, and this becomes the nucleus of the movement. A good example is the rise and spread of the socialist movement in nineteenth-century Europe, with socialist parties eventually being established in most countries.

Statuses Up to this point in our discussion of social structure, we have considered only the *horizontal* dimension of societies, the functional differences between roles and between groups. There is a second dimension, however—a *vertical* dimension. Individuals, roles, and groups can be ranked in a variety of ways, such as by income, wealth, or education. This ranking is the *status* of the unit in the society. Sociologists are especially concerned with statuses that reflect the power, privilege, or prestige of units, since these are extremely important in the life of societies.

As a rule, the various statuses of a unit are fairly consistent. People who are wealthy and well educated, for example, also tend to be powerful and to have considerable prestige. There are exceptions, however, and these are often interesting and important. A leader of the Mafia, for example, may enjoy great power and wealth in the community at large but have little prestige except in the Mafia itself. Or a member of an ethnic minority who has low status in that role may enjoy high status in the occupational system. A person, a role, or a group exhibiting such characteristics is said to have *inconsistent status.*

The status of a unit often changes with the passage of time. When this occurs, the unit is said to be *upwardly mobile* or *downwardly mobile.* For example, when an individual is promoted, he or she is upwardly mobile; when a family fortune is dissipated, the family is downwardly mobile.

Classes The term *class* is used in two different, though related, ways.[33] Sometimes it refers to an aggregation or group of people whose *overall* status is fairly similar. In this case, we usually speak of upper, middle, and lower classes; or, if we divide the hierarchy more narrowly, of upper-middle, lower-middle, and so on.

"Class" can also be applied to an aggregation or group of people who are in a similar position with respect to some specific resource that affects their access to power, privilege, or prestige. These resources include wealth, education, occupation, political position, and so on. This usage of the concept is generally more precise and less ambiguous than when it is used to refer to middle, upper, and lower classes. It permits us to identify such specific entities as the managerial class, the working class, the governing class, and the propertied class, for example, and to refer to the nobility and peasantry of the past or the rich and poor of contemporary societies.

One question that arises at this point is whether classes are groups. The answer is both yes and no. In many instances, classes are simply aggregates whose members, though in a similar position with respect to some important resource, have no sense of common identity, have no common behavioral expectations, and do not act together to satisfy common, or complementary, needs. This is true, for example, of American office workers, a rapidly growing occupational class. On the other hand, American blacks, a racial-ethnic class, *are* a group: they have long been a cultural community with a strong sense of common identity.

Taken together, all the classes of a given type (e.g., all the occupational classes in a society) form what is known as *a class system*. And all the class systems of a society taken together (e.g., the occupational system, the racial-ethnic system, and the wealth system) form what sociologists have come to call *a system of stratification*. The basic function of such systems is to distribute the things of value that people produce through the relationships they form with one another. These "valuables" include not only *material products* but, equally important, *services* (e.g., education and medical care) and *psychic gratifications* (e.g., prestige and popularity).

Because no society has yet been able to produce enough of all these things to satisfy fully the needs and desires of every individual, systems of stratification often generate serious conflict among the members of a society. This problem is impossible to resolve to everyone's satisfaction, because there is no obviously "right" way to distribute things that are produced by the cooperative actions or efforts of many different people. It is equally reasonable to argue, for example, that a given product should be distributed on the basis of (1) how much a person needs it, (2) how much effort a person put into producing it, or (3) how much skill a person contributed, to name only three possibilities.

Even if the group settles on one of these principles, disputes are still likely. If the members apply the principle of effort, for example, they must still decide how to measure it. Should it be calculated by the hours spent on the job, by the foot-pounds of energy expended, or by how hard a person tries? Or, if the group adopts a different criterion, how do they measure such dissimilar skills as those of a nurse, a statesman, and a computer programmer? In brief, there is no simple way, no one "right" way, to handle distribution in human societies, and arbitrary standards are inevitable. But arbitrary or not, fair or not, there must *be* standards. Given our natural tendency to put the satisfaction of our own needs and those of our immediate families ahead of other people's, the only alternative is anarchy.

Not surprisingly, the subject of social stratification and inequality has given rise to one of the major controversies in modern sociology.[34] The issue is whether distributive systems develop in response to the needs and requirements of society as a whole or in response to the power of elite

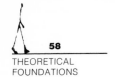

groups within society. One school of sociologists stresses the inevitability of inequality, sometimes arguing that inequality is needed to motivate the abler members of society to seek the more important positions, sometimes arguing the social necessity of unequal authority. A second group argues that most inequality is simply the result of force and fraud on the part of the more powerful and clever. A third group sees elements of truth in both views and tries to synthesize them. Though we cannot hope to resolve this controversy here, there will be materials in later chapters that should help readers form their own views on the subject.

Conclusion   By way of conclusion, we can say that social structures are built on two principles: (1) the principle of the division of labor and (2) the principle of stratification. Because it is more efficient and more rewarding for the members of a society to divide up the tasks that are necessary for their survival and well-being, a system of functionally differentiated roles and groups gradually evolves. But as this process of *functional* differentiation takes place, it is accompanied by a process of *status* differentiation. Thus, individuals, roles, and groups come to be differentiated in terms of status as well as in terms of the functions they perform. This, in turn, leads to the formation of classes. In some human societies, these possibilities have been realized in only the most limited way, but in others, social structures have become immensely complex.

REASSEMBLING THE SYSTEM

When we began this chapter, we observed that a system is not so much a matter of parts per se as of *relationships among parts*. Thus, although it is necessary to separate the parts of a system in order to study them, as we have done in this chapter, it is important to remember that they do not normally exist except in relation with one another. We must not, in other words, become so intrigued with the components that we lose sight of the system.

Strange as it may seem, this can happen. Modern scientists have frequently been content merely to dismantle and dissect systems (biological, social, and other varieties), in the apparent belief that this would ultimately tell them everything they want to know. In his book *So Human An Animal*, the distinguished biologist René Dubos maintains that the philosophical heroes of modern science have been Democritus and Descartes, both of whom "taught that the way to knowledge is to separate substances and events into their ultimate components and reactions."[35] According to Dubos, this process, known as *reductionism*, leads the scientist

> . . . to become so involved intellectually and emotionally in the elementary fragments of the system and in the analytical process itself, that he commonly

loses interest in the phenomena or the organisms which had been his first concern. For example, the biologist who starts with a question formulated because of its relevance to human life is tempted, and indeed expected, to progress seriatim to the organ or function involved, then to the single cell, then to subcellular fragments, then to molecular groupings or reactions, then to the individual molecules and atoms. He would happily proceed, if he knew how to do it, until he reached the ultimate aspects of nature in which matter and energy become indistinguishable.[36]

Maintaining that this has been a profound mistake, Dubos argues that:

The most pressing problems of humanity . . . involve . . . situations in which systems must be studied as a whole in all the complexity of their interactions. This is particularly true of human life. When life is considered only in its specialized functions, the outcome is a world emptied of meaning.[37]

Dubos goes on to say that to be fully relevant to life, the biological sciences must deal with the responses of total biotic systems to their total environments.

Dubos's advice, though aimed at biological scientists, is equally applicable to social scientists. It is easy for us, too, to become so absorbed in "the elementary fragments of the system"—individuals, roles, symbols, norms, classes, and all the rest—that we neglect sociocultural systems themselves. To say this is not to minimize the importance of understanding these components. It only means that we cannot stop with them. We must "reassemble the system" and turn to the study of *total* societies in their *total* environments. And this leads us directly to the subject of sociocultural evolution.

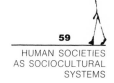

CHAPTER 3 SOCIOCULTURAL EVOLUTION

Approximately 3.5 billion years ago, a bit of cell-like material apparently crossed the threshold between life and nonlife. From its remote origins in the sea, life spread into increasingly diverse environments—on the earth's surface, beneath it, and in the air. In the process of relating to their dissimilar environments, living things developed a fascinating variety of attributes, including mechanisms to utilize energy sources, communicate, reproduce, and defend themselves. One of these mechanisms is social organization, and this, too, varies greatly among species. All this diversification was accomplished through the process of biological evolution.*

Our species, too, is a product of biological evolution, and still subject to its operation. But genetic change can occur only slowly in organisms with a generation span as long as ours. For at least 35,000 years, in fact, our species has experienced no genetic change that has significantly altered its mode of relating to the environment.[2]

And yet, during that time our species has developed capabilities and

---

*More than 1 million living species of animals, and more than 300,000 plants, have already been identified. It is believed that, as knowledge of the earth's flora and fauna grow, twice these numbers will be recognized.[1]

adaptive mechanisms that are remarkably like those produced by major genetic changes. What is more, these "new traits" vary *within* our species the way genetic traits vary only *among* species. We live in almost every kind of terrestrial environment, burrow into the earth, probe the ocean's depths, and soar into space. We utilize highly varied resources, communicate by a variety of methods, and protect ourselves in amazingly dissimilar ways. We possess more strength and speed, heavier armament, and deadlier poison than any other species, and we have even created nonliving things—machines—that perform some of the functions of our own bodies. We live in very small, simple social organizations, and we live in extremely large, complex, and behaviorally differentiated ones.

What has happened to our species is called *sociocultural evolution*, a process as important to an understanding of human societies as biological evolution is to an understanding of plants and animals.

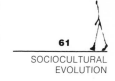

BIOLOGICAL AND SOCIOCULTURAL EVOLUTION COMPARED

There is probably no better way to begin the study of sociocultural evolution than by asking how it is related to biological evolution. In what ways do the two processes resemble one another? How do they differ?

Sociocultural evolution, like biological, is a process of gradual change and development that is based on experience. The two forms of evolution are not different facets of a single phenomenon, of course, but separate and distinct processes. Their study requires different training, focuses on different materials, and uses different methods—which is why the biological and social sciences have developed largely independently of one another.

At the same time, there are important links between the two modes of evolution. As we have seen, biological evolution produced the species, Homo sapiens, that creates and uses symbol systems to build cultures. Thus, in a sense, sociocultural systems, and their evolution as well, are *products* of biological evolution.

But something more links sociocultural evolution to biological evolution: a fundamental similarity in the way they operate. This similarity has become evident only in recent years and is a fascinating subject in its own right. We are concerned with it here, however, only because of the light it can shed on human societies and their development. And it can shed a great deal. For this similarity provides the key to the riddle of how our species accomplished such drastic change in such a short span of time.

Basic Similarities

The most fundamental similarity between the process of biological evolution and the process of sociocultural evolution is that *both are based on systems of coded information*. This fascinating parallel between the biotic world and the

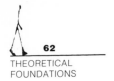

cultural world has become evident only during the last several decades. Although biologists used the concept "gene" to refer to the basic unit of heredity as long ago as the 1860s, they had no idea what a gene actually was. Now, however, geneticists have determined that a gene is composed of minute bits of deoxyribonucleic acid (DNA), a chemical molecule structured as a helical chain from four nucleotide bases. The DNA of every species is made up of only these four components, and yet, because they are capable of such varied and complex combinations, they can form an infinite number of unlike genes.[3] In other words, these nucleotides (adenine, thymine, guanine, and cytosine, which geneticists refer to as A, T, G, and C) are very much like human symbol systems—our alphabet, for example, or the Morse code, which with only *two* components can be used to convey virtually unlimited amounts of information. With those four nucleotides, a fantastic amount of information is recorded in *genetic code* within the cells of every living thing, and it is this which is translated into the chemical "messages" that guide and control an organism's development and behavior.*

The four letters of the genetic alphabet have, to paraphrase a noted geneticist, written all the words and all the sentences that comprise billions of years of biological history.[5] During much of that time, this was the *only* form in which information was available to living things. Then, as we saw on page 16, some species acquired the ability to *learn* : drawing on individual experience, they could obtain information beyond what was genetically programmed in them, and store this new information in memory systems by means of electrochemical codes. Later, some of these species became genetically structured in such a way that they could *communicate* what they learned with others of their kind, using coded information in the form of signals. But because genes control both the basic form and meaning of signals, the scope and usefulness of signaled information was greatly restricted.

Finally, a species evolved that could create and use symbol systems and, in so doing, attained a potential for adaptive change without parallel in the biotic world. The explanation of this lies in the fact that symbol systems are *like* the genetic alphabet in their capacity for handling an unlimited amount and variety of information; but symbols and their meanings, *un*like the genetic alphabet, are determined by humans themselves, and not by natural forces over which we have no control.

We can pull all this together by saying, first of all, that both the genetic alphabet and symbol systems provide a population with the means of acquiring, storing, transmitting, and using information; and, second, that both are mechanisms through which change occurs in a population. In brief, *symbol systems are the functional equivalent of the genetic alphabet.*

It should hardly be surprising, then, that the two evolutions operate in

---

*A single human sex cell, for example, is conjectured to contain between 10,000 and 100,000 information-laden genes.[4]

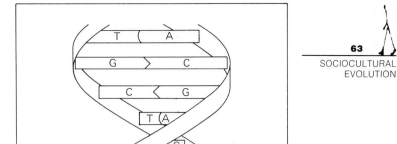

FIGURE 3.1 Symbol systems are the functional analogue of the genetic alphabet. Both provide the means for acquiring, storing, transmitting, and using information, and both are mechanisms through which change occurs in a population. The Greek alphabet and the structure of the DNA molecule.

comparable ways and produce comparable results. First of all, both involve the interaction of populations and their environments. We saw in Chapter 1 that this is what shapes genetic evolution. And in Chapter 2 we saw that it is through precisely this same population-environment interaction that social and cultural change is produced.

Second, both evolutions have produced comparable results. Biological evolution has meant an incredible increase in genetic information. This is evident whether we compare the simplest organisms with the most complex (the genes of the simplest known virus, for example, hold only one-millionth as much information as a human's[6]) or compare the era when life was new on this planet with the diversity and variety of life today. One biologist summed it up by declaring that genetic codebooks have gradually evolved from little notebooks to multivolume encyclopedias.[7]

The pattern is strikingly similar in sociocultural evolution. We see this when we compare the simplest contemporary societies with advanced industrial nations. And we see it when we turn from this present age of social and cultural diversity and complexity to that era hundreds of thousands of years ago when every human society was a small band of nomadic hunters and gatherers with relatively little to distinguish it from other human societies—or, for that matter, from the societies of other anthropoids.

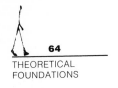

Furthermore, our species has responded in the course of its sociocultural evolution very much the way species respond when they acquire new *genetic* information—by displaying new behavioral capabilities, moving into new environments, using previously unused materials, and, in the process, altering the environment. In summary, evolution, whether biological or sociocultural, involves *an increase in information.*[8]

Basic Differences

Perhaps the most important difference between the two modes of evolution is the way information is transferred and spread. The only way genetic information can be transmitted is through the process of reproduction.* Because different species cannot interbreed, they cannot share genetic information with one another.† Thus, biological evolution is characterized by continued differentiation and diversification, a process biologists often compare to the branching of a tree or shrub. Cultural information, by contrast, is easily exchanged between the members of different sociocultural systems. Not only can human societies exchange information, but two or more can merge into a single system—the equivalent, were it possible, of the merging of separate species in biological evolution. Thus, sociocultural evolution is likely to eventuate in fewer and less dissimilar societies than exist today.

A second basic difference involves a population's ability to incorporate into heritable form the useful information its members have acquired through the process of individual learning. In sociocultural systems, this is easily done; it is, in fact, the basis of their evolution. But it has no counterpart in biological evolution. Actually, most biologists prior to Darwin believed that something analogous *did* occur in the biotic world. Jean Baptiste Lamarck argued that if an organism continually repeats a certain behavior, not only will this produce structural change in the organism, but the change will be inherited by its offspring.[10] It has long since been clear that biological evolution does not work that way: giraffes do not have long necks because their ancestors stretched day after day to reach high leaves, but because long necks were such an asset in their ancestors' environment that the genes responsible for long necks were selected for. In the cultural world, however, a kind of Lamarckian evolution does occur. Just about anything a population learns and considers worth preserving can be incorporated into its sociocultural heritage.

Springing from the easy flow of cultural information among societies and the ease with which it is incorporated into heritable form is yet another way in

*A group of researchers at the National Cancer Institute has recently claimed that viruses have occasionally been responsible for transferring genetic material from one species to another, but this is still highly speculative.[9]

†Closely related species do occasionally interbreed, as when lions and tigers produce "ligers" or "tiglons." Hybrids are usually sterile, however, at least in the animal kingdom, and therefore their importance in the total process of biological evolution has been minor.

which sociocultural evolution differs from biological: it has a capacity for much higher rates of change. An evolution whose mechanism is genetic change is necessarily a slow process in a species like ours that has a long generation span and relatively few offspring. But sociocultural information, relative to genetic, can be rapidly acquired, exchanged, recombined, and accumulated; and substantial alterations in a group's culture are possible within a single generation. Moreover, sociocultural evolution does not require that every society go through step-by-step sequential stages of development, which are the essence of biological evolution. Rather, societies may compress or even skip stages. In the Third World today, for example, some nations have gone directly from human porters and pack animals to trucks and airplanes as the primary movers of goods, largely bypassing the stage of dependency on wagons and railroads that was part of the evolutionary experience of those societies in which these methods of transportation were first developed.

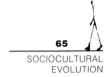

Yet another important difference involves the conditions under which major evolutionary change occurs. In the biotic world, most *major* change happens during the process of speciation (see page 13), which depends on a population being reproductively isolated and therefore not in a position to receive new information from other populations. By contrast, human societies that are isolated almost invariably experience a *low* rate of cultural change. In short, isolation tends to have opposite effects in the two modes of evolution.

Finally, sociocultural evolution, unlike biological, has a potential for being at least partially controlled by the species that experiences it. Up to this point in history, however, the developmental process of human societies has been largely accidental and unplanned. One of the most urgent tasks of this century is to improve our understanding of sociocultural evolution and to find means of bringing the process under rational control.

INFORMATION IN SOCIOCULTURAL EVOLUTION

Evolution, whether biological or sociocultural, depends on an increase in information—genetic in the one case, cultural in the other. But what *kind* of cultural information? Have all varieties been equally important? Or have some been more important than others in shaping the basic patterns of societal development and change? To answer this question, we must turn to the historical record.

Basic Historical Trends in Sociocultural Systems

Although there are still many unanswered questions about the origin and early history of our species, on a number of essential points there is virtually no doubt. To begin with, prior to the last 10,000 years, all human societies

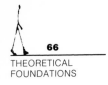

obtained their food by hunting wild animals and foraging for wild fruits and vegetables.* Tools and weapons were made of wood, stone, bone, or other materials that were readily available in the environment. Populations were invariably small: they probably averaged only a few dozen people and seldom if ever was one larger than a few hundred. Societies rarely remained long in one location; typically, they moved every few weeks or months as the supply of game and other resources in the immediate area was depleted. With so few people and such primitive conditions, social structures were simple, except possibly for kinship systems.

As human societies spread out over more of the earth, they encountered new environmental challenges and new resources, and gradually diversified. In cold regions, for example, societies might respond by appropriating the skins of animals or by using branches and skins to construct shelter. Differences in language also evolved, as well as variations in norms, values, and beliefs. But there was little change in the fundamental characteristics of human societies: they all remained small, structurally simple, and dependent on the most readily available resources of their immediate environments.

Then, about nine or ten thousand years ago, a number of societies in what is now the Middle East mastered the techniques of plant cultivation and animal domestication and things began to change.† Populations grew in size and in density, settlements became more permanent, material goods accumulated, and social structures became more complex. The first urban communities appeared during this period and, although small by modern standards (the largest had only a few thousand people), they were enormous by the standards of their day. The most striking thing about these urban settlements, however, was the fact that many of their inhabitants were not involved in producing their own food. Instead, for the first time in human history, people were engaging in a variety of specialized occupations and satisfying their subsistence needs by bartering with neighboring farmers.

The most revolutionary consequences of all, however, were for technology itself. These initial innovations—plant cultivation and animal domestication—created a set of social conditions and an informational foundation that resulted in a rapid succession of further innovations. Within 5,000 years, Middle Eastern societies had discovered the basic principles of metallurgy, invented the plow and the wheel, harnessed the energy of horses and oxen, invented writing and the alphabet, developed numerical systems and a calendar, produced sailing ships, and done a great many other new things. In brief, more technological advances happened in those 5,000 years than had happened during the preceding millions of years of hominid‡ history.[11]

*Supporting evidence for this and other generalizations in this section will be provided in later chapters, beginning with Chapter 5.

†For a more detailed review of those changes, see Chapters 6 and 7.

‡"Hominid" refers to the members of the genus Homo, which includes not only our own species but other closely related species that are now extinct.

In the societies affected by these technological advances, the conditions of human life were transformed. By 2500 B.C., the first great civilizations were firmly established in the Middle East. Societies were larger and more powerful by far than any that had preceded them, with towns and even small cities, considerable occupational specialization and division of labor, and striking social inequality. Monumental temples, palaces, and pyramids still survive to bear witness to the impressive new capabilities of those human societies. The developments of that era can only be characterized as revolutionary.

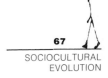

Subsequently, sometimes at a slower pace, sometimes more swiftly, the process of sociocultural evolution continued. By the time of Christ, for example, a number of societies surpassed the leading societies of 2500 B.C. in size, complexity, and power. But the most striking changes of all have come during the last 200 years, in the wake of the Industrial Revolution. Advances in technology, including the use of new materials and new energy sources, have once again been the catalyst in the process, triggering changes in every area of human life. With the new technology, societies today produce goods and services undreamed of even 100 years ago, and the very fabric of societal life has been transformed. Populations are more mobile, more urban, more specialized, more interdependent, more bureaucratized than ever before. To appreciate the magnitude of the changes that have occurred, one only need contemplate the emerging megalopolis that stretches in an almost continuous belt from Boston to Washington, D.C., or the supersonic flights that make it possible for an individual to work in London in the morning and Washington in the afternoon.

Technology's Revolutionary Role

We reviewed these basic trends in human societies to determine what type of cultural information has been most important in sociocultural evolution. The answer is clear. Technological information—information about the utilization of the material resources of the environment to satisfy human needs—has been far more important than any other in shaping the most basic processes of development and change in human societies. Had there been no technological innovations during the last 10,000 years, all societies would be small, nomadic populations of hunters and gatherers, living much the way our Stone Age ancestors did. Instead, technological advance has propelled us rapidly (by evolutionary standards) from Stone Age to Atomic Age. Thus, we must define sociocultural evolution as *the process of development and change that results from the acquisition and use of new cultural information, especially technological information.*

The basic causal relationships in general evolution are summarized in Figure 3.2. Starting at the left-hand side, we see that the interaction of the human population with the biophysical environment has produced a growing

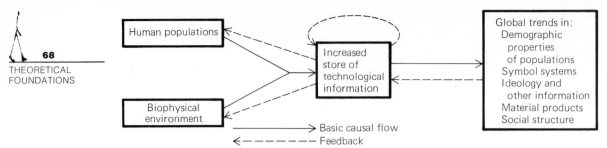

FIGURE 3.2   Basic model of general evolution.

store of technological information. This, in turn, has produced the basic trends in the other components of sociocultural systems. In other words, technological advance has been responsible for the growth in numbers of the human population, the growth in the average size of societies and communities, the creation of new kinds of symbol systems (e.g., written languages, musical notation), the growth of vocabularies, the development of new kinds of ideologies, the increased production of material goods, the growing complexity of social structures (e.g., increased division of labor among individuals, among communities and associations, and even among societies), and other related developments.

These global trends have, in turn, influenced technology. For example, growth in the size of the human population produced an accelerated rate of technological innovation because the latter is, in part, a function of the number of people involved in using technological information and looking for more of it (see page 78). It is important to note, however, that this is a *feedback* effect: it happened only because technological advance first caused population growth.

The model of general evolution shown in Figure 3.2 also indicates feedback from technology to both the biophysical environment and the human population, as well as feedback on itself. Each of these requires comment. The impact of technological advance on the biophysical environment is probably self-evident, since it is a subject of great concern to so many people today. The impact of technological advance on the human population itself is not as often recognized, although an interesting body of evidence on this subject is beginning to emerge.* Finally, as the brief survey of historical

*For example, there is evidence that the incidence of color blindness increases in societies the farther they are removed technologically from the traditional way of life of hunters and gatherers, who require normal color vision to survive.[12] In other words, the selective forces at work on the human population as a whole have altered as technological advance has altered the conditions of human life. Similarly, the use of machines to replace human muscle power, the use of x-rays and other agents capable of causing mutations, and medical advances that extend more people's lives into the reproductive stage will undoubtedly also prove to have consequences for the gene pool of the human population.

trends made clear, technological advance stimulates further technological advance, and we will shortly consider the reasons why this is so.

The impact of new technological information on the development of sociocultural systems can best be understood in the light of its functional similarity to new *genetic* information, which changes the way *biotic* systems relate to the environment and utilize its material resources. When a society experiences an important modification in its technology, it is as if there had been an important modification in the genetic makeup of its members. The acquisition of sonar bestows on a society the navigational ability of the bat, thermal clothing confers on it the heat insulation of arctic birds, and planes give it the capacity for flight of both kinds of animals.

Comparisons between technological and genetic mechanisms are limited, however, because technology has produced many capabilities that far exceed any found in the biotic world. This is true, for example, of our vision, which has been dramatically extended a number of times by such inventions as the telescope, the microscope, and television. Similarly, our ability to utilize a wide variety of energy sources; the range of our habitat; our endurance, speed, strength, mobility, hearing, and numerous other characteristics have been rendered not only unique in the biotic world, but incomparable. And, just as major genetic differences between species are responsible for major differences in their ways of life, so major technological differences between human societies are responsible for major differences in societal life.

Technology does not determine all a society's characteristics, of course. It does, however, determine two fundamental things. First, it determines the *range of what is possible* in the various parts of the system. A society with a very simple technology, for example, could not possibly develop large communities, labor unions, universities, or a nuclear capacity. Second, its technology determines *the relative costs of its options*, that is, the relative costs of the things within its "range of the possible." Thus, a typical Third World nation may find that, although free education for all its youth is not actually an impossibility, the cost of such a program, with the resulting diversion of resources from more immediate needs (e.g., mechanization of farms, or population-control programs), renders that option hopelessly impractical. It is because of constraints like these that societies with comparable technologies resemble one another in so many fundamental ways.

Ideology's Contribution

Even among societies with similar technologies, there are, of course, many differences, including differences in their ideologies. Moreover, it is their ideologies that are responsible for many of the other differences among societies. For it is the beliefs, values, and norms of a society that

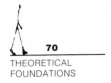
determine—within the limits of the possible and the practicable defined by technology—the patterns that actually develop.

Consider material products, a component of every sociocultural system. A society's technology necessarily restricts the variety, complexity, and quantity of material goods that can be produced. But a society's ideology largely determines the choices that are made within those limits—whether there will be better housing for the masses or more pyramids; more guns or more butter; more art or more highways; more nonessentials or cleaner air. Similarly, anything from a moderate to a great degree of social inequality may be possible for societies at a certain level of technological development, but their ideologies determine how much inequality actually develops in each of them.

Despite its important influence on the characteristics of individual societies, ideology has not played a major role in sociocultural evolution as a whole. In effect, ideology has not been capable of effecting the kind of change that produces responsive changes *throughout* the system. Even in instances when it appears that ideology *has* been responsible for a major evolutionary trend, the appearance proves to be deceptive. Consider the growth in population size. As recently as 8000 B.C., the human population numbered only 10 million or less; it is now 4,000 million, or 4 billion. But despite the fact that the admonition to "be fruitful and multiply" has been the most widely observed religious injunction in history, not ideology, but technology, has been responsible for this tremendous growth in numbers. For it was technological advance that made it possible for human societies to spread into new territories, produce greater quantities of food per acre, and overcome famines and disease.

This is not to minimize the importance of ideology, for there are always choices confronting every society, and their beliefs and values enable people to evaluate the alternatives (such as having only a few well-fed children in this life or a great many of them in the next) and establish their priorities. But just as ideology did not cause the historical trend in population growth, so it does not determine the limits of the possible for any society. Those are set by technology.

PROCESSES WITHIN THE PROCESS

Evolution is anything but a simple process. As sociocultural systems change and develop, they are actually experiencing several processes simultaneously. First, there is *continuity*: some social and cultural elements remain precisely as they were. Second, there is *innovation*: some new social and cultural elements are created or borrowed from another society. Third, there is *extinction*: some social and cultural elements are partially or totally discarded. We will look at each of these in turn.

Continuity

Regardless of how rapidly a society appears to be changing, most of its cultural elements are *not* changing. Most of its symbols and the meanings they convey, most of its store of information, and most of the ways in which its information is combined and used continue unaltered. For sociocultural evolution is essentially *cumulative* change: it involves the gradual addition of new elements to a continuing base.

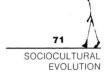

Evidence of cultural continuity is all around us. The alphabet and the modern processes of papermaking, printing, and bookbinding used to produce this book, for example, contain numerous elements that originated hundreds of years ago, while the concept of books is itself over three thousand years old. Other elements in our culture, such as the calendar, the concept of God, certain tools and techniques of cultivation and metallurgy, to name only a few, are even older than that.

Not surprisingly, a process as widespread and pervasive as sociocultural continuity is the result of a number of factors, with perhaps the most fundamental being the intrinsic value of the cultural elements themselves. Every society preserves its spoken language, its basic medical, military, and subsistence technologies, and many of its laws, for example, for the simple reason that these are its best or only answers to some very important needs, both of the system itself and of its members. Some elements may be preserved for a rather different reason. Certain norms, for instance, are valued not because they provide superior solutions but simply because they

FIGURE 3.3 Sometimes no particular solution to a society's problem is superior, yet a standardized solution is necessary. British law requires that vehicles travel on the left.

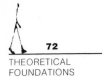

provide standardized behavioral responses in situations where, without them, there would be serious problems, even chaos. For example, although driving a car on the right side of the road is inherently neither safer nor easier than driving on the left, this choice cannot be left to the individual. Every society must have a norm to ensure that all its drivers follow the same procedure. Other cultural elements as diverse as literature, history, art, customs, belief systems, fads, and even dangerous norms (such as speeding and using drugs) persist in a society because they satisfy a diversity of needs, of the system or of its members.

But continuity is by no means simply the result of people's conscious and deliberate efforts to keep things as they are and avoid change. There is, to be sure, an element of purposefulness in the process of continuity, but for the most part, it operates without conscious intent, even without the possibility of control by the group. Rather, in every society, for good and for ill, a number of potent and largely impersonal forces work against change. Some of these forces lie in our common genetic heritage. The fact that this heritage does not change appreciably from one generation to the next is itself conducive to a considerable amount of continuity.

The *process of aging* is another barrier to change. At any age, new information can threaten an individual's view of life to the extent that one may well find it easier to ignore the information than to restructure one's thinking to accommodate it. As we grow older, changing our views tends to become even more difficult, with the result that the elderly usually have a conservative bias, relative to the young. Yet it is older people who, for various reasons, occupy the seats of power in most societies, and their conservative tendencies are greatly reinforced by the kind of bias that naturally attaches to positions of power (i.e., those in power usually prefer to maintain the status quo). The result is a considerable resistance to change on the part of those who control a society.

Not only can change exact a psychic toll on people: it also consumes time and energy to learn new ways, new rules, and new techniques. It may also be expensive financially, especially when existing investments have to be scrapped and heavy new expenditures incurred.

Perhaps the greatest single contributor to continuity is *the socialization process.** During their prolonged period of dependency, children are obliged to master the basic elements of their culture. This is essential for their survival and their only route to independence. Before they learn to talk, for example, children are almost totally dependent on other people; afterwards, however, they have at their disposal an invaluable tool to help them obtain the things they want. The same is true of other elements of culture: it pays the child to master them. Thus, the desire of the older generation to preserve

*See also pages 35–36 on socialization, social control, and sanctions.

FIGURE 3.4 Socialization occurs in play as well as in situations where adults attempt to train the young.

culture by transmitting it to their offspring is more than matched by their offspring's eagerness to learn it, especially during the formative years.

These efforts to pass culture on to the next generation are reinforced by most *ideologies.* One of their chief functions in a society is to preserve for the future the basic insights of the past. Since these insights usually include the belief that the existing social order is a moral order and ought to be preserved, a society's values, norms, and leadership all acquire an aura of the sacred and are thus less vulnerable to efforts to alter them. Ironically, even revolutionary ideologies like Marxism eventually acquire a sacred and conservative character: once they win acceptance, they, too, become a force for continuity—and against change.

Another basic force for cultural continuity lies in *the systemic nature of human societies.* Most elements are linked to other elements in such a way that change in one necessitates change in many others. For example, when

Sweden decided to shift to driving on the right-hand side of the road, a supposedly simple change, cars and buses had to be redesigned, traffic signals and highway signs moved, and traffic laws changed. All this took months of planning and cost millions of dollars. Similar linkages are found throughout every sociocultural system.

Society's systemic nature manifests itself most clearly, however, in *social institutions*. A social institution is essentially *a system of social relationships and cultural elements that has developed in a society in response to some set of basic and persistent needs.* These cultural elements are such things as rules, laws, customs, role definitions, and values that serve to regulate people's behavior and organize their activities in certain basic areas of life.

The consequences of this become clear when we look at kinship institutions. They organize and regulate our behavior in certain aspects of our lives and cause us to form the kinds of relationships that help satisfy society's needs for the production and early socialization of new members. Similarly, economic institutions are essentially systems of relationships in which people participate as producers and consumers, and they help answer society's needs for the production and distribution of goods and services.

A British sociologist once referred to social institutions as "frozen answers to fundamental questions."[13] Although "frozen" is too strong a characterization, institutions are associated with conservatism and resistance to change precisely because they do provide workable, if imperfect, answers to fundamental and persistent problems. Their value to a society is impressed on its members from an early age, through the socialization process. Institutions also resist change because, as systems (more precisely, as subsystems within more inclusive sociocultural systems), their elements are intricately intertwined, not only within but between institutions.

Because institutions are so important in the life of societies, much of our analysis of societal types in Chapters 5 to 13 will focus on them. We will be especially concerned with the variations among societies in five institutional spheres: kinship (or the family), the economy, the polity, religion, and education.

Innovation

The introduction of a new cultural element into a system may occur in response to either external (i.e., environmental) or internal forces. In the first instance, change in any of the characteristics of a society's environment tends to generate pressure for compensatory change within the society itself. For example, several times in history, societies have had to make major innovations in response to changes in their *biophysical* environments. This was the case at the end of the last Ice Age. Up to that time (about 10,000 years ago), societies in Europe had depended for subsistence on the hunting of reindeer which grazed in great numbers on what were then open plains. As the climate grew warmer, however, forests sprang up, the reindeer retreated toward the arctic regions, and new and very different species of plants and animals replaced the former Ice Age varieties. Societies had either to innovate or perish.

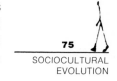

The *social* environment, too, can force a society to innovate. Sometimes a major change in one society will trigger a chain reaction of adjustment and innovation in many others. During the last 5,000 to 10,000 years, the social environment has been much less stable than the biophysical environment, and consequently it has provided the greater stimulus for innovation. Even under relatively stable conditions, however, neighboring societies are a source of innovation because they normally exchange at least some cultural elements with one another.

The rate of innovation in human societies would not have been what it has, however, if all the forces responsible for it were in the environment. There are also potent *internal* causes, rooted in our genetic makeup and in the societal way of life. To begin with, people, being fallible, do not always learn perfectly what their elders try to teach them, and errors occur in the transmission of cultural information from one generation to the next. What is more, people seem to be naturally motivated to try new ways of doing things. Sometimes they experiment with alternatives because they are bored by routine and feel the need for new experiences. Sometimes the motivation is sheer curiosity, or it may simply be self-interest, such as the desire for material things or for power. In any case, experimentation and innovation appear to be inevitable.

Problems that are generated by societal life also provide stimulus for innovation. Population growth, for example, may force a society to improve its subsistence technology; or its numerical increase may produce problems in the area of social control that call for new legal or organizational solutions. Any such change in one part of a sociocultural system may then generate pressure for further innovations in other parts.

Technological Innovation   Technological innovations are introduced into a sociocultural system in three basic ways: through *diffusion*, *discovery*, and *invention*. Diffusion is the transmission of existing information from one society to another. The ease with which diffusion occurs is one of the chief reasons why sociocultural evolution moves so much faster than organic evolution.

Discoveries and inventions, in contrast, involve information that was not borrowed but was acquired by a society independently. A discovery provides the members of a society with information they did not previously have; an invention is essentially a useful new combination of information the group already possessed. Thus, Columbus was a discoverer, while Gottlieb Daimler,

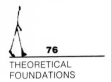
the creator of the first automobile, was an inventor. Daimler combined in a novel way a number of technological elements that were already part of the cultural heritage of Western nations (e.g., the gasoline engine, running gears, drive shaft, carriage body, etc.). The "only" thing new was the *combination* of elements.

People have been exploring the environment and experimenting with new methods of doing things from the earliest times. In the ensuing process of discovery and invention, purposive behavior and accident—or chance—have often been curiously intermingled. For example, the great scientist Louis Pasteur discovered the principle and technique of immunization only after he accidentally injected a stale bacterial culture of chicken cholera into some animals. When, unexpectedly, they survived, it occurred to Pasteur that a weakened culture might immunize against the disease.[14] Similarly, a key problem in the development of photographic techniques was solved when Louis Daguerre put a bromide-coated silver plate into a cupboard where, unknown to him, an open vessel of mercury was standing. When he returned the following day, he found that the latent image had begun to develop and surmised that fumes from the mercury were responsible.

Although chance has played an important part in the process of innovation, *knowledge*, *intelligence*, and *purpose* have also been essential, for without them the value of new information would go unrecognized. It was more than accident that led Pasteur to discover the process of immunization and Daguerre the process of developing pictures. Both men had already acquired the knowledge that enabled them to appreciate the import of their accidental discoveries. Furthermore, both were actively seeking new information.

Considering our evolutionary history, this is exactly what we would expect. We stand in an evolutionary line that has relied on learning as a basic means of adaptation, and the chief function of that learning is to enhance the value of experience. This experience comes to us both by chance and by purposive action.

Chance played a greater role in technological innovation during the earlier stages of human history than is the case today. Although we have no record of how important discoveries of the past occurred (e.g., fire-making, animal domestication, plant cultivation), we can be sure that accident was an important element. As we already noted, accidental changes in the information being transmitted were also common. Subsequently, however, writing and other methods of record keeping have greatly improved the accuracy with which information is conveyed. And in the last 100 years, science, with its systematic methods of research and organized bodies of information, has further reduced the role of chance.

Technological innovation has now become, in many societies, a highly purposeful and even predictable process. For example, numerous modern

FIGURE 3.5 "If this doesn't result in one or two first-class inventions, nothing will."

inventions, including rocket ships and submarines, were predicted years before the first working model was constructed, and the existence and properties of most of the "newer" elements in the periodic table of chemistry were predicted long before scientists actually discovered them. This decline in the importance of chance and the corresponding increase in purposeful action are natural by-products of the steady growth of the store of technological information.

But what determines how rapidly that store of information will grow in a particular society? In some societies, the rate of technological advance has been so slow as to be virtually imperceptible; in others, it has been extremely high. Why is this? The answer to this question is very important, for as we have seen in our examination of the general model of sociocultural evolution (see Figure 3.2, page 68), technological advance is not a matter that concerns only inventors, engineers, and business executives. On the contrary, it is the most basic force for change in every area of human life, and thus a matter of vital concern to all of us.

Of all the factors involved in the rate of innovation, probably none has been more important than *the magnitude of the existing store of technological information in the population.*[15] The reason is simple. Invention, as we have seen, is one of the basic modes of innovation, and inventions are essentially *combinations of existing elements of the culture.* It follows, therefore, that a society's potential for invention is a simple mathematical function of the number of elements available for combination. This is easily illustrated. Table 3.1 shows the number of combinations that are possible for various numbers

TABLE 3.1 Number of combinations possible for various numbers of units

No. of Units	Total Number of Combinations									
	2 at a Time	3 at a Time	4 at a Time	5 at a Time	6 at a Time	7 at a Time	8 at a Time	9 at a Time	10 at a Time	Total
2	1	0	0	0	0	0	0	0	0	1
3	3	1	0	0	0	0	0	0	0	4
4	6	4	1	0	0	0	0	0	0	11
5	10	10	5	1	0	0	0	0	0	26
6	15	20	15	6	1	0	0	0	0	57
7	21	35	35	21	7	1	0	0	0	120
8	28	56	70	56	28	8	1	0	0	247
9	36	84	126	126	84	36	9	1	0	502
10	45	120	210	252	210	120	45	10	1	1,013

of units or elements. Though two units can be combined in only one way, three units can be combined in four ways, and four units in eleven ways. In other words, *the addition of each new unit more than doubles the number of possible combinations.* Thus a mere fivefold increase in the number of units from two to ten leads to a thousandfold increase in the number of possible combinations, and when the number of units reaches twenty, over a million combinations are possible!

Of course, many technological elements cannot be combined in a useful way. It is difficult, for example, to imagine a useful combination of the hammer and the saw. The number of potential combinations, therefore, is much greater than the number of *fruitful* ones. Nevertheless, the amount of available information is a major factor in a society's rate of innovation.

A second cause of difference in the rate of technological innovation is *the size of the society's population.*[16] The more people aware of a problem and looking for a solution, the more quickly it will be found, other things being equal. Since societal populations vary so greatly in size, this is another factor of considerable importance.

A third factor affecting the rate of innovation is *the stability of the environment to which the society must adapt.* The greater the rate of environmental change, the greater the pressure on the society to modify its technology. In the social environment, anything that upsets the balance of power among societies (e.g., large-scale migrations, empire building, new weapons systems, and so on) is a potent force for technological innovation.

A fourth factor influencing the rate of innovation in a society is *the extent of its contact with other societies.* The greater the amount of peaceful interaction, the greater its opportunities to appropriate their discoveries and inventions. In short, sociocultural contact enables a society to take advantage of the brainpower and cultural information of other societies through diffusion.

The importance of diffusion was beautifully illustrated by Ralph Linton, a

ading anthropologist of the last generation. Analyzing American culture, he
rote:

Our solid American citizen awakens in a bed built on a pattern which originated
in the Near East but which was modified in Northern Europe before it was
transmitted to America. He throws back covers made from cotton, domesticated
in India, or linen, domesticated in the Near East, or wool from sheep, also
domesticated in the Near East, or silk, the use of which was discovered in China.
All of these materials have been spun and woven by processes invented in the
Near East. He slips into his moccasins, invented by the Indians of the Eastern
woodlands, and goes to the bathroom, whose fixtures are a mixture of European
and American inventions, both of recent date. He takes off his pajamas, a
garment invented in India, and washes with soap invented by the ancient Gauls.
He then shaves, a masochistic rite which seems to have been derived from either
Sumer or ancient Egypt.

Returning to the bedroom, he removes his clothes from a chair of southern
European type and proceeds to dress. He puts on garments whose form
originally derived from the skin clothing of the nomads of the Asiatic steppes,
puts on shoes made from skins tanned by a process invented in ancient Egypt
and cut to a pattern derived from the classical civilizations of the Mediterranean,
and ties around his neck a strip of bright-colored cloth which is a vestigial
survival of the shoulder shawls worn by the seventeenth century Croatians.
Before going out for breakfast he glances through the window, made of glass
invented in Egypt, and if it is raining puts on overshoes made of rubber
discovered by the Central American Indians and takes an umbrella, invented in
southeastern Asia. Upon his head he puts a hat made of felt, a material invented
in the Asiatic steppes.

On his way to breakfast he stops to buy a paper, paying for it with coins, an
ancient Lydian invention. At the restaurant a whole new series of borrowed
elements confronts him. His plate is made of a form of pottery invented in China.
His knife is of steel, an alloy first made in Southern India, his fork a medieval
Italian invention, and his spoon a derivative of a Roman original. He begins
breakfast with an orange, from the eastern Mediterranean, a cantaloupe from
Persia, or perhaps a piece of African watermelon. With this he has coffee, an
Abyssinian plant, with cream and sugar. Both the domestication of cows and the
idea of milking them originated in the Near East, while sugar was first made in
India. After his fruit and first coffee he goes on to waffles, cakes made by a
Scandinavian technique from wheat domesticated in Asia Minor. Over these he
pours syrup, invented by the Indians of the Eastern woodlands. As a side dish he
may have the egg of a species of bird domesticated in Indo-China, or thin strips
of the flesh of an animal domesticated in Eastern Asia which have been salted
and smoked by a process developed in northern Europe.

When our friend has finished eating he settles back to smoke, an American
habit, consuming a plant domesticated in Brazil in either a pipe, derived from the
Indians of Virginia, or a cigarette, derived from Mexico. If he is hardy enough he
may even attempt a cigar, transmitted to us from the Antilles by way of Spain.
While smoking he reads the news of the day, imprinted in characters invented by
the ancient Semites upon a material invented in Germany. As he absorbs the

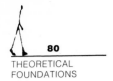

accounts of foreign troubles he will, if he is a good conservative citizen, thank a Hebrew deity in an Indo-European language that he is 100 per cent American.[17]

A fifth factor in a society's rate of technological innovation is *the character of its biophysical environment*. The potential for development and change in some societies has been severely limited by environmental factors over which they have no control. Thus, desert and arctic societies have been unable either to develop the techniques of plant cultivation themselves or to learn them from others. The absence of vital resources, such as an adequate water supply or accessible metallic ores, can also hinder innovation, as can endemic diseases and parasites.[18] Topography has also played an important role in shaping patterns of intersocietal communication. Such features as oceans, deserts, and mountain ranges have prevented or seriously impeded the flow of information between societies, while other features, such as navigable rivers and open plains, have facilitated it. Considering how crucial the flow of information is in the evolutionary process, enormous differences in sociocultural development can be explained by this factor alone.

Sixth, the rate of innovation is greatly influenced by *"fundamental" discoveries and inventions*. Not all discoveries and inventions are of equal importance: a few open the way for literally thousands of other innovations, while the majority have no such effect.[19] The invention of the plow and the steam engine and the discovery of the principles of plant cultivation, animal domestication, and metallurgy were all fundamental innovations.

Sometimes a fundamental innovation will cause the rate of innovation to rise because it involves a principle that can be applied, with minimum effort and imagination, to hundreds, even thousands, of problems. This was true of both the steam engine and metallurgy. Sometimes, however, an invention or discovery earns the label "fundamental" because it so drastically alters the conditions of human life that hundreds or thousands of other changes become either possible or necessary. This was the case with the discovery of the principles of plant cultivation, which, as we shall see in a later chapter, led to a host of major sociocultural changes.

Before leaving the subject of fundamental innovations, we should note that they have an impact that follows the pattern of the so-called S-curve, or logistic curve, shown in Figure 3.6. Their immediate effect is a period during which derivative innovations occur at an accelerating rate. In time, however, as the number of possible derivations begins to be exhausted, this rate begins to decline. How soon this happens depends on the nature of the fundamental innovation: some have a more limited number of possible derivatives than others. In every case, however, the long-term trend involves some approximation of the S-curve.

A seventh factor influencing the rate of innovation is *the society's attitude*

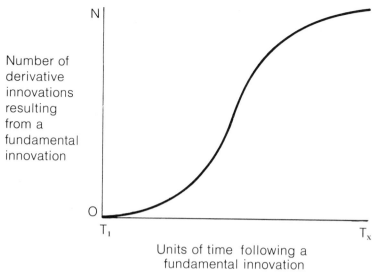

FIGURE 3.6   S-curve pattern of derivative innovations resulting from a fundamental innovation.

toward innovation. In many societies, there has been such a powerful ideological commitment to the past and to traditional ways of doing things that interest in innovation of any kind—even technological—has been discouraged. Perhaps the strongest justification for doing something in a particular way in such a society has been to say one's parents did it that way, and their parents before them. By contrast, most modern societies have a much more positive attitude toward innovation.

Though the problem has not been studied as systematically as it deserves, a society's attitude toward innovation is apparently greatly influenced by its prior experience with change. A society that has undergone an extended period of change and benefited from it will almost always be more receptive to innovation than a society that has not. Attitudes toward innovation also vary according to the nature of the dominant ideology in the society. Some ideologies generate a very conservative and anti-innovative outlook; Confucianism is a classic example of such a faith. Christianity and communism, by contrast, have been much more supportive of sociocultural innovation.

One of the most important facts of human history is the tremendous *increase in the rate* of technological innovation since early prehistoric times. Though one might suppose that such a trend began only recently, it has actually been going on for tens of thousands of years. Figure 3.7 shows the pattern for the past 900 years, and, as we will see in Chapter 5, archaeological evidence extends the trend far into the past.[20]

This is not to say there has been a constantly accelerating rate in every

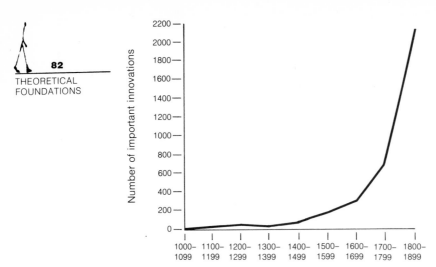

FIGURE 3.7 Number of important inventions and discoveries, by century, 1000 to 1900 A.D.

society, or even that there has been an accelerating rate for the world as a whole in every century. At several points in history the rate of innovation remained fairly stable or even declined for a period, but the rate invariably turned upward again and became greater than ever before.

The reasons for this should be evident by now. Technological information is cumulative, and each new bit of useful information increases the probability of getting more. Also, technological advance makes possible larger populations (which means more people are looking for solutions to problems), and it leads to increased contacts between societies and to the more rapid diffusion of knowledge. Finally, the benefits resulting from all these developments gradually undermine historic prejudices against change and contribute to the emergence of new change-oriented ideologies.

Where will this trend end? No one can really say at this time. We can say only that sooner or later acceleration must cease. But this is getting ahead of our story and is a subject we will examine in more detail in a later chapter.

Other Cultural Innovation   To a large extent, nontechnological innovations are a result of prior technological innovations. For technological change virtually always makes changes in other areas *possible*, and it frequently *stimulates* or *necessitates* them. Most of the achievements in the arts, for example, were made *possible* by prior technological advances. Bach and Beethoven could not have produced the music they did had they lived in Roman times, or even in the Middle Ages.[21] Their works depended on a technological foundation that did not exist in those days.

Some technological innovations not only permit, but actually *stimulate* innovations in other areas. The inventions that created the television industry, for example, led to innumerable innovations in literally dozens of areas, including advertising, education, fine arts, regulatory laws, political campaigning, family life, and even diet (e.g., TV dinners). Finally, technological innovations may *necessitate* other kinds of change. The technology that reduced the death rate in the last century, for example, led inevitably to new norms and values in many societies on such subjects as ideal family size, birth control, and abortion.

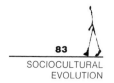

Innovations in art, morals, fashions, and other nontechnological areas can be introduced into a sociocultural system in several ways. Some are borrowed (i.e., diffused) from another system, either intentionally or unintentionally. Some are created by members of the society—and again, they may be the result of purposeful action or they may be unintentional consequences of societal life. The latter are especially interesting, for they arise entirely as a result of people living and working together and gradually developing, through their interactions, new ways of doing things and new expectations of one another. In fact, this is how most new norms are established: through a protracted process of social interaction involving large numbers of individuals with divergent ideas on a subject.

Most innovations, nontechnological as well as technological, have adaptive value, either for the society as a whole or for groups within it, but their benefits are not always obvious. For example, one might ask how anyone can possibly benefit from the special vocabularies developed by many youth groups and minority groups. Yet this kind of innovation is very useful to such groups when one of their goals is to keep outsiders at a distance. Later, if the larger society adopts some of these same linguistic innovations, it, too, benefits, because it thereby weakens or eliminates a barrier that tended to divide its members.

There are some innovations, however, that appear to have no adaptive value at all. Among them are those that result from the faulty transmission of information from one generation to the next. Stories, songs, legends, and histories that are communicated solely by word of mouth are often altered in the process. Similarly, gradual shifts occur in the forms of symbols and in patterns of speech. This is the reason for the diversity of words for "mother" in the various Indo-European languages, for example. These languages all evolved from a single source, and in the course of their evolution variations developed in the pronunciation of words. Thus, what is mother in English is *mère* in French, *mutter* in German, *matka* in Polish, *mater* in Latin, *mētēr* in Greek, and *matar* in Sanskrit.

Extinction

Extinction is the process whereby social and cultural elements disappear from a society. This can happen abruptly, as when a law is repealed by a government; or the process may be drawn out over an extended period, as in the gradual replacement of the horse and carriage by the automobile. Many

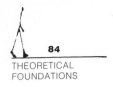

FIGURE 3.8 A case of intrasocietal selection: early automobiles in competition with horse-drawn carriages.

factors are involved in the process of extinction, but it is largely a matter of *selection* among available alternatives by the members of the society, by groups within it, or by its leaders.

Unlike its counterpart in the biotic world (and even in comparison with the process of *inter*societal selection, where societies themselves are the units selected for survival or extinction), *intra*societal selection can be a fairly rational and deliberate process. This is especially true in the area of technology. For one thing, emotional attachments to traditional elements of technology are normally not great (e.g., few women wept when scrub boards were replaced by washing machines). For another, it is often possible to obtain good measures of the relative efficiency of competing alternatives (e.g., measures of the gasoline consumption of different models of automobiles).*

---

*This is not to deny that accurate comparisons can be difficult even in the realm of technology. As we have discovered in recent years, technological innovations may have hidden costs and side effects that cannot be anticipated. Or, side effects may be anticipated but almost impossible to assess in advance, such as the magnitude of the risk involved in building a nuclear power plant near an urban community.

The situation is different where the selection of *non*technological elements is concerned, however. It is usually difficult to evaluate ideological alternatives accurately and objectively. Not only may strong emotions be involved, but the members of a society may be unable even to agree on the criteria. Should competing ideologies be judged on their contribution to people's happiness here and now, to the happiness of future generations, or to happiness in a future life? Similarly, people often find it difficult to agree on criteria in evaluating art, morality, and so on. Selection among nontechnological elements depends a great deal on the experiences of different individuals, and much less on the intrinsic value of the cultural elements themselves. As a result, there is often no well-defined trend in the intrasocietal selection of them. Instead societies often change course, and even reverse direction.

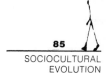

This is yet another reason why technological innovation usually defines the basic patterns of sociocultural change and development. Even groups and individuals with radically different ideologies (e.g., communists and capitalists) can agree that the clock is superior to the sundial, and the telephone to the pony express.

SPECIFIC EVOLUTION AND THE DIVERSITY OF SOCIETAL OUTCOMES

Growth, expansion, and development that result from an increasing store of cultural information—this has been the experience of human societies as a whole over the course of their history, and it is this we have referred to as *general evolution* (see page 68). But this is not the complete story. Not every society has grown in size and complexity, or possessed an expanding store of information. Many, in fact, have gone for centuries virtually unchanged, and some have actually regressed. Because the patterns of sociocultural evolution in individual societies may differ radically from the basic trends of general evolution, sociologists and anthropologists use the term *specific evolution*[22] to refer to the experience of a single society, or a particular set of societies (e.g., European societies). The best way to understand specific evolution is to consider the several outcomes that are possible.

Societal Survival

In the final analysis, there are only two outcomes possible for a sociocultural system: it survives, or it becomes extinct. A system that survives, however, may have three quite different experiences. First, it may develop, as its store of useful information expands. Second, it may remain stable. Third, it may regress.

Development Until the last 10,000 to 20,000 years, societal development was apparently the exception rather than the rule. Even since then, many

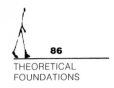
human societies have shown little evidence of technological advance or its consequences for long periods of time. And yet, the history of human societies as a whole (i.e., general evolution) has been influenced far more by the minority of societies that *have* experienced development. The reason is clear: sociocultural development has meant power—economic power, political power, military power. Thus, more developed societies have often conquered and absorbed their less developed neighbors, or, if they have not done this, they have penetrated them culturally, infusing them with new information and new ideas, thereby causing them to develop also.

Stasis   Stasis is a word borrowed from the ancient Greeks, for whom it meant the condition of standing still. Societies to which this term applies are those that, for considerable periods of time or for their entire history, neither acquire useful new cultural elements nor lose what they have and, as a consequence, experience no appreciable change or development.

Typical of societies in this state are most of the small, isolated, and technologically primitive societies that until recently existed in such areas as the Canadian Arctic, the Amazonian rain forest, and most of the continent of Australia. The basic technology of these groups had changed little if at all for thousands of years prior to their first contacts with European explorers, missionaries, and merchants. As we saw in our discussion of the basic trends of history, the vast majority of human societies were largely static up until 20,000 years ago. In Chapter 5, we will explore societies like these in more detail.

Regression   Regression refers to the condition of societies that lose important cultural elements and as a consequence become less well adapted than they were before. This has happened in small, primitive societies in which a particular kind of technological information was traditionally kept as the closely guarded secret of a single individual or family. The death of such individuals can have dire consequences. One society is known to have lost the technique of canoe making this way, another the ability to make stone adzes.[23]

Regression can also happen in larger, more advanced societies. When the Roman Empire collapsed, for example, it was not conquered by a society at a comparable level of development, but was brought down by a number of smaller, less technologically advanced groups. Without a strong central government to protect them, the merchants of that region could no longer move safely from town to town, and trade and commerce became increasingly unprofitable. As commerce declined, the skilled craftsmen and artisans who had produced a great variety of specialized products began to turn to other activities, especially farming and soldiering. With the elimination or drastic reduction of merchants and artisans, the economic base of urban communities was so undermined that they declined drastically in size or disappeared completely. In short, there was a reversion to a more primitive level of development, and societies in that part of the world were deprived for centuries of important information, both technological and other kinds.*

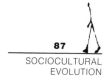

Societal Extinction

The most drastic societal outcome of all has also been the most common: extinction. The pages of history and ethnography are filled with reports of societies that are no more; contemporary societies are but a tiny fraction of the total that ever existed. In short, a process of selection has been operating among, as well as within, societies.

Societal extinction occurs when, for any reason, a society is no longer able to maintain its autonomy. This may come about because of some devastating natural calamity. An epidemic or earthquake, for example, might so decimate a population that it could no longer function, and survivors would be absorbed by neighboring groups. More societies have been eliminated by other societies, however, than by natural disasters, and they have usually been technologically and organizationally less developed than the societies that destroyed or conquered them.

Although the process by which a biotic species becomes extinct is unrelated to the process by which a human society becomes extinct, there is an important parallel between the two. The extinct species and the extinct society both possessed stores of information—genetic in the one case, cultural in the other—that inadequately equipped them to cope with the particular environmental circumstances that confronted them.

Specific versus General Evolution

Because the developmental experience of human societies has been so varied, it is imperative that we differentiate between specific and general evolution. Stasis has been the "normal" state of the vast majority of individual societies throughout history, and yet the most striking feature of general evolution has been *advance*. This paradox is explained by the fact that, over many thousands of years, large numbers of the least developed societies have gradually been eliminated. Thus, the *upper limit* of the curve of societal development has been steadily rising, and so has the *average*. Only the lower limit has remained constant, and even it is destined to rise as modern industrial societies absorb or destroy the last surviving Stone Age peoples.

*For example, virtually all the once numerous copper mines of Western Europe were shut down by the beginning of the sixth century and not reopened until the tenth; and brass, an alloy of copper and zinc, was apparently not manufactured again until the fifteenth century![24]

CHAPTER 4 TYPES AND VARIETIES OF SOCIETIES

Science is built on a foundation of comparisons. To understand anything in the world of nature—a plant, a star, a society, a rock formation—we are forced to compare it with other things, noting how it resembles them and how it differs.

Over the years, this process of comparison has led to the discovery of many orderly patterns. This, in turn, has laid the foundation for a variety of classificatory systems, such as the Linnaean taxonomy and its successors in biology, the periodic table in chemistry, and the typology of market systems in economics.*

Classification systems are essential in every area of study, because they enable us to order and organize the kaleidoscopic welter of our experiences. Without them, it would be impossible to develop general propositions about many aspects of the world of nature—propositions that help us anticipate, and sometimes control, the forces of nature and the behavior of living things.

*The most basic classificatory systems of all are the vocabularies of languages.

CLASSIFYING HUMAN SOCIETIES

The origins of evolutionary theory in sociology lie in the work of seventeenth-
and eighteenth-century European scholars who responded to the discovery
of less advanced societies in the New World, Africa, and Asia by rethinking
the age-old questions about our species' origins and early development. This
led, quite naturally, to comparisons of societies and efforts to differentiate
among them and classify them. As early as the eighteenth century, a number
of scholars recognized the crucial importance of *subsistence technology* (i.e.,
the technology used to provide a livelihood) and based their systems of
classification on it.[1] These writers frequently classified societies on the basis
of their dependence on hunting or herding or farming.

The system of classification used in this volume follows in that tradition.
The next eight chapters will be devoted to an examination and analysis of ten
basic types of societies that are defined by their basic mode of subsistence:[2]

Hunting and gathering societies
Simple horticultural societies
Advanced horticultural societies
Simple agrarian societies
Advanced agrarian societies
Fishing societies
Maritime societies
Simple herding societies
Advanced herding societies
Industrial societies

There are also a variety of *hybrid* types, but we need to consider the basic
types first.

Figure 4.1 illustrates how the various types of societies are related to one
another. The vertical dimension indicates the degree of overall technological
advance: the higher the societal type, the greater its store of information
about how to utilize the material resources of its environment. Hunting and
gathering societies are the least advanced in this respect, industrial societies
the most. As the diagram indicates, societies may reach comparable technological levels by following different evolutionary paths, that is, by developing
different but equally advanced subsistence technologies. Because of this, the
categories cannot all be neatly ranked, one ahead of the other. Maritime and
agrarian societies, for example, are roughly equal in terms of technological
progress even though they employ very different subsistence technologies.

For a typology to be useful, it must be as simple and unambiguous as the
data permit. For this reason, the criteria used to classify societies have been
held to a minimum. In most instances, a single criterion is used to differenti-

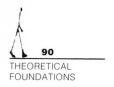

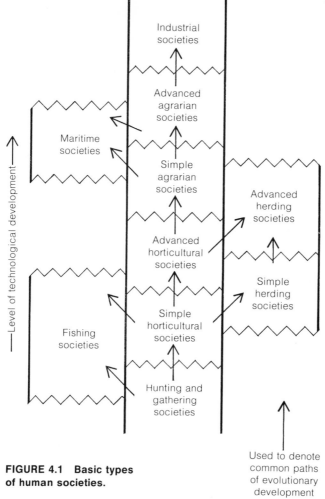

**FIGURE 4.1   Basic types
of human societies.**

Used to denote
common paths
of evolutionary
development

ate between two adjacent categories (i.e., categories with a common bound-ary in Figure 4.1). For the same reason, the criteria are features whose presence in a society can be easily ascertained—the use of plows, for example.

A society is classified as hunting and gathering when this is its primary mode of subsistence. This classification does not mean that the group never gets any of its material necessities by other means. Most of the hunting and gathering societies studied in the last century have, in fact, relied on fishing or part-time horticulture to some degree. But when hunting and gathering is the *primary* mode of subsistence, that is the basis of classification.

The four categories of horticultural and agrarian societies constitute an evolutionary sequence of societies that depend primarily on plant cultivation.

FIGURE 4.2 Bushmen of Southwest Africa: members of a contemporary hunting and gathering society.

We could lump them all together, but in doing so we would lose many valuable insights into the nature of the evolutionary process. The best way to describe the relationship among the four types is to list the minimal criteria for each. As Table 4.1 indicates, horticultural societies have no plows, but work the soil with hoes and digging sticks. Advanced horticultural societies, however, have metal tools and weapons, while simple horticulturists have only wooden ones. All agrarian societies have plows, but advanced have *iron* for tools and weapons, while simple have only copper and bronze, which are softer metals and less plentiful.

TABLE 4.1   Minimal criteria for classification of horticultural and agrarian societies

Type of Society	Plant Cultivation*	Metallurgy*	Plow*	Iron*
Simple horticultural	+	−	−	−
Advanced horticultural	+	+	−	−
Simple agrarian	+	+	+	−
Advanced agrarian	+	+	+	+

*The symbol + means that the trait is present in the type of society indicated; the symbol − means it is not.

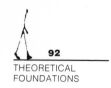

Fishing, herding, and maritime societies differ from the rest in that they are *environmentally specialized types.* They are distinguished from other societies at comparable levels of development, not so much in terms of the technological repertoire they *possess*, but rather in terms of the parts of it they *use.* They naturally rely disproportionately on those elements in their technology which are especially suited to the distinctive features of their unusual environments. Thus a fishing society relies primarily on the part of its technology that is most useful to a people located on a body of water. A herding society relies disproportionately on those elements of its technology which enable it to subsist on open grasslands with limited rainfall. Maritime societies, like fishing societies, utilized their proximity to water, though in a different way: being technologically more advanced, they adapted their technology to the use of waterways for trade and commerce at a time when the movement of bulky goods was much cheaper by water than by land.

Technologically, there is more variation among herding societies than either of the other specialized types. For this reason, the category is divided into simple and advanced types. The basic distinction is that the latter employ horses or camels for transportation in work and warfare, while the former lack this important resource.

Industrial societies were the most recent to appear. The key development marking their emergence was the harnessing of new energy sources. Previously, the major sources were human and animal power, water, wind, and wood. Beginning in the eighteenth century, first coal, then petroleum, natural gas, hydroelectric power, and, most recently, nuclear power came into use. When these sources are dominant in a society and industrial production becomes its chief source of wealth and income, the society is classified as industrial.

The jagged lines along the upper and lower boundaries of the various societal types in Figure 4.1 indicate that a few of the most advanced groups within one type may be a bit more advanced overall than the least advanced societies in the next higher type. This apparent contradiction exists because of our decision to base the system of classification on the fewest possible criteria. As a result, a society that lacks a key differentiating element (e.g., the plow) may possess enough other technological elements to make it somewhat more advanced *overall* than a few of the least advanced societies that have the key element. Despite occasional incongruities of this kind, the benefits of this method of classification far outweigh the drawbacks.*

*The chief advantages are that (1) the information needed to classify a society is most likely to be available when few criteria are used and (2) with fewer criteria, fewer categories are required and fewer societies will be unclassifiable because of contradictory characteristics (i.e., some characteristics pointing to one classification, others to another).

Finally, a word about *hybrid* societies. These are omitted from Figure 4.1 because they would clutter the diagram and make it difficult to read. Hybrid societies are those that rely substantially on two or more basic modes of subsistence. In some cases these societies are on the boundary between adjacent societal types. For example, a society might rely as much on fishing as on hunting and gathering. In another society, at a certain time in its history, a basic innovation like the plow may have spread to the point where roughly half the population uses it, while the other half still relies on the hoe. Neither society can be put in a single category, and we have to classify them as hybrids.

In other instances, the pattern of hybridization is more complex. This is particularly true when highly advanced societies come into contact with substantially less developed groups and crucial elements of technology diffuse from the former to the latter. Most contemporary African societies south of the Sahara are good examples of this: they can only be described as industrializing horticultural societies (see Chapter 13).[3]

FIGURE 4.3 Hybrid societies rely substantially on elements of technology from two or more basic societal types. Contemporary India, an industrializing agrarian society, combines elements of the older agrarian technology and the newer industrial.

Throughout most of our species' history, the entire human population lived in hunting and gathering societies. This period of relative technological uniformity ended only within the last 10,000 to 12,000 years. The first new kind of society to emerge was probably fishing. Though the practice of fishing seems to have developed some thousands of years earlier, the invention of true fishhooks, nets, traps, boats, and paddles was required before any society could make the shift from hunting and gathering to fishing and gathering as its primary means of subsistence.[4]

Simple horticultural societies probably came next, first appearing in the Middle East around 7000 B.C.[5] Though people began to use copper within the next 1,500 years,[6] it was not until nearly 4000 B.C. that metal tools and weapons became common enough to permit us to call any of these societies *advanced* horticultural.[7]

The plow was invented late in the fourth millennium, and this innovation, too, occurred in the Middle East.[8] By 3000 B.C. it was used widely enough by societies in Mesopotamia and Egypt to justify calling them simple agrarian.

Iron was discovered early in the second millennium B.C. but, like copper, did not become the dominant material in tools and weapons for a long time.[9]

FIGURE 4.4   Societal types from 12,000 B.C. to the present.

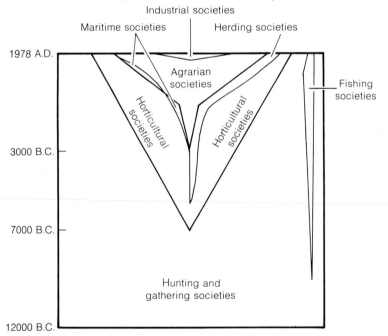

Thus, the first *advanced* agrarian societies did not appear until the early years of the first millennium B.C.

The origin of herding societies remains something of a mystery. Evidence of animal domestication dates from about 9000 B.C., but the findings from the earliest site suggest a hybrid technology.[10] While we cannot say for certain when people first relied on herding as their chief means of subsistence, it was probably sometime after horticultural societies appeared.

Maritime societies date from the end of the third millennium B.C. The Minoans on the island of Crete were apparently the first to rely on overseas commerce as their primary economic activity.[11] Unlike other major societal types, maritime societies have not had a *continuous* history. After flourishing in the Mediterranean world for 2,000 years, they were wiped out by the growth of Roman power. During the Middle Ages, they enjoyed a revival for a number of centuries, only to disappear once more.

The last major societal type is the industrial. Although the basic inventions that mark the beginning of the modern technological revolution occurred in the eighteenth century, it was not until early in the nineteenth that Britain, pioneer in industrialization, reached the point where it could be classified as a truly industrial society. Since then numerous others have followed Britain's lead.

HISTORICAL ERAS

As Figure 4.4 makes clear, the types of human societies in existence have been changing constantly during the last 10,000 years. There was a time when every society was at the hunting and gathering level of development; today, we have everything from hunting and gathering to industrial societies.

To understand the problems confronting a given society, it is not always enough to know what type of society it is. It may be equally important to know when it existed, since this tells us a great deal about its social environment and its chances for survival. For example, the situation of hunting and gathering societies today is far more precarious than the situation of hunting and gathering societies 10,000 years ago. In the modern world such a group usually finds itself in the unenviable position of interacting with far more advanced, and hence far more powerful, societies. No matter where it is located, agents of industrialism are likely to be penetrating, using their vast resources to transform the conditions of life for the less advanced group. This may be done with the best of intentions—as in the case of medical, educational, or religious missions—but that makes little difference. The ultimate effect is to transform and eventually destroy the sociocultural systems of technologically primitive peoples.

For analytical purposes, therefore, it is often necessary to identify the

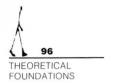

historical era. Combining the era with what we know about the society itself, we can discuss problems and patterns much more intelligently.

Reduced to essentials, there have been four major eras in human history (all dates are approximate):

Hunting and gathering (to 7000 B.C.)
Horticultural (from 7000 B.C. to 3000 B.C.)
Agrarian (from 3000 B.C. to 1800 A.D.)
Industrial (since 1800 A.D.)

Until about 7000 B.C., hunting and gathering societies were the most advanced technologically.* They were then replaced by horticultural societies, which remained dominant until around 3000 B.C. At this point, agrarian societies emerged as the dominant form of societal organization, a position they held until the early part of the last century, when industrial societies appeared on the scene. With each new era, the position of less advanced societies became increasingly precarious. Because of the process of intersocietal selection, their chances of survival went steadily down.

CORRELATES OF SOCIETAL TYPE AND CONSEQUENCES OF TECHNOLOGICAL ADVANCE

Beginning in Chapter 5, we will examine the major societal types one by one. First, however, we will look at some basic comparative data that will prepare us for the kinds of differences we can expect to find between them. Later, we will have occasion to refer back to some of these data.

The richest source of systematic information on preindustrial societies is the Ethnographic Atlas published in a journal entitled *Ethnology.* This journal, founded by George Peter Murdock, provides a wealth of coded data on hundreds of societies in all parts of the world, dealing with everything from a people's subsistence technology to the kinds of games they play.[12]

The tables that follow are based on information on the first 915 societies recorded in the Ethnographic Atlas. These societies were distributed as follows among the basic societal types:[13]

Hunting and gathering	151
Simple horticultural	76
Advanced horticultural	267

*Although fishing societies made their appearance prior to 7000 B.C. and were a somewhat more advanced form of societal organization, we do not speak of a "fishing era" for the simple reason that fishing can never be a dominant mode of subsistence except in very limited areas.

Agrarian (both simple and advanced)	96
Fishing	44
Herding (both simple and advanced)	60
Hybrids, maritime, industrial, and unclassifiable	221

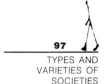

In our survey in this chapter, we will omit hybrid societies in order to concentrate on the more basic types, and we will omit maritime and industrial societies because they are so few in number and Murdock's data concerning them are sometimes questionable.[14]

Population Size

One of the most important consequences of technological advance is population growth, which can take two forms. First, when higher densities can be sustained in a given area, larger communities become possible. Second, when more communities can be united within a single political system, overall societal size increases.

Table 4.2 shows both of these patterns. In hunting and gathering societies, communities are extremely small, averaging only about forty people each. Since these local groups are nearly always autonomous—that is, independent societies in their own right—the average hunting and gathering society also contains only about forty people. In simple horticultural societies, communities average nearly a hundred, and there, too, local groups are usually autonomous, so that community and society are the same

TABLE 4.2 Median size of communities and societies, by societal type

Type of Society	Median Size of Communities	Median Size of Societies	No. of Societies*
Hunting and gathering	40	40	93–62
Simple horticultural	95	95	48–45
Advanced horticultural	280	5,800	107–84
Agrarian	†	Over 100,000	58–48
Fishing	60	60	20–22
Herding	55	2,000	17–22

*Data are seldom available on a given subject for all 915 societies. This column indicates the number of societies for which data were available and on which the statistics are based. The first of the two figures indicates the number of cases on which the median size of communities is based, the second, the number for the median size of societies.

†Murdock's method of coding community size does not permit one to give a precise figure for the median size of communities in agrarian societies, since 57 per cent fall in a category labeled "one or more indigenous cities with more than 50,000 inhabitants." In other words, the content of the code shifts from a measure of central tendency to a measure of the upper limit of the range. It should also be noted that averages are much less meaningful in agrarian societies than in simpler societies owing to the greater range of size.

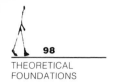

size. Among advanced horticultural societies, however, the picture changes. Not only are communities larger, but multicommunity societies are the rule. Thus, though the average advanced horticultural *community* is only three times larger than its simple horticultural counterpart, the average advanced horticultural *society* is sixty times larger than its counterpart. The trend continues in agrarian societies, where urban communities are common and the average society covers an even wider area. Since 60 per cent of the agrarian societies for which we have data fall into Murdock's top category of "100,000 or more,"[15] it is not possible to give an exact figure for them. But it is clear that they are substantially larger on the average than even their nearest rivals among the less advanced types.

Table 4.2 is also pertinent to our earlier discussion of the relative technological levels of fishing, herding, and horticultural societies. Fishing societies stand between hunting and gathering and simple horticultural societies in size. In community size, so do herding groups, but for societal size, which is more important, they stand between simple and advanced horticultural. It may seem strange that although herding communities are no larger than fishing communities, herding *societies* are more than thirty times the size of fishing societies. The explanation seems to be that fishing communities generally occupy unusually favorable environmental niches with respect to food, enabling them to build up local population densities higher than are normal for communities at their level of technological development, while herding peoples' environments are just the opposite. At the societal level, however, the technological superiority of herding societies permits them to expand geographically and develop politically to an extent impossible for the less advanced fishing groups. Moreover, political expansion is easier in the open steppe and prairie environments of herders than in the coastal and river territories of fishing peoples, where there are often a multitude of natural barriers.

These data direct our attention to an important qualification concerning the relationship between technological and structural development in a society. The latter tends to be a function of the former, but only to the extent that environmental conditions are held constant. To put it another way, *the level of structural development in a society is a function both of its technological information and of its environment.*

Permanence of Settlements

Technological advance also leads to more permanent settlements. Hunters and gatherers are generally nomadic; more advanced groups (except for herders) are more settled. This is because hunting and gathering usually so depletes the supply of plants and animals in a small area that it becomes

TABLE 4.3 Frequency of craft specialization,* by societal type (in percentages)

Type of Society	Metal Working	Weaving	Leather Working	Pottery	Boat Building	House Building	Average
Hunting and gathering	†	0	0	0	0	0	0
Simple horticultural	†	0	3	2	4	2	2
Advanced horticultural	100	6	24	24	9	4	28
Agrarian	100	32	42	29	5	18	38
Industrial‡	100	100	100	100	100	100	100
Fishing	†	0	0	0	9	4	2
Herding	95	11	22	†	†	0	21

*The term "craft specialization" as used here includes Murdock's category of industrial specialization.
†The activity in question is seldom found in this type of society.
‡The figures for industrial societies are not from Murdock's data but are added simply for comparative purposes.

impossible to feed even a few dozen people on a permanent basis. Murdock's data show this clearly. Of 147 hunting and gathering societies, 90 per cent were nomadic,[16] in contrast to only 4 per cent of 377 horticultural and agrarian societies.

Division of Labor

Another result of technological advance is an increased division of labor. Table 4.3 shows how often certain tasks are performed by specialists in each of the major types of societies. Such specialization is virtually unknown in hunting and gathering and simple horticultural societies. In advanced horticultural societies, it occurs with some frequency, becoming more prominent still in agrarian societies. Fishing societies closely resemble simple horticultural societies, while herding societies again are located between the simple and advanced horticultural types.

Religious Beliefs

Religion is one area where we might suppose technology and societal type would have little effect. Yet, as Table 4.4 indicates, the basic beliefs typical of the simpler societies are quite different from those of the more advanced. Few hunting and gathering, simple horticultural, or fishing societies believe in a Creator God who is actively interested in his creation and in the moral aspects of human life. Few of these societies, in fact, have even conceived of a Supreme Creator, and those that do usually assume him to be indifferent to humans. In advanced horticultural societies, however, the pattern is quite

TABLE 4.4   Beliefs concerning God, by societal type (in percentages)

Type of Society	Beliefs*				Percentage Total	No. of Societies
	A	B	C	D		
Hunting and gathering	60	29	8	2	99	85
Simple horticultural	60	35	2	2	99	43
Advanced horticultural	21	51	12	16	100	131
Agrarian	23	6	5	67	101	66
Fishing	69	14	7	10	100	29
Herding	4	10	6	80	100	50

*A—no conception of Supreme Creator; B—belief in a Supreme Creator who is inactive or not concerned with human affairs; C—belief in a Supreme Creator who is active in human affairs but does not offer positive support to human morality; D—belief in a Supreme Creator who is active and supports human morality.

different, and a majority of societies believe in an otiose (i.e., inactive) Creator God. Belief in a Supreme Creator who is actively interested in his creation and supports moral conduct is a common pattern only in agrarian and herding societies.[17] This subject will be discussed further on page 237.

Social Inequality

Another aspect of life that we might expect to be relatively immune to variations in subsistence technology is social inequality. Yet here, too, the evidence indicates that different types of societies have quite different patterns.

Slavery is extremely rare in both hunting and gathering and simple horticultural societies, as Table 4.5 indicates. In fishing and agrarian societies, however, it is found about half the time, while among advanced horticultural and herding societies it occurs five times out of six. The fact that agrarian societies are less likely to practice slavery than advanced horticultural and herding societies is interesting, because it indicates that evolutionary patterns sometimes assume a curvilinear form (i.e., they involve a reversal in direction). We will find other instances of this later on.

The decline in slavery associated with the rise of agrarian societies did not mean a reduction in social inequality as a whole, however. On the contrary, class systems are actually more common in agrarian societies than in any other. The trend shown in Table 4.5 certainly indicates a change in the *nature* of social stratification, but not a general movement toward greater social equality.

We could easily add more tables of correlates, but these suffice to show how substantial and varied the consequences of technological advance have been. This will become even more evident when we examine the major societal types individually, beginning in Chapter 5.

TECHNOLOGICAL DETERMINISM?

Today, as in the past, efforts to understand the role of technology in human affairs have been hindered by the tendency of some scholars to take extreme positions on the subject. Over the years, one group has argued the case for technological determinism, saying, in effect, that technology explains almost every sociocultural pattern.[18] To combat this exaggerated view and to uphold the importance of ideological factors, others have minimized or denied the importance of technology.[19] The unreasonableness of *both* positions has apparently escaped many social scientists, with the result that sociology and anthropology have been slow in coming to a realistic assessment of technology's role in the evolutionary process.

Much of the confusion results from the failure to think in *probabilistic* and *variable* terms. Few, if any, significant social patterns are determined by a single factor. Where human societies are concerned, one rarely can say that A, and A alone, causes B. Usually B is due to the combined effect of a number of factors, and, although A may be the most important, it alone is not likely to be strong enough to determine the outcome. The most we can say, as a rule, is that if A is operative, B will be present *with some degree of probability.*

The problem is further complicated because so many of the B's we deal with are *variables.* For example, when we talk about a society's population, we are not interested in whether it exists, but in its relative size. The same is true of most of the phenomena we are concerned with—the *degree* of occupational specialization, the *frequency* of warfare, the *extent* of the authority vested in leaders, and so forth. To think in categorical, either-or terms about such things is bound to be misleading.

Clearly, then, the controversy over technological determinism has been a false issue. Technological factors are obviously incapable of explaining all

TABLE 4.5 Percentage of societies with slavery and with class systems, by societal type

Type of Society	Percentage Having Slavery	Percentage Having a Class System*	No. of Societies†
Hunting and gathering	10	2	142–143
Simple horticultural	14	17	66–69
Advanced horticultural	83	54	243–224
Agrarian	54	71	84–89
Fishing	51	32	43–41
Herding	84	51	50–49

*This includes those societies which Murdock codes as having "complex class systems," "dual stratification," and "elite stratification."
†The first column of figures refers to slavery, the second to class systems.

TABLE 4.6 Range of differences (in percentages) for selected variables in six basic types of societies*

Variable	Range
Specialization in metal working	100
Leather working: wholly or largely a female activity	96†
Boat building practiced	91
Nomadic communities	87
Median size of communities 100 or more	80
Belief in God as active and moral force	78
Slavery practiced	74
Leather working practiced	71
Two or more levels of government above the local community	71
Pottery made	71
Class stratification	69
Games of strategy	68
Patrilocal residence	68
Urban communities of 5,000 or more	67
Bride price or bride service required	56
Weaving practiced	56
House construction: predominantly male activity	51
Patrilineal clans	51
Games of chance	50
Premarital virginity enforced for women	49
Weaving: predominantly male activity	46†
Specialization in leather working	42
Extended family system	33
Gathering: predominantly female activity	31
Specialization in pottery making	29
Specialization in fishing	29
Fishing: predominantly male activity	22†
Matrilineal clans	18
Specialization in house construction	18
Dowry system	15
Games of physical skill	13
Specialization in boat building	9
Boat building: predominantly male activity	8†
Specialization in hunting	7
Polyandry	1
Hunting: predominantly male activity	0†

*The societal types are those shown in Table 4.5.
†Percentage difference based on those societies in which the specified activity is carried on and for which data on sexual specialization are available.

social phenomena. On the other hand, the evidence indicates that they explain a great deal. How much they explain varies from subject to subject. We can see this in Table 4.6, which is a measure of the explanatory power of the sixfold societal typology we have used in analyzing Murdock's data.

To understand what this table means, turn back to Table 4.5. In the column "percentage having slavery," note that the highest figure is 84 per cent (for herding societies), the lowest only 10 per cent (for hunting and gathering). The difference between these two extremes is 74 percentage points, which is recorded as the range for that particular variable in Table 4.6 (see "slavery practiced," line seven). Similarly, the difference between the two extremes for "class stratification" is shown in Table 4.5 to be 69 points (between hunting and gathering and agrarian societies) and this information is on line 11 of Table 4.6.

The data shown in Table 4.6 are all based on tables similar to Tables 4.3 through 4.5, but they cover many additional topics. Industrial societies were not included in the calculations, since Murdock's data on them are inadequate. The basic point demonstrated by Table 4.6 is that *the differences between societal types cover the entire range of possibilities from 0 to 100 per cent.* At the lower level, variations in technology are obviously irrelevant or of little importance. In nearly every case this is because the activity in question is either found in almost every society, or in almost none. Hunting, for example, is predominantly a male activity in every society in Murdock's sample, while, at the other extreme, polyandry (i.e., several men married to one woman) is practiced in less than 1 per cent of the societies. In such cases, there is little or no variance to be explained by technology—or by anything else.

By contrast, where the values are large in Table 4.6, there is considerable variance to be explained, and technological differences appear to be of major importance. In still other instances, the variance may be considerable, but subsistence technology is of little help in explaining it. To ignore or minimize such differences would both misrepresent and oversimplify the complexities of the real world.

In summary, modern evolutionary theory does *not* take a deterministic view of technology's role: it views subsistence technology as but one force in a field of forces that, together, determine the total pattern of societal characteristics. Its position can be stated briefly in two propositions:

1. Technological advance is the chief determinant of that constellation of global trends—in population, culture, social structure, and material products—which defines the basic outlines of human history.
2. Subsistence technology is the most powerful single variable influencing the social and cultural characteristics of societies, individually and collectively—not with respect to the determination of each and every characteristic, but rather with respect to the total set of characteristics.

These propositions suggest that the first step in analyzing any society should be to determine its basic technology. This assures that we take into account, at the start of our analysis, the most powerful single factor influencing the life of that society.

Our basic task for the rest of this volume will be to apply these propositions in a broadly comparative study of human societies. We will examine each of the major societal types that have emerged in the course of history, seeing how technological innovations have influenced developments in population, culture, social structure, and material production, and how developments in these areas have fed back on technology and influenced its development. We will, for obvious reasons, give special attention to the industrial and industrializing societies of our own day. Our ultimate goal is to understand the basic forces responsible for sociocultural evolution, in the hope that this will help us understand and even control the process of change that is such a striking, and at times threatening, feature of the contemporary world.

PART TWO
PREINDUSTRIAL
SOCIETIES

CHAPTER 5 HUNTING AND GATHERING SOCIETIES

Hunting and gathering societies are unique, for they alone span the whole of human history. From the emergence of our first hominid ancestors down to the present, there have always been societies obtaining their livelihood in this way, but the effects of industrialization make it unlikely that any will survive into the twenty-first century. Because these peoples add so much to our understanding of the development of human societies, we must be grateful that they survived long enough for trained observers to live among them and record their way of life.

These modern hunting and gathering societies were for decades the focus of a major controversy among social scientists. Some scholars saw these groups as the living counterparts of prehistoric hunting and gathering societies. Others denied the legitimacy of any such comparison, arguing that these modern groups are products of an evolutionary process as extended as that of any modern industrial society.

Though the latter view prevailed for a time, there has been a reversal. Many archaeologists now refer to the hunting and gathering peoples of

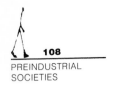

prehistoric and modern times as "analogous peoples" and acknowledge the benefits to their discipline of inferences drawn from ethnographic studies (i.e., studies of contemporary primitive societies).[1] A leading British archaeologist summed up the current view when he wrote that the archaeologist learns from the ethnographer

> how particular peoples adapt themselves to their environments, and shape their resources to the ways of life demanded by their own cultures: he thus gains a knowledge of alternative methods of solving problems and often of alternative ways of explaining artifacts resembling those he recovers from antiquity. Study of ethnography will not as a rule . . . give him straight answers to his queries. What it will do is to provide him with hypotheses in the light of which he can resume his attack on the raw materials of his study. In fact, the great value of ethnography to the prehistorian is that it will often suggest to him what to look for. . . . By constant reference to the culture of living or recently living societies, the prehistorian should be able to enrich and fortify his interpretation of the past, as well as bring into the open problems calling for further research.[2]

In our analysis we will follow the conservative procedure of presenting the findings of archaeology and ethnography separately. Only after we have done this will we explore the question of whether they provide consistent or contradictory images of hunting and gathering societies.

THE ARCHAEOLOGICAL EVIDENCE

Human Origins

It is easy to speak of "the dawn of human history," but it is not so easy to assign a date to it, or even to say precisely what it means. The same evolutionary process that produced our species (Homo sapiens) first produced a number of others (e.g., Australopithecus and Homo erectus) that were, to widely varying degrees, "humanlike." Thus, it is impossible to say that human history began at some particular point. What *is* possible is to identify the patterns that gradually began to form during the long era of "morning twilight" that ultimately produced *fully* human creatures and *truly* human societies.

Our species, Homo sapiens, is part of the genus *Homo*, which is, in turn, part of the family *Hominidae*, better known as the hominids. This family split off from the ancestors of the modern chimpanzees and gorillas about 15 million or more years ago, according to the best available evidence,[3] and has subsequently pursued a separate, distinct, and increasingly unique evolutionary course. The process of natural selection, operating on the populations of a succession of hominid species, gradually shaped this line in certain fundamental and important ways that culminated in Homo sapiens—the sole surviving member of the hominid family.

If we could look across space and time to a grass-covered plain in Africa about 10 million years ago, we would see that hominids were already on an evolutionary course headed in a new direction. At that early date, they had been altered, according to fossil evidence, from their ancestors' arboreal and herbivorous way of life to a bipedal, terrestrial, and carnivorous one.[4] In short, our ancestors had come out of the trees, were walking on two feet and moving about much as we do, and were hunting small game. This drastic set of changes had involved many genetic modifications, especially in cranium, dentition, and the rest of the skeleton, the limbs in particular. One of the most critical changes was the new upright stance, for this meant that hominids' hands were no longer required to propel their bodies through trees or across the ground, but were free to handle such things as sticks and stones used as tools, and eventually to fashion tools.[5]

During that early era, and subsequently as well, other important characteristics were also being selected as elements in the basic genetic heritage of the hominids. Among the attributes that developed, not independently but more or less in concert, were larger size;* greater brain size and mental capacity; increased cooperation and communication; improvements in eye-hand coordination; and a variety of other advances in the nervous system.[6]

As the ages passed, hominids came to be more like humans, both in appearance and in behavior. Their capacity for tool use developed until they were using pieces of stone to skin animals, cut off chunks of meat, and sharpen wooden tools and weapons. But progress was slow. The crude chopper that was the chief hominid tool at one stage of their history, for example, went virtually unaltered for hundreds of thousands of years.[8] Prehistorians, not surprisingly, have spoken of the "almost unimaginable slowness of change" during that period.[9] Eventually, however, as a consequence of their increasing use of, and dependence on, tools and further evolution of their brains, hominids reached a point when, as the "brainiest" of the mammals, they began to make more effective use of the resources of their environment.

One of the most significant things that happened in this connection was the beginning of big-game hunting about half a million years ago.[10] Prior to that time, hominids obtained their meat by hunting small game or by scavenging. A shift to the pursuit of larger animals would have required a greater capacity for planning, maneuvering, remembering, communicating, and cooperating; and individuals who did these things best would have been most likely to survive. Thus there appears to be a link between big-game

*The earliest hominids appear to have weighed only about fifty pounds.[7]

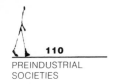
hunting and further evolution of the hominid brain, especially in its development of more memory units and interconnecting nerve cells.[11] Big-game hunting would not have been possible except for creatures that already used symbols to some degree. And that activity would almost certainly have stimulated greater symbol use and been an important factor in the selective process shaping the hominid capacity in this regard.

There is also reason to believe that the greater degree of cooperation demanded by big-game hunting strengthened the social bonds that united the adult members of hominid societies. Adult males could no longer be as independent of one another as they tend to be in most primate societies. Big-game hunting probably also increased the interdependency of the sexes by intensifying the division of labor between them. This trend had begun long before. For example, the female's hips had widened as the size of the newborn hominid's brain had increased, making running slower and more awkward for her. Such physical differences, combined with the limitations on her mobility imposed by pregnancy and lactation, probably led to the historic distinction between men as hunters and women as foragers of wild fruits and vegetables. But this distinction could well have remained fuzzy and ill-

FIGURE 5.1 Artist's conception of cave-dwelling, fire-using hunters near Peking, China, about 500,000 B.C.

defined until the beginnings of big-game hunting greatly increased requirements for mobility. From that point on, however, the division of labor between the sexes must have been rather well defined. One of its consequences has been a strengthening of the ties between males and females, ties which are usually weak among the primates.

The use of fire was another significant technological innovation of this period. Fire was the first great natural force to be, in any sense, brought under control. Although hominids probably could not generate fire during this era, they preserved it after it was started by natural causes. And fire did far more than warm these societies. It set them apart from all other animals, giving them some control over the cycle of day and night, and giving them a little more freedom of movement. It was also important for protection, and was a powerful weapon for driving predators away from camp or out of an especially good cave that hominids wanted to use. Fire was also used to harden the points of wooden spears, and possibly to kill large animals by driving them over cliffs or into swamps.

The use of fire for cooking may have affected the evolution of our teeth, and even the shape of our faces, since cooked food requires so much less chewing than raw. It was probably also involved in the beginnings of religious experience, as a basis of ritual, even as an object of worship. But most important, fire strengthened the network of interrelationships within these societies. It brought males back from the hunt to eat with females and young, rather than at the scene of the kill. It drew the group together at the end of a day to communicate, to remember, and to plan.

Despite their advances, living was precarious for these people, and their life expectancy short. An authority who analyzed the remains of forty individuals who lived approximately fifty to a hundred thousand years ago found that only one of them apparently reached the age of fifty, and only 10 per cent the age of forty. Half of them died before their twentieth year.[12]

Within the last 100,000 years, hominids began to bury their dead, frequently placing in the grave with them artifacts that strongly suggest belief in life after death: food, flowers, implements, and red ocher, which some scholars suspect was felt to have the life-giving properties of blood.[13] At least one grave held animal bones and cinders, suggesting either burnt offerings or the remains of a funeral feast. This era also provides us with our first evidence of intraspecies violence. Several skeletons have been found with wounds that were almost certainly inflicted by other hominids (e.g., a flint projectile in a rib cage and a pelvis with a spear hole in it).[14]

Although human societies of this era were clearly becoming more dependent upon culture, cultural change was apparently still not as important to them in the adaptive process as genetic change. This has altered in the last 35,000 years, however, since the emergence of Homo sapiens

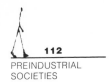

sapiens, a subspecies within Homo sapiens and the sole surviving hominid. Since then, there has been no major genetic change in our species, and cultural change has become the basic mode of adaptation.

Hunting and Gathering Societies from 35,000 to 7000 B.C.

The clearest indication of the quickening pace of sociocultural evolution is the rapid proliferation of new and improved tools and weapons. The spear, for example, had been in use for hundreds of thousands of years, with no significant improvements except for the use of fire to harden the point. Then, in the period from 35,000 to 7000 B.C., hunters made several further improvements. First, they developed the spear-thrower, which, because it applies the principle of the lever, doubles the distance a spear can be hurled.[15] Second, at the other end of the spear they began using sharpened bone points to increase the penetrating power. Finally, they added barbs to the spear head to create a much more serious wound.[16]

The most important innovation in weapons, however, was the bow and arrow. Utilizing the principle of the concentration of energy, hunters in this period created a weapon of great usefulness and versatility. Its effective wounding range is roughly four times that of the spear and twice that of the spear thrown with the aid of a spear-thrower.[17] Furthermore, an arrow travels two and a half to three times faster than a spear. This is important not only because of the time advantage it affords the hunter but also because the force of the blow is a function of the speed of the missile.* Finally, in contrast

*These advantages are partly offset by the greater weight   the spear, which means that it might remain best for hunting animals with thick hides.

FIGURE 5.2 **Two comparisons of the spear and bow and arrow.**

Effective wounding range:

Spear

Bow and arrow

Speed of missile:

Spear

Bow and arrow

FIGURE 5.3 Reconstruction of settlement of mammoth hunters in Czechoslovakia.

with the spear, the bow and arrow permits the hunter to sight the missile at eye level, which greatly increases the accuracy of his aim.

Though less dramatic, the development of other tools was no less important. As one writer puts it, people of this era "began to make the tool fit the task with an altogether new precision."[18] Innovations included such diverse tools as pins or awls, needles with eyes, spoons, graving tools, axes, stone saws, antler hammers, shovels or scoops, pestles and grinding slabs (for grinding minerals to obtain coloring materials), and mattocks.

In colder regions, people usually lived in caves. This was not always possible, however, as in the case of the mammoth hunters who ranged from Czechoslovakia to Siberia and whose way of life forced them to remain in caveless country even during the winter. Figure 5.3 shows a modern reconstruction of one of their settlements. Some groups also built true earth houses.[19]

The discovery of such settlements has provided us with information on the size of human communities in that era. In general, they were quite small, many with as few as six to thirty persons. One, spread out along a two-mile stretch of river in France, may have housed as many as 400 to 600 persons, but this was exceptional and probably reflected unusual fishing opportunities.[20]

The best-known innovation of that period is its art. The drawings on the walls of caves in Western Europe (see Figure 5.4) are world famous, but they are only one of the art forms developed then. There was sculpture of various kinds (Figure 5.5), as well as bone and ivory carvings, often on the handles of weapons and tools (Figure 5.6).[21]

It would be hard to exaggerate the importance of these artistic remains, for they provide many insights into the life of that era. Drawings of men dressed to resemble animals strongly suggest magical or religious practice and a belief in sympathetic magic. This belief—that anything done to an image, or a part, of a person or animal will affect that person or animal—is further suggested by the fact that a great number of the drawings have spears or darts drawn or scratched into animals' flanks.[22] Sympathetic magic was

FIGURE 5.4   The stag hunt, cave painting, Spain.

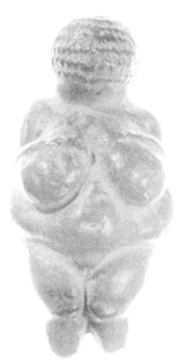

FIGURE 5.5   The Venus of
Willendorf, Germany.

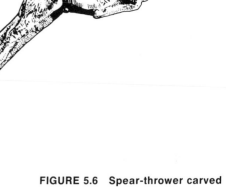

FIGURE 5.6   Spear-thrower carved
in form of horse, France.

apparently also used to produce fertility, in both humans and animals. At least this is the most likely explanation for the numerous female figures with exaggerated evidences of pregnancy (see Figure 5.5). Most scholars think it is no coincidence that the artist ignored the facial features and devoted all his attention to the symbols of fertility.

Many examples of the art of this period indicate the development of ceremonies or rituals. These are suggested by the drawings of men dancing and by engravings of processions of men standing before animals, heads bowed and weapons resting on their shoulders in a nonthreatening position. It has been suggested that they are following the practice of some modern hunters and are asking the forgiveness of the animals they plan to kill.[23] In short, the art of this era reveals the growth of human consciousness and people's efforts to understand and control their environment, and it attests to the gulf developing between them and the animal world.

By the close of the hunting and gathering era (about 7000 B.C.), human societies possessed a far greater store of cultural information than they possessed thirty thousand years before. They had, in fact, acquired more information in those last thirty thousand years than in all the fifteen million years of prior hominid history.

Table 5.1 makes clear just how dramatic this change in the rate of innovation was, over the course of hominid history. It lists all the known technological innovations of importance from the beginnings of the hominid family to the end of the hunting and gathering era. The four time intervals involved correspond to the periods which archaeologists label the Lower Paleolithic, Middle Paleolithic, Upper Paleolithic, and Mesolithic, and it should be noted that they differ tremendously in their duration (from 3,000 years to 14.9 *million* years). By dividing the number of innovations by the approximate time required to produce them, and by adjusting the results to make the earliest figure unity, or one, we arrive at the figures in the right-hand column, which are measures of the relative rate of innovation during the successive periods.

The 16,000-fold acceleration shown in this table cannot be explained by genetic change. Our genus, *Homo*, had already appeared at least half a million years before the end of the first time period, and our species, *Homo sapiens*, existed throughout the whole of the second time period. We must look elsewhere for an explanation of this remarkable acceleration—at the nature of technological innovation itself. When we do this, we are reminded that inventions are essentially recombinations of existing cultural elements and that the rate of invention is therefore a function of the size of the store of accumulated information (see pages 77 to 78). What we see in Table 5.1, then, is a striking demonstration of this principle—and evidence of the beginnings of a trend that has continued to this day.

TABLE 5.1   The rising rate of technological innovation: 15,000,000 to 7,000 B.C.

Time Periods and Their Major Technological Innovations		Number of Major Innovations	Rate of Innovation*
15,000,000 to 100,000 B.C.		5	1
Hand ax	Wooden spear		
Use of fire	Constructed shelters		
Fire-hardened spear point			
100,000 to 35,000 B.C.		3	140
Use of bone for tools	Skin clothing (probable)		
Built-in handles on tools			
35,000 to 10,000 B.C.		16.5†	2,000
Spear-thrower	Bow and arrow		
Lamps	Harpoon heads		
Fish gorgets	Pins or awls		
Needles with eye	Antler hammers		
Shovels or scoops	Mattocks		
Stone saws	Graving tools		
Spoons	Stone ax with hafted handle		
Separate handles	Pestles and grinding slabs		
Boats (?)			
10,000 to 7,000 B.C.		16.5†	16,500
Boats (?)	Fishhooks		
Fish traps	Fish nets		
Adzes	Sickles		
Plant cultivation	Domestication of sheep		
Basketry	Domestication of dog		
Grinding equipment	Leather-working tools		
Paving	Sledge		
Ice picks	Combs		

Sources: This table is based on data in Grahame Clark and Stuart Piggott, *Prehistoric Societies* (New York: Knopf, 1965); S. A. Semenov, *Prehistoric Technology* (New York: Barnes and Noble, 1964); John Pfeiffer, *The Emergence of Man*, 2d ed. (New York: Harper & Row, 1972); and Jacquetta Hawkes, *Prehistory*, UNESCO History of Mankind, vol. 1, part 1 (New York: Mentor, 1965).
*All rates are calculated as multiples of the rate for the earliest period, which is set arbitrarily at one.
†Since the date for the invention of boats is uncertain, half credit has been assigned to each of the latest periods.

THE ETHNOGRAPHIC EVIDENCE

After the emergence of more advanced types of societies, hunting and gathering societies continued to flourish in many parts of the world. A hundred years ago, there were still large numbers of them in both the New World and Australia, and smaller numbers in Southwest Africa, parts of the rain forest in central Africa, certain remote areas in Southeast Asia and neighboring islands, and in Arctic Asia.[24] As recently as 1788 there were probably 5,000 hunting and gathering societies in Australia alone[25] and almost certainly as many more in North America. Although the settlement of these areas by Europeans and the spreading influence of industrialization are finally destroying the last of them, we have detailed descriptions of many of these groups.

In our review, we will concentrate on hunting and gathering groups whose way of life has been least affected by contact with agrarian and industrial societies. Our primary concern will be with the more remote and isolated groups, and with groups that were studied before social contacts and cultural diffusion transformed or destroyed their traditional social patterns.

Even with these limitations, our sample of societies is by no means homogeneous. Of the 151 hunting and gathering societies in Murdock's sample, 13 per cent relied on hunting and gathering for their entire subsistence, while 11 per cent relied on these techniques for only about half. Most groups (80 per cent) depended on fishing to some extent, and a few (15 per cent) obtained nearly half their food from this source. A minority (23 per cent) derived part from horticulture, and a few (less than 5 per cent) almost half. In short, some were pure hunting and gathering societies, but most of them incorporated limited elements of fishing or horticulture or both.

Population Density and Size

Despite these variations, modern hunting and gathering societies* have a lot in common. None of them can support a large or dense population. Even in the most favorable environment, such as north central and northern California prior to white settlement, the population density for small localities rarely reaches 10 people per square mile and, over larger areas, seldom exceeds 3 per square mile. In less favorable environments, such as Australia, much of which is desert, population density drops well below 1 person per square mile.[26] Communities, therefore, are necessarily small. And, since communities are almost always autonomous, societies are equally small. The average size of those that survived into the modern era is somewhere between twenty-five and forty.[27]

Nomadism

Modern hunting and gathering societies are usually nomadic. Some groups are reported to remain in an area for periods as short as a week.[28] On the other hand, a few communities occupy permanent settlements, but all these

---

*When referring to "modern" hunting and gathering societies, we mean both those now in existence and those which survived into the modern era (i.e., the last several hundred years). In writing about these societies, the present tense is usually used for convenience.

either rely on fishing or horticulture as important secondary sources of subsistence or are located in unusually favorable environments.[29]

The nomadic character of most hunting and gathering communities is an inevitable result of their subsistence technology. One anthropologist described the basic problem when he said of a group of African Pygmies that "after a month, as a rule, the fruits of the forest have been gathered all around the vicinity of the camp, and the game has been scared away to a greater distance than is comfortable for daily hunting."[30] He went on to say that since "the economy relies on day-to-day quest, the simplest thing is for the camp to move."

Hunters and gatherers may also change camp sites for other reasons. A recent study of the Hadza in east Africa, for example, indicates that they often move to the place where a large animal has been killed simply to avoid carrying the meat.[31] Since their possessions are few, such moves require little effort. The Hadza also move to a new site when someone dies, or even when a member becomes sick or has a bad dream.

Many hunting and gathering groups disperse for a part of the year, with individual families striking out on their own. This pattern has been observed in such widely scattered groups as the Bushmen of Southwest Africa, the Eskimo, and the Australian aborigines. The reasons for this seem to be of two kinds. Sometimes seasonal changes in flora and fauna make it more advantageous for the group to split up and do their hunting and foraging in smaller groups. Other times, the splitting up of the group seems to be in response to controversies and conflicts in the larger group which require a cooling-off period—after which the attractions of greater opportunities for socializing bring the group back together again.[32]

Despite their nomadism, hunters and gatherers usually restrict their movements to fairly well-defined territories. When they move, they usually settle in or near some former camp site. There may even be a regular circuit of sites that the group uses year after year. Groups are deterred from entering new territories if only because they are usually occupied already. Moreover, they normally have a strong attachment to their own historic lands, which have often acquired a sacred or semisacred character through song and legend.

Economic Conditions

The combination of a primitive technology and a nomadic way of life makes it impossible for most hunting and gathering peoples to accumulate many possessions (see Figure 5.7). In describing the Negritos of the Philippines, one observer reports that "the possessions of a whole settlement would not be a good load for a sturdy carrier."[33] The situation is virtually the same among the Bushmen of southwestern Africa. "It is not advantageous to

FIGURE 5.7 Home and possessions of Paiute hunter in southern Utah in the 1870s.

multiply and accumulate in this society. Any man can make what he needs when he wants to. Most of the materials he uses are abundant and free for anyone to take. Furthermore, in their nomadic lives, without beasts of burden, the fact that the people themselves must carry everything puts a sharp limit on the quantity of objects they want to possess."[34] The few hunting and gathering groups able to establish permanent settlements may accumulate more possessions, but even they are greatly limited by their primitive technology.[35]

The quest for food is an important activity in every hunting and gathering society. Since most of these societies have no way to store food for extended periods, the food quest is fairly continuous. Moreover, unlike our situation, every member of the group must participate and make a contribution.

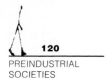

Until recently, most studies of hunting and gathering societies emphasized the uncertainty of the food supply and the difficulty of obtaining it.[36] A number of more recent studies, however, paint a brighter picture. Reports from the Pygmies of the Congo, the aborigines of Australia, the Tasaday of the Philippines, and even the Bushmen of the Kalahari Desert in southwestern Africa indicate that they can all secure an ample supply of food without an undue expenditure of time or energy.[37] This has led some anthropologists to swing to the other extreme and refer to hunters and gatherers as "the most leisured people in the world" and to their way of life as "the original affluent society."[38]

Neither view does justice to the diversity and changeability of the situations reported by the numerous observers who have lived among these peoples. Conditions vary considerably from group to group, and within a group they may vary from season to season. For example, the Indians of northern California usually had an abundance of food, and yet they occasionally encountered a shortage so severe that some of them starved.[39]

A very few societies, such as the recently discovered Tasaday, do not practice hunting. For the rest, hunting usually provides less food, in terms of bulk, than gathering. Yet hunting is valued more highly in virtually all these groups. There are several reasons for this. To begin with, meat is generally preferred to vegetables.[40] Whether this reflects a genetically based need or preference, we do not know; certainly not everyone feels this way. In some groups, preference for meat may simply reflect its scarcity. Hunting may also be valued because it provides excitement and challenge and an opportunity for the individual to excel. Added to all this is the fact that meat, unlike vegetables, is commonly shared beyond the immediate family, so success in hunting may be rewarded by widespread respect and deference. One leading anthropologist even suggests that sharing meat "is basic to the continued association of families in any human group that hunts."[41]

Because of the primitive nature of their technology, the division of labor in hunting and gathering societies is largely limited to distinctions based on age and sex. Hunting and military activity fall to the male, as do most political, religious, ceremonial, and artistic activities. The collection and preparation of vegetables and the care of children are women's responsibilities.[42] Some activities, such as constructing a shelter, may be defined as either men's or women's work, depending on the society.[43] Still other activities may be considered appropriate for both sexes. Further division of labor results because the very young and the aged are both limited in their capabilities.

There are no full-time occupational specialties in hunting and gathering societies, although there is usually some part-time specialization. For example, most groups have at least a headman and a shaman or medicine man. When their services are required, they function in these specialized capacities, but, as one writer says of the headmen of the Bergdama and the

FIGURE 5.8   Bushman hunter, Southwest Africa.

Bushmen, "when not engaged on public business they follow the same occupations as all other people."[44] He adds that this is most of the time.[45]

Within hunting and gathering groups, the family or kin group is normally the only significant form of economic organization. Sometimes, when the practice of sharing is widespread and hunting and gathering are carried on as communal activities, even the family group ceases to be economically important.

With respect to subsistence, each society is virtually self-sufficient. Some trade does occur, but except where contacts have been established with more advanced societies, the bartered items tend to be nonessentials, primarily objects with status or aesthetic value. Trade between two hunting and gathering societies usually involves things that are scarce or non-existent in one group's territory but fairly abundant in the other's (e.g., certain kinds of shells, stones, feathers, etc.).

Trade with advanced societies is more likely to involve technologically important items. For example, many groups obtain metal tools and weapons this way.[46] In the past, these imports were seldom important enough to alter

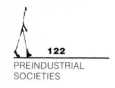

seriously the basic character of these societies.* In recent years, however, as contacts with industrialized and industrializing societies have increased, the volume and importance of the imports have often greatly distorted traditional patterns of life and helped undermine the sociocultural system.

Kinship and Marriage

Ties of kinship are vitally important in most hunting and gathering groups. It is hard for members of modern industrial societies to appreciate the tremendous significance of these ties, because so much of our own social interaction is organized in terms of *non*kinship, and often impersonal, roles (as in relations between lawyer and client, teacher and student, or clerk and customer).

In contrast, social interaction in hunting and gathering societies is usually organized around kinship roles. A student of the Australian aborigines reports that "in a typical Australian tribe it is found that a man can define his relations to every person with whom he has any social dealings whatever, whether of his own or of another tribe, by means of the terms of [kinship]."[47] Another writer goes so far as to say of these people that "every one with whom a person comes in contact is regarded as related to him, and the kind of relationship must be ascertained so that the two persons concerned will know what their mutual behavior should be."[48] He adds that kinship ties are the anatomy and physiology of aboriginal society and "must be understood if the behavior of the aborigines as social beings is to be understood." Though there are exceptions to this, *kinship is usually the basic organizing principle in hunting and gathering societies.*[49]

Viewed in evolutionary perspective, the family has often been described as the matrix, or womb, from which all other forms of social structure have evolved. Although this may be an exaggeration, it points to a basic truth: in hunting and gathering societies, kin groups perform many of the functions that are performed by schools, business firms, governmental agencies, and other specialized organizations in larger, more advanced, and more differentiated societies.

Kin groups in hunting and gathering societies are of two types, nuclear and extended families. A nuclear family includes a man, his wife or wives, and their unmarried children. Polygyny is widespread; only 12 per cent of the hunting and gathering groups in Murdock's Ethnographic Atlas are classified as monogamous. It does not follow, of course, that 88 per cent of *families* are polygynous: this is impossible, given the roughly equal numbers of men and women. Usually only one or two of the most influential men have more than one wife, and they seldom have more than two or three. This limited polygyny

*The introduction of the horse and the gun among the Plains Indians of the United States was an important exception to the usual pattern.

is possible because girls usually marry earlier than boys, and some men are forced to remain bachelors. Multiple wives appear to be an economic asset in these societies and, to some extent, a status symbol as well.

Divorce is permitted in virtually all hunting and gathering societies and is fairly common in some.[50] In others, however, it is made relatively difficult.[51] The most we can say is that there is great variability in this matter.

The nuclear family is usually part of a larger, more inclusive, and more important kin group known as the extended family.[52] The extended family typically includes a group of brothers and their families or a father and his married sons with their families; in any event, it is usually organized around kinship ties among *males*. This practice probably reflects the peculiar requirements of hunting.[53] Successful hunting often calls for extremely close cooperation—cooperation that presupposes years of close association in the activity and enables every individual to anticipate the moves of every other. Gathering has no such requirement. Since plants are stationary, no cooperation is required; if women go foodgathering in groups, it is largely for companionship. Furthermore, since animals, unlike plants, move about, hunters must have an intimate knowledge of the local environment. This kind of familiarity is acquired from early childhood on, and it is not readily

FIGURE 5.9 Bushman girl gathering berries.

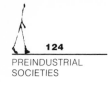

transferable from one locale to another. Finally, the practice of keeping married sons within the family probably reflects, to some extent, simple male dominance and male preference.

The extended family is also important economically, for the ties of kinship among its members encourage the practice of sharing. When the daily acquisition of food is as uncertain as it is in many hunting and gathering societies, a nuclear family could easily starve if it had to depend exclusively on its own efforts. A family might be surfeited with food for a time and then suddenly have nothing. Or all the adult members of the family could be ill or injured at the same time. In either case the family would be dependent on the generosity of others. Although sharing can, and does, take place between unrelated persons, kinship ties reinforce the tendency. In this connection, it is noteworthy that many hunting and gathering peoples create what we would call fictional ties of kinship when there is no "real" relationship by blood or marriage. These ties are just as meaningful to them as "true" kinship ties and serve to tighten the bonds within the group.

By marrying outside the local group (a practice known as exogamy), a society gradually establishes a web of kinship ties with neighboring groups. According to one anthropologist, "One of the important functions of exogamy is that of opening territories so that peaceful movements can take place among them, and particularly so that any large temporary variations in food resources can be taken advantage of by related groups."[54] Related to this is the custom of wife lending, practiced by hunting and gathering peoples as diverse as the Eskimo and the Australian aborigines.[55] As in the case of exogamy, the purpose seems to be to strengthen, restore, or create bonds between the men involved. Thus, if two individuals or two groups have had a quarrel, they may settle it by lending one another their wives. The practice is predicated on the assumption that women are prized possessions that one does not share with everyone. It would be a mistake to suppose, however, that women are merely property in these societies; they often have considerable influence in the life of the group and are far removed from the position of chattels.

Political Patterns

Politically, modern hunting and gathering societies are extremely primitive. As we have seen, most local communities are autonomous and independent entities even though they have an average population of less than fifty. The primitive nature of their political systems is also evidenced by the limited development of specialized political roles and the very limited authority vested in them. In most cases, there is simply a headman, who provides minimal leadership for the group.[56] The late Allan Holmberg, an anthropologist who lived among the Siriono of eastern Bolivia, wrote a description of their headmen that is close to being a portrait of the "typical" headman in a hunting and gathering society.

> Presiding over every band of Siriono is a headman, who is at least nominally the highest official of the group. Although his authority theoretically extends throughout the band, in actual practice its exercise depends almost entirely upon his personal qualities as a leader. In any case, there is no obligation to obey the orders of a headman, no punishment for nonfulfillment. Indeed, little attention is paid to what is said by a headman unless he is a member of one's immediate family. To maintain his prestige a headman must fulfill, in a superior fashion, those obligations required of everyone else.
>
> The prerogatives of a headman are few. . . . The principal privilege . . . if it could be called such, is that it is his right to occupy, with his immediate family, the center of the [communal] house. Like any other man he must make his bows and arrows, his tools; he must hunt, fish, collect, and plant gardens. He makes suggestions as to migrations, hunting trips, etc., but these are not always followed by his [people]. As a mark of status, however, a headman always possesses more than one wife.
>
> While headmen complain a great deal that other members of the band do not satisfy their obligations to them, little heed is paid to their requests. . . .
>
> In general, however, headmen fare better than other members of the band. Their requests more frequently bear fruit than those of others because headmen are the best hunters and are thus in a better position than most to reciprocate for any favors done them.[57]

There are similar reports on most other hunting and gathering societies.[58] In a number of instances it is said that the headman "held his place only so long as he gave satisfaction."

Occasionally the headman enjoys a bit more power and privilege. For example, among the Arunta of Australia the headman "has, *ex officio*, a position which, if he be a man of personal ability, but only in that case, enables him to wield considerable power. . . ."[59] Among the Bergdama of southwestern Africa, the headman "is treated with universal respect, being specified as a 'great man' by adults and 'grandfather' by children; he usually has the most wives (sometimes three or more); he has the pick of all wild animal skins for clothing himself and his family, and only his wives wear necklaces or girdles of ostrich eggshell beads; and he receives portions of all game killed in the chase, and tribute from men finding honey."[60]

At the opposite extreme are a number of groups that do not even have a headman. (This is true of 12 per cent of the hunting and gathering societies in the Ethnographic Atlas sample.) In these societies, decisions that affect the entire group are arrived at through informal discussions among the more respected and influential members, typically the heads of families.[61]

The limited development of political institutions in hunting and gathering societies stands in sharp contrast to the situation in more advanced societies

TABLE 5.2   Degree of power of political leaders, by societal type

Societal type	Degree of power (in percentages)			No. of Societies
	Substantial	Moderate	Slight	
Hunting and gathering	9	18	73	11
Horticultural	50	33	17	24
Herding	88	13	0	8

Source: Derived from data in Leo Simmons, *The Role of the Aged in Primitive Society* (New Haven, Conn.: Yale, 1945).

(see Table 5.2). It stems from the primitive nature of the groups' subsistence technology and their resultant small size and relative isolation, which make it possible for them to handle their political problems very informally. Consensus is achieved much more readily in a small, homogeneous group of a few dozen people (of whom only the adults, and often only the adult males, have a voice) than in a larger, more heterogeneous community of hundreds or thousands. A headman is valuable to such a small group only if he contributes special knowledge, insight, or skills.

Even if the leader of a hunting and gathering band were ambitious and eager to increase his power, he would not get very far. Unlike leaders in technologically more advanced societies, he would find it impossible to build and maintain an organization of dependent retainers to do his bidding, or to obtain a monopoly of the more powerful weapons. Every man is able to provide for his own material needs. The materials for making weapons lie ready at hand, and every man is trained to make and use them. If worse comes to worst, a man can usually leave the band he is in and join another.[62] Thus, there are no opportunities for building political empires, even on a small scale.*

Given the rudimentary nature of political institutions in hunting and gathering societies, one might suppose that there are few restrictions on an individual. In one sense this is true; there *are* few imposed by political authorities—no court, no police, no prisons. The individual is hardly free, however, to do as he wishes. To begin with, his freedom is limited by the nature of his society's technology. Compared with members of more advanced societies, hunters and gatherers are very restricted in where they can go and what they can do.

There are also social restraints. No society can afford to be indifferent to the actions of its members, and even in the absence of formal political authority, the group controls their conduct. Though there are minor variations from one hunting and gathering society to another, we find the same

*The limiting effects of a hunting and gathering technology will become clearer in subsequent chapters, as we observe the growth of political systems in horticultural and agrarian societies.

basic patterns of social control in groups as far apart as the Kaska Indians of the Canadian Northwest, the Andaman Islanders of Southeast Asia, the Bushmen of Southwest Africa, and the Punan of Borneo.[63] First, there is blood revenge, whereby an injured person, aided, perhaps, by his kinsmen, punishes the offender himself. As one student of the Bushmen put it, "when disputes arise between the members of the band . . . there is no appeal to any supreme authority [since] . . . there is no such authority. . . . The only remedy is self-help."[64] But this mode of social control is usually invoked only when the victim of the offense is a single individual or a family. When an entire band suffers because of a member's actions, group pressure is used. For example, if a man refuses to do his fair share in providing food, he is punished by losing the respect of others.[65] In the case of more serious offenses, the penalty may be ostracism or even banishment. The third method of control is a deterrent that applies primarily to ritual prescriptions. In such cases, the group's fear of spontaneous supernatural sanctions provides the needed restraint. Bushmen, for example, believe that girls who do not observe the restrictions imposed on them at puberty turn into frogs.[66] All three methods of social control are very informal and would not be sufficient except in small, homogeneous groups in which ties among the members are intimate and continuous, and contradictory ideas are absent.

Equality and Inequality

The rudimentary nature of the political system and the primitive nature of the technological system contribute to yet another distinctive characteristic of modern hunting and gathering societies: minimal inequality in power and privilege. Differences between individuals are so slight, in fact, that a number of observers have spoken of a kind of "primitive communism." To some extent this is justified. As we have seen, political authority with the power to coerce is virtually nonexistent. Differences in *influence* exist, but only to the degree permitted by those who are influenced, and only as a result of their respect for another individual's skills or wisdom. Should he lose this respect, he also loses his influence.

The chief exceptions to the near equality in wealth and economic privilege occur among the handful of nonnomadic groups, where some modest inequalities are reported.[67] In most societies, differences in wealth are very minor. Many factors are responsible for this. For one thing, as we have seen, the nomadic way of life prevents any substantial accumulation of possessions. Moreover, the ready availability of most essential resources (e.g., wood for bows, flint for stone tools, etc.) precludes the need to amass things, while technological limitations greatly restrict what can be produced. Finally, there is the widespread practice of reciprocity, or sharing, in most of these groups.

TABLE 5.3   Frequency of private ownership of land, by societal type

Societal type	Frequency of Private Ownership of Land (in percentages)				No. of Societies
	General	Frequent	Rare	Absent	
Hunting and gathering	0	0	11	89	9
Horticultural	36	23	23	18	22

Source: Derived from data in Leo Simmons, *The Role of the Aged in Primitive Society* (New Haven, Conn.: Yale, 1945).

As a general rule, the concept of private property has only limited development among hunting and gathering peoples. Things that an individual uses constantly, such as his tools and weapons, are always recognized as his, but fields and forests are the common property of the band (see Table 5.3). The territorial rights of bands, however, are often taken quite seriously, and outsiders are frequently obliged to ask permission to enter another group's territory to seek food.[68] Animals and plants are normally considered the common property of the band until they are killed or gathered, when they become the property of the individual. Even then, his use of them is hedged about by the rule of sharing.[69]

A successful hunter does not normally keep his kill for himself alone or even, in most cases, for his family.[70] The reason for this is the same as the one that underlies the popularity of insurance in industrial societies: *it is an effective method of spreading risks*. As we have seen, poor hunting conditions, ill health, or just a streak of bad luck can render any individual or family incapable of providing for itself, and sharing food greatly enhances the entire group's chances of survival. Most of the societies that failed to develop this practice have simply been eliminated.

Despite the near equality of power and wealth, there is inequality in prestige in most hunting and gathering societies. The interesting thing about this, from the viewpoint of a member of an industrial society, is the extent to which prestige depends on the *personal* qualities of an individual rather than on such impersonal criteria as the offices or roles he occupies or the possessions he controls. This is, of course, a natural consequence of the limited development of specialized offices and roles and the limited opportunities for accumulating possessions and wealth. But it sharply differentiates these societies from our own.

Writing of the Andaman Islanders, A. R. Radcliffe-Brown reports that they accord honor and respect to three kinds of people: (1) older people, (2) people endowed with supernatural powers, and (3) people with certain personal qualities, notably "skill in hunting and warfare, generosity and kindness, and freedom from bad temper."[71] Though he does not say so explicitly, men are apparently more likely than women to become honored members of the group. These same criteria are usually employed by other hunting and gathering peoples, with skill in oratory often honored as well.[72]

Because personal criteria are so important, the systems of stratification in these groups have an openness about them not found in more advanced societies. Almost no organizational or institutional barriers block the rise of talented individuals. For example, even where the office of headman is inherited, as it is in approximately half the societies,[73] others can surpass him in achieving honor, and he himself may fail to win even a modicum of it. The study of the Siriono Indians quoted earlier tells of a headman who was a very poor hunter and whose status, as a result, was low. The importance attached to age also contributes to the openness of the system. Almost anyone who lives long enough will probably end up with a fair degree of honor and respect.

Tribal Ties

As we have noted a number of times, local hunting and gathering bands are usually autonomous. Rarely are even two of them brought under a single leader, and when it happens, it usually involves groups no longer completely dependent on hunting and gathering.

Despite the virtual absence of formal political structures beyond the level of the local community, there are often structures based on other kinds of social and cultural ties. The most inclusive of these, and one that is nearly universal, is the *tribe*—a group of people who speak a distinctive language or dialect, share a culture that distinguishes them from other peoples, and know themselves, or are known, by a definite name.[74] Unlike a society, a tribe is not necessarily organized politically. On the contrary, few are, at least among hunting and gathering peoples.

Most tribes appear to have been formed by the process of societal fission. When the population of a hunting and gathering band grows too large for the resources of the immediate area, it divides. Division may also occur because of conflict within a band.[75] In either case, although a new group is formed, its members will naturally continue to share the culture of the parent group. Normally the new group locates somewhere near the old one, if for no other reason than because their technology and accumulated experience become less relevant the further they move and the more the environment differs from the one they have been used to. As this process of fission occurs, a cluster of autonomous bands with the same language and similar stores of information will emerge, forming a new tribe.

As this suggests, among hunters and gatherers the tribe is more important as a cultural unit than as a social unit. One writer, describing the Bushmen, reports that the tribe "has no social solidarity, and is of very little, if

any, importance in regulating social life. There appears to be no tribal organization among the Bushmen, nothing in the nature of a central authority whose decisions are binding on all the members of the tribe, nor is collective action ever taken in the interests of the tribe as a whole. The tribe, in fact, is merely a loose aggregate of hunting bands which have a common language and name."[76] This description applies to most tribes of hunters and gatherers. Occasionally, as in Australia, an entire tribe comes together for some important event, but this is not typical.

From the structural standpoint, the chief significance of these tribal groupings lies in their evolutionary potential: with technological advance, they may become political units. Even among societies still on the hunting and gathering level, there is some evidence of movement in this direction. In a few of the more favorably situated sedentary groups, for example, several villages have been brought together under the leadership of a single individual.[77] Such a step would be impossible, of course, without the common cultural heritage.

FIGURE 5.10 Bushman shaman in trance.

Religion

Few facets of primitive life have received as much attention in the last hundred years as religion. Yet, paradoxically, there are few areas where our understanding is less satisfactory. One reason is that too many writers have twisted the facts to fit preconceived theories.[78] As a result, we have many very plausible but mutually contradictory theories and a minimum of systematic analysis. Another reason is the great diversity of religious beliefs among hunting and gathering peoples. This is an area where a primitive technology appears not to restrict too greatly the development of ideas.[79]

In almost every carefully studied hunting and gathering society of the modern era, there is evidence that people have grappled with the problems of ultimate causation and meaning.[80] In myths and legends, they have developed explanations for most of the recurring features of life. Most of these peoples believe the world is populated with countless unseen spirits that influence the course of events in the world around them.[81] These spirits can be responsible for the success or failure of the hunt, for unexpected deaths or accidents, for illness, for births, or for unexpected good fortune. Many, perhaps most, of these spirits reside in material objects such as plants, animals, rocks, or other natural phenomena (a belief known as *animism*).

Although these beliefs may appear crude and unscientific, scholars who have studied them carefully have found that they sometimes embody profound insights and moving sentiments.[82] Above all, these religions proclaim that the world is far more complex and mysterious than it appears on the surface—a belief shared not only by the major world religions but by modern science as well.

Linked to the basic beliefs of a group of hunters and gatherers is a set of moral values that undergirds the life of the society. These values define basic standards of good and evil for members of the group and are the basis for the norms and roles that govern their conduct in daily life.

Because religious differentiation within a hunting and gathering society is minimal, religious conflict is negligible. The one really important religious distinction is the role of shaman or medicine man, an individual who is believed to have special powers as a result of his distinctive relationship with the spirit world. While a shaman uses his powers in various ways, one of the most common is in healing.[83] He may also use them to ensure the success of hunting expeditions, to protect the group against evil spirits and other dangers, and generally to ensure the group's well-being. Shamans do not always use their special powers for the benefit of others, however. Sometimes they employ them to punish people who have personally offended them.[84]

Because of their role, shamans usually command respect and often are more influential than the headman.[85] Sometimes, as with the Northern Maidu

**FIGURE 5.11 Siberian shaman of the
eighteenth century, as seen by Dutch
traveler.**

in California, the headman "was chosen largely through the aid of the
shaman, who was supposed to reveal to the old men the choice of the
spirits."[86] The role of shaman tends to be profitable, since others are usually
happy to offer gifts in exchange for help or to maintain goodwill. One early
observer of the Indians of Lower California wrote that successful shamans
were able "to obtain their food without the trouble of gathering it . . . for the
silly people provided them with the best they could find, in order to keep
them in good humor and to enjoy their favor."[87] Though the shaman is
normally a man, a woman may become one if she has had psychic experiences and if, like other shamans, she can prove her power through healing and
other feats.

Socialization and Education

Socialization of the young in hunting and gathering societies is largely an
informal process in which children learn both through their play and through
observing and imitating their elders. Colin Turnbull, who lived among the
Pygmies of the Congo, writes:

> For children, life is one long frolic interspersed with a healthy sprinkle of
> spankings and slappings. Sometimes these seem unduly severe, but it is all part
> of their training. And one day they find that the games they have been playing are

not games any longer, but the real thing, for they have become adults. Their hunting is now real hunting; their tree climbing is in earnest search of inaccessible honey; their acrobatics on the swings are repeated almost daily, in other forms, in the pursuit of elusive game, or in avoiding the malicious forest buffalo. It happens so gradually that they hardly notice the change at first, for even when they are proud and famous hunters their life is still full of fun and laughter.[88]

At a relatively early age, boys are allowed to join the men on the hunt, participating in any activities of which they are capable. Fathers commonly make miniature bows as soon as their sons can handle them, and encourage the boys to practice. Girls assist their mothers in their camp-site duties and in gathering vegetables and fruits. Thus the children prepare for their future roles.

This informal socialization is often supplemented by a formal process of initiation that marks the transition from childhood to manhood or womanhood.[89] Initiation rites vary considerably from one society to another, though girls' ceremonies are usually linked with their first menstruation. The rites for boys commonly involve painful experiences (e.g., circumcision, scarification, or knocking out a tooth), which prove their courage and thus their right to the privileges of manhood. As a rule, these rites are also the occasion for introducing young men to their group's most sacred lore, and this combination of experiences helps to impress on them its value and importance.

Compared with horticultural and herding societies, hunting and gathering societies put more stress on training the child to be independent and self-reliant, less on obedience (see Table 5.4). This is apparently an adaptation to a subsistence economy in which it is imperative to have "venturesome, independent adults who can take initiative in wresting food daily from nature."[90] By contrast, venturesomeness and independence are less necessary—and may even be harmful to the group—in technologically more advanced horticultural and herding societies.

TABLE 5.4 Emphasis in child rearing, by societal type

| Societal Type | Child-rearing Emphases (in percentages) | | | | | | No. of Societies |
	A*	B	C	D	E	Total	
Hunting and gathering	36	36	14	14	0	100	22
Horticultural and herding	3	8	3	36	51	101	39

Source: Based on Herbert Barry III, Irving L. Child, and Margaret K. Bacon, "Relation of Child Training to Subsistence Economy," *American Anthropologist,* 61 (1959), table 2.
* A—Self-reliance stressed much more than obedience; B—Self-reliance stressed somewhat more than obedience; C—Self-reliance and obedience stressed equally; D—Obedience stressed somewhat more than self-reliance; E—Obedience stressed much more than self-reliance.

FIGURE 5.12 Contemporary cave art by Australian hunter: the water-snake pattern illustrates a religious legend.

The Arts and Leisure

Modern hunting and gathering peoples in widely scattered parts of the world have produced a variety of artistic works. Some are strikingly similar to the cave drawings and carvings of hunters and gatherers of the prehistoric era. The motivation behind these efforts is not always clear, but in some cases it is plainly religious, in others, magical.[91] And sometimes it appears to be purely aesthetic.

Music, too, plays a part in the lives of at least some hunters and gatherers. Turnbull has written in detail of Pygmy hunter festivals, in which songs and the music of a primitive wooden trumpet are central.[92] These festivals have great religious significance and express the people's devotion to, and trust in, the forest. Or, as with the visual arts, music may be purely for enjoyment.[93] Dancing is another valued feature in the life of many of these societies, and, again, the motives for it are varied.

Another popular leisure activity is storytelling. Turnbull reports that the Pygmies "are blessed with a lively imagination," and he provides several delightful examples.[94] Stories range from accounts of the day's hunt (often embellished to hold the listeners' attention) to sacred myths and legends

SONG OF THE ELEPHANT HUNTERS

The following song was sung by Pygmy hunters just before they set out on an elephant hunt. The headman was joined in the choruses by the entire group. The song was recorded by a visiting French missionary.

In the weeping forest, under the evening wind,
The night, all black, lies down to sleep, happy.
In the sky the stars escape trembling,
Fireflies flash and go out,
Up high, the moon is dark, its white light is out.
The spirits are wandering,
   Elephant hunter, take up your bow!
     Chorus: Elephant hunter, take up your bow!

In the timid forest the tree sleeps, the leaves are dead,
The monkeys have closed their eyes, hanging high from the branches,
The antelopes glide by with silent steps,
They nibble the cool grass, cocking their ears, alert,
They raise their heads and listen, a little frightened,
The cicada falls silent, cutting off his grating sound,
   Elephant hunter, take up your bow!
     Chorus: Elephant hunter, take up your bow!

In the forest that the great rain lashes,

Father elephant walks heavily, baou, baou,
Carefree and fearless, sure of his strength,
Father elephant whom nothing can vanquish,
Among the tall forest trees that he breaks, he stops and moves on,
He eats, trumpets, and searches for his mate,
Father elephant, we hear you from afar,
   Elephant hunter, take up your bow!
     Chorus: Elephant hunter, take up your bow!

In the forest where nothing moves through but you,
Hunter, lift up your heart, glide, run, leap, and walk,
The meat is in front of you, the huge piece of meat,
The meat that walks like a hill,
The meat that rejoices the heart,
The meat that will roast at your hearth,
The meat your teeth sink into,
The beautiful red meat and the blood that we drink steaming,
   Yoyo, Elephant hunter, take up your bow!
     Chorus: Yoyo, Elephant hunter, take up your bow!

From Carleton S. Coon, *The Hunting Peoples* (Boston: Little, Brown, 1971), pp. 114–115. Reprinted by permission of Little, Brown and Company in association with the Atlantic Monthly Press.

passed down over many generations. Legends commonly deal with the origins of the world and the group, which are often considered identical. Stories about the exploits of great heroes of the past are popular and often help explain the group's customs. Sacred myths and legends, as we have seen, frequently enter into initiation rites, especially for boys, and they are sometimes accompanied by music and dance. This complex interweaving of art, religion, entertainment, and education provides a strong foundation for tradition and for sociocultural continuity.

Hunters and gatherers, like people everywhere, also enjoy gossip, small

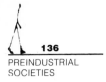

TABLE 5.5   Types of games, by societal type

Type of Society	Percentage of Societies Having Games of:			No. of Societies
	Physical Skill	Chance	Strategy	
Hunting and gathering	96	83	0	117
Simple horticultural	83	33	7	30
Advanced horticultural	90	37	68	41
Agrarian	92	60	60	25
Fishing	93	63	3	30
Herding	89	44	56	9

Source: George Peter Murdock's Ethnographic Atlas sample of 915 societies.

talk, and other nonessential activities. Games are played in virtually all these groups, but it is interesting to note that games of strategy are rare or unknown, while games of chance are more common than in any other type of society (see Table 5.5). If a society's games reflect the experiences its members have in their everyday lives, this strongly suggests that hunters and gatherers feel that they have less control over the events in their lives than members of more advanced societies do.

Demographic Patterns: Birthrates and Death Rates

The basic determinants of population size are birthrates and death rates. These, together with the rates of in- and out-migration, are the only immediate determinants of population change in a society. All other factors (e.g., famines, wars, etc.) make their influence felt through one of these four.

It is usually difficult to determine these rates in hunting and gathering societies, because ethnographers have generally been more interested in such things as the details of childbirth rituals and the intricacies of marriage rules than in the birthrate or typical family size. Such evidence as we have, however, indicates that birth and death rates are usually quite high. In Greenland, from 1922 to 1930, the average annual birthrate among the Eskimo was 42.3 per thousand inhabitants, more than twice that of modern industrial societies.[95] In a Canadian Eskimo group that had minimal contact with the outside world, the average number of births per married woman was 5, and the average for women forty-five or older was over 10. Among the Bushmen, it is reported, pregnancies "follow in rapid succession during the course of married life, and it often happens that another child, or even two, may be born while the first is still at the breast."[96] The Negritos of Malaya have apparently been somewhat less prolific, if we may judge from one small study: a group of thirty-two men aged forty and over had already had 151 children, an average of nearly 5 apiece, with the prospect of more to come.[97] Finally, among the Punan of Borneo "large families are the rule; a family with as many as eight or nine children is no rarity."[98]

One should not assume, however, that these societies are swarming with children. Mortality rates are high, especially among infants. For example, over 40 per cent of the 151 children born to the thirty-two Negrito fathers were already dead at the time of the study, and a recent study of the Bushmen found that 40 per cent died before the age of fifteen.[99]

Infanticide and abortion are widely practiced in hunting and gathering societies.[100] Children often cannot be weaned until the age of two-and-a-half or three, because of the lack of suitable foods, and when a mother with a child still at the breast gives birth to another child, the parents have little choice but to dispose of it.[101] Accidents, illness, and periodic food shortages also take their toll, often causing premature aging and early death. An ethnographer who lived among the Siriono of South America, for example, estimates that the average life-span of those who survive infancy is only thirty-five to forty years, by which time the stresses of their way of life have rendered most people decrepit.[102] At one time, it was believed that death rates were uniformly high for all hunting and gathering societies, but more recent evidence indicates that there are at least some exceptions.[103]

ARCHAEOLOGICAL AND ETHNOGRAPHIC EVIDENCE COMPARED

Now that we have completed our review of both the archaeological and ethnographic evidence, we can consider the relationship between prehistoric hunting and gathering groups and contemporary ones. Though indiscriminate comparisons of the two can be misleading, our evidence indicates that careful comparisons are not only valid but extremely valuable.[104] To begin with, we must recognize that we cannot equate modern hunters and gatherers with early hominid hunters and gatherers of a million or more years ago—before *Homo sapiens sapiens* had evolved and before the basic tools and weapons of modern hunters and gatherers had been invented. We can, however, reasonably compare modern hunters and gatherers with those that lived during the last 15,000 years.

We can see why, now that we are familiar with both sets of evidence. The similarities between these two sets of hunters and gatherers are many and basic; the differences are fewer and much less important.* Similarities occur

*We are excluding here those modern hunting and gathering groups that have been socially and culturally overwhelmed in recent years by contact with more advanced societies. Thus we must rely heavily on older (especially pre–World War II) studies of such peoples.

in such crucial matters as technology and mode of subsistence, size of local groups, relative equality,* and minimal occupational specialization. In addition, similarities in art suggest similarities in religious belief and practice.

The differences are largely of three types. First, in many modern hunting and gathering societies there are certain elements that originated in more advanced societies (e.g., metal tools and some religious ideas). Second, modern hunters and gatherers have no opportunity for territorial expansion, which means that population growth is impossible and deaths and births must balance. Prehistoric hunters and gatherers, happily, were not always subject to this harsh restriction. Finally, technologically advanced societies have often forced modern hunters and gatherers out of territories suited to farming and herding.†

As we have seen, the archaeological record is much less complete than the ethnographic, being silent on many subjects about which the latter provides a wealth of information. Therefore, when the ethnographic record shows patterns that are consistent for all or most modern groups and when these patterns do not depend on conditions peculiar to the modern era, archaeologists now tend to regard them as applicable to most of the hunting and gathering societies of the last 15,000 years. This is a consequence of the growing awareness of the *limiting* nature of a hunting and gathering technology and economy.[105] Such a primitive technology and economy make it utterly impossible to have large settlements, highly developed governments, literacy, schools, a high degree of occupational specialization, a market economy, a complex class system, and a host of other things.

What *is* possible are small communities, usually autonomous, usually nomadic, led by headmen who have almost no authority and govern by persuasion. These groups are likely to be composed of a number of nuclear families linked by ties of kinship. These ties will probably be of vital importance to both the individual and the community. The division of labor is likely to be almost entirely along the lines of age and sex, with very limited occupational specialization a possibility. Possessions are certain to be few, near equality in wealth the rule. Finally, birth and death rates will both be high by the standards of modern industrial societies.

Certain limited variations on these themes are possible. Societies in very

---

*This is indicated by the absence of differentiation in burial remains prior to about 5000 B.C. By contrast, in more advanced societies of later eras one finds clear evidence of distinctions between rich and poor, the former having many rare and obviously costly objects buried with them.

†The importance of this may not have been as great as we would imagine, however, because territory that farmers and herders consider marginal may provide a good living for hunters and gatherers. Moreover, hunters and gatherers in both the New World and Australia still occupied good farming and herding lands until fairly recently, so we are not entirely without information on societies that existed under such conditions.

favorable locations and those with a somewhat more advanced technology (e.g., those able to supplement their food supply by fishing or horticulture) will probably be a bit larger, somewhat less nomadic, a little more developed politically and specialized occupationally, and a bit wealthier and less egalitarian. The differences, however, will not be great.

By contrast, there are certain aspects of life where the hunting and gathering technology seems completely irrelevant. Observations of modern hunters and gatherers indicate that this is true of divorce. Every possibility, ranging from the complete absence of divorce to the most casual practice of it, has been noted.

Between the extremes, there are a number of areas where a hunting and gathering technology neither determines the pattern nor is irrelevant. Rather, it seems to predispose the group to adopt a particular alternative without completely precluding the others. Marriage practices are a case in point: a minority of modern hunting and gathering societies (12 per cent of those in the Ethnographic Atlas sample) are monogamous, for example, even though the great majority permit polygyny. Apparently, a hunting and gathering technology and the characteristics that accompany it are not strong enough to preclude either of these possibilities, but neither are they irrelevant. In statistical terms, one would say that the characteristics of hunting and gathering societies increase the probability of polygyny and reduce the probability of strict monogamy.

Since there is no reason to think that relevant conditions were different in late Upper Paleolithic or Mesolithic times, it is reasonable to suppose that roughly comparable probabilities prevailed then. In short, except where there is no distinctive pattern for modern hunting and gathering societies (as in the case of divorce) or where relevant conditions have changed (as in the case of metal tools), we can probably assume substantial similarity between the advanced hunting and gathering societies of the late prehistoric era and those of recent centuries.

THE LAST HUNTING AND GATHERING SOCIETIES

In the summer of 1975, death came to the last full-blooded member of the Ona, a tribe of hunters and gatherers that had inhabited the southern tip of South America since at least the days of Ferdinand Magellan, the famed sixteenth-century explorer, and probably for centuries or even millennia before that.[106] It is estimated that in Magellan's day there were 2,000 Ona, divided into about thirty societies. Despite the remoteness and harshness of their homeland, the Ona were destroyed by their contacts with technologically more advanced societies. Disease, loss of territory, and loss of members

FIGURE 5.13 One of the last photographs of the Ona of Tierra del Fuego, a now extinct tribe of hunters and gatherers.

through intermarriage with other groups all took their toll. The last Ona society died years ago; now the last member is also dead.

The experience of the Ona has been the experience of tens of thousands of hunting and gathering societies during the 9,000 years since hunters and gatherers first began competing for territories and other resources with technologically more advanced societies.* Hunters and gatherers have had only one defense: retreat to lands that other groups regarded as worthless or inaccessible.

Today, even this defense has begun to crumble and the last outposts of this ancient way of life appear doomed. The speed of the process is demonstrated by the experience of an anthropologist who pioneered in the study of the Bushmen of the Kalahari Desert in Southwest Africa. She reports that to reach them in 1951 required an arduous trip across the desert by truck, lasting eight days from the final outposts of civilization until she made contact with the Bushmen.[108] There was no road of any kind, not even a track across the sand and bush country. When she returned in 1962, only eleven years later, she reached them in one day over a well-cleared track. As

---

*Scholars today estimate the world population of hunters and gatherers at 5 to 10 million around 7000 B.C.[107] This would indicate a minimum of 100,000 hunting and gathering societies.

Bushmen come more and more in contact with and under the influence of horticultural and industrial societies, their traditional way of life is crumbling. According to a recent report, less than 5 per cent of the 30,000 Kung Bushmen are still hunters and gatherers.[109] By the end of the century, perhaps before, the world will probably have seen the last true hunting and gathering society, and an irreplaceable link to our past will have vanished.

CHAPTER 6
HORTICULTURAL
SOCIETIES

By the end of the hunting and gathering era ten thousand years ago, human populations had accumulated substantial stores of information about plants and animals. People were as familiar with the behavior patterns of some animals as they were with their own, and probably understood them almost as well. They had also identified hundreds of varieties of edible plants and become familiar with their processes of growth, fructification, and decay. What is more, archaeological research has shown that some hunters and gatherers in the Middle East were harvesting wild grains with stone sickles. Thus, it is clear that the shift from hunting animals to herding them and from gathering fruits and vegetables to cultivating them was not as great as one might imagine.[1] The people involved in the transition, which was spread over many generations, almost certainly had no idea that they were initiating a major social revolution. Yet they were laying a foundation for basic changes in the conditions of human life, for the rise of towns and cities, the creation of empires, and the emergence of civilization.

There are many questions about the origins of plant cultivation and animal domestication to which we would like answers. When, where, and precisely how did they begin? Were the new techniques devised independently by societies in many different parts of the world, or were there only a few centers from which the crucial information spread? Archaeologists, geneticists, and other scholars have been searching for the answers to such questions for years, but they remain elusive. On several points, however, there is general agreement. First, as we have already indicated, horticulture developed very gradually. Second, even if the basic techniques of plant cultivation and animal domestication originated in only a few societies, many other societies subsequently contributed to the new technology by learning to cultivate new varieties of plants and domesticate new kinds of animals. Finally, since in both hunting and gathering and horticultural societies, women are generally concerned with plants and men with animals, there is good reason to believe that plant cultivation was primarily the innovation of women, animal domestication of men.[2]

The nature of the social revolution that resulted from the new technology is far clearer than the origins of the technology itself, and it will be the primary focus of this chapter. As with hunting and gathering societies, our discussion of horticultural societies begins with the evidence from archaeology. Then, provided with an historical perspective, we will move on to the evidence from ethnology, which answers a number of questions archaeology cannot.

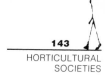
THE ARCHAEOLOGICAL EVIDENCE

Simple Horticultural Societies in Prehistoric Asia and Europe

In Asia Minor, Palestine, and the hill country east of the Tigris River, archaeologists have found the remains of ancient settlements, dating from about 7000 B.C., in which horticulture was apparently the primary means of subsistence.[3] From this area, horticultural techniques spread both east and west until horticultural societies were eventually established at points as distant as Britain and China.

During recent years our knowledge of these early horticultural societies has been advanced substantially by developments in the field of archaeology, including the excavation of new sites and the more extensive exploration of older ones. Biologists and geologists have contributed a great deal to our understanding of the environmental conditions of that era. Most important of all, a new technique for dating archaeological remains was developed after World War II. With this technique, known as radiocarbon dating, prehistoric materials up to about 50,000 years of age can now be dated with a substantial degree of accuracy, and many once unanswerable questions can now be resolved.[4]

Characteristics of the Societies In traditional archaeological usage, the period in which simple horticultural societies were dominant in a region is known as the Neolithic, or New Stone Age. This name was chosen because in early research in Europe and the Middle East, some strata in excavated sites yielded distinctive stone axes, adzes, and hammers that had been smoothed by grinding or polishing. Prior to the discovery of radiocarbon dating, these tools were one of the best indicators of the relative age of the stratum and its place in evolutionary history.

As research progressed, however, and more and more sites were excavated, it became increasingly clear that these tools were neither the most distinctive feature of Neolithic societies nor their greatest technological achievement. Rather, their most important innovations were in the area of subsistence technology: for the first time in history, people were *producing* their food, and hunting and gathering were relegated to a secondary role.

In this connection, it is important to recognize that these early horticultural societies had a mixed economy. Horticulture was their basic means of subsistence, but it was supplemented by herding, hunting, or gathering in various combinations.[5] The presence of livestock in many of these early societies was especially important, as we will soon see.

Archaeologists have come to recognize that the term "Neolithic" focuses attention on the wrong thing, and some now refer to the period in which these societies were dominant as "the era of effective food production."[6] We will call it simply "the horticultural era."

Although scholars today describe the emergence of horticultural societies as the first great social revolution in human history, it would be wrong to assume that the rate of change seemed revolutionary to those involved. As far as we can judge today, the process was so gradual that the changes occurring during a lifetime were neither very numerous nor overwhelming. For example, people in the Middle East had been relying on cereal grains for a thousand years or more before the horticultural era began. Techniques of harvesting, storing, grinding, and cooking grains were well established long before the techniques of cultivation were developed. Furthermore, as we have noted, hunting, and to some extent gathering, continued to play an important part in the lives of the early horticulturists. We may also assume that there was considerable continuity in other areas of life, especially kinship, religion, and politics. The survival of fertility cults, indicated by the widespread presence of female figurines in Neolithic remains, is one evidence of this.[7]

Our use of the term "revolutionary" in connection with the rise of horticultural societies, then, is based primarily on our awareness of the eventual consequences of the change. For example, the shift to horticulture meant settlements were more permanent. No longer did groups have to move about constantly in search of game and other food. On the contrary, the

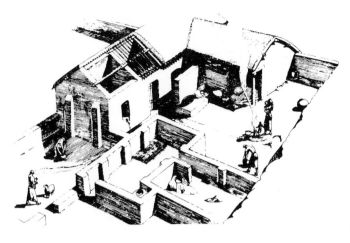

FIGURE 6.1 Reconstruction of a farmhouse of the early horticultural era, Hassuna, Iraq (5500 to 5000 B.C.).

practice of horticulture forced them to stay in one place for extended periods. In the Middle East and in southeastern Europe, truly permanent settlements seem to have been established. Elsewhere, simple horticultural-ists usually have had to move their settlements every few years, because their primitive methods of cultivation seriously depleted the soil.[8] Why this was not necessary in the Middle East and in southeastern Europe is still a mystery, since modern research indicates that only fertilization (by alluvial deposits or by man), irrigation, the use of the plow, or crop rotation permits land to be kept under continuous cultivation,[9] and so far there is no evidence of any of these practices. We do know, however, that these early horticulturalists kept livestock, and it is possible that the value of manure was discovered at an early date.[10] This practice may not have spread simply because of the greater availability of arable land elsewhere.

In any case, the shift from hunting and gathering to horticulture substan-tially increased the permanence of human settlements, enabling people to accumulate many more possessions than ever before. This is evident in the archaeological remains left by horticulturalists of the Neolithic era. Tools and weapons are much more numerous and varied than in older sites, and for the first time there are large, bulky objects such as stone cups and bowls and pottery.[11] Dwellings also became more substantial. Some buildings con-tained several rooms and a small courtyard (see Figure 6.1) and were made of materials like sun-dried clay blocks, capable of lasting for as long as two generations.[12] Even more noteworthy is the appearance of such things as religious shrines or ceremonial centers, village walls, and occasional paved or timbered (corduroy style) roadways or alleys; though none of these is typical of simple horticultural communities, neither are they rare.[13]

The change from hunting and gathering to horticulture also resulted in larger settlements and denser populations. Jarmo, one of the oldest horticul-tural villages yet discovered, contained twenty to twenty-five houses and an

FIGURE 6.2 Archaeological excavation at Çatal Hüyük.

estimated population of 150,[14] nearly four times that of the average hunting and gathering band. Neolithic villages in Europe had from eight to fifty houses, suggesting populations ranging up to at least 200.[15] In several cases there were even more striking concentrations of population. One of the most famous was a town located on the site of Jericho 5,000 years before the days of Joshua. Excavations there uncovered a community that apparently housed 2,000 to 3,000 inhabitants.[16] More recent excavations of Çatal Hüyük in Asia Minor revealed a community occupying an even larger area and, presumably, with a larger population.[17]

These two communities, though obviously exceptional, illustrate another development associated with the rise of horticultural societies—the rapid expansion and growing importance of trade and commerce.[18] Modern scholars feel that the "great" size of Jericho and Çatal Hüyük was not simply the result of the practice of horticulture. As one writer has put it, "It is . . . most unlikely that [horticulture] should have flourished more at Jericho, 200 metres below sea-level, than elsewhere in Palestine. Some other resource must have existed, and this was probably trade."[19] As he points out, Jericho commanded the resources of the Dead Sea, notably salt, bitumen,* and sulfur, all useful materials in simple horticultural societies and not

*Bitumen was used to fix blades in handles, mend pottery, etc.

available everywhere. This view of Jericho as an early center of trade is supported by the discovery there of products such as obsidian from Asia Minor and cowrie shells from the Red Sea. In the case of Çatal Hüyük, obsidian (i.e., volcanic glass, a material much sought after for use in weapons and other things) seems to have been the key local resource responsible for its growth. Even in small villages far removed from such centers as Jericho and Çatal Hüyük, there is evidence of trade. For example, shells from the Mediterranean have been found in the sites of Neolithic villages and in graves throughout the Danube Basin and far down the Oder, Elbe, and Rhine river valleys in northern Europe.[20]

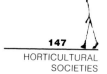
The growth of trade and commerce suggests an increase in occupational specialization, at least in the chief commercial centers. Direct evidence of this has been found at several sites. For example, a community south of Jericho yielded a number of small workshops where such specialized craftsmen as a butcher, a bead maker, and a maker of bone tools worked.[21] This kind of specialization, however, was limited.[22] Most communities remained largely self-sufficient, and most families still produced nearly everything they used.[23] Important innovations continued in the domestic arts, the most notable being the invention of pottery and weaving.[24]

There is little evidence of warfare during the early Neolithic. Graves rarely contain weapons, and most communities had no walls or other defenses.[25] Some, it is true, had ditches and fences, but these were more suitable for protection against marauding animals than against human enemies. Later in the Neolithic the picture changed drastically and warfare became increasingly common. In this period battle-axes, daggers, and other arms appear in the grave of every adult male. The reason for this change is not clear, but some scholars think it was linked with the growth of population and the resulting scarcity of new land suitable for horticulture. It may also have been related to declining opportunities for hunting, a traditional male activity. Warfare, with its demands for bravery and skill in the use of arms, would be a natural substitute, and if women were doing most of the work of tending the gardens, as is the case in most contemporary horticultural societies, men would have had substantial time on their hands to spend in this activity. Moreover, the frictions created by growing pressure for land would provide a ready-made justification. Finally, some experts suspect that the increase in warfare was linked with the increase in wealth, especially in the form of cattle, which could be stolen so easily.[26]

Diffusion Gradually, the new way of life spread until simple horticultural societies were established throughout most of Europe and North Africa. It spread more irregularly in Asia, where large areas of land unsuited for plant cultivation made the development of horticulture impossible.[27]

From an evolutionary standpoint, the new technology spread rather

rapidly, but from the perspective of an individual lifetime, the pace was extremely slow. If China's horticulture came by diffusion from the Middle East (as opposed to some nearer, and undocumented, place of origin), the process required at least 3,000 years to cover approximately 5,000 miles. The movement westward was even slower: 2,500 years were required to reach Britain, 3,000 miles away. In other words, the new way of life spread only a mile or two per year on the average.

Various factors contributed to the spread of horticulture, but one of the most important was the growth of population. Because human populations, like all others, tend to increase unless checked by the limitation of resources, population pressures would naturally build up in the original area of horticultural practice. This would lead to the formation of new settlements on the outer fringes as horticulturalists moved into territory occupied by hunters and gatherers. When this happened, the horticulturalists would almost certainly displace the hunters. By remaining in one place for a number of years, they would reduce the supply of game to the point that it could no longer support the hunters. And should the latter be tempted to fight for their "rights," they would typically find themselves outnumbered by a ratio of more than 2 to 1, if the populations of contemporary groups are any indication.[28]

In the process of diffusion, there was a definite tendency for the whole cluster of horticultural traits to spread together, but there were exceptions. Weaving, for example, apparently never reached horticultural Britain, and large trading centers like Jericho and Çatal Hüyük were limited to the Middle East.[29] On the other hand, certain elements of the horticultural way of life were adopted by some groups that still relied primarily on hunting and gathering. In parts of northeastern Europe and northern Asia, for example, pottery and polished stone axes, both innovations of horticulturalists, came to be widely used by hunting and fishing peoples.[30] Developments such as these demonstrate the need for those irregular boundaries between societal types shown in Figure 4.1 (page 90).

The spread of horticulture to China is especially interesting, because it reached China late enough, and writing developed there early enough, for some memory of the horticultural era to be preserved in legends that were eventually written down. For a long time scholars thought this material was entirely fictional, but modern archaeological research has substantiated enough of it that it is now regarded as an intermingling of fact and fiction.[31]

According to legend, China's earliest inhabitants were hunters, but the increase of population eventually forced a shift to horticulture. As one source recounts, "The ancient people ate meat of animals and birds. At the time of Shen-nung [an early legendary ruler and culture hero] there were so many people that the animals and birds became inadequate for people's wants and

FIGURE 6.3   Reconstruction of the Ubaid temple at Tepe Gawa.

therefore Shen-nung taught the people to cultivate."[32] Other legends relate
that Shen-nung introduced pottery and describe the era as a period of peace
and self-sufficiency. "During the Age of Shen-nung people rested at ease and
acted with vigor. They cared for their mothers, but not for their fathers. They
lived among deer. They ate what they cultivated and wore what they wove.
They did not think of harming one another." This preference for mothers is
intriguing, because it is so contrary to the later Chinese tradition yet
conforms to one of the distinctive features of contemporary horticultural
societies (see page 162 below). Finally, there is a legend describing the Age
of Shen-nung as the last era in which people were free from coercive political
authority. "People were administered without a criminal law and prestige was
built without the use of force. After Shen-nung, however, the strong began to
rule over the weak and the many over the few."

Technological Advance   During the horticultural era, technological progress was almost continuous, especially in the Middle East. In addition to the

invention of pottery making and weaving, metals were discovered and the basic principles of working them were developed. Thus the simple horticultural societies of the latter part of the era were appreciably more advanced than their predecessors three thousand years earlier. The societies that flourished throughout Mesopotamia around 4000 B.C. are a good example of this. These groups apparently shared a common culture, called the Ubaid culture after one of the sites where its remains are found.

Ubaid culture was notable in many ways. To begin with, large settlements were relatively common. This is indicated by the size of cemeteries (one of which contained more than 1,000 graves) as well as by the large temples that dominated these communities.[33] A variety of technical skills were highly developed. Some copper tools and weapons were used, at least in the northern area, while in the south, sickles and other tools were made from clay fired at high temperatures, a process that produced a remarkably efficient substitute for stone, which was unavailable in that area.[34] Trade became extensive throughout Mesopotamia, facilitated by simple sailboats plying the myriad waterways.[35] This undoubtedly contributed to the wide diffusion of Ubaid culture. As one writer says, "Never before had a single culture been able to influence such a vast area, if only superficially."[36]

Advanced Horticultural Societies in Prehistoric Asia and Europe

Each of the inventions and discoveries of the horticultural era increased human control over the environment to some degree. None, however, had such far-reaching effects as the use of metal in weapons and tools. This is why we use metallurgy as the basic criterion for differentiating between simple and advanced horticultural societies. To be more specific, we classify societies as advanced horticultural only when the use of metal weapons and/or tools was widespread. Societies in which they were rare, or in which metals were used only for artistic and ceremonial artifacts (as in some South and Central American Indian groups where gold was the only metal known), are better classified as simple horticultural, since the impact of metallurgy on societal life was so limited.

Middle Eastern Beginnings To the nontechnically inclined, the shift from stone to metal may suggest a radical break with the past and the introduction of something completely new. Actually, however, the use of metals evolved from the use of stone by a series of surprisingly small steps.

For thousands of years, people had been aware of differences among rocks and stones. They had learned that some were better for tools and weapons because they were harder and held a cutting edge longer. They were also aware of the colors in rocks and used the more unusual for beads and other ornaments, and also as a source of pigments.

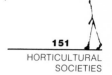

This interest in unusual rocks undoubtedly attracted people to copper. In its native form, copper appears as purplish green or greenish black nuggets which, when scratched or rubbed, show the yellowish kernel of pure copper. At first, copper was simply hammered cold into small tools and ornaments such as awls, pins, and hooks. A few articles made by this method have been found in Middle East sites dating from the sixth millennium B.C.[37] Later, people discovered the technique of annealing.[38] By alternately heating and hammering the metal, they made it less brittle and thus could use it for a wider variety of purposes. The heat from a simple wood fire was sufficient for this process. Later still, people discovered techniques for extracting copper from various kinds of ores by means of smelting, as well as ways to melt ''pure'' copper and cast it in molds.[39]

These discoveries illustrate again the cumulative nature of technological progress. Both smelting and melting copper require higher temperatures than a simple wood fire can produce. This strongly suggests that these important discoveries came after the invention of pottery and the pottery kiln.[40] And these inventions, in turn, presupposed settled communities where heavy and bulky objects could be accumulated.

As far as we can judge, the use of copper tools and weapons increased rather slowly, for a variety of reasons.[41] For one thing, until smelting was discovered, the supply of copper was extremely limited, and it often had to be carried some distance by primitive and costly methods of transportation. Second, metal working (particularly smelting and casting) was probably mastered by only a few specialists, who may have treated their skills as a kind of magic (as smiths in modern horticultural societies often do) to protect a lucrative monopoly. Finally, since any man could make his own tools and weapons out of stone, people were undoubtedly reluctant to switch to the costlier product.[42] Thus, though copper was discovered as early as the middle of the sixth millennium B.C., no truly advanced horticultural society (i.e., one in which metal tools and weapons were widespread) seems to have developed until about 4000 B.C.[43] What is more, the archaeological record provides an inadequate picture of European and Middle Eastern societies at this stage of development. To see what the widespread adoption of metal tools and weapons meant for the life of a horticultural society, we turn to China.

The Chinese Experience Advanced horticultural societies flourished in China from the middle of the second millennium B.C. to the middle of the first.[44] The plow, for reasons that are unclear, was slow to reach China, thus delaying the appearance of agrarian societies. The resultant prolongation of the advanced horticultural era was undoubtedly a factor in the achievement in China of an overall level of technological development that surpassed most other horticultural societies.

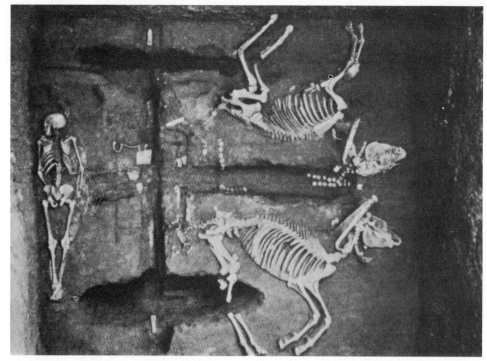

FIGURE 6.4 Chariots, together with bronze weapons, gave the advanced horticulturalists of China a great advantage over their simple horticultural neighbors. Burial remains of a warrior with his horses and chariot, from the eleventh century B.C.

One indication of this is the fact that the dominant metal in China during most of this era was not copper, as in the Middle East and Europe, but bronze. This is significant, because bronze, whose manufacture represents an important advance in metallurgy (involving, as it does, the principle of alloying), is a great deal harder than copper and thus can be used for many purposes for which copper is unsuitable. In the Middle East, the technique of making bronze was not really understood until the early part of the third millennium B.C., some time *after* the first agrarian societies had made their appearance.[45] These variations in the sequence of such major innovations as bronze and the plow warn us of the inadequacy of *unilinear* theories of evolution, which assume that all societies follow exactly the same evolutionary path. Some variation is the rule, not the exception.

When the advanced horticultural era in China is compared with the simple horticultural period, the differences are striking. During the earlier era, northern China was covered with numerous small, largely self-sufficient, autonomous villages. In the later period, the villages were no longer autonomous, and a few had become urban centers of some size and substance.

The emergence of these urban centers was largely the result of the military success of village leaders who had one important advantage: the possession of bronze weapons. As one scholar summarized this period, "In the course of a few centuries the villages of the plain fell under the domination of walled cities on whose rulers the possession of bronze weapons, chariots, and slaves conferred a measure of superiority to which no [simple horticultural] community could aspire, however populous and well fed."[46]

The importance of this development can hardly be exaggerated. For the first time in Chinese history, people found the conquest of other people a profitable alternative to the conquest of nature. Much the same thing happened in other parts of the world during this stage in societal development. Thus, beginning in advanced horticultural societies and continuing in agrarian, we find almost as much energy expended in war as in the more basic struggle for subsistence. One might say that bronze was to the conquest of people what plant cultivation was to the conquest of nature. Both were decisive turning points.

From the military standpoint, China's advanced horticulturalists enjoyed a great advantage over the simple horticulturalists. Recently excavated burial remains show that their warriors wore elaborate armor, including helmets, carried shields, and were equipped with spears, dagger-axes, knives, hatchets, and reflex bows capable of a pull of 160 pounds.[47] In addition, they used horse-drawn chariots carrying teams of three men.

These peoples also enjoyed *numerical* superiority over less advanced groups in the land: every victory brought more people under their control, enabling them to enlarge their armies still further.[48] This could not have been accomplished by a hunting and gathering society, where primitive technology made it impossible for conquerors to incorporate a defeated people into their group. At that level of development, the economic surplus (i.e., production in excess of what is needed to keep the producers healthy and productive) was too small and irregular. But with the introduction of horticulture, the situation changed dramatically. For the first time in history, the conquest, control, and exploitation of other societies became possible—*and profitable*. All that remained to transform this possibility into a reality was an advance in military technology that would give one society a definite advantage over its neighbors. That advance was bronze. It tipped the balance of military power decisively in favor of the advanced horticulturalists.

The earliest advanced horticultural society in China of which we have any archaeological knowledge was established around 1600 B.C., and its structure was basically feudalistic.[49] In most regions, especially those remote from the capital, effective power was in the hands of feudal lords, who paid

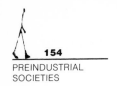

tribute to the king and supported him militarily but otherwise enjoyed great autonomy.[50] They were so independent, in fact, that they often waged war among themselves.

Marked social inequality was the rule in these societies. There were two basic classes, a small warrior nobility and the great mass of common people.[51] The warrior nobility was the governing class and lived in the walled cities, which served as their fortresses, and it was they who enjoyed most of the benefits of the new technology and the new social system. The chief use of bronze was to manufacture weapons and artistic and ceremonial objects for the exclusive benefit of this elite class. Almost none of this relatively scarce material was made available to the common people for farm tools.[52] Much the same situation existed in the Middle East and Europe for 2,000 years or more. As one writer put it, this was a world in which metals played a major role in the military, religious, and artistic spheres but not in the economic.[53]

Kinship ties were extremely important in the political systems of advanced horticultural China. Membership in the governing class was largely hereditary, and as far as possible leading officials assigned the major offices under their control to kinsmen.[54] The origins of these noble families are unknown, but it seems likely that such families were descended from the village headmen of the simple horticultural era and from the close associates of early conquerors.

The walled towns where the aristocracy lived, small by modern standards, were nonetheless an important innovation. One recently excavated town, probably the capital of an early state, covered slightly over one square mile.[55] The size of the walled areas, however, does not tell the full story of these towns, especially in the earlier period, for many of the common people had their homes and workshops outside the protected area and cultivated nearby fields.

The walled area, while basically a fortress and place of residence for the governing class, was also a political and religious center. Religious activities were quite important and were closely tied to the political system—so closely, in fact, that one writer describes the state as "a kind of theocracy."[56] Though this is an overstatement, ancient inscriptions prove that the ruler did perform major religious functions and was what we today would describe as head of both church and state.

The physical structure of those early urban centers was impressive and reflected the evolution of the state and its newly achieved ability to mobilize labor on a large scale. One scholar estimates, for example, that it required the labor of 10,000 men working eighteen years to build the wall around the capital of an early state. Such massive undertakings apparently utilized large numbers of captives taken in war, many of them subsequently used as human sacrifices.[57]

FIGURE 6.5 The Great Wall of China. This 1,500-mile-long fortification, begun late in China's horticultural era, illustrates the growing ability of societies to mobilize labor on a large scale.

Not much is known about the daily life of the common people, but their chief functions were obviously to produce the economic surplus on which the governing class depended and to provide the manpower for the various projects and military campaigns. Not all labor was of the brute, physical type, however. Some people were craft specialists who provided the new and unusual luxury goods that the governing class demanded for display and for ceremonial purposes; others produced military equipment.[58] Although many of these specialists were probably part-time farmers, the growth of occupational specialization was undoubtedly accompanied by a significant growth in trade.

Despite their increasingly exploitative character, the advanced horticultural societies of China made important progress in a number of areas. The more important innovations included writing, money, the use of the horse, probably irrigation, and possibly the manufacture of iron just before the first agrarian society. In addition, there were lesser innovations too numerous to mention, some of them Chinese inventions or discoveries, others the result of diffusion. In most cases, it is impossible to determine which are which.

FIGURE 6.6 Mayan temple at Tikal, Mexico. Some horticultural societies in the New World achieved a level of technological sophistication comparable to that of ancient Mesopotamia and Egypt.

Horticultural Societies in the New World

No one knows for certain when humans first settled the New World. Until recently, evidence indicated that it was no more than 20,000 to 25,000 years ago. New evidence, not yet fully evaluated, suggests that people were living in what is now California as early as 46,000 B.C.[59] In any case, the original settlers were almost certainly hunters and gatherers who had migrated from Asia by means of the land bridge that once connected Siberia and Alaska.

When the last Ice Age ended and the waters locked in the glaciers were largely freed, the level of the oceans rose and the land bridge was submerged. As a result, the inhabitants of the New World were cut off from the inhabitants of the Old World during those crucial millennia associated with the horticultural revolution. Thus, there was no way that information about the techniques of plant cultivation could spread to the Americas.

Despite this, horticultural societies did develop in the New World, and some of them achieved a level of technological sophistication comparable to that of Mesopotamia and Egypt around 2500 B.C. Space limitations prevent us from tracing these developments in detail, and much of the account would be repetitive if we did. But in the New World, as in the Old, the shift from hunting and gathering to horticulture led to more permanent settlements, larger and denser populations, more substantial dwellings, increased wealth and possessions, the development of pottery and later of metallurgy, the beginnings of full-time craft specialization, the appearance of permanent markets and increased trade, the beginnings of urbanism, the establishment of permanent religious centers, the construction of massive temples and temple complexes, and a marked increase in both militarism and imperialism.[60]

There were also some differences: New World horticulturalists were not as successful in domesticating animals, for example, nor was their metallurgy as advanced. On the other hand, they developed a numerical system that included the concept of zero centuries before this was invented in the Old World. But overall, the similarities far outweigh the differences.

The fact that horticulture developed at all in the isolated New World is the crucial point, however, for it provides an independent test of some basic ideas. For a long time, scholars debated whether the similarities between the developmental process in the Middle East, China, and Europe were the result of the operation of basic laws of sociocultural evolution or merely the result of diffusion (i.e., the spread of social and cultural patterns from one area to another). The issue proved impossible to resolve when only Old World societies were involved, because the possibility of diffusion could never be ruled out. The New World, however, is a different matter. Its contacts with the Old ended several thousand years before horticulture began in the Middle East, and contact was not resumed until about 1000 A.D., when Leif Ericson briefly visited Vinland, somewhere on the coast of North America.*

---

*Though attempts have been made to prove other contacts, they have not been very successful. Moreover, careful studies of the evolution of plant cultivation in the New World convince scholars that this was entirely an indigenous process. (For example, the transformation of maize, or corn, from a wild plant to a cultivated plant took much longer than one would expect if the process had been guided by information on the techniques of plant cultivation brought from the Old World.)

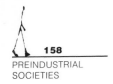

In short, the New World has been a kind of "Second Earth," where ideas about sociocultural evolution suggested by studies of the Old World can be put to the test. And the remarkable parallels between developments in the New World and the Old strongly indicate that much more was involved than mere accident or human choice. There is, apparently, a necessary sequence in the progression of basic technological innovations. People must know certain things about both fire and rocks, for example, before metallurgy is possible, and a society must possess the hoe before it can invent the plow. In addition, major technological innovations have fairly predictable consequences for other aspects of sociocultural systems—especially for social structure, the demographic variables, and material production.

This is not to say that sociocultural evolution compels societies to march in lock-step. But it does indicate that there is a considerable element of predictability in the critical early stages of societal development beyond the hunting and gathering level. Marvin Harris, a leading proponent of

FIGURE 6.7 Sixteenth-century sketch of a village of simple horticulturalists in North Carolina.

ecological-evolutionary theory, stated the matter as well as anyone when he wrote, "Similar technologies applied to similar environments tend to produce similar arrangements of labor in production and distribution, and these in turn call forth similar kinds of social groupings, which justify and coordinate their activities by means of similar systems of values and beliefs."[61]

THE ETHNOGRAPHIC EVIDENCE

Horticultural Societies in the Modern Era

In recent centuries, horticultural societies have been found in four parts of the world—the islands of the Pacific, southern Asia, Africa below the Sahara, and the New World. Most of those in the Pacific and the New World were simple horticultural societies; those in Africa and Asia were generally advanced. Before European expansion and colonialism in the sixteenth century, horticultural societies occupied about as much of the earth's surface as any societal type. Since then, however, they have declined greatly, not only as a result of conquest and absorption by more advanced societies but also because of hybridization resulting from cultural diffusion. Except in hybrid form (i.e., as industrializing horticultural societies), it is doubtful that they will survive much longer.

Simple Horticultural Societies All simple horticultural societies practice some version of *slash-and-burn* or *swidden* horticulture. This involves the periodic clearing of new land to replace gardens that have lost their fertility and have been abandoned. Clearing is typically done by girdling or cutting trees and undergrowth and, after they have dried, setting fire to them. The ashes fertilize the ground, and the garden is then planted amid the stumps and debris (see Figure 6.8). The basic tools are wooden hoes and digging sticks. In many horticultural societies, women have the primary responsibility for the routine tasks of gardening, men for the occasional and more strenuous tasks, such as clearing the land. Usually within a few years weeds take over and the soil loses its fertility, so new gardens must be cleared. The old ones are allowed to revert to jungle or forest and remain unused for decades until nature restores the soil's fertility. Then, the villagers return to the area and repeat the cycle all over again.

In most matters where comparisons are possible, the simple horticultural societies of modern times are strikingly similar to those of prehistoric times. In other words, they are usually small, largely self-sufficient, politically autonomous villages with populations ranging from a few dozen to a few hundred.[62] Compared with modern hunting and gathering societies, their settlements are much more permanent; most groups move only every few years, when the soil is exhausted.[63] As in prehistoric times, their relative

FIGURE 6.8 Women planting taro in a simple horticultural society in New Guinea. Note the tree stumps in the cultivated area: most horticulturalists do not clear land as thoroughly as agriculturalists, who use the plow.

permanence results in a greater accumulation of goods and the construction of more substantial buildings.[64] These developments are associated with a more diversified production of goods and services and an increase in trade.[65]

Finally, as in the simple horticultural societies of the later Neolithic, warfare is fairly common.[66]

As with hunting and gathering societies, the ethnographic record not only supports the view provided by archaeology but broadens and enriches it. For example, modern studies show that kinship ties are extremely important in simple horticultural societies. In many instances, especially in the less advanced societies, these ties provide the basic framework of the social system.[67] This is hardly surprising in view of the small size of these groups: almost everyone is related in some way to many, or perhaps most, of those with whom he comes into contact and must consider his kinship obligations in all his dealings with them. The virtual absence of competing social structures (e.g., craft guilds, political parties, etc.) further enhances the importance of kinship.

Kinship systems in these societies are sometimes very complex, with intricate systems of rules governing relations between numerous categories of kin. Extended kin groups, or clans, are common and usually very important, since they perform a number of essential functions for their members.[68] Above all, they function as mutual aid associations, providing the individual with protection against his enemies and with economic support. Although both these functions are important, the former is critical, for the political system is too primitive at this level to provide police services. Clans also perform important regulatory functions in the area of marriage, and they sometimes have important religious functions as well. Finally, the most powerful or respected clan often assumes leadership functions for the entire community, with its head serving as headman for the village.

In horticultural societies, both simple and advanced, the concept of the kin group includes the dead as well as the living. This manifests itself in many ways, but especially in the form of religious rituals designed to appease the spirits of dead ancestors. Nowhere is ancestor worship more common than in horticultural societies. In one recent study of 110 preindustrial societies, the incidence of ancestor worship was as follows:[69]

Hunting and gathering societies	17%
Simple horticultural societies	71%
Advanced horticultural societies	82%
Agrarian societies	27%

The reason for such a high incidence of ancestor worship among horticulturalists, relative to hunters and gatherers, is probably tied to the greater permanence of their settlements. Because of this, the living not only remain in close physical proximity to their buried dead, they also carry on their daily activities in the very same settings in which their ancestors once lived. Under

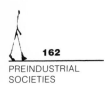

FIGURE 6.9 Leisure among the Yanamamö of South America. The man in the hammock is the boy's maternal uncle, and the relationship between them is an especially intimate one, as in many horticultural societies.

such circumstances, ancestors are less easily forgotten. In agrarian societies, more awesome and more powerful polytheistic and monotheistic deities usually displace ancestors from the central position they occupy in most horticultural societies, but ancestor worship has been important in many of them (e.g., China, Rome).

Another distinctive feature of kinship systems in horticultural societies is the importance many of them attach to ties with the mother's relatives. This can be seen clearly in the Ethnographic Atlas sample, where the percentage of societies having matrilineal kin groups (i.e., descent traced through the maternal line) is as follows:[70]

Hunting and gathering societies	10%
Simple horticultural societies	26%
Advanced horticultural societies	27%
Agrarian societies	4%

TABLE 6.1 The division of labor between the sexes in horticultural and agrarian societies

Type of Society	Percentage Distribution				
	Cultivation Primarily a Female Responsibility	Both Sexes Share Equally	Cultivation Primarily a Male Responsibility	Total	Number of Societies
Simple horticultural	37	49	14	100	51
Advanced horticultural	50	27	23	100	142
Agrarian	7	37	56	100	43

Source: George Peter Murdock's Ethnographic Atlas sample of 915 societies.

This unusual pattern is apparently linked with women's contribution to subsistence in horticultural societies: in many of these groups, women do most of the work of cultivation (see Table 6.1). Where men also make a substantial contribution to the subsistence of the group—by hunting or herding, for example—matrilineal patterns are not as likely to develop. But where the men do not make a significant contribution, these patterns are much more common (see Table 6.2).[71]

Though village autonomy is still the rule, multicommunity societies are more common than at the hunting and gathering level.[72] When societies do consist of more than one community, there are usually only a handful, seldom more than ten.[73] Typically, they were formed by a process of confederation involving villages that belonged to the same tribe,[74] with military considerations providing the motivation.

Despite the formation of these larger, multicommunity societies, the

TABLE 6.2 Matrilneality and matrilocality among simple horticultural societies, by percentage of subsistence obtained by hunting and herding

Percentage of Subsistence Obtained by Hunting and Herding*	Percentage of Societies Matrilineal	Percentage of Societies Matrilocal	Number of Cases
26 per cent or more	13	6	16
16 to 25 per cent	25	17	28–29†
Less than 15 per cent	39	22	23

Source: George Peter Murdock's Ethnographic Atlas sample of 915 societies.
* These figures are estimates made by Murdock and his associates and are based on qualitative statements in ethnographic reports.
† Information was available on matrilineality for 28 societies, on matrilocality for 29.

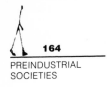

power of political leaders remains quite limited in nearly all simple horticultural societies. Except in matters of war and relations with other societies, local villages enjoy virtual autonomy. Both the village headman and the tribal chief depend more on persuasion than on coercion to achieve their goals. This is partly because of the limited development of the governmental system: a leader has few subordinates so dependent on him that they are obliged to carry out his instructions. Also important is the fact that there are no weapons of the kinds that a governing class could monopolize to control the rest of the population; bronze weapons, for example, because they are expensive and must be made by specialists, lend themselves to monopolization by a wealthy minority, as happened in China.

In some simple horticultural societies, shamans also serve as headmen or chiefs because of the awe or respect in which they are held;[75] in some, secular leaders assume important religious functions and become quasi-religious figures. As one writer notes, a "chief's influence is definitely enhanced when he combines religious with secular functions."[76] In short, in many simple horticultural societies of the modern era, just as in the prehistoric past, church and state are closely linked and sometimes almost become one.

The only other important basis of political power in these societies is membership in a large and prosperous kin group. As we noted previously, the senior member and leader of the largest, most powerful, or most respected lineage group often becomes the village headman or the tribal chief.[77] He can usually count on the support of his kinsmen at least, a substantial political resource in a society with such limited political development.

Social inequality is generally rather limited, though societies differ in this. Although extremes of wealth and political power are absent, substantial differences in prestige are not uncommon. Political and religious leaders usually enjoy high status, but this depends far more on their achievements than on mere occupancy of the office. There are few sinecures in these societies. Other bases of status include military prowess (which is highly honored in nearly all societies), skill in oratory, age, lineage, and in some

TABLE 6.3   Incidence of warfare, by societal type (in percentages)

Type of Society	Perpetual	Common	Rare or Absent	Number of Societies
Hunting and gathering	0	27	73	22
Simple horticultural	5	55	41	22
Advanced horticultural	34	48	17	29

Source: Derived from data in Gregory Leavitt, "The Frequency of Warfare: An Evolutionary Perspective," *Sociological Inquiry*, 14 (January, 1977), appendix B.

FIGURE 6.10 Combat may serve as a psychic substitute for hunting. Yanamamö men intoxicated on ebene, an hallucinogenic drug, prepare for a "friendly" duel with a neighboring village with which they are allied. Such duels often turn violent and lead to war.

cases wealth in the form of wives, pigs, and ornaments.[78] Each society has its own peculiar combination of these criteria.

The more advanced the technology and economy in one of these groups, the greater social inequality tends to be. Societies that practice irrigation, own domesticated animals, or practice metallurgy for ornamental and ceremonial purposes are usually less egalitarian than groups that have not taken these steps. We can see this when we compare the villagers of eastern Brazil and the Amazon River basin with their more advanced neighbors to the north and west who, in pre-Spanish days, practiced irrigation and metallurgy (since they used gold, which is too soft for tools and weapons, they cannot be considered advanced horticulturalists). Hereditary class differences were absent in the former groups but quite common in the latter, where a hereditary governing class of chiefs and nobles was set apart from the larger class of commoners.[79]

Modern ethnographers have found warfare to be much more common among horticulturalists than among hunters and gatherers (see Table 6.3). This finding parallels the evidence from archaeology, where all the signs

FIGURE 6.11 The Jivaro Indians of South America collected heads as trophies of their prowess and developed a special technique for shrinking and preserving them. The skin was removed from the skull and hot sand was repeatedly poured in to dry and shrink it, after which the lips were sewn together.

indicate that warfare increased substantially during the horticultural era. Now, as in the past, combat may serve as a psychic substitute for the challenge and rewards of hunting. Moreover, skill in warfare is probably essential in areas where population pressures and more stable settlement patterns combine to create a deadly game of musical chairs, whose losers often face societal extinction.

As warfare grows in importance in a society, several new patterns develop. Above all, there is the cult of the warrior, which heaps honors on successful fighters. Record keeping and publicity are no less important to these warrior heroes than to modern athletes, and, in the absence of statisticians and sports writers, they invent techniques of their own—especially trophy taking. Some of the more popular trophies are skulls and shrunken heads, which are preserved and displayed like modern athletic trophies.[80]

Ceremonial cannibalism, a surprisingly widespread practice among simple horticultural societies, may have developed as a by-product of trophy collecting. Utilitarian cannibalism, or eating other humans to avoid starvation, is an ancient practice, traceable to distant prehistoric times, but ceremonial cannibalism seems to be a more recent invention. The basic idea underlying it is that one can appropriate the valued qualities of a conquered enemy by eating his body.[81] Ceremonial cannibalism is usually surrounded by a complex, and often prolonged, set of rituals, as the following account from South America indicates.

> The prisoners taken by a Tupinamba war party were received with manifestations of anger, scorn, and derision, but after the first hostile outburst, they were not hampered in their movements nor were they unkindly treated. Their captors, whose quarters they shared, treated them as relatives. The prisoners generally married village girls, very often the sisters or daughters of their masters, or, in certain cases, the widow of a dead warrior whose hammock and ornaments they used. They received fields for their maintenance, they were free to hunt and fish, and they were reminded of their servile condition by few restrictions and humiliations.
>
> The period of captivity lasted from a few months to several years. When, finally, the date for the execution had been set by the village council, invitations were sent to nearby villages to join in the celebration. The ritual for the slaughter of a captive was worked out to the most minute detail. The club and cord which figured prominently in the ceremony were carefully painted and decorated in accordance with strict rules. For three days before the event, the village women danced, sang, and tormented the victim with descriptions of his impending fate. On the eve of his execution a mock repetition of his capture took place, during which the prisoner was allowed to escape but was immediately retaken; the man who overpowered him in a wrestling match adopted a new name, as did the ceremonial executioner.
>
> The prisoner spent his last night dancing, pelting his tormentors, and singing songs which foretold their ruin and proclaimed his pride at dying as a warrior. In the morning he was dragged to the plaza by old women amidst shouts, songs, and music. The ceremonial rope was removed from his neck and tied around his waist, and it was held at both ends by two or more men. The victim was once more permitted to give vent to his feelings by throwing fruit or potsherds at his enemies. The executioner, who appeared painted and dressed in

a long feather cloak, derided the victim, who boasted of his past deeds and predicted that his relatives would avenge him.

The actual execution was a cruel game. The prisoner was allowed sufficient freedom of movement to dodge the blows aimed at him; sometimes a club was put in his hands so that he could parry the blows without being able to strike back. When at last he fell, his skull shattered, everyone shouted and whistled. Old women rushed in to drink the warm blood, children were invited to dip their hands in it, and mothers smeared their nipples so that even infants could have a taste. While the quartered body was being roasted on a babracot the old women, who were the most eager to taste human flesh, licked the grease running from the sticks. Certain delicate or sacred portions, such as the fingers and the grease around the liver, were given to distinguished guests.[82]

The high incidence of warfare in simple horticultural societies serves to keep the channels of vertical mobility open. Almost every boy becomes a warrior and thus has a chance to win honors and influence. At the same time, however, the channels of vertical mobility are narrowed in horticultural societies, because status advantages can more easily be passed from parent to child than in hunting and gathering societies. This is partly due to the greater amount of private property among horticulturalists, and its increased importance. In addition, there are the beginnings of inequality among kin groups: it is a distinct advantage to be born into a large, powerful, and wealthy clan. Finally, the institutional structures of these societies frequently evolve to the point where they can, to some extent, supplement the personal attributes of leaders. No longer need a headman be the best man in his group; he need only be competent, because he now has assistants who can act in his stead. As a consequence, it becomes easier for such positions to be inherited. This growth in the heritability of status, though modest in scope and of limited importance in simple horticultural societies, marks the beginning of a trend destined to become of tremendous importance in more advanced societies.

Advanced Horticultural Societies   For several centuries, advanced horticultural societies have been limited to two parts of the world, sub-Saharan Africa and Southeast Asia. Until recently, they occupied almost all of sub-Saharan Africa; other types of societies—hunters and gatherers, herders, and fishers—were relatively scarce. In Southeast Asia, on the other hand, agrarian societies occupied most of the land.

These advanced horticulturalists of modern times differ in one important respect from their prehistoric predecessors: the dominant metal in their societies has been iron, not copper or bronze. This fact is important, because iron ore is so much more plentiful than copper and tin that it can be used for ordinary tools as well as weapons. However, because it is so much more difficult to reduce the ore to metal, the manufacture of iron was the last to develop.

FIGURE 6.12 Basket weaver, an occupational specialist, at work beside his home in Guinea.

The history of Africa proves once again that the evolutionary process does not compel societies to follow exactly the same pattern of development. Bronze was never the dominant metal in most of Africa below the Sahara. During the period when bronze was dominant in the Middle East, cultural contacts between Egypt and the territories to the south were minimal. By the time there was sufficient contact to permit diffusion of specialized skills like metallurgy, iron had become dominant.[83]

Compared with hunting and gathering or simple horticultural societies, advanced horticultural societies are usually larger and more complex. Table 4.2 (page 97) summarizes the evidence from Murdock's sample. Communities in advanced horticultural societies are three times larger than those in simple horticultural societies and seven times larger than those in hunting and gathering societies. A comparison of societies is even more striking: on the average, advanced horticultural societies are 60 times the size of simple horticultural and 140 times the size of hunting and gathering societies.

As one would expect, advanced horticultural societies are also structurally more complex. Of those in Murdock's sample, some have as many as *four* layers of government above the local community; no simple horticultural

FIGURE 6.13   Woman spreading rice to dry in the sun in Liberia.

society in the sample has more than *two*. These data also show that village autonomy is the rule in simple horticultural societies, the exception in advanced. In 79 per cent of the former, villages are autonomous; in 71 per cent of the latter, they are *not*.

Another evidence of structural complexity is the extent of occupational specialization. Table 4.3 (page 99) shows that craft specialization is much more common in advanced horticultural societies than in simple ones. In six basic areas, craft specialization occurred an average of only 2 per cent of the time in simple horticultural societies, but 28 per cent of the time in advanced.

Murdock's data also show that social inequality increases markedly with the emergence of advanced horticultural societies. Class stratification was reported in only 17 per cent of the simple horticultural societies, as opposed to 54 per cent of the advanced (see Table 4.5, page 101). In addition, the class systems of the latter are generally more complex, involve greater degrees of inequality, and are more often hereditary.[84] The presence of slavery in 83 per cent of the advanced but only 14 per cent of the simple horticultural societies is a striking illustration of this.

One consequence of the more fully developed economy and stratification system in advanced horticultural societies is their increased emphasis on the economic aspect of marriage. In almost every one of these societies, marriageable daughters are viewed as a valuable economic property, and men who want to marry them must either pay for the privilege or render extended service to their prospective in-laws. Fortunately for young men with limited resources, extended kin groups usually view marriage as a sensible investment and are generally willing to loan suitors part of the bride price. This economic approach to marriage is much more common in advanced horticultural societies than in either hunting and gathering or simple horticultural societies (see Table 6.4).

The growth in social inequality is closely linked with the growth of government. A generation ago, Meyer Fortes, one of the pioneer students of African political systems, argued that most traditional African societies fell into one of two basic categories: those "which have centralized authority, administrative machinery, and judicial institutions—in short, a government—and in which cleavages of wealth, privilege, and status correspond to the distribution of authority" and those which have none of these attributes.[85] Though recent studies suggest that this twofold division is something of an oversimplification, they confirm that African societies differ in the ways Fortes described and that there is a strong relationship between the development of the state and the growth of social inequality.[86]

African societies afford a valuable opportunity to study the early stages of political development. A leading student of East African political systems suggests that a critical step in the process occurs when the head of some strong extended kin group begins to take on, as retainers, men who are not related to him, thus breaking out of one of the traditional limitations on power and its expansion.[87] These retainers are usually individuals who have been expelled from their own kin groups for misconduct or whose groups have been destroyed in war or some natural disaster, and they offer their allegiance and service in exchange for protection and a livelihood.

Since there is a natural tendency for men in this position to turn to the strongest families, power begins to pyramid. This is reinforced by the wealth

TABLE 6.4 Association of economic transaction with marriage, by societal type

Type of Society	Percentage of Societies Requiring Economic Transaction with Marriage	Number of Societies
Hunting and gathering	49	148
Simple horticultural	61	74
Advanced horticultural	97	265

Source: George Peter Murdock's Ethnographic Atlas sample of 915 societies.

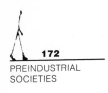

of such a group, which permits it to buy more wives to produce more sons and warriors, and by the development of myths that explain the group's success by attributing magical powers to its leader. The final link in this chain of state building is forged when less powerful families, and even whole communities, are brought under the control of the head of a strong kin group—either by conquest or by the decision of the weaker groups to put themselves under the strong group's protection. When this happens, each of the subordinate groups is usually allowed to retain its land, and its leader his authority within the group, but the group is compelled to pay tribute. The leader of the dominant group then uses these revenues to support his kinsmen and retainers, thereby increasing their dependence on him and, it is hoped, their loyalty to him as well.

Sometimes the state-building process is stimulated by intrafamily and interfamily feuds that get out of hand. Where strong political authority is lacking, feuds are a serious matter. Individuals and families are forced to settle their own grievances, which often sets off a deadly cycle of action and reaction. More than one East African group has voluntarily put itself under the authority of a strong neighboring leader just to break such a cycle and reestablish peace among its members.

One might suppose that these processes, once set in motion, would have continued until eventually all Africa came under a single authority. But powerful countervailing forces prevented this. Technological limitations, especially in transportation and communication, were most important. Advanced horticulturalists in Africa, as in the New World, had no knowledge of the wheel and used no draft animals until contact with Europeans. As a result, the farther a ruler's power extended into outlying areas, the weaker it became. These areas were vulnerable to attack by foreign enemies, and, even more serious, they were likely to revolt. From the territorial standpoint, Songhay was probably the largest kingdom that ever developed in sub-Saharan Africa. In the early fourteenth century, it controlled approximately 500,000 square miles in the western Sudan (i.e., twice the size of present-day France).[88] Most African kingdoms were much smaller.

By the standards of modern industrial societies, the governments of Africa's advanced horticultural societies were extremely unstable. Revolts were a common occurrence, not only in outlying provinces but even in the capitals. These were seldom, if ever, popular risings. Rather, they were instigated by powerful members of the nobility, often the king's own brothers, a pattern so common that the Zulus developed a proverb that "the king should not eat with his brothers lest they poison him."[89]

In virtually every politically advanced society of horticultural Africa there was a sharply defined cleavage between a hereditary nobility and the mass of common people. Historically, this distinction grew out of the state-building process.[90] Nobles were usually descendants either of past rulers and their chief lieutenants or of hereditary leaders of subordinated groups. They comprised a warrior aristocracy supported by the labors of the common people. Below the commoners there was often a class of slaves, many of them captives taken in war, and, as in other horticultural societies, they were frequently slaughtered as human sacrifices.

In the advanced horticultural societies of Africa, as in the New World and elsewhere, religion and politics were intimately related. In many instances the king was viewed as divine or as having access to divine powers.[91] This undoubtedly served to legitimate tyrannical and exploitative practices. And it helps explain why no efforts were made to establish other kinds of political systems: given the ideological heritage of these societies, such a thing was inconceivable. This ideology did not protect a ruler against attacks from his kinsmen, however, because they shared his special religious status and were also qualified to assume the duties and privileges of the royal office—if they could seize it.

A comparison of the politically advanced societies of sub-Saharan Africa with those which remained autonomous villages shows that the former were more developed in other ways as well. They were far likelier to have full-time craft specialization, for example, and they were also more likely to have urban or semiurban settlements—a few with populations of 20,000 or more.[92]

Before concluding this discussion of advanced horticultural societies in the modern era, a brief comment on those in Southeast Asia is necessary.

FIGURE 6.14 Early bronze casting of Dahomean chief and his entourage of relatives and retainers. Note the fine workmanship. This is a native art form in West Africa, predating European contact. For a modern scene similar to that depicted here, see Figure 13.11.

FIGURE 6.15 Contemporary view of the old city of Kano in northern Nigeria. Kano has been an important commercial and political center for more than 500 years. Although the photograph is recent, the style of architecture remains much as it was centuries ago.

The striking feature of these societies is their relative backwardness, especially from the standpoint of political development. In most instances they remain on the level of village autonomy, and when multicommunity societies do develop, they invariably are small.[93] Urban or semiurban settlements are absent.

The reason appears to be ecological. Centuries ago, after this region came under the domination of more powerful agrarian societies, horticultural societies usually survived only in hill country where transportation was difficult and the land unsuited for the plow and permanent cultivation. This combination of more powerful neighbors and the deficiencies of their own territories apparently prevented all but the most limited development and caused these groups to be looked down upon, and often exploited, by their agrarian neighbors. Ecological factors of a different type had a similar effect in certain parts of Africa: political development was quite limited in the tropical rain forests. Apparently the lush vegetation and other hindrances to the movement of armies and goods made it impossible to build and maintain extensive kingdoms.[94]

HORTICULTURAL SOCIETIES IN EVOLUTIONARY PERSPECTIVE

Few events in human history have been as important as the discovery of the principles of plant cultivation. It is no exaggeration to say that the discovery of horticulture in the realm of technology was comparable to the invention of symbols in the realm of communication. Each was a decisive break with the animal world. Hunting and gathering, like the use of signals, are basically techniques our species inherited from its prehuman ancestors. Horticulture and symbols, by contrast, are uniquely human.

Of all the changes in human life that resulted from the horticultural revolution, the most fundamental—the one with the greatest repercussions for other change—was the creation of *a stable economic surplus.* Hunting and gathering societies were rarely able to create such a surplus: food producers and their dependents usually consumed all the calories those groups were able to provide. With nothing left over to support *non*producers of food, only the most limited occupational specialization was possible. There could be no governments or religious institutions staffed by full-time officials and priests, nor could there be full-time artisans and merchants. And this, in turn, ruled out the development of towns and cities, since these are based on populations that are freed from the necessity of producing their own food.

The shift from hunting and gathering to plant cultivation provided societies with the means of establishing an economic surplus *if* the growth in productivity was not nullified by a corresponding growth in population size. To translate the potential for a stable surplus into a reality, a society needed an ideology that would motivate the people producing food to put part of their harvest under the control of someone else.

Religious beliefs sometimes answered this need. In a number of societies, people were already accustomed to offering sacrifices, and nothing was more natural than that they should continue this practice as they shifted to plant cultivation. With greater productivity, rituals became more elaborate and more frequent, and priestly activities became full-time, for one man at first, and eventually for others. In this way, small proto-urban communities began to develop around important shrines—communities whose existence was predicated on the maintenance of a stable economic surplus.

In other societies, development of such a surplus appears to have evolved out of a prior tradition of turning over to the headman a portion of the fruits of the hunt to distribute to families of hunters who were unsuccessful that day. Here, too, the increase in productivity resulting from the shift to

FIGURE 6.16 Human sacrifice, from carving on the Mayan Temple of the Jaguars, Chichén Itzá, Mexico.

plant cultivation made full-time employment possible, first for a headman, later for aides. Thus, the foundation was laid for the emergence of the state as a specialized entity, in some sense separate from the society it served—and would later govern.

In either case, the outcome was the same: the potential of an economic surplus became a reality, opening up important new possibilities for the organization of societal life. All those possibilities would not be realized in horticultural societies, however. The most dramatic and the most revolutionary would be realized only in agrarian and industrial societies, where the size of the economic surplus would be many times greater.

Before concluding this summary, a brief comment on the ethical consequences of the horticultural revolution is needed, lest anyone still suppose that the technological and structural progress of horticultural societies implies ethical progress. As numerous scholars have noted, it is one of the great ironies of evolution that progress in technology and social structure is often linked with ethical *regress*. Horticultural societies provide several striking examples. Some of the most shocking, by the standards of our own culture, are the increases in headhunting, cannibalism, human sacrifice, and slavery, all more common in the technologically progressive horticultural societies than in the more primitive hunting and gathering groups.

Another development many would regard as ethical regression is the decline in the practice of sharing and the growing acceptance of economic and other kinds of inequality. This is not as simple a matter as it seems on the surface, however. Although inequality is an inevitable accompaniment of an economic surplus, the establishment of that surplus seems to have been a prerequisite for the development of civilization—with all that implies—and for improvement of the standard of living. In other words, without an economic surplus, all the benefits of technological advance would have been consumed by population growth, and there would simply be more people living at the subsistence level. Our judgment of this growth in inequality, therefore, depends largely on whether we take a short-term or a long-term view.

CHAPTER 7 AGRARIAN SOCIETIES

"The thousand years or so immediately preceding 3000 B.C. were perhaps more fertile in fruitful inventions and discoveries than any period in human history prior to the sixteenth century, A.D."[1] So wrote V. Gordon Childe, the most influential archaeologist of the last fifty years. The innovations of that period included the invention of the wheel and its application to both wagons and the manufacture of pottery, the invention of the plow, the harnessing of animals to pull wagons and plows and their use as pack animals, the harnessing of windpower for use in sailboats, the invention of writing and numerical notation, and the invention of the calendar.[2]

Collectively, these innovations were the basis for a revolutionary transformation of the conditions of life in the Middle East, and ultimately for societies throughout the world. With these new cultural resources, societies expanded their populations, increased their material products, and developed social structures far more complex than anything known before.

Though it is difficult to single out any one of these innovations as more important than the rest, a good case can be made for the plow. To a modern city dweller, the plow may not sound very exciting, yet without it, we would still be back in the horticultural era. To appreciate the importance of the

177

plow, we need to keep in mind two basic problems that confront farmers everywhere: controlling weeds and maintaining the fertility of the soil.[3] With traditional horticultural tools and techniques, both these problems grow more severe the longer a plot is cultivated. Weeds multiply faster than horticulturalists with their hoes can root them out, while the soil's nutrients seep deeper into the ground, below the reach of plants and too deep to be brought back to the surface with hoes or other simple tools. Within a few years, the yield usually becomes so small that the cultivator is forced to abandon the plot and move elsewhere.*

The plow, if it did not eliminate these problems, at least reduced them to manageable proportions. Because it turns the soil over to a greater depth than the hoe, the plow buries weeds, not only killing them but adding humus to the soil. Deeper cultivation also brings back to the surface the nutrients that have seeped below root level. This made permanent cultivation of fields a common practice for the first time in history and led to the replacement of horticulture (from the Latin *hortus*, or garden) by agriculture (from *ager*, or field).

The invention of the plow also paved the way for the harnessing of animal energy.[4] As long as the digging stick and hoe were the basic tools of cultivation, men and women had to supply the energy. But the plow could be pulled, and it did not take long for people to discover that oxen could do the job. The importance of this discovery can hardly be exaggerated, since it established a principle with broad applicability. As Childe has stated, "The ox was the first step to the steam engine and the [gasoline] motor."[5]

More immediately, however, the harnessing of animal energy relieved people of one of the most exhausting forms of labor required by the new mode of food production and led to greatly increased productivity. With a plow and a pair of oxen, a farmer could cultivate a far larger area than was

---

*In a few instances, horticulturalists have been able to maintain continual cultivation because of irrigation (natural or artificial) or fertilization.

FIGURE 7.1 Early Egyptian ox-drawn plow (about 2700 B.C.). Note the primitive method of harnessing the animals—a simple bar attached to the horns.

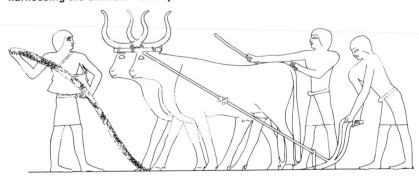

possible with a hoe.[6] In addition, the use of oxen led, in many societies, to stall feeding, and this in turn led to the use of manure as a fertilizer.[7] In short, the shift from hoe to plow not only meant fields kept permanently under cultivation and larger crops; it also meant the potential for a much larger economic surplus and new and more complex forms of social structure.[8]

SIMPLE AGRARIAN SOCIETIES

The earliest evidence of the plow comes from Mesopotamian cylinder seals and Egyptian paintings dating from a little before 3000 B.C.[9] Modern research indicates that the plow, like so many other innovations since the Paleolithic, presupposed certain earlier inventions and discoveries— underlining again the cumulative nature of technological change. The first plows of the Mesopotamians and the Egyptians were simply modified versions of the hoe, the basic farm implement of all advanced horticultural societies. In the earliest period, the plow was probably pulled by men, but before long, cattle and oxen began to be used.

As in the case of horticulture, the techniques of agriculture spread by diffusion or borrowing until agrarian societies were eventually established throughout most of Europe and much of North Africa and Asia. For reasons that are still not fully understood, use of the plow never spread to sub-Saharan Africa until the period of European colonialism. In the New World, too, it was unknown until introduced by Europeans.

The full impact of the new technology was not felt immediately in either Mesopotamia or Egypt. Nevertheless, the shift to agriculture was quickly followed by several important developments, notably the invention of writing, the rise of urban communities,[10] and the beginnings of empire building (which in Egypt led to the unification of the entire country under a single ruler for the first time in history). This was the period that historians have often referred to as "the dawn of civilization."

As we have seen, similar developments occurred (though at later dates) in horticultural societies in China and Mexico, proving that an agrarian economy was not a necessary precondition for literacy, urbanism, and large-scale imperialism. But the rarity of these phenomena in horticultural societies and their frequency in agrarian societies indicate that the shift to agriculture, by increasing productivity, greatly increased the probability of their occurrence.

The Role of Religion in the Formation of a Surplus

In early Mesopotamia and Egypt, religion was an extremely powerful force. Mesopotamian theology held that "man was . . . created for one purpose only: to serve the gods by supplying them with food, drink, and shelter so that

FIGURE 7.2 **The temple of Luxor, Egypt.**

they might have full leisure for their divine activities."[11] Each temple was believed to be, quite literally, the house of a particular god, and each community had its own special deity. Priests and other attendants constituted the god's court or household, and their chief task was to minister to his needs. Another responsibility was to mediate between the god and the community, trying to discover his will and appease his anger. In order to perform these tasks, temples and their staffs had to be supported by a steady flow of goods. Over the years, the temples were continually enlarged and became increasingly costly. In fact, they became, in many respects, substantial business enterprises, a development that apparently provided the stimulus for the invention of writing, which was originally a means of recording the temple's business activities.[12] Many scholars have described the early Mesopotamian city-states as theocracies, since the local deity was regarded as the real ruler and the king merely as his "tenant farmer."[13]

Egypt was also a theocracy, but of a different type. One scholar compared the Egyptian and Mesopotamian patterns this way:

> Egypt's theocracy was of a totally different kind from that of [Mesopotamia]; instead of the earthly ruler being but the chosen representative and the "tenant farmer" of the sovereign deity, Pharaoh was himself a god, and his government was divine simply because it was Pharaoh's. The other gods did not and could not dispute his authority. To whatever deity of the Egyptian pantheon the local temple might be dedicated, yet Pharaoh's statues adorned it, and, likely as not, the reliefs on the walls celebrated Pharaoh's exploits.[14]

To his subjects Pharaoh "was the incarnation, the living embodiment, of the god of any district he happened to be visiting; he was their actual God in living form, whom they could see, speak to, and adore."[15] Like the gods of the Mesopotamian city-states, he was theoretically the owner of the land and entitled to a portion of all that was produced, and, as in Mesopotamia, his revenues supported a small army of specialists (e.g., officials, craftsmen, soldiers, etc.).

In later years there was a secularizing trend, especially in Mesopotamia.[16] By then, however, societies had developed other institutional arrangements—notably political ones—to ensure the continued transfer of the economic surplus from the peasant producers to the governing class. Nevertheless, religion continued to play an important role as a legitimizing agency: it provided a rationale to justify the operation of the political system and its economic consequences.

The experience of Mesopotamia and Egypt thus supports the impression gained from horticultural societies concerning the importance of religion in the formation of an economic surplus. Technological advance creates the *possibility* of a surplus, but to transform that possibility into a *reality* requires an ideology that motivates farmers to produce more than they need to stay alive and productive and persuades them to turn that surplus over to someone else. Although this has sometimes been accomplished with secular and political ideologies, a system of beliefs that explained people's obligations in terms of the supernatural was better suited to play this critical role in societies of the past.

Scale of Organization

In the first few centuries after the shift to agriculture, there was striking growth in the size of a number of communities, especially in Mesopotamia.[17] These became the first full-fledged cities in history. The largest of them were the capitals of the largest and most prosperous societies. Although it is impossible to obtain accurate figures on the size of the cities and towns of the third and second millennia B.C. and scholars disagree on the interpretation of the evidence, some believe that one or more of these cities passed the 100,000 mark.[18]

Egypt was the largest of the simple agrarian societies of ancient times and politically the most stable. She enjoyed the unique distinction of surviving as a united and independent nation throughout most of the simple agrarian era. This achievement was due to her unique environmental situation: no other society had such excellent natural defenses and was so little threatened by powerful neighbors.

In the second half of the second millennium, Egypt embarked on a program of expansion that brought under her control all the territory from Syria to the Sudan. There were also other important empires in this era, especially those established by the Babylonians in the eighteenth century B.C. and the Hittites in the thirteenth century B.C. Babylonia succeeded briefly in uniting most of Mesopotamia, while the Hittites conquered much of what is now Turkey and Syria.

Organizational Development: Growth of the State

These conquests posed serious organizational problems for the rulers of early agrarian societies. Traditional modes of government organized around an extended kin group proved totally inadequate for administering the affairs of societies whose populations now sometimes numbered in the millions. Though rulers continued to rely on relatives to help them perform the most essential tasks of government, they were forced to turn increasingly to others. One expedient was to incorporate a conquered group as a subdivision of the state, leaving its former ruler in charge, but in a subordinate capacity. Eventually, however, all of the more successful rulers found it necessary to create new kinds of organizational structures, not based on kinship.

We can see these newer patterns evolving in both military and civil affairs. The first armies, for example, were simply organizations of all the able-bodied men in the society.[19] During this period, wars were of short duration and were fought only after the harvest was in. In fact, the period following the harvest came to be known as the "season when kings go forth

FIGURE 7.3 Egyptian painting of soldiers attacking a fortress (about 1940 B.C.).

to war." This limitation was essential because, with the shift to agriculture, the male's responsibilities in farming had greatly increased.

As long as wars were brief and limited to skirmishes with neighboring peoples, this arrangement was adequate. But once rulers became interested in empire building, the traditional system proved unworkable. As early as the middle of the third millennium in Mesopotamia, would-be empire builders established small, but highly trained, professional armies. For example, Sargon, the famous Akkadian king, had a standing army of 5,400 men who "ate daily before him."[20] As far as possible, recruits were sons of old soldiers, and thus a military caste was gradually created. The Egyptians followed a similar policy except that they relied chiefly on foreign mercenaries. These new armies soon came to be royal, rather than national, armies. Their expenses were paid by the king out of his enormous revenues, and the profits resulting from their activities were his also. Not only were these armies useful in dealing with foreign enemies, they also served as a defense against internal threats.[21]

In civil affairs, too, the casual and informal practices of simpler societies proved inadequate. As states expanded and the problems of administration multiplied, new kinds of governmental positions were created, and a governmental bureaucracy began to take shape.[22] In addition to the many officials who comprised the royal court and were responsible for administering the king's complex household affairs, there were officials scattered throughout the countryside to administer the affairs of units ranging from small districts to provinces with hundreds of villages and towns. Each official had a staff of scribes and other lesser officials to assist him, and written records became increasingly important as administrative problems grew more complex.[23]

Throughout most of the history of the simple agrarian societies of antiquity, writing was a specialized art mastered by only a few individuals after long apprenticeships.[24] This is easily understood, considering the

FIGURE 7.4   Model of a royal granary, found in an Egyptian tomb (about 2000 B.C.). Note the scribes and other officials recording the deliveries of grain.

complex, prealphabetic systems of writing then in use. Even after a process of simplification that lasted over 2,000 years, cuneiform script still had between 600 and 1,000 distinct characters. Before a person could learn to read or write, he had to memorize this formidable array of symbols and learn the complex rules for combining them. The Egyptian hieroglyphic and hieratic scripts were equally complicated. Thus, those who could write formed a specialized occupational group in society—the scribes—and their services were much in demand. For the most part this occupation was filled by the sons of the rich and powerful, since only they could afford the necessary education.[25] Because of the political importance of their skill and the limited supply of qualified personnel, most scribes were at least marginal members of the governing class.

   One consequence of the growth of empires and the development of bureaucracy was the establishment of the first formal legal systems. Over the centuries every society had developed certain concepts of justice, as well as informal techniques for implementing them. The most common solution seems to have been to rely on blood revenge by the injured party and his relatives. Recognizing the anarchic tendencies inherent in this system, people began to seek settlement by arbitration, turning quite naturally to the most respected and most powerful members of the community. In this way, headmen and other political leaders gradually acquired judicial powers. Then, as empires grew, peoples of diverse cultures were brought within the framework of a single political system. In many instances, the official appointed to rule over an area was not a native and was therefore unfamiliar with local conceptions of justice (which varied considerably from place to place). This generated pressure to clarify and standardize judicial practice, which eventually led to the promulgation of formal codes of law. The most famous of these was the Code of Hammurabi, the great Babylonian empire builder of the early second millennium.

The Development of Monetary Systems

Money as we know it was absent in the first simple agrarian societies. There were, nevertheless, certain standardized media of exchange. Barley served this function in ancient Mesopotamia, wheat in Egypt. Wages, rents, taxes, and various other obligations could be paid off in specified quantities of these grains.[26]

As media of exchange, grains were less than ideal, since they were both perishable and bulky. So, from a fairly early date, various metals, particularly silver and copper, were used as alternatives.[27] Initially, they were circulated in the form of crude bars of irregular size and weight, and their use was restricted to major transactions, since metal was still relatively scarce. Later, as metals were easier to obtain, smaller units were made to facilitate local trade, and their sizes and weights were gradually standardized. As the last stage in the process, governments assumed the responsibility for manufacturing metallic currencies, and full-fledged monetary systems appeared. This did not occur, however, until the very end of the simple agrarian era.

The growth of monetary systems had tremendous implications for societal development. Money has always acted as a lubricant, facilitating the movement, the exchange, and ultimately the production of goods and services of every kind. A money economy greatly enlarges the market for the things each individual produces, because products can be sold even to people who produce nothing the individual wants in exchange. Thus the effective demand for goods and services is maximized.

One immediate consequence of the emergence of a money economy is the growth of opportunities for merchants, or middlemen, who purchase goods which they do not want for themselves, but which they know are in demand. Once a class of merchants has come into being, they serve not only to satisfy existing demands but to create new ones. By displaying new and uncommon articles, they generate needs and desires that did not exist before and thereby stimulate economic activity.

In the long run, a money economy subverts many of the values of simpler societies, especially the cooperative tendencies and traditionalism inherent in extended kin systems. In their place it fosters a more individualistic, rationalistic, and competitive orientation and lays a foundation for many of the attitudes and values that characterize modern industrial societies.

These developments were very limited, however, in the simple agrarian societies of the ancient Middle East. The newly emerging monetary economies barely penetrated the rural villages, where most of the people lived. Even in the cities and towns, the role of money was quite limited compared with what we are accustomed to. The major impact of money still lay in the future.

Sociocultural Cleavages

In the simple agrarian societies of the ancient world, there were several important lines of cleavage. First, there was the cleavage between the small governing class and the much larger class of people who, having no voice in political decisions, had to turn over all or most of their surplus to the governing class. Second, there was the division between the urban minority and the far more numerous peasant villagers. Finally, there was the cleavage between the small literate minority and the illiterate masses.

As Figure 7.5 indicates, these three lines of cleavage tended to converge. As a result, the small governing class lived in a very different world from that of the illiterate, rural, peasant majority—despite the fact they were members of the same society. One historian has pointed out that the invention of writing intensified the great social cleavage between the governing class and the governed and led to the formation of two increasingly distinct subcultures.[28] The subculture of the common people was a mixture of primitive superstition and the kinds of practical information they needed in their daily lives. It was extremely parochial in outlook and knew little of the world beyond the village. The subculture of the governing class, by contrast, incorporated many of the refinements we identify with "civilization." It included elements of philosophy, art, literature, history, science, and administrative techniques, and above all, a contempt for physical labor of any kind (except warfare) and for those who engage in it. In short, the governing class possessed a body of cultural information that differed radically from that of the peasant class.

In many respects the differences *within* simple agrarian societies were greater than those *between* them. An Egyptian peasant in the latter half of the second millennium B.C. could have adapted far more easily to the life of a Babylonian peasant than to the life of a member of the governing class of his own society. As this gulf widened, members of the governing class found it increasingly difficult to recognize the ignorant, downtrodden peasants as

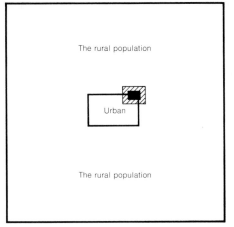

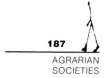

The governing class

The literate population

**FIGURE 7.5 Important cleavages in simple
agrarian societies of the ancient world.**

fellow human beings. The scribes of ancient Egypt were fond of saying that
the lower classes were "without heart" (meaning that they lacked intelligence) and therefore had to be driven with a stick like cattle.[29]

Slowdown in the Rate of Technological Innovation

Another significant development in these societies was a marked slowdown
in the rate of technological innovation and progress, beginning within a few
centuries after the shift from horticulture to agriculture. Childe described the
change this way:

> Before the [agrarian] revolution comparatively poor and illiterate communities
> had made an impressive series of contributions to man's progress. The two
> millennia immediately preceding 3,000 B.C. had witnessed discoveries in applied
> science that directly or indirectly affected the prosperity of millions of men and
> demonstrably furthered the biological welfare of our species by facilitating its
> multiplication. We have mentioned the following applications of science: artifi-
> cial irrigation using canals and ditches; the plow; the harnessing of animal
> motive-power; the sailboat; wheeled vehicles; orchard husbandry; fermentation;
> the production and use of copper; bricks; the arch; glazing; the seal; and—in the
> earliest stages of the revolution—a solar calendar, writing, numerical notation,
> and bronze.
>
> The two thousand years after the revolution—say from 2,600 to 600 B.C.—
> produced few contributions of anything like comparable importance to human
> progress. Perhaps only four achievements deserve to be put in the same category
> as the fifteen just enumerated. They are: the "decimal notation" of Babylonia

(about 2,000 B.C.); an economical method for smelting iron on an industrial scale (1,400 B.C.); a truly alphabetic script (1,300 B.C.); aqueducts for supplying water to cities (700 B.C.).[30]

Childe went on to note that two of these four innovations, the smelting of iron and the development of the alphabet, "cannot be credited to the societies that had initiated and reaped the fruits of the urban revolution" but rather were the products of somewhat less advanced neighboring societies.[31]

On first consideration, this slowing of the rate of technological advance seems an unlikely development. Larger populations, improved communications, and the greater store of information available to potential innovators should have produced still higher rates of innovation. The fact that they did not poses an interesting problem.

As scholars such as Childe have seen, the explanation lies in the transformation of the social structure and ideology of the societies involved.[32] Specifically, the development of the state and the growth of social inequality that followed the shift from horticulture to agriculture created a situation in which those who were engaged in the daily tasks of production were gradually reduced to the barest subsistence level, and held there, by their more powerful superiors. Thus these peasant producers lost the normal incentive for creativity; any benefits that might result from an invention or discovery would simply be appropriated by the governing class.* At the same time, the governing class, though it had a vested interest in a more productive economy, no longer had the necessary knowledge of, and experience with, subsistence technology and thus was in no position to make creative innovations. In short, expertise and incentive were inadvertently divorced, with disastrous results for technological progress.

Under the circumstances, it is hardly surprising that the governing class turned increasingly to warfare and conquest as a more promising means of increasing its wealth. Warfare was something it understood; moreover, in its system of values it was one of the few occupations considered appropriate for members of its class. The energies of this powerful and influential class were thus turned from the conquest of nature to the conquest of man.[33] And this, thanks to the new, more productive technology, could be a highly profitable enterprise. With the peasants producing much more than they needed to survive and remain productive, there was a steady flow of taxes, tithes, and rents to support the host of servants and artisans that catered to the whims of the governing class, as well as the army of soldiers and officials that obeyed its commands.

These developments help explain the advances in social organization made during this period. Having cut themselves off from the sweaty world of

*It is possible that the problem was more complicated and that the mental capacities of many peasants were impaired by protein-deficient diets and limited learning opportunities in early childhood.

work and directed their efforts instead to conquest, the governing class found a new challenge for their creative talents in the area of social organization. The exercise of power and the manipulation of others were activities in keeping with their dignity. Furthermore, they were rewarding: the better organized an army or government, the greater its chances of success in struggles with other groups.[34]

ADVANCED AGRARIAN SOCIETIES

During the period in which simple agrarian societies dominated the Middle East, the most important technological advance was the discovery of the technique of smelting iron. Prior to this, bronze was the most important metal. But since the supply was always limited* and the demands of the governing class always took precedence over the needs of peasants, bronze was used primarily for military and ornamental purposes. It never really replaced stone and wood in ordinary tools, particularly agricultural tools, and so its impact on the economy was limited.

People knew of iron at least as early as the first half of the third millennium B.C., but apparently only in its meteoric form, which is very scarce.[35] Sometime during the second millennium, the Hittites of Asia Minor discovered iron ore and invented a technique for smelting it. For centuries they kept this a closely guarded secret, which brought them both economic and military advantage. Then, about 1200 B.C., their nation was destroyed. This led to the rapid dispersal of both the Hittite people and the technique of iron smelting.

As one would expect, in view of the nature of the class structure of simple agrarian societies, the initial use of iron was limited largely to the governing class. Some of the earliest iron objects recovered from Egypt were a dagger, a bracelet, and a headrest found in the tomb of the pharaoh Tutankhamen. Prior to the military collapse of the Hittites, iron was five times more expensive than gold, forty times more than silver. Only later, perhaps during the eighth century B.C., did it come into general use for ordinary tools. Thus, not until this period were there true advanced agrarian societies—though the Middle Eastern societies of the previous three or four centuries were certainly transitional types.

During this transitional period two further discoveries greatly enhanced the value of iron. First it was found that if the outer layers of the iron absorbed some carbon from the fire during the forging process, the metal was somewhat hardened. Later it was discovered that this carburized iron could be hardened still further by quenching the hot metal in water, thus producing

*This was because of the scarcity of tin, an essential component.

steel. With these developments, iron became not only more common than bronze but also more useful for both military and economic purposes. As one writer has said, "After the discovery of quench-hardening, iron gradually passed into the position from which it has never subsequently been ousted; it became the supremely useful material for making all the tools and weapons that are intended for cutting, chopping, piercing, or slashing."[36]

From its point of origin in the Middle East, iron-making spread until eventually it was practiced in nearly all of the Old World, even in many horticultural societies. By the time of Christ, advanced agrarian societies were firmly established in the Middle East, throughout most of the Mediterranean world, and in much of India and China. Within the next thousand years, the advanced agrarian pattern spread over most of Europe and much of Southeast Asia and expanded further in India and China. Still later it was transplanted to the European colonies in the New World. Advanced agrarian societies still survive in hybrid form in much of Asia, the Middle East, and Latin America, where they constitute the majority of the problem-ridden, underdeveloped nations of our own day. We will examine these partially industrialized agrarian societies in Chapter 13.

Technology

Compared with simpler societies, advanced agrarian societies enjoyed a very productive technology. Unfortunately, however, the same conditions that slowed the rate of technological advance in simple agrarian societies continued to operate. As a result, their progress was not nearly what one would expect on the basis of their size, the degree of communication among them, and, above all, their store of accumulated information.[37]

Nevertheless, over the centuries quite a number of important innovations were made. A partial list would include the catapult, the crossbow, gunpowder, horseshoes, a workable harness for horses, stirrups, the wood-turning lathe, the auger, the screw, the wheelbarrow, the rotary fan for ventilation, the clock, the spinning wheel, porcelain, printing, iron casting, the magnet, water-powered mills, windmills, and, in the period just preceding the emergence of the first industrial societies, the workable steam engine, the fly shuttle, the spinning jenny, the spinning machine, and a number of other power-driven tools. As a result of these and other innovations, the most advanced agrarian societies of the eighteenth century A.D. were considerably superior, from the technological standpoint, to their predecessors of 2,500 years earlier.

The level of technological development was not uniform throughout the agrarian world, despite diffusion. Information still spread slowly in most cases, and some areas were considerably ahead of others. During much of the advanced agrarian era, especially from 500 to 1500 A.D., the Middle East,

FIGURE 7.6 Throughout the agrarian era, societies remained dependent on humans and animals as their chief sources of energy: peasants in India raise water from ditch to irrigate field.

China, and parts of India were technologically superior to Europe.[38] In part, this was simply a continuation of older patterns: the Middle East had been the center of innovation for more than 5,000 years following the horticultural

revolution. Even more important, however, were the effects of the collapse of the Roman Empire. For centuries afterward, Europe was divided into scores of petty kingdoms and principalities that had only enough resources to maintain the smallest urban settlements and the most limited number of occupational specialists. Therefore, Europeans were inactive on many of the most promising and challenging technological frontiers of the time. Though they made relative gains during the later Middle Ages—thanks largely to the diffusion of knowledge from the East—they did not really catch up until the sixteenth century and did not take the lead until even later.

Scale of Organization

In any comparison with simple agrarian societies, the greater organizational development of the advanced is evident on both the societal and the communal levels. On the societal level, there is roughly a tenfold difference between the largest society in each of the two categories. The largest simple agrarian society was probably Egypt in the latter half of the second millennium, at which time it controlled roughly 800,000 square miles.[39] By contrast, the Russian empire in the mid-nineteenth century covered nearly 8 million square miles; even as early as the reign of Peter the Great (1689–1725), it covered nearly 6 million square miles.[40] Several other advanced agrarian societies built empires that far surpassed that of the ancient Egyptians. These include the Spanish empire in the eighteenth century (5 million square miles), the Chinese empire at various times since the first century B.C. (up to 4 million square miles), the Umayyad empire in the eighth century (3 million square miles), and the Roman Empire in the second century (2 million square miles).[41]

Populations, too, were much larger. The most populous simple agrarian society, Egypt, probably had fewer than 15 million members.[42] By contrast, the largest advanced agrarian society, mid-nineteenth-century China, had approximately 400 million.*[43] While that was exceptional, India reached 175 million in the middle of the nineteenth century, and the Roman and the Russian empires each had at least 70 million people.[44]

Similar differences are found at the communal level. The populations of the largest cities in simple agrarian societies were probably not much over 100,000, if that. By contrast, the upper limit for cities in advanced agrarian societies may have been as high as 1 million (see Table 10.4, page 295)—although, as with all population figures from earlier times, there is considerable uncertainty.[45] Only the capitals of great empires ever attained such a size, and they maintained it but briefly. Cities of 100,000 were more numerous than in simple agrarian societies, though still quite rare.

*Growth in China's population *after* the middle of the nineteenth century was increasingly due to the beginnings of industrialization. The same is true of India.

FIGURE 7.7 Montepeyroux, France: a provincial town of the agrarian era, now almost deserted.

Differentiation of Parts

Growth in the scale of organization was accompanied by an increasing differentiation of the parts. For the first time, there was significant economic specialization by regions and by communities, and it was accompanied by increased occupational specialization.

The Roman Empire provides a good illustration of both regional and local specialization. North Africa and Spain were noted as suppliers of dried figs and olive oil; Gaul, Dalmatia, Asia Minor, and Syria for their wine; Spain and Egypt for salted meats; Egypt, North Africa, Sicily, and the Black Sea region for grain; and the latter for salted fish as well.[46] The tendency toward specialization at the community level is illustrated by a passage from a manual for wealthy farmers, written in the second century B.C., which advised:

> Tunics, togas, blankets, smocks and shoes should be bought at Rome; caps, iron tools, scythes, spades, mattocks, axes, harness, ornaments and small chains at Cales and Minturnae; spades at Venafrum, carts and sledges at Suessa and in Lucania, jars and pots at Alba and at Rome; tiles at Venafrum, oil mills at Pompeii and at Rufrius's yard at Nola; nails and bars at Rome; pails, oil urns, water pitchers, wine urns, other copper vessels at Capua and at Nola; Campanian baskets, pulley-ropes and all sorts of cordage at Capua, Roman baskets at Suessa and Casium.[47]

Similar patterns are reported in other agrarian societies.[48] Even at the village level a measure of specialization was not uncommon. In the agricul-

FIGURE 7.8 Occupational specialization in an advanced agrarian society: Middle Eastern silversmith in his shop.

tural off-season, peasants often turned to handicrafts to make ends meet, and certain villages gradually developed a reputation for a particular commodity.

In the larger urban centers, occupational specialization reached a level that surpassed anything achieved in simpler societies. For example, a tax roll for Paris from the year 1313 lists 157 different trades, and tax records from two sections of Barcelona in 1385 indicate a hundred occupations (see Table 7.1).[49] The clothing industry alone contained such specialized occupations as wool comber, wool spinner, silk spinner (two kinds), headdress maker (seven kinds, including specialists in felt, fur, wool and cotton, flowers, peacock feathers, gold embroidery and pearls, and silk), and girdle maker. Though such specialization could be found only in the largest cities, smaller cities often had forty or fifty different kinds of craftsmen, and even small towns had ten or twenty.[50] In addition to craft specialists, urban centers contained specialists in government, commerce, religion, education, the armed forces, and domestic service. The list should also include specialists engaged in illegal occupations, since they were a normal part of urban life in advanced agrarian societies.

TABLE 7.1 Occupations of householders in two sections of Barcelona in 1385 A.D.

Sailors	227	Longshoremen	50	Silversmiths	29
Merchants	151	Inn-keepers	49	Curriers	29
Shoemakers	108	Brokers	45	Notaries	28
Tailors	96	Carpenters	43	Tavern-keepers	27
Fishermen	94	Bakers	40	Spicers	26
Seamen	73	Janitors	39	Bargemen	25
Wooldressers	70	Hucksters	36	76 other occupations	525
Weavers	63	Butchers	34		
Tanners	61	Scriveners	32	Total	2000

Source: Adapted from Josiah Cox Russell, *Medieval Regions and Their Cities* (Bloomington: Indiana University Press, 1972), p. 170.

The Polity

In nearly all these societies, the state was the basic integrative force. It was inevitable in any society created by conquest and maintained for the benefit of a tiny governing class that coercive power would be required to hold the natural antagonisms of its subjects in check. In exercising this power, a state

FIGURE 7.9 Occupational specialization in an advanced agrarian society: Middle Eastern baker rolling dough.

welded together formerly disparate groups, unifying them politically and often, over a period of time, culturally as well.

At the head of nearly every advanced agrarian state was a single individual, the king or emperor. Monarchy was the rule, republican government an infrequent exception limited almost entirely to the least powerful and least developed societies and to those on the margins of the agrarian world.[51] The prevalence of monarchical government seems to have been the result of the militaristic and exploitative character of societies at this level. Governments were constantly threatening, or being threatened by, their neighbors. At the same time, they were in danger from internal enemies—dissatisfied and ambitious members of the governing class, eager to seize control for themselves, and restless, hostile members of the numerically dominant lower classes. Under such conditions, republican government was nearly impossible.[52]

Because of a tendency to romanticize the past, many people today are unaware of the frequency of both internal and external conflict in the great agrarian empires. In Rome, for example, thirty-one of the seventy-nine emperors were murdered, six were driven to suicide, four were forcibly deposed, and several more met unknown fates at the hands of internal enemies.[53] Though Rome's record was worse than most, internal struggles occurred in all advanced agrarian societies.[54]

Peasant risings were also indicators of internal stress. One expert states that "there were peasant rebellions almost every year in China," and an authority on Russia reports that in the short period from 1801 to 1861, there were no less than 1,467 peasant risings in various parts of that country.[55] Most of these disturbances remained local only because authorities acted swiftly and ruthlessly. Had they not, many would have spread as widely as the famous English revolt of 1381 or the German Peasants' War of 1524–1525.[56]

External threats were no less frequent or serious, and warfare was a chronic condition. A survey of the incidence of war in eleven European countries in the preindustrial period found that, on the average, these countries were involved in some kind of conflict with neighboring societies nearly every second year.[57] Such conditions obviously required strong centralized authority. Societies without it were eliminated in the selective process, unless they happened to occupy a particularly remote and inaccessible territory.

Most members of the governing class considered political power a prize to be sought for the rewards it offered rather than an opportunity for public service, and the office of king or emperor was the *supreme* prize. This is the only interpretation one can put on the perennial struggle for power within agrarian states or the use made of it after it was won. Efforts to raise the living standards of the common people were rare, efforts at self-aggrandizement commonplace.[58] In many of these societies, government offices were bought and sold like pieces of property, which purchasers used to obtain the greatest possible profit. Office holders demanded payment before they would act on any request, and justice was typically sold to the highest bidder. No wonder the common people of China developed the saying "To enter a court of justice is to enter a tiger's mouth."[59]

These practices reflected what is known as the *proprietary* theory of the state, which defines the state as a piece of property that its owners may use, within broad and ill-defined limits, for their personal advantage.[60] Guided by this theory, agrarian rulers and governing classes saw nothing immoral in the use of what we (not they) would call "public office" for private gain. To them, it was simply the legitimate use of what they commonly regarded as their

FIGURE 7.10 One use of the economic surplus in an agrarian society: the Taj Mahal, a tomb erected by the Mogul emperor Shah Jahan in memory of his favorite wife.

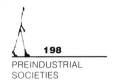

"patrimony." It is said of the Ptolemies of Egypt, for example, that they showed the first emperors of Rome "how a country might be run on the lines of a profitable estate."[61] In the case of medieval Europe, we read:

> The proprietary conception of rulership created an inextricable confusion of public and private affairs. Rights of government were a form of private ownership. "Crown lands" and "the king's estate" were synonymous. There was no differentiation between the king in his private and public capacities. A kingdom, like any estate endowed with elements of governmental authority, was the private concern of its owner. Since "state" and "estate" were identical, "the State" was indistinguishable from the prince and his personal "patrimony."[62]

The proprietary theory of the state can be traced back to horticultural societies and, in a sense, even to hunting and gathering bands. In those simpler societies, the private and public aspects of political leadership were undifferentiated. When a surplus first began to be produced, at least part of it was turned over to the leader, who held it as trustee for the group. As long as the surplus was small and in the form of perishable commodities, there was little the leader could do with it except redistribute it, thereby winning status for his generosity. Eventually, however, as we saw in Chapter 6, it grew large enough to permit him to create a staff of dependent retainers who could be used to enforce his wishes. At this point, the proprietary theory of the state was born. Later rulers merely applied it on an ever-expanding scale, as productivity and the economic surplus steadily increased.

Recent research provides a good picture of the extremes to which rulers and governing classes have carried the proprietary principle. In late nineteenth-century China, for example, the average income for families not in the governing class was approximately 20 to 25 taels per year. By contrast, the governing class averaged 450 taels per year, with some receiving as much as 200,000.[63] The emperor's income, of course, was considerably larger than even this. To cite another example, the English nobility at the end of the twelfth century and early in the thirteenth had an average income roughly 200 times that of ordinary field hands, and the king's equaled that of 24,000 field hands.[64] Putting together the evidence from many sources, it appears that the combined income of the ruler and the governing class in most advanced agrarian societies equaled not less than half of the total national income, even though they numbered 2 per cent or less of the population.[65]

Despite their many similarities, the political systems of advanced agrarian societies did vary in a number of ways, the most important being the degree of political centralization. In some societies the central government was very strong; in others its powers were severely limited. In the main, these differences reflected the current state of the perennial struggle between the ruler and the other members of the governing class. Kings and emperors naturally wanted the greatest possible control over their subordinates, and the latter just as naturally wanted to minimize it. When the ruler was dominant, the political system was despotic, autocratic, or absolutist; when the governing class was relatively free from monarchical control, the system tended to be feudalistic or oligarchic.

Since land (including the peasants who worked it) and political office were the most valuable resources in agrarian societies, struggles between rulers and the governing class usually revolved around their control. In a few instances, extremely powerful rulers like the Ottoman emperor Suleiman and the Mogul emperor Akbar managed to gain almost complete control over

FIGURE 7.11 Working equipment for member of the governing class in sixteenth-century Europe.

FIGURE 7.12 Armor of a Japanese nobleman of the sixteenth century.

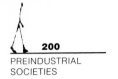

these resources. During their reigns, both land and offices were held at the ruler's pleasure and were subject to instant confiscation should the services of the holder be judged unsatisfactory.[66] A Dutch traveler of the early seventeenth century left a vivid picture of the situation in the Mogul empire at that time.

> Immediately on the death of a lord who has enjoyed the King's [favor], be he great or small, without any exception—sometimes even before the breath is out of the body—the King's officers are ready on the spot and make an inventory of the entire estate, recording everything down to the value of a single piece, even to the dresses and jewels of the ladies, provided they have not concealed them. The King takes back the whole estate absolutely for himself, except in a case where the deceased has done good service in his lifetime, when the women and children are given enough to live on, but no more.[67]

In Turkey under Suleiman, the chief officers of state were recruited from the ranks of specially trained slaves over whom the sultan held life-and-death power.[68] At the other extreme, during much of the medieval period, Europe's feudal lords were virtually autonomous. Though their lands were typically royal grants given in exchange for pledges of service, rulers usually lacked the power to enforce these pledges.[69]

Although examples of both extremes can be found, the usual pattern was something in between. Typically, the powers of the ruler and the governing class were fairly evenly balanced. Various factors influenced the balance and determined the location of a society on what might be called the autocracy-oligarchy scale. In general, the larger a state and the poorer its transportation and communication, the easier it was for members of the governing class to infringe on royal prerogatives.[70] A great deal also depended on the personal qualities of the ruler. Ruthless, energetic, and intelligent men were usually able to improve their positions, while those who lacked these qualities were apt to see them weakened. A ruler who was successful in foreign wars was especially likely to dominate his governing class, since conquests provided him with new resources to distribute and these always strengthened the bonds of "loyalty." The case of William the Conqueror is a classic example.

Patterns of inheritance and succession also greatly influenced the balance of power. A system of primogeniture in the governing class tended to prevent the breakup of large estates, keeping this crucial base of power intact.[71] Rules governing succession to the throne were equally important. Where there was a principle of automatic succession, as in most European countries, children and other weak individuals could become rulers, providing the governing class with an excellent opportunity to increase its powers.[72] By contrast, where there was an open contest, there were few weak rulers. To become ruler of the Mogul empire, for example, a prince had to kill his own brothers. This system produced a succession of strong emperors who held the rights of the governing class to the barest minimum.[73]

Finally, the balance of power depended on the unity of the governing class. When it presented a united front, it could exert far more pressure than when it was torn by internal conflicts. Skillful rulers recognized this and typically sought to exploit differences in rank, wealth, ethnicity, region, and religion for their own advantage.[74]

The Economy: An Overview

Because politics and economics were always tightly intertwined in advanced agrarian societies, those who dominated the political system also dominated the economic system. The leading office holders in government were usually the chief landholders as well, and in these societies land was the most important economic resource. As one economic historian expressed it, "In pre-market societies [among which he includes agrarian], wealth tends to follow power; not until the market society [does] power tend to follow wealth."[75]

As this statement suggests, in resolving the central economic questions—how resources should be used, what should be produced and in what quantities, and how the products should be distributed—the basic market forces of supply and demand were much less important than the arbitrary decisions of the political elite. These were *command* economies, not market economies.[76]

The economy of an advanced agrarian society consisted of two distinct parts: its rural-based agricultural sector and its urban-based commercial and industrial sector. These were not of equal importance, however: one historian has estimated that the Roman state derived approximately twenty times more tax revenue from agriculture than from trade and industry. He went on to say that "this appointment of the burden of taxation probably corresponded roughly to the economic structure of the empire. All the evidence goes to show that its wealth was derived almost entirely from agriculture, and to a very small extent from industry and trade."[77] The same could be said of every other agrarian society. It does not follow, however, that the urban economy was of little interest to the governing class. On the contrary, it was of tremendous interest because it provided the luxuries they valued so highly. The urban economy, however, depended on the rural economy and on its ability to produce a surplus that could support the urban population.

In many respects the economy of the typical agrarian society resembled a tree with roots spreading in every direction, constantly drawing in new resources. Graphically, the pattern was that shown in Figure 7.13. At the economic center of the society was the national capital, controlled by the king or emperor and the leading members of the governing class. Surrounding it were various provincial or regional capitals controlled by royal governors and other members of the governing class. Each of these, in turn, was surrounded by smaller county seats and market towns, controlled by

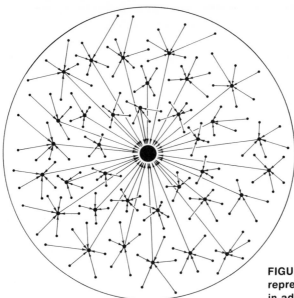

FIGURE 7.13 Graphic
representation of the flow of goods
in advanced agrarian societies.

lower-ranking members of the governing class. Finally, each of these towns was surrounded by scores of small villages. In the larger empires, there was often another layer interposed between the county seats and the regional capitals.

In this system, there was a steady flow of goods from smaller units to larger, or from villages to county seats and from there to regional and national capitals. Basically this flow was through taxation, but it was supplemented by rents, interest on debts, tithes, and profits, all of which helped transfer the economic surplus from the peasant producers to the urban-based governing class and their allies and dependents.

Some scholars have argued that this was actually a symbiotic relation-ship in which the villagers freely exchanged the goods they produced for goods and services produced in the urban centers. Although there was an element of this, the historical record shows that basically it was a one-sided, coercive relationship in which the peasants were forced to give far more than they received. The peasants recognized this, even if some modern scholars do not, and they greatly resented it, as indicated by the frequency of their protests and hopeless revolts.[78]

With what they retained of their surplus after paying taxes, rents, interest, and other obligations, peasants could go to the urban centers and trade for commodities that were not available in their villages (e.g., certain metal tools, salt, etc.). Towns and cities were also religious centers in many cases, and the peasants often used these facilities. Finally, the peasants benefited to some degree from the maintenance of law and order provided by urban-based governments, even though the law was used disproportionately to protect the rights of the governing class and keep the peasants in their place. The maintenance of order is especially important in an agrarian society, where so much depends on the success of each harvest and each harvest

FIGURE 7.14 The city as a religious center: Hindu temple complex in Nepal.

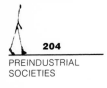

depends on months of effort. Disruption at any point in the agricultural cycle can be disastrous for everyone.

The Rural Economy

In most advanced agrarian societies, the ruler and the governing class (including religious leaders) owned a grossly disproportionate share of the land. Though there are no precise figures for earlier times, the traditional pattern can still be seen in many parts of Latin America, the Middle East, and Southeast Asia. In recent years, a minority of 1 to 3 per cent of the population

TABLE 7.2 Landholdings of the governing class in selected nations in the mid-twentieth century

Nation	Percentage of Population	Percentage of Arable Land Owned
Chile	1.4	63
Northeast Brazil	2	48
Portugal	0.3	39
Southern Spain	1.8	50+
Egypt	0.4 3	34 56
Jordan	3.5	37
Lebanon	0.2 1.4	50 65
Iraq	3	67
North-central India	1.5 3.3	39 54
South Vietnam	2.5	50

Sources: Chile—Federico Gil, *The Political System of Chile* (Boston: Houghton Mifflin, 1966), p. 148; Northeast Brazil—Josue de Castro, *Death in the Northeast* (New York: Random House, 1966), p. 154; Portugal—Herminio Martins, "Portugal," in Margaret Archer and Salvador Giner (eds.), *Contemporary Europe* (New York: St. Martin's, 1972), p. 66; Spain—Salvador Giner, "Spain," in Archer and Giner, p. 134; the Middle Eastern nations—Morroe Berger, *The Arab World Today* (Garden City, N.Y.: Doubleday Anchor, 1964), pp. 196–199; North-central India—Baljit Singh and Shridhar Misra, *Land Reforms in Uttar Pradesh* (Honolulu: East-West Center Press, 1964), p. 28; South Vietnam—*The Washington Post*, October 17, 1965, p. A 8.

FIGURE 7.15   Peasant using the traditional wooden plow in Iran.

has owned from one-third to two-thirds of the arable land in these countries, as shown in Table 7.2.

Not only did the governing class usually own most of the land, but it often owned most of the peasants who worked it. Systems of slavery and serfdom have been common in agrarian societies, with large landholdings and large numbers of slaves or serfs normally going hand in hand. Thus it was only natural that a nineteenth-century Russian nobleman who owned 2 million acres of land also owned nearly 300,000 serfs.[79] Rulers, understandably, had the largest holdings. Prior to the emancipation of the serfs in Russia, the czar owned 27.4 million of them.[80]

But even when the peasant owned his own land and was legally free, he usually found it difficult to make ends meet. A bad crop one year, and he had to borrow money at usurious rates, sometimes as high as 120 per cent a year.[81] In any event, there were always taxes, and these usually fell more heavily on the peasant landowner than on his wealthier neighbor, either because of special exemptions granted the latter or simply because of his greater ability to evade such obligations.[82] If a peasant did not own his land, he had to pay rent, which was always set high. In addition, he was often subject to compulsory labor service, tithes, fines, and obligatory "gifts" to the governing class.[83]

Because the number and variety of obligations were so great, it is difficult to determine just how large the total was, but in most societies it appears to have been not less than half the total value of the goods the peasants produced.[84] The basic philosophy of the governing class seems to have been to tax the peasants to the limit of their ability to pay.[85] This philosophy is illustrated by a story told of a leading Japanese official of the seventeenth century who, returning to one of his estates after an absence of ten years and finding the villagers in well-built houses instead of the hovels he remembered, exclaimed, "These people are too comfortable. They must be more heavily taxed."[86]

Living conditions for most peasants were very primitive, and it is doubtful that they were as well off as hunters and gatherers. For example, the diet of the average peasant in medieval England consisted of little more than the following: a hunk of bread and a mug of ale in the morning; a lump of cheese and bread with perhaps an onion or two to flavor it and more ale at noon; a thick soup or pottage with bread and cheese in the evening.[87] Meat was rare and the ale usually thin. Household furniture consisted of a few stools, a table, and a chest to hold the best clothes and any other treasured possessions.[88] Beds were uncommon; most peasants simply slept on earthen floors covered with straw. Other household possessions were apparently limited to cooking utensils.

In some cases, the lot of the peasant was worse than this. Conditions frequently became so oppressive that it was impossible to eke out a livelihood and the peasants were forced to abandon their farms.[89] In China, conditions were so wretched that female infanticide was widely practiced. One nineteenth-century scholar indicated that in some districts as many as a quarter of the female infants were killed at birth.[90] Sometimes signs were posted in these areas: "Girls may not be drowned here."

To compound the misery created by their economic situation, peasants were often subjected to cruel treatment. Families were sometimes split up if it served their master's economic interests.[91] Peasants often found it difficult to defend their wives and daughters from the amorous attentions of the governing class, and in some areas the lord of the manor maintained the notorious *jus primae noctis*.[92] Finally, peasants were subject at all times to the whims and tempers of their superiors, who could invoke severe punishments even for minor offenses. Petty thievery was often punished by death, frequently by cruel and frightful means.[93]

To the governing class, all this seemed only natural, since most of them, like their predecessors in simple agrarian societies, viewed peasants as essentially subhuman. In legal documents in medieval England, a peasant's children were not his *familia*, but his *sequela*, meaning "brood" or "litter."[94] Estate records in Europe, Asia, and America often listed the peasants with the

FIGURE 7.16 Peasant household in Colombia.

livestock.[95] Even so civilized a Roman as Cato the Elder argued that slaves, like livestock, should be disposed of when no longer productive.[96]

As shocking as these views seem today, they were not completely illogical. So divergent were the ways of life of the governing class and the peasantry, and so limited their contacts (normally a class of officials and retainers stood between them[97]), it is perhaps more surprising that some members of the privileged class recognized their common humanity than that the majority did not.

Despite the heavy burdens laid on them, not all peasants were reduced to the subsistence level. By various devices, many contrived to hide part of their harvest and otherwise evade their obligations.[98] A small minority even managed, by rendering special services to the governing class or by other means, to rise a bit above their fellows, operating larger farms and generally living a bit more comfortably.[99]

For the majority, however, the one real hope for a substantial improvement in their lot lay, ironically, in the devastation wrought by plagues, famines, and wars. Only when death reduced their numbers to the point

TWO VIEWS OF PEASANT LIFE

The rural past often evokes nostalgia. People familiar with the ills of modern industrial societies sometimes covet the "quiet, happy, wholesome way of life" of an earlier era. To a large extent, this image of the past reflects a heritage bequeathed us by romantics who used their pens and paints to create a world that rarely existed. Oliver Goldsmith (1728–1774) was such a poet. Excerpts from his poem, "The Deserted Village," are followed by a few lines from Edwin Markham's remarkably prophetic poem, "The Man With the Hoe," written in 1899—eighteen years before the Russian Revolution and half a century before the Chinese and Cuban revolutions.

From "The Deserted Village," by Oliver Goldsmith

Sweet Auburn! loveliest village of the plain,
Where health and plenty cheered the laboring swain. . . .
How often have I loitered o'er thy green,
Where humble happiness endeared each scene!
How often have I paused on every charm,
The sheltered cot, the cultivated farm,
The never-failing brook, the busy mill,
The decent church that topped the neighboring hill. . . .
How often have I blest the coming day,
When toil remitting lent its turn to play,
And all the village train, from labor free
Led up their sports beneath the spreading tree. . . .
A time there was, ere England's griefs began,
When every rood of ground maintained its man;
For him light labor spread her wholesome store,
Just gave what life required, but gave no more;

---

where good workers were scarce was the governing class forced to bid competitively for the peasants' services, raising their income above the subsistence level.[100] Normally, however, high birthrates kept this from happening or, when it did, soon brought about a return to the former situation.

The Urban Economy

When we think of the great civilizations of the past, most of us conjure up images of Rome, Constantinople, Alexandria, Jerusalem, Damascus, Baghdad, Babylon, and the other great cities that loom so large in the historical record. Thus it is with a sense of shock that we discover that rarely if ever did all the urban communities of an advanced agrarian society contain as much as 10 per cent of its population, and they usually contained much less.[101]

His best companions, innocence and health;
And his best riches, ignorance of wealth.

From "The Man With the Hoe," by Edwin Markham

Bowed by the weight of centuries he leans
Upon his hoe and gazes on the ground,
The emptiness of ages in his face,
And on his back the burden of the world.
Who made him dead to rapture and despair,
A thing that grieves not and that never hopes,
Stolid and stunned, a brother to the ox? . . .
Whose breath blew out the light within this brain? . . .

Through this dread shape the suffering ages look;
Time's tragedy is in that aching stoop;
Through this dread shape humanity betrayed,
Plundered, profaned and disinherited,
Cries protest to the Judges of the World,
A protest that is also prophecy. . . .

O masters, lords and rulers of all lands,
How will the future reckon with this man?
How answer his brute question in that hour
When whirlwinds of rebellion shake all shores?
How will it be with kingdoms and with kings—
With those who shaped him to the thing he is—
When this dumb terror shall rise to judge the world,
After the silence of the centuries?

How can this be? The explanation is that we have been victims of an illusion. Because history was recorded by literate men—men who nearly always lived in cities and towns and regarded the life of the rural villages as unworthy of their attention—the record is primarily of city life, particularly the life of the governing class.

The most striking feature of the cities and towns of these societies was the great diversity of people who lived in them. Urban residents ranged from the most illustrious members of the governing class to beggars and other destitute people who barely managed to stay alive. Unlike so many cities and towns in modern industrial societies, these were not primarily industrial centers. Though considerable industrial activity was carried on in them, their political and commercial functions, and frequently their religious ones, were more important.

Since the cities and towns were the centers of government, and social

FIGURE 7.17 Class distinctions in ancient Rome: slaves transporting a wealthy woman.

and cultural centers as well, most members of the governing class preferred to live in them.[102] As a result, urban populations included not only the necessary complement of civil and military officials, but the extensive households of the governing class as well. Servants were far more numerous in these societies than in ours, both because of the absence of labor-saving devices and because the governing class viewed manual work of any kind as degrading. Furthermore, one of their chief forms of status competition was to see who could maintain the most luxurious household. The household staff of the head of one small kingdom, Edward IV of England, numbered 400.[103] A more important ruler, such as the Roman emperor at the height of empire, had thousands. As one historian put it, one "is dumbfounded by the extraordinary degree of specialization [and] the insensate luxury."[104] One group of servants was responsible only for the emperor's palace clothes, another for his city clothes, another for those he wore to the theater, yet another for his military uniforms. Other servants attended strictly to eating vessels, a different group to those used for drinking, another to silver vessels, and still others to gold vessels and those set with jewels. For entertainment, the emperor had his own choristers, an orchestra, dancing women, clowns, and dwarfs. Lesser members of the Roman governing class obviously could not maintain household staffs as elaborate as this, but many had staffs of hundreds, and some had a thousand or more.[105] All this was made possible by the labors of the peasantry.

Part of the peasants' surplus also went to support two important groups that were allied with the governing class yet separate from it. The first of these was the clergy, of whom more will be said shortly. The second was the

FIGURE 7.18 Merchants worked to obtain their wealth, and this, by the values of the governing class, was unpardonable: merchants loading boat on the Rhine as shown in a fifteenth-century woodcut. Note the guards hired to protect the merchants from robbers.

FIGURE 7.19 Like modern advertisers, merchants sought to create a demand for their goods, especially luxuries: market scene in Morocco.

merchant class. Merchants were a peculiar group in the structure of agrarian societies. Although some of them were extremely wealthy, they were rarely accepted as equals by members of the governing class—even by those less wealthy than they. For merchants worked to obtain their wealth, and this, by the values of the governing class, was unpardonable.[106] Nevertheless, the latter avidly sought the goods that the merchants sold and coveted their wealth, acquiring it whenever they could by taxes, marriage, or outright confiscation.[107] The attitude of the merchants toward the governing class was equally ambivalent: they both feared and envied them, but, given the chance, they emulated their way of life and sought to be accepted by them.

Like modern advertising men, the merchants of agrarian societies often created the demand for their goods, thereby spurring productivity. And like modern advertisers, they were primarily interested in creating a demand for luxuries. One reason for this was the high cost of moving goods. With the primitive transportation available, only lightweight luxury items, such as silks, spices, and fine swords, could be moved very far without the costs becoming prohibitive. A report on China shortly after World War II indicates the enormous differential between traditional and modern methods of transportation there. To ship one ton of goods one mile, the costs were as follows (measured in United States cents):[108]

Steamboat	2.4	Animal-drawn cart	13.0	Pack donkey	24.0
Rail	2.7	Pack mule	17.0	Pack horse	30.0
Junk	12.0	Wheelbarrow	20.0	Carrying by pole	48.0

Figures from Europe are strikingly similar: in 1900, for example, it cost ten times more to move goods by horse-drawn wagon than by rail.[109] In short, modern methods of transportation have slashed this expense by 80 to 95 per cent.

The prosperity of the merchant class was due in no small measure to the labors of another, humbler class with which they were closely affiliated—the artisans, who numbered approximately 3 to 5 per cent of the total population.[110] Except for the peasantry, this class was the most productive element in the economy. Most artisans lived in the urban centers and, like the rest of the urban population, were dependent on the surplus produced by the peasants. Craft specialization was rather highly developed in the larger urban centers, as we have seen.

The shops where artisans worked were small by modern standards and bore little resemblance to a modern factory. In Rome in the first century B.C., a shop employing fifty men was considered very large.[111] A pewter business employing eighteen men was the largest mentioned in any of London's medieval craft records, and even this modest size was not attained until the middle of the fifteenth century.[112] Typically, the shop was also the residence of both the merchant and his workmen, and work was carried on either in the living quarters or in an adjoining room.[113]

The economic situation of the artisans, like that of the merchants, was variable. In Peking at the time of World War I, wages ranged from $2.50 a month for members of the Incense and Cosmetic Workers Guild to $36 a month for members of the Gold Foil Beaters Guild.[114] Those in highly skilled trades and some of the self-employed fared moderately well by agrarian standards. Apprentices and journeymen in less skilled trades, however, worked long hours for bare subsistence wages. In Peking, for example, a seven-day workweek and ten-hour workday were typical, and many artisans remained too poor ever to marry.

Merchants and artisans in the same trade were commonly organized into guilds. These organizations were an attempt to create, in an urban setting, a functional approximation of the extended kin groups of horticultural societies. Many guilds spoke of their members as brothers, for example, and functioned as mutual aid associations, restricting entry into the field, forbidding price cutting, and otherwise trying to protect the interests of their members.[115] But because a guild included merchant employers as well as artisan employees, the former were dominant, controlling key offices and formulating policies that benefited them more than the artisans.[116]

Beneath the artisans in the class structure of the cities were a variety of other kinds of people, including unskilled laborers who supplied much of the animal energy required by the system. The working conditions of these men were usually terrible, and injuries were common. As a result, their work life was short. For example, early in the present century, the average Peking rickshaw man was able to work only five years, after which he was good for little except begging.[117] The class of unskilled laborers shaded off into still more deprived groups—the unemployed, the beggars, and the criminals. The high birthrates of agrarian societies resulted in a perennial oversupply of unskilled labor, and such people drifted to the cities, hoping to find some kind of employment. As long as men were young and healthy, they could usually get work as day laborers. But after they were injured or lost their youth and strength, they were quickly replaced by fresh labor and left to fend for themselves, usually as beggars or thieves. No agrarian society found a solution to this problem. But then, the leading classes were not especially interested in finding one. The system served their needs quite well just as it was.

Many of the sisters of the men who made up the urban lower classes found their livelihood as prostitutes. Moralists have often condemned these women as though they elected this career in preference to a more honorable

---

WHEN THE RICE CROP FAILED

This story in *The Washington Post,* April 27, 1972, reports a recent recurrence of a practice that was once moderately widespread in agrarian societies.

Dork Kham Tai, Thailand—Like the golden acacia, after which it is named, this northern Thailand country town has lost its blossoms and gone to seed.

Its golden flowers were its daughters. By count of its own district's embarrassed and chagrined officials, 100 girls aged 14 to 20 years, mostly belonging to poor rice-farmer families, were sold to madams and pimps last year for service in Bangkok's red-light district known as Sukhothai.

A drought had struck the rice crop, and many families in this lean countryside were desperate for food, as well as for seed and fertilizer for

next season's crop. Their teenage daughters were the most salable commodity, for northern Thailand women have a reputation for prettiness and for docility.

The selling price ranged, depending on youth and beauty, from $50 to $250. The servitude in the world's oldest profession ends only after they have worked off their bond, plus sizeable "interest and upkeep."

Excerpted from a report by Jack Foisie.
©*Los Angeles Times.* Reprinted by permission.

one. The record indicates, however, that most of them had little choice: their only alternative was a life of unrelieved drudgery and poverty as servants or unskilled laborers, and many could not even hope for that.[118] The men they might have married were too poor to afford wives, and the system of prostitution was often, in effect, a substitute for marriage forced on many men and women by society. To be sure, the poor were not the only ones to avail themselves of the services of prostitutes, nor were all girls in the "profession" because of poverty. But economic factors were clearly the chief cause of its high incidence.

The number of profitable working years for prostitutes was hardly longer than that for the rickshaw boys, porters, and others who sold their animal energies for a meager livelihood. As a result, the cities and towns in agrarian societies often swarmed with beggars. Estimates by observers and officials suggest that beggars comprised from a tenth to as high as a third of the total population of urban communities.[119] The proportion was not so high for the society as a whole, of course, since many of the rural poor migrated to the cities and towns in the hope of finding greater opportunities.

Demographic Patterns

As we have noted, the population potential of advanced agrarian societies far surpassed that of simpler societies, rising slowly over the centuries in response to technological advances in food production. Thus China's population gradually increased from about 50 million in the middle of the second century A.D. to around 240 million in the late eighteenth century and then, more rapidly, to 400 million by the middle of the nineteenth.[120] Japan's grew from about 10 million in the thirteenth century to 35 million in 1875, and Britain's from 1 million in the eleventh century to 6 million in the early eighteenth.[121]

Birthrates have always been high in advanced agrarian societies, averaging about 40 births per 1,000 population per year, more than double that of modern industrial societies.[122] In general, there seems to have been little interest in limiting the size of families, since large families, particularly ones with many sons, were valued for both economic and religious reasons. From the economic standpoint, children were viewed by peasants as an important asset, a valuable source of cheap labor.[123] As members of a modern industrial society, we are often ignorant of the amount of work required on a peasant farm. Children were also important as the only form of old-age survivor's insurance available to peasants. Religion added another incentive for large families, either by encouraging cults of ancestor worship in which perpetuation of the family line was essential or simply by declaring large families to be a sign of God's favor.[124] The chief deterrent to large families was probably the reaction of women to the strains and risks of repeated pregnancies; but

FIGURE 7.20 The streets of medieval towns were generally little more than alleys that effectively excluded all but a minimum of light and air: view from the city wall of an old Yugoslav city.

because they were subordinate to their husbands, who generally desired large families, their views were usually ignored.[125]

Despite their high birthrates, advanced agrarian societies grew slowly. Sometimes they failed to grow at all or even declined in size. The reason, of course, was that death rates were almost as high as birthrates and sometimes higher. Wars, disease, accidents, and famine all took their toll. Infant mortality was especially high before the development of modern sanitation and medicine. Recent studies show that the average child born in Rome 2,000 years ago could not expect to live more than twenty years.[126] Even as recently as the seventeenth century, the children of British queens and duchesses had a life expectancy of thirty years, with nearly a third dead before their fifth birthday. Youngsters of the elite who survived the dangerous infant years still had a total life expectancy of only a little more than forty years.[127] For the common people, conditions were even worse. With death rates averaging nearly 40 per 1,000 per year, life expectancy could not have been much over twenty-five years.

The larger cities were notoriously unhealthy places, especially for the common people. The citizens of Rome, for example, had a shorter life expectancy than those in the provinces.[128] England in the early eighteenth century presented a similar situation. During the first half of that century, there were an estimated 500,000 more deaths than births in London.[129] Some of the reasons for this become clear when we read descriptions of sanitary conditions in medieval cities. As one historian depicts them:

> The streets of medieval towns were generally little more than narrow alleys, the overhanging upper stories of the houses nearly meeting, and thus effectually excluding all but a minimum of light and air. . . . In most continental towns and some English ones, a high city wall further impeded the free circulation of air. . . . Rich citizens might possess a courtyard in which garbage was collected and occasionally removed to the suburbs, but the usual practice was to throw everything into the streets including the garbage of slaughter houses and other offensive trades. . . . Filth of every imaginable description accumulated indefinitely in the unpaved streets and in all available space and was trodden into the ground. The water supply would be obtained either from wells or springs, polluted by the gradual percolation through the soil of the accumulated filth, or else from an equally polluted river. In some towns, notably London, small

FIGURE 7.21   Sanitation standards were minimal in most agrarian societies: an open-air butcher shop in the Middle East.

streams running down a central gutter served at once as sewers and as water supply. . . . In seventeenth century London, which before the Fire largely remained a medieval city, the poorer class house had only a covering of weatherboards, a little black pitch forming the only waterproofing, and these houses were generally built back to back. Thousands of Londoners dwelt in cellars or horribly overcrowded tenements. A small house in Dowgate accommodated 11 married couples and 15 single persons. . . . Another source of unhealthiness were the church vaults and graveyards, so filled with corpses that the level of the latter was generally raised above that of the surrounding ground. In years of pestilence, recourse had to be made to plague pits in order to dispose of the harvest of death.[130]

This account calls attention to one of the striking demographic characteristics of advanced agrarian societies: the disasters that periodically overtook them and produced sharp peaks in the death rates.[131] The most devastating of all, the Black Plague that hit Europe in the middle of the fourteenth century, is said to have killed a third of the population of France and England, half that of Italy, and to have left the island of Cyprus almost depopulated.[132] Crop failures and famines seldom affected such large areas, but they were much more frequent and could be just as deadly where they struck. One Finnish province lost a third of its population during the famine of 1696–1697, and many parts of France suffered comparable losses a few years earlier.[133] Even allowing for a considerable margin of error in the reports of such disasters, it is clear from other kinds of evidence—for example, the severe labor shortages and the abandonment of farms that followed plagues and famines—that the number of deaths was huge. Because of these disasters, the growth of advanced agrarian populations was anything but continuous.

Religion

During the era in which advanced agrarian societies were dominant, a number of important changes occurred in the religious sphere. The most important by far was the emergence and spread of three new religions, Buddhism, Christianity, and Islam. Each proclaimed a supranational or universal faith, and each succeeded in creating a community of believers that transcended societal boundaries. In all the older faiths, religious belief and affiliation were determined by the accidents of birth and residence. Where one lived determined the god or gods one worshiped, for the prevailing view was that there were many gods and that, like kings, each had his own people and territory.

The ancient Israelites were perhaps the first to reject this view and move toward a more universalistic outlook. Centuries before the birth of Christ, the prophets proclaimed that there was only one God and that He ruled over the

FIGURE 7.22 Islam is one of the universalistic faiths that emerged in the agrarian era: worshipers listening to a sermon in a Pakistani mosque.

entire world. For a time, Judaism was a missionary religion and won converts in many parts of the Roman world.[134] This phase ended, however, when the early Christian missionaries won most of these Gentile converts over to their faith. After this, the implementation of the universalistic vision became the mission of Christians and Muslims, who eventually converted, at least nominally, most of the population of Europe, North Africa, and the Middle East and some of the people of India, Central Asia, China, and Southeast Asia.

Buddhism, the other great universal faith, began in India as a heretical offshoot of Hinduism and spread through most of Southeast Asia, China, Korea, and Japan, though it later died out in the land of its origin. Older ethnic faiths, such as Hinduism, Confucianism, and Shintoism, still survived in much of Asia, but even they now incorporated some elements of universalism in their thought.

The spread of the new universal faiths reflected the broader social and intellectual horizons opened up by improved transportation and the spreading web of trade relations. Empire building, too, helped weaken parochial or "tribal" views. As people's knowledge of other societies increased, and with

FIGURE 7.23   Religious procession in Venezuelan village.

it their awareness of the essential unity of mankind, the basic postulate of the older ethnic faiths was gradually undermined.

Another important development was the growing separation of religious and political institutions.[135] Compared with the situation in advanced horticultural and simple agrarian societies, the state had become much more secular. Kings and emperors were still said to rule "by the grace of God," the divine right of kings was generally accepted, and occasionally a ruler claimed to be a god; but few rulers functioned as high priests, and theocracies (i.e., states in which a priesthood rules in the name of a god) were almost unknown. This separation was part of the more general trend toward institutional specialization that is so basic in the evolutionary process from the horticultural era on.

Despite the growing organizational separation of politics and religion, the two systems continued to work closely together, and political and religious leaders were normally allied. This was especially evident in struggles between the governing class and the common people. When rebellious voices challenged the right of the governing class to control the economic surplus produced by the peasants, the clergy usually defended the elite, asserting that their power had been given them by God and any challenge to it was a challenge to His authority.[136] By legitimizing the actions of the governing class in this way, the clergy reduced the need for costly coercive efforts.

In appreciation for this, and also because of their own religious beliefs, agrarian rulers were often extremely generous with religious groups, giving them large grants of land and special tax exemptions. In effect, a symbiotic relationship was established, with religious groups legitimizing the actions of the governing class in return for generous financial support. Modern research indicates that religious groups frequently owned as much as a quarter or a third of a nation's land.[137]

Despite such profitable alliances, most religions fostered some concern for distributive justice. This is especially evident in Judaism and Christianity.[138] One historian captured the contradictory nature of the medieval church in this discerning characterization: "Democratic, yet aristocratic; charitable, yet exploitative; generous, yet mercenary; humanitarian, yet cruel; indulgent, yet severely repressive of some things; progressive, yet reactionary; radical, yet conservative—all these are qualities of the Church in the Middle Ages."[139]

FIGURE 7.24 This eighteenth-century French cartoon bitterly satirizes the clergy and nobility for "riding on the back" of the peasantry.

Magic and Fatalism

Before we leave the subject of ideology, two other aspects of the world view of agrarian societies deserve comment: (1) the widespread belief in the efficacy of magic and (2) the equally widespread attitude of fatalism.[140] Logically, these are contradictory. If magic really works, people do not need to be fatalistic, and if they are true fatalists, they should have no confidence in magic. But people are seldom completely logical in their view of life. In their more optimistic moments they often hope for things they know are impossible. Considering the tremendous pressures operating on the masses of common people in agrarian societies, and their limited sources of information, it is hardly surprising that so many of them held these mutually contradictory views.

The prevalence of these beliefs, however, was another factor that contributed to the slow rate of technological advance in agrarian societies. Neither belief was likely to motivate people to try to devise better tools and techniques. On the contrary, one encouraged them to look to magic for the solutions to their problems, and the other convinced them that success was, after all, simply a matter of fate.

Kinship

Kinship ties continued to be important for the individual in advanced agrarian societies. Their importance for society, however, was greatly diminished compared with their importance in hunting and gathering or horticultural societies. The explanation for this lies in the growth in the scale of organization. As long as communities and societies were small, the kinship system could serve as an integrative force for the entire population. Later, when the growth of population made this impossible, the largest and most powerful clan in a society, supplemented perhaps by its dependent retainers, could still provide enough men to staff the political system. By the time the level of advanced agrarian societies was reached, however, even this became impossible. Civil and military offices were so numerous that not even the largest extended family could fill them all. Thus, the kinship system could no longer provide the structural basis for the political system.

Family ties still played a significant role in politics, however. Many civil and military offices in agrarian societies were a family's patrimony, handed down from father to son like any other family possession. The classic case of this was the royal office itself in most societies, but the pattern was much more widespread than that. When offices were not privately owned, they were often closed to anyone who was not a member of the nobility or whose family did not qualify by less formal criteria as one of "the right families." Even when these criteria were not invoked in the allocation of offices, family ties were still important. Family funds might be needed to purchase an office, for example; and those who had it in their power to assign an office were naturally influenced by their own family's interests. Although similar practices still occur in modern industrial societies, they are usually a violation of the law and lack public approval. But in advanced agrarian societies, these practices were usually an accepted part of life, and there was little criticism, and still less punishment, of those who engaged in them.

In the economic realm, the family was usually the basic unit of organization. This was equally true in urban and in rural areas. Businesses were almost always family enterprises; the corporate form of enterprise, owned jointly by unrelated persons, was virtually unheard of, even in the largest cities. And in rural areas the basic work unit was the family.

It is not unfair to say that in these societies the family was largely an economic and political organization. While this can be demonstrated in many ways, some of the best examples are associated with marriage practices. For instance, because of its economic implications, marriage was considered much too important to be decided by young people, and marriages were usually arranged by the parents, often with the aid of marriage brokers.[141] Sometimes the young couple did not even meet until the ceremony itself. In selecting spouses for their children, parents were primarily concerned with the economic and status implications of the match and only secondarily with other matters. Marriage arrangements often involved an outright economic transaction, either the payment of a bride price (i.e., payment for the bride) or a dowry.[142] Among members of the governing class, marriages were usually arranged with an eye to their political implications: by skillful management of its children's marriages, a family could do a great deal to improve its political position.

As one would suppose, marriages contracted in this way did not always produce psychological or sexual compatibility between the spouses, but then, this was not necessarily expected. For those pleasures, wealthier men often turned to mistresses and concubines. Despite this, marriage ties were usually quite durable because of the strong economic or political bonds between the partners.

Within the family, male dominance was the rule. Obedience was generally held to be the highest ideal for women and children.[143] This was but part of the general authoritarian pattern of life in agrarian societies.

Leisure and the Arts

In describing the life of the peasant masses in thirteenth-century England, the British historian H. S. Bennett has written:

FIGURE 7.25 *Peasant Wedding*, by Pieter Breughel the Elder (1520?–1569).

> The land is always there: harsh, exacting, insatiate, and rapidly overcoming the puny efforts man can put into it unless he is constantly fighting. And the fight is unending—the harvest is but the signal for the autumn plowing; and the autumn plowing for the sowing, and so on. Season follows season: the rhythmic passage of the year drags in its wake the rural society.[144]

But Bennett also notes that there were occasional opportunities for leisure and recreation.[145] Weddings and religious festivals, for example, were important occasions for people to get together for a good time, with singing and dancing their basic entertainment and alcoholic beverages adding to the merriment in most societies. People also amused themselves with games and contests, courtship and lovemaking, gossiping and storytelling, and a host of other activities.

Class distinctions were evident in leisure activity as in any other, with falconry, jousting, and chess among the activities generally identified with the governing class. But some forms of entertainment, such as archery and dice, had a universal appeal. Gambling in particular was popular with every class.

The rise of professional entertainers was part of the general trend toward occupational specialization. Actors, minstrels, jesters, clowns, acrobats, jugglers, prostitutes, and geishas are a few of the more familiar. In general, the status of such people was extremely low, probably because of their economic insecurity and their excessive dependence on the favor of others. Yet an entertainer who had a powerful patron might find his or her work quite lucrative.

Recreation was frequently raucous and crude; it could also be brutal and violent. In the latter respect, the Romans were probably unsurpassed. In their so-called games, first in the Circus Maximus, later in the Colosseum, tens of thousands came to watch wild animals devour helpless victims, and armed gladiators maim and kill one another. When the Colosseum was first opened in 80 A.D., the Emperor Titus promised the people of Rome 100 consecutive days of such games, with fights to the death between more than 10,000 prisoners and 5,000 wild animals (including lions, tigers, and elephants), and a naval battle between 3,000 men in an arena flooded for the occasion.[146]

In agrarian Europe, cockfights and dogfights were very popular and public hangings often drew large and exuberant crowds. Wedding parties and other festivities frequently ended in drunken brawls. In fact, violence typically followed drinking. From what we know of life in agrarian societies, it would appear that alcohol simply removed a fragile overlay of inhibitions, revealing people's frustrations and bitterness.

FIGURE 7.26   Recreation was frequently brutal and violent in agrarian societies, and the Romans were probably unsurpassed. In their so-called games, tens of thousands came to watch wild animals devour helpless victims, and armed gladiators maim and kill one another.

SONG OF THE TROUBADOUR

I love the gay Eastertide, which brings forth leaves and flowers; and I love the joyous songs of the birds, re-echoing through the copse. But also I love to see, amidst the meadows, tents and pavilions spread; and it gives me great joy to see, drawn up on the field, knights and horses in battle array; and it delights me when the scouts scatter people and herds in their path; and I love to see them followed by a great body of men-at-arms; and my heart is filled with gladness when I see strong castles besieged . . . and the warriors . . . [with] maces, swords, helms of different hues, shields that will be riven and shattered as soon as the fight begins; and many vassals struck down together; and the horses of the dead and the wounded roving at random. And when battle is joined, let all men of good lineage think of naught but the breaking of heads and arms; for it is better to die than to be vanquished and live. I tell you, I find no such savour in food, or in wine, or in sleep, as in hearing the shout "On! On!" from both sides, and the neighing of steeds that have lost their riders, and the cries of "Help! Help!"; in seeing men great and small go down on the grass beyond the fosses; in seeing at last the dead, with pennoned stumps of lances still in their sides.

Attributed to Bertrand de Born, a petty nobleman and troubadour of the twelfth century. From Marc Bloch, *Feudal Society*, p. 293. By permission of The University of Chicago Press.

But if the agrarian world at play was often unattractive, its artistic accomplishments were quite the opposite. In their sculpture, their painting, their architecture, these societies left monuments of lasting beauty. Thousands of cathedrals, churches, mosques, pagodas, temples, and palaces, and all the treasures within them, testify to an impressive development of the arts during that era. Achievements in literature were probably no less impressive, though language barriers make it difficult for us to appreciate them as fully.* Developments in music during most of the agrarian era seem to have been less spectacular than in the other arts. Toward the end of the era, however, the invention of new instruments and the genius of composers like Bach, Mozart, Beethoven, and Chopin combined to produce an outburst of magnificent music that has transcended societal boundaries in unprecedented fashion.

Most artists were subsidized by the governing class or the religious elite, drawing on the economic surplus extracted from the peasant masses. Thus, the artistic achievements of agrarian societies were a product of the harshly exploitative social system. Yet, if the peasants had been allowed to keep the surplus, the result would simply have been more poor people. Again, as with

*Robert Frost once said that "poetry is what gets lost in translation," and anyone who has ever tried seriously to translate a poem understands the complexity of the language problem.

horticultural societies, this link between an exploitative class system and cultural achievements reminds us of the difficulty we face in passing ethical judgments on complex sociocultural systems.

Cleavages and Conflicts

The sociocultural cleavages dividing advanced agrarian societies were similar to those in simple agrarian societies. Most important of all was the division along class lines. In advanced agrarian societies, however, this could no longer be described simply as a cleavage between the governing class and the rest of the population. The class structure had become more complex. Some merchants were now wealthier than some members of the governing class, for example, and between these privileged classes and the mass of common people was a growing middle class of self-employed artisans, small merchants, minor officials, lesser members of the clergy, and well-to-do peasants. In conflicts with the poor, the wealthy merchants and the middle class usually aligned themselves with the governing class, but at other times they did their best to advance their own interests at the expense of the governing class.

The cleavage between city people and country folk was still there, intensified, if anything, by greater urbanization. Towns and cities could no longer be described as overgrown villages. They had developed their own distinctive way of life, one that seemed completely alien to the visiting peasant or the migrant from a rural area. And because of the concentration of the literate and privileged classes in the urban centers, the villages seemed to city dwellers to be social and cultural backwaters, their residents ignorant and uncouth. There was a great deal of barbed humor by city people at the expense of country "yokels," and by country people at the expense of city "slickers" who were not quite as smart as they thought they were when confronted with the problems of rural life.

The cleavage between literate and illiterate continued, the chief difference being that in advanced societies most of the privileged class were literate. Writing was no longer a craft specialty. In most societies, this spread of literacy was greatly facilitated by the invention of the alphabet, though the Chinese experience shows that the alphabet was not essential.

Religion was the basis of an important new cleavage in many advanced agrarian societies. Although religious conflicts existed in simple agrarian societies, they were largely power struggles within the governing class, and most people had little interest in their outcome. With the rise of the new universal faiths, however, the common people were often drawn into these struggles. In many areas, especially in the Middle East and India, this led to the formation of largely endogamous (that is, inbred), culturally differentiated, and hostile religious groups. Each group sought control of the machinery

of government in order to protect and further its own special interests. Members of religious minorities were often discriminated against politically, economically, and legally.

On the whole, the divisions within advanced agrarian societies were more serious than those within simple agrarian societies. In particular, they were more likely to lead to violence. Earlier, we noted the frequency of peasant risings. Though most of these were local incidents involving small numbers of people, some spread and became large-scale insurrections. In either case, they were something new in history. Nor was it only the peasants who revolted against the governing class. The artisans followed suit on a number of occasions, as did the merchants.[147] And these groups, unlike the peasants, sometimes emerged victorious. In Europe, the merchants were so successful in their challenges to the governing class that eventually *they* became the governing class in many cities and towns. From the evolutionary perspective, this proved to be a very important development indeed.

Sociocultural Variations

In surveying societies at the same level of development, it is natural to emphasize those characteristics which are found in all of them, or are at least widespread, and to slight the differences, thus giving an impression of greater uniformity than really exists. Obviously there have been variations in every area of life in advanced agrarian societies, and we have noted many of them—or hinted at them in qualifying phrases, saying that a particular pattern was found in "most" or "many" of these societies.

Technologically, for example, the first advanced agrarian societies were much more like their simple agrarian predecessors than like the advanced agrarian societies of Europe on the eve of the Industrial Revolution. Furthermore, the size of societies in this category ranged all the way from tiny principalities to great empires. Most were monarchies, but a few were republics. Similar variations occurred in almost every area of life.

Clearly, then, variation is to be expected among societies at the advanced agrarian level—indeed, at *every* level of societal development. There is, however, one important difference: in the simple societal types (i.e., hunting and gathering, fishing, and simple horticultural), intratype variation results primarily from differences in the biophysical environment. We see this clearly when we compare the Eskimo with the Australian aborigines, or the Bushmen of the Kalahari Desert with the Pygmies of the rain forest. In advanced agrarian societies, on the other hand, differences in biophysical environment have been much less responsible for intratype variation. This is exactly what evolutionary theory would lead us to expect, since the further a society advances on the evolutionary scale, the greater its ability to overcome the limitations imposed by the biotic and physical world.

Differences in the *social* environment of advanced agrarian societies, however, have sometimes been responsible for rather important intratype variation. This is especially evident when we compare frontier societies with other advanced agrarian societies. A frontier society is one that is in the process of expanding into the territories of technologically simpler societies. The most familiar example for Americans is the European settlement of the New World; other instances include the British settlement of Australia and New Zealand, the Dutch or Boer settlement of South Africa, and Russia's settlement of Siberia.

Frontiers are especially interesting because they provide a unique opportunity for departures from the sociocultural patterns so deeply entrenched in agrarian societies. Those who respond to the challenges of the frontier, to its dangers and its opportunities, are primarily people with little to lose, with little stake in the established order. Thus they are likely to possess a willingness to take great physical risks and a proclivity for independence and innovation. As a result, new ways of life commonly develop in frontier areas, innovations are readily accepted, and older rigidities give way.[148]

One of the most significant changes that occurs is the breakdown of the traditional class system. Except where the native population is enslaved or enserfed—as in much of Latin America—or where slaves are imported—as occurred in the Caribbean and the southern United States—a highly egalitarian system of small farms is likely to develop. This is what happened in Canada, the United States outside the southern region, Australia, New Zealand, and Siberia. In such areas, there is always a serious shortage of labor; workers are suddenly much more valuable than they were in the older, settled areas with their typical surplus of labor. On the frontier, there are neither enough farmers to cultivate the newly opened land nor enough fighters to defend it. It is not surprising, then, that frontier life produces a striking independence of spirit and a stubborn resistance to authority. Having risked their lives to establish themselves in a new territory, frontiersmen are not prepared to hand over their surplus to anyone. Thus, frontier conditions often break down the sharp inequalities and exploitative patterns characteristic of agrarian societies.

This condition is usually temporary, however. As the resistance of the native population comes to an end and the land begins to fill up with people, as roads are built and governmental authority is established, there is a waning of the spirit of independence and individualism, opportunities for resistance decline, and the traditional system begins to assert itself. To be sure, this does not happen overnight. On the contrary, it is likely to take a century or more. But in the end, the typical agrarian pattern prevails.

Only one thing has ever prevented this from happening—the onset of industrialization. In a number of instances during the last century and a half, the Industrial Revolution generated a new demand for labor before the

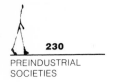

demands of the frontier had been satisfied and thus aborted the rebirth of the old system. This happened in the United States in the nineteenth century and subsequently in Canada, Australia, and New Zealand. All these societies were thus spared the agony of slowly sliding into the classic agrarian pattern in which a massive, impoverished peasantry is dominated and exploited by a small, hereditary aristocracy.

In the United States, this process actually got fairly well under way in much of the South with its system of slavery. But the Confederacy's defeat in the Civil War and the South's eventual industrialization halted the process. In other parts of the country, the process had not really developed very far before the forces of industrialization intervened.

Looking back, it seems clear that the frontier experience was excellent preparation for the Industrial Revolution. Most important, perhaps, it established a tradition of innovation and a receptivity to change that were lacking in other agrarian societies. Also, by creating a more egalitarian class system, the frontier prepared the way for the more open and fluid class systems of modern industrial societies. These developments help explain the relative ease with which the overseas English-speaking democracies made the transition to the industrial era and also why they have been in the forefront with respect to productivity, standard of living, and political stability. It is interesting to speculate, however, how different the situation in these societies might be had they been settled a thousand years sooner and a more typical agrarian social system taken root.

CHAPTER 8
SOME
EVOLUTIONARY
BYPATHS AND A
RECAPITULATION

SPECIALIZED SOCIETAL TYPES

Up to this point in our survey of human societies, we have concentrated on those types which are in the mainstream of evolutionary history, those which developed their technologies around the resources of fields and forests. The types of societies to which we now turn have adapted to more specialized, less typical environments—two to aquatic conditions, the third to semidesert grasslands and other marginal environments. Though these specialized societies have contributed to sociocultural evolution in many ways, their overall contribution has been more limited than that of the mainstream societies. This is chiefly because of the specialized nature of the problems with which they have dealt in their subsistence activities. Because of this, we will not examine them in the same detail as the others.

FIGURE 8.1 African fishing village, Dahomey.

Fishing Societies

Actually, it is something of a misnomer to call any group a "fishing" society, for none ever depended exclusively on fishing for its food supply.[1] Except in the Arctic, nearly all fishing peoples obtain fruits and vegetables by foraging or cultivation. Many of them also supplement their diet by hunting or, occasionally, by raising livestock. To call a society a fishing society, then, simply indicates that fishing is its most important subsistence activity.

In recent centuries, fishing societies have been found in many parts of the world, but they have been most common in the northwestern part of North America—Oregon, Washington, British Columbia, Alaska, and the arctic regions of Canada. They have occurred less frequently in northern Asia and among the islands of the Pacific (most of the Pacific peoples have been simple horticulturalists) and in scattered parts of Africa, South America, and elsewhere.

Historically, fishing societies are probably the second oldest type, emerging about a thousand years before the first horticultural societies. The actual practice of fishing is, of course, even older and more widespread and has provided a supplementary source of subsistence in most societies for at least 12,000 years.

In some ways fishing societies might be regarded simply as specialized hunting and gathering societies, adapted to aquatic environments rather than terrestrial. One might argue that the chief difference is simply that fish, rather than land animals, are the object of the chase and that the technology of the group is modified accordingly. But this ignores a crucial fact: fishing economies usually have a potential for supporting larger, more sedentary populations than hunting and gathering economies. There are two reasons for this. First, because fish have much higher reproductive rates than most land animals, especially the larger animals on which hunters so often depend, primitive fishing people are less likely to deplete the food resources of their territory. As a result, it is easier for them to establish permanent settlements, with all this implies for the accumulation of wealth and the growth of social inequality.

A second basic difference is that fishermen usually work only a small fraction of the food-producing territory. When primitive people fish a large body of water, such as an ocean, a sea, or a large lake, their simple boats prevent them from going very far. As a result, even if they catch all the fish in the territory they work, the supply is quickly replenished by the great surplus spawned in adjacent areas. Nothing like this can happen on land, at least not after hunting and gathering bands occupy all the habitable territory in an area. This second difference reinforces the effects of the first.

Thus, although fishing societies are only a bit more advanced technologically than hunting and gathering societies, we would expect them to be somewhat larger, more sedentary, and more complex.[2] This is, in fact, precisely what we find. With respect to size, they are half again as large: Murdock's sample shows that the average size of fishing communities is approximately 60, the average size of hunting and gathering groups only 40.[3] With respect to sedentariness, only 10 per cent of the hunting and gathering societies live in permanent settlements, compared to 49 per cent of the fishing societies.

Their political systems also indicate the greater potential inherent in a fishing economy. Less than 10 per cent of hunters and gatherers are organized into multicommunity societies, in contrast to nearly a quarter of the fishing societies. Social inequality, too, is more pronounced and more common: slavery is reported in slightly over half of the fishing societies. A system of hereditary nobility is also much more common in fishing societies than in hunting and gathering societies (32 per cent versus 2 per cent). Finally, as another indication of their greater economic development and wealth, fishing peoples are much more likely to link marriage with some economic transaction. This happens in 77 per cent of these groups but in only 48 per cent of hunting and gathering societies.

In terms of structural development, fishing societies have about as much in common with simple horticultural societies as with hunting and gathering societies.[4] Depending on the criterion, they sometimes lean more toward

FIGURE 8.2 The Shui-jen, or water people, of South China are descended from fishing peoples of an earlier time. They still depend on fishing for their livelihood and remain separate from the mainland population.

one, sometimes the other. For example, in community size they more closely approximate hunting and gathering societies,[5] in permanence of settlements they are midway between hunting and gathering and simple horticultural,[6] and in frequency of multicommunity societies they are almost indistinguishable from simple horticultural.[7]

From an evolutionary standpoint, the line of development represented by fishing societies has been something of a blind alley. Unlike hunting and gathering societies, fishing groups did not evolve into a more advanced type.[8] The reasons for this are quite simple. To begin with, the areas suited to a predominantly fishing economy are not only very limited, they are scattered and strung out along thin coastal strips, so that it has been virtually impossible to consolidate several groups into one large political entity.[9] Instead, when neighboring horticultural societies became powerful enough, fishing societies were usually conquered and absorbed. Then, even though fishing continued in the area, it was only a minor part of the economy of the larger society, and the leaders of the fishing groups were reduced to the status of minor officials, too weak to hold onto the local surplus for local use. As a result, fishing communities in agrarian societies have often been socially and culturally less advanced (except in subsistence technology) than fishing communities in more primitive fishing societies. Typically, their situation was no better than that of peasant villages, and for the same reason—their surplus was confiscated by the more powerful elements in the society.[10]

Though fishing societies did not give rise to more advanced societal types, they were not evolutionary blind alleys in the same sense as animals which become extinct and whose unique genetic characteristics are thereby lost. The technological contributions made by fishing societies, far from being lost, have become part of the cultural heritage of almost every advanced society.

Herding Societies

Herding societies, like fishing societies, represent an adaptation to specialized environmental conditions. Other than that, the two have little in common. Their environments are radically different, and their technologies, although overlapping somewhat, are basically on different levels.

Technologically, herding groups cover the same range of development as horticultural and simple agrarian societies. Animals were first domesticated about the same time plants were first cultivated, and the two practices typically went hand in hand in the horticultural and agrarian societies of the Old World.* In some areas, however, crops could not be cultivated because of insufficient rainfall, too short a growing season (in northern latitudes), or mountainous terrain. This was true of much of central Asia, the Arabian peninsula, and North Africa, and parts of Europe and sub-Saharan Africa. Because it was often possible to raise livestock in these areas, however, a new and different type of society gradually come into being.†

A pastoral economy usually necessitates a nomadic or seminomadic way of life.[11] In fact, "nomad" comes from an early Greek word meaning a "herder of cattle."[12] In the sample of herding societies in the Ethnographic Atlas, more than 90 per cent are wholly or partially nomadic. In this respect they closely resemble hunters and gatherers.

Herders are also like hunters and gatherers in the size of their communities. On the average, they are a bit smaller than fishing communities and much smaller than simple horticultural, as the following population figures show.

---

*This was not true in most of the New World, where there were almost no domesticated animals.

†Usually these societies have also had some secondary means of subsistence, frequently horticulture or agriculture on a small scale.

FIGURE 8.3 Bedouin herders drawing water from well near Al Kharj, Saudi Arabia.

Hunting and gathering communities	40
Herding communities	55
Fishing communities	60
Simple horticultural communities	95

The explanation for this is primarily environmental. Given the sparse resources of their territories, large and dense settlements are impossible.[13]

Despite the small size of their communities, herding *societies* are usually fairly large. Whereas the typical hunting and gathering, fishing, or simple horticultural society contains but a single community, the average herding society contains several dozen.[14] Thus the median population of herding societies far surpasses those of the other three types.

Hunting and gathering societies	40
Fishing societies	60
Simple horticultural societies	95
Herding societies	2,000

The size of herding societies results from the combined influence of environment and technology. Open grasslands, where the majority of herders live, present few natural barriers to movement and, therefore, to political consolidation. Furthermore, since early in the second millennium B.C., many of the herding peoples have mastered the art of horseback (or camel) riding, which greatly facilitates military conquest and political expansion.

The basic resource in these societies is livestock, and the size of the herd is the measure of a man. Large herds signify not only wealth but power, for only a strong man or the head of a strong family can defend such vulnerable property against rivals and enemies. Thus, in most of these societies, and especially in the more advanced (i.e., those with horses or camels and herds of larger animals such as cattle), marked social inequality is the rule. Hereditary slavery, for example, is far more common in herding societies than in any other type.[15] Other kinds of inequality are also very common, especially inequality of wealth.[16]

With respect to kinship, herding societies are noteworthy on at least two counts. First, they are more likely than any other type of society to require the payment of a bride price or bride service.[17] Second, they are the most likely to require newly married couples to live with the husband's kinsmen.[18]

These strong patriarchal tendencies have several sources. To begin with, they reflect the mobile and often militant character of pastoral life. Raiding and warfare are frequent activities, and, as we have noted before, these activities stimulate the growth of political authority. Moreover, the basic economic activity in these societies is man's work. In this respect they stand in sharp contrast to horticultural societies, where women so often play the dominant role in subsistence activities. It is hardly coincidence that horticultural societies are noted for their frequent female-oriented kinship patterns, herding societies for the opposite.

Herding societies are extremely interesting from the religious standpoint. Their concept of God corresponds to the Jewish and Christian concept more closely than any other group's. In forty of the fifty herding groups for which the Ethnographic Atlas has data, there is a belief in a Supreme Deity who created the world and remains actively concerned with its affairs, especially with man's moral conduct. This combination of beliefs is rare in other societies, except agrarian, where it occurs in two-thirds of the cases.[19] But even there, as Table 8.1 makes clear, its occurrence varies directly with the importance of herding activities to the particular group.

For those familiar with religious history, this relationship is not surprising. The Hebrews, who played such an important role in the rise and spread of monotheism, were originally a herding people. And Islam, the most uncompromisingly monotheistic of faiths, enjoyed most of its early successes among the herding peoples of the Arabian peninsula.

Why this relationship developed is far from clear, but the relation itself is undeniable. One can find repeated evidence of the affinity between the pastoral way of life and these religious concepts in Biblical texts that describe God as a shepherd and his people as sheep. The shepherd's relationship with his flock may have suggested answers to the perennial questions about humanity's nature and destiny and the power that ultimately controls them. These answers have not been obvious to all herding peoples,

TABLE 8.1 Religious beliefs of agrarian societies, by percentage of subsistence derived from herding

Percentage of Subsistence from Herding	Percentage Believing in Active, Moral Creator God	Number of Societies
36–45	92	13
26–35	82	28
16–25	40	20
6–15	20	5

Source: George Peter Murdock's Ethnographic Atlas sample of 915 societies.

however; a number of pastoral groups in Asia and Africa have come up with very different ones. The most we can say is that pastoral life increases the probability that people will arrive at these kinds of answers.

One of the most important technical advances made by herding peoples was utilizing the energy of horses, and later camels, for transportation. This practice originated in the eighteenth century B.C., when certain herding groups in the Middle East began to harness horses to chariots.[20] This gave them an important military advantage over their less mobile agrarian neighbors and enabled them to win control of much of the Middle East—at least until the new technology was adopted by the more numerous agrarian peoples. Herders later learned to *ride* their horses, which led to a new wave of conquests, beginning in the ninth century B.C.[21] During the next 2,500 years, a succession of advanced herding groups attacked agrarian societies from China to Europe and frequently conquered them. The empires and dynasties they established include some of the largest and most famous in history—the great Mongol empire, for example, founded by Genghis Khan early in the thirteenth century A.D. and expanded by his successors. At the peak of its power, the Mongol empire stretched from Eastern Europe to the shores of the Pacific and launched attacks against places as far apart as Austria and Japan. Other famous empires and dynasties founded by herding peoples include the Mogul empire, established in India by one branch of the Mongols, the Manchu dynasty in China, the Ottoman empire in the Middle East, and the early Islamic states established by Muhammad and his followers.

Despite their frequent military victories, herding peoples were never able to destroy the agrarian social order. In the end, it was always they, not the agrarian peoples, who changed their mode of life. There were a number of reasons for this, but it was primarily because the herders were motivated chiefly by greed. They saw agrarian societies as rich prizes and coveted the luxuries that their governing classes enjoyed. After a few early conquerors tried to turn fields into pastures, they realized they were, in effect, killing the goose that lays the golden eggs, and abandoned the effort. Thus, despite many impressive victories, the limits of the herding world were never enlarged.

Although herding continued to be an important secondary source of subsistence in the agrarian world, it was the primary source only in areas not suited to cultivation. In recent centuries, even these areas have, in most cases, been brought under the control of agrarian or industrial societies, and herding societies, like other preindustrial types, are vanishing.

Maritime Societies

Maritime societies have been the rarest of all the major societal types. Not one survives today. Yet they once played an important role in the civilized world.

Technologically, maritime societies had a lot in common with agrarian societies. What set them apart was the way they used their technology to take advantage of the opportunities afforded by their environmental situation. Located on large bodies of water in an era when it was cheaper to move goods by water than by land, these peoples found trade and commerce far more profitable than either fishing or the cultivation of their limited land resources and gradually created societies in which overseas trade was the chief economic activity.

The first maritime society in history was probably developed by the Minoans on the island of Crete, late in the third millennium B.C. We are told that the wealth and power of the Minoan rulers "depended more upon foreign trade and religious prerogative than upon the land rents and forced services."[22] The island location of Minoan society was important not only because it afforded access to the sea but also because it provided protection against more powerful agrarian societies. Maritime societies always required the absence of powerful neighboring societies, and for this reason they usually developed on islands or peninsulas that were difficult to attack by land (see Figure 8.4). Their only military advantage was in naval warfare.

During the next 1,500 years a number of other maritime societies were established in the Mediterranean world. These included the Mycenaeans, or pre-Hellenic Greeks of the second millennium B.C., the Phoenicians, the Carthaginians, and the Corinthians. The spread of the maritime pattern was largely, perhaps wholly, the result of diffusion and the migration of maritime peoples.

Eventually, all these groups were conquered by societies of other types and either destroyed or absorbed as subunits. This was not the end of overseas trade and commerce, of course, since these remained important activities in advanced agrarian societies. It was, however, a temporary end to

FIGURE 8.4 Maritime societies usually developed on islands or peninsulas: aerial view of Tyre, once an important maritime society. When Tyre was a leading Phoenician city-state, no land bridge connected it to the mainland.

societies in which they were the *dominant* economic activities. Then, more than a thousand years later, there was a revival of maritime societies during the Middle Ages. Venice and Genoa are the best known, but there were others (e.g., Danzig and Luebeck in northern Europe). The last important maritime society was Holland, which in the seventeenth and eighteenth centuries apparently derived the major part of its income from overseas trade. England moved far in this direction in the seventeenth, eighteenth, nineteenth, and early twentieth centuries but probably never quite reached the point where her dependence on overseas commerce exceeded her dependence on, first, agriculture and, later, industry. Nevertheless, because of the great growth of overseas commerce, she took on some of the characteristics of maritime societies.

In many ways maritime societies resembled advanced agrarian societies, particularly their urban centers. But there were also a number of important differences. To begin with, most maritime societies were much smaller, often containing only a single city and its immediate rural hinterland. Only two maritime societies ever developed empires worthy of the name, and, significantly, both of these (the Carthaginian and Dutch) were *overseas* empires.[23] In each case the empire was created more as an adjunct of commercial activity than as a militaristic venture.

This curious feature is linked with other, more basic peculiarities of maritime societies. In a largely agrarian world in which monarchy was the normal—almost universal—form of government, maritime societies were usually republics. Although monarchies were not unheard of, this was most common in the earlier period of a maritime society's history, suggesting a carryover from a premaritime past.

The explanation for the republican tendency in maritime societies seems to be that commerce, rather than warfare and the exploitation of peasant masses, was the chief interest of the governing class. Being less involved in military activities than the typical agrarian state, these nations had less need for a strong, centralized, hierarchical government. An oligarchy of wealthy merchants could do the job, since their primary responsibilities would be to regulate commercial competition and to provide naval forces to defend their access to foreign ports. The fact that navies were the chief military arm of maritime states was also important, for navies, unlike armies, are usually busy in places far from the seat of government. This affords considerable protection to civilian leaders, for it greatly reduces the risk of military coups.

Another peculiarity of maritime societies was their unusual system of values and incentives. As we saw in the last chapter, the governing class in agrarian societies typically viewed work of any kind as degrading. Since this

FIGURE 8.5 Venetian room showing the wealth which commercial activities brought to merchants and officials of maritime societies.

was the class that all others emulated, their view of economic activity rubbed off on the rest. This was especially evident in the case of merchants, who, when they became wealthy, usually gave up their commercial activities. As we noted, this antiwork ethic undoubtedly contributed to the slowdown in the rate of technological innovation and progress. In maritime societies, by contrast, the merchants were the dominant class, and a very different view of economic activity prevailed. Though much more research is needed on the subject, there is reason to believe that the rate of technological advance was greater in maritime societies than in agrarian and that maritime societies made disproportionate technological and economic contributions to the emergence of modern industrial societies. Moreover, the rate of technological advance in *agrarian* societies seems to have been correlated with the sociopolitical strength of their merchant class. In other words, the greater their social status and political influence, the higher the society's rate of technological and economic innovation.[24]

SOCIOCULTURAL EVOLUTION TO THE EVE OF THE INDUSTRIAL REVOLUTION: A PRELIMINARY RECAPITULATION

Having completed our survey of the various types of preindustrial societies, we are ready to consider the three types of societies that are most important today—industrial, industrializing agrarian, and industrializing horticultural. Before we turn to them, however, it may be well to pause and look back over the long evolutionary span and see how some of the more crucial developments in human history relate to our basic theoretical framework.

Beginnings

Our species is the product of a tremendously complex evolutionary process. While we can identify a number of critical steps in this process, the most basic was the growing hominid ability to create and use first tools and later symbols. Hominids eventually became so dependent on these adaptive mechanisms that they could no longer survive without them. Eventually, about 35,000 years ago, our own hominid subspecies (*Homo sapiens sapiens*) emerged, and cultural change soon became far more important in the adaptive process than genetic change.

Throughout most of the prehistoric period, technological progress was painfully slow. There were fewer advances during all the hunting and gathering era than in the last century alone. This was due to the very small number of people, the paucity of information they had to work with, and the poor communication among societies. Later, as population and information increased, the rate of technological advance gradually accelerated. Even so, progress was infinitely slower than it is today.

Diversification and Development

Until about ten thousand years ago, every human group was a hunting and gathering society. They were hardly carbon copies of one another, however. Because of their gradual spread over the earth, societies were forced to adapt to many kinds of environments, ranging from arctic to tropical. There probably were also many differences in marriage patterns, religious practices, and other aspects of life, but the archaeological record is silent on this. Since there is considerable variation in these areas among modern hunters and gatherers, however, there is no reason to suppose it was any different then.

The emergence of the first fishing societies during the Mesolithic was an important new step. Humans had at last devised techniques and tools that enabled them to take advantage of the resources of a radically different kind of environment, one that could support population growth, more permanent settlements, and multicommunity societies. These, in turn, made possible the production of new kinds of goods and services, the accumulation of property, and the elaboration of ritual and ceremony—in short, a significant enrichment of human life.

Not long afterward, an even more revolutionary development occurred when people discovered the basic techniques of plant cultivation and animal domestication. For the first time, relatively permanent settlements could be maintained in a variety of environments. The larger populations and greater permanence of settlement that fishing groups enjoyed were now possible for other societies, and to an even greater degree. But from the evolutionary standpoint, the most important development was the formation of an *economic surplus*, since this opened up so many structural and cultural possibilities.

Forming a surplus was not, however, an automatic by-product of horticulture; many horticultural societies, and even a few agrarian ones, did not take this step (see Figure 8.6). Horticulture, though *necessary* for the formation of a surplus, was not enough: people had to be motivated to produce more than their families required, and ideologies provided the necessary incentive.

Once an economic surplus was established, some people could forget about subsistence activities and devote all their time and energy to other things. Although some specialization occurs without it, an economic surplus has been essential for any significant increase in a society's division of labor.

The surplus also led to increased status and class differentiation. Those who were powerful enough to control the surplus became the governing class in a society and were supported by the mass of common people, whose duty it was to produce all they could.

As the productive capacity of a society increased, there gradually emerged an intermediate class of specialists who catered to the governing class and helped them produce, and dispose of, the surplus. Servants,

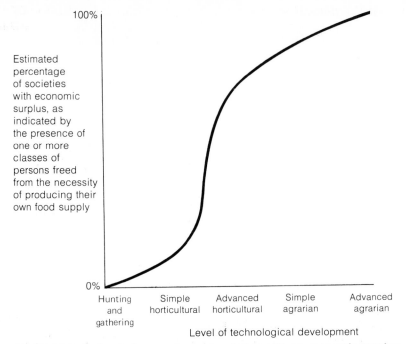

FIGURE 8.6 **Estimated percentage of societies with an economic surplus, as indicated by the presence of one or more classes of persons freed from the necessity of producing their own food.**

retainers, officials, merchants, craftsmen, soldiers, and clergy formed most of the new class. As a rule, they lived near the governing class, often in the same households, and these clusters of people became the nuclei of what evolved into urban communities.

With the creation of stable surpluses, warfare became increasingly profitable. No longer were powerful and aggressive groups limited to hit-and-run raids and plundering expeditions. Now they could establish permanent control over weaker groups and take their surplus, in the form of tribute or taxes, on a regular basis. In short, conquest and empire building became feasible for the first time in history, opening up a road to wealth that soon proved far more attractive to rulers and governing classes than the more pedestrian route of technological innovation.

These developments made the process of intersocietal selection even more important than it had been before. Since military advantage lay with the larger, technologically more advanced, and organizationally more efficient societies, these generally survived at the expense of their opposites. Similarly, militaristic and exploitative societies had an advantage over more peaceful and humane ones.

Meanwhile, despite many developments that should have stimulated technological advance, the rate of innovation actually began to *slow* after the rise of the first agrarian societies. This appears to have been the first major break in the long process of acceleration that began far back in the prehistoric past. The new ideologies and the exploitative social structures generated by the agrarian revolution were primarily responsible.

As societies grew in size and complexity, ties of kinship became increasingly unsatisfactory as the basis for social organization and had to be supplemented and replaced by more formal ties. From the standpoint of societal cohesion, political ties between a ruler and his subjects were the most significant addition. These were supplemented by an expanding network of commercial ties generated by economic institutions, and by ideological and communal ties created by religious institutions. These newer integrative forces, however, could no more prevent the development of intrasocietal antagonisms and conflict than kinship bonds could. If anything, antagonisms were more serious, since they now involved groups and classes of people, rather than individuals, and the issues were much more complex.

This points up a basic irony of sociocultural evolution: in the process of solving one problem, people usually create others. Sociocultural evolution is thus not only a problem-solving process but a problem-producing one. Sometimes, in fact, it almost seems to be a process whereby people trade old problems for new ones.

Why, then, have people tried so hard to achieve progress if its fruits are not sweeter? To begin with, we must remember that much of this progress has not been a matter of choice. Many hunting and gathering groups would probably have preferred to continue their traditional way of life, but their lands were confiscated by societies with a more advanced technology. Other groups have had the same experience. The process of intersocietal selection, then, has not been a voluntary one.

But this is not the whole answer. Many individuals and many societies have voluntarily, even eagerly, adopted more efficient tools and techniques and new ways of doing things, because they believed the gains would outweigh the costs. And they were right—up to a point. Technological advance usually has meant more food, better health, longer life, less exhausting labor, and greater leisure for most people in the generation that initially adopted the advance—and often for their children and grandchildren as well. But those who took this step had no way of knowing that their technological advance would lead to such an increase in population that all the gains would be wiped out in just a few generations, leaving their descendants little or no better off than people were before the innovation. And, even if they had known, they would not have chosen differently.

Until recently, there was only one way to halt this chain of events: a social organization that ruthlessly appropriated everything the common people could spare and gave it to the governing class.* No dramatic increase in population was likely to ensue under this system; death rates and birthrates remained about equal. In this way, some of the benefits of technological advance were preserved, if only for a tiny minority of the population. For the masses, however, conditions seldom improved.

Once this system was firmly established in a society, it was virtually impossible to turn back to a less sophisticated technology. For one thing, with the population larger and denser than it had been in the past, such a reversion would mean starvation for large numbers of the common people. Nor would the governing class have allowed it; from their viewpoint, technological advance was a fine thing. The elites in agrarian societies have almost always been better off than their counterparts in less advanced groups. Most agrarian societies thus found themselves virtually "locked into" the technological status quo. They could not afford to turn back, and they could move forward only very slowly.

This, then, was the situation that prevailed on the eve of the Industrial Revolution.

*Population growth might also have been controlled by abortion, infanticide, monasticism, prostitution, and the like; but these techniques never were adopted widely enough to solve the problem.

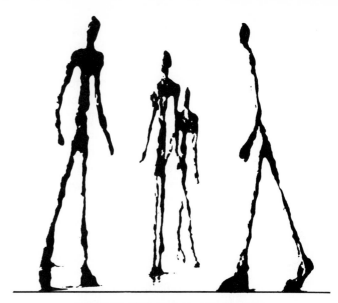

CHAPTER 9
THE INDUSTRIAL
REVOLUTION

Toward the end of the nineteenth century, economic historians began using the term "Industrial Revolution" to refer to the series of dramatic technological and economic innovations that occurred in England during the period from about 1760 to 1830.[1] In their view, the mechanization of the textile industry, technical advance and expansion in the iron industry, the harnessing of steam power, the establishment of the factory system, and other, related developments of that period revolutionized the English economy. What had still been essentially an agrarian society (or agrarian-maritime hybrid) in the middle of the eighteenth century had become an industrial society by the middle of the nineteenth.

The time limits assigned the Industrial Revolution by early writers have subsequently been questioned by scholars who believe it is a mistake to put a terminal date on a revolution that is still continuing.[2] Other scholars argue that the starting date is too late, that the acceleration in industrial activity began not in the middle of the eighteenth century but in the middle of the sixteenth.[3]

Both these criticisms have some merit. The rate of technological advance did, in fact, begin to accelerate at least two hundred years before 1760. But it does not follow that we are justified in treating those earlier developments as part of the Industrial Revolution. To be meaningful, this term must be reserved for developments that led directly to a rapid and substantial increase in the economic importance of industrial activity. Refinements and improvements of older techniques do not qualify unless they significantly increased the proportion of the population dependent on industrial activity or the percentage of the gross national product obtained from this source.[4] Using these criteria, we cannot put the start of the Industrial Revolution much, if any, before the middle of the eighteenth century.[5] The earlier events, however, obviously contributed to the later ones.

The other criticism of the dates is sounder: the Industrial Revolution definitely was not over by 1830. Only its first phase ended at that time. Subsequently, there have been three other phases, and each has contributed substantially to the importance of industrial activity in the societies involved and to their general transformation.

We cannot assign precise dates to these phases, since they are all rather arbitrary divisions in what is essentially a continuous process of development. However, the use of even approximate dates can help us to see more clearly the progression of events. In the initial phase, which began in mid-eighteenth-century England, the revolution was centered in the textile, iron, and coal industries, and the invention of the first true steam engine was probably the most important innovation. The second phase got its start in the middle decades of the nineteenth century and was characterized by rapid growth in the railroad industry, the mass production of steel, the replacement of sailing ships by steamships, and application of the new technology to agriculture. Around the turn of the century, the Industrial Revolution entered a third phase, whose areas of rapid growth were the automobile, electrical, telephone, and petroleum industries. World War II marked the beginning of the fourth phase, distinguished by remarkable development in aviation, aluminum, electronics, plastics, nuclear power, computers, and automation.

Our review will deal with the Industrial Revolution from the perspective of general evolution (i.e., as it has developed in the world as a whole, not as it has developed in individual societies). The phases are not stages that each society must pass through to become industrialized. On the contrary, latecomers tend to skip over certain phases, or at least parts of them, and to combine elements from different phases. For example, an underdeveloped nation today will often develop its railways, highways, and air transportation system simultaneously. But a review of the way things happened *initially* enables us to "get inside" the process of technological advance and see how one innovation makes further innovations possible—or imperative.

A BRIEF HISTORY OF THE INDUSTRIAL REVOLUTION

First Phase

The first phase of the Industrial Revolution, as we just noted, began in the middle of the eighteenth century and lasted about a hundred years. Geographically, it was centered in England, where there was a great burst of technological innovation. Many of the best-known innovations occurred in the textile industry and were of two kinds—machines that increased the efficiency of human labor and machines that harnessed new sources of energy. The flying shuttle is a good example of the first—and a good example, too, of the way one invention stimulated others. Because it enabled one weaver to do the work formerly done by two, spinners could no longer keep up with the demand for yarn. This disruption of the traditional balance between spinning and weaving triggered a succession of additional inventions. First, the traditional spinning wheel was replaced by the spinning jenny, which enabled a worker to spin 4 threads simultaneously and, after a number of modifications, 120 threads! But although the spinning jenny was a tremendous improvement from the standpoint of speed, its yarn was so coarse and loose that flax had to be mixed in with the cotton to produce a satisfactory fiber. This was remedied with the water frame, a machine that could satisfactorily spin pure cotton, and later with the spinning mule, whose cotton threads were stronger and finer. All these advances in spinning reversed the earlier situation: now weaving was the bottleneck in the industry—until a new series of innovations in weaving machines helped restore the balance.

**FIGURE 9.1 James Hargreaves'
spinning jenny.**

By the end of the eighteenth century, the new looms were so large and heavy that they were almost impossible to operate. To work the treadle of one machine even at a slow speed, for example, required two powerful men—and they had to be spelled after a short time.[6] This led to a search for alternative sources of power. One possibility was waterpower, which had already been used for a variety of purposes for many centuries. But England was poorly supplied with suitable streams and rivers, and the wheels and troughs used in water systems were extremely inefficient.[7] Eventually, James Watt developed the first true steam engine,[8] a source of power that could be employed anywhere, and by the end of the century it had been adapted for use in the textile industry.

The net effect of these innovations was such a rapid expansion of the British textile industry that between 1770 and 1845 its contribution to the national income increased more than fivefold.[9] Though unspectacular by more recent standards, this was a striking rate of growth by traditional agrarian standards. Remember, too, that the actual increase in production was even larger, since per unit costs of production dropped considerably during this period.

Another industry that expanded greatly during the first phase of the Industrial Revolution was iron manufacturing. Despite an increasing demand for iron by the textile industry and the military, technical difficulties held its manufacture back until late in the eighteenth century. One problem was England's growing shortage of wood, which was needed to make charcoal for smelting and refining. This problem was partially solved early in the century, when someone found that coke could be substituted for charcoal, at least in the smelting process. But a serious bottleneck remained. Because it is hard and brittle, pig iron must be converted into wrought, or malleable, iron before it can be used for most purposes. Again, the process required charcoal, and it was very slow—until development of the double process of puddling and rolling. These innovations opened the way for rapid expansion: in 1788, England produced only 68,000 tons of iron; by 1845, twenty-four times that.[10]

Between them, the iron industry and the steam engine substantially increased the demand for coal. The steam engine also helped alleviate the ancient problem of flooding in coal mines, providing power to pump out the water that constantly seeped into shafts and tunnels. The growth of the coal industry, though not quite so dramatic as that of the iron industry, was still impressive: in 1760, Britain produced barely 5 million tons; by 1845, the figure had risen over ninefold.[11]

No discussion of developments in this period would be complete without mention of the machine-tool industry. Although it never achieved the size or financial importance of the textile, iron, and coal industries, it was crucial for technological progress, because it produced the increasingly complex in-

FIGURE 9.2 Model of the DeWitt Clinton, built in New York in 1831. On its first run between Albany and Schenectady, it covered twelve miles in less than an hour.

dustrial machinery. This industry, which began undramatically with the invention of the first practical lathe, was soon producing machines capable of precision work to the thousandth of an inch.[12] For many years a single tool was used for drilling, boring, grinding, and milling; but, gradually, specialized tools were designed for the various operations.

Another basic advance in the eighteenth century was the production of machines with interchangeable parts. This greatly facilitated industrial growth, since damage to one part of a complex machine no longer meant that the entire machine had to be discarded or a new part specially manufactured. Spare parts could now be kept on hand and replacements made on the spot by mechanics with limited skills and equipment.

During this initial phase of the Industrial Revolution, shortly after 1800, Britain became the first nation in which industry replaced agriculture as the most important economic activity and thus became the first industrial society.[13] The United States would not reach this point until 1870.[14]

Second Phase

The second phase of the Industrial Revolution began in the middle decades of the nineteenth century. Expansion continued at a rapid pace in the textile, iron, and coal industries, but now there were breakthroughs in a number of others as well. By the end of the century industrialization had occurred in most segments of the British economy. Meanwhile, the Industrial Revolution began to play a significant role in some of the other countries of northwestern Europe and in the United States.

One of the most important developments during this phase was the application of the steam engine to transportation, something inventors had been trying to accomplish for decades. Finally, about 1850, most of England was linked together by a network of railroads.[15] The results were tremendous: the lower cost of moving goods by rail contributed to a reduction in the price of many heavy, bulk commodities, and this, in turn, led to greater demand. In addition, railroads helped break down local monopolies and

oligopolies (i.e., markets with only a few sellers), which added to the competition and further lowered prices. Thus, England gradually became a single giant market for an increasing number of commodities, a development destined to have far-reaching consequences.

Even before the steam engine was adapted to land transportation, it had been used on water. For many years, however, it was limited to coastal and river shipping, both because inefficient engines made it impossible to bunker enough wood or coal for long voyages and because paddle wheels worked poorly in high seas. Then, in only a few decades, efficient compound engines solved the problem of bunkering fuel; iron and steel began to replace wood in ship construction, permitting longer and larger ships with greater carrying capacity (the upper limit in length for wooden vessels was only about 300 feet); and the screw propeller replaced the cumbersome and easily damaged paddle wheel.[16] After this, steamships increased so rapidly that by 1893 world steam tonnage exceeded sailing tonnage.

In the iron industry, meanwhile, a way was finally found to produce steel cheaply and in large quantities, making it available for many new purposes.[17] Between 1845 and the early 1880s, Britain's production of iron and steel increased more than fivefold.[18] This meant that in less than a century, the increase was 100-fold, and the quality of the product was vastly superior.

The tremendous growth in railroads and use of steamships and the expansion of the iron industry all combined to increase the demand for coal. Though there were no spectacular breakthroughs in mining techniques, improved engines and other products of the steel industry pushed production up fivefold.[19]

A number of new industries emerged in addition to the railroads, none as important at the time, but some destined to surpass them later on. The rubber industry developed after Charles Goodyear's discovery of the technique of vulcanization, which prevented rubber goods from becoming sticky in hot weather, stiff and brittle in cold. About the same time, Samuel Morse and several others invented the telegraph, and this quickly became the basis of another new industry. A method for making dyes from coal tar helped establish the chemical industry. Then, in the 1860s, the electric dynamo was invented, and the door was opened for the use of electricity in industry. A second crucial development in this field, the invention of the transformer, helped alleviate one of the greatest impediments to the use of electricity: the loss of energy during long-distance transmission. The petroleum industry also got its start in these years, chiefly by providing a substitute for whale oil in lighting homes.

The Industrial Revolution began to make an impact even on agriculture, through improved equipment (e.g., sturdier steel plows), new kinds of machines (e.g., threshing machines, mowers, reapers, steam plows, etc.), and synthetic fertilizers from the growing chemical industry. The result was a substantial increase in productivity. In Germany, for example, production per acre rose 50 per cent in only twenty-five years.

All during this period, industrialization was spreading rapidly in northwest Europe and in North America. Before the century closed, Britain had lost her position of economic and technological leadership. The iron and steel industry illustrates the trend: although Britain nearly doubled her production of pig iron between 1865 and 1900, her share of the world market dropped from 54 to 23 per cent.[20] Her chief rivals were the United States and Germany, whose production of pig iron increased more than sixteenfold and eightfold respectively. The American share of the market jumped dramatically from 9 to 35 per cent, while the German share rose from 10 to 19 per cent.

As these figures indicate, though industrialization was spreading, it was still largely limited to a few countries. The United States, Britain, Germany, and France, for example, produced 84 per cent of the world's iron in 1900. A similar picture emerges when we look at national shares of all manufacturing activity. In 1888, the percentages are estimated to have been as follows:[21]

United States	32%
Britain	18%
Germany	13%
France	11%
All other countries	26%

The fact that "all other countries" contributed more to *all* types of manufacturing than they did to iron production alone reflects the more rapid spread of the new technology in light industries, such as textiles, than in heavy industries. This resulted both because light industries required less capital and because their pace of development had already slowed considerably, reducing the need for highly skilled and innovative personnel.

The last factor points up a final characteristic of this phase of the Industrial Revolution: the growing dependence on science and engineering. Before 1850 most of the major advances were made by simple craftsmen, or by gentlemen amateurs. After that, key inventions came primarily from people with formal technical or scientific training. This was especially true in the chemical industry, but it was evident in others as well.

Third Phase

Around the turn of the century, the Industrial Revolution entered a phase that lasted until the beginning of World War II. One of its most dramatic and significant developments was the expansion of the automobile industry. Just as remarkable as this industry's rate of growth were the repercussions it had on other industries: in 1937, for example, the American automobile industry

FIGURE 9.3 Early assembly line: dropping the engine into the Ford Model T chassis, Highland Park, Michigan.

consumed 20 per cent of the nation's steel, 54 per cent of its malleable iron, 73 per cent of its plate glass, 80 per cent of its rubber, and 90 per cent of its gasoline.[22] The key inventions, of which the gasoline engine was the most important, were all made some years before the industry actually began production at the end of the century. In 1900 no more than 20,000 automobiles were produced in the entire world, with France the largest producer.[23] By 1913, annual world production had risen to 600,000, with the United States turning out more than 80 per cent; by 1929 annual world production passed the 6 million mark, with the United States' share 85 per cent.[24]

The electrical industry was another that mushroomed during the third phase. Between 1900 and 1940 the capacity of all the generating plants in the world increased 200-fold.[25] Again the United States led the way, producing 40 to 45 per cent of the world's electrical power.

The proportional growth of the petroleum industry was less dramatic, because it had already enjoyed substantial growth before 1900. Even so, production in 1940 was thirteen times larger than it was in 1900.[26]

The telephone industry, too, grew rapidly in this period. Between 1900 and 1940, the number of telephones in the United States increased from 1.4 million to 20.8 million, and by the latter date, the industry had investments valued at $5 billion.[27]

During this phase, as during the second, the Industrial Revolution was felt not only in new sectors of the economy but in new parts of the world as well, which meant some change in the relative ranking of nations. While the United States continued in the lead, Britain, Germany, and France all lost ground relatively (see Table 9.1) despite substantial growth in absolute terms. The chief gains were registered by nations that were just beginning to industrialize. The gains by Russia and Japan were especially noteworthy.

Fourth Phase

No previous war had ever been as dependent on industrial activity as World War II, and every major nation made tremendous efforts to increase its output of military supplies. One of the most important long-term consequences of this was the great stimulus it gave the aviation industry. In the United States, the production of aircraft rose from 3,600 in 1938 to more than 96,000 in 1944.[28] Though the rate fell when the war ended, the air transport industry expanded rapidly. Between 1940 and 1974, the number of passenger-miles flown by scheduled airlines rose from 1.2 billion to 163 billion, and the number of ton-miles flown in hauling freight and mail rose from 14 million to over 4.7 billion.[29] Despite somewhat slower growth, European airlines flew more than 45 billion passenger-miles in 1969.[30] The year 1958 marked a significant shift in transportation patterns: for the first time, planes covered more passenger-miles in the United States than trains, and they also replaced steamships as the chief carriers of transatlantic passengers.

Just as automobiles spurred the petroleum industry, so aviation spurred

TABLE 9.1 Percentage distribution of world industrial output (excluding handicrafts), by nation, in 1888 and 1937

Nation	1888	1937
United States	32	34
United Kingdom	18	10
Germany	13	10.5
France	11	5
Russia	8	10
Japan	No data	4
All others	18	26.5

Source: Calculated from W. S. Woytinsky and E. S. Woytinsky, *World Population and Production: Trends and Outlook* (New York: Twentieth Century Fund, 1953), pp. 1003–1004.

aluminum. Though it was first manufactured in the nineteenth century, its production was quite limited until Germany and Italy started building their air forces in the 1930s. In three and a half decades (from 1938 to 1973), world production increased more than twenty-five times, and it is still increasing as new uses continue to be found.[31] As in most of the rapidly expanding industries of the third and fourth phases, American production was a major share, about half of the world's aluminum output since World War II.

The plastics industry is another that came into its own during this fourth phase. Its origins go back to 1861, when nitrocellulose was plasticized with camphor to produce artificial ivory and used as a substitute for horn in spectacle frames. Thanks to many subsequent developments, plastics have become the most versatile of modern materials: they can now be manufactured to almost any set of specifications. Not surprisingly, the industry has mushroomed: as recently as the late 1930s, world output was under 200,000 tons; by 1969, it was nearly 28 million and growing, with American production half of the total.[32]

Electronics is another industry with a spectacular rate of expansion, and its impact on daily life has been as dramatic as its growth. Its products include radio and television equipment, tape recorders, high-fidelity systems, computers, calculators, testing and measuring equipment, industrial control equipment, and microwave communications systems, to name a few of the more familiar. With the development of servomotors—small power units that respond instantly to signals of various kinds (e.g., a temperature change)—machines that not only act but *react* became possible, and the foundation was laid for automation.

The invention of the computer may well be the most revolutionary technological innovation of all time, since it is, in effect, the equivalent of a radical advance in our species' most valuable tool—its brain. The first electronic digital computer was built at the University of Pennsylvania in 1946, only thirty years ago.[33] A massive piece of equipment occupying 15,000 square feet and weighing thirty tons, it had a memory capacity of only twenty ten-digit numbers. In the last twenty years, the speed of the fastest computers has increased 10,000 times,[34] and new approaches to circuitry may soon raise this to 10 million or more.[35] Such rates of change dwarf all the earlier advances of the Industrial Revolution. So far, we can only speculate about the possible consequences for humans and for their societies.

Nuclear energy is one more industry that has grown tremendously since World War II. Although the Atomic Age began with Hiroshima, the world's first nuclear power facility did not begin operating until 1955, when the Soviet Union opened a small installation with a 5,000-kilowatt capacity.[36] By 1975, there were, in the United States alone, more than fifty reactors with a capacity of 36 million kilowatts, or nearly 9 per cent of the nation's total electrical capacity.[37] Furthermore, government planners expect this to increase to

TABLE 9.2 World industrial output, by nation, 1973, as indicated by consumption of energy

Nation	Percentage Share of World Industrial Output
United States	32
Union of Soviet Socialist Republics	16
Germany (West and East)	6
China	6*
Japan	5
United Kingdom	4
Canada	3
France	3
All others	25

Source: Derived from *Statistical Abstract, 1975*, table 1403.
*The figure for the People's Republic of China is based on a report for 1969. See United Nations, *Statistical Yearbook, 1970*, table 138.

more than 50 per cent by the year 2000. Although the opposition of environmentalists may prevent this, the United States, and other nations as well, appear to be expanding their nuclear facilities as fast as their resources permit.*

Several of the rapid-growth industries of the third phase maintained their high rate of growth during the fourth. Between 1940 and 1973, world output of electricity increased twelvefold, world production of motor vehicles and petroleum tenfold.[39] The United States was still a major producer, but its contribution to total world production in these industries had declined considerably. For example, its share of world automobile production dropped from 85 per cent in 1929 to 27 per cent in 1973.

Table 9.2 reveals some of the important changes that have occurred in the world's industrial output in the twentieth century. As a comparison with Table 9.1 indicates, Britain's share of world production has dropped precipitously, and, to a lesser extent, France's and Germany's. By contrast, the Soviet Union, China, and Japan have made impressive advances.

Although Table 9.2 tells us which nations have the largest industrial output, it does not tell us which are the most highly industrialized. For this we need a *per capita* measure—a type of measure that does not penalize countries with small populations. Several per capita measures are available, but the best is probably the one based on energy consumption.

As a comparison of Tables 9.2 and 9.3 shows, the picture changes dramatically when we take account of a society's size: populous nations like

---

*As this goes to press, reports are appearing of a possible uranium shortage developing toward the end of the century. Efforts to locate new deposits of reasonably high quality ore have been disappointing in recent years.[38]

TABLE 9.3 Per capita energy consumption in kilograms of coal equivalent consumed per person per year, by nation, 1973

Nation	Energy Consumption	Nation	Energy Consumption	Nation	Energy Consumption
United States	11,960	New Zealand	3,225	Syria	469
Canada	11,237	Israel	2,868	Liberia	338
Czechoslovakia	6,694	South Africa	2,815	Thailand	303
Belgium	6,253	Italy	2,737	Egypt	294
Sweden	6,110	Spain	1,993	Vietnam	274
Australia	5,956	Argentina	1,908	Bolivia	214
West Germany	5,792	Greece	1,828	India	188
United Kingdom	5,778	Yugoslavia	1,709	Ghana	155
Denmark	5,547	Chile	1,458	Pakistan	149
Norway	4,979	Mexico	1,355	Kenya (1969)	148
Soviet Union	4,927	South Korea	908	Indonesia (1969)	98
Poland	4,575	Portugal	898	Burma	64
France	4,389	Lebanon	848	Ethiopia	35
Japan	3,601	Peru	641	Afghanistan (1969)	26
Ireland	3,569	Brazil	566	Nepal (1969)	11
Hungary	3,461	China (1969)	505	Upper Volta (1969)	10

Sources: *Statistical Abstract of the U.S., 1975,* table 1403; and United Nations, *Statistical Yearbook, 1970,* table 138.

China and the Soviet Union prove to be less industrialized than many smaller nations. For example, although Canada, Czechoslovakia, Belgium, and Sweden consume far less energy and have far smaller outputs, they consume far more energy *per capita* than China or the Soviet Union, indicating a much higher level of industrialization.

Per capita energy consumption is not a perfect measure of industrialization, however. There are certain distortions that creep in, and these should be noted. For one thing, societies in colder climates inevitably consume more energy per capita than societies with the same level of industrialization in warmer climates. Second, the large gap in the level of energy consumption between the United States and Canada on the one hand and Western Europe on the other is largely due to the vast armada of oversize, gas-guzzling private automobiles in the two North American countries and the large distances between cities and towns, and hence almost certainly exaggerates the difference in level of industrialization.

Despite such problems, per capita energy consumption is probably as good a single measure of industrialization as any available today. Since a minimum of 2,000 to 2,500 kilograms of coal equivalent per person per year appears to be required to sustain a modern industrial society, it is clear that industrial societies are concentrated primarily in Europe and North America. The only industrial societies outside these continents are Australia, Japan,

New Zealand, Israel, and South Africa—and several of these are barely across the threshold. Some other societies—notably Spain, Argentina, Greece, and Yugoslavia—are approaching the threshold, but the great majority of the societies of the world are, at most, industrializing agrarian or industrializing horticultural societies.

CONSEQUENCES OF THE INDUSTRIAL REVOLUTION

From an early date it was clear that the Industrial Revolution meant far more than a change in techniques of production, that it had enormous implications for every aspect of life. Though our chief concern is with the long-run consequences of the revolution, we cannot ignore its immediate effects on the lives of those who first experienced the transition from the agrarian way of life to the industrial.

FIGURE 9.4   Early English industrial town, Staffordshire.

Immediate Consequences

The first indication of serious change came with the invention of the new spinning and weaving machines in the late eighteenth century. Because of their great size and weight, they could no longer be operated in people's homes, as they had been before, but required specially constructed buildings and an inanimate source of power, such as a steam engine or waterfall. In short, the new technology forced the creation of the factory system.

Factories required a concentrated supply of dependable labor. A few of the early factories were built in open countryside, but their owners quickly found they could not hire enough workers unless they built adjoining tenements, which in effect created new urban settlements. Most factories were built in or near existing towns, and the cry that went out from them for workers coincided with the declining need for labor on the farms.

Although the ensuing migration into urban areas was not a new phenomenon, its *magnitude* was, and most communities were unable to cope with the sudden influx. The migrants themselves were badly prepared for their new way of life. Sanitary practices that had been tolerable in sparsely settled rural areas, for example, became a threat to health, even to life, in crowded urban communities.

Equally critical problems resulted from the abrupt disruption of social relationships. Old ties of kinship and friendship were severed and could not easily be replaced, while local customs and institutions that had provided rural villagers at least a measure of protection and support were lost for good. Thus, it was an uprooted, extremely vulnerable people who streamed to the towns and were thrown into situations utterly foreign to them and into a way of life that often culminated in injury, illness, or unemployment. A multitude of social ills—poverty, alcoholism, crime, vice, mental and physical illness, personal demoralization—were endemic.

Town magistrates and other local officials had neither the means nor the will to cope with rampant problems in housing, health, education, and crime. Cities and towns became more crowded, open space disappeared, and people accustomed to fields and woodlands found themselves trapped in a deteriorating situation of filthy, crowded streets and tenements, polluted air, and long workdays, rarely relieved by experiences of either hope or beauty.[40]

The misery of the new urban dwellers was compounded by the harshness of the factory system, which often operated along quasi-penal lines.[41] Regardless of how hard life had been before, country folk had at least had some control over their own hour-to-hour movements; but now, work was, if anything, longer, more arduous, more confining. Women and children, though they had always worked extremely hard in their homes and fields, now worked in factories with dangerous, noisy machinery or in dark and dangerous mines.

CHILDREN AND THE FACTORY SYSTEM

The following testimony was given to a Parliamentary committee investigating working conditions in 1832 by Peter Smart. Similar testimony was provided by numerous others.

Q. Where do you reside?
A. At Dundee.
Q. Have you worked in a mill from your youth?
A. Yes, since I was 5 years of age.
Q. Had you a father and mother in the country at the time?
A. My mother stopped in Perth, about eleven miles from the mill, and my father was in the army.
Q. Were you hired for any length of time when you went?
A. Yes, my mother got 15 shillings for six years, I having my meat and clothes.
Q. What were your hours of labor, as you recollect, in the mill?
A. We began at 4 o'clock in the morning and worked till 10 or 11 at night; as long as we could stand on our feet.
Q. Were you kept on the premises constantly?
A. Constantly.
Q. Locked up?
A. Yes, locked up.
Q. Night and day?
A. Night and day; I never went home while I was at the mill.
Q. Do the children ever attempt to run away?
A. Very often.
Q. Were they pursued and brought back again?
A. Yes, the overseer pursued them and brought them back.
Q. Did you ever attempt to run away?
A. Yes, I ran away twice.
Q. And you were brought back?
A. Yes; and I was sent up to the master's loft, and thrashed with a whip for running away.
Q. Do you know whether the children were, in point of fact, compelled to stop during the whole time for which they were engaged?
A. Yes, they were.
Q. By law?
A. I cannot say by law; but they were compelled by the master; I never saw any law used there but the law of their own hands.

Source: *Parliamentary Papers, 1831–32*, vol. XV.

Minor infractions of complex rules, such as whistling on the job or leaving a lamp lit a few minutes too long after sunrise, led to fines, more serious infractions to floggings. One observer of the period wrote poignantly of hearing children, whose families could not, of course, afford clocks, running through the streets in the dark, long before time for the mills to open, so fearful were they of being late.[42]

The immediate effects of industrialization have been traumatic for vast numbers of people in virtually every society that has made the transition from agrarianism. The details vary, but the suffering was no less acute in the Soviet Union than in England. Whether life for the new urban working class was better or worse than it had been for the peasants and the urban lower classes of the old agrarian societies is still a matter of debate.[43] But one point is not debatable: the transition to an industrial economy has exacted a cruel price

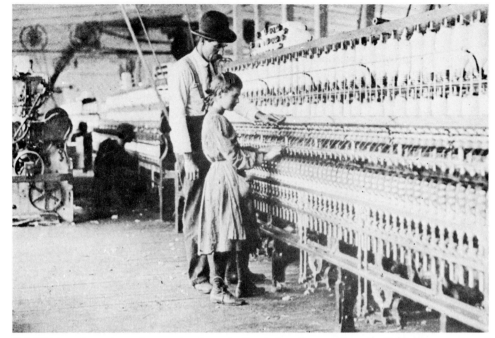

FIGURE 9.5 Superintendent and spinner in North Carolina textile mill, 1909. One quarter of the employees in this mill were as young as this girl, or younger.

in terms of human suffering and demoralization for countless millions of people.

Long-Run Consequences

In subsequent chapters, we will examine in detail the new societies and the distinctive life patterns that have resulted from two centuries of industrialization. For the moment, however, we will note just a few of the most important and most striking consequences outside the realm of technology. Collectively, these changes in population, social structure, ideology, and language add up to a revolution without parallel in human history, from the standpoint of scope as well as speed:*

1. World population has multiplied nearly sixfold (from 725 million to 4 billion) just since 1750, a rate of growth at least seven times higher than the rate during the agrarian era.
2. The rural-urban balance in advanced industrial societies has been completely reversed: agrarian societies were approximately 90 per

*Documentation for these assertions will be found in Chapters 10 to 13.

cent rural; advanced industrial are approximately 90 per cent urban.

3. The largest communities of the industrial era are already ten times the size of the largest of the agrarian era.
4. Women in industrial societies have only about a third as many children as women in preindustrial societies.
5. Life expectancy at birth has almost tripled in advanced industrial societies.
6. The *per capita* production and consumption of goods and services in advanced industrial societies is at least ten times greater than in traditional agrarian societies.
7. The division of labor is vastly more complex.
8. Hereditary monarchical government has almost disappeared in industrial societies.
9. The functions of government have been greatly enlarged.
10. Free public educational systems have been established and illiteracy largely eliminated in all industrial societies.
11. New ideologies have spread widely (notably socialism and capitalism), while older ones inherited from the agrarian era either have been substantially modified or have declined.
12. Worldwide communication and transportation networks have been created that have, for all practical purposes, rendered our entire planet smaller than the England of the agrarian era.
13. A global culture has begun to emerge, as evidenced in styles of dress, music, language, technology, and organizational patterns (e.g., bureaucratic work organizations, small families).
14. The family has ceased to be a significant unit of production in industrial societies.
15. The role of women in the economy and in society at large has changed substantially.
16. The role of youth has also changed, and youth groups and youth cultures have become a significant factor in the life of industrial societies.

All this in only 200 years!

CAUSES OF THE INDUSTRIAL REVOLUTION

For more than a century, scholars have debated the causes of the modern social and cultural revolution, especially why it occurred where and when it did. Much of the controversy has centered on the relative importance of technological and economic determinants on the one hand, and ideological

determinants on the other. This is probably an irresolvable issue because the Industrial Revolution, like every sociocultural revolution, depended on a number of highly interrelated factors.

The Accumulation of Information in the Agrarian Era

Perhaps the least heralded of the major causes of the Industrial Revolution was the gradual accumulation of technological information during the long agrarian era. That era was, it is true, marked by a slowdown in the rate of innovation; but inventions and discoveries did not come to a halt by any means. The sum of human knowledge about the material world and how it could be manipulated for human advantage had been increasing all the while and, as a result, the chances of an Industrial Revolution were greater in the seventeenth century than they had been in the twelfth, and greater in the eighteenth than in the seventeenth.

The development of printing provides a good illustration of the importance of this gradual accumulation of information. Printing has been tremendously important to sociocultural evolution because it facilitates the flow of new information and thereby increases the likelihood that there will be further innovation of one kind or another. As far as can be determined today, printing was invented in the fifth century A.D., or earlier, by the Chinese, who used wooden blocks engraved in relief for the purpose.[44] Since the process of engraving is an extremely slow one requiring considerable skill, the products of the printer's art were limited and expensive.

By the fourteenth and fifteenth centuries, printing had spread from China to the Middle East and Europe, and printers as far apart as Korea and Germany were looking for a way to avoid the separate engraving of the materials for every printed page. The first to devise a workable system was Johann Gutenberg, a German printer skilled in both metallurgy and engraving.[45] By 1440, he was engraving letters on hard steel punches of a kind already employed in the manufacture of coins and using the punches to cut the images of letters into a plate of softer, but durable, alloy made of lead, tin, and antimony. He then cut the plate up into individual pieces of type that could be used repeatedly.

Gutenberg's new system of printing spread rapidly, and an enormous increase in the volume of books and pamphlets was accompanied by a dramatic reduction in their cost. Historians have long credited this technological advance with much of the success of the Protestant Reformation in the sixteenth century, because without printing presses, the new doctrines could not possibly have spread so quickly or so widely.

The use of the new printing press was not limited to religious materials, however. From an early date, it was used to disseminate information of other

FIGURE 9.6 The earliest
illustration of a printing press,
dating from 1499. The typesetter
is reading copy on the left; the
press and pressmen are on the
right. The large figures to the
rear symbolize the constant
presence of death, a recurring
theme in medieval art.

kinds. In the sixteenth and seventeenth centuries, it was used to circulate the
new scientific theories of Copernicus and Galileo. And in eighteenth-century
England a number of books were published to advise farmers on new
techniques of animal breeding, crop rotation, and farm management.[46] This
literature produced a significant revolution in farming, and that, in turn,
contributed to the Industrial Revolution by freeing more people to work at
jobs other than food production. It was rather like a "domino effect," with
advances in one area (printing) leading to advances in a second area
(agriculture), and both, in turn, contributing to advances in manufacturing.

Printing and agriculture were only two of the areas in which there was
significant technological advance prior to the Industrial Revolution. New
information was accumulating on a broad front, even if the rate was slow by
contemporary standards. As a result, the informational foundation of
eighteenth-century England far surpassed anything ever known before.

Discovery of the New World

The discovery of the New World at the end of the fifteenth century also made
important contributions to the Industrial Revolution. The impact of this event
on Europe was enormous. In less than half a century after Columbus' first
landfall, the Spaniards had conquered the two leading empires of the New

FIGURE 9.7 Indian laborers in Peruvian silver mines working for their Spanish masters, with candles as their only illumination.

World (i.e., the Incan and Aztec) and were shipping back to Europe vast quantities of gold and silver.[47]

One important consequence of this was to enlarge the scope of the cash economy and hasten the demise of the old barter system. Though money had been used for more than 2,000 years, the supply of precious metals had been so limited that many payments were still made in kind rather than in cash—especially in rural areas, but by no means only there.

This situation had seriously hindered both economic and technological advance, because an economy that operates on the basis of barter is not flexible and the flow of resources from areas of oversupply to areas of short supply tends to be sluggish. Furthermore, it is difficult to calculate economic advantage in a barter system. The more widely money is used, however, the easier it is for people to calculate their costs and income and determine which of the alternatives open to them is likely to yield the greatest profit. This is extremely important in breaking down barriers to technological innovation. In a society where technological progress has been halting and uncertain for centuries and where there is no efficient accounting system, people with money to invest will generally conclude that traditional forms of investment are best. Also, where money is scarce, people tend to state obligations (wages, rents, debts, and so on) in relatively inflexible and traditional terms, which makes the economy less responsive to changing conditions and new opportunities. But all this began to change in Western Europe during the sixteenth and seventeenth centuries because of the flow of precious metals from the New World.

This gold and silver had a second important effect: it produced inflation. This was a natural consequence of the greatly increased supply of money together with the much more limited increase in the supply of goods. Prices doubled, tripled, even quadrupled within a century. As is always the case under such conditions, some people prospered and others were hurt. In general, those with fixed incomes, notably the landed aristocracy and wage-earners, were hurt. But entrepreneurs of all sorts tended to benefit. This meant a marked improvement in the position of the merchants relative to the governing class. More of the economic resources of European societies began to wind up in the hands of men who were interested in, and knew something about, both economics and technology. More than that, these were men oriented to rational profit making (a far from typical orientation in agrarian societies) and therefore motivated to provide financial support for technological innovations that would increase the efficiency of people or machines. The rise in prices in the sixteenth century was "at once a stimulant to feverish enterprise and an acid dissolving all customary relationships."[48]

The benefits to Europe that resulted from the discovery of the New World were even greater in the eighteenth and nineteenth centuries than they had been before. The New World provided a marvelously rich and fertile territory to which Western European nations could export their surplus populations. Opportunities that do not normally exist in traditional agrarian societies, with their perennial labor surpluses, began to open up for people with talent and energy. Trade quickly developed between Europe and the Americas, with the New World supplying raw materials and the Old World supplying manufactured goods.[49] In the period from 1698 to 1775, Britain's trade with its colonies increased more than fivefold.[50] And this was only the beginning. The center of world trade had begun to shift from the Middle East to the Atlantic.

Immense new territories, vast new resources, rapidly growing markets, unparalleled opportunities for upward mobility and wealth—it is little wonder these conditions overcame the historic deterrents to innovation and change that had characterized agrarian societies for 5,000 years and set in motion *new* forces that hastened the Industrial Revolution and ensured its success.

TABLE 9.4 Median energy consumption for groups of nations classified by dominant traditional religion

Dominant Traditional Religion	Median Energy Consumption[a]	No. of Nations
Protestant[b]	5,141	10
Eastern Orthodox[c]	3,060	4
Roman Catholic[d]	914	31
Islam[e]	208	24
Eastern religions (Buddhism, Hinduism, etc.)[f]	193	13
Preliterate tribal faiths[g]	70	25

Sources: United Nations, *Statistical Yearbook, 1970*, table 138; and Bruce Russett et al., *World Handbook of Political and Social Indicators* (New Haven, Conn.: Yale, 1964), tables 73–75.

[a] Kilograms of coal equivalent consumed per person per year in median nation in each category.

[b] United States, United Kingdom, Australia, New Zealand, Scandinavia (including Iceland), and East Germany.

[c] U.S.S.R., Bulgaria, Romania, and Greece.

[d] Most of Latin America, Southern and Eastern Europe (except Greece, Yugoslavia, and Albania), Ireland, Belgium, France.

[e] Middle East (except Israel and Lebanon), Indonesia, Pakistan, Afghanistan, Iran, North Africa, Sudan, Chad, Niger, Mali, Mauritania, Senegal, Guinea, and Somalia.

[f] Southern and eastern Asia (except Indonesia and Malaysia).

[g] Sub-Saharan Africa (except South Africa, Rhodesia, and Muslim nations indicated in note e).

Note: Nations of mixed background (e.g., West Germany, Canada, Ethiopia, Yugoslavia) and very small nations (e.g., Mauritius, Malta, Kuwait) were omitted.

The Protestant Reformation

Only twenty-five years after Columbus discovered the New World, Martin Luther took the first decisive steps in what came to be known as the Protestant Reformation. For more than half a century, scholars have debated the nature of the relationship between this epoch-making religious revolution and subsequent developments in economics and technology. On one point, however, there is no room for argument: Christian nations in general, and Protestant nations in particular, are unique in the modern world by virtue of their high level of economic development (see Table 9.4). Added to this is the fact that the Industrial Revolution got its start in a predominantly Protestant nation, which remained the leader in industrialization until another predominantly Protestant nation took over.

The modern controversy over the relationship between Protestantism and economic development stems largely from the work of Max Weber. Reacting against what he regarded as the overly economic Marxian interpretation of history, Weber sought to show that the rise of capitalism, one of the most important economic developments of modern times, owed a great deal to the new religious outlook promoted by the reformers, the Calvinists and the Puritans in particular.[51] Although the reformers did not intend to produce an economic revolution, Weber believed that this had been a by-product of their labors and that various aspects of the new Protestant teachings had, in several ways, contributed to it.

In the first place, Weber noted, the reformers taught that work is a form of service to God. Luther, for example, insisted that all honest forms of work are Christian callings just as truly as the ministry or priesthood. This challenged both the medieval Catholic view of work as a penalty for sin and the traditional aristocratic view of work as degrading and beneath the dignity of a gentleman. At the same time, it supported the merchants and craftsmen in their efforts to upgrade their status. Second, the new Protestant faiths undermined traditionalism and trust in magic and encouraged the growth of rationalism. Though the reformers dealt with these things only in the area of religion—and even there only imperfectly—they strengthened a trend that ultimately had broad ramifications. Some branches of Protestantism, for example, encouraged their adherents to plan their lives in rational terms rather than simply live from day to day, as the name Methodist reminds us. Third and finally, many of the newer Protestant faiths emphasized the value of denying the pleasures of this world and living frugally, a practice that led those who were economically successful to accumulate capital. To the extent that they followed these teachings, Weber argued, people developed a new outlook on life: they worked harder, acted more rationally, and lived more thriftily. Thus, personalities were remolded by the Reformation in ways that helped undermine the traditional agrarian economy and stimulate economic and technological innovation. In later years, Weber modified his views to the extent of recognizing that the roots of what he called the "Protestant Ethic" lay in *pre*-Reformation Christianity and ancient Judaism.

Weber's work has been attacked from many quarters,[52] particularly for his neglect of *the prior effects of economics on religion*. Probably none of Weber's critics has been more influential and perceptive than the English economic historian R. H. Tawney, who pointed out that Calvinism and Puritanism were influenced from the very beginning by the fact that their leaders were townsmen and city dwellers, with a heavy representation of merchants and craftsmen. He wrote:

As was to be expected in the exponents of a faith which had its headquarters at Geneva, and later its most influential adherents in great business centers, like Antwerp with its industrial hinterland, London, and Amsterdam, its leaders addressed their teachings, not of course exclusively, but none the less primarily, to the classes engaged in trade and industry, who formed the most modern and progressive elements in the life of the age. In doing so they naturally started from a frank recognition of the necessity of capital, credit and banking, large-scale commerce and finance, and the other practical facts of business life. They thus broke with the tradition which, regarding a preoccupation with economic interests "beyond what is necessary for subsistence" as reprehensible, had stigmatized the middleman as a parasite and the usurer as a thief. They set the profits of trade and finance, which to the medieval writer, as to Luther, only with difficulty escaped censure as *turpe lucrum*, on the same level of respectability as

the earnings of the laborer and the rents of the landlord. "What reason is there," wrote Calvin to a correspondent, "why the income from business should not be larger than that from landowning? Whence do the merchant's profits come, except from his own diligence and industry?"[53]

Calvinism and Puritanism did not condone all forms of business activity. But they did accord business in general a measure of legitimacy and respectability denied it by traditional agrarian ideologies. Wherever Calvinist thought became dominant, profit seeking was viewed not as a necessary evil but as a legitimate and socially useful activity.

Tawney also pointed out that Calvinism gradually changed after its founder's death, neglecting some of his teachings while emphasizing those that were more congenial with the needs and aspirations of the commercial class. For example, the corporate elements in Calvinism were weakened and the individualistic elements strengthened. Thus the group abandoned the practice of excommunication, which had previously been an important means of discipline, and left discipline more and more to the conscience of the individual—enlightened, presumably, by Calvinist teaching. This in turn led to a gradual withdrawal of the church from the realm of economics and the elimination of even those few restraints on economic activity which Calvin had retained. In Tawney's view, the social teachings of the Puritans and other later Calvinists were a complex mixture "derived partly from the obvious interests of the commercial classes, partly from [their] conception of the nature of God."[54]

In the judgment of the majority of social scientists today, the Protestant Reformation was not the principal cause of either the Industrial Revolution or the rise of capitalism, but rather a facilitating force. The new Protestant ideology, like the discovery of the New World, helped weaken traditional agrarian social structure and ideology, which were barriers to innovation and change. In particular, it encouraged a new respect for work and planning, and diminished faith in magic. To a considerable degree, however, that new ideology was a consequence of prior changes in the economic life of Europe and its technology. Thus, the Reformation's influence on the economic life of Europe was largely feedback, rather than an independent and autonomous source of change.

CAUSES OF THE CONTINUING INDUSTRIAL REVOLUTION

As Weber noted more than half a century ago, any explanation of the modern social and cultural revolution must address itself to two problems. After we have dealt with its origin, we still must explain its *continuation*.

Although the origin has easily been the more controversial of the two, we cannot simply take the continuing revolution for granted, as though it were inevitable or its causes self-evident. On the contrary, because we live in the midst of that continuing revolution, we have a special interest in the forces changing our societies and our lives.

The Institutionalization of Innovation

Modern industrial societies have not been content to remove impediments to technological advance; they have consciously tried to stimulate it. The democratization of educational systems and the extension of educational opportunities to citizens of every class has been an extremely important step in this process. Another has been the changing function of educational institutions: whereas their sole function used to be the transmission of the cultural heritage of the past, in the last century institutions of higher education have increasingly become centers of research and innovation.

More recently, business groups and government agencies have discovered the importance of research and have set up research units within their own organizations. Expenditures for scientific research and development in the United States rose from $166 *million* in 1930 to more than $34 *billion* in 1975.[55] For the first time in history, human societies are systematically searching for solutions to their problems.

Modern research becomes more fruitful every year, thanks to increasingly sophisticated methods of observation and measurement, which run the gamut from the electron microscope to public-opinion polling. Far more precise comparisons are now possible between the performances of proposed innovations and the older technologies they are designed to replace, while newer methods of cost accounting provide more accurate comparisons of relative costs and profits.* These comparisons naturally speed the acceptance of useful innovations and thus contribute to the continuing revolution in modern technology.

The Changing Nature of Warfare

Although there are many reasons for the growing emphasis on research, one of the most important (as gauged by financial support) is the changing nature of warfare.[56] Prior to the Industrial Revolution, military technology changed slowly. Among nations on the same level of development, victory was usually

---

*Critics have noted, however, that these modern methods of accounting fail to take account of human values that are not monetized. For example, they make no allowance for the high value most people place on clean air, water that is safe for swimming, or highways that are free from the clutter of billboards.

determined by the sizes of the armies and the organizational and tactical skills of their commanders.

Today, this is largely changed. Military technology becomes obsolete in a few years. The sizes of armies and the skills of their commanders are usually less important than the productive capacity of a nation's economy and the skills of its engineers and scientists. To maintain their relative military status, the leading nations must invest increasing amounts in military research— biological, chemical, and space, as well as the more traditional kinds.

Population Control

Another enormously important factor in the continuing revolution is the control of population growth. By now it should be clear that population growth can easily offset any gains in productivity that result from technological advance. Unless that is prevented, most people are doomed to live at or near the subsistence level—and life at that level is not conducive to technological innovation and progress.

Over the centuries, societies have used a wide variety of mechanisms to help control population growth. These range from norms that permit infanti-

FIGURE 9.8 Prior to the twentieth century, children were usually an economic asset to the poor: a nineteenth-century English family sewing uniforms for the British army under the domestic, or putting-out, system that preceded the factory system.

cide or discourage early marriage to religious beliefs that encourage celibacy. In addition, all agrarian societies have known techniques for preventing either conception or live births.

Until well into the Industrial Revolution, however, these techniques were, at best, inconvenient and less than reliable; in the case of abortion, they were also dangerous. The extent to which population control was practiced in a given society was related to such things as the existing food supply, the demand for labor, and prevailing moral norms. It is clear from the sizes of families, however, that most members of agrarian societies were not sufficiently motivated to use the population control techniques available to them. This was both because children were perceived as economic assets in an agrarian economy and because of high death rates, especially among the young.

In the last hundred and fifty years, as advances in sanitation and medicine drastically reduced mortality and as more people survived into the reproductive years, the need for population control became acute. Simultaneously, technological advances eliminated the need for child labor and increased the need for education, with the result that children became an economic liability (i.e., their economic costs to their parents exceeded their economic benefits).[57] France, in the 1830s, became the first industrializing nation to lower its birthrate and begin the remarkable demographic transition that ultimately included all industrial societies (see pages 290 to 292). As one writer has put it, the early date at which this trend began proves that "if motivation is high enough, fertility reduction can occur in the absence of convenient contraceptive methods . . . [and] in the face of restrictive legislation, religious opposition, and public denunciation of birth control."[58]

Subsequently, the new technology that makes population control imperative for societies also made it easier to achieve. From 1844, when rubber was first vulcanized, on up to the most recent innovations in chemical contraceptives, sterilization procedures, and abortion, population control has become safer, more convenient, more effective, and more acceptable to members of industrial societies. As a consequence, couples no longer require extreme economic pressure to be motivated to limit births. Other concerns, such as the state of the environment, the wife's career, or simply the desire for a higher standard of living, are sufficient.

The substantial reduction of birthrates in modern industrial societies has meant that the growth in productivity has, for the first time in history, far outrun the growth in population. This in turn has made it possible—again, for the first time—for all segments of the population to share in the benefits of technological advance: the historic necessity of keeping millions of people at the subsistence level has been eliminated. Lower birthrates also make it possible to educate more children and youth. All these factors combine to produce a population that is physically and intellectually equipped, and psychologically motivated, to contribute to the ongoing process of change.

Increased Information and Improved Communications Facilities

The continuing technological revolution is also a consequence of the increased store of information and the improved facilities for transmitting it within and between societies. Since inventions are recombinations of existing elements of information, the larger the store of such elements, the greater the potential for further innovation. Thus, advances made back in the early stages of the Industrial Revolution laid the foundation for inventions occurring now, as well as for ones yet to come.

Today, millions of books and technical publications disseminate information quickly and widely, and the growing use of computers promises to accelerate the process even more. Telephones and modern transportation are also crucial, facilitating contacts between people working on related problems.

Neophilia: A New Value

Not surprisingly, the changes of recent centuries have resulted in a radical shift in human values. In the past, people generally looked on innovation and change as undesirable, even dangerous, and departures from tradition were usually considered wrong until proved otherwise. This attitude seems almost to have been reversed in industrial societies, where *neophilia*, the love of novelty, is becoming an important factor in more and more areas. In the arts, for example, innovation is often praised simply for its own sake, without regard to aesthetic criteria. Many people are so ready to applaud the artist who does something—anything—no one has done before, that entries submitted as hoaxes have been known to win prizes. In education, too, a higher value is now placed on innovation. Rote learning is scorned by many educators, and "creativity" is one of the qualities most sought in students, particularly in leading colleges and universities. Even in religion and family life, there is a tendency to value the new above the old, regardless of its merits by other standards.

Whatever else its consequences, this shift in values makes it easier for technological innovators to gain a hearing for their ideas. Ideology, which once slowed the rate of innovation, has now become a stimulant.

Future Prospects

Since the middle of the eighteenth century, the western world has been caught up in a technological revolution that has radically transformed the conditions of human life. Any thoughtful person, after surveying this period of history, is bound to wonder, "What next?"

Before we tackle that question, however, we must take a careful look at contemporary industrial and industrializing societies, since they are the products of the revolution thus far. They will be our chief concern in the next four chapters. After we have examined them, we will be in a much better position to consider that most difficult question of all—the question of the future.

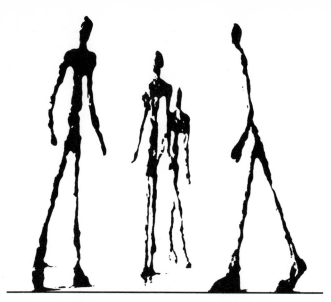

CHAPTER 10 INDUSTRIAL SOCIETIES: PART I

In the century and a half since England became the first industrial society, she has been joined by a score of other nations, including all the English-speaking democracies overseas, most of the other European nations, Japan, Israel, and South Africa. Some of these societies, however, have barely crossed the threshold separating agrarian from industrial societies, and many elements of their old way of life persist. For this reason, our primary concern in the next three chapters will be with those societies that have moved well beyond their industrial beginnings and therefore provide the best picture of what industrialization means for a society.

THE INFORMATIONAL BASE

The same kinds of cultural information that are most important in shaping the patterns of life in other human societies are also dominant in industrial societies. First, there is technological information, which defines "the limits of the possible" for a society and the costs of the various alternatives within those limits. Since the technological bases of advanced industrial societies are all fairly similar, their "limits" and their "cost calculations" are not too different. In this respect they are set apart from all *other* societies. Second, there is ideological information, the basic system of beliefs and values that a society or its leaders use in selecting from among their viable alternatives. And, since their ideologies are quite *dissimilar*, industrial societies are, in a number of important ways, set apart from *one another*.

Technology

The best way to appreciate the dramatic difference between an agrarian society and an industrial one is to look at some of the measurable changes that occur during the shift from the older technology to the new. Take such a basic matter as the source of the energy that is used to do a society's work, for example.* In agrarian societies, people and animals are the chief source of this energy, supplemented to some extent by wind and water. These traditional sources supplied over 87 per cent of the energy used in work in the United States as recently as 1850. Today, they account for less than 1 per cent.†[2] In their stead, industrial societies use the energy of coal, petroleum, natural gas, hydroelectric power, and nuclear power. Except for coal, these sources were still untapped in 1850, and even coal was not used in performing work until the invention of the steam engine.

Not only have energy sources changed, but the quantities used have multiplied enormously. In 1850, all the prime movers in the United States (i.e., human bodies, work animals, steam engines in factories, sailing ships, etc.) had a capacity of less than 10 million horsepower; by the middle nineteen-seventies, this had risen to 25 *billion*—a 250-fold increase in per capita terms in only a little more than a century.[3]

This remarkable jump in the production and consumption of energy was closely linked with increases in the production and consumption of a wide variety of raw materials. Consider iron and steel, for example: British production rose nearly 7,000-fold between 1750 and 1970,[4] while American production increased 12,000-fold between 1820 and 1974.[5]

Equally dramatic growth is evident in the production and consumption of many other raw materials. In one recent year, the United States produced 4.9

Work in this context refers to the kind of labor that has been, or conceivably could be, accomplished by human muscle power—activities like pulling, pushing, digging, lifting, and cutting, in other words, but not providing heat, light, or refrigeration.[1]

†In this discussion, we will draw heavily on data concerning the United States because of the excellent statistical materials that are available for the nineteenth as well as the twentieth century.

FIGURE 10.1 The Krupp steel works at Rheinhausen, Germany, operates twenty-four hours a day, producing two million tons of steel a year.

tons of stone for every man, woman, and child in the population, 4.6 tons of sand and gravel, 3.2 tons of coal, 2.4 tons of crude petroleum, 900 pounds of iron ore, 780 pounds of cement, 575 pounds of clay, 440 pounds of salt, 430 pounds of phosphate rock, 220 pounds of uranium ore, 200 pounds of lime, 115 pounds of gypsum, and 85 pounds of sulfur, to cite but a few items.[6] Altogether, mineral production equals 17 tons per person per year!

Statistics like these document the radically new relationship that advanced industrial societies have established with the biophysical environment. Their ability to mobilize energy and information has increased so rapidly that they are literally able to level mountains, redirect rivers, erase forests, and remove mineral deposits from deep below the surface of the earth and the sea. They can even moderate the effects of climate with modern systems of heating, cooling, and irrigation.

As environmentalists continually remind us, this enormous power to manipulate the biophysical environment has been anything but a simple success story and may yet turn into a major disaster. Certainly we are all painfully aware of rivers converted into sewers, giant lakes unable to support marine life, even oceans beginning to show signs of trouble, and we are conscious that in areas around the globe our life-sustaining atmosphere is becoming life-threatening. Many forms of plant and animal life have been, and are being, irrevocably destroyed, and such critical resources as fossil fuels are being depleted at a rate that threatens the security of future generations. In short, modern technology, in the process of solving many historic problems, has emerged as an alarming source of new ones.

Since this unprecedented use of the earth's resources is at the very heart of the technological revolution, a society's rate of energy consumption is, as we have seen (Table 9.3, page 260), a good indicator of its technological development. Unfortunately, data on energy use prior to World War II are not available for most societies. We do have an alternative, however, because a society's *per capita income* is highly correlated with its energy consumption. Using this measure, we can estimate the magnitude of the change that occurs when a society moves from the agrarian to the advanced industrial level.

Per capita personal income in the United States underwent a dramatic increase—from approximately $500 per person per year in 1871 to approximately $5,500 in 1974 (the 1871 figure and all figures for earlier decades used in this section have been adjusted to take account of inflation in the intervening years).[7] As striking as this elevenfold increase is, it actually understates the magnitude of the difference between a typical advanced agrarian society of the past and American society today, because this country was already well on the road toward industrialization by 1871. In fact, as we noted in the last chapter, the value of its industrial production surpassed its agricultural production as early as the 1880s. To get an accurate idea of the productive level of traditional agrarian societies, we must turn either to European nations during much earlier stages of industrialization, or to the underdeveloped nations of more recent years. In the first category, both Britain and Sweden can provide us with good data. In Britain, per capita income in 1801 seems to have been somewhere near $210 per year, in Sweden in 1861, approximately $230 (in 1974 dollars).[8]

Data from societies still predominantly agrarian in the twentieth century are remarkably similar. In 1938, the earliest year for which reliable estimates are available for most of them, per capita income was estimated to have been as follows:[9]

Greece	$265
Colombia	$248
Egypt	$217
Peru	$212
Turkey	$207
Mexico	$201
Brazil	$173
India	$117
China	$ 58

Like the United States in 1871, Britain in 1801, and Sweden in 1861, these societies had already experienced some degree of industrialization, which

**FIGURE 10.2   Diesel
works, Denmark.**

suggests that if this influence could be stripped away, the figure for the typical agrarian society prior to the Industrial Revolution would not be much in excess of $150 per person per year. Even if we double this to allow for the likelihood that production was underreported in rural areas, the current American figure represents almost a twentyfold increase.

Yet even this figure fails to do justice to the magnitude of the economic transformation. Modern industrial societies not only provide a higher income per capita, they also support much larger populations within a given territory. In England, for example, the population has multiplied more than sevenfold since 1750.[10] To get a more meaningful estimate of the effect of the Industrial Revolution on the productive capacity of societies, then, we have to multiply the increase in per capita income by the increase in population. When we do this, we find that the most advanced modern industrial technology has a productive capacity approximately *100 times greater* than that of traditional agrarian societies of the recent past.* Small wonder that such an increase in the economic surplus triggered a social and cultural revolution!

Ideology

During the last five centuries, the bounds of human knowledge have expanded enormously. The voyages of exploration that began in the fifteenth century gave humans their first accurate picture of the earth as a whole. Astronomers of the sixteenth and seventeenth centuries did the same for the solar system. More recently, science has given us a vision of a universe of infinite complexity, whose age must be measured in billions of years and whose size can be expressed only in billions of light-years. Finally, in the last hundred years, the social sciences have begun the task of demythologizing the social order, challenging ancient theories about the nature of humanity and subjecting virtually every aspect of human life to systematic scrutiny.

Not surprisingly, this flood of new information about ourselves and the world we live in has shaken and unsettled many traditional beliefs, and the institutional systems based on them. This is most evident in the area of theistic religion. The thought forms of all of the great historic faiths—Judaism, Christianity, Islam, Hinduism, and Buddhism—bear the imprint of the agrarian era during which they evolved. But beliefs about the natural

*Some of this fantastic expansion has been due to the utilization of the resources and labor of nonindustrial societies, but this does not alter the basic point: technological advance has bestowed on the most industrialized societies a 100-fold increase in productive capacity. It is *because* of their new technology that these societies are able to utilize resources far beyond the boundaries of their own territories.

TABLE 10.1   Religious beliefs in fourteen industrial societies plus India, in percentages

Society	Belief in "God or Universal Spirit"	Belief in Life after Death	Religious Beliefs "Very Important"
India	98	72	81
United States	94	69	56
Canada	89	54	36
Italy	88	46	36
Australia	80	48	25
Belgium, Netherlands	78	48	26
United Kingdom	76	43	23
France	72	39	22
West Germany	72	33	17
Sweden, Norway, Denmark, Finland	65	35	17
Japan	38	18	12

Source: Gallup Poll report, Sept. 9, 1976.

world and the social order that were "self-evident" to members of agrarian societies often appear alien and inadequate to members of industrial societies. This has created an acute theological crisis for all theistic faiths in industrial societies (see Table 10.1). Their intellectual leaders must somehow translate the valid elements of their traditions into modern terms, while steering a course between irrelevant orthodoxy and heretical innovation. The turmoil within the Roman Catholic Church since Vatican Council II is but the latest in a series of intellectual crises that began with the theories of Copernicus and the research of Galileo.

Beginning in the eighteenth century, a number of new ideologies were established with the intent of replacing older belief systems with ones that were more consistent with the newly emerging view of the world. Deism was probably the most successful of these newer faiths for a time, and it served as something of a stepping-stone between the faiths of the agrarian era and those that emerged in the nineteenth century. Deists retained the concept of God, but they regarded Him as a remote and unapproachable figure who created the universe and set it on its course, subject to impersonal physical and moral laws. Unlike the Christian God, He could not be moved by prayers or sacrifices, for this would be contrary to His basic nature.

The most important of the newer ideologies of the industrial era, however, have been *capitalism, socialism,* and *nationalism.* Each of them has attracted great numbers of adherents during the last two centuries, often at

FIGURE 10.3 Adam Smith, spiritual father of modern capitalism.

the expense of the older faiths of the agrarian era. And each of them has been of tremendous significance in sociocultural evolution during the twentieth century.

Adam Smith, a Scottish professor of moral philosophy who combined a keen analytical mind and a crusading nature, was the father of modern capitalist thought.[11] In his book, *An Inquiry into the Nature and Causes of the Wealth of Nations*, published in 1776, Smith made a powerful case for the thesis that the intervention of government into a society's economic life will only retard its growth and development. The only useful function of government in the economic sphere, according to Smith, is to enforce contracts that individuals enter into of their own free will. Anything more than this is harmful. Smith backed up his argument with an impressive analysis designed to show that the law of supply and demand, operating in a truly free market situation, would ensure that "the private interests and passions of men" are led in the direction "most agreeable to the interest of the whole society."[12] It would be a self-regulating system, but it would function, said Smith, as though an "invisible hand" were at work, ensuring the best possible outcome.

Smith's work laid the foundation for the emerging academic discipline of modern economics. More important than that, however, his basic beliefs about the harm done by governmental intervention in the economy became the basis of a powerful new ideology that for a hundred and fifty years has exercised a profound influence on societies around the globe. Above all, it has provided much-needed moral justification for governmental policies that minimize public control of businessmen and business enterprises. In societies where capitalism is the dominant ideology, the term "free enterprise" has become a sacred symbol that is often invoked with considerable success to manipulate public opinion.

As we will see in Chapter 11, the realities of contemporary capitalism are strikingly different from the ideals proclaimed by the ideology. The same thing is true, of course, of every ideology from Christianity to socialism. It does not follow from this, however, that ideologies are unimportant to societal life. On the contrary, they are badly needed in every society to undergird its system of social control, especially in societies in which injustice and inequality are widespread. More than that, ideologies are useful because they help identify policy alternatives and make it easier for a society's leaders to choose among the options open to them.

The second important new ideology of the industrial era is socialism. While some simpler societies have applied its underlying principle for thousands of years, the modern concept dates from the nineteenth century and was an explicit response to, and reaction against, the realities of capitalism. Socialists argued that the basic economic resources of a society should be the common property of all the members and used for the benefit

FIGURE 10.4 Karl Marx, spiritual father of modern socialism.

of all. Where proponents of capitalism praised free enterprise for the growth in productivity it generated, socialists attacked it for its harsh working conditions, its low wages and great economic inequality, its unemployment, its child labor, its boom and bust cycles, and its alienating and exploitative character. Where capitalists advocated the private ownership of the means of production, socialists favored public ownership. Where capitalists argued for economic inequality to provide incentives for people to work productively, socialists insisted that a more egalitarian distribution would achieve that result.

Karl Marx, while he was by no means the first to espouse the principles of socialism, has come to be recognized as the most significant of socialism's Founding Fathers.[13] In most socialist societies today, in fact, he occupies a status not unlike that accorded Muhammad in Islamic societies or Gautama in Buddhist. Pictures and images of him abound, and his writings are cited by leaders of state to justify their policies.

Marxist socialism is an extremely comprehensive ideology and, for that reason, is functionally similar to the great historic faiths. Like them, it provides answers to the ultimate questions of human existence and guidance for the individual perplexed by the problems of life. Friedrich Engels, Marx's lifelong collaborator, commented on this when he wrote:

> The history of early Christianity has notable points of resemblance with the modern working class movement. Like the latter, Christianity was originally a movement of oppressed people: it first appeared as the religion of slaves and emancipated slaves, of poor people deprived of all rights, of peoples subjugated or dispersed by Rome. Both Christianity and the workers' socialism preach forthcoming salvation from bondage and misery; Christianity places this salvation in a life beyond, after death, in heaven; socialism places it in this world, in a transformation of society. Both are persecuted and baited, their adherents are despised and made the objects of exclusive laws, the former as enemies of the human race, the latter as enemies of the state, enemies of religion, the family, social order. And in spite of all persecution, nay, even spurred on by it, they forge victoriously, irresistibly ahead. Three hundred years after its appearance Christianity was the recognized state religion in the Roman world empire, and in barely sixty years socialism has won itself a position which makes its victory absolutely certain.[14]

This was written in 1894, twenty-three years before the Russian Revolution. More recently, the Soviet poet Evgeny Evtushenko, in his autobiography written for Western readers, referred to Communism as "my religion." And Svetlana Alliluyeva, Stalin's daughter, spoke of her conversion to belief in God as marking the end of her belief in Communism, indicating the functional equivalence of the two competing belief systems in her life.[15] Finally, countless non-Communist scholars have observed the striking functional similarities between Communism and the great historic faiths. Maurice Duverger, the French political scientist, is typical of these. He writes:

> The party not only provides [the militant Communist] with organization for all his material activities, more important still it gives him a general organization of ideas, a systematic explanation of the universe. Marxism is not only a political doctrine, but a complete philosophy, a way of thinking, a spiritual cosmogony. All isolated facts in all spheres find their place in it and the reason for all their existence. It explains equally well the structure and evolution of the state, the changes in living creatures, the appearance of man on the earth, religious feelings, sexual behavior, and the development of the arts and sciences. And the explanation can be brought within the reach of the masses as well as being understood by the learned and by educated people. This philosophy can easily be made into a catechism without too serious a deformation. In this way the human spirit's need for fundamental unity can be satisfied.[16]

Today, Marxism is the official creed of societies in which a third of the world's people live. In addition, some societies have adopted non-Marxist versions of socialism, while others—societies in which capitalism is the prevailing ideology—have active socialist parties. Socialist ideology provides an alternative model to capitalism for organizing a modern industrial or industrializing society. Such a society—its members as a whole, or its governing elite—can make choices of a kind that have never been made before. Within the limits imposed by their technologies, they can follow the path advocated either by the followers of Adam Smith or by the followers of Karl Marx. And even within these two basic alternatives, they find further options available, as is clear when we compare capitalist Britain or Sweden* with the United States, or socialist Yugoslavia with the Soviet Union.

*Though socialist parties have often held office in Britain and Sweden, neither is a socialist society because ownership and control of the means of production remain largely in private hands. A socialist government in a basically capitalist society is thus one of the many possible options open to modern industrial societies. In practice, this alternative usually means a higher level of governmental expenditures for public welfare than would otherwise be the case, as well as greater regulation of business enterprises.

FIGURE 10.5 Adolph Hitler, German nationalist leader.

A third new ideology of importance in the industrial era is nationalism.[17] As with socialism, some of its elements existed long ago: group loyalty and tribalism are certainly not new. During the agrarian era, however, the peasant masses, who made up 80 per cent or more of the population, had little understanding of politics beyond the village level and took no interest in them. The rise and fall of empires meant little to the peasants—unless, of course, they were drawn into the struggle against their will. This was a natural consequence of the theory which viewed the state as the private property of the sovereign.

With industrialization, the situation changed. Expanded educational systems and the mass media, combined with shortened workweeks and an improved standard of living, have brought politics within the sphere of concern of the average citizen. With this has come a heightened sense of identification with one's nation-state, especially in times of international tensions and conflict. Nationalism has been an especially potent ideology in colonial territories ever since the American Revolution.

In recent years, nationalism and socialism have combined to form a potent force in a number of nations. In others, an older faith of the agrarian era has sometimes combined with one or more of the newer faiths. In the United States, for example, Christianity, capitalism, and nationalism are often brought together to form what some have called this nation's "civil religion."[18]

Despite their differences, the new ideologies of the industrial era have one striking feature in common: *they are all predicated on the assumption that the destiny of human societies is, to a substantial degree, under the control of humans.* This is in strong contrast to the situation in preindustrial societies. Their ideologies emphasized societies' dependence on forces beyond human control—fate, destiny, God, the gods—and prescribed magic, ritual, and tradition as the best means of appeasing those forces.

Modern societies, armed with the information and resources acquired in recent centuries, are not so passive. In effect, the technology that has provided human societies with new concepts of how they *can* adapt has generated ideologies with new concepts of how they *should* adapt. Societies now rely increasingly on these newer ideologies, and less on traditional ones, in their continuing efforts to interpret human experience and order societal life.

In recent decades, the most important ideological choice made by societies, or by their governing elites, has been the choice between capitalism and socialism, or some version of them. For this reason, our examination of industrial societies in the next two chapters will frequently focus on elements that clearly reflect the differences between these two ideologies. First, however, we will look at some trends and traits that characterize all industrial societies, regardless of ideology.

Growth in Numbers

On the eve of the Industrial Revolution, during the early years of the eighteenth century, the population of the entire world was about 725 million.[19] Today, less than three centuries later, it is more than 4 billion.[20] To many people, there is nothing startling about a sixfold increase in a 250- to 300-year period. But to demographers, such a rate of change is revolutionary. Throughout most of the agrarian era, world population appears to have grown about 0.1 per cent per year;[21] today, it is averaging 1.9 per cent, nearly twenty times the traditional rate.[22] At the lower rate, the population doubled every 700 years; at the present rate, it doubles every 37 years.

Although the long-term population growth has been greatest in industrial societies, the hybrid societies of Asia, Africa, and Latin America are growing more rapidly now that modern sanitation and medical technology have eliminated many of their historic scourges. Unfortunately, other aspects of the new technology, notably techniques of contraception and of production, have not spread so readily, with the result that many of these nations now face a demographic catastrophe (see Chapter 13).

In Europe, the birthplace of the Industrial Revolution, population has increased "only" about fivefold since 1700. This is partly due to the heavy migration of Europeans to the New World and Oceania. If we take the whole area of European settlement into account, the increase is almost twice as great. And were it not for their lowered birthrates, the combined populations of Europe, the Americas, and Oceania alone would almost certainly be 3 billion, possibly more. The rate of growth of industrial societies is clearly no measure of their *potential* for sustaining numbers. If Europeans were willing to live at the subsistence level, as millions do in Asia, Europe alone might support a population of several billion.

Fertility and Mortality: Shift to a New Equilibrium

To understand the modern demographic revolution, we have to look beyond the figures on total population to those on fertility and mortality. They reveal the striking fact that the great increase in population during recent centuries was achieved without any increase in the birthrate. In fact, it occurred in spite of a substantial *decline* in many parts of the world.

Throughout most of history, human societies maintained a demographic equilibrium, with their birthrates and death rates roughly balancing each other. Over the long run, the birthrate was usually a little higher than the death rate, with the result that there was a slow increase in population.[23] This

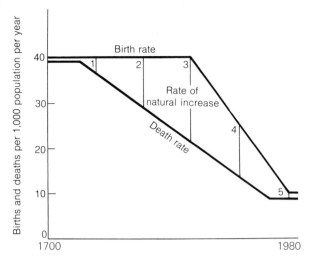

FIGURE 10.6 The demographic cycle experienced by advanced industrial societies: trends in fertility, mortality, and natural increase. The vertical lines measure the rate of natural increase in different years.

modest growth was made possible by technological advance. In the short run, of course, the death rate often exceeded the birthrate because of wars, famines, and plagues. Most societies apparently established an equilibrium at about 40 births and 40 deaths per 1,000 population per year.

Then, during the eighteenth century, the death rates of some societies began to drop as a result of their increased productivity, improved transportation (which eliminated localized famines resulting from crop failures, formerly an important cause of death), and advances in sanitation and medicine. The trend continued until, in recent years, the death rate in a number of the more advanced industrial societies dropped below 10 per 1,000 per year.

The decline in the birthrate was much slower. In most of the new industrial societies, there was no permanent reduction until the end of the nineteenth century. This combination of a traditional birthrate and a steadily declining death rate naturally resulted in a sharply rising rate of natural increase, as shown by the growing length of the first three vertical lines in Figure 10.6.

Now, at last, a number of industrial societies seem to be establishing a new equilibrium between birth and death rates (see Table 10.2). In the case of the two Germanies, zero population growth has already been achieved. In fact, the number of deaths in both countries now slightly exceeds the number of births. Equally important, a number of other industrial societies have already brought their birthrates down to 13 to 14 per year, a level that will shortly produce an equilibrium. Unless medical science produces in the near future some unanticipated advances that substantially increase life expec-

TABLE 10.2 Crude birth and death rates for selected industrial societies, 1973

	Crude Birthrate*	Crude Death Rate*	Rate of Natural Increase
West Germany	10.2	11.8	−1.6
East Germany	10.6	13.7	−3.1
Finland	12.2	9.3	2.9
Austria	13.0	12.3	0.7
Sweden	13.5	10.5	3.0
United Kingdom	13.9	12.1	1.8
Hungary	15.0	11.8	3.2
United States	15.0	9.4	5.6
Canada	15.7	7.4	8.3
Italy	16.0	9.9	6.1
France	16.5	10.7	5.8
Poland (1972)	17.4	8.0	9.4
U.S.S.R.	17.7	8.7	9.0
Czechoslovakia	18.8	11.5	7.3
Australia	18.9	8.4	10.5
Japan	19.4	6.6	12.8
New Zealand	20.5	8.5	12.0
Ireland	22.5	11.0	11.5
Israel (1972)	27.8	7.2	20.6

Source: *Statistical Abstract of the U.S., 1975*, p. 839.
*The terms "crude birthrate" and "crude death rate" refer to the number of live births and the number of deaths per thousand population per year.

tancy, or unless there is a considerable migration of young people into these countries, their death rates will rise to the same level as their birthrates and zero population growth will be achieved.* In most other industrial societies, the probabilities are that population growth will continue, but at a very modest pace. The only industrial societies for which anything like substantial increases seem likely are the few in which underpopulation may be a problem, such as Australia and New Zealand; marginal industrial societies, such as Ireland; and societies with large, nonindustrial ethnic groups within their borders, such as the Soviet Union, Israel, and South Africa.

*In a numerically stable population (i.e., one that is neither growing nor declining), the crude death rate equals 1,000 divided by the average expectancy of life at birth in years. Thus, if the average expectancy is 70 years, the crude death rate will be 14.3. If the average life expectancy rises to 80 years, the crude death rate will drop to 12.5. The very low crude death rates (i.e., 10 or less) that have been achieved in a number of industrial societies in recent years are a temporary phenomenon resulting from the earlier period when birthrates were much higher than death rates. This caused populations to have an abnormally small proportion of older people in the years when death takes its heaviest toll. As the balance between births and deaths is restored (through the decline in the birthrate), the proportion of older people will increase and death rates will rise to the level of 13 or 14 per year—unless the medical "miracle" referred to above occurs.

SOCIAL STRUCTURE: INTRODUCTION AND OVERVIEW

Despite their great technological achievements, or actually because of them, industrial societies have not set any spectacular records for size. From the demographic standpoint, China, an industrializing agrarian society, remains the largest society that ever existed. Its present population, which is believed to be approaching 900 million, puts it far ahead of the largest industrial society, the Soviet Union, with approximately 260 million. India, another hybrid society, also far surpasses the Soviet Union. Its present population is over 600 million.

Industrial societies are not especially impressive from the geographical standpoint either. As we noted in Chapter 7, czarist Russia built an empire covering nearly 8 million square miles. Under Communist leadership, the boundaries have been enlarged to embrace 8.6 million square miles, hardly a remarkable increase.

But comparisons such as these are misleading. Industrial societies have a capacity for expansion, both demographic and geographic, that far exceeds the potential of agrarian societies. Inventions like the radio and the airplane have made it possible to communicate with people on the other side of the world in a matter of seconds, and meet them in a matter of hours. From the technical standpoint, it would be easier to govern the entire world today than it was to govern most small kingdoms in the not far distant past.

So far, however, industrial societies have been extremely zealous in guarding their national sovereignty. Moreover, the new military technology has made war an increasingly costly and risky road to expansion. Nations now stand to gain much more by peaceful economic development than by wars of conquest. In this respect, industrialization has reversed a relationship that existed throughout most of the agrarian era.

If societal expansion does come, then, it may well be because of pressures generated by economic competition. In the modern world, the low cost of moving goods has forced firms in every country to compete with their foreign counterparts. In this situation, firms based in the small countries are usually at a serious disadvantage: having a smaller volume of sales to begin with, they cannot spread their fixed costs over as many units, and as a result they wind up with higher prices. (In the automobile industry, for example, the design costs for a new model are essentially fixed costs: they will be the same whether millions of cars are produced, or only a few hundred thousand. By contrast, the costs of the materials that go into the cars are variable costs: the more cars produced, the greater the expenditures for these items.) Since the price of most commodities is a function of both fixed and variable costs, the producer with the largest volume of sales enjoys an advantage over his competitors, especially in an industry where fixed costs are a significant part of the total (see Table 10.3). In this situation, the largest producer usually increases his share of the market at the expense of the other firms, because he can consistently underprice them or offer a better product at the same price. In the end, he will probably drive them into bankruptcy unless they have some offsetting advantage, such as greater organizational efficiency, lower labor costs, tariff protection, or the like.

In response to this problem, a number of countries have established customs unions, which eliminate tariffs on goods shipped between member nations. This was tried first by Belgium, the Netherlands, and Luxembourg (the Benelux Union); later, by most of the nations of Western Europe (the European Economic Community). Although these new arrangements have helped West European firms compete with American firms in world markets, they have not been achieved without some loss of national sovereignty, and undertakings of this sort may prove to be the first step toward political unification.

The most striking development with respect to the scale of organization in the industrial era has been the formation of global political entities—first the League of Nations, now the United Nations. Though their powers have been minimal, the very fact of their existence is indicative of the changes wrought by the Industrial Revolution. A few centuries ago, organizations like these could not have functioned. Today, despite the limitations imposed on the United Nations, there is a real possibility that it may yet evolve into a more inclusive kind of political system than the world has ever seen.

TABLE 10.3 Illustration of how fixed costs contribute to the growth of monopoly in a free enterprise system

Time Period and Firm	Number of Units Sold	Variable Costs*	Fixed Costs*	Total Costs	Cost per Unit[†]
Time I:					
A	10,000	$10,000	$5,000	$15,000	$1.50
B	9,000	9,000	5,000	14,000	1.56
C	8,000	8,000	5,000	13,000	1.63
Time II:					
A	11,500	11,500	5,000	16,500	1.43
B	8,500	8,500	5,000	13,500	1.59
C	7,000	7,000	5,000	12,000	1.71
Time III:					
A	13,000	13,000	5,000	18,000	1.38
B	8,000	8,000	5,000	13,000	1.63
C	6,000	6,000	5,000	11,000	1.83

*Variable costs need not be exactly proportional to sales volume, and fixed costs need not be exactly identical for all firms, but they have been shown this way to make the essential principles clearer.
†Cost per unit equals total cost divided by number of units sold.

TABLE 10.4 The world's largest cities, from 3000 B.C. to 1968 A.D.

Date	City	Population*	Date	City	Population*
3000 B.C.	Memphis	40,000	620 A.D.	Constantinople	500,000
2000 B.C.	Memphis	100,000	900 A.D.	Baghdad	900,000
1700 B.C.	Babylon	?	1100 A.D.	Kaifeng	440,000
1360 B.C.	Thebes	100,000	1300 A.D.	Hangchow	430,000
650 B.C.	Nineveh	120,000	1500 A.D.	Peking	670,000
430 B.C.	Babylon	250,000	1700 A.D.	Constantinople	700,000
200 B.C.	Patna	350,000	1800 A.D.	Peking	1,100,000
100 A.D.	Rome	650,000	1900 A.D.	London	6,480,000
360 A.D.	Constantinople	350,000	1968 A.D.	Tokyo	20,500,000

Source: Tertius Chandler and Gerald Fox, *3000 Years of Urban Growth* (New York: Academic Press, 1974), pp. 300–341 and 362–363.
*Population includes suburbs.

Industrialization also means growth in the size of organizations at the community level. In agrarian societies, the largest communities never had much over a million inhabitants. Prior to the Industrial Revolution, this figure was attained only a few times, and then only by the capitals of empires that controlled the resources of vast territories. Today, approximately 125 cities have populations of 1 million or more, and only a minority are national capitals.[24] Moreover, 17 cities have more than 5 million; and Greater New York, Tokyo, and Shanghai have already passed the 10 million mark and are still growing. By the end of the century, some students of urbanism expect to see the cities on the east coast of the United States linked up in a giant megalopolis stretching from Boston to Washington. Although this is by no means a certainty, most of the technology needed to maintain such a community is already available. If these expectations are not realized, it will probably be because people *choose* not to live that way—not because they are unable to.

Differentiation of Parts

From the structural standpoint, industrial societies are by far the most complex that have ever existed. No other type of society has contained such a variety of differentiated subunits. This is true both of the roles individuals fill and of the groups of which these roles are a part.

Nowhere is this complexity more evident than with respect to occupational roles: the U.S. Department of Labor has identified more than 35,000 different kinds of jobs in this country.[25] The meat-packing industry nicely illustrates the extremes to which occupational specialization has been carried. Here are a few of the more specialized jobs in that industry, each a full-time, forty-hour-a-week job:

aitchbone breaker	jowl trimmer
belly opener	leg skinner
bladder trimmer	lung splitter
brain picker	rump sawyer
gland man	side splitter
gut puller	skull grinder
gut sorter	snout puller
head splitter	toe puller

("What does your daddy do?" "Oh, he's a snout puller over at the packing house.")

In recent years, automated machinery has replaced human labor in many highly specialized blue-collar jobs, but this has been more than offset by the growing number of equally specialized white-collar jobs. In the medical profession, for example, the general practitioner is rapidly being replaced by a growing variety of specialists.[26] The same thing is happening in the academic world: the general historian is being replaced by the specialist in eighteenth-century German history or nineteenth-century French history. This pattern is repeated in most other professional and managerial occupations.

FIGURE 10.7 Extreme occupational specialization is characteristic of industrial societies: IBM assembly line.

Specialization is also evident in the tremendous variety of associations found in every industrial society. Here is a small sample of nationwide groups in the United States today, with their membership figures:

Aaron Burr Association (600)
Abortion Action Rights League (10,000)
Acoustical Society of America (5,000)
Actors Equity Association (18,500)
Administrative Management Society (15,500)
Adult Education Association of the U.S.A. (6,500)
Aerospace Industries Association of America (49 companies)
Aerospace Medical Association (4,064)
African Violet Society of America (14,000)
Agricultural History Society (800)
Ahepa Order (26,000)
Air Force Association (130,000)
Air Force Sergeants Association (34,000)
Air Lines Pilots Association (30,000)
Air Pollution Control Association (6,700)
Aircraft Owners and Pilots Association (180,000)
Alcoholics Anonymous (650,000)
Altrusa International (17,950)
Aluminum Association (70 companies)
American Anthropological Association (9,150)
American Federation of Labor and Congress of Industrial Organizations
　(14,300,000)
American Legion Auxiliary (900,000)
American Medical Association (210,000)
Amputation Foundation (2,000)

A recent issue of *The World Almanac* listed over a thousand such groups, even though it omitted most religious groups, labor unions, and political parties.[27]

Community specialization is also common in industrial societies, with the production of automobiles, textiles, tobacco, recreation, educational services, or governmental services, to name a few, often concentrated in a single city or group of cities. We find specialization even at the national level. In a world dominated by advanced industrial societies, some countries concentrate on oil, others on rubber, coffee, sugar, or manufactured goods. Were the world not still divided into autonomous nation-states that are concerned with maintaining balanced economies, this tendency would be even more pronounced, for greater national specialization is technically feasible and would certainly be more rewarding for humanity as a whole.

Increased Social Interaction

The amount of social interaction in a modern industrial society would stagger the imagination of the members of societies of the past. To a large extent, this unprecedented level of interpersonal contact is the natural result of increasing urbanization: communities are larger, people live closer together, and increased contact is inevitable. Industrialization also has an effect: home is now the workplace of only a small minority of men; children spend half their days in crowded schools; and women are increasingly drawn outside the home by paid employment, as well as a variety of other responsibilities and opportunities.

Revolutionary advances in communication and transportation have played a major role in breaking down former barriers to social contact. Political leaders often travel over 100,000 miles in a single year (Democratic presidential candidate George McGovern traveled 200,000 miles during the 1972 campaign). Ordinary citizens, too, travel more than ever before: Americans have recently been averaging *at least* 10,000 miles every year.[28] In addition, hundreds of millions of contacts are made daily by telephone and mail. On a typical day in the United States, there are currently more than 600 million telephone conversations and 250 million communications by mail.[29]

The mass media have opened up yet another avenue of interaction, one available even to people whose other contacts are limited by lack of transportation, poor health, or geographical isolation. Although the flow of communication is in only one direction, and the image at best only two-dimensional, the impact is tremendous. This was strikingly illustrated following President Kennedy's assassination: millions of people all over the world watched the television coverage of events, many of them weeping openly and later reporting that they had experienced a depth of involvement and a sense of loss comparable to what they felt after a death in their own family.

One consequence of the growth of social interaction has been the steady erosion of *localism* and *local subcultures*. Local dialects, customs, and loyalties, so pronounced in agrarian societies, are being replaced by national norms and national loyalties. From the standpoint of cultural diversity, this is a great loss, as evidenced by the tiresome similarity of most American cities and towns.

A more serious consequence of the rise of the mass media has been the increased opportunity for tiny elites to manipulate people's thinking. This problem is especially critical with television and movies, for not only are they the most vivid and dramatic of the media, they also appeal disproportionately to that part of the population with the fewest alternative sources of information. What is more, the impact of the audiovisual media is such that it is easy for the uncritical, unsophisticated viewer to come away believing he has been an eyewitness to events, when, in fact, he was exposed to a severely limited, or even badly distorted, representation. During peace demonstrations in the 1960s, for example, camera crews often zeroed in on the most unkempt and unattractive participants, with the result that many viewers were sure they knew precisely the type of person who was questioning America's involvement in Vietnam.

Where television and the press are operated as commercial enterprises, there is a natural tendency for them to focus on the bizarre, the dramatic, and the startling, since this ensures larger audiences and larger audiences ensure higher profits. Thus, exciting but trivial events usually receive far more coverage than more important events conducted in a lower key. In politics, for example, personalities are likely to be featured, issues played down.

When the mass media are operated by governments, deliberate attempts to manipulate public thinking are even more frequent. One-party states are notorious for introducing distortions, though French experience demonstrates that the problem can also arise in multiparty states. Though the desire to change other people's thinking and persuade them to new ideas is neither new nor inherently bad, there is real reason for concern when a few individuals can so directly and so subtly influence the minds of so many.

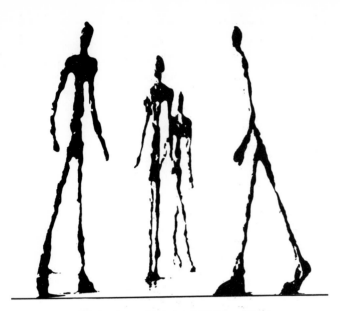

CHAPTER 11 INDUSTRIAL SOCIETIES: PART II

THE POLITY

The Democratic Trend

People who are sensitive to the undemocratic elements in the political systems of all modern industrial societies are usually surprised to learn that one of the more striking changes associated with the rise of industrial societies has been the growth of political democracy. Yet this is clearly the case. The agrarian societies from which most modern democratic nations evolved were, as we have seen, largely monarchical, and popular participation in political decision making was negligible. Maritime societies, although often republican, were oligarchic at best. In brief, popular involvement in political decision making in most industrial societies today, imperfect though it is, represents a substantial change from the situation in the agrarian era.

Not all industrial societies have been democratic, of course. Dictatorial regimes flourished in a number of these societies in the past, and they still exist, though somewhat modified, in Eastern Europe today.* Also, the government of South Africa, though moderately democratic where its white minority is concerned, denies virtually all political rights to the nonwhite majority. In addition, Britain, the Scandinavian countries, the Low Countries, and Japan retain certain monarchical trappings. But even these countries, in most instances, reflect the democratic drift that is linked with the industrialization process. In the case of the constitutional monarchies, the real power lies in the hands of elected officials; kings and emperors are now little more than ceremonial heads of state. As for dictatorships, some of them have been eliminated (e.g., Germany and Italy), while others have been liberalized so that a somewhat larger proportion of the population has at least a little influence in the political process (e.g., Hungary, Poland, and even, to some degree, the Soviet Union).[1] Though the level of democratic participation achieved in these nations falls far short of what exists in most other industrial societies, the *trend* is important. In recent years, significant reversals have occurred in only two industrial societies, South Africa and Czechoslovakia, and even in these cases there are some prospects of an eventual resumption of the earlier trend. Furthermore, in the case of Czechoslovakia, the reversal resulted from foreign intervention, while South Africa is a marginal industrial society with a very unusual ethnic-racial structure. There has been no significant reversal of the democratic trend in any truly advanced industrial society as a result of internal developments, with the single exception of Germany in the 1930s, a country struggling with a most unusual combination of problems.

In discussions of political systems, democracy is often treated in categorical, rather than variable, terms. Too often we simply say that nations are, or are not, democracies, ignoring variations in the degree of citizen participation in the political process. This is a serious mistake, for no large society has ever enjoyed pure democracy. This would mean, in effect, equal participation of every citizen in every decision—a practice that would result in utter chaos and the abandonment of every other useful activity. Even the most democratic nations achieve no more than representative democracy, a system in which most of the adult population are permitted, at infrequent intervals, to cast ballots for a limited number of candidates for public office and, between elections, to voice support or criticism of the actions of elected officials. Without denying the democratic elements in such a system, it is clear that everyone does *not* have an equal voice in political decisions. Professional politicians and party functionaries always have disproportionate influence, and so, as a rule, do the wealthy who finance election campaigns and otherwise subsidize and influence elected officials.[2]

Once we recognize the impossibility of pure democracy in large organi-

*Dictatorships also exist in Chile, Brazil, Cuba, North Korea, and a number of other countries that cannot yet be considered industrial societies.

TABLE 11.1 Percentage of the British population aged twenty-one and over eligible to vote

1831	5.0
After First Reform Act, 1832	7.1
After Second Reform Act, 1867	16.4
After Third Reform Act, 1884	28.5
After 1918	74.0
After Equal Franchise Act, 1928	96.9

Source: Judith Ryder and Harold Silver, *Modern English Society: History and Structure, 1850–1970* (London: Methuen, 1970), p. 74.

zations, it is easier to distinguish the varying degrees of democracy attained by different societies, or by a particular society at different times. The United States, for example, enjoys a much greater degree of democracy today than it did at the beginning of the nineteenth century. The elimination of property restrictions on the franchise and on the right to hold office, the direct election of senators, women's suffrage, the voting provisions in recent civil rights legislation, the "one man, one vote" decisions of the Supreme Court, and the vote for eighteen-year-olds—all these have increased either the percentage of Americans allowed to participate in the electoral process or the effectiveness of their participation. Similar trends can be observed in the recent history of other highly democratic nations, such as Britain and Sweden (see Table 11.1).[3]

Causes of the Democratic Trend

The democratic trend resulted primarily from the Industrial Revolution and the forces that gave rise to it. We have already seen how the discovery of the New World weakened the power of the traditional governing class in Western Europe and strengthened the power of the merchant class. Both in maritime societies and in the urban centers of agrarian societies, this class had long been known for its republican tendencies. Then, during the seventeenth and eighteenth centuries, merchants in Britain, France, and the United States moved to acquire a greater share of political power for themselves. A key element in this struggle for power was a new ideology which maintained that the powers of government are derived from the consent of the governed. This challenged the ancient belief in the divine right of rulers and served to legitimize the struggle of the merchants and their allies and provide a moral justification for their actions. Without this ideological justification, they might well have failed completely.

Among the various factors that contributed to the rise and spread of the new democratic ideology, Protestantism looms large. Whatever else the

Reformation accomplished, it proved that established authority *could* be challenged and overthrown. But beyond that, the Protestant doctrine of the priesthood of all believers—that all believers are equal in God's sight and can relate directly to Him without the mediation of the clergy—had political implications of a revolutionary nature. Though Luther and Calvin did not recognize that fact, others soon did, and the bitter German Peasants' Revolt of 1524–1525 and the Leveler movement a century later in England were both stimulated by it. That doctrine also led to the adoption of democratic or semidemocratic polities by many of the more radical Protestant groups, such as the Anabaptists, Mennonites, Baptists, Quakers, Puritans, and Presbyterians. It is no coincidence that democratization began in ecclesiastical (i.e., church) governments some generations before it began in civil governments and that when it did begin in civil government, its early successes were

FIGURE 11.1 Luther's doctrine of the priesthood of all believers had revolutionary political implications; though Luther did not recognize this, others soon did.

chiefly in countries where ecclesiastical democratization had already made considerable headway. The first major and enduring victory of the democratic movement was in the United States, a country which since colonial days had been a refuge for the more radical and more democratic Protestant groups.

The rise of the new democratic ideology was also aided by the discovery of the New World. From an early date Europeans were fascinated by stories of the American Indians, and many believed their way of life revealed the condition of people living in a "state of nature." A myth, or mystique, quickly developed about "the noble savage," who, free from the fetters of autocratic government, achieved true nobility of character.[4] The monarchical form of government was increasingly depicted by intellectuals as a corrupting and unnatural institution. Building on this view, political theorists like John Locke and Jean Jacques Rousseau propounded the "social contract" theory of government, which maintained that government is the creation of the people and therefore answerable to them. These ideas, together with the democratic outlook stimulated by Protestantism, successfully mobilized popular sentiment against monarchical governments and hastened their decline.

As important as these influences were, it is doubtful that the democratic movement would have succeeded without the Industrial Revolution. To begin with, industrialization eliminated the traditional need for large numbers of unskilled and uneducated workers living at or near the subsistence level, and as new sources of energy were tapped and new machines invented, societies had to produce more skilled and educated workers. Such people, however, are much less likely to be politically apathetic and servile. On the contrary, they tend to be self-assertive, jealous of their rights, and politically demanding.[5] Such characteristics are essential in a democracy, for they counterbalance and hold in check the powerful oligarchical tendencies present in any large and complex organization.

Industrialization also made possible the remarkable development of the mass media. To a great extent, this has been a response to the spread of literacy and to the increased demand for information generated by the rising level of education. Through newspapers, magazines, radio, and television, the average citizen of a modern industrial society is vastly more aware of political events than his counterpart in agrarian societies. Although much of the information he receives is extremely superficial and distorted, it nevertheless generates interest and concern. Thus the media not only satisfy a need, they also stimulate it.[6]

Finally, industrialization, by stimulating the growth of urban communities, further strengthened democratic tendencies. Isolated rural communities have long been noted for their lack of political sophistication and for their patriarchal and paternalistic political patterns. Urban populations, by contrast, have always been better informed and more willing to challenge

FIGURE 11.2 The rise of industrial societies has produced a totally new kind of political organization, the mass political party: British Labour Party assembled in convention.

established authority. Thus, merely by increasing the size of urban populations, industrialization contributed to the democratic trend.

Political Parties

The growth of democracy and the rise of industrial societies have produced a totally new kind of political organization, the mass political party, which serves to mobilize public opinion in support of political programs and candidates. Wherever there are more candidates than offices, there is a process of selection, and the candidates supported by organizations are usually the ones who survive.

At the present time, party organizations differ in several respects. Some, including the Republican and Democratic parties in the United States, are largely pragmatic, brokerage-type parties. This means they have no strong ideological commitments and no well-defined political programs. Their chief goal is to gain control of public offices in order to trade favors with special-interest groups, giving preferential legislative treatment in exchange for electoral and financial support. This cannot be said publicly, of course, and so party rhetoric takes the form of glittering generalities about service to the nation. In this type of party, discipline is weak or nonexistent, since each elected official is a free agent, permitted to work out his own "deals." Some degree of party unity is maintained, however, because once an interest group establishes close ties with the officials of a certain party, it usually prefers to continue working with them. This unity is reinforced by the tendency of the more ideologically inclined to separate into opposing camps, liberals gravitating toward one party, conservatives toward the other. Sometimes the more ideologically inclined win control of the party machinery, as the Goldwaterites did in 1964 and the McGovernites did in 1972, but these periods are usually short-lived.

In contrast to the brokerage-type parties, most of those formed in the latter part of the nineteenth century and the twentieth had strong ideological commitments. Such parties, including both the Fascist parties of the right and the Socialist and Communist parties of the left, usually had well-developed programs for what they regarded as the rehabilitation of society and, in most instances, were willing to be defeated again and again rather than compromise with principles they held sacred.

Since World War II, however, many of these parties have become less ideological and more pragmatic. The Communists of Yugoslavia are a good example of the newer trend. This reversal seems to be rooted in the high rate of technological and social change characteristic of industrial societies. Political programs devised in the last century, or even in the early decades of this one, have become obsolete in many respects, especially in their more specific prescriptions. Modern Socialists and Communists, therefore, increasingly find themselves obliged to innovate, both politically and economically. Most West European Socialist parties, for example, have abandoned, or substantially modified, their former objective of nationalizing all basic industries, while East European Communist parties have introduced the profit mechanism into their economies and even, in some cases, elections between competing candidates into their polities.[7]

In addition to pragmatic, brokerage-type parties and ideological parties, two other types deserve mention. The first is based on subgroup loyalties, sometimes ethnic, more often religious. The Catholic parties of Western Europe are the best example. The other major type is the nationalistic party, of which the German National Socialist, or Nazi, Party is a classic example. Nationalist parties are quite common today in underdeveloped countries, especially in those recently freed from colonial rule; but they are very rare in industrial societies. It is not hard to see why this is so: a nationalist party cannot prosper unless there is some overriding national concern. Germany developed such a concern as a result of the harsh Versailles Treaty following

World War I, and the Nazis capitalized on it. This pattern was not repeated after World War II despite Germany's second loss, perhaps because of the disclosure of the many Nazi atrocities. Widespread feelings of national guilt, together with the postwar economic boom, effectively blunted any sense of grievance.

Though nationalistic parties are rare in industrial societies today, nationalistic elements occur, in varying degrees, within other parties. This is especially true of the more conservative parties, most of which have a long tradition of nationalistic concerns.* This tendency will undoubtedly continue as long as international tensions and conflicts remain.

Political Conflict and Stability

Every social system generates internal conflict, and industrial societies are no exception. Nevertheless, they are remarkable for their success in channeling it into nonviolent forms. Compared with agrarian societies in particular, they are much less prone to revolution and serious political upheavals. This is especially true of those societies which are past the transitional or early phase of industrialization. In fact, a recent study of sixty-two nations found a strong, positive correlation of .965 (see Glossary) between level of political stability and level of socioeconomic development.[8]

There are a number of reasons for this. First, the greater productivity of these societies and the resultant higher standard of living give the majority of the population a vested interest in political stability. Revolution and anarchy are costly for most members of advanced industrial societies. Second, the democratic ideology strengthens the allegiance of most segments of the population to the government and weakens support for revolutionary movements. Especially noteworthy in this connection is the loyalty shown the government by the military and the absence of military coups in the more advanced industrial societies.† Finally, the very complexity of the structure of industrial societies seems to generate a readiness to compromise controversial issues. This is partly because there are so many people in intermediate positions between the contending groups (e.g., people with modest property holdings standing between those with great wealth and those with little or none). These people are likely to benefit more from peaceful compromise and to shy away from extreme or violent solutions. Contrary to Marxian predictions, this has been true of the great majority of blue-collar workers. Moreover, since the complexity of industrial societies means that each

*This is the result of the dominant role of the upper classes in these parties. Members of upper classes find it easy to identify their own private interests with the national interest, since they benefit disproportionately from national prosperity.

†Though military coups have been common in many parts of the world in recent decades, it is impossible to find a pure case in a truly advanced industrial society.

TABLE 11.2 Party preferences of the British population by economic class, in percentages (average of four samples)

Class	Labour	Liberals and Conservatives	Total
Upper and middle classes	27	73	100
Working class	61	39	100

Sources: Adapted from Robert Alford, *Party and Society* (Chicago: Rand McNally, 1963), p. 136; and Richard Rose, "Class and Party Divisions: Britain as a Test Case," *Sociology*, 2, (1968), pp. 129–162.

individual simultaneously fills a number of roles and often belongs to a variety of groups, people who are opponents in one controversy are likely to be allies in the next. For example, middle- and working-class blacks who are divided over labor-management controversies find themselves allies on racial issues. This, too, has a moderating effect.

Although political conflicts are restrained in industrial societies, they are still there in a variety of forms and involve a wide range of issues. The most common type of conflict is between the "haves" and the "have-nots," and, in most democratic, multiparty nations, this conflict is the most important single factor defining the basic framework for partisan politics. Typically, some parties appeal to the working class and other disadvantaged elements in the population, promising improved conditions if they are elected. Opposing parties rely for support on the more privileged elements in the population,

TABLE 11.3 Strength of relationship between occupational class and party preference in eleven industrial societies

Society	Percentage Point Difference*
Finland (average of 3 surveys)	50
Norway (average of 3 surveys)	46
Denmark (1 survey)	44
Italy (males only, 1 survey)	37
Sweden (average of 5 surveys)	35
Australia (average of 7 surveys)	35
Britain (average of 4 surveys)	34
West Germany (average of 2 surveys)	26
France (average of 2 surveys)	22
United States (average of 9 surveys)	17
Canada (average of 10 surveys)	7

Sources: See footnote 9, page 473.
*Specifically, the figures are the difference between the percentage of urban upper- and middle-class people who support Labor, Socialist, and Communist parties and the percentage of urban working-class people who do so. Canada's Liberal Party and the Democratic Party in the United States are also included, since there are no mass socialist parties in those societies.

FIGURE 11.3 Canada has been divided for years by struggles between its large French-speaking minority and its English-speaking majority: French-Canadian separatists demonstrating in Montreal.

though they usually avoid stressing this in their campaign rhetoric. Nevertheless, the relationship is recognized by most people.

Britain provides a good example of the typical relationship between economic class and party preference. As Table 11.2 shows, support for the Labour Party is more than twice as strong in the working class as in the middle and upper classes. The strength of the relationship between party preference and economic class is quite variable in industrial societies, and Britain's position is intermediate. The relationship is most pronounced in the Scandinavian countries, least pronounced in the North American, as Table 11.3 shows. The limited relation between class and party preference in the latter is due in part to the absence of working-class parties with strong ideological commitments. All the major parties in the United States and Canada are pragmatic, brokerage types, which tend to play down class-related issues rather than emphasize them.

Another factor that influences the relation between economic class and party preference is the presence of important ethnic and religious divisions

within the population. It is probably no coincidence that the countries in Table 11.3 with the strongest relation between class and party preference are also generally the most homogeneous from an ethnic and religious standpoint. By contrast, Canada has for years been torn by struggles between an English-speaking Protestant majority and a very large French Catholic minority. In both Canada and the United States, religion and ethnicity are at least as powerful as economic class in determining party preference. In a number of countries, religious groups even sponsor their own political parties. The most powerful of these are the predominantly Catholic parties in Italy, Germany, Austria, Belgium, and the Netherlands. In the Netherlands, three of the four major parties are organized along religious lines (one Catholic, one conservative Calvinist, and one liberal Calvinist), though there are signs that this is changing.

Modern industrial societies differ dramatically from traditional agrarian societies by virtue of their willingness to permit ethnic and religious minorities and the economically disadvantaged to participate in the political process. In agrarian societies, such groups had little or no political power. In industrial societies, by contrast, these groups have sometimes won control of the machinery of government, or at least a share in it, as the Socialists have done in Scandinavia and Britain, the French Catholics in Canada, and the Catholics in the Netherlands.

The Growth of Government

Apart from the rise of democracy, the most important political change associated with industrialization is the great growth of government. The range of the activities and the diversity of the functions performed by government are much greater in modern industrial societies than in any other type of society. In a traditional agrarian society, the government's chief functions were the preservation of law and order, defense, taxation, and the support of religion. In modern industrial societies the last has sometimes been dropped, but dozens of new ones have been added.

The broader scope of government in industrial societies is closely linked with their increasing democratization. As the masses of common people gain a voice in government, they demand services seldom, if ever, provided in agrarian societies. They want educational opportunities, job training, assistance when they are old or sick or unemployed, protection against dishonest businessmen, recreational facilities, and many other things. The provision of such services further strengthens democratic tendencies, since an educated, economically secure population usually participates more intelligently and effectively in the democratic process and is less likely to be attracted to antidemocratic programs than an illiterate and economically insecure population.[10]

Another factor contributing to the growth of government in an industrial society is the greater interdependence of its population. Occupational specialization has progressed to the point where virtually everyone is engaged in specialized work. Everyone, therefore, is dependent on the labors of others and on the maintenance of the complex system of exchange by which goods and services reach the ultimate consumer. In a society like this, a disruption at any point in the economy has adverse consequences for almost everyone.

Similarly, in a society geared to a high degree of interaction among its members, dependable systems of transportation and communication are essential. And in its urban centers, where people live cheek by jowl, well-organized fire, police, and health services are imperative. Private individuals and organizations are unable to assume these responsibilities: only government can commandeer the resources and exercise the authority needed to deal with such fundamental problems.

The Growth and Transformation of Government Bureaucracies

One of the best measures of the growth of a government's activity is the size of its bureaucracy. In the United States, for example, the number of civilian employees of the federal government has gone steadily up for the last century and a half.[11]

1821	7,000
1861	37,000
1901	239,000
1941	1,438,000
1974	2,866,000

This increase far outdistanced the growth of the population as a whole. While the latter increased 20-fold, the number of federal employees shot up 400-fold. Contrary to what a lot of people think, it is not only the federal bureaucracy that has been growing: between 1940 (the earliest year for which national totals are available) and 1974, the number of employees in state and local government increased more than 300 per cent, while the general population grew only about 60 per cent.[12]

The great growth in the powers of governments and the size of their bureaucracies has made top administrative officials (i.e., civil servants) powerful figures in every industrial society. Although this might be interpreted as simply a perpetuation of the old agrarian pattern with its dominance by a hereditary governing class, it is not. Government offices are no longer regarded as private property to be bought and sold and transferred to one's children. Rather, they are usually assigned on the basis of competitions in which technological competence, training, and experience are the chief criteria. Furthermore, in the exercise of office, officials are expected to act on the basis of the public interest rather than private advantage. Although this ideal is obviously not fully achieved, there is still a marked contrast between the practices of officials in most modern industrial societies and the practices of those in traditional agrarian societies. For example, the United States has discovered this in dealing with the officials of many of the governments of Southeast Asia, the Middle East, and Latin America.

In large measure, the explanation for this change lies in the new democratic ideology, which asserts that the powers of government are derived from the people and should therefore be used for their benefit. This is in sharp contrast to the traditional ideology of agrarian societies, which defined the state as the property of the ruler. When modern officials use public office for private advantage, they are subject to severe censure and, in some cases, even to guilt feelings. Such restraints were largely lacking in agrarian societies.

Despite the less venal behavior of public officials in industrial societies, the great power they exercise is a matter of concern. In the first place, where brokerage-type parties are dominant, plenty of leaders are willing to accept bribes and "honest graft," as they call it, if they think they can get away with it. But even when leaders are basically decent and responsible, a problem still exists, for their conception of what constitutes a wise and responsible use of power is not necessarily shared by others. Like everyone else, they have biases. The fact that most high officials are recruited from the more prosperous segments of society creates one kind of bias.[13] The fact that they are exposed, with increasing frequency, to specialized professional training creates another (e.g., a common criticism of American city managers is their preoccupation with technical efficiency, which they often promote at the expense of democratic values).[14]

So far the critics of official power have not come up with any feasible alternative. The sheer size and complexity of government in a modern industrial society makes mass participation in decision making impossible. A substantial delegation of power, therefore, is inevitable, and those to whom the power is delegated will generally do what they deem appropriate. In short, there are decided limitations to the applicability of democratic principles in any large-scale organization.

Warfare

Compared to some of the wars of the agrarian era (e.g., the Thirty Years' War), wars among industrial societies have been of rather short duration. This is an indication not of pacifism, but of the awesome power of industrial technology. World Wars I and II alone caused over 23 million military deaths, maimed and killed many millions of civilians, and destroyed so much property that a reliable estimate is virtually impossible.[15]

FIGURE 11.4   Center of the city of Hiroshima, one year after the bomb.

Since the Second World War, weapons technology has advanced at a startling pace. The atomic bomb that fell on Hiroshima was the equivalent of 13,000 tons of TNT, while a single hydrogen bomb today may be the equivalent of 59 *million* tons.[16] Any future conflagration involving the major military powers would clearly cause far more suffering and devastation than wars of the past. In fact, many experts believe that full-scale war between the United States and the Soviet Union would be brief and would either destroy humanity or, at a minimum, cause industrial societies to regress to a preindustrial state.

The tremendous destructive power of the modern military machine is simply a corollary of the tremendous productive power of the modern industrial economy. The invention of the automobile led inevitably to the tank, the invention of the airplane to fighter planes and bombers. While the relationship is sometimes reversed, with advances in weapons technology leading to important civilian innovations (as was the case with radar, for example), the point is the same: industrial societies, like societies before

them, are unable to segregate or separate the military and nonmilitary components of their technology. As a consequence, technological advance always carries with it the potential for greater destruction.

Unfortunately, industrial societies, again like their predecessors, have not developed adequate alternative methods for settling their disputes. Some kind of world government is the obvious solution, but such a system will not emerge as long as the leaders of most nations continue to believe that war can be avoided, and their own interests protected, within the framework of the present multination system. In effect, in this area as in so many others, industrial societies, although technologically well equipped to solve their problems, are ideologically and organizationally ill equipped to do so.

THE ECONOMY

Urbanization of Production

In agrarian societies, productive activities were centered in the rural villages, agriculture was the dominant industry, and farmers were a substantial majority of the labor force. In addition to farming, the rural population often engaged in a variety of crafts during the off-season, welcoming the chance to supplement their meager incomes. Urban populations were small, and many urban residents, leisured members of the governing class, were not gainfully employed, while those who were, often produced nonessential or luxury goods and services for the upper class.

The Industrial Revolution changed all this. As we saw in the last chapter, the new machines that were invented required factories and large concentrations of people living nearby. While the new industries generated a growing demand for workers in the cities and towns, advances in agriculture reduced the need for farm workers. And so, before the end of the eighteenth century, a massive migration began which only now shows signs of having run its course.

Today, in the more advanced industrial societies, the historic distribution of population has been reversed. Whereas less than 10 per cent of the people in agrarian societies lived in urban areas, 90 per cent or more of the people in advanced industrial societies do so. Yet even that dramatic comparison understates the difference, for the city dwellers of modern industrial societies are much more urban than the city dwellers and townspeople of the agrarian era. Their communities, of course, are much larger on the average (e.g., more than two-fifths of the American population now lives in communities of 1 million or more).[17] But it is more than that: they are much farther removed culturally from the historic rural way of life. For example, during harvests city dwellers of the agrarian era often suspended their activities to go work in the fields.[18] In industrial societies today, that would be inconceivable.

FIGURE 11.5 City dwellers in modern industrial societies are much more urban than city dwellers and townspeople of the agrarian era: view from the top of the RCA Building, New York City.

Rural life, too, has been transformed far beyond anything the simple statistical reversal could indicate. One sign of this is the fact that since 1970 most American farmers earned more from *non*farm activities than from selling crops, livestock, and other products.[19] Only about one farmer in three reports that he derives more than half of his income from farm activities. Similar trends are being reported in other countries.[20]

The traditional family farm is a dead or dying institution in most industrial

FIGURE 11.6   The traditional family farm is a dead or dying institution in most industrial societies: harvesting wheat in North Dakota.

societies. In the Soviet Union and in most East European societies, it was eliminated fairly quickly by government edict and replaced with large agricultural cooperatives and state farms. In most other industrial societies, the process has been more gradual and market forces have been primarily responsible for the demise of this institution. In both cases, however, the underlying cause has been the technological revolution, which has made large, highly mechanized farms more productive than small, traditional ones. Today, in the United States, for example, a single tractor may cost as much as $100,000, while the minimum investment in land and buildings required for a profitable farm is several hundred thousand dollars in many areas.[21] Unable to raise this kind of capital (and the need for new capital is continuous, since not only must equipment be replaced but the acreage required to break even keeps rising), most farm families have been forced to sell out. Their places are increasingly taken by agribusinesses—highly capitalized and mechanized, even automated, corporate enterprises run by salaried managers and employing wage labor.

Changing Patterns of Employment

The decline in the farm population is only part of the massive shift in employment patterns that accompanies industrialization. In traditional preindustrial societies, as we have seen, the vast majority of people are employed in what are known as *primary industries*, those which produce raw materials (such as farming) or extract them (such as mining). Then, in the early stages of industrialization, there is a rather rapid shift of manpower to *secondary industries*, which process the raw materials and turn out finished products, and to *tertiary industries*, which perform services (such as retail trade, education, government). As industrialization progresses, the secondary industries grow less rapidly and eventually begin to decline in relative numbers, while the service industries continue their rapid growth (see Table 11.4).

The Rise of Market Economies

In *The Making of Economic Society*, Robert Heilbroner writes:

> Looking not only over the diversity of contemporary societies, but back over the sweep of all history, [the economist] sees that man has succeeded in solving the production and distribution problems in but three ways. That is, within the enormous diversity of actual social institutions which guide and shape the economic process, the economist divines but three overarching *types* of systems which separately or in combination enable humankind to solve its economic challenge. These three great systemic types can be called economies run by Tradition, economies run by Command, and economies run by the Market.[22]

In a traditional economy, the basic questions of production and distribution—what shall be produced? in what quantities? and for whose benefit?—are answered by simply preserving the patterns of the past. In a command economy, the opinions and values of those who control the government provide the answers. In a market economy, the basic economic decisions are made through a complex interaction of the forces of supply and demand, reflecting the opinions and values of all the individuals and organizations in the society, *but in proportion to their wealth.*

The economies of most societies are actually a complex blend of all three

TABLE 11.4 Changing patterns of employment in the American labor force, 1840 to 1975: percentages employed in primary, secondary, and tertiary industries

Year	Primary Industries	Secondary Industries	Tertiary Industries	Total
1840	69	15	16	100
1870	55	21	24	100
1900	40	28	32	100
1930	23	29	48	100
1960	8	30	62	100
1975	4	26	70	100

Sources: Calculations based on *Historical Statistics of the U.S.: Colonial Times to 1957* (Washington, 1960), ser. D 57-71; *Statistical Abstract of the U.S., 1975*, p. 343; and *World Almanac, 1976*, p. 103.

of these elements, but the majority of modern industrial societies are unique by virtue of the strength and importance of the market element. Prior to the Industrial Revolution there was no society with what could properly be called a *market economy*—that is, an economy in which the basic problems of production and distribution were settled primarily by the free play of market forces.[23]

Several conditions must exist before there can be a true market economy.[24] To begin with, the economy must be monetized: money must become a pervasive element in the daily life of society, and most of the goods and services people value must be available for a price. Further, land, labor, and capital must be mobile; traditional restraints on their use or transfer have to be eliminated. People must be free to sell ancestral lands if that is profitable; workers must be free to leave their jobs and take new ones if they can get higher wages; and owners of businesses must be free to use their capital however they wish. Restraints on economic activity based on family sentiments, religious taboos, social customs, or organizational restrictions (guild restrictions on output, for example, or legal restrictions on the migration of serfs and slaves) must be minimal. In short, individual economic advantage, as measured in monetary terms, must be the decisive determinant of economic action.

As we have seen, the discovery of the New World gave a powerful impetus to the first requirement: the great flow of bullion from the Spanish colonies increased the supply of precious metals in Western Europe several-fold. At the same time, the Protestant Reformation and the ideological changes that followed it, such as eighteenth-century deism and the Enlightenment, weakened traditional social bonds that had immobilized both men and property. These same factors also sparked the Industrial Revolution. Once that was under way and the economy had begun to change, the effect tended to be cumulative. Each change stimulated further change; the more resources that came under the control of Western Europe's entrepreneurial class, for example, the better they were able to promote further change.

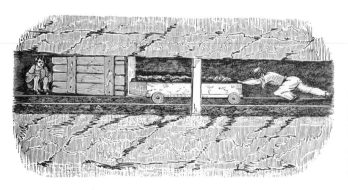

FIGURE 11.7 Children working in a British mine in the nineteenth century: the Mines Act of 1842 prohibited the employment of boys under the age of ten in mines.

By the end of the nineteenth century, it looked as if every industrial society would soon have a largely market economy. Industrial societies were coming increasingly under the control of political parties dominated by businessmen committed to the philosophy of laissez-faire capitalism or free enterprise. Following the teachings of Adam Smith, the pioneer economist, this new governing class argued that the most productive economy, and the most beneficial, was one that was free of governmental restrictions. They were firm believers in the principle that "that government governs best which governs least."

Shift Toward a Mixed Market-Command Economy

It was not long, however, before it became evident that the new market economy was not the unmitigated blessing its enthusiasts made it out to be. In the pursuit of profits, businessmen adopted practices that were obviously harmful to others. In an attempt to cut labor costs, many employers fired adult workers and replaced them with children, simultaneously creating adult unemployment and endangering the health and safety of children. In other instances, efforts to reduce costs resulted in dangerous working conditions and the production of shoddy, even unsafe, merchandise.

Protests soon began to be raised, sometimes by social reformers like Robert Owen, sometimes by poets and novelists like Thomas Hood and Upton Sinclair. Even before the middle of the last century, the British Parliament began enacting legislation to protect society against the extremes of free enterprise. The Factory Acts of 1833 and 1844, the Mines Act of 1842, and the Ten Hour Law of 1847 prohibited the employment of children under the age of nine in textile factories, restricted children under thirteen to six and a half hours' work per day in factories, forbade the employment of women or of boys under ten in the mines, limited women and young people aged thirteen to eighteen to ten working hours per day, and provided for inspectors to enforce these laws.[25] By 1901, the minimum age for child labor in England was raised to twelve, and in 1908 limitations were finally imposed on the working hours of men. Other legislation forced employers to provide for the safety of their employees in dangerous industries and established the first minimum wage. In Germany, under Bismarck, new laws provided for sick leave and for workmen's compensation in the case of injuries sustained on the job. The crowning achievement of German legislation in this period was the Old Age and Security Law of 1889.

Before the end of the century, another major defect in the market system became evident: its tendency to lose its competitive character and evolve in the direction of monopolistic enterprise. This danger was especially apparent in industries where fixed costs were a significant part of total costs (see page 294). A large company, because it could spread its fixed costs over a larger volume of sales than its competitors could, was thus in a position either to undersell them or to match their price but offer a superior product. Either way, the larger company would gradually win its rivals' customers, further increasing its advantage. Were market forces allowed to operate without any restriction, smaller competitors would eventually be driven out of business.

In some instances, monopolies seemed preferable to competition. In the telephone industry, for example, rival firms operating within the same territory would complicate communications and increase costs. In a number of other industries—public utilities—a monopoly or, at most, limited competition seemed preferable to free enterprise and an unregulated market system. Such monopolies could not be permitted, however, to set their own prices and conditions of service: governmental controls were imperative. Thus, beginning in the nineteenth century, local, state, and national governments established regulative agencies. In the United States, the first such agency at the national level was the Interstate Commerce Commission, established in 1887 to regulate the operation of the railroads.

In most industries, however, monopolies were considered undesirable in the United States. Congress passed the Sherman Antitrust Act in 1890 to prevent their formation. Although it has not been very vigorously enforced, this Act has served as a deterrent. A number of industries might now be dominated by a single company had not the managers of the leading firms been fearful of the legal consequences. For example, economists have testified before Congress that economies of scale have long made it possible for General Motors to substantially undersell all its competitors. But rather than face antitrust action, its managers have chosen to price their cars competitively, offering, perhaps, a bit more for the money and taking advantage of the situation primarily through higher profits.

The situation in which a market is dominated by a very few sellers—known as oligopoly—is a common occurrence in many nations. Table 11.5 provides some indication of the current situation in the U.S. As a rough rule of thumb, economists consider an industry oligopolistic when as few as four companies control 50 per cent or more of production.[26] This standard can be deceptive, however, because degree of national concentration means different things in different industries, depending chiefly on whether the market is local, regional, or national. The newspaper industry, for example, might appear highly competitive, because according to government statistics the four largest companies produce only 16 per cent of the papers. But a moment's reflection reminds us that most newspapers produce for a local market, and in a typical community, over 90 per cent of them, in fact, the paper or papers are owned by a single person or firm.[27] Thus Table 11.5 *understates* the extent of oligopoly in this country.

Where oligopoly prevails, the law of supply and demand often stops functioning, primarily because collusion between firms is so easy. Collusion

TABLE 11.5 Percentage of production accounted for by the four largest companies in selected industries in the United States

Industry	Percentage	Industry	Percentage
Motor vehicles	92	Radio and TV receivers	49
Steam engines	88	Steel mills	48
Cereal preparation	88	Metal office furniture	38
Typewriters	81	Petroleum refining	33
Cigarettes	81	Textile machinery	31
Home refrigerators	73	Meat packing	26
Tires	70	Pharmaceuticals	24
Soap and detergents	70	Frozen fruits and vegetables	24
Aircraft	69	Fluid milk	22
Thread mills	62	Paints	22
Synthetic rubber	61	Newspapers	16
Phonograph records	58	Soft drinks	13
Distilled liquor	54	Women's dresses	7
Roasted coffee	53	Fur goods	5

Source: U.S. Bureau of the Census, *Census of Manufacturing, 1967* (Washington: 1971), vol. 1, chap. 9, table 5.

can take a variety of forms. A fairly common practice in the construction industry is the rigging of bids, whereby firms get together and decide among themselves which one will take which job and then bid accordingly, with the "low" bid set as high as they dare. Price leading, a perfectly legal practice, appears to be standard procedure in several major industries: one firm, usually the largest, sets its prices at a level that ensures profits for all and maximum profits for the larger firms. In this situation, competition is largely restricted to such secondary matters as design and advertising.

Another development that has weakened the role of market forces has been the increase in what is known as vertical integration, the process by which a company gets control of companies in other industries that either supply it with materials or buy its products.[28] A furniture manufacturer, for example, buys up a number of lumber companies and sawmills to provide his raw materials and then buys into retail establishments that handle the furniture he turns out. In this way, he eliminates a lot of the uncertainties of the market situation. Another device with a similar purpose is to establish interlocking directorates, which bring the top officials or directors of a company on which one depends for some essential commodity onto the controlling board of one's own company. This device is widely used to bring officers of financial institutions on the boards of firms that require ready access to large amounts of capital.[29]

Finally, the market system has been weakened by the changing nature of warfare. World War II demonstrated beyond any doubt that success in all-out modern war requires the mobilization of all of a nation's economic resources.[30] Obviously this effort cannot begin with the outbreak of hostilities: it must be planned and implemented far in advance. In societies that wish to maintain a strong military position, this inevitably leads to the development of a military-industrial complex from which most of the elements of free enterprise are eliminated. For one thing, there is only one buyer for the product, the government. Often there is only one producer as well, and seldom more than a handful, for a particular weapons system. The situation is prejudicial to an open market in yet another way: the military is disinclined to shop around for bargains ("more bang for the buck"), because this increases security risks and truly competitive bidding might cause companies to cut corners and turn out defective products. Also, so long as the military has the taxing power of the government behind it, it has little motivation to economize. Finally, when major weapons systems are involved, there are usually few companies in a society that have both the equipment and the engineering skills required. Thus, there is a natural tendency for market forces to be replaced by the principles of command in the vast and important area of military procurement, even in a society whose leaders constantly affirm their commitment to the principles of free enterprise.

We could summarize most of the foregoing by saying that the last two hundred years have revealed three basic flaws in the market mechanism. First, not only does it fail to protect the weaker and more vulnerable members of society, such as the industrial worker and the consumer, it compels the strong to act ruthlessly if they wish to remain strong. Second, the market system has what might be called a built-in self-destruct element, which causes most free competitive markets to evolve into monopolistic markets unless checked by governmental intervention. (Marx saw this more than a century ago when he argued that capitalism contains the seeds of its own destruction.) Finally, the market system cannot respond adequately to many or most of the *corporate* needs of society (as contrasted with the needs and desires of individuals).

This final weakness is particularly evident during societal crises, such as wars, depressions, or environmental crises. As long as individuals and organizations are free to act according to what they perceive as their own best interests, the more short-sighted tend to win out. Corporations that respond to the environmental problem by installing expensive antipollution devices, for example, find themselves at a disadvantage in competition with firms that do not.

For a variety of reasons, then, even those societies whose members are ideologically most committed to free enterprise have been edging away from the market system. Public rhetoric to the contrary, the economies of these societies can now be described only as a highly complex mixture of market and command economies. And trends like the one shown in Table 11.6 make it almost inevitable that the command component of these economies will

TABLE 11.6   Oligopolistic trends in the United States and Sweden

	Percentage Share of All Business Activity*	
United States	1947	1967
50 largest companies	17	25
200 largest companies	30	42
Sweden	1942	1964
50 largest companies	16	21
200 largest companies	25	32

Sources: U.S. Bureau of the Census, *Census of Manufacturing, 1967* (1971), vol. 1, chap. 9, table 1; Swedish Finance Department, State Public Investigations (SOU), *Ägande och inflytande inom det privata näringslivet: Koncentrationsultredningen, V* [Ownership and influence in the private sector of the economy] (Stockholm, 1968), p. 7.
*The measure of business activity used for the United States is total value added; the measure used for Sweden is industrial employment.

continue to gain at the expense of the market component. There seems little danger, however, that the market component will disappear altogether: the experience of the socialist societies of Eastern Europe suggests that would not be a rewarding alternative.

The Economies of Socialist Societies

In the industrialized socialist societies of Eastern Europe, with the exception of Yugoslavia, market forces have been relegated to a very secondary position in the economy.[31] With the private ownership of the means of production largely (though not entirely) eliminated, the basic questions of production and distribution are decided through central planning. The famous Five-Year Plans of the Soviet Union are the classic example of this.

Prior to the Russian Revolution, many critics of socialism argued that it would be impossible to operate an economy successfully without private ownership and the operation of market forces. Today, however, this argument is no longer heard, since the Soviets and other socialist societies have proved that there is nothing incompatible about a socialized economy and economic growth. In fact, compared to other societies that, like themselves, were not among the early industrializers, their record has been very good. The Soviet Union has now surpassed every nation except the United States in total productivity, and the rates of economic growth in East Germany, Poland, Hungary, Czechoslovakia, and Yugoslavia are also high.

In addition, socialist economies have overcome one of the great scourges of capitalist economies, namely, *unemployment*. In part, this is achieved by the creation of "busywork" jobs (e.g., the women who ride the escalators of the Moscow subway system, hour after hour, wiping the handrails with a rag), and often at the expense of economic efficiency. Nevertheless, it is a significant accomplishment. Closely related to this, socialist societies have generally been successful in eradicating abject poverty, especially in urban areas (rural populations have been slower to benefit from economic innovations). Finally, socialist societies have been quite successful in reducing the degree of economic inequality—partly by a reduction in wage inequalities, partly by the virtual elimination of the private ownership of the means of production.

We need to beware, however, of exaggerating the differences between socialist and capitalist economies. Supermarkets in Warsaw, for example, function in a manner strikingly similar to those in Washington D.C.; visitors from capitalist societies are likely to have to remind themselves that the former are not private, but state, enterprises. Even in factories, where we might expect greater differences, the similarities are striking. Jan Szczepański, Poland's leading sociologist, made this point recently when he wrote:

> . . . the workers are still hired labor. The socialist revolution does not change the relation of the worker to the machine, nor does it change his position within the technological system of the factory . . . his relation to the machine and the organizational system of work requires his subordination to the foreman and the management of the factory. He receives wages according to the quantity and quality of work performed, and he must obey the principles and regulations of work discipline.[32]

In the last twenty years, Communist Party leaders have become increasingly aware of the limitations inherent in a completely planned economy. Effective planning must take account not only of all the thousands of commodities produced but also of *all the interrelations among them*, since the production of one commodity is always contingent on the availability of others. One Soviet economist is reported to have argued that a sound plan for the Soviet machine industry alone would require provision for more than 15 billion interrelations.[33] Because it is impossible to coordinate successfully such a fantastic number of relationships, shortages have repeatedly developed in some commodities, surpluses in others.

The great virtue of the market system is its automatic mechanism for balancing supply and demand. When the demand for a product goes up, so does the price, giving producers an incentive to turn out more of it. Conversely, a slump in the demand lowers prices and reduces incentives. All of this is accomplished without costly centralized planning. But despite this attractive feature, the market system had always been so closely identified with capitalism that it was unthinkable for Soviet leaders.

During recent decades, however, East European economists have been able to demonstrate that the market mechanism is not necessarily linked to private enterprise and that its introduction into socialist economies would

FIGURE 11.8 State-operated supermarket, Warsaw.

not stimulate a revival of capitalism. With this point clarified, and with the more pragmatic orientation of the new generation of Communist leaders, the way was cleared for experimentation. First in Yugoslavia, then in the Soviet Union, and eventually in all of Eastern Europe, elements of the market system have been reintroduced into areas of the economy from which they had been excluded for years.

The introduction of market mechanisms into socialist economies suggests that in the future there may be somewhat less variation in this important aspect of industrial societies than there has been in the past.[34] Both socialist and nonsocialist societies are moving toward a more balanced type of economy, in which both market and command will play important roles. Market forces will be used to achieve greater efficiency, while command will be used to protect the corporate interests of society and to limit the degree of social inequality. This is not to say, of course, that differences between economic systems will be eliminated (East European Communist leaders seem determined to prevent the reestablishment of privately owned enterprises, for one thing), but they will probably be reduced.[35]

New Types of Economic Organizations

The economies of agrarian and maritime societies were usually organized around three types of units—family enterprises, guilds, and state enterprises. Of these, only state enterprises play a major role in modern industrial societies. Guilds have vanished entirely and family enterprises have declined to the point where they play at best a secondary role and in some nations not even that. In their stead, a number of new kinds of organizations have emerged, among them corporations, cooperatives, labor unions, and professional and industrial associations. These, together with state enterprises, constitute the major economic units in industrial societies.

Corporations   The modern business corporation easily ranks as one of the most important inventions of modern times, and, like many major innovations, it evolved gradually. Its origins go back to the middle of the sixteenth century, when English and Dutch merchants, trading with remote areas, banded together in what came to be known as joint stock companies.[36] This form of organization had several advantages over family enterprises and partnerships. Above all, it permitted people to pool their capital, to spread their risks. This was extremely important in ventures where risks were great and large investments essential. In addition, a joint stock company, unlike a family enterprise or a partnership, was not disrupted by the death of one of the owners. Either the heirs inherited the stock, or, if they wanted to get the money out of the enterprise, they could sell the stock to someone else. This was not possible in a partnership, since the law required (as it still does) that if one of the partners died or wished to withdraw, the partnership had to be dissolved and the assets distributed.

During the next several centuries, the joint stock company, or corporation, gradually spread to new fields of enterprise. More important, a series of changes made this form of organization safer and more attractive to investors. For one thing, the development of preferred stock (i.e., shares that had first claim on profits and assets in the case of bankruptcy) provided a safer form of investment, and the organization of stock markets facilitated the exchange of stock. Most important of all, however, was the adoption of the principle of *limited liability*. Prior to the nineteenth century, stockholders in most corporations, like owners of family businesses and members of partnerships, had unlimited liability in case of bankruptcy. This meant that they stood to lose not only their investment in the company but all their other possessions as well if these were needed to satisfy the claims of creditors. This naturally made investors extremely cautious; unless they had firsthand knowledge of a business and those running it, they were taking a great risk. The passage of laws limiting the liability of stockholders to the investment itself greatly stimulated the flow of capital into this new form of enterprise.

In today's industrial societies, nearly all the largest and most powerful private enterprises are organized as corporations. In the United States in 1972, for example, 85 per cent of all business was done by corporations, and among larger concerns (i.e., those with annual receipts of $1 million or more), they accounted for 95 per cent of the total.[37] The very largest concerns, those with annual profits in the hundreds of millions or billions of dollars, are all corporations. A single firm, American Telephone and Telegraph, has assets totaling $74 billion, and in 1974 Exxon had receipts in excess of $45 billion.[38]

As corporations have grown, their character has changed substantially. Most important, control of the largest ones has passed from the owners to the top managers.[39] As one observer put it more than a decade ago, "Almost everyone now agrees . . . that, typically, control is in the hands of management; and that management normally selects its own replacements."[40] The chief cause of this shift is the fragmentation of stock ownership, an almost inevitable by-product of enormous corporate growth. In AT&T, for example, not a single one of its 3 million stockholders owns as much as 1 per cent of the stock, and most own only a minute fraction of 1 per cent. Furthermore, the stockholders are scattered around the world. Mobilizing a majority of the voting stock to wrest control from the managers would be extremely difficult.

The growing power of managers in industry is part of a larger trend in modern societies. In government, education, religion, labor, and other areas as well, organizations have become so large, and administrative problems so complex, that those who constitutionally hold ultimate power (e.g., the voters, stockholders, trustees, or members) cannot possibly exercise more than the most limited control over the administrators and managers.[41] Under the circumstances, most of the responsibility for day-to-day decisions gravitates into the hands of the latter.

Labor unions One of the most striking differences between agrarian and industrial societies is the development of organizations designed to advance the interests of the common people. The two most obvious examples are working-class political parties and labor unions.

The origins of modern labor unions can be traced back to the latter part of the eighteenth century, when small groups of workingmen, in both England and the United States, banded together to negotiate with their employers on wages, hours, and working conditions. During the nineteenth century the movement had many ups and downs, but over the long run the gains outweighed the losses. Laws forbidding union organization and strikes were gradually repealed and more stable organizations established, until, by 1900, there were 2 million union members in Britain and nearly a million each in the United States and Germany. Today, labor unions claim approximately 20 million members in the United States; and union-backed political parties hold office, or have held or shared office, in Britain, Scandinavia, the Low Countries, France, Italy, Austria, the United States, and Australia.

As corporations have grown in size, so have unions: the United Auto Workers, for example, currently has about 1.4 million members. Size is essential in bargaining with corporate giants like General Motors, whose profits in one recent year were more than $2 billion.

With their growth in size and power, and with their increasing respectability, labor unions have lost a lot of their former idealistic and reformist fervor. Under the leadership of often elderly administrators and bureaucrats, they tend to play a rather cautious and conservative role, both economically and politically. Many of them now see their chief task as simply maximizing the wages of their own members, thus assuring them a larger share of the benefits of an affluent society.

The function of labor unions in one-party societies has been quite different from what it is in democratic nations.[42] In both communist and fascist nations, unions have been used by the dominant party as an instrument of social control. In theory, the unions are instruments of the workers, in practice, largely instruments of the Party and the governing elites. Recently there have been some indications that unions may play a more independent role in the future, but so far this is more promise than reality.

Professional associations Another new form of economic organization is the professional association. With increasing frequency, professional people (e.g., doctors, lawyers, teachers, chemists, accountants, architects, etc.) have organized into associations ostensibly designed to ensure high standards of performance in their fields but, in practice, functioning largely to advance their economic and other interests. The most publicized, and most controversial, of these organizations in the United States has been the American Medical Association. As a result of its aggressive efforts, the medical profession has become the most lucrative single occupation in the country. In one-party nations, these associations, like unions, are primarily instruments of the Party, though the fact that professionals need long training, and are thus hard to replace, has sometimes made their organizations more difficult for the Party to control and manipulate.

Cooperatives A fourth organizational innovation is the cooperative. Its development is related to that of socialism and trade unionism. It, too, grew out of the efforts of workingmen to improve their situation.

In its earliest stages, leaders of the cooperative movement tried to establish cooperative communities, like the one Robert Owen founded in New Harmony, Indiana, in the 1820s. Very soon, however, the energies of the movement were channeled into consumers' and producers' cooperatives. Consumers' cooperatives were retail stores owned by groups of consumers,

FIGURE 11.9   Cooperative housing development, Sweden.

with the profits either shared by the members or turned back into the movement to help establish other cooperative ventures. Producers' cooperatives were associations of craftsmen or farmers who banded together, formed their own businesses in competition with privately owned enterprises, and shared the profits among themselves.

In many industrial societies, including the United States, the cooperative movement has had only limited success, with cooperatives accounting for no more than a small percentage of the total volume of business in any industry except agriculture. This is not the situation everywhere, however. In Scandinavia in particular, cooperatives are an important element in the economy: at least a third of the wage-earners in these countries belong to a cooperative, with the ratio highest in Denmark.[43] Farmers' cooperatives have been an important element in the Danish economy since the latter half of the nineteenth century, with nine-tenths of the farm population organized into one large cooperative by 1939. In recent years, Sweden's cooperatives have controlled much of her agricultural production and urban housing, a third of her retail trade, and a tenth of her wholesale trade and nonfarm production. In general, cooperatives have been most successful in agriculture, housing, and retail and wholesale trade—industries whose capital requirements are not so great as in, say, manufacturing, and in which small enterprises are not at such a serious competitive disadvantage.

FIGURE 11.10 Collective farm workers in the Ukraine.

Cooperatives have also found a place in the economies of East European nations. In the Soviet Union they have functioned primarily as a transitional arrangement during the shift from private to state enterprise, especially in agriculture, where collective farms, a form of cooperative, have played a major role for a long time.[44] Even as recently as 1965, cooperatives still produced 42 per cent of the nation's farm products.[45]

Over the years, state enterprises have grown so at the expense of cooperatives that one might well predict the eventual elimination of cooperatives in East Europe. But this may be premature. Housing cooperatives seem to be growing in popularity in urban areas throughout most of Eastern Europe. Moreover, the Yugoslav system of workers' self-management is essentially an application of the principles of the cooperative movement, if not its name.[46] Though opposition by Soviet leaders has prevented the spread of the self-management system, there is considerable evidence to suggest strong interest in it in other socialist societies, and sooner or later this may have an effect.

Continuing Forms of Organization

Along with these newer kinds of economic organization, certain older ones have managed to survive and, sometimes, to flourish. These include *the family-owned enterprise*, which survives in most industrial societies, even in some of the East European nations. In Poland and Yugoslavia, for example, there are still privately owned farms and small businesses, though they are hedged about with many restrictions, particularly on their size. In nonsocialist societies, family businesses operate in a wide variety of fields, though they are being crowded out by newer forms of organization, especially the corporation. Farming was the last major industry to remain predominantly under family control, but even there, as we have seen, corporations and cooperatives are taking over.[47]

An older form of organization that has fared far better is *the state-operated enterprise*, which for thousands of years flourished in agrarian societies and even in some advanced horticultural societies. In modern industrial societies, the role of state enterprises varies considerably. In some, notably the East European nations, they are dominant. For example, state enterprises in the U.S.S.R. account for 98 or 99 per cent of nonagricultural production, and nearly half of agricultural.[48] Their role is much smaller in the United States; yet even here they operate the postal system, many electric and water companies, some hospitals and other health facilities, many insurance programs, most educational institutions, some housing facilities, quite a few recreational facilities, many transportation facilities (e.g., highways, ports, passenger trains, etc.), and many banking services.

West European nations stand somewhere between the United States and the East European nations with respect to the scope of state enterprises. Railroads there, for example, are 90 to 100 per cent government-owned.[49] Of the scheduled airlines in Western Europe, only Swissair is less than half government-owned, and radio and television broadcasting are entirely government enterprises in every country but the United Kingdom and Luxembourg. The state also plays a major role in Europe's electric, gas, insurance, banking, mining, iron, and steel industries, and, in some countries, in the automobile, chemical, and machine-tool industries as well. In short, state-owned enterprises are thriving and apparently increasing in modern industrial societies, capitalist and socialist alike, and primarily as a consequence of those inherent limitations of the market system that we noted earlier.

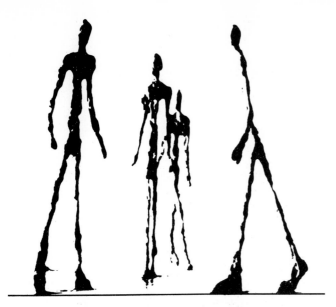

CHAPTER 12
INDUSTRIAL
SOCIETIES:
PART III

SOCIAL STRATIFICATION

Prior to the Industrial Revolution, every major technological advance led to an increase in social inequality. This was true of the horticultural revolution, and it was true of the agrarian. During the early stages of the Industrial Revolution, it seemed that the historic pattern would be repeated once again and that industrial societies would emerge as the least egalitarian in history.

More recently, however, as a number of societies have reached a more advanced stage of industrialization, this trend toward greater inequality, which began ten thousand years ago, has begun to falter, even to show signs of a reversal. This has not meant a return to the highly egalitarian patterns of hunting and gathering societies. Far from it. But it has meant a somewhat more equitable distribution of power, privilege, and prestige within advanced industrial societies than was characteristic of either early industrial or advanced agrarian societies.

As we saw in Chapter 2, the basic function of any society's system of stratification is to distribute the things of value that people produce in their life together in society. These include not only material goods but also power and prestige. An individual's access to these things depends to a great degree upon his own, or his family's, status with respect to such key resources as occupation, education, wealth, ethnicity, political status, age, and sex. We cannot hope to understand the distributive process in advanced industrial societies without taking into account all these separate, but interrelated, class systems.

It is important to note at the outset that the distributive process in an industrial society is affected, to a significant degree, by the ideological commitments of its politically dominant group. In East European societies, the dominant class consists of people who occupy key positions in the Communist Party and are committed to a socialist ideology. In most other industrial societies, the dominant class is made up of people who manage giant private corporations or own great fortunes and who are committed to a capitalist ideology. Socialist societies have put more emphasis on economic equality than nonsocialist societies, while the latter have been more concerned with political equality. But as important as the differences are, they should not be allowed to obscure basic underlying similarities: in every industrial society, for example, people with advanced education are highly rewarded, as are those in key managerial and political offices. Similarly, power tends to be concentrated in older male hands, and minority ethnic groups tend to be disadvantaged.

Occupational Stratification

For the vast majority of people the most obvious determinant of their access to society's rewards is their position in the occupational system of stratification. In the United States today, there are a number of persons who hold positions that pay a million dollars or more a year in salary, bonuses, and fringe benefits. Meanwhile, others are unable to find employment of any kind. Between these extremes, the great majority have jobs that provide anything from bare subsistence to substantial affluence.

In the socialist societies of Eastern Europe, occupational inequality is generally not as great as in nonsocialist societies, but it is still substantial. At the lower extreme, workers on poor collective farms and many pensioners barely eke out an existence, while at the upper extreme, high Party and government officials, scientists, writers, and entertainers enjoy great affluence, including multiple homes, servants, vacations in exclusive resorts, and so forth.[1] A Soviet writer recently reported that in the last years of Stalin's reign, the incomes of some high-ranking officials, though not the very highest, were a hundred times the average worker's, several hundred times the most poorly paid worker's.[2] Since then, however, there has been a

FIGURE 12.1 One of the basic divisions in the occupational structure of industrial societies is the one that separates manual from nonmanual workers.

deliberate effort to reduce this differential, with current differentials in wages being no more than 50 to 1.[3]

The basic structure of the occupational system of stratification is remarkably similar in socialist and nonsocialist societies. In both, managerial and professional occupations are the most highly rewarded, skilled technicians and skilled manual workers come next, then the lower echelons of nonmanual workers (such as clerks) and semiskilled manual workers. And—again in both societies—unskilled manual laborers, small farmers, and farm laborers have the lowest incomes and the least power and prestige. The chief difference between the two systems is the position of self-employed businessmen. In nonsocialist societies their status depends on the amount of capital they control, but generally they rank high (usually on a par with managers and professionals). In socialist societies their position is very ambiguous: they often enjoy large incomes, but they also run the risk of imprisonment and are viewed by much of the public as engaged in morally questionable activities.[4] Their extreme status inconsistency resembles that of racketeers and others involved in illegal or immoral activities in nonsocialist societies.

One of the most basic divisions in the occupational hierarchy is that separating manual from nonmanual workers. This is, of course, the basis for the popular distinction between the working and middle classes: people in families headed by manual workers usually think of themselves, and are thought of by others, as members of the working class, while people who belong to families headed by nonmanual, or white-collar, workers are thought of as middle class. Nonmanual jobs tend to be more rewarding not only in terms of income, but working conditions, job security, chances for upward mobility, and prestige as well.

Neither of these classes is a homogeneous entity: each has significant internal divisions. In nonsocialist countries there is an upper-middle class composed of proprietors, managers, officials, and professionals, and a lower-middle class consisting of people like clerks, salespeople, and secretaries. The division in socialist societies is similar, except for businessmen, as we noted, but what we will call the upper-middle class is usually referred to there as the intelligentsia (a reflection of historic educational prerequisites for entry into the class).[5]

In both types of societies, the working class has at least three fairly distinct skill levels. Its elite are highly skilled workers who have usually served long apprenticeships to master their trades. Included are such people as tool-and-die makers, electricians, and plumbers. Beneath them is a stratum of semi-skilled workers of the kind found on assembly lines, and on the bottom are those with minimal skills, such as laborers, domestic servants, and many other service workers.

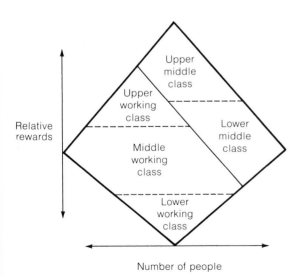

FIGURE 12.2 **Many skilled manual workers are more highly rewarded than many clerks and other members of the lower-middle class in industrial societies. This is especially common in socialist societies.**

But the occupational system of stratification is more complex than this breakdown reveals. For example, as Figure 12.2 illustrates, many skilled members of the upper segment of the working class are more highly rewarded than many clerks and other members of the lower-middle class. For socialist societies, the line dividing the middle and working classes would be tilted a bit more toward the vertical to reflect the more favored position of the upper working class; for nonsocialist societies it might be tipped a bit more toward the horizontal. Fifty or seventy-five years ago, that line would have been even closer to the horizontal for *all* industrial societies. Since then, however, the middle and upper segments of the working class, through the efforts of labor unions and working-class parties, have substantially improved their position, while the largely unorganized lower-middle class has lost ground relatively.

An even more significant change in the occupational system of stratification has been the great proportional increase of higher-status occupations. As Table 12.1 shows, in the United States, white-collar workers, who comprised only 17 per cent of the labor force at the turn of the century, are now 51 per cent. Even if one considers the occupations of men only (on the assumption that their jobs are usually the chief determinant of family economic status), the trend is still impressive: from 17 to 42 per cent. These gains have been accompanied by a reduction in the least rewarding occupational categories, unskilled manual work and farming. Industrialization and technological advance have thus effected a drastic restructuring of the occupational hierarchy, eliminating many low-status occupations, which are physically so demanding, and replacing them with higher-status positions with greater rewards.

It is no longer valid, as it was in agrarian societies, to depict the

TABLE 12.1 Frequency distribution of adult population among occupational classes, United States, 1900 and 1975 (in percentages)

Occupational Class	Both Sexes		Males Only	
	1900	1975	1900	1975
Upper white-collar	10	26	10	29
Lower white-collar	7	25	7	13
Upper blue-collar	11	13	13	20
Middle blue-collar	13	15	10	18
Lower blue-collar*	21	18	18	16
Farmer and farm laborer	38	3	42	5
	100	100	100	101

Sources: Figures based on data in U.S. Bureau of the Census, *Historical Statistics of the United States: Colonial Times to 1957*, ser. D 72-122 (1960); and U.S. Bureau of the Census, *Statistical Abstract of the United States, 1975*, table 586.
*Includes service workers.

TABLE 12.2 Distribution of wealth and investment assets in the United States

Net worth Category*	Percentage of Population	Percentage of Wealth Owned	Percentage of Investment Assets Owned
Under $2,000	25	0.04	0.05
$2,000–$9,999	17	2	0.3
$10,000–$19,999	14	5	0.9
$20,000–$49,999	24	19	7
$50,000–$99,999	11	19	10
$100,000–$199,999	5	16	17
$200,000–$999,999	2	20	35
$1,000,000 or more	0.3†	19	29
Total	98.3‡	100	99.3‡

Source: Based on data in *Federal Reserve Bulletin* (March 1964), pp. 285–293.
*All values have been doubled to take account of inflation since 1962.
†This is our estimate; officially listed as "less than 0.5 per cent."
‡These columns do not add up to 100 per cent because of rounding procedures.

occupational hierarchy as more-or-less a pyramid, with the masses of people concentrated at or near the bottom. In advanced industrial societies, the structure more nearly approximates a diamond, with the largest concentrations in the middle levels (see Fig. 12.2).

Property Stratification

The most basic difference between the stratification systems of socialist and nonsocialist societies involves the locus of power. In the socialist nations of Eastern Europe, power is concentrated in the hands of those who dominate the *political* system of stratification, the leaders and key officials of the Communist Party. In nonsocialist societies, power tends to be concentrated, though not nearly to the same degree, in the hands of those who dominate the *property* system of stratification, the wealthy, propertied elite.

Virtually everyone in nonsocialist nations owns some property: even the poorest usually have a few possessions. But most of the wealth belongs to a strikingly small minority. Data on this subject are hard to come by: the most recent for the United States were gathered for the Federal Reserve Board in the 1960s and show that a mere 7 per cent of the population owned over half of the wealth (see Table 12.2). More striking still, barely 2 per cent owned a majority of the nation's investment assets.

Recent research by a specially appointed Royal Commission on the Distribution of Income and Wealth yields a similar picture for Britain, though their much more thorough examination of the subject brought out the many difficulties involved in any effort to obtain reliable measures of the distribu-

TABLE 12.3   Distribution of wealth in Britain

Percentage of Population	Percentage of Wealth Owned	
	Excluding Pension Rights	Including Pension Rights
Top 1 per cent	28	17
Top 5 per cent	54	35
Top 10 per cent	67	46
Top 20 per cent	82	59
Bottom 80 per cent	18	41

Source: Royal Commission on the Distribution of Income and Wealth, Report No. 1, *Initial Report on the Standing Reference* (London: H. M. Stationery Office, 1975), tables 36 and 39.

tion of wealth. For example, as Table 12.3 indicates, when one takes into account the accumulated equity which workers have built up in governmental and private pension systems, the concentration of wealth is not nearly as great as it appears when this is ignored (as in the American data).[6] Nevertheless, it is still considerable.

If the power of the very wealthy were confined to the economy, it would be impressive; but when it spills over into the polity, as it frequently does, it becomes awesome. This situation arises in part because of the tremendous costs of modern election campaigns. A recently published analysis of the 1972 elections in the United States indicates that they cost $425 million.[7] The more powerful the office, the greater the costs: candidates for the office of the presidency alone spent $138 million. As a consequence, candidates for important public office tend to be either very wealthy individuals themselves (see Table 12.4) or indebted to such individuals. The only alternative is financial support of candidates by broadly based mass organizations, such as labor unions, public interest groups, or political parties themselves (though the latter often become financially dependent on a limited number of wealthy donors).

Because of their great political power in capitalist societies, the propertied elite are able to secure many striking political advantages. In the United States, for example, many provisions of the tax laws have been written for their special benefit. For example, while large salaries can be taxed at rates up to a maximum of 50 per cent, capital gains can be taxed only to a limit of 25 per cent, and even this could be avoided until recently if the individual did not sell the property, but passed it on to his or her heirs. In that case, the federal government asked no income tax at all,* even when the capital gains

*There was, of course, usually an inheritance tax, though that is applied to every large estate, no matter how it was acquired. Also, sympathetic lawmakers have created sufficient loopholes to provide ample opportunities for wealthy individuals to minimize, or even avoid, the impact of inheritance taxes as well.

amounted to tens of millions of dollars. United States Treasury Department statistics indicate that the special treatment accorded capital gains under present tax laws is the equivalent of a $5-billion-a-year subsidy of the propertied elite.[8]

Because of their political power, many members of the propertied elite are legally able to avoid income tax payments *entirely*. In 1970, for example, Ronald Reagan and Nelson Rockefeller, both multimillionaires, managed to find sufficient loopholes in the federal tax laws to avoid any income tax obligation at all—despite the fact that people with incomes of less than $5,000 per year were being taxed an average of 9 per cent. And Reagan and Rockefeller had considerable company. Reports from the Department of the Treasury show that every year hundreds of people in the upper brackets manage to do the same thing. In fact, Benjamin Bradlee, Executive Editor of *The Washington Post* and a close personal friend of the late President Kennedy, reports that the President once examined the income tax returns of J. Paul Getty, reputed to have had a net worth of $2 billion, and found that he paid only $500 in federal income tax in 1962—and did this quite legally because of class-biased tax legislation.[9]

The dominance of the propertied elite is not reflected only in tax benefits, of course. In countless ways, subtle and not so subtle, their influence pervades the life of society. Government policy on education, health care, environmental pollution, and even relations with other nations is affected by the fact that so many of those who make the decisions are members of the propertied elite or obligated to it. Thus, they cannot decide issues of war and peace simply on the ground of justice or national security; they must also take into account the implications for giant corporations whose profits depend on a continuing demand for costly weapons systems. In finding solutions to the health needs of the nation, they must consider the special

TABLE 12.4 The distribution of wealth among members of the United States Senate as compared to the American population as a whole

Net Worth Category	Percentage of U.S. Senate	Percentage of U.S. Population
Less than $20,000	0	56
$20,000–$49,999	5	24
$50,000–$199,999	38	16
$200,000–$999,999	28	2
$1,000,000 or more	28	0.3
	99	98

Sources: Table 12.2 above, plus summary of Ralph Nader's Citizen Action Group report as summarized by Lloyd Shearer, "The Richest Men in the U.S. Senate," *Parade*, May 23, 1976, p. 7. The percentages for the U.S. Senate are based only on the seventy-eight Senators for whom reliable data were available.

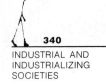

interests of the American Medical Association and the drug industry. The United States is not unique in all of this; the situation in France, Italy, Japan, Canada, West Germany, and other nonsocialist nations is similar in many respects.[10]

Yet despite its immense power in most nonsocialist societies, the propertied elite does not have anything approaching total control in any of them. The democratic political system ensures at least some measure of influence for the more numerous, but less wealthy, segments of the population, provided they organize effectively. Groups as dissimilar as Common Cause and Welfare Rights Mothers and techniques as disparate as running candidates for office and organizing protest rallies can be used by members of democratic societies to fight the propertied elite and protect their own interests.

The most effective opposition to the power of the propertied class, however, has come from working-class parties. In some countries, such as Sweden, Norway, and Denmark, these parties have held office much of the time since the 1930s. In other countries, such as the United States, there is no real working-class party, and both major parties are substantially under the control of the propertied elite. Table 12.5 provides some indication of the difference this can make in the distribution of wealth within societies.[11]

Political Stratification

According to democratic theory as taught in public schools and extolled by politicians, the members of society are all made politically equal by giving each of them a single vote. But most people soon learn that this is not the way

TABLE 12.5 Distribution of wealth in the United States and in Sweden compared

Wealth Category	Percentage of Wealth Held	
	United States	Sweden
Top 2 per cent	39	20
Top 10 per cent	61	39
Top 25 per cent	80	56
Top 50 per cent	96	75
Bottom 50 per cent	4	25

Sources: *Federal Reserve Bulletin* (March 1964), pp. 285–293; and Swedish Finance Department, State Public Investigations (SOU). *Ägande och inflytande inom det privata näringslivet: Koncentrationsultredningen, V* [Ownership and influence in the private sector of the economy] (Stockholm, 1968), 7, table 6/4b. Minor corrections were required in United States data to make them comparable to the Swedish data.

**FIGURE 12.3 Leonid Brezhnev,
chief of the *apparatchiki* in the
Soviet Union.**

democracy works, either in nonsocialist or in socialist societies (all East European societies profess to be democratic and regularly hold elections).[12] In George Orwell's felicitous phrase, some people are more equal than others. There is, in other words, a political hierarchy, just as there are hierarchies of wealth and occupation, and an individual's status in this hierarchy affects his access to rewards. This is especially true in one-party societies.

The political system of stratification so important in the socialist societies of Eastern Europe has a structure both simpler and more sharply defined than that of nonsocialist societies. The top stratum in the political hierarchy, and the dominant class in these societies, consists of full-time Party workers, or functionaries, and their families. In the Soviet Union they are known as the *apparatchiki* (literally, "members of the apparatus or machine"; in effect, organization men). Milovan Djilas, Communism's famous heretic, denounced this group, calling it "the new class" to direct attention to its striking similarity to the power-wielding, privilege-seeking, exploitative classes of other societies.[13]

Numerically, the *apparatchiki* and their immediate families are only a small fraction of 1 per cent of the population;[14] but their near monopoly of political and economic power gives them a strength far out of proportion to

their numbers. When the class first came to power, idealists and political zealots dominated it; but once its position was secure, careerists began to infiltrate, and the class became increasingly concerned with its own special interests, as Djilas noted.

Beneath the Party functionaries is the much larger class of ordinary Party members. In the Soviet Union, it includes about 9 per cent of the adult population. A minority of these members are volunteer activists who provide leadership in the lower echelons of Party affairs; the majority play a much more limited role, like most church members in this country.

Still lower in the political class system of a one-party state are those who, though outside the Party, are not regarded as hostile to it: people who would like to join the Party but lack relevant qualifications, others who are covertly hostile to the Party and stay outside as a matter of principle, and still others who are politically apathetic. This class normally includes the vast majority of the population.

Finally, at the bottom of the system are people who are regarded as enemies of the Party. The size of this class varies considerably from time to time and from country to country, and the circumstances of its members vary from mere police surveillance to imprisonment, torture, and execution.[15]

The effects of one's status in this hierarchy are substantial, although they have sometimes been surprisingly inconsistent. For instance, shortly after World War II, when 2,000 former Soviet citizens were asked their opinion of thirteen occupations within the Soviet Union, the position of Party secretary ranked first in terms of material benefits—ahead of doctor, scientist, engineer, officer in the armed forces, or factory worker—but only eighth with respect to safety from arrest.[16] Since Stalin's death, the role of *apparatchik* has become much safer, so this inconsistency has largely disappeared.

The ordinary Party member, too, enjoys advantages. The most important of these today is probably access to good jobs. As one writer puts it, "Although there are a few exceptions, managers generally can not move up even to the plant-director level without first becoming Communist Party members."[17] The situation is the same in the professions, though not quite to the same degree.[18] One consequence of this has been a disproportionate representation of managers and professionals in Party ranks, an ironic development in a party committed to the dictatorship of the proletariat. In fairness, however, we should note that the post-Stalinist leadership has tried to correct the imbalance, and the proportion of white-collar workers in the Party has been reduced a bit, from 51 to 45 per cent since 1956.[19]

Democratic multiparty societies also have political class systems, but they lack the extremes of reward and punishment and they are not as important in the life of the nation. In their general structure, they resemble the political class system of one-party states. At the top is a class of people for whom politics is a vocation. Although many of these professionals depend on politics for their livelihood, others, like the Kennedys and

Rockefellers, are people of wealth who are involved for other reasons. In a number of countries, including the United States, party activity can be extremely lucrative. For example, in 1964 President Johnson's family had a fortune valued at $9 to $14 million, "amassed almost entirely while Mr. Johnson was in public office; mainly [after] he entered the Senate and began his rise to national power in 1948."[20] His is not an isolated case, at least not among politicians in brokerage-type parties. Typically, these men seem to feel they are entitled to use their public offices for private gain and regard the income as a kind of "broker's fee" paid by the special interests they serve.[21] Though the ethics of such practices are dubious, to say the least, most political leaders stay carefully within the law (as interpreted by fellow members of the political class).

In ideologically oriented democratic parties, such as the Social Democrats in Scandinavia or the Labour Party in Britain, leaders are much less likely to use their positions for private financial advantage. Their rewards are chiefly power, fame, and the satisfaction of implementing their beliefs.

A second important political class in most multiparty nations is composed of wealthy individuals and business leaders who take an active interest in politics but do not make it their vocation. These people, the so-called fat cats, provide political organizations with one of their most essential ingredients—money. Some of them seem to want only the excitement of political participation and other psychic benefits, but most are interested in more substantial rewards (e.g., special tax advantages, lucrative government contracts, etc.).

Beneath the professional politicians and wealthy contributors is a class of volunteer workers. This is a very mixed group and includes people motivated by political ideals, by private ambition (such as the hope of joining the ranks of the professionals), or by a combination of both. This class is always small, seldom more than a few per cent of the population, and it has a high rate of turnover.[22]

The lowest rung in the political system in multiparty states is occupied by the great majority of citizens whose political activity is limited to voting and a vague identification with one or another of the parties. As voting records show, many people do not take even this much interest in the political process: nearly half of the adult population does not bother to vote even in presidential elections in the United States.[23]

In the political class system, as in some of the others, an individual tends to benefit in proportion to his investment of time and money. For this reason, a disproportionate share of the benefits accrues to the professional politicians and their wealthy allies. Fortunately, their opportunities for self-aggrandizement are at least somewhat limited by the widespread right of suffrage, which serves as a check on their self-seeking tendencies: they know that if they push their private advantage too far, they can be voted out of office.

Educational Stratification

The roots of educational stratification go far back in history. Even in hunting and gathering societies, shamans enjoyed greater power and prestige because of their special knowledge. After the invention of writing and the formation of schools early in the agrarian era, educational stratification became increasingly important. As we saw in Chapter 7, only a minority learned to read and write, because the costs of education were prohibitive for peasants. The literate were primarily children of the middle and upper classes, and this skill ensured that they would remain at that level. For the top positions in society, education was seldom of crucial importance; at most, literacy was required, sometimes not even that. Because these positions were usually filled by inheritance, the best-educated men tended to occupy the middle levels of the governmental and religious establishments and used their skill in the service of the elite.

Some elements of the older system have carried over into modern industrial societies. Above all, an individual's educational opportunities and attainments are still linked with the class position of his or her parents, and children of the powerful and wealthy stand a better chance of obtaining a university education, especially at the best institutions, than children of the poor. (This is true even in socialist societies.) But it is easy to exaggerate the similarity between the old system and the present one. Both the new technology and the new democratic ideology have created a need for a populace that is, at least, literate. Literacy is imperative for participation in a modern bureaucratized economy, and it is equally important for the effective operation of a democratic political system. Fortunately, as technology and ideology have created this need, they have provided the means and the motivation for meeting it: technology has become so productive that child labor is no longer needed, and the new ideology has made education a basic right of every child.

As a result, there is no longer the traditional cleavage between a literate minority and an illiterate majority.* Illiteracy has almost disappeared in advanced industrial societies. At the same time, other educational distinctions have become important, particularly those based on amount of education. In the United States, an individual is often categorized according to whether he has less than a high school education, a high school diploma, a college diploma, or an advanced degree. As a result of the bureaucratization of government and industry, the great majority of jobs in the United States, and increasingly in other industrial societies as well, have educational prerequisites, and the individual who lacks them is automatically ineligible.

---

*In the United States, however, there are a large number of persons who, though technically literate (i.e., they can sign their names and read or write a few simple words), cannot read and write well enough to use these skills in their work. Such persons are often referred to as "functional illiterates."

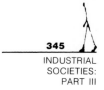
THE INDUSTRIAL SYSTEM   THE MILITARY SYSTEM

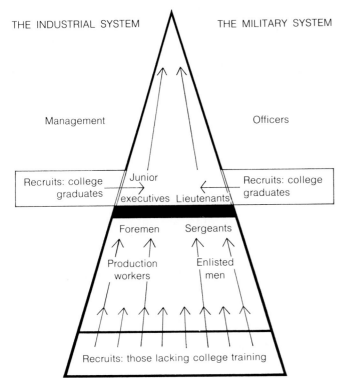

Management   Officers

Recruits: college / Junior → ← Lieutenants \ Recruits: college
graduates / executives   graduates

Foremen   Sergeants

Production   Enlisted
workers   men

Recruits: those lacking college training

FIGURE 12.4 Recruitment and promotional patterns in modern industry compared with those in the military.

This affects not only a person's chances of being hired but also chances for promotion.[24] In this respect, modern bureaucratic personnel practices have created a civilian counterpart of the military caste system, with its sharp cleavage between officers and enlisted men. Just as the ceiling for the promotion of privates is normally the rank of sergeant, so the ceiling for production workers tends to be the rank of foreman or possibly plant superintendent. Higher ranks are reserved for people with more education, and they are recruited outside the organization. Figure 12.4 illustrates this pattern.

A good measure of the importance of education today is found in recent census data on the relationship between education and income. In 1972, lifetime incomes of American males, classified by years of formal education, were as follows:[25]

0–7 years of education	$280,000
8 years of education	$344,000
1–3 years of high school	$389,000
4 years of high school	$479,000
1–3 years of college	$543,000
4 years or more of college	$758,000

The educational elite today appear to have more influence on public policy than their counterparts in the past. This is not to suggest that they have become politically dominant or that advanced academic degrees are necessary for top political office. However, college or university training has become almost a prerequisite for top office, while political leaders are increasingly forced to rely on the educational elite for help in making major decisions.[26] The role of physical scientists and engineers in planning military and space programs, and of social scientists in economic and social policies, is taken for granted today. This pattern is by no means limited to the United States. In the Soviet Union, for example, the reintroduction of market mechanisms was due in no small measure to the efforts of economists, and physical and medical scientists have had comparable influence in other areas of public policy.[27] Although the political elite are interested only in the information these experts can provide, it is hard to get it in pure form; almost invariably, the personal values of the experts intrude, but often so subtly as to be unrecognized even by the experts themselves. Because of this, today's educational elite have a much larger voice in high-level decision making than their predecessors in agrarian societies ever had.

Racial, Ethnic, and Religious Stratification

Most industrial societies have racial, ethnic, or religious cleavages. Canada, for example, has a serious cleavage between its French- and English-speaking groups, Italy between Catholics and Marxists, and the United States between whites and blacks—to name but a few of the more important ones. As long as groups like these have no effect on how goods and services and other benefits of a society are distributed, they are not really a part of the system of social stratification. But when membership in such a group has an appreciable influence on an individual's access to those things, the group becomes a part of the system. In that case, the group becomes, in effect, a class: it is an aggregation of people who stand in a similar position with respect to a resource that influences their access to power, privilege, or prestige. It is obviously a special kind of class, however. For one thing, the resource involved is the individual's *membership in a group*, rather than his or her personal wealth, occupation, etc. For another thing, classes like these have a greater degree of group or class consciousness than most others, more, say, than people with a high school diploma, more even than manual workers as a whole. Finally, it is often more difficult to move into or out of such a class. Because of these differences, some sociologists call this type of class a *status group*; and in instances where movement into or out of the group is virtually impossible the label *caste* is often used.

The most striking example of this type of stratification in the United States involves the two major racial groups. Since early in this country's history, blacks have been a subordinated group. Before the Civil War this was

FIGURE 12.5 So much basic learning occurs while a child is small: learning opportunities in Harlem.

underlined by the legal position of the majority of blacks, who were slaves and the property of members of the white group. Even before the Emancipation Proclamation, some blacks achieved considerable success in the occupational, educational, and property systems of stratification, but despite this they continued to suffer from handicaps imposed on them because of their identification with the black group. Their access to clubs, churches, housing, and services of almost every kind was much more limited than that of whites with comparable status in other systems of stratification.

Today, many of these limitations have been removed. Civil rights legislation ensures blacks equal treatment in stores, hotels, restaurants, and other business establishments, at least in most sections of the country. But racial discrimination continues in housing, club membership, and some other areas. Even more important, the general cultural and economic deprivation of recent centuries has left many blacks unable to take full advantage of the new opportunities. So much basic learning occurs while a child is small that large numbers of black children with poorly educated, low-income parents are already badly handicapped when they begin school. These youngsters generally make slow progress and leave school poorly equipped to compete in the occupational system. As a result, the median income of black families has not been much more than half that of white in recent years ($7,800 versus $13,350 in 1974).[28]

Although the white population is sometimes thought of as a unit, it is, of

course, divided along both ethnic and religious lines. From the ethnic standpoint, people of British extraction enjoy the highest status, then those of other northwestern European ancestry, followed by those of Southern and Eastern European ancestry.[29] Among religious groups, Protestants rank first, followed by Catholics, then by Jews. These rankings reflect the historic dominance of the Protestants of British ancestry who first settled this country. Until about 1830, most of the white population were Anglo-Saxon and Protestant, and these people occupied the dominant positions in all the major institutions. Since most of the later immigrants were poor, had little education, and were unable to speak English, they tended to fill the more menial positions. The more they had in common with the older stock, the more readily they were accepted in marriage and in the better jobs, clubs, and neighborhoods. Northwestern European Protestants were thus accepted more readily than Southern and Eastern European Catholics and Jews.

Ever since the Civil War, the Democratic Party has been the political instrument for most of the groups that have felt discriminated against by the nation's political, economic, and social elite (i.e., wealthy Northern Protestant families of British origin). This is the reason the Democratic Party has attracted such diverse groups as Southern whites, blacks, Catholics, Jews, and the working class. The Republican Party, by comparison, has tended to be the political instrument for the historically dominant groups and has sought to protect their advantages.

In Canada, the most serious cleavage is along ethnic lines, dividing French-speaking Canadians from English-speaking. Although the French settled the country first, they were conquered by the British, who dominated the political system from the eighteenth century on. The problem was further aggravated because the English industrialized while the French clung to the agrarian way of life. As a consequence, the English also dominated the economy, even in Quebec, the home province of the French.[30] In recent years the French have succeeded in eliminating many discriminatory practices through political action, but many of them still favor political independence for Quebec.[31]

Age and Sex Stratification

Age and sex have been bases of social differentiation in every society throughout history. The social roles of men and women have differed, as have the roles of children, adults, and the aged. In almost every case, these role differences have been linked to status differences in power, privilege, and prestige.

The ultimate basis of these distinctions lies in human biology.* Children are both physically and intellectually less developed than adults. Having had

---

*This is not to minimize the tremendous influence of culture on age and sex status systems.

fewer chances to acquire experience and information, they are at a competitive disadvantage. For women, the primary handicap has been quite different. Throughout most of human history, the limitations imposed by frequent pregnancy, lactation, and the care of small children prevented women from competing with men in political and military activities, traditionally the basic determinants of power and prestige.

There are elements of both continuity and change in the systems of age and sex stratification in industrial societies. Middle-aged and older people continue to be dominant in the political, property, and occupational systems. In recent years, for example, the median age of United States Senators has been fifty-six, and, with the Senate's system of seniority, committee chairmen have been even older.[32] One national study of business leaders indicated a median age of fifty-four; another, limited to the managerial elite, showed a median of sixty-one.[33] A study of American military leaders found their average age was fifty-four; and a study of the very wealthy showed that the average age of men with estates valued at $5 million or more was sixty-nine.[34] The situation is similar in other advanced industrial societies, including the Soviet Union.[35] On the other hand, younger people are now challenging the authority of their elders to a degree that was unthinkable in agrarian societies.

As far as sex stratification is concerned, although men continue to be dominant both politically and occupationally, women have made substantial gains in the property and educational systems. Laws that restricted their right to own property have been eliminated in most industrial societies, and in the United States women now own much of the wealth.[36] Similarly, former barriers to higher education have been largely eliminated. Even in the political arena, women have made substantial gains. As recently as 1900, women were permitted to vote only in New Zealand and four states in this country.[37] Today they enjoy this right in every advanced industrial society.

In the occupational world, the historical distinction between men's work and women's work has begun to blur. This has been made possible by the great reduction in the birthrate and the changing nature of work activities. In some societies women now enter the labor force in almost the same numbers as men. In one recent year, women constituted 48 per cent of the labor force in the Soviet Union.[38] This figure was inflated somewhat as a result of the heavy death toll among Soviet men in World War II; but even if there had been equal numbers of both sexes in the population, women would still have made up 43 per cent of the labor force. In the United States, too, the percentage of gainfully employed women has steadily risen. In 1890 only 14 per cent of women between twenty-five and sixty-four years of age worked outside the home.[39] Today more than half of the women in this age category are employed outside the home, and women make up 39 per cent of the labor force.[40]

**FIGURE 12.6 Female
locomotive engineer,
U.S.S.R.**

Despite these increases, women are still far from achieving occupational equality and are disproportionately concentrated in the less remunerative occupations. In 1974, only 9 per cent of Americans with incomes of $15,000 or more per year were women.[41] A similar situation prevails in other industrial societies.[42] To some extent this is because women are handicapped during the early, and often critical, years of employment, when childbearing and child rearing interrupt their careers. In addition, some women prefer full-time homemaking. These factors have traditionally led most employers to favor men for the more responsible and demanding positions. This, in turn, reinforces the disinclination of many women to compete in the job market.

Consequences of Social Stratification

The unequal distribution of power, privilege, and prestige divides the members of industrial societies as surely as it did the members of agrarian societies. Those who have similar resources and backgrounds tend to associate with one another and to stand apart from the rest. This inevitably leads to the formation of class-based subcultures and class-based communities.

The differences that divide the classes are partly economic. The poor obviously cannot afford many of the things that are an integral part of the middle-class way of life, and the middle classes cannot afford many of the things that are essential to the upper-class way of life. But it is not only material differences that are divisive. Differences in values and beliefs, in experience and information, in social norms (especially the etiquette of daily life), and even in speech, are equally important.

It would be impossible to describe here all the differences that sociologists have found between the classes in modern industrial societies. The subject fills volumes.[43] Suffice it to say that hardly any aspect of life is untouched. Even one's chances for survival are influenced by class membership: white babies born in the United States today can expect to live six years longer than nonwhite babies.[44] Class also affects many personality traits, since its influences begin to operate immediately after birth. To a large degree, a person's needs and desires, goals and ambitions, and even self-image are molded by the system of stratification. And not least of all, class affects an individual's chance of success both in school and in the world of work. Sometimes these influences are extremely subtle: children of the poor, for example, sometimes suffer permanent mental impairment because their mothers' diet during pregnancy, or their own early diet, was deficient in protein.

Despite our physical proximity to people of other classes, most of us never have the opportunity to see their lives "from the inside." At best, we are spectators who watch from a distance—and often misunderstand what we see. (This is what black militants mean when they say that whites are unable to "think black.") Talented novelists and other writers have often helped to bridge this gap by sharing insights or their own experiences, and sociologists and anthropologists now add to our understanding of what it means to live in other classes.[45] But it is important to remember that vicarious experiences are no substitute for direct, personal, life-long experience.

From the standpoint of society, one of the most important consequences of stratification is the dissension it generates between individuals and between classes. Where there is opportunity for upward mobility, competition will result; this is a natural consequence of basic tendencies in our common nature. Where status is primarily ascribed, however, class conflict often ensues. People born into classes to which many of the good things of life are denied are likely to join with others in the same situation and try to force society to make more rewards available to them, while those in the favored classes usually resist these efforts. We see this in struggles between workers and employers, in racial conflicts, and in student efforts to get more power in the affairs of universities and colleges and in the larger society.

The stakes in struggles like these can be extremely high. In industrial

societies, the outcome, more often than not, has favored the *less* advantaged class, resulting in a gradual reduction in social, economic, and political inequality. Even if this is not always evident in short-run comparisons, it becomes clear whenever we compare the more advanced industrial societies of the modern world with agrarian societies of the past (see *Social Inequality: Two Trends*, below).

Vertical Mobility

Compared with agrarian societies, industrial societies afford far more opportunities for individuals to better themselves. In the agrarian era, birthrates ensured an oversupply of labor in almost every generation. At every social level, a certain percentage of the children were forced to work in an occupation less rewarding than their fathers' or to join the ranks of the beggars, outlaws, prostitutes, and vagabonds. Though some did improve their situations, the downwardly mobile were much more numerous.

In industrial societies, conditions are strikingly different. While birthrates have been falling, technology has been increasing the proportion of high-status occupations (see Table 12.1). As a result, the situation has been reversed: there is now more upward than downward mobility. A recent survey by the U.S. Bureau of the Census compared the occupations of men today with those of their fathers and found that two and a half times as many had risen from blue-collar occupations to white-collar as had dropped from white-collar to blue-collar.[46] Even if we divide the urban occupational hierarchy into three or four levels, the ratio of upward to downward mobility is about the same. This ratio is higher than in most other countries (owing, apparently, to the more rapid expansion of higher-status occupations here), but nearly every industrial society has eliminated the excess of downward mobility.[47]

This has undoubtedly been a factor in reducing the threat of the working-class revolution predicted by Marx and Engels. If, in every generation, a quarter or more of the children of workingmen are able to rise into the ranks of the middle class, resentment against the system is almost certain to be less than if only a few per cent move up the ladder, as Marx and Engels expected. Furthermore, since those who rise are generally some of the most talented and ambitious members of their generation, a lot of potential leadership for protest movements is permanently lost to the working class.

It is probably no coincidence that a great deal of the leadership and support for protest movements in advanced industrial societies has come from members of racial, ethnic, or religious minorities. Upward mobility for such people is more difficult, sometimes impossible. Unable to escape the limitations society imposes on them, many turn their energies to social protest, especially programs designed to eliminate the differential between their own group and more favored ones.

Social Inequality: Two Trends

When we began our examination of systems of stratification, we noted the trend toward increasing social inequality that started with the horticultural revolution 10,000 years ago and continued down to the early stages of the Industrial Revolution. We also noted that with further industrialization this trend was halted, even reversed. Before concluding our review of stratification, we need to take a closer look at this important development and at one other critical trend as well.

In advanced agrarian societies of the past, systems of inequality were often built right into the legal codes. There was no pretense that people were equal: some were legally recognized as privileged nobility, some as commoners, others as slaves or serfs, and legal rights and privileges varied accordingly. Democracy as we understand it was unknown in these societies. Political decisions were the God-given prerogative of a tiny elite; the rest of the population had no influence. The only thing that set limits on the actions of the elite was the knowledge that, if conditions became too oppressive, the masses would revolt. Economically, the ruler and the governing class usually received not less than half of the national income, sometimes as much as two-thirds.[48]

In advanced industrial societies, the legal bases of inequality have been virtually eliminated. In Britain and a few others, titles of nobility remain, but the special rights that were once attached to them have been largely stripped away. It is true, of course, that people still receive unequal treatment in courts of law, in both socialist and nonsocialist societies,[49] but the situation has improved greatly since the time when the poor were often hanged for the theft of an egg or a loaf of bread.

Except in the one-party states of Eastern Europe, opportunities for participation in the political decision-making process have been increased substantially. The right of franchise has gradually been enlarged until virtually the entire population is able to vote (see Table 11.1, page 302). Though the value of such limited participation may seem questionable at times, the record of the Scandinavian democracies shows what is possible; and even in countries like the United States and Canada, much of the legislation reflects the influence of less advantaged segments of the population. Although no society has anything approaching pure democracy, a much larger percentage of the population in industrial societies has some voice in political decision making.

While socialist societies lag in terms of political equality, they are ahead in terms of economic equality. Substantial differences in income still exist, but they are, as we have seen, less than in nonsocialist societies, and far less than in traditional agrarian. Even in nonsocialist societies, the upper 2 per cent of the population does not appear to receive more than 25 per cent of the national income, and usually less than that.[50] Though far more than their

FIGURE 12.7   Public housing project for low-income families, Denmark.

proportionate share, it represents a significant reduction in inequality. But far more important than this is the fact that, in all advanced industrial societies, the majority of people live somewhere *between* wealth and poverty, and their living standards, though greatly varied, would all be judged comfortable by traditional agrarian standards.

The factors responsible for the egalitarian trend are primarily the same ones that led to the democratic trend (see page 302), which is simply part of the larger movement away from the extreme social inequality that developed in agrarian and early industrial societies.[51] But one other point should be emphasized—the speed and magnitude of the increase in productivity in industrial societies. When national income is rising rapidly and promises to continue to rise as long as political and economic stability are maintained, the dominant classes find it in their interest to make some concessions to the lower classes to prevent costly strikes, riots, and revolutions. Even though they give ground in *relative* terms, they come out far ahead in *absolute* terms in an expanding economy. For example, an elite would enjoy a substantially greater income if it settled for "just" 25 per cent of the national income in a $1,500 billion economy than if it stubbornly fought to preserve a 50 per cent share and, in the process, provoked so much internal strife that the economy stalled at the $100 billion level. In short, the new technology has provided the elites of industrial societies with an option undreamed of in agrarian societies; and judging by the results, it has proved highly attractive.

But as the new technology has helped to reduce the level of inequality *within* industrial societies, it has had the opposite effect for the world as a whole. The gap between rich and poor nations has been widening ever since the start of the industrial era. One expert estimates that in the 100 years between 1860 and 1960, the wealthiest quarter of the nations increased their share of the world's income from 58 to 72 per cent, while the share of the bottom quarter fell from 12.5 to 3.2 per cent.[52] With the new technology gradually eroding the barriers between societies, this trend is bound to grow in relevance for everyone. We will return to this subject in Chapter 13, when we examine the complex problems of societies that are struggling to industrialize in the shadow of far wealthier and more powerful societies.

KINSHIP AND MARRIAGE

Declining Functions of Kin Groups

In the simplest societies, almost every aspect of life was centered within the family. Kin groups were all-purpose organizations that provided for their members' political, economic, educational, religious, and psychic needs.

As societies grew in size and complexity, this could not last. Relationships had to be established between individuals who were not related to one another. And people who were related had to become involved in relationships that violated the norms of the kinship system—for example, an individual of inferior rank in a family might find himself in a position where he exercised political authority over kinsmen of higher rank.

Although the functions of kin groups began to change thousands of years ago, no other type of society ever altered them as drastically as modern industrial societies. In agrarian societies, the family was still the basic unit of production, and the state was normally the property of the royal family. Education, too, was still predominantly a family responsibility; most boys learned the male role by assisting their fathers, and girls the female role by assisting their mothers. Even when a boy was apprenticed to a master craftsman, he lived in the craftsman's household in a kind of pseudofamilial relation.

By contrast, in advanced industrial societies, ties of kinship are greatly reduced. The family is often so scattered that meaningful relations among its members are nearly impossible. The nuclear family is no longer the basic unit of production, as it was in agrarian societies. In politics, family ownership of the state has been eliminated; and nepotism, though it still occurs occasionally, is no longer accepted as normal or legitimate. Finally, the schools have assumed many of the family's responsibilities of training and supervising children.

Today the family's basic function is to order the private and personal aspects of the lives of its members. This means continued responsibility for some of its historical functions—reproduction, child rearing, and the channeling of sexual activity—as well as new or enlarged responsibilities with respect to personality development, affective relationships, and the consumption of goods and services.

One of the clearest indications of the change is in the area of courtship and marriage. In most horticultural, herding, agrarian, and maritime societies, marriage was thought of largely in economic terms (and in the governing class, in political terms as well). This was reflected in the practice of arranged marriages, in which the parents took the major responsibility for deciding whom their son or daughter would marry, and in the requirement of a bride price or a dowry. For companionship, men looked to other men, women to other women. For love and sexual satisfaction, the more prosperous men often kept mistresses or concubines, whom, unlike their wives, they were able to choose.

By contrast, people in industrial societies view marriage largely in

TABLE 12.6   Number of children born to British couples married around 1860 and 1925

Number of Children Born	Percentage of Marriages	
	Marriages Around 1860	Marriages Around 1925
None	9	17
One	5	25
Two	6	25
Three	8	14
Four	9	8
Five	10	5
Six	10	3
Seven	10	2
Eight	9	1
Nine	8	0.6
Ten	6	0.4
Over ten	10	0.3
Total	100	101

Source: Royal Commission on Population, *Report* (London: H. M. Stationery Office, 1949), p. 26.

romantic terms. As our movies, magazines, and music testify, it is the union of a man and a woman who are attracted to one another physically and psychologically and who expect to find continuing pleasure in one another's company. Parents may offer advice, but as likely as not it will be ignored. Bride price and dowry are irrelevant, and mistresses have lost their former respectability. On the other hand, if the marriage fails to live up to expectations, there are far fewer economic, moral, or legal impediments to its dissolution.

The fact that the divorce rate is not higher than it is suggests, however, that it is easy to underrate the real functional importance of the nuclear family. In societies where people move so frequently and are involved in such a variety of organizations, they have plenty of opportunity to develop superficial relationships. Yet their mobility makes it harder for them to achieve sustained, intimate relations of the kind that involves all aspects of an individual's personality—including the memory of shared experiences. If sustained primary-group ties are essential for the development of emotionally mature and stable personalities, as social psychologists believe, then this function of the family is actually growing in importance.

Changing Composition of the Nuclear Family

The Industrial Revolution has changed not only the family's functions, but its composition as well. Above all, there has been a drastic reduction in the number of children, as Table 12.6 indicates. British marriages contracted around 1860 produced a median of six children. Only two generations later, the median had dropped to two. Families with eight or more children declined from 33 per cent of the total to only 2 per cent. Although the decline was more rapid in Britain than in most industrial societies, the general pattern has been quite similar.[53]

Comparisons like the one in Table 12.6 are misleading if we assume that they reflect differences in the number of children actually living within a family at the same time. For one thing, in the earlier period the death rate among children was much higher than it is today. Table 12.7 shows how the rate for Swedish children has declined since the eighteenth century (these figures are used because Sweden has some of the oldest reliable statistics on the subject). In the middle of the eighteenth century, 43 per cent of Swedish children died before they reached the age of five.* Of those who survived, 14 per cent died before they were twenty. In other words, half of the children died before their twentieth birthday. By contrast, in the middle of the twentieth century, 97 per cent of the Swedish children lived to age twenty.

---

*The figure of 43 per cent is arrived at by taking the average annual death rate of 86.6 per 1,000 shown in Table 12.7, multiplying by 5 (for the first five years of life), and dividing by 1,000 (the base against which the annual death rate was calculated).

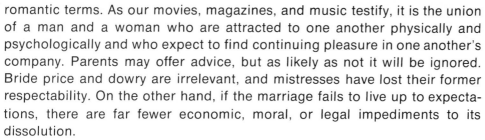

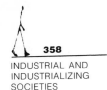
TABLE 12.7   Average annual death rates, by age, Sweden, 1751–1959 (rate per 1,000 population)

Age	1751–1780	1881–1910	1955–1959
0–4	86.6	36.3	4.2
5–9	13.8	5.9	0.5
10–14	7.2	3.6	0.4
15–19	7.0	4.6	0.7

Source: From *Statistical Abstract of Sweden,* as cited in Warren Thompson and David Lewis, *Population Problems,* 5th ed. (New York: McGraw-Hill, 1965), p. 374.

Obviously, with so many deaths in the first years of life, there were considerably fewer children *living* in an agrarian family than were *born* into it.

Another factor that reduced the number of children living with their parents at any given time was the long duration of the childbearing period. Women who had eight, ten, or more children often bore them over a twenty-year period or longer. By the time the youngest child was five or ten, many of its older brothers and sisters had left home or died. Thus, although the nuclear family was certainly larger in agrarian societies, the number of its members who actually lived together at one time was not as different as the birthrates suggest.

A second noteworthy change in the composition of the family is the elimination of the last vestiges of polygyny. Industrial societies are the only major type in which polygyny has never been socially approved. Among preliterate societies, only 13 per cent insist on monogamy;[54] in agrarian societies, monogamy is more common, though still far from universal (until recently, polygyny was practiced throughout the whole of the Islamic world extending from the East Indies to Morocco). The shift in industrial societies reflects the changing character of the family, especially the growing importance of affective ties between husband and wife and the declining importance of economic functions. And at least one writer has argued that the norm of monogamy in industrial societies is an expression of democratic, egalitarian values and a reaction against the obvious inequalities inherent in polygynous marital systems.[55]

Finally, the modern family includes fewer relatives outside the nuclear group; households today seldom accommodate aged grandparents, unmarried aunts and uncles, or even grown children. This is no longer necessary in most families because modern urban communities provide so many alternative facilities—apartments, nursing homes, restaurants, laundries, and so on. Moreover, as these facilities have developed, changes have occurred in societal values: most members of industrial societies are extremely jealous of their privacy and apparently regard it more highly than they do the advantages that go with more inclusive households.

Changing Role of Women

Nowhere can the effects of industrialization on society's norms, values, and sanctions be seen more clearly than in the changing role of women.[56] Throughout most of human history most women were destined to spend the prime years of their lives bearing children, nursing them, caring for them when they were sick and dying, rearing them if they survived, doing domestic chores, tending a garden, and often helping in the fields. It is hardly surprising, therefore, that women seldom played significant roles outside the home or made outstanding contributions to the arts. (Read Virginia Woolf's fascinating little fable about Judith Shakespeare.[57])

The first signs of change came early in the Industrial Revolution when the new economic conditions caused children to be perceived less as economic assets and increasingly as liabilities. People's efforts to reduce fertility were soon aided by innovations in the area of birth control. During the nineteenth century, however, the average woman still produced a large family, still had babies for whom there was no real alternative but prolonged breast feeding, still carried the full burden of child care and housework, and, at the same time, was increasingly forced to work outside the home.

Because women were normally supplementary wage-earners for their families, they were not trained for skilled jobs and were relegated to those that paid the least. Their availability for work at low wages posed a threat to

FIGURE 12.8   During the nineteenth century, large families were still the rule.

the emerging labor movement and, as a consequence, women were virtually excluded from it. That was, in effect, a working*man's* movement, and its goal was to wrest a fair share of the new economic surplus from the upper classes.

In contrast, the early women's movements were dominated by the better educated, more leisured, and economically more secure women of the upper classes, and their goals were primarily to obtain for women some of the legal and civil rights that already belonged to upper- and middle-class men: the right to vote, to hold public office, to own property, and to enter universities. Late in the nineteenth century, they also became concerned with the situation of the working mother and sought to have her working hours shortened and night work eliminated.

By the early years of the twentieth century, these initial goals had been accomplished and the movement virtually died out. Changes continued in women's role, however, and these, too, were consequences of continuing technological and economic change. One of the most significant was the development of an alternative to breast feeding, which freed the mothers of infants from the need to be constantly available. Women's educational levels also continued to rise. Meanwhile, the growing needs of industrial societies for people in service industries (e.g., nursing, social work, teaching) and the growth of organizations requiring large numbers of secretarial and clerical workers (business and government) opened up new occupational possibilities for women from every social class. By the middle of the century, not only were more women in the labor force, but more of them were married women, a trend that still continues.

The newer women's movement that got under way in the 1960s has a diversity of goals, but one underlying objective: to break the restrictive molds in which societies continue to cast women. This goal is based on the premise that with a single exception—women's capacity for childbearing—the differences between the sexes no longer provide a valid basis for the division of labor. Modern technology compensates for those differences that are physical (e.g., strength, lactation), while those that are psychological (e.g., emotional responses, competitiveness) are to an indeterminate degree the result of socialization rather than genetics.

The women's movement also emphasizes the fact that power and prestige in modern societies derive from activities outside the family and that if women are to have equal access to these rewards and share equally in shaping society's institutions they must participate fully in the occupational system. But women probably cannot have equal access to the more interesting and demanding jobs, promotions, higher pay, political offices, or other opportunities outside the home unless the burden of responsibilities *within* the home is divided equally. Thus, the women's movement in the United States is currently seeking both to increase men's participation in household responsibilities and child care and to spread the burden of child care by tax

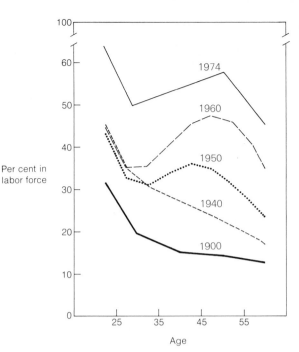

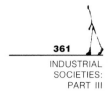

**FIGURE 12.9   Female labor force
participation in the United States,
by age: 1900 to 1974.**

rebates for working parents and by the creation of tax-supported child-care
centers.

Although it is impossible to predict how this issue will ultimately be
resolved, one thing seems apparent: increasing numbers of women in
industrial societies do not think raising a family is rewarding enough to be
the principal productive activity of a lifetime. We can assume, therefore, that
women will turn in growing numbers to activities outside the home. Some
women will decide against motherhood in order to devote themselves fully to
careers, some will have husbands who are willing to assume equal responsibility for running the household and raising the children, and some will
devote part of their lives to young families and accept the ensuing handicaps
should they return to school or work. In this area, as in so many others, the
new technology has opened up an ever-widening range of possibilities. The
only certain consequence is greater participation by women in every sphere
of societal life.

Broken Marriages: Divorce and Widowhood

During the last century, the divorce rate in the United States has risen
substantially. In 1890 it was 0.5 per 1,000 population per year; by 1974 it had
risen more than ninefold to 4.6.[58] Partly as a consequence of this trend, more
than half of all black schoolchildren and more than a quarter of all white

FIGURE 12.10 Prior to industrialization, a large percentage of marriages were broken during the child-rearing years by the death of one or both parents.

schoolchildren now live in one-parent homes, in homes with one or more stepparents, or apart from both parents.[59]

It would be a mistake to suppose, however, that children were spared the trauma of broken marriages in agrarian societies of the past. While it is true that divorce was rare in most agrarian societies,* a large percentage of marriages were broken by the death of one or both parents before all of the children reached adulthood. In mid-eighteenth-century Sweden, for example, this happened in about half of all marriages, in late eighteenth-century France in approximately 60 per cent, and in early twentieth-century India in approximately 70 per cent.[60]

In most countries, this pattern resulted in frequent remarriages. Individuals who survived to old age had often had several spouses. Marriages between widows and widowers were common and led to merged families with complicated combinations of half-brothers and half-sisters. Fairy tales about cruel stepmothers and stepfathers bear witness to the unhappy situations that often resulted.

In modern industrial societies, widowhood before middle age is relatively infrequent. In the United States, the probability that one spouse will die before the age of forty-five is now only 10 per cent.[61] This means that the

---

*In Islamic societies, divorce was much easier to obtain than in Christian or Buddhist societies.

likelihood of a nuclear family's disruption before the children are grown was actually considerably greater in agrarian societies despite the rise in the divorce rate in many industrial nations.

SOCIETIES:
PART III

Loosening of Ties

Another basic change in family life is the loosening of ties among the members. The agrarian family, as we have seen, was usually a work group. This was almost invariably the case among peasants, who were a substantial majority of the population, but it was typical of artisans, too. The place of work and the place of residence were normally the same, and all the members of the family, including children, shared in the work.

In industrial societies the pendulum has swung to the opposite pole. Very few men work at home, and most work too far away to return even for the midday meal. Many married women also work outside the home or are away for other activities, while the schools draw children out of the family for a major part of their waking hours. As a result, family members spend much less time together than they did in agrarian societies. A child in the lower grades may be with his teacher more than with his mother. Similarly, teenagers often spend more time with their friends than with their parents, and a businessman may see more of his secretary than of his wife. This situation is bound to have an effect on family ties.

A classic illustration of the problem is the familiar dinner table dialogue in which the parents ask the children, "What happened at school today?" or the wife asks her husband, "What happened at work?" The standard answer is, "Oh, nothing." This does not really mean that nothing happened but rather that nothing happened that could be easily explained or that would be meaningful to people unfamiliar with the setting. The frequency with which this response is given is a good measure of the loosening of family ties.

This is not necessarily bad, however, even from the standpoint of its effect on family solidarity. Family ties were frequently *too* close in the past, and as likely to generate hate and resentment as love and goodwill. In an industrial society, family unity rests more on a foundation of common interests and mutual attraction than it did when social and economic necessity offered people so few alternatives. Despite its negative aspects, then, the new situation seems about as conducive to harmonious relations within the family as the old.

The Changing Role of Youth

In preindustrial societies, the transition from childhood to adulthood occurred rather swiftly and at an early age. Children were typically given chores to do while they were still quite young, and their responsibilities gradually increased. By the time they were in their middle teens, sometimes earlier,

TABLE 12.8 Growth of the student population in the United States, 1871–1971

Date	Enrollment in Public Schools, Grades 9–12	Enrollment in Colleges and Universities	Total	Percentage of American Population Enrolled
1871	80,000	50,000	130,000	0.3
1900	520,000	240,000	760,000	1.0
1930	4,400,000	1,100,000	5,500,000	4.4
1971	14,060,000	8,090,000	22,150,000	10.1

Sources: U.S. Bureau of the Census, *Historical Statistics of the United States: Colonial Times to 1957* (1960), pp. 207, 210, and 211; and U.S. Bureau of the Census, "School Enrollment in the United States, 1971," *Current Population Reports*, ser. P-20, no. 234 (March 1972), tables 2 and 3.

they were doing much the same work as their parents and other adults. Traces of this older pattern still survive in the rites of passage of certain religious groups (e.g., confirmation rites and bar mitzvahs), which occur around the age of thirteen. In an earlier era, these commonly signaled the end of childhood and the beginning of adulthood, a period in which the individual would be obliged to earn his or her own way and contribute to the support of others.

With the rise of industrialization, however, the need for human labor was reduced to such an extent that children came to be viewed as a threat on the job market, and labor unions fought to make child labor illegal. Their efforts were reinforced by the passage of legislation to make school attendance compulsory, and young people were gradually edged out of the labor force or into marginal, part-time jobs. In short, their opportunities for participation in the adult world were drastically curtailed. As a consequence, a new age role was, in effect, created. Whereas most people in their teens, and certainly those in their early twenties, had previously been viewed as young adults, they increasingly came to be seen as occupying an intermediate role, a role that is neither that of adult nor that of child.

Most of the individuals in this new age role are students. Table 12.8 shows how rapidly the school population in the United States increased over the last hundred years. By the mid-1970s, 93 per cent of Americans aged fourteen to seventeen were in school, and 32 per cent of those aged eighteen to twenty-four.[62] As this suggests, advanced industrial societies have expanded their educational institutions far beyond what is required to equip their members for roles in the economy, or even for roles as citizens in a democratic society.[63]

Unfortunately, many of these societies have failed to take account of the fact that all individuals are not equally disposed to be students for such a protracted period. Many young people have little interest in the liberal aspect of education, or even in its vocational aspect (which is often inadequate), but would rather move on into adult roles. They frequently discover, however, that there are no viable alternatives. Many who drop out of secondary school, or even out of college, have trouble finding work and often drift into street gangs, communes, and similar groups whose members are recruited almost entirely from this age stratum.

As always happens when one segment of a population is cut off for an extended period from full participation in the life of the larger society, young people have developed their own subculture. Many of its more distinctive features (e.g., music, sports, experimentation with sex and drugs, etc.) are a natural consequence of some of the distinctive attributes of youth, such as great vitality, curiosity about life, the desire for fun and excitement, and resistance to adult authority. The high rate of innovation that occurs in areas like music, language, and dance, however, is to some extent the result of deliberate efforts to establish a boundary between the youth community and the adult community. The faster such things change, the harder it is for outsiders to keep up with them, thereby forcing adults to keep their distance and preventing their moving in and dominating the youth scene.

At a more fundamental level, though, youth culture simply reflects some of the most distinctive characteristics of industrial societies themselves: their high rate of innovation, their affluence, their increased leisure, their emphasis on individuality, and their tendency to specialize. The preoccupation of young people with changing fads and fashions, for example, is just one more expression of their society's enormous economic surplus and its attitude toward the new and different (see *Neophilia*, page 276).

The differences between the norms and values of young people and those of the older generation sometimes cause very serious problems, because decisions with major consequences for the adult years are made while one is still part of the youth community. The qualities that a teenager considers most desirable in a date, for example, may have little to do with the qualities desirable in a marriage partner, yet many marriages are initiated while one is still subject to the values of youth culture. Similarly, some boys make a heavy investment in athletics at the expense of their studies because their peer group regards success in sports far more highly than success in academics, only to find that their skills are no longer in demand once they are through high school or college. As Table 12.9 shows, no more than one-tenth

TABLE 12.9 Number of men and boys playing basketball and football in high school, college, and professional sports

Level of Competition	Basketball	Football
High school	700,000	1,100,000
College	18,000	43,000
Professional	264	1,194

Source: Adapted from Leonard Shapiro and Donald Huff, "The Games Always End," *Washington Post*, Mar. 20, 1977, p. D4.

FIGURE 12.11   Hare Krishna festival, San Francisco.

of 1 per cent of high school varsity athletes make it into the ranks of the professionals.

In most industrial societies, socialist and capitalist alike, youth culture has flourished to the extent that great numbers of specialized youth groups have developed, each with its own distinct subculture. In the United States, these include a wide variety of religious cults; urban communes; back-to-the-land communes; black separatists; ghetto gangs; motorcycle gangs; political groups of various persuasions; environmentalist, women's movement, and homosexual groups.

It is possible that the importance of youth cultures will decline in industrial societies as declining birthrates produce a growing proportion of older people. Counterbalancing this trend, however, is a continued expansion of the youth role to include people beyond their early twenties, and even in their thirties, who are still outside the labor force. Some of these are students who have returned to school, or who never left because their fields require such extended study; others are unemployed because of society's declining need for human labor; and still others are unemployed, permanently or for varying periods of time, by their own choice.

LEISURE AND THE ARTS

No preindustrial society ever offered such varied opportunities for filling leisure hours as modern industrial societies provide. With electronic aids, one can vicariously explore the moon, follow sports events in distant places, or enjoy "command" performances by the world's greatest artists, dead as well as living, all in the privacy of one's own living room. If one is inclined to physical activity, the affluent society offers everything from miniature golf to skydiving.

Industrial societies are also unique with respect to the commercialization of their recreation, the vicarious nature of so much of their leisure-time activities, and their dependence on manufactured aids in the search for pleasure. Both entertainment and the production of equipment for leisure activities are major industries. Ironically, even when members of industrial societies "return to nature," they often take along every conceivable substitute for the conveniences of urban life they can cram into their trailers and campers.

One of the happier features of leisure in modern societies is its relative democracy. Many of the gross inequalities of agrarian societies have been drastically reduced. The shorter workweek of the average citizen furnishes the time, and mass production and general affluence the means, for participation in a wide variety of sports, hobbies, and other activities. Unattractive as it is in many respects, the commercialization of entertainment has expanded opportunities for new kinds of careers, thus enabling far more people to develop their abilities more fully.

FIGURE 12.12   The modern symphony orchestra is a triumph of technology as well as of art: the New York Philharmonic at Avery Fisher Hall, Lincoln Center, New York.

Although the influence of the new technology is most obvious in things like water skiing and photography, its impact on the fine arts has also been substantial. The modern symphony orchestra is a triumph of modern technology, and trends in painting reflect the influence of materials and processes not available to artists of an earlier era. But perhaps the most important consequence of the new technology in this area is an indirect one: traditional standards have given way to the belief that "newer is better." This could not occur except in societies inured to, and favorably disposed toward, change in other areas.

INTRATYPE VARIATION: TRENDS AND PROSPECTS

In recent decades there has been a great deal of variation among industrial societies. The differences have been especially pronounced between the one-party socialist nations of Eastern Europe with their command economies, on the one hand, and democratic-capitalistic nations, on the other. Twenty-five years ago it seemed that these were fundamentally different kinds of industrial societies, both stable and durable, both with excellent chances of surviving for the indefinite future.

But the picture has changed somewhat. Signs of some convergence have been increasing for a number of years. Since Stalin's death in 1953, and even more since the Twentieth Party Congress in 1956, there has been a definite, though slow and halting, movement away from the extremes of totalitarianism and political repression in the U.S.S.R. Compared with the Stalin years, the present system seems almost liberal, even though political dissent is still likely to lead to prison sentences, exile, or commitment to a mental institution.[64] In the economic area, there has been a clearly discernible shift away from more extreme forms of the command economy. For a number of years, market forces have been permitted to operate in certain areas of the economy, and the role of centralized planning has been somewhat curtailed. These trends, as we have noted, are not limited to the Soviet Union, but extend throughout most of East Europe.*

The capitalist democracies, meanwhile, have taken steps to increase governmental intervention in their economies and to restrict the free play of market forces. Even as conservative a President as Richard Nixon found it expedient to introduce wage and price controls of a sort, as did the British Prime Minister, Edward Heath, a Conservative. These are only two developments in a trend toward a mixed command-market economy that began

---

*Czechoslovakia is clearly a special case, though it should be noted that its difficulties since 1968 were the result of an effort by Czech and Slovak Communists to push political and economic liberalization much more rapidly than the more cautious Soviet leaders would tolerate. Thus, there has been no lack of liberalizing forces within Czech society.

decades ago. Politically, revelations of the activities of the FBI and CIA during the Kennedy-Johnson-Nixon years warn us of the dangers of assuming that capitalist democracies are necessarily free of police-state tactics or that criticism of a democratic government is always safe.

Signs of convergence are not restricted to the political and economic areas. A declining birthrate, the movement of women into the labor force, the growth of urban populations, the growing importance of education, the growth of tertiary industries, the generation gap, the emergence of a distinctive youth culture—all these and many more are common trends in industrial societies.

These societies are not, of course, moving toward a single, uniform pattern. Differences will certainly remain; but they will probably be less marked than those which separated Hitler's Germany or Stalin's Russia from the still largely laissez-faire, capitalistic western democracies of the 1930s. The reason for this seems to be that the social, psychological, economic, and political costs inherent in these more extreme systems are more than most citizens are willing to pay. Public pressure thus led to the gradual erosion of both laissez-faire capitalism in the West and totalitarian rule in socialist societies. Although future crises might cause some industrial societies to return to the extremes of totalitarianism, this does not seem likely at present. A return to the older forms of capitalism, meanwhile, seems even less likely.

PROGRESS AND PROBLEMS

In many ways modern industrial societies can be regarded as the crowning achievement in humanity's long struggle to build a better life. Never before have we had such a store of accumulated information or been able to harness such powerful forces in our own behalf. Never has a group of societies been as secure from the threat of starvation.

Yet for all their achievements, modern societies are not free from problems—not even from the threat of extinction. The problems we face today, however, differ from our earlier ones in one respect at least: they are increasingly problems of our own making, by-products of the material progress of which we are so proud. Today more than ever, we can appreciate the reversal of an old saying: invention has, indeed, become the mother of necessity—and with a vengeance. Examples of this are everywhere. The internal combustion engine solved many transportation problems, but created problems of air pollution; DDT brought troublesome insects under control on farms, but introduced a dangerous carcinogenic element into the food chain; nuclear power offers a valuable alternative to fossil fuels, but involves a number of deadly risks.

And it is not only the new technology that creates problems. New, highly bureaucratized systems of social organization, with their impersonal—

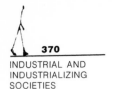

sometimes mindless—operation, are the source of plenty of others. People whose needs do not fall neatly into one of the prepackaged routines that these systems are programmed to handle can wind up horribly frustrated. Even those who manage to avoid this are alienated by the organization's impersonality.

Yet for all the shortcomings of modern industrial societies, it is doubtful that many people would elect the traditional agrarian way of life, with its widespread poverty, hunger, injustice, ignorance, exploitation, and disease. When people talk about the superiority of the great civilizations of the past, they reveal either an ignorance of the past or an unusual set of values. Taken *as a whole*, the agrarian way of life is decidedly inferior to the industrial. One indication of this is the eagerness with which most members of agrarian societies industrialize or migrate to industrial societies when they have the chance[65] and the reluctance of members of industrial societies to migrate to agrarian societies.

The inescapable conclusion, therefore, is that industrial societies, for all their defects, represent a significant advance over agrarian societies—and not only in technological terms. While some individuals may not share this judgment, the vast majority clearly do.

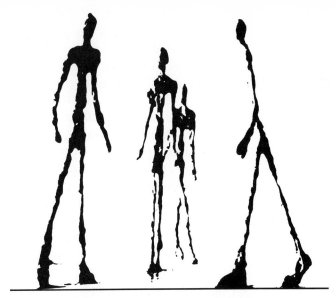

CHAPTER 13
INDUSTRIALIZING SOCIETIES

Despite the rapid spread of industrialization during the last two centuries, less than a third of the world's population live in societies that can be called "industrial" as we have defined the term. The great majority, however, do live in societies that have been substantially influenced by the Industrial Revolution—either by the diffusion of modern industrial technology or by its products obtained through trade. These influences have produced a large number of hybrid societies that are best described as *industrializing agrarian* and *industrializing horticultural* societies—the ones we commonly refer to as the underdeveloped, or developing, nations of the Third and Fourth Worlds.*

These nations are in a transitional phase, moving from the older agrarian or horticultural way of life to the modern industrial. Social scientists usually refer to this as the *modernization* process, a process that involves *all* aspects of the life of society, not just the technological. Unfortunately, the transitional

*The term "Fourth World" was coined a few years ago to call attention to the fact that some underdeveloped nations were in a far worse situation than others. Nations with very low per capita GNPs and poor prospects for improvement came to be known as the Fourth World, to distinguish them from developing nations with more favorable prospects. Sometimes, however, the term "Third World" is still used to refer to underdeveloped nations as a whole.

period is proving to be longer and more difficult than most scholars had expected. For both theoretical and practical reasons, then, these societies merit careful study.

In most analyses, industrializing agrarian and industrializing horticultural societies are lumped together indiscriminately. This is a serious mistake, since the two types differ in a number of important respects. In this chapter, therefore, we will deal with them separately.

First, however, a word concerning the place of other preindustrial types in the contemporary world. As we noted earlier, quite a number of hunting and gathering, fishing, and simple horticultural societies did survive into the modern era in remote and isolated areas. But recent advances in transportation have opened up most of these areas and removed this once effective source of protection. As a result, most of these groups have either been destroyed or herded onto reservations where they live as wards of their conquerors, usually under conditions that make their traditional way of life impossible. Even the few groups that still preserve a high degree of autonomy have usually adopted some tools and other elements from more advanced societies and thus are no longer pure types. This does not make them *industrializing* societies, of course; that implies something utterly beyond their adaptive capacities. Groups with such a primitive subsistence base could not possibly evolve into anything so advanced in the little time that is still available to them. They are, at best, unusual hybrids with a very limited future.

Maritime societies disappeared years ago, most of them absorbed by expanding agrarian societies. Herding societies have been more resistant, but in recent years they, too, have been largely absorbed into expanding industrial, industrializing agrarian, or industrializing horticultural societies. Though tribes of herdsmen remain distinct subgroups in many societies (Iraq, Iran, Morocco, Kenya, etc.), because they are minority groups they do not set the tone for the society as a whole. There are a few societies in which herding peoples are dominant or nearly so—for example, Mongolia, Somalia, and Upper Volta—and others where herding is of major importance—including Jordan, Mauritania, and Afghanistan—but research on these societies has been very limited, and they are not, as a group, very important on the world scene. Therefore we will not attempt to examine their special characteristics and problems here.

INDUSTRIALIZING AGRARIAN SOCIETIES

Today, industrializing agrarian societies comprise most of Latin America, South and East Asia, the Middle East, and North Africa, and are also found in parts of Southern and Eastern Europe. To speak of industrializing agrarian societies is to speak of China, India, Egypt, Greece, Spain, Brazil, Cuba, and Mexico, as well as several dozen other nations in these same areas.

Naturally, these societies differ from one another in many ways, reflecting differences in their histories, in the environments to which they must adapt today, and in their precise level of technological advance. Yet despite their differences, they share a number of important characteristics, for they all combine elements of the agrarian past and the industrial present. Recognition of this fact can be enormously helpful to us as we try to understand them and their problems.

By one criterion, at least, industrializing agrarian societies are the most important type in the world today: more people live in them than in any other type of society. But this is not the only reason for their importance. These societies have, for decades, been struggling with problems that constantly threaten to overwhelm them. Despite a measure of industrialization, the majority of their citizens are as poor as the common people ever were in

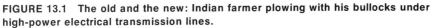

FIGURE 13.1 The old and the new: Indian farmer plowing with his bullocks under high-power electrical transmission lines.

traditional agrarian societies. At the same time, improved education and the mass media have raised their hopes and expectations and given them a sharp awareness of a better kind of life. This contradiction has created a revolutionary situation that threatens to involve the entire world.

Sometimes it is suggested that the basic problem of the underdeveloped countries is simply their technological and economic backwardness. Actually, however, their problems are much more complex than that and involve all their major social institutions—polity, economy, family, religion, and education—as well as the attitudes and values of their people.

TABLE 13.1 An industrial and an industrializing society compared: the United States and India

	U.S.	India
Population (in millions)	210	574
Area (in millions of square miles)	3.6	1.3
Population density (population per square mile)	58	454
Birthrate per 100 population	15	42.8
Death rate per 100 population	9.4	16.7
Rate of natural increase (per cent per year)	0.56	2.61
Infant mortality per 1,000 live births	18	139
Life expectancy at birth: males	67.4	41.9
Life expectancy at birth: females	75.1	40.6
Hospital beds per 1,000 population	7.2	0.6
Doctors per 1,000 population	1.6	0.2
Secondary school students per 1,000 population	94	16
Percentage growth annually in GDP,* 1960–1970	4.6	3.5
Percentage growth annually in GDP per capita, 1960–1970	3.3	1.2
UN cost-of-living index (Washington versus New Delhi)	92	77
Percentage of population in manufacturing	8.5	0.8
Thousands of kilograms of energy consumed per capita per year	12	0.2
Petroleum production per capita, in tons annually	2.16	0.13
Coal production per capita, in tons annually	2.52	0.13
Steel production per capita, in tons annually	0.65	0.01
Pounds of wheat, rice, and corn production per capita per year	2,024	352
Pounds of meat and fish production per capita per year	194	31
Pounds of milk production per capita per year	550	88
Pounds of fiber production per capita per year	31	4
Passenger cars per 1,000 population	481	1
Telephones per 1,000 population	657	3
Newspaper circulation per 1,000 population	297	16
Radios per 1,000 population	1,750	220
Televisions per 1,000 population	520	1

Source: Calculations based on data in *Statistical Abstract of the U.S., 1975,* sec. 32.
*Gross domestic product equals gross national product minus net income from abroad.

Technology and Productivity

Technologically, an industrializing agrarian society is a bewildering mixture of the ancient and the modern. Peasant farmers using techniques and tools very much like those their forefathers used 2,000 years ago work in sight of such marvels of modern technology as the Aswan Dam in Egypt or the Tata Iron and Steel Works in India.

Unfortunately from the developmental standpoint, the old technology is much more common, especially in the agricultural sector of these economies. In one recent year, an average of 55 per cent of the labor force of forty-six industrializing agrarian nations was engaged in agriculture, and yet produced only 26 per cent of the gross domestic product.[1] This differential would have been even greater if many of these countries did not have income from relatively modern plantations (tea, rubber, etc.) operated by foreigners from industrial societies.

There are marked differences in the level of technological and economic development of industrializing agrarian societies. With per capita income as a measure, levels range from only $81 per person per year in Cambodia to $1,816 in Greece. Unfortunately, the average for all industrializing agrarian societies is closer to Cambodia's: in 1974 the median for fifty-one of them was only $459.

In general, the level of technological development is higher in Latin America and the Middle East than in North Africa and southern and eastern Asia. Median figures for per capita income in these areas were as follows:[2]

Latin America	$630
Middle East	$580
North Africa	$260
Southern and eastern Asia	$110

These figures do not include the industrial societies in those areas (e.g., Japan and Israel).

Many discussions of the underdeveloped countries give the impression that they are technically and economically stagnant or, at the very least, developing less rapidly than industrial societies. But data assembled by the United Nations show that this is not the case. Since 1938, the productivity of the industrializing societies has increased at almost exactly the same rate as that of industrial societies.[3] Unfortunately, however, they have far surpassed industrial societies in population growth (see below), and this has often kept gains in per capita income small, or been responsible for losses. During the period from 1960 to 1970, for example, India's real per capita income (i.e., income measured in terms of purchasing power) rose a meager $2 for the entire decade, from $69 per person per year to $71, while the Philippines experienced a modest $20 increase, and Egypt $31. In Algeria, per capita

income dropped from $272 to $225, in Haiti from $273 to $243, and in Indonesia from $77 to $75. By comparison, real per capita income during this same period increased $714 in the United States, $831 in Japan, and $890 in West Germany.[4]

Demographic Patterns

With the introduction of modern medicine and sanitation, death rates have been cut drastically in almost every industrializing agrarian society. But except in a few cases, birthrates have remained high, often over 40 per 1,000 population annually (see Table 13.2). Year in, year out, the populations of the underdeveloped nations continue to swell, consuming most of their hard-won gains in productivity.

Table 13.3 shows in detail the cost of uncontrolled population growth for the industrializing nations of southern and eastern Asia and Latin America. Had they been able to maintain a balance between births and deaths from 1938 to 1961, their per capita income would have grown at a faster rate than industrial societies experienced during that period. Instead, they fell further behind, even in Latin America, where the average annual increase in gross national product was greater than in industrial societies.

Uncontrolled population growth is a serious problem for industrializing

TABLE 13.2   Crude birthrates, death rates, and rates of natural increase for selected industrializing agrarian societies, 1973

Nation	Crude Birthrate*	Crude Death Rate*	Rate of Natural Increase
Peru	48.8	11.1	37.7
Mexico	43.2	8.9	34.3
Colombia	44.6	10.6	34.0
Philippines	44.7	12.0	32.7
Thailand	42.8	10.4	32.4
Indonesia	48.3	19.4	28.9
Iran	45.4	16.6	28.8
Brazil	37.8	9.5	28.3
India	42.8	16.7	26.1
Turkey	39.6	14.6	25.0
Sri Lanka	29.5	7.7	21.8
Egypt	34.8	13.1	21.7
China	33.1	15.3	17.8
Portugal	20.1	11.1	9.0
Greece	15.3	8.7	6.6

Source: *Statistical Abstract of the U.S., 1975*, p. 839.
*The terms "crude birthrate" and "crude death rate" refer to the number of live births and the number of deaths per 1,000 population per year.

TABLE 13.3 Increases in gross domestic product and in per capita gross domestic product for three sets of societies, 1950–1969

Set of Societies	Percentage Increase in GDP, 1950–1969	Percentage Increase in *per Capita* GDP, 1950–1969
Industrial societies, except Communist bloc	141	93
Industrializing societies:		
East and Southeast Asian	134	53
Latin American and Caribbean	160	57

Source: Adapted from United Nations, *Statistical Yearbook, 1970,* table 4.

societies not only because it means so many more mouths to feed but also because it complicates the entire process of societal development. For one thing, mass public education is prohibitively expensive in these nations, and yet without it the population is not equipped for most kinds of jobs in modern industry. This forces large numbers of people to find employment in traditional industries, especially farming. But even there they cannot be accommodated except by subdividing already small farms to the point where they are hopelessly inefficient and the introduction of modern machinery is impossible. In Egypt, for example, 70 per cent of the farm owners had less than half an acre in 1950.[5] As one writer observed, "Most of those who are working the land work not because the land requires their labor but because they require the work."[6] He went on to say that as early as 1939 it was estimated that 10 per cent of Egypt's farmers could have supplied all the necessary labor if Egypt's farms had been even half as mechanized as America's were. The story is much the same in other industrializing agrarian societies.

Another complication results from the fact that the surplus population is too poor to buy anything but the most basic traditional commodities. Thus they do not generate a demand for the many kinds of industrial products that are an essential component of the economy of every industrial society. Finally, this surplus population compounds all the other problems by its own productive achievements: an abundance of children. The society is thus trapped in a vicious circle.

In view of all this, it is hardly surprising to learn that there is a correlation of −.49 (see Glossary) between the birthrate and the average annual growth of per capita productivity. This indicates a strong relationship between high birthrates and low rates of economic progress.[7]

In recent years the leaders of a few of these industrializing societies have finally begun to grasp the seriousness of the population problem and its relation to economic growth, and have encouraged the use of modern

FIGURE 13.2   Squatters' settlement, Lima, Peru.

methods of contraception. Their efforts have not been very successful, however, largely because children are still perceived as an economic asset by the average peasant farmer. While they are growing up, they are cheap labor, and when their parents are too old to work, the children can support them. If too many children survive to adulthood, they can always go to the cities to work. Unfortunately, modern sanitation and medicine are keeping so many children alive that they frequently migrate to the cities in search of jobs that do not exist, or jobs they can fill only while they are young and vigorous. After that, they drift into the growing ranks of the underemployed and the unemployed and become a drain on the economy. According to a recent United Nations study, people like these largely comprise the squatter settlements and shantytowns that contain from one-fourth to two-thirds of the populations of most Third World metropolises.[8] Moreover, these settlements are growing at an annual rate of 12 per cent a year, which means they will double in size in less than seven years.

By the middle 1970s, there began to be signs of a new urgency with regard to population control, especially in India. Early in 1976, the state of Maharashtra, which has a population of 55 million, adopted a law that provides jail sentences and fines for couples of childbearing age who have three or more children and refuse sterilization.[9] Introducing the legislation, the state's minister of health said, "If the alarming rate of growth is not checked it will be impossible to remove poverty and realize the fruits of economic development." The state assembly approved the bill by a vote of 75 to 1, and two other states have since adopted similar measures. The national government, meanwhile, has announced that in the case of food and other shortages, preferences will be given to those who have limited the size of their families. In Mrs. Gandhi's words, "I do not believe in compulsion, but if there is a shortage it is obvious that what is available must go to those who follow our policies and not to others."[10] India hopes to reduce its birthrate to 25 per 1,000 by 1984; and Maharashtra hopes to achieve zero population growth by 1991. Not long ago, these goals would have sounded much too optimistic to be taken seriously, but the latest reports by the Indian government indicate that 2.6 million men and women were sterilized in a recent twelve-month period.[11]

Taiwan is another industrializing society that has recognized the need for vigorous governmental action. The Taiwanese have created a system whereby couples with two children receive a credit of $25 a year for a period of ten years, with the accumulated funds plus interest later made available for the children's education. If a third child is born, the annual payments are cut in half, and a fourth child disqualifies the family.[12] The most recent figures on the birthrate in Taiwan indicate striking success: 23.8 births per 1,000 population per year, a figure closer to those in advanced industrial societies than in traditional agrarian.[13] If other Third and Fourth World nations are willing to initiate measures comparable to India's and Taiwan's, there is reason to hope that the era of runaway population growth is drawing to a close and that standards of living in these nations may soon begin to improve.

The Economy

The economies of industrializing societies can be divided into two basic parts. The traditional component is very similar to the economy of the typical agrarian society of the last 2,000 years. The tools and techniques are much the same, and so, unhappily, is the level of productivity. In contrast, the modern—or at least modernizing—component uses tools, techniques, and patterns of economic organization that have, for the most part, been borrowed from industrial societies.

Obviously, this division results in tremendous internal variation within each developing nation. The people in some areas are living just about the way their forebears did a thousand years or more ago, while other areas are already well on the way to industrialization. Table 13.4 shows the situation in Greece, but a similar situation exists in most societies of this type.

But the modernizing sector of these societies is not simply a scaled-down version of the economy of the average industrial society—a few small steel mills, a small automobile plant or two, some textile mills, wholesale and

TABLE 13.4 Some indicators of regional differences in Greece

Indicators	Attica or Greater Athens	Thrace
Per capita consumption of electric energy in kilowatt-hours	833	34
Private cars per 10,000 inhabitants	168	8
Percentage of households with inside baths or showers	30	2
Percentage of households with drinking water installation	72	21
Number of doctors per 10,000 inhabitants	33	3
Number of hospital beds per 10,000 inhabitants	142	17

Source: Centre of Planning and Economic Research, *Draft of the Five Year Economic Development Plan for Greece* (Athens, 1965), p. 147, cited by Nikos Mouzelis and Michael Attalides, "Greece," in Margaret Archer and Salvador Giner (eds.), *Contemporary Europe* (New York: St. Martin's, 1972), p. 187.

retail distributors, and so forth. Compared with more advanced economies, the modern sector in the average underdeveloped country is very one-sided or imbalanced and very highly specialized.

To understand why this is so, we have to recognize the tremendous difference between the circumstances under which these nations are industrializing and those under which Western Europe and the United States industrialized. Today's developing nations have to make the transition in a world dominated politically and economically by *already industrialized* nations, nations that have well-established home markets with high volumes of sales, nations that have become the builders of industrial machinery for the rest of the world. Add to this the relatively low cost of moving goods today, and the industrializing countries are left without much of a competitive advantage *even in their home markets*; European, American, and Japanese firms can easily undersell Latin American and Asian manufacturers in a wide variety of fields, especially in heavy and technologically advanced industries.

As a result, many of the industrializing societies have been forced into a peculiar ecological niche: they have become the producers of the world's raw materials. Furthermore, because of pressures generated by world markets and by their own desire to maximize income, they often become dangerously specialized (see Table 13.5).

Any nation that depends so heavily on just one commodity is highly vulnerable to shifts in the world economy that affect its specialty. Technological innovations in particular (e.g., synthetic fibers, coffee or sugar substitutes) may permanently reduce, or even eliminate, demand for the product. This sensitivity to change creates an unstable "boom or bust" atmosphere, hardly conducive to rational economic planning and development by businessmen or government. Instead, it encourages a speculative attitude whose goal is to make quick profits and then transfer capital to less risky ventures.

FIGURE 13.3 Two views of an industrializing society: peasants plowing near Karlovac, and city scene in Belgrade.

TABLE 13.5 Leading exports of selected industrializing agrarian societies and percentage dependence on these exports for foreign exchange

Society	Commodity	Percentage Dependence
Iran	Petroleum	86
Cuba	Sugar	77
Chile	Copper	75
Jamaica	Bauxite	65
Bolivia	Tin	52
Colombia	Coffee	50
Indonesia	Petroleum	50
Pakistan	Textiles	47
Egypt	Cotton	44
Malaysia	Rubber	27
India	Textiles	26
Brazil	Coffee	22
Thailand	Rice	15

Source: Adapted from United Nations, *Yearbook of International Trade Statistics, 1974*, vol. I.

Despite their drawbacks, these specialized industries are an important source of income for developing nations and help them accumulate the capital that is so essential for industrialization. They also help to increase the number of people with modern skills and a modern economic orientation.

It is still too early to say whether the benefits of specialized industries will, in the long run, outweigh the costs. A lot will depend on the attitude of the more advanced nations. If countries like the United States, Japan, the Soviet Union, and the members of the European Economic Community regard industrializing nations simply as pawns to be manipulated and exploited for economic and political advantage, the long-term benefits for the developing nations are likely to be small. On the other hand, if the leading nations act responsibly, they may be able to set the less developed ones on a more hopeful course.

Several Third World nations have decided that the risks of involvement in the world economy outweigh the benefits and are trying to hold their participation in world markets to a minimum. The People's Republic of China has been the pioneer and chief exemplar of this strategy. The decision to strive for economic self-sufficiency was made in the late 1950s. When Chinese leaders concluded that Soviet leaders were using the foreign aid they were then supplying as an instrument of political control, they sent their advisers back to the U.S.S.R. The Soviets retaliated by cutting off virtually all aid.

Since that time, China has made remarkable progress with minimal involvement in the world economy. From the late 1950s to the early 1970s,

China's gross national product appears to have increased at an average annual rate of 4.5 to 5 per cent, even as its foreign trade declined from about 9 per cent of GNP in the 1950s to under 5 per cent in the 1970s.[14] Meanwhile, China has discovered important deposits of oil, which have raised its level of petroleum production from virtually zero to more than half a billion barrels a year. In fifteen years, it is expected that China will be producing 2.8 billion barrels of crude oil annually—a level that will make it one of the world's major producers, comparable to Saudi Arabia and Iran and only slightly behind the United States and the Soviet Union.[15] Western experts feel that these new developments assure China's capacity for continued economic growth and development for decades to come.

Compared to other Third World nations, China is unusually fortunate in that it has not only a wealth of natural resources, but huge domestic markets as well, which means fixed costs can be spread out much farther than in smaller nations. Thus, the prospects for a successful strategy of self-sufficiency are probably greater in China than in any other Third World nation. But others will be watching the Chinese experiment closely and, if it is successful, will be strongly inclined to follow her lead. At least one nation has already done so, in fact: after the new Communist regime took power, Cambodia closed its doors to the outside world. Its first priority appears to be to establish self-sufficiency with respect to food. Once this is assured, it will presumably turn its attention to industrial development.

FIGURE 13.4   State-operated department store in Peking.

The Polity

In industrializing agrarian societies, one of the greatest hindrances to modernization and industrialization has been the kind of governing class they inherited from the past. This class had a good thing going for centuries, and its contemporary members have usually seen no need for change. The ideal society, for them, is the kind that flourished before intellectuals, students, and the common people ever heard of liberty, equality, democracy, socialism, and communism. From their perspective, change is something to be feared and fought—or occasionally, as in the case of aid programs sponsored by industrial societies, exploited for their private benefit.

In the last hundred years, however, a growing number of voices have been raised against the old order and its backward-looking, exploitative character. In some instances proponents of modernization have seized control of the government, with the idea of using the power of the state as a force for political, economic, and social change. These modernizers have been a heterogeneous lot. Some have been military men with a strong spirit of nationalism, like Ataturk and Nasser; some, civilians and democratic socialists, like Nehru. A number have been Communists, like Lenin, Tito, Mao Tse-tung, and Castro, while in at least one case—Iran—the monarch himself played this role.

Would-be modernizers have usually found, however, that it is not enough simply to win control of the government. To implement their plans, they must have the support of thousands of lower- and middle-level officials who are both efficient and honest. Unfortunately, such people are hard to find in societies that for centuries have neglected education and viewed government office as a means for self-aggrandizement. As a result, the efforts of the top leaders are often frustrated by the incompetence and corruption of lesser officials.[16]

One of the most basic questions confronting the leaders of industrializing societies today concerns what role the state should play in the industrializing and modernizing process. In recent decades there have been two radically different models for them to choose from, one provided by western capitalist democracies, especially Britain, France, and the United States, the other by the socialist nations, the Soviet Union and China in particular. In practical terms, the choice has been between a society in which the state plays a limited role in the economy and other areas of life and there are free elections and parliamentary rule, and a society in which the state directs and controls the economy and other areas and a strong political elite dominates the government without permitting free elections.

Until World War II, most would-be modernizers chose the western democracies for their model. Parliamentary government and free elections looked as if they were the key to progress. The adoption of democratic forms by underdeveloped nations, however, seldom produced the expected results. Democratic governments were often toppled by military juntas representing the old order. Even the ones that survived such threats rarely experienced the economic progress they had anticipated.

In recent decades, the rapid advances made by the Soviet Union and China and the promises contained in Marxist theory have made that model an attractive alternative. The key to progress in the socialist model has been the systematic, and if necessary ruthless, mobilization of a society's resources by a regime with a definite plan for the future.

For some years now, leaders in underdeveloped countries have found the choice difficult. On the one hand, they have been attracted by the liberal, humane, and pragmatic principles of the democratic model. On the other hand, they have been impressed by the ability of an authoritarian system to mobilize resources and by its promise of greater political stability and economic progress. Most leaders have come to doubt that a full-fledged democratic system can be both politically stable and economically progressive in a society characterized by widespread poverty and illiteracy among the common people, exploitative traditions among the old upper class, and a critical shortage of technical skill and capital.

As a result, many leaders are experimenting with various hybrid forms, incorporating elements from both of the new models while retaining some elements of their own societies' traditional systems. Egypt's Nasser stated the goals and methods of these hybrid types as well as anyone. The six objectives of the Egyptian revolution, according to him, were "elimination of imperialism and its helpers, elimination of feudalism, elimination of monopoly and its domination of the government, the establishment of universal social justice, the formation of a strong, patriotic, national army, and the creation of sound democratic life."[17] In his view, however, democracy could not be put first, for the effort to establish it would undermine the whole revolutionary effort. In an address to the nation in 1954, he said, "There will be democracy and freedom, but we must first be free from exploitation, despotism, and slavery. I cannot understand how there can be freedom if I am not free to find my bread and make a living, and free to find employment."

In recent years, a growing number of western social scientists have reluctantly concluded that truly democratic regimes are less well equipped to survive the terrible political stresses in these societies and at the same time provide the rate of economic growth essential for their future.[18] The most serious deficiency of democratic regimes in industrializing nations has been their inability to keep up with the nondemocratic and mixed types in the vital area of economic growth. Table 13.6 shows the record of the 1950s and 1960s. As the figures in the right-hand column indicate, the gap between democratic and nondemocratic societies steadily grew. A 1.4 per cent annual growth rate versus a 3.8 per cent growth rate may look unimpressive, but it

TABLE 13.6 Median annual growth rates of per capita real gross domestic product in democratic and nondemocratic industrializing agrarian societies compared, 1950–1969 (in percentages)*

Time Period	Democratic Societies	Nondemocratic Societies	Difference
1950–1959	1.4[†]	2.4	1.0
1960–1964	0.9[‡]	2.3	1.4
1965–1969	1.4[§]	3.8	2.4

Sources: United Nations, *Statistical Yearbook, 1965*, tables 183 and 184; and United Nations, *Statistical Yearbook, 1970*, table 178.
*"Real" indicates the amounts are measured in constant dollars (i.e., the effects of inflation are controlled).
[†]The democratic nations in this period were Brazil, Ceylon, Chile, India, Pakistan, the Philippines, and Uruguay.
[‡]The democratic nations in this period were Brazil, Ceylon, Chile, Greece, India, Jamaica, the Philippines, and Uruguay.
[§]The democratic nations in this period were Ceylon, Chile, Colombia, India, Jamaica, the Philippines, and Uruguay.

means the difference between doubling a nation's per capita income in *fifty* years as opposed to only *twenty*. For people who no longer accept poverty as inevitable, that extra thirty years makes democratic government an insupportable luxury.

Social Stratification

Systems of stratification in industrializing agrarian societies are as varied as the polities and economies with which they are linked. In a number of them, the class structure is still very much like that of agrarian societies of the past, though modified in varying degrees by the influences of industrialization. In others, the traditional class structure has been modified not only by industrialization, but by socialism as well.

In societies of the first variety, the upper class is still largely an aristocracy of long-established, wealthy, land-owning families that dominate the government, army, church, and other basic social institutions. The middle class is relatively small and made up of merchants, lesser officials, lesser members of the religious establishment, and a few prosperous peasants. In addition, it includes increasing numbers of business and professional people with modern education and skills, members of the civil service with modern educational qualifications, and teachers trained in the newer disciplines (e.g., science and engineering). As industrialization and modernization progress, some members of the new middle class even penetrate into the upper classes by virtue of their wealth or political success. In effect, there tend to be two separate systems of stratification in these societies. One, dominant in rural areas, reflects the old order; the other, dominant in urban areas, reflects the new. With the passage of time, the system of stratification based on the new ways tends to become dominant throughout the country as a whole.

In societies where socialist regimes have gained control, the transformation of the system of stratification is quicker and more ruthless. Often, many members of the old upper class are killed, the remainder dispossessed. They are replaced by a new elite made up largely of leading Party cadres (many of whom, ironically, are sons of members of the former upper and middle classes). Merchants and private entrepreneurs are also eliminated from the system of stratification, and their replacements, the managers of state enterprises, make up a significant portion of the new middle and upper strata.

Overall, the system of stratification in these societies closely resembles that in more advanced socialist societies, with two exceptions. First, the proportion of peasants is much greater. Second, under the influence of Maoist ideology, many of these societies are trying to break down some of the historic barriers between the middle class on the one hand and workers and peasants on the other. Their efforts go beyond those of the Soviet Union and East Europe, whose workers and peasants are given job security and salaries that are more like those of the middle strata than is the case in nonsocialist societies. In Maoist nations, however, Party cadres, managers, and professionals are actually required to engage in physical labor periodically, to prevent them from losing touch with the working class and its conditions of life. Because these societies have not given foreign scholars and journalists much opportunity to observe them, it is impossible to say how successful these efforts have been. But this is a major innovation in social structure, and the experiment should be watched closely in the years ahead.

The value of modern education, especially training in engineering and science, is substantial in almost all industrializing societies. This has had one interesting, though almost certainly temporary, consequence: it places the younger generation in a relatively advantageous position. This advantage is often reinforced by the effects of political revolutions. Because they are usually the work of young people who distrust the older generation and prefer to surround themselves with their age peers, revolutions tend to be followed by a period in which youth is an asset and young people are promoted much faster than they would be otherwise. As the Chinese, Russian, and Cuban revolutions demonstrate, however, this is a temporary phenomenon, and revolutionary elites often become gerontocracies.

The major variations in the composition of the lower classes in these societies are the result of differences in level of economic development. The less development, the larger the peasant class and the smaller the urban working class, especially those in factories and other modern industries. Conversely, the more development, the fewer peasants and the more urban workers. At one extreme, 80 to 95 per cent of the labor force in Nepal,

FIGURE 13.5 Life is grim for large numbers of the lower classes in many industrializing agrarian societies: lower-class housing in Rio de Janeiro.

Afghanistan, and Ethiopia are still engaged in agriculture, and only a small percentage in industry. At the opposite extreme, countries like Mexico, Chile, Portugal, Greece, and Bulgaria have less than half of their workers in agriculture and 15 to 25 per cent in manufacturing.[19]

Life is grim for large numbers of the lower classes in many industrializing agrarian societies. High birthrates, moderate and declining death rates, and inadequate educational systems combine to ensure a constant oversupply of unskilled labor, and the situation is naturally aggravated by the economy's shift from men to machines. The excess population typically migrates from rural areas to the cities, where there are at least some employment opportunities for the young and able-bodied. But, as in agrarian societies of the past, aging, accidents, and illness soon deprive them of their economic value, especially when there is a steady stream of fresh labor continually moving into the cities.

The only industrializing agrarian societies that seem to have solved this problem are socialist nations, such as the People's Republic of China and Cuba. There, according to almost all reports, beggary, prostitution, and widespread unemployment and underemployment have been eliminated by drastic authoritarian measures. In effect, the leaders of these nations have traded the political liberties and many of the economic privileges of the small middle class and the elite for the economic benefit of the much more numerous lower classes.

Cleavages and Conflict

Few societies in history have had such serious internal divisions as the majority of those now undergoing industrialization. Most of them are torn not only by the ancient cleavages that have always existed in agrarian and horticultural societies, but by some which are peculiar to societies industrializing at this particular time.

Most basic of the older cleavages in industrializing agrarian societies is that between the few who control the nation's resources and the vast majority who supply the labor and get little more than the barest necessities in return. The traditional cleavages between urban and rural populations and between the literate minority and the illiterate majority are also present, though they may be less pronounced now that advances in transportation and communication have reduced the isolation, and hence the ignorance, of the rural and the illiterate.

FIGURE 13.6   Large numbers of the poor in Calcutta have no place of residence and are compelled to cook, eat, and sleep on the sidewalks.

OH! CALCUTTA!

Modern Calcutta is a city of outrageous paradoxes: a hell hole of filth and disease, whose poor curse it and their bad luck in living there; a city of matchless fascination for its richest citizens, who would not live anywhere else, and for prosperous foreign visitors.

Satahu Sahni, one of its poorer citizens, pulls a rickshaw for a living. He works from 6 A.M. to midnight, earning 52 cents a day. He lives in a one-room hut with his wife and two children. They spend about 40 cents a day for food alone, which provides tea and cookies for breakfast, a wheat cake for lunch, and rice and dried peas for supper. Satahu says of his work, "This job shouldn't be done by any human being, but I couldn't find any other thing to do."

Up and down hills, through broiling molten tar, across rough cobblestones, hauling heavy carts often loaded with more than one passenger as well as freight, Satahu and his fellow rickshaw men run day after day. Summer temperatures that are often above 100, and high humidity, cause a few each day to simply slip from between the shafts of their carts and drop dead. "It's really quite awful lately," said a British-educated Calcuttan, who has his own air-conditioned Mercedes and never rides in a rickshaw. "Not only do the poor runners die, but many passengers are injured when the rickshaws tip over backwards. Quite awful." But Satahu is fortunate compared to the hundreds of thousands of jobless persons and beggars in Calcutta who have no home at all and are forced to sleep on the open sidewalks at night and beg for a little food each day.

Adapted from a copyrighted story by Myron Belkind of
the Associated Press, April 19, 1970, by permission.

As we have already seen, the struggle to industrialize and modernize creates its own cleavages and conflicts. There is a split within the more favored classes, for example, between those educated along traditional lines and those with modern scientific and technical training. These groups have difficulty understanding one another and are mutually prejudiced. Another new cleavage separates the landowning aristocracy and the new elite of industrial entrepreneurs, who frequently surpass the older group in wealth.

As the patrimonial, monarchical system found in most agrarian societies breaks down, many new groups become politically active and many new issues become politically relevant. For example, the political unrest and other changes associated with industrialization often exacerbate historic tensions between religious and ethnic groups. One can see this in such widely scattered countries as Vietnam, Indonesia, India, Lebanon, Iraq, and Guyana, to name but a few whose interethnic or interreligious conflicts have been especially serious. The breakdown of the older political system and efforts to establish a modern regime can also produce serious tensions between civilian political leaders and the military. Struggles between these groups have caused crises in many Latin American, Middle Eastern, and Asian nations. In more democratic countries, mass political parties have introduced yet another cleavage. Although support for the various parties tends to follow other lines of cleavage, it is seldom a perfect reflection of them. Therefore, it creates further divisions within an already badly divided population.[20]

Finally, the rapid rate of change characteristic of industrializing societies invariably creates a cleavage between the generations. Though there are no valid measures, this gap appears to be more serious than the generation gap in societies that have already industrialized. This conclusion is suggested both by the frequency and bitterness of the conflicts between students and political authorities in these nations and by the frequency of revolutionary activity by "young Turks" (the Kemalists in Turkey after World War I, Nasser's associates in Egypt, the Fidelistas in Cuba, Ben Bella in Algeria, the early Apristas in Peru, etc.). We would expect such a split, of course, in societies changing so rapidly. The experiences of the different generations, and thus the information and values on which they base their actions, are so dissimilar that conflict is almost inevitable. Universities are often the centers of discontent, because they bring together large numbers of people who have maximum exposure to new ideas but very little power to implement them. The result, not surprisingly, is often explosive.

Authoritarian governments of both the right and left generally manage to suppress these conflicts so they are not visible to the outside world. Yet as the Chinese experience indicates, suppressing is not the same as eliminating them. When Mao mistakenly assumed in the 1950s that the masses were solidly behind his revolution and announced a new policy of greater political freedom ("Let a hundred flowers bloom, let a hundred schools contend"), the situation quickly threatened to get out of hand. Cleavages within the People's Republic were again revealed during the Great Cultural Revolution of the middle 1960s and its aftermath, with violent conflicts between students and Party cadres, workers and managers, soldiers and civilians, young and old. Then, following Mao's death in 1976, dissension surfaced once more. The fact of the matter is that industrialization and modernization are extremely stressful processes and when the cleavages they generate are added to the historic cleavages inherent in an agrarian social order, the choice is between harsh repression and chronic and endemic conflict.

Education and Economic Development

The importance of education for economic growth is abundantly clear: the most prosperous nations are those that have invested heavily in education. In

FIGURE 13.7   Dissension has surfaced repeatedly within the People's Republic of China: supporters of Chairman Hua demonstrate against radicals following Mao's death.

the United States, Japan, and the Soviet Union—three of the most striking examples of economic growth—"high levels of national expenditure on education preceded industrialization."[21] In czarist Russia as early as the end of the last century, 44 per cent of the men between thirty and thirty-nine were literate, and in urban areas the figure was as high as 69 per cent. In Japan, half the male population was literate a generation before that; and in the United States, 90 per cent of white adults were literate as early as 1840.

Other studies of the relation between education and economic progress reinforce this conclusion. A recent survey of sixty-eight nations found a correlation of .42 (see Glossary) between the rate of annual growth of per capita production and the percentage of children aged five to nineteen attending school, and a correlation of .49 between that growth and the literacy rate.[22]

Developments in a number of industrializing countries, however, suggest that it is not enough simply to provide more education regardless of content. Many of these nations have seriously overemphasized the humanities and classical forms of higher education at the expense of the sciences and engineering. In both Eastern and Western Europe, from one-third to one-half of university students study science or engineering, compared to only 23 per cent in Asia and 16 per cent in Latin America.[23]

These figures are important not only because industrializing societies so urgently need technical and engineering skills but because they have so much trouble absorbing the nontechnical professionals their universities turn out. In India, for example, where, recently, 58 per cent of the students were enrolled in the humanities, fine arts, and law,[24] many graduates simply cannot find jobs that utilize their skills. Unwilling to accept lesser employment (a reflection of the traditional value system of agrarian elites and would-be elites), they become a kind of intellectual proletariat with deep-seated hostilities toward the existing social order. Because such people are easily attracted to revolutionary movements, there is increased political instability, and this in turn hampers economic progress. In short, far from aiding economic growth, an oversupply of nontechnically trained students in a society can actually hinder it.

One might ask why the leaders of these societies allow this kind of educational imbalance to develop. There are several reasons. First, in allowing the humanities to dominate their educational systems, they are following the example of the oldest and most prestigious educational institutions in the world—Oxford, Cambridge, and the famous Continental universities—as well as their own native traditions. Second, it costs much more to provide technical education, and these nations have very limited resources. Finally, it has not been very long since the nature of this problem first became evident. Perhaps in the light of experience these nations will begin to revise their educational programs.

Belief Systems and Ideologies

Most leaders of modernizing movements are convinced that social and economic progress require more than increased capital and improved techniques of production. New creeds and new gods are needed to arouse and mobilize the common people, who, after centuries of frustration, are so often apathetic and take a fatalistic view of life. Ironically, even such a dogmatic and supposedly orthodox Marxist as Mao Tse-tung came to place the spiritual struggle for men's minds and souls on a par with, or even ahead of, the struggle to transform the economy.

Today, in all but the most backward parts of the industrializing agrarian world, there is an intellectual ferment and clash of ideas between the advocates of traditional belief systems and the proponents of newer ones. The situation is often extremely complicated, because both traditionalists and modernizers are themselves divided on many points, while other people favor various blends of the old and the new.

A lot of the intellectual and ideological resistance to modernization has come from advocates of the traditional faiths. In southern and eastern Asia, this means Buddhism, Hinduism, and sometimes Islam; in the Middle East,

FIGURE 13.8   Two faiths.

Islam; in Latin America, Spain, and Portugal, Roman Catholicism. In all these areas, religious leaders have often been the leaders of conservative and traditionalist movements. This is hardly surprising, considering the historical role of these groups in agrarian societies and the nature of their beliefs. In general, they believe that the quest for truth is essentially complete: what people need to know has already been revealed—in the Vedas, or in the Koran, or to the Sangha, or to the Church. True wisdom, in their opinion, lies in turning to religious authorities for guidance and following their directions. In describing the traditionalist approach to education in the Middle East, one writer has said, "Education, as far as it is under the control of the ulema [the spiritual leaders of the Muslim community], is still bound up with authoritarianism, rote learning, and a rigid devotion to ancient authorities—providing only already known solutions to already formulated problems."[25] Traditionalist education in Latin America and southern and eastern Asia is very similar. This approach sees little need for change, unless it is to root out whatever modernizing influences have crept in.

In the late nineteenth and early twentieth centuries, many western intellectuals thought these older faiths would simply die out as their adherents came to recognize the "obvious" superiority of western creeds such as Protestantism, humanism, and socialism. All three of these newer faiths were then winning converts, especially among the better educated, and it looked as if it were only a matter of time until the older faiths would vanish altogether.

Since World War I, however, and even more since World War II, the situation has changed drastically in many areas. With the development of nationalist movements and a growing resistance to colonialism of every kind, many of the traditional faiths have experienced a remarkable reinvigoration. After Sri Lanka won its independence, for example, a significant number of Christian converts there reconverted to Buddhism. In India, Hindu traditionalist forces became strong enough to pass laws forbidding the entry of foreign missionaries. In Egypt, Nasser imprisoned or executed most of the leaders of the Communist Party.

In some instances, this reinvigoration resulted from reform movements within the religious group itself. Vatican Council II, for example, provided a powerful impetus to modernizers within the Roman Catholic Church in Latin America, giving the church renewed vigor in a number of countries.[26] Though professional religious leaders have often been the most conspicuous proponents of traditionalism, they have usually had strong support from the old governing class, especially the large landowners. In fact, the rural population as a whole, emotionally involved in traditional religion and unfamiliar with alternatives, has generally supported them. Members of the old "professions," such as herbalists and practitioners of traditional medicine, have also been strong supporters of traditionalist ideologies and belief systems, because they know their skills would be obsolete and their labor unnecessary in a more modern setting.

Ranged against people like these are individuals and groups who by virtue of educational, occupational, or other experience have been converted to the newer faiths. Early in a modernization movement, a disproportionate number of the leaders are people who were won over to a new outlook during visits to industrialized societies, either as students or as workers.[27] Later, however, most of the leaders are people who were converted by experiences in their own countries. Frequently they are children of members of the old governing class, gravitating, after conversion, to positions of leadership because of their superior training and other resources.

As we noted earlier, there are usually competing movements within the camp of modernizers, some advocating western-style democracy, others the authoritarian socialist model, still others some kind of hybrid system. The liberal western model was the first to be tried in most industrializing agrarian nations. It has had its greatest support from the more prosperous segments of the new middle class—professional men, managers in new industries, and others with modern education. Socialist and communist movements were usually introduced next. Their support has been greatest among intellectuals, students, and the economically insecure—landless peasants, underemployed or unemployed urban workers, and the like.

The hybrid approach to modernization is the most recent and reflects the fact that many of the current generation of leaders have reacted negatively to both of the older models. Their idea is to synthesize not only liberalism and authoritarianism but modernism and traditionalism as well. Most of the nationalist ideologies that have flourished in the industrializing agrarian world since World War II have had a strong element of traditionalism. To some extent, nationalism is a reaction against colonialism, and crucial in the process of nationbuilding, especially in countries that were under foreign control until very recently.

There is more to modern nationalism than this, however: it is also an effort to reassert the importance of the cultural traditions of non-European peoples (in the case of Latin America, of peoples not in the Anglo-American tradition). This helps heal the breach between traditionalists and modernists by providing a position that is more or less acceptable to both. Moreover, it gives dignity to a nation's leaders in their relations with European (or Anglo-American) peoples. In this respect, the function of these nationalist movements is similar to that of the "black nationalist" movement in the United States, which seeks to increase the self-respect of blacks by emphasizing the worth of the black cultural tradition.

Unfortunately, the deliberate cultivation of nationalist sentiments easily leads to the hatred of other nations. Even when this is not a spontaneous development, leaders of industrializing nations may encourage it solely to divert criticism from themselves and their policies. It can be very useful to blame foreigners for all the defects and shortcomings, inevitable and otherwise, of one's own policies. A number of leaders in industrializing nations have succumbed to this temptation, but as the experiences of Sukarno in Indonesia and certain Arab leaders in the Middle East demonstrate, this policy is not without risks of its own.

INDUSTRIALIZING HORTICULTURAL SOCIETIES

Prior to the modern era, advanced horticultural societies were found in several locations in the New World, most of Africa south of the Sahara, and some parts of Southeast Asia. But during the last several centuries, more advanced societies conquered many of these groups and destroyed others by sociocultural assimilation (the fate of many hill tribes in India).[28]

In Africa south of the Sahara, however, things have been different. There, much of the traditional horticultural way of life has survived into the second half of the twentieth century, apparently because the period of European colonial rule was so brief and its impact on most of the native societies relatively limited. It is easy to forget that the period of European rule in most of sub-Saharan Africa did not begin until the last decades of the nineteenth century and ended early in the second half of the twentieth. Thus the process of institutional disintegration and transformation in these societies was just beginning when colonialism ended. By contrast, many of the horticulturalists in the New World and Southeast Asia have been under alien control since the sixteenth century or longer. For this reason, the concept of industrializing horticultural societies is really applicable only in Africa south of the Sahara.

The problems of these societies are similar in a number of respects to those of industrializing agrarian societies. Both are confronted with a variety of radically new social and cultural elements introduced by diffusion from technologically more advanced societies. Both find that these new elements throw their traditional relations out of kilter and create serious tensions. Furthermore, both experience an almost continuous state of crisis because things are changing so fast.

At the same time, there are a number of important differences between them that reflect their horticultural and agrarian backgrounds and often cause them to react differently to the impact of industrialization. To avoid unnecessary repetition, we will focus mainly on these differences, referring only briefly to the points of similarity. Unless this is kept in mind, the differences between industrializing agrarian and industrializing horticultural societies may appear to be greater than they actually are.

Technology, Productivity, and Demographic Patterns

Technologically, industrializing horticultural societies are much less advanced than industrializing agrarian, especially in their indigenous (native) technology. This is revealed in a number of ways. For one thing, they are much less urbanized: in one recent year, industrializing agrarian societies had an average of 27 per cent of their populations in cities of 20,000 or more, while industrializing horticultural societies had only 9 per cent in cities that large.[29] This is important, because the size of the urban population is a good measure of the size of the economic surplus and of the growth of specialized crafts and trade and commerce.

Another indication of the technological and economic lag of horticultural societies is their low level of productivity. The extent of this lag is not usually revealed by the standard measures of productivity, such as per capita income. Using this measure, countries like Ghana, Liberia, Zaire, and Kenya appear to be at least as productive as China, India, and Burma and most of the other industrializing agrarian societies of Southeast Asia. But *per capita* measures of productivity fail to take into account the fact that agrarian technologies and economies are sustaining larger and denser populations. With per capita measures, we actually destroy much of the evidence of the technological superiority of industrializing agrarian societies.

A better way to compare the technological development of societies that are still in the process of industrializing is by *per area* income. The question

then becomes, How much can the society produce per square mile of territory? (There is some distortion even in this measure, because of the influence of large deserts and other unproductive territories, but while such things may appreciably affect the figures for a particular society, their effect on large groups of societies is not great.) Figures on gross national product show nearly a fivefold difference in the productivity of the two types of societies. In forty-nine industrializing agrarian nations, the median value of the gross national product was $10,400 per square mile; in sixteen industrializing horticultural nations, it was only $2,200.[30]

Despite its inferior technological development, the typical industrializing horticultural society has a standard of living roughly comparable to that of the typical industrializing agrarian society. Although its economy is only a fifth as productive, its population is only a fifth as dense.

This low density could turn out to be an extremely valuable asset. Modern methods of birth control are available to these societies at an earlier, more opportune point in their development than in the case of industrializing agrarian societies. Thus, they do not have to become saddled, as most other developing nations are, with huge surplus populations that must be put to work even when their employment reduces the level of productive efficiency (as in the case of peasants working excessively subdivided farms). In the race to industrialize and modernize, most of the advantages—literacy, skilled manpower, commercial experience, urbanization, and so on—lie with industrializing agrarian nations. But low population density is one plus on the side

TABLE 13.7   Crude birthrates in selected industrializing horticultural societies

Society	Crude Birthrate*
Niger	52.2
Rwanda	51.8
Togo	50.9
Dahomey	50.9
Malagasy	50.0
Liberia	49.8
Nigeria	49.6
Kenya	47.8
Guinea	47.2
Ghana	46.6
Zaire	44.1
Uganda	43.2
Gambia	42.5

Sources: United Nations, *Demographic Yearbook, 1974,* table 9.
*Number of births per 1,000 population per year.

of industrializing horticultural nations. Considering how serious the effects of overpopulation are, it is just possible that this single advantage could eventually outweigh all the others.

Unhappily, the current demographic signs in sub-Saharan Africa are discouraging. Birthrates in most of its societies are running close to the human maximum (see Table 13.7). Death rates, meanwhile, have dropped considerably from the old equilibrium level: though there is little reliable evidence, they are estimated to be around 20 per 1,000. The average rate of increase, then, appears to be about 2.5 per cent per year—in other words, dangerously high.

The Economy

Because the urban sector of the economy in horticultural societies is much less developed than in agrarian societies, the urban population has had even less experience with such fundamentals of modern life as money, trade and commerce, markets, occupational specialization, literacy, and bureaucracy. This makes it very difficult for modernizing governments and businesses to find skilled personnel to staff their organizations. The problem is especially serious in an era of nationalism (and nationalism is just as strong in these societies as in industrializing agrarian societies), because national pride often demands that businesses and government be staffed with local personnel, even at the expense of organizational efficiency.[31]

Data on literacy provide some idea of the relative magnitude of this problem for the two types of industrializing societies. In the late 1950s, 44 per cent of the adult population in the average (median) industrializing agrarian society was literate; in industrializing horticultural societies the comparable figure was 7.5 per cent.[32] Assuming literacy as a minimum requirement for effective participation in modern economic life and assuming also that these nations will not be able to increase their rate of literacy any faster than other nations have, it will take industrializing agrarian societies at least fifty years to develop a fully qualified labor force and industrializing horticultural societies at least ninety.[33]

Horticultural societies face still other problems in economic development. We can see why when we consider the nature and meaning of work in traditional settings. Not long ago, the Inter-African Labour Institute characterized work traditions in horticultural Africa this way:

1. Work is viewed in its relation to the basic institution of family or clan; within the family, it is divided on the basis of age and sex.
2. Work is linked with religious rites.
3. Work activities are considered and evaluated in the light of a subsistence economy rather than a profit economy (i.e., one oriented

to the production of the necessities of life rather than to the maximization of profits in a market economy).

4. Work requires neither foresight nor planning.
5. Time is largely irrelevant in work activities; no time limits are set for most tasks.
6. There is little specialization.
7. For men, work is episodic; when a task has to be done, men often do it without a break, but intervals of inactivity are long and frequent.
8. Men hardly ever work alone; work activities (e.g., hunting parties and work parties) often resemble a collective leisure activity in modern industrial society.[34]

These traditions do little to prepare the members of these societies, especially the men, for work in a modern industrial society. A parallel list of the characteristics of work in industrial societies would, in fact, be an almost perfect contradiction.

One of the biggest problems is suggested by item 7. In analyzing horticultural societies, we saw how often farming is primarily women's work. The men's responsibility may be limited to the occasional clearing of new fields. Where women do the sustained, tedious chores—planting, cultivating, and harvesting crops—men are free to do more interesting and exciting things—hunting, fighting, politicking, socializing, and participating in ceremonial activities. The disciplined, routinized forms of work so typical of an industrial economy are seldom encountered by men in these societies. In this respect, the peasant farmers of agrarian societies are far better prepared for industrialization. Yet even they have found the transition difficult.[35]

There is tremendous economic and social variation in sub-Saharan Africa today. At one extreme, a few tribes and villages remain virtually untouched by the influences of industrialization; at the other, the older patterns have been all but destroyed in cities like Dar es Salaam, for example.[36] In between is every conceivable combination of the old and the new—such as the woman in Nairobi who practiced witchcraft in order to earn the down payment on a truck so she could go into the trucking business.[37] (A more common practice is for a person to work part-time in a factory while continuing to practice traditional horticulture.)

One observer reports that there have been four basic economic patterns in Africa in recent years.[38] The first, which is now extremely rare, is a pure subsistence economy in which the local village consumes only what it produces or obtains through barter with its neighbors. The second pattern he calls "taxed subsistence," which means that a village raises a cash crop or sends its young men out to work for cash so it can pay the taxes levied by the government. The third might be called a mixed economy: villagers still rely on a subsistence economy for their basic necessities, but they simultaneously work for cash—not only because of taxes but so they can buy modern consumer goods. The fourth pattern is a predominantly cash economy in which even food is bought and laborers are hired to work on the farms.

These patterns, which typically follow one another in sequence, show how internal and external forces combine to transform a society's economy.

FIGURE 13.9 **Harvesting in a cocoa grove, Ghana. Like many industrializing nations, Ghana is heavily dependent on a single crop; in recent years as much as 60 per cent of its foreign exchange has come from cocoa.**

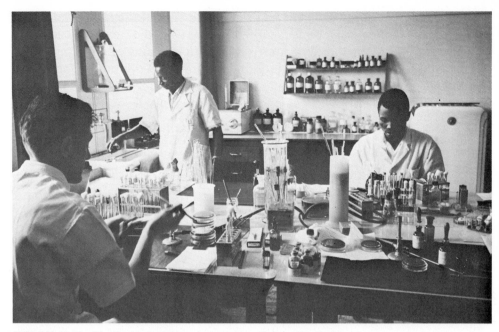

FIGURE 13.10   Medical laboratory, Louvanium University, Zaire.

On one side, there are the preferences and desires of the villagers themselves; on the other, the demands made, and attractions offered, by alien groups and institutions. It is easy to underestimate the power of the internal forces and interpret economic development as a process that is simply forced on reluctant villagers who want only to be left alone to live as their fathers did for centuries. But the problem is far more complex than this romanticized view suggests. Given a choice, most horticultural peoples prefer the industrial way of life—not knowing, it is true, all the implications and ramifications of their choice. Sometimes they adopt it *in toto*, like the family that migrates to the city; sometimes in part, like the couple who stay in the village but earn all the cash they can to buy modern tools, cloth, soap, a sewing machine, a radio, a bicycle, and the other products of an industrial economy.

The Polity

One of the striking features of sub-Saharan Africa is how new most of its societies are: almost without exception, they were established in the late nineteenth or the twentieth century. Most of them are the products of European colonialism, and their boundaries are largely the result of the rivalries of missions or colonial governments, the outcomes of battles, the location of rivers, and a variety of other things that had little to do with the

FIGURE 13.11   Tribal chief on visit to Monrovia, capital of Liberia.

boundaries of the societies they replaced. Actually, the process was not too different from the one that produced most of the modern nations of Europe, Asia, and the New World.

Because of their newness, most African societies suffer from serious internal divisions that stem from traditional tribal loyalties. The colonial powers seldom destroyed the older tribal groups. On the contrary, in most cases they consciously preserved them as instruments of administrative control, allowing tribal rulers to serve as lower-echelon officials in the new colonial societies. Colonial governments often pretended these groups were autonomous in order to put the burden, and the onus, of political control on their leaders. They also encouraged tribal rivalries, applying the ancient principle "Divide and rule." As a result, even after independence was won, there was a fundamental tension between tribal loyalties and national loyalties in most parts of Africa. This is one problem that few industrializing agrarian societies have had to contend with.

The consequences have been serious for sub-Saharan societies, howev-

TRIBAL LAW VERSUS NATIONAL LAW:
THE CASE OF THE MARAKAWET ELDERS

On March 17, 1971, Kap sirir rap Koech, better known as Chelimo, a member of the Marakawet tribe in Kenya, had a quarrel with his wife and beat her to death. He then fled into the bush, but his brothers, following tribal custom, hunted him down and brought him before village elders, who, after deliberation, rendered the verdict of death, a judgment that was accepted by both of the families involved. Chelimo was then tied face down on the ground, and his older brother and the father of his murdered wife together brought large stones and smashed the back of his head. Word of their action came to government authorities, and Kibor, the brother, and Kirop, the father, were brought to trial under national law, which is based on English law, and were themselves condemned to death for murder.

In discussing the case, a reporter for the *Los Angeles Times* wrote, "In more developed countries, like Britain and the United States, the law has evolved naturally, coming out of the folkways of the people. But in Africa, the law has been imported from an alien country and imposed upon a host of traditional laws of many different tribes.

"At independence, the new African leaders could have thrown out the colonial law and reverted to the old tribal laws. But they did not. Mainly because they feared chaos. The leaders want to create unified states, and unity would be held back if each small tribe practiced a law of its own.

"Selecting one tribal law and imposing it on all the others might even be more divisive. So the leaders decided to retain the foreign law that had become common to all tribes during colonial days.

"There was another reason. The new leaders consider themselves modern, educated men, and in their view much of traditional tribal law was not 'civilized.' They did not want justice governed by such law.

"But the use of European law has not been absolute. There has been an attempt, both in colonial days and now, to bend the European law to accommodate some of the traditional tribal law. In some cases, in fact, tribal law or, as it is called in the courts, 'customary law,' guides the decision of judges. If this were not the case, the legal system would be so alien that the people would attempt to ignore it."

er. In Zaire and Angola, tribal divisions nearly destroyed the new nations after independence. In Nigeria and Burundi, the fuse burned more slowly, but the results were even worse. In most other countries, tribalism remains an important divisive force, sometimes with the potential for civil war.[39] When they were fighting for independence, many African leaders (as well as their friends in the western academic world) ignored or minimized the importance of these tribal loyalties, thinking that their countrymen valued them as little as they did and that the old ties were rapidly losing their vitality. Although this seems to be true in a few countries, it has proved a serious misjudgment in most.[40] Even in cities and towns, tribal loyalties are still meaningful to some degree.[41] In the light of American experience with ethnic loyalties, and considering the virtual absence of national institutions in Africa until recently, this is hardly surprising. With increasing urbanization, with the establishment of schools that indoctrinate children in a nationalistic outlook, and with the growth of the mass media to reinforce these early lessons, tribal loyalties will eventually disappear. But this will probably take decades, and in the meantime these allegiances will produce many bitter conflicts.

In other respects, the polities of industrializing horticultural societies have a lot in common with those of industrializing agrarian societies. Planning efforts, even basic administrative activities, are often hamstrung by the lack of trained personnel and by commitments to rapid Africanization of the civil service. This is especially serious because most of these governments are also committed to programs of economic planning and development, a notoriously difficult and complex business.[42]

Another important similarity is the trend that one writer has referred to as "the erosion of democracy."[43] Prior to independence, most political leaders in these countries professed to be democrats in the West European sense, in other words, to believe in parliamentary government, a multiparty system, free elections, and so forth. Very soon, however—confronted by opposition that threatened to turn them out of office or by incipient chaos resulting from the tribalization of politics and the return to power of tribal chiefs and other proponents of traditionalism—most of them shifted to advocacy of a one-party state with control largely or wholly in the hands of a strong executive (i.e., themselves). In a number of countries, civilian government was terminated and leadership assumed by the military.

Although many of the new governments have survived thus far, the pressures on them are often intense. One British observer has outlined the process that commonly develops in the wake of independence:

As a new African government first assumes power, there seems to be much in its favor. There is enthusiasm, there are congratulations and good wishes from the world; many promotions to make, ambassadorships to be filled, national development plans to occupy energies and give a sense of progress and achievement. Above all, it is an African government, it is "ours."

But there is a debit side. Naturally, the age-old frustrations of being governed were turned against the colonial power over years of agitation and electioneering. The anti-colonial struggle had aroused much expectation of greater freedom from restraint which is not compatible with the other goals of the nationalist movement. Nervous [foreigners] had often quoted the wilder expectations of the uneducated ("We shall print more bank notes"; "The Bank will be nationalized and forced to give us loans") and as caricature these stories are not important. But there is a more serious side. In rural areas there could be great impatience with continuing agricultural reform; and in the modern sector much expectation of a quick inheritance of opportunities and profits of expatriate trade [i.e., businesses owned by foreigners]. And there are other reversals. The Trade Unions, once a weapon of anti-colonialism, may seem to be sabotaging the national effort.[44]

He goes on to describe the problems national leaders face in their attempts to control the self-seekers within their party organizations and concludes that "The imposition of a standard of conduct and discipline is a trying task for a victorious party."

But these problems are all secondary compared with the really serious ones. Although they take different forms in different countries, these are common to most: "tribalism; the conflict between traditional and modern— the old authority and the new democratic forms; the control and status of land; the whole system of local administration; and ultimately, the moral standards and social norms which are to be established in society."[45] With the elimination of the colonial regime, all the hostilities are now focused on the new national governments—and this is sometimes more than they can handle without repressive measures.

Social Stratification

Most of the new nations in sub-Saharan Africa profess socialist ideals. In practice, however, this usually means a concern with economic development combined with a commitment to the principles of central planning. There has been much less concern about social inequality, probably because the level of inequality, until recently at least, was low compared to that found in industrializing agrarian and industrial societies.[46] Also, there was not the grinding poverty for millions that has been characteristic of agrarian and early industrial societies.

With the elimination of the colonial powers, a new upper class is emerging. In some areas, such as northern Nigeria, the upper class is made up of the rulers of the old society: the chiefs, kings, or emirs, together with their ministers and retainers. Where the modernizers are in control, the more typical situation, the upper class is largely composed of the new political and intellectual elite and, in most countries, the new entrepreneurial elite.

**FIGURE 13.12 Where
modernizers are in control,
the upper class is made up
largely of the new political
and intellectual elite: Jomo
Kenyatta, first prime
minister of Kenya,
graduate of the London
School of Economics and
author of the highly
regarded ethnography,
*Facing Mt. Kenya.***

Beneath the economically and politically dominant class, there are two
fairly distinct systems of stratification. In the rural areas, where traditional
patterns prevail, an individual's status is largely a function of his own or his
family's relation to traditional authorities (the village headman, the tribal
chief, etc.). In urban areas, where the modern system of stratification is
centered, education, occupation, income, and connections with the new
political authorities become the crucial criteria.

Cleavages and Conflict

By now it should be clear that industrializing horticultural societies are as
badly divided as industrializing agrarian societies. They, too, are heir to

nearly all the cleavages of traditional societies, and most of those of modern industrial societies as well. In one respect, however, their situation is even worse than the agrarian: because they are such young nations, they are still divided along tribal lines. This is a powerful divisive force, because it involves deep emotional commitments, always difficult to control by rational, political procedures. But time is on the side of the advocates of national unity: with each passing decade, the older loyalties weaken. Therefore, if civil war can be avoided for the next several decades, the problem will probably be resolved in most of these societies.

Religion and Ideology

The traditional religions of sub-Saharan Africa were relatively undeveloped, both organizationally and intellectually. There were no complex organizations of priests or monks, as in the major religions of the agrarian world, no body of sacred writings to serve as the core of a common faith, no tradition of religio-philosophical speculation, and, most important of all, no supranational faith uniting the members of different societies. As a result, these faiths could not easily defend themselves against the inroads of Islam and Christianity, especially when these were being introduced by peoples who were politically and economically stronger and whose way of life, therefore, seemed so obviously worthy of emulation.

Africans who still cling to the older tribal faiths are usually residents of the more isolated rural areas or the less educated residents of the towns. Since this describes the majority of the people in these societies, adherents of the older faiths are obviously still numerous. In Zaire, for example, only 30 per cent of the people are even nominally Christian or Muslim, in Zambia 13 per cent.[47] In the cities, however, the picture is very different. In Dar es Salaam, a city of 100,000 in Tanzania, 99.8 per cent of the population claim to be either Muslim or Christian—and this in a country still 60 per cent non-Muslim and non-Christian.[48] Similarly, in Monrovia, the capital of Liberia, 72 per cent regard themselves as either Christian or Muslim, although in the country as a whole, only 9 per cent do so.[49]

Conversions to Islam and Christianity are frequently for nonreligious reasons. For many, conversion is simply a status symbol, an effort to identify with modern ways and avoid being regarded as an ignorant, backward countryman. In Dar es Salaam, for example, many pagan tribesmen "on arrival in town call themselves Muslims—some few call themselves Christians—in order to conform, not to be conspicuous in a [community] where Islam is supreme and where to 'have no religion,' as people put it, is the mark of the uncivilized. Some go so far as to be circumcised and to be formally admitted to Islam: most merely use a Muslim name instead of a tribal one; some have two names, a Christian and a Muslim, to cover all eventualities."[50] Under the circumstances, it is hardly surprising to find that "the outward observances of religion are strikingly absent in Dar es Salaam: it is rare to see an African Muslim praying his daily prayers [and] in Ramadhan [the Muslim month of fasting] people may be seen anywhere eating and drinking publicly during the daily hours [a forbidden practice]," and the consumption of alcohol, also forbidden, is almost universal.[51] In Monrovia, where Christianity is dominant, the pattern is not quite so pronounced, but even here "the professing of Christianity remains a basic requirement of 'civilized' status," and "for a great many of the civilized, church membership has become largely a question of social status, and has little more significance than membership [in] other types of associations."[52] In many areas, both urban and rural, even those who have adopted Christianity or Islam continue traditional pagan practices.[53]

In the early years of colonial rule, Christian missions were an important force for modernization. This was primarily due to the mission schools, which introduced literacy and elements of western culture and, most important of all, opened up channels of communication with the larger world. As a result, the areas that came under Christian influence advanced more rapidly than those where paganism or Islam prevailed. In discussing Tanzania, one writer asserts:

> Mission schools and mission hospitals have been very important factors in changing tribal society, although their influence has been felt much more strongly in some areas than others. Very nearly a one-to-one correlation exists between mission influence, the cash-crop economy, fertile land, education, and the general desire for progress.[54]

Similarly, many visitors to Africa have commented on the singular success of the Christian Ibo of southeastern Nigeria compared with the Muslim and pagan tribes to the north.

With the rise of the independence movement after World War II, identification with Christianity became an ambiguous social attribute. Christianity was linked with colonialism, and colonialism was, by definition, a force detrimental to Africa. The missionaries came under heavy attack for dominating the churches and refusing to let native Christians assume positions of leadership. Furthermore, in an era of great social change and uncertainty, mission-brand Christianity often seemed too tame and too western. In many areas, native leaders founded new sects, some basically Christian, others largely pagan, many a mixture of the two.[55] These sects have their greatest appeal for individuals who are in midpassage in the difficult transition from traditional culture to modern. Such people are subject to great insecurity, both economically and intellectually, and the sects often provide an element of reassurance. They also are popular because they accept polygyny and other traditional African practices condemned by the missionaries.

In sub-Saharan Africa, as in other industrializing areas, nontheistic faiths also compete with the older faiths. The most important of these is nationalism. In many cases, nationalism functions simply as a secular ideology. But sometimes, when it demands supreme loyalty, it assumes a truly religious character. In Ghana, for example, President Nkrumah assumed messianic titles, and his political party took on quasi-religious functions.[56] This tendency is so marked that some students of the modernization process now speak of *political* religion in contrast to *church* religion.[57] Whether nationalism will survive in this extreme form no one can say. Its chances are probably linked with the new nations' efforts to modernize: the quicker and easier the modernization process, the poorer the chances for an extreme nationalism; the slower the change, and the more painful, the likelier it becomes.

Kinship and Family

In the traditional horticultural societies of precolonial Africa, kin groups were extremely important. As one writer put it, in Africa "the [kin group] was the basic building block of society."[58] More than that, it was psychologically the center of the individual's world, establishing his identity and defining most of his basic rights and responsibilities.

Now the historical bases of power of the kin group are being destroyed. In the modern sector of the economy, the kin group no longer controls its members' access to the means of livelihood as it traditionally did through its control of the land. Similarly, family ties lose much of their political value when there is an increasingly impersonal governmental bureaucracy to be dealt with. Last but not least, the cult of the ancestors, centered in the kin group, declines in importance as Christianity and Islam grow.

Under the old system, most of the advantages of the kin group were enjoyed by the older generation, while the disadvantages fell disproportionately on the younger. Before the growth of cities and towns, young people had no choice but to accept the burdens and patiently await the day when they would become the privileged elders. Industrialization changed all this: at the very least, it offered youth a way to escape the authority of the elders, at best, a rise to fame and fortune beyond the wildest dreams of those who stayed in the villages.

We get some idea of this change from the following excerpt from a document written by an African townsman explaining to a European why Africans leave the villages. In it, he describes a typical conversation between two young villagers, one of whom says:

> Lucas, old boy, we have a very hard life here in the country; the authorities—I don't know if it is the chief or his assistants—have their knives into us. And as for Father and even Mother! . . . Listen, it was only the other day, you've seen the

maize, cucumbers, and vegetables, all ripe? Well, this day hunger followed me around all day, I ran away from it but my feet wouldn't get me away, so I thought it best to go to our field and help myself to some cucumber. I admit I took one and swallowed it down without chewing. Then I got a mad desire to eat some maize and broke off three and went home to roast them. Presto, as the first was ready I began to eat it, then the second, when in come my parents from visiting. They see me and start straight in to abuse me, tell me never to darken their door again. That evening there was a big storm with lightning, one bolt of which struck a tree in that field and it fell and ruined a stretch of crops: then in the morning everyone said: Ah, yes, Juma ate unblessed food before we had sacrificed, that's why their field was destroyed. So the news spread and they sent me to expiate it, and when I got there the omens were against me and I was an outcast to the whole village. My father is an old man but he has no gratitude; since he was exempted from tax he has been to work for the chief only five times, every time it is his turn it's me that goes. . . .

I hate it here, better get a change of air—town air—even if it kills me. I am lucky enough to have borrowed the fare down, though I haven't enough to come back. But every day they sit on me, and now there is nothing for it but to disappear and give myself a break; in the town there are many people and many jobs, but here what job can a chap get? It's just the messenger coming in the morning, early, with a little bit of paper summoning me to the court; you get there and they tell you, you are charged by the agricultural inspector for not having a cassava field; if you ask who the inspector himself is, you're told, "That child over

FIGURE 13.13   The lure of the city: Lagos, capital of Nigeria.

there." If you ask who is prosecuting and where he is they'll say, "So you are one of these bush lawyers are you? Do you suppose a full agricultural inspector will tell lies?"

Elders like this are not to be borne, in the end you may be had up for murder, better go to town where nobody knows me, and nobody will say what's that you're eating, what's that you're wearing, every man for himself and mind his own business: but here! You've only to cough and somebody ticks you off for getting your feet wet.

Last week I returned from safari with the dresser, carrying his loads, and only a little later they volunteered me again to carry the [District Commissioner's] loads, nothing but work, any time there's loads to be carried it's always me. . . . Well now, the rains are starting and lorries won't pass, off I go again. Soon I'll develop wheels and be a public service vehicle. Go to town any day.[59]

Family life in the village was obviously not the idyllic experience that those who romanticize simpler societies make it appear. For thousands of young Jumas, the choice is clear.

Actually, the break with one's family and kin is seldom as sharp as Juma's musings suggest. When they get to town, young men usually search out their kinsmen, who help them find employment and get settled. But in the long run the ties with family and kin group are seriously weakened, and industrializing horticultural societies have not yet developed any real substitute for them.[60] This is a fairly serious source of social instability, yet the experience of industrial societies suggests it is inevitable.

Another problem confronting these societies is the shift from polygyny to monogamy. Polygyny was practiced in almost all the traditional horticultural societies of sub-Saharan Africa, while monogamy, as we have seen, is the rule in all modern industrial societies. Although the Christian missions fought polygyny vigorously, they had only limited success. Their opposition to it is, in fact, reputed to be one of the major reasons many Africans have been reluctant to be baptized. Eventually, however, the same forces responsible for monogamy in other industrial and industrializing societies will probably prevail here.

Considering the historical importance of kinship in horticultural Africa, such revolutionary changes are bound to be unsettling. Their effects will be felt at both the individual and the societal levels for a long time to come.

INDUSTRIALIZING SOCIETIES: PROSPECTS AND PROBLEMS

Not too many years ago, the prospects for industrializing societies looked bright and promising. All they had to do, apparently, was follow in the path blazed by the industrial nations of Western Europe and North America. In fact, by coming along later, they could profit from the others' experience, avoid many of their problems, and speed up the entire modernization process.

So it seemed.

A quarter of a century later, this prediction seems ludicrous. Far from occupying a favored position in history, industrializing societies today are in a singularly disadvantageous one. They are increasingly drawn into a global economic system in which industrial societies hold almost all of the high cards. If they want to participate, they have to abide by rules the others lay down, and one of those rules is that they play the restrictive and hazardous role of supplier of raw materials, often of a single commodity. Thus they become economically dependent on countries that know little, and care less, about the consequences of this dependency.

An economy evolving under these conditions is naturally going to develop differently than Europe's and the United States' economies did in the nineteenth century. Instead of starting out producing things like textiles, iron, coal, and machine tools, which led those nations to develop skilled labor forces and balanced economies, the nation industrializing today starts out by furnishing bananas or coffee, rubber or petroleum, in a highly competitive world market. And in most cases these things are not even produced by native firms, but by firms from industrial nations, firms whose interest in their

TABLE 13.8 Nations and corporations: a comparison of the gross national products of selected industrializing nations and the annual sales volumes of selected corporations, 1974, in billions of dollars

Nation or Corporation	GNP or Sales	Nation or Corporation	GNP or Sales
Mexico	$48.7	Philips Gloeilampenfab	$9.4
Exxon	45.0	U.S. Steel	9.2
General Motors	31.5	Egypt	9.1
Austria	27.9	Israel	9.0
AT&T	26.2	Nippon Steel	8.8
Iran	25.6	Pakistan	8.3
Ford	23.6	Hoechst	7.8
Turkey	22.0	Chile	7.6
Norway	18.8	Nestle Chocolate	5.6
British Petroleum	18.3	Morocco	5.0
Standard Oil of California	17.9	Lockheed Aircraft	3.3
Greece	16.3	Ghana	2.9
Sears Roebuck	13.1	Colgate-Palmolive	2.6
South Korea	12.4	Burma	2.4
Portugal	11.2	Chicago Pneumatic Tool	0.3
ITT	11.2	Dahomey	0.3

Sources: *The World Almanac, 1976*, pp. 84 and 681–682; and *Moody's Handbook of Common Stocks*, Summer 1976.

host nation is restricted to its raw materials and its unskilled labor. This is as likely to foster the growth of a depressed rural proletariat as it is to encourage the development of a skilled labor force and a balanced economy.

Then, as the developing nation tries to establish industries really its own, to build factories and branch out into something beyond raw materials, it is confronted by another hard fact: because most secondary industries are dominated by huge, immensely wealthy corporations based in industrial societies, small, new firms simply cannot compete. A single corporation, Exxon, has annual sales six times greater than *the entire gross national product* of a country the size of Chile (see Table 13.8). Because of the vast resources at their disposal, and because of the vast markets they control, such corporations can afford to adopt the latest technology as soon as it becomes available. Small firms with limited sales cannot: they must keep old equipment in use much longer in order to write off their investment in it. As we have seen before, the market system favors larger units at the expense of smaller ones.

Meanwhile, the one real gift of advanced nations to their industrializing cousins has backfired. Modern methods of sanitation and preventive medicine have worked—too well. Death rates have dropped dramatically, but birthrates have not. As a result, populations in industrializing nations are growing alarmingly.

Like so many other problems of development, this one was not nearly so severe for societies that industrialized earlier. The reason is simply that no one handed those societies any ready-made death preventives. In this area,

TABLE 13.9 Average annual rates of population growth of industrializing societies in three periods

	Population Growth Rate 1815–1870		Population Growth Rate 1870–1925		Population Growth Rate 1963–1969
Great Britain	1.1	Romania	1.3	Philippines	3.5
Scandinavia	1.1	Poland	1.1	Iraq	3.5
Germany	1.0	Russia	1.1	Brazil	3.0
Netherlands	1.0	Balkans	0.8	Kenya	2.9
Belgium	0.9	Hungary	0.7	Ghana	2.7
Switzerland	0.8	Italy	0.6	India	2.5
France	0.4	Spain and Portugal	0.5	Indonesia	2.5
				United Arab Republic	2.5
				Pakistan	2.1
				China	1.4

Sources: The data for 1815–1925 were computed from Helmut Haufe, *Die Bevolkerung Europas* (Berlin, 1936) by Bert Hoselitz and are reported in "Advanced and Underdeveloped Countries: A Study in Development Contrasts," in William B. Hamilton (ed.), *The Transfer of Institutions* (Durham, N.C.: Duke, 1964), p. 39; the data for 1963–1969 are from United Nations, *Statistical Yearbook, 1970*, table 18.

**FIGURE 13.14 Hunger and
starvation remain serious
problems in much of the Third
and Fourth Worlds: resident in
the Home for the Dying
Destitute, Calcutta.**

as in others, there was a more coordinated pattern of development among the various parts of the sociocultural system. But the industrializing nation today has been given a powerful assist in increasing its population—without a comparable boost in other critical areas of development.

As Table 13.9 indicates, when the nations of Europe were in the process of industrializing, they had an average annual population growth rate of only 1 per cent. By contrast, most societies industrializing today are growing more than 2 per cent a year. This means, quite simply, that much of the potential for increased capital investment and for improvements in the standard of living is being swallowed up in the effort to feed, clothe, and house more and more people whose labor is not needed.

Runaway population growth portends a serious food crisis for many of these countries, and in the not too distant future. New techniques of farming (e.g., the use of new high-yield varieties of cereal grains, heavy use of fertilizers, etc.) have increased agricultural productivity. But they are also expensive, and it is doubtful whether many of these countries will be able to afford the increased investments that further increases in food production will require. In fact, the United Nations Food and Agriculture Organization

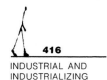

predicts that by 1985 there will be thirty-four nations with a combined population of 800 million that will be unable to afford either to produce or to purchase the minimum food required by their members.[61]

What, then, does the future hold for these societies? For most of them, the prospects are certainly not good. Given present world political and economic conditions, a few of them may make the breakthrough to full-fledged industrialization. The nations with the best chance of doing so are of three types: (1) nations like Argentina, Spain, Greece, and Yugoslavia, which are already semi-industrialized; (2) nations like Iran and Venezuela, which, though less industrialized, have an immensely valuable resource (petroleum) that can supply the capital to create the necessary infrastructure of highways, schools, factories, etc.; and (3) nations like China, which are both willing and able to isolate themselves to a great extent from the advanced industrial world and develop their own resources independently. The latter option is probably viable only for rather large countries that contain within their own borders the full range of mineral resources required by a modern industrial economy.

For the majority of industrializing societies, the only real hope for rapid modernization lies in the formation of a new kind of world political system—some kind of world government with the authority to transfer financial, informational, material, or any other kinds of resources from advanced industrial societies to those in greatest need. Politically, this sounds utopian, but technologically, it is quite feasible.

In the final analysis, the resolution of this enormous problem will depend on how the leaders of nations assess the relative costs and benefits of the various alternatives. Without substantially increased international cooperation, the fate of many Third and Fourth World nations is not pleasant to contemplate.

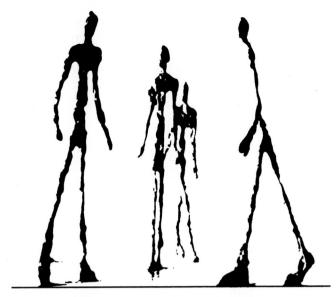

CHAPTER 14
RETROSPECT
AND PROSPECT

The study of societal evolution is a lot like the study of a giant mural. In both cases, we are easily overwhelmed by the many small details. To grasp the picture as a whole, we have to step back from time to time and look at it in its entirety.

We began this volume with the larger view, but for the last nine chapters we have concentrated on different parts of the panorama. Now we must again step back for another look at the basic outlines and the overarching patterns. This time, however, we will try to discover the extent to which technological progress has been accompanied by progress toward humanity's other goals—freedom, morality, justice, and happiness.

We will also consider the fascinating and important question of the future. If sociology is to help us understand the societies we live in and depend on, it cannot limit its concern to those of the past and present. It must also try to see where the process of societal evolution is taking us. Because the rate of change promises to make tomorrow's world strikingly different from today's, predictions are risky. But that is not sufficient reason to avoid the subject. As one social scientist commented recently:

It is an intellectually and morally intolerable state of affairs that we plan twenty and thirty years ahead when we take a mortgage on a house . . . but pretend that in the matters of war and peace, or in the matters of the life and death of mankind, we can't see further ahead than two years at most.[1]

LOOKING BACK

For millions of years, our early hominid ancestors gave little indication that they were anything more than another variety of primate. There was nothing to suggest that they would one day evolve into the dominant form of life, a species capable of overcoming many of the limitations imposed by the environment, and even able to alter that environment in major respects.

Today, we take all this for granted. With the wisdom of hindsight, we see that our species was destined for a unique role. We see, moreover, that the key to this was the ability to use symbols to mobilize information. We also understand how our ancestors gradually escaped some of the restraints of their genetic makeup, and how sociocultural evolution finally replaced biological evolution as the dominant mode of human adaptation.

The significance of this is hard to exaggerate. Sociocultural evolution, unlike biological evolution, has a natural tendency to snowball. Despite occasional reversals of relatively short duration, this tendency has persisted throughout history. As a result, we find ourselves today in the most revolutionary era of all, and change has become the central fact of life.

Distortions

In our survey of human societies, certain distortions were unavoidably introduced. For example, because there is so little nontechnological evidence from the prehistoric era, our description may exaggerate the importance of subsistence activities in the daily life of Stone Age societies. Similarly, because we took an evolutionary approach to the study of human societies and incorporated the whole span of human history into our analysis, we had to concentrate on the more basic patterns. Such a survey can never do justice to the human scene. However, we are all aware of the richness and complexity of human life, and its amazing variety. Not only is this part of our daily experience, but history and the arts continually remind us of it. For most of us, then, an overemphasis on the basic patterns comes as a badly needed corrective.

The Question of Progress

Whenever we have discussed sociocultural evolution in this book, it has been in terms of progress, or advance, in one sense only: growth in the store of cultural information—especially technological—and the consequences for human societies of its use. This accumulation of information has not, of course, been humanity's ultimate goal. Rather, people have valued new information because they believed it would, in some way, contribute to their well-being. Thus, it is appropriate in this final chapter to ask whether progress in the restricted sense of an increased store of cultural information has, in fact, contributed to progress in the sense of an increase in human freedom, justice, morality, and happiness.

Freedom The high value that the affluent members of modern industrial societies attach to freedom is revealed in the growing challenge to all forms of authority, not only in the liberal democracies of the West but in the authoritarian nations of East Europe as well. Even those who are not in the forefront of the libertarian movement are likely to consider the degree of freedom accorded the individual one of the basic measures of the attractiveness, and hence the progress, of a society, and they would deny that a technologically advanced, politically repressive society is truly progressive.

But human freedom is more than the absence of repressive social controls; it is also freedom from the restraints imposed by nature. People who must spend most of their waking hours in an exhausting struggle to produce the necessities of life are not truly "free"—even if there are few social restraints on them. A woman whose life is one long succession of pregnancies is not "free"—regardless of the kind of society she lives in. Disease, physical and mental handicaps, geographical barriers, and all the laws of nature restrict people and deny them freedom. For freedom does not exist where there is no alternative; and freedom can be measured only by the range of choices that are available. The fewer viable choices, the less freedom—and it matters little, from the standpoint of freedom, whether the restrictions are imposed by nature or by other people.*

Once we recognize this, it becomes clear that humanity's long struggle to advance technologically is not irrelevent to the desire for freedom. Every technological innovation reflects the desire to overcome natural limitations on human actions. Thanks to this struggle, some of us are now free to talk across oceans, even from a ship in space, free to travel faster than sound, free to live longer lives in better health while enjoying a range of experiences that far surpass in richness and variety what was available to the greatest kings and emperors of the past.

There has been a price to pay, of course: technological progress has necessitated larger and more complex social systems. If we want the option of flying to another part of the country instead of walking there, or of watching the day's events on a screen in our home instead of hearing about

*Psychologically, it seems easier for people to accept restrictions imposed by impersonal physical forces than those imposed by other people, but this does not make the individual any more free.

them weeks later, we have to accept certain social controls. The goods and services essential for those options can be produced only where there are organizations with rules and with sanctions to enforce the rules, and individuals with authority to exercise the sanctions. And these organizations can function efficiently only within the context of a society with rules to govern the relationships between them, and an authority system to enforce the rules. The only alternative is anarchy—and the loss of all the freedoms that modern technology affords.

Critics of modern society often say that the price has been too high, that the increased social restrictions outweigh the gains in freedom we derive from modern technology.[2] They may be right—this is a matter each of us must decide for himself. In thinking about it, however, we need to beware of romanticizing the past. Before deciding that people are less free than they used to be, we should read the records of peasant life in agrarian societies and of the life of horticultural and hunting and gathering peoples. In doing this, we must resist the temptation to abstract the attractive features and ignore the appalling ones. We must remember that slavery and serfdom were not accidental characteristics of agrarian societies but reflections of basic, inescapable conditions of that way of life, as were the high mortality rate and short life span of many hunting and gathering peoples. Finally, we must keep in mind that the restraints in those societies were not all physical ones; there were often powerful social restrictions operating too.

Once we recognize the danger of comparing some rosy version of life in

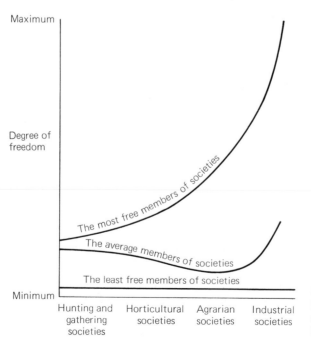

FIGURE 14.1 Degree of freedom for various categories of persons in four basic types of societies.

less advanced societies with the negative side of life in industrial societies, we are in a better position to consider whether freedom is a correlate of technological advance. We can say, first of all, that technological progress has clearly raised the *upper* level of freedom in human societies. People with the greatest measure of freedom in modern nations—that is, members of the upper classes—have a far wider range of choice than people with the greatest measure of freedom in agrarian societies, and the elites of agrarian societies had more freedom than the elites of less advanced societies. This has been true with respect to everything from the individual's use of a leisure hour to the use of a lifetime. In this limited sense, then, there is a high positive correlation between technological progress and gains in human freedom.

The relation between technical progress and freedom for the *average* member of society is more complicated. If we compare the typical peasant in an agrarian society with a typical hunter and gatherer, it is not at all clear that there were any gains. In fact, the peasant had to live with a lot of new social controls, while gaining very little freedom from natural controls. Thus, during much of the course of evolutionary history—especially after the formation of the state—the average person probably experienced a decline in freedom. With industrialization, however, the pattern changed: once the difficult period of transition is past, technological progress and freedom for the average person *do* begin to be positively related, as Figure 14.1 illustrates. Whether people in industrial societies have more freedom than hunters and gatherers is a moot point. Clearly they have more social restraints, but far fewer biophysical ones.

For the *least* free members of society, there appears to have been little change through the years. If we compare the least free members of modern societies—the inmates of many medical, mental, and penal institutions and the very poor—with the least free members of other societies, it is hard to see much difference: both are severely restricted. The chief difference is that in the least advanced societies (i.e., hunting and gathering) the restrictions are usually imposed by nature, while in the more advanced, they are more often imposed by society.

Before leaving the subject of freedom, we should take note of the popular misconception that governmental activity necessarily results in a loss of freedom for the members of society. This is at best a half-truth. Laws do, of course, place restrictions on people, but often this is done in order to increase freedom, not reduce it. For example, when the United States established the death penalty for kidnapping in the 1930s, this restricted the freedom of a tiny predatory minority, but it increased the freedom of millions of children and parents. Similarly, the Pure Food and Drug Act was designed to restrict the freedom of businessmen who were willing to sell spoiled food and dangerous drugs for profit, but it increased the freedom of the rest of the population. Sometimes laws restrict everyone's freedom in one area—the freedom to proceed at will through a busy intersection, for example—in order

to enlarge it in others. In short, most governmental regulations *redistribute* freedom.

The crucial question, therefore, is whether the gains outweigh the losses. With the growth of democratic government, there have been efforts to increase the freedom of the less favored majority, and this often necessitates transferring some of it from traditionally favored groups and classes. In an effort to defend their privileges, such groups (e.g., the National Association of Manufacturers, the Chamber of Commerce, the American Medical Association) argue frequently and with remarkable success that proposed legislation is a threat to everyone's freedom. They do not mention the fact that most modern social legislation, such as minimum wage laws or Medicare, has been adopted because the gains in freedom for those who benefit are judged to be more significant than the losses for others. This is, of course, only what we should expect in a democratic society. Admittedly, there is also a great deal of legislation that denies freedom to the majority in order to make those in office more secure or to benefit the elite. But in balance, the great growth in the power of government in modern democratic societies has increased freedom for the average person far more than it has restricted it.*

Morality   Morality is a difficult subject. For one thing, it concerns so much of human life, ranging from personal behavior like sexual conduct to corporate acts of society like war. For another, judgments about what is good and what is evil have varied throughout history—not only from society to society but from group to group and individual to individual within the same society. Finally, the way we evaluate other moral codes is naturally influenced by our own. In order to simplify matters, we will limit this discussion to a single, critical area, one in which a new moral consensus may be emerging— violence against other human beings. Among better-educated people in every industrial society, there seems to be a growing agreement that, except in self-defense, violence is wrong, and this provides a standard against which we can try to measure the historical trend. This ignores many other important dimensions of morality, of course, but we could not do justice to them all in this brief space.

In the simplest human societies, hunting and gathering groups, the incidence of violence is strikingly low. Certainly in those which have survived into the modern era, warfare is uncommon (see Table 6.3, page 164), and violence between members of the same group is infrequent.

In horticultural societies, the situation is quite different. As we observed in Chapter 6, the cult of the warrior was prominent in many of them, with warfare encouraged and such violence as torture and human sacrifice common. These were not the acts of deviant individuals, taken in defiance of

---

*The situation is not necessarily the same in nondemocratic societies. On the contrary, the increased power of government may be used to reduce the freedoms of the majority.

group norms, but expressions of some of the most deeply held values of the society.

With the rise of agrarian societies, warfare became the concern of a specialized occupational group. The cult of the warrior declined in importance, human sacrifice gradually vanished, and the mutilation and torture of captives became much less common. But this does not mean that warfare became more humane: on the contrary, as the technological resources of armies increased, so did their devastation. The pillage and destruction of conquered towns and villages was commonplace, although the morality of these things was no longer unquestioned. Intragroup violence was also widespread in agrarian societies, and much of it was socially approved. The beating of women and children, for example, was often regarded as a necessary part of the father's role, while masters could usually beat serfs and slaves with impunity for minor transgressions. Minor crimes were punished with death in many cases, and executions were regarded as public entertainment. In the schools, physical punishment was considered the best stimulus to learning.

Since the rise of industrial societies, there has been a sharp decline in the incidence of socially approved violence within societies. For example, a gradual reduction in the number of crimes for which the death penalty could be imposed was followed by a decline in the frequency with which it actually *was* imposed; and more recently there has been a widespread movement toward its total abolition. Within families and schools, violence against women and children no longer has public approval. And there is no longer physical abuse of the lower class by the elite.

Even war has lost some of its respectability: skepticism about it is more widespread than ever before—not so widespread, obviously, as to prevent war entirely, but prevalent enough to make governments more cautious in undertaking military commitments. On the other hand, the destructive power of the modern military machine has grown even more awesome, as the horrors of the recent Indochina War testify. And the ability of political leaders to sustain broad public support for a venture of this kind suggests that the change in popular thinking can easily be exaggerated.

Putting all this together, it seems that once again we have a curvilinear trend, with a declining standard of morality (as reflected by patterns of violence) after the hunting and gathering era but some reversal more recently. So far, however, the newer trend has been felt in intrasocietal relations more than in intersocietal.

Justice Basically, justice has to do with the fairness of a society in its treatment of its members. Although no one would quarrel with that as an objective, we run into trouble as soon as we try to define what "fairness" means. Should a society reward its members on the basis of how much they contribute to the common good, or according to their individual needs and capacities? Should the handicapped person, for example, be rewarded as generously as those who outproduce him? What about those unable to make any productive contribution at all? And what is a "fair" evaluation of the relative contributions of people in radically dissimilar activities—a symphony conductor, a bricklayer, a mother, a garbage collector, a student?

Questions like these point up the difficulty of measuring progress with respect to justice. An adequate treatment of the subject would require volumes. All we can hope to do here is call attention to basic trends and offer some tentative conclusions.

To begin with, as we observed in earlier chapters, social inequality became more pronounced as societies advanced technologically and status became increasingly dependent on the family into which one was born. The result of these developments was a weakening of the relationship between a person's efforts and his rewards. Whereas every boy in a hunting and gathering group had a chance of becoming the best hunter (and hence the most important man) in his society, a peasant's son had little hope of advancing even a notch above his father's social level, no matter how hard he tried.

The relationship between a person's natural ability and his rewards also declined with societal advance. For one thing, societies beyond the level of simple horticultural frequently excluded segments of their populations from access to rewards on the basis of religion or ethnicity, thereby denying many people the opportunity to use all their abilities. In addition, increasingly rigid stratification systems locked people into roles and situations where they could neither develop nor use their gifts, while whose with few or none to use might occupy positions they were grossly unsuited for—even thrones. Societies also tended to hand out punishments the way they did rewards: on the basis of social status. This is especially evident in the criminal codes of many agrarian societies.

In general, then, it appears that societies became less just, less fair, as they advanced technologically. However, there are signs of a reversal in this trend too. Industrialization has resulted in some decline in the level of social inequality. Industrial societies are more solicitous of their poor, their handicapped, and their minorities than the typical agrarian society. Criminal justice is less harsh: people are no longer hanged for stealing an egg, for example. Public education provides at least some chance for practically every child to develop his or her abilities. And women are gradually gaining opportunities that were long denied them. In short, after a long period of declining justice, there is finally some movement in the other direction.

Happiness Of all the possible measures of progress, happiness is the most elusive, for it depends so much—perhaps primarily—on the quality of interpersonal relations, whether there is love, mutual respect, cooperation, and so forth. And these things do not seem to depend on the level of technological development. Studies of modern hunting and gathering groups indicate that the most primitive people develop these qualities as often as members of modern industrial societies do.[3]

There are several respects, however, in which technological progress is definitely relevant to this kind of happiness. To begin with, some of life's greatest tragedies involve the premature death of a loved one—a cherished child, a father or mother, or a partner in a happy conjugal relation. We saw how common this was in most societies prior to the Industrial Revolution and can therefore appreciate what the recently expanded life-span has meant for human happiness.

Health, too, contributes to happiness. When we are seriously ill, life may not seem worth living. Disease was very poorly understood through most of human history, and it would be hard to argue that technological advance prior to the Industrial Revolution had any real impact in this area. More recently, however, advances in sanitation and medicine have dramatically improved the physical well-being of the members of advanced societies. Unfortunately, modern medical technology has also had a negative effect: it has been used to keep alive individuals who, in simpler societies, would mercifully be allowed to die. Still, the net result has undeniably been positive.

Hunger, another cause of enormous human misery, has been drastically reduced in a large number of societies by industrialization. Table 14.1 shows two measures of the change that has occurred. Not only do the members of

TABLE 14.1 Daily meat consumption and caloric intake per person, by society

Society	Grams of Meat	Calories	Society	Grams of Meat	Calories
United States	310	3300	Brazil	84	2820
New Zealand	301	3380	Peru	64	2190
Australia	294	3160	Kenya	57	2200
France	256	3270	Mexico	55	2620
West Germany	220	3180	Japan	48	2470
United Kingdom	209	3170	China	47	2050
Denmark	170	3250	Tanzania	40	1700
Hungary	158	3190	Iran	37	2030
Israel	155	2990	Morocco	37	2130
Sweden	142	2850	Egypt	31	2770
Italy	136	3020	Syria	31	2450
South Africa	113	2730	Nigeria	28	2290
Spain	112	2770	Haiti	22	1930
Soviet Union	106	3180	Indonesia	10	1920
Yugoslavia	93	3130	India	4	1990

Source: Food and Agriculture Organization of the United Nations, *Production Yearbook, 1971*, tables 135 and 136.

modern industrial societies have a high average caloric intake, but their diet is rich in fats and proteins, amazingly varied in content, and remarkably free from periodic shortages. As with health, it is easy to take these benefits for granted and lose sight of this link between technological advance and happiness.

The increased production of other kinds of goods and services, especially nonessential ones, has probably had much less effect on happiness. The absolute quantity of luxuries we enjoy is certainly not as important in this regard as how they compare with what people around us have. Thus the headman in a simple horticultural society may be quite content with his few special possessions, because they are more than his neighbors own and as good as anything he knows about, while middle-class Americans, surrounded with goods and services the headman never dreamed of, may feel terribly deprived when they compare themselves with more prosperous neighbors. In other words, insofar as happiness depends on material possessions, the degree of inequality is probably more important than anything else.

When we take into account the advances in health, the greater abundance and improved quality of food, and the drastic reduction in premature deaths, it is clear that the Industrial Revolution has eliminated the sources of much of the misery of earlier eras. Putting it all together, we are again led to the tentative conclusion that the long-term trend for the average individual has been curvilinear. Conditions seem to have been more conducive to human happiness for the average individual in hunting and gathering societies than in horticultural, and better in horticultural than in agrarian, or even in early industrial. But with further advances in industrialization, the situation of the average individual seems to have improved considerably, reversing the long-term trend.

Recently published evidence, the first of its kind, tends to support this conclusion. In a study of almost seventy nations, containing two-thirds of the world's population, the Gallup Poll and its associates found a striking relationship between the level of happiness expressed by the people they interviewed and the level of technological advance of the societies in which they lived (see Table 14.2). The same relationship was found between societal development and people's satisfaction with various aspects of their lives (e.g., family life, health, housing, work). The results of this survey led George Gallup to comment: "For centuries, romantics and philosophers have beguiled us with tales of societies that were 'poor but happy.' If any such exist, the survey failed to discover them."

Concluding Thoughts   In an earlier chapter we asked, in effect, why people have invested so much of themselves in the struggle for technological advance when it has not been more consistent in producing happiness and justice. We answered that people have always been more concerned with the

TABLE 14.2 Degree of happiness and satisfaction with life expressed by members of societies around the world

	Per Cent Very Happy or Fairly Happy	Per Cent Highly Satisfied with Their Lives*
North America	91	50
Western Europe	80	41
Latin America	70	40
Africa	68	15
Far East	48†	11

Source: Adapted from George H. Gallup, "Human Needs and Satisfactions: A Global Survey," *Public Opinion Quarterly,* 40 (Winter, 1976–1977), tables 2 and 6, pp. 465 and 467.
*The values shown in this column are the arithmetic mean of responses to questions about satisfaction with ten specific areas of life (see Table 6 of Gallup's article).
†The Far East includes both Japan and India, and Gallup notes that "the differences between Japan [an advanced industrial society] and India [a Fourth World society] with respect to personal happiness are very large."

immediate consequences of their choices and actions than with the long-term results and that the latter often do not become evident until it is too late for society to reverse its course. We also said that people are rarely motivated by a desire to gain happiness and justice for humanity as a whole, but concentrate their energies on achieving these things for themselves and those closest to them. Since what is advantageous for one group is so often achieved at the expense of others, the costs of progress have frequently outweighed the benefits for an entire society or for human societies as a whole. Moreover, intersocietal selection has helped ensure that societies which are primarily oriented toward technological advance and political expansion will survive, and that societies with other orientations will not.

Idealists may well ask, therefore, whether technological advance has not been, in fact, a bitch goddess. Had human history come to an end a thousand years ago, one would have been forced to answer affirmatively. But recent technological developments, especially those of the last hundred years, have begun to make a positive contribution to the attainment of humanity's higher goals. Whether or not this will continue to be the case in the future is a question for the next section. We can certainly say this, however: technology has at last brought into the realm of *the possible* a social order with more freedom, justice, morality, and happiness than any society has yet known.

Whatever our judgment about the wisdom of our species' pursuit of technological advance, one thing is clear: *sociocultural evolution cannot be equated with progress except in the highly restricted sense of growth in cultural information, and the consequences of its use.*

For thousands of years, hoping for a glimpse into the future, people turned to shamans and oracles, prophets and astrologers. Despite the sorry record of predictions made by such people, interest in the subject has not abated. Never, in fact, has it been greater than in modern industrial societies, as evidenced not only by the serious books and articles produced on the subject, but by the revival of interest in astrology.

The reason for this concern is clear: culture makes us aware of the relation between events of the present and those of the future, and the increased pace of social change in recent decades has heightened our perception of that relationship. But despite our desire to see into the future, and our need to do so, prediction remains a hazardous business. Only a hundred years ago, for example, Friedrich Engels wrote that warfare had reached the point where no significant advances in weapons could be expected. As he put it, "The era of evolution is therefore, in essentials, closed in this direction."[4]

There have been so many unsuccessful attempts to forecast the future that prediction might appear to be entirely a matter of luck. Successful prediction does, in fact, involve an element of luck, for the future depends on the interaction of so many factors that no one can possibly assess them all correctly. Besides, the most critical factor in a situation may be so poorly understood that it upsets the most carefully reasoned analysis of the others. This is the case, for example, with certain aspects of the biophysical environment, on which all life depends. We simply do not have the ability to predict such things as major shifts in climate or the appearance of new and deadly strains of bacteria.

As we attempt to see what lies ahead for human societies, we need to keep two basic guidelines in mind. First, the shorter the time interval involved, the greater the chance of success. Predicting events far in the future greatly increases the probability that some important but unforeseeable factor will intervene and completely upset one's calculations. It also increases the chance that minor errors will be compounded, through repetition, into major ones. The safest predictions, therefore, concern the very near future. But these are also the least interesting and the least valuable. Because of this inverse relationship between accuracy and value, it makes sense to concentrate on predictions geared to an intermediate time span.

Second, the more thoroughly a prediction is grounded in an analysis of the past, the better its chance of success. This means we cannot simply extrapolate current trends into the future. Rather, we must know what conditions gave rise to a particular trend and what forces sustained it—or caused it to waver or accelerate—so that we can anticipate reversals and other shifts. For example, the birthrate in the United States dropped 40 per cent during a twenty-year period, starting in the middle 1950s; but it would be as irresponsible simply to project that trend to the end of the century as it would be to ignore it.

This approach does not lead to flat, unqualified predictions, the kind everyone would prefer. Rather, it results in statements which say that, under conditions X, Y, and Z, outcome A is likelier than B, which in turn is likelier than C. The virtue of discussing the future this way is that it puts the assumptions on which predictions are based out in the open where other people can examine them, and challenge or modify them as new information or insights become available. Hopefully, this will lead to progressively better predictions about human societies.

Applying the first guideline, we will focus on the next two decades. The period around the year 2000 takes us beyond the point where we can simply say, "Things will be pretty much the way they are today," yet it does not get us into the realm of science fiction. Applying the second guideline, we will base our predictions of societal change on our analysis of sociocultural evolution up to the present. We will start with the fundamentals in the basic model of general evolution (see Figure 3.2, page 68): the biophysical environment, the genetic makeup of the human population, and technology. Once we know what can reasonably be expected with regard to these factors, we can move on to consider prospects for the other elements in sociocultural systems.

Prospects: The Environment and Human Genetics

Change in the biophysical environment during the next two decades is inevitable, but most of it will probably be the result of feedback from technology. Independent or autogenous change of any significance is unlikely to occur in such a short time span, and even if it should, contemporary science cannot predict it.

The situation is similar with respect to our species' genetic heritage. Not only has there been no major change in it for more than 30,000 years, but the principles of biological evolution make it clear that spontaneous alteration would happen too slowly to be noticeable by the year 2000.

Thus, by a process of elimination, our attention is directed to technology as the most likely initiator of major changes in the next several decades. We have to keep in mind, of course, that we are not starting with a world in equilibrium: a major revolution has been under way in human societies for years, and its effects will carry over into the future. The situation is something like that on a billiard table soon after a shot has been made: the balls are still bounding and rebounding, their total impact and ultimate resting places uncertain. Thus, we cannot concentrate exclusively on the effects of future advances in technology; we must also watch for the still unregistered consequences of *past* advances.

Prospects: Technology

Benjamin Franklin once said that nothing is certain in this world but death and taxes. Were he alive today, he might add technological advance. A prediction of continuing advance at an accelerating rate does not depend simply on an extrapolation of the current trend. The basic factors responsible for the trend—the magnitude of the existing store of information, the great size of societal populations, and the amount of communication between societies—are still operative and they give every indication of providing even stronger impetus in the near future than they do today. Furthermore, advanced industrial societies are engaging, for the first time in history, in a systematic, large-scale pursuit of new information. Investments in scientific and technological research and development have grown immensely, while computers and other devices that increase our ability to acquire and analyze data add their own boost to the rate of change.

At present, only two things seem at all likely to halt this trend in the next two decades. First, a nuclear holocaust could destroy the fabric of modern industrial societies, in which event there might well be a permanent reversion to the agrarian level. In a provocative volume entitled *The Challenge of Man's Future*, geophysicist Harrison Brown noted that the emergence of industrial societies depended on a combination of circumstances that no longer exist, thus making a second emergence unlikely. Brown argues the case this way:

> Our ancestors had available large resources of high-grade ores and fuels that could be processed by the most primitive technology—crystals of copper and pieces of coal that lay on the surface of the earth, easily mined iron, and petroleum in generous pools reached by shallow drilling. Now we must dig huge caverns and follow seams ever further underground, drill oil wells thousands of feet deep, many of them under the bed of the ocean, and find ways of extracting elements from the leanest ores—procedures that are possible only because of our highly complex modern techniques, and practical only to an intricately mechanized culture which could not have been developed without the high-grade ore resources that are so rapidly vanishing.
>
> As our dependence shifts to such resources as low-grade ores, rock, seawater, and the sun, the conversion of energy into useful work will require ever more intricate technical activity, which would be impossible in the absence of a variety of complex machines and their products—all of which are the result of our intricate industrial civilization, and which would be impossible without it. Thus, if machine civilization were to stop functioning as the result of some catastrophe, it is difficult to see how man would again be able to start along the path of industrialization with the resources that would then be available to him. . . .
>
> Our present industrialization, itself the result of a combination of no longer existent circumstances, is the only foundation on which it seems possible that a future civilization capable of utilizing the vast resources of energy now hidden in

rocks and seawater, and unutilized in the sun, can be built. If this foundation is destroyed, in all probability the human race has "had it." Perhaps there is possible a sort of halfway station [agrarian society?] in which retrogression stops short of a complete extinction of civilization, but even this is not pleasant to contemplate. . . .[5]

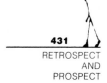

The second threat to a rising rate of innovation comes from the environmental crisis created by industrialization. Should a series of environmental disasters occur, as some environmentalists predict, advanced industrial societies might suddenly be forced to revert to a simpler way of life (something closer to the patterns of life in the nineteenth century), and the resources available for research and innovation would be reduced drastically. It seems unlikely, however, that the situation will deteriorate to that point before the end of the century. Rather, increasing efforts to find technological solutions to the environmental crisis will probably *step up* the rate of innovation.

There is a third development which, though unlikely in the next twenty years, could eventually cause a slowing in the rate of technological innovation. At some point, the rate of change in society may reach a point where it becomes socially and psychologically intolerable.[6] On the other hand, it should prove possible for societies, through planning, to concentrate their innovative efforts in areas selected for their capacity to produce needed improvements with minimum social and psychological disruption. Thus, emphasis might be placed on innovations whose primary objective is to simplify life. For example, high priority might be given to creating clean, dependable public transportation systems to replace the millions of automobiles whose owners pay dearly—fighting traffic, weather, an inadequate maintenance system, and rising costs—and often end up feeling guilty for contributing to pollution and consuming gas.

The possibilities for technological change that would entail a minimum of adjustment and a maximum of simplification are tremendous. But they presuppose a more rational ordering of national priorities than is characteristic of most industrial societies, especially democratic-capitalistic ones.

The Content of Change   Turning from the rate of future technological innovation to its content, we encounter a subject so vast and so technical that we can do no more than call attention to a few of the highlights. The authors of one volume that looks ahead to the year 2000 listed 100 areas in which, in their judgment, important technological innovations are "very likely" during the last part of this century. They also noted 25 developments they consider "less likely, but important possibilities," and another 10 "far-out possibilities." Table 14.3 gives examples from all three categories.

The 100 "very likely" developments are little more than an enumeration of fairly obvious applications of inventions and discoveries that have already

TABLE 14.3   Examples of possible and probable technological innovations in the last third of the twentieth century, according to Herman Kahn and Anthony Wiener

Innovations Rated as "Very Likely"

1. Multiple applications of lasers and masers for sensing, measuring, cutting, heating, welding, power transmission, communication, illumination, destructive (defensive), and other purposes
2. New or improved materials for equipment and appliances (plastics, glasses, alloys, ceramics, intermetallics, and cermets)
3. New sources of power for ground transportation (storage battery, fuel cell, propulsion or support by electromagnetic fields, jet engine, turbine, and the like)
4. Major reduction in hereditary and congenital defects
5. Extensive use of cyborg techniques (mechanical aids or substitutes for human organs, senses, limbs, or other components)
6. New or improved uses of the oceans (mining, extraction of minerals, controlled "farming," source of energy, and the like)
7. Three-dimensional photography, illustrations, movies, and television
8. Automated or more mechanized housekeeping and home maintenance
9. Extensive and intensive centralization (or automatic interconnection) of current and past personal and business information in high-speed data processors
10. Other new and possibly pervasive techniques for surveillance, monitoring, and control of individuals and organizations
11. Capacity to determine the sex of unborn children
12. More extensive use of transplantation of human organs
13. Chemical methods for improving memory and learning
14. Practical large-scale desalinization
15. Artificial moons and other methods for lighting large areas at night

"Less Likely, but Important Possibilities"

1. Artificial growth of new limbs and organs (either in situ or for later transplantation)
2. Effective chemical or biological treatment for most mental illnesses
3. Chemical or biological control of character or intelligence
4. Conversion of mammals (humans?) to fluid breathers
5. Automated highways

"Far-out Possibilities"

1. Life expectancy extended to substantially more than 150 years
2. Major modification of human species (no longer *Homo sapiens sapiens*)
3. Interstellar travel
4. Lifetime immunization against practically all diseases
5. Laboratory creation of artificial live plants and animals

Source: Adapted from Herman Kahn and Anthony Wiener, *The Year 2000: A Framework for Speculation on the Next Thirty-three Years* (New York: Macmillan, 1967), tables XVII–XX.

been made. The first item, for example, simply involves the application of recently invented lasers and masers to a variety of tasks. All the details have not yet been worked out, but the important point is that the fundamental innovations—the laser and the maser—are accomplished facts. By 1967, almost every corporation and major university in the nation already had a laser for research purposes.[7] That same year more than 100 specific applications of lasers were being investigated, though only a handful had actually been adopted (e.g., "spotwelding" detached retinas).[8]

Several areas with exceptional promise for the next few decades involve fundamental innovations still so new that only a fraction of their potential has been explored. But equally important change is expected from major improvements in earlier inventions. Computers are a good example: since the early 1950s, computer performance has doubled every eighteen months on the average. Though we cannot expect this pace to continue indefinitely, computers will be able, by the end of the century, to handle problems far beyond their present capacity.[9]

Not all innovations will be in the form of refinements and applications of existing information. New *fundamental* innovations are virtually certain, although it is impossible to anticipate what they will all be. We should not exaggerate their unpredictability, however, for we do know the areas where societies are investing the most money and effort, and we also know which areas seem to have been "mined out."

One area where less guesswork is required is the field of energy. Because modern industry requires such tremendous inputs of energy and has already consumed so much of the limited supply of petroleum and natural gas,* a massive search is under way for alternative sources of energy. For a time, nuclear fission seemed to be the answer, though serious problems have arisen (e.g., disposal of the highly poisonous radioactive wastes, unanticipated shortage of uranium ore, serious security hazards) and many scientists are now focusing their attention on three other possibilities: (1) solar energy; (2) nuclear *fusion* (which produces less radioactive wastes than fission); and (3) geothermal energy (i.e., harnessing the heat under the earth's surface). Most experts do not expect that any of these will be in wide use by the year 2000, but growing demands for new and better energy sources may speed up the process of innovation. In fact, practical devices for harnessing solar energy have already appeared. Thus, it would be rather surprising if we reached the year 2000 without one or more fundamental innovations in the energy area.

Technology's Feedback on the Biophysical Environment   Over the course of evolutionary history, our species' relation to the biophysical environment has changed dramatically. Hunting and gathering societies simply adapted to environmental conditions; there was nothing they could do to alter them. Following the horticultural revolution, human societies gradually began

*The United States has already consumed more than half of both the onshore and offshore petroleum resources of the original forty-eight states, and is expected to have consumed 90 per cent by the year 2000.[10] With respect to natural gas, the situation is even worse.

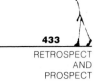

making changes on the earth's surface, clearing forests and planting gardens in their place. Although the balance of nature was affected wherever this happened, the impact was not great, for horticulturalists usually had to move every few years, and their abandoned gardens reverted to wilderness. The agrarian revolution, however, changed this. From that point on, fields became permanent and the land no longer reverted to forest.

But all the changes of the past were as nothing compared with the impact of industrial societies. Modern technology has enabled us to rearrange the landscape and adjust the earth's natural features so drastically that entire areas that once teemed with life have been destroyed, while complex ecosystems that required millions of years to evolve have been damaged almost beyond repair in a matter of years, even months. Not even polar regions, oceans, or atmosphere has escaped.

Environmentalists have been warning us for years that our biophysical environment does not have an unlimited capacity for renewing itself. Some of the resources on which human societies depend, fossil fuels, for example, are produced so slowly that for all practical purposes the supply can be considered nonreplenishable. Others, such as oxygen, are renewed much more rapidly but are nonetheless vulnerable. Yet, even as we have heard these warnings, our demands on the environment have risen at a fantastic rate. Between 1950 and 1975, an infinitesimal period of time by geological standards, the gross world product rose from just over $1 trillion to approximately $4 trillion. If we consider what this represents in terms of the plunder of our planet, environmental crises of increasing number and severity should come as no surprise.

The simple fact is that the biophysical environment can sustain neither an infinite growth of the human population nor the endless demands of an advancing technology. There are limits to what it can provide for humans or any other species. And for their part, human societies have a very limited repertoire of responses: they can control their numbers and they can control their technology. The more quickly they do one, the more leeway, relatively, they will have in the other. But at some point, societies will have to stop all growth—in numbers and in material production—or the environment will do it for them, *its* way.

One thing that makes it extremely difficult to be optimistic about the environmental situation for the remainder of this century is the slow response of the major industrial nations. These are the nations that can best afford to apply pollution control devices and take the other steps necessary to protect their own environments and the air and water they share with the rest of the world's peoples. Because societies that are still industrializing can hardly be expected to invest in expensive pollution control devices when it is already so difficult for them to compete in the world market, it is imperative that industrial nations take the step first, and soon. But even if they do, it is

ONE VISTA: TWO VIEWS

Above Wheeling, West Virginia, the Ohio River flows past low forested bluffs and . . . on a hot summer day the smog from the steel factories and electric power plants hangs heavy over the river, obscuring the view of more smokestacks and more piles of coal farther upstream.

It is a vista industrialized America has come to abhor.

"What a beautiful sight," exclaimed Yeh Chih-hsiung [a newsman from the People's Republic of China], as we rounded a bend in the Ohio and saw two enormous chimneys belching white smoke. We stopped for a picture.

For China, eager to achieve total industrialization, it was an impressive spectacle, Mr. Yeh explained.

From Fox Butterfield, "Reporter's Notebook: Chinese on Tour," the *New York Times*, Sept. 3, 1972, p. 2. © by The New York Times Company. Reprinted by permission.

---

doubtful that the year 2000 will find the problem less severe on the global level than it is now.

The limited steps industrial societies have taken to alleviate this problem do, at least, prove the situation is not hopeless. The British, adopting stringent legislation and applying new technologies, have almost eliminated London's deadly smogs, while the Thames abounds with fish for the first time in decades. This experience suggests that damage to the environment can be halted, even reversed, if policy makers in industrial nations will only recognize the seriousness of the problem. Britain's solution serves as a reminder, however, that new technology will be required to help solve problems that were brought on, in the first place, by new technology.

A great deal of attention will have to be focused on recycling in the decades ahead. As John Ruskin noted a hundred years ago, industrialization is as productive of "illth" as of wealth. In the last half century, America's daily refuse increased sixfold.[11] At this rate, we will soon bury ourselves in our own wastes. Fortunately, the technological problems of recycling appear generally tractable, and this could become an important area of technological advance in the next few decades.

Technology's Feedback on Our Genetic Heritage   In the distant past, technology apparently had a significant effect on our species' common genetic heritage. As we noted in earlier chapters, most modern scholars agree that the use of tools and big-game hunting contributed, through natural selection, to the enlargement of our brain and to the development of the other parts of

our physiology on which the use of symbols and the development of culture depend. We also know that technological advance subsequently affected our genetic heritage by fostering the growth of some genetic strains at the expense of others (e.g., the increase in color blindness in populations beyond the level of hunting and gathering).

But whatever technology's impact on human genetics in the past, the fact is that it may be considerable in the near future, for we are now entering an era in which deliberate genetic manipulation will be possible. There are several ways this could occur. First, societies could deliberately control reproduction along the lines that eugenicists have advocated for years. For example, to ensure that only its healthier members reproduced, a government might require couples to be licensed to have children and levy heavy fines or other penalties for violations. Even if the requirement were not perfectly enforced, the genetic composition of a population could be substantially affected in only a few generations. A second, and far more drastic, potential for genetic manipulation lies in the process of "cloning." This is an asexual method of reproduction whereby an exact genetic copy of a plant or animal is generated from a single cell taken from any part of it. This makes it possible to produce literally thousands of exact replicas of a single specimen in a relatively short time. So far the process is confined to experimental laboratories, but it has already been applied to frogs, and most scientists are convinced there are no insurmountable barriers to cloning humans: all they need is time and money.[12] Other products pouring out of the "cornucopia" of modern science include the still largely untried weapons of nuclear, biological, and chemical warfare, any of which might adversely affect our species' genetic heritage. Although the politicians who finance these innovations and the scientists who produce them constantly reassure us that they have only the public interest at heart, a healthy degree of skepticism seems warranted.

Fortunately, many scientists are concerned, even alarmed, by the potentials inherent in advances such as these.[13] In addition to the obvious danger that they may be misused by authorities more interested in social control than in human welfare, there is the danger of unintended consequences. Consider, for example, the insurance factor built into the present genetic diversity of the human population. Should the biophysical environment change significantly at some time in the future, either because of human activity or through spontaneous natural processes, genetic characteristics that are currently of little adaptive value to a population might suddenly become the difference between survival and extinction for the human race. As biologists have come to recognize, anything that reduces the genetic diversity of a population increases its risk of extinction. Thus, well-intentioned efforts to breed or clone a race of supermen could actually prove disastrous. Recognizing the dangers and implications of innovations before they are put into use is probably our best protection against their abuse.

Prospects: Ideology

Through most of history, human societies had little control over their future. It was shaped for them by a mysterious complex of forces that they understood poorly or not at all and over which they had little or no control. In such a world, people were not inclined to plan ahead. They did not so much attempt to control life or shape their future as to adapt to it. Ideologies reflected this fatalistic attitude: they helped people accept the inevitable.

The situation today is different. Most people have a far better comprehension of the natural forces that surround them and, to a greater or lesser extent, shape their destiny. What is more, they feel much less vulnerable before these forces because technology enables them to exert some measure of control over nature and over their own lives. These changes are reflected in the trends in ideology. Systems of beliefs are less passive and fatalistic, more active and manipulative, than they were in an earlier era. This is evident even in theistic religions, as reflected in changing values and norms relating to birth control, abortion, suicide, and euthanasia.

From the standpoint of societal evolution, however, the most significant change in ideology has been in the beliefs and values of governing elites. Socialist ideology is already the official creed in a large number of countries. Perhaps more significant is the fact that the governments of virtually all nations have accepted, to a greater or lesser degree, certain fundamental socialist principles. While they may not bear the label "socialist," new ideas and new ideals are at work regarding the ability of societies to shape their future, and the need to shape it to benefit more than a small elite. This ideology appears certain to spread further in the decades ahead, especially in the nations of the Third World. In short, the process of change and development in human societies is going to depend increasingly on conscious decisions based on the ideas and the ideals of their members.

What we are witnessing is essentially the same thing that has happened throughout human history: technological change making change in other components of sociocultural systems possible. As we saw in Chapters 6 and 7, this once had extremely important consequences for ideology. When technological advance first made an economic surplus possible, it also made possible new kinds of ideologies that legitimized a controlling elite, ideologies that had tremendous repercussions for subsequent societal development. Now technological advance is once again having dramatic implications for ideology, and for its role in sociocultural evolution. Industrialization has produced societies with such enormous informational stores and economic surpluses that those in control have a far wider range of ideological options than societies of the past ever had. Because industrialization is such a recent occurrence, these dissimilar ideological choices are only now beginning to have a significant influence on societal development. But the potential exists for them to play a far greater role in the future.

It should be noted, however, that while planning based on ideological choice has become an increasingly important element in the life of most individual societies, it has not been accepted at the global level. At the global level, *political anarchy* and *economic capitalism* prevail.[15] Literally, there *is* no government, and comprehensive planning is therefore impossible. This is an increasingly dangerous situation, both politically and economically, and it is wasteful as well. To make matters worse, the prospects for improvement do not seem bright. Thus, in judging the stage that has been reached in the evolutionary process, we must not be fooled into thinking we have moved further than, in fact, we have.

Prospects: Demographic Variables

According to the latest estimates, world population in the year 2000 will be approximately 5.4 billion.[16] This will mean many more mouths to be fed, and many more needs of every kind to be met, even without any improvement in standards of living. The problem is the equivalent of finding global resources to support another China and another India—approximately one-third of the world's present population—within twenty years!

As we have seen, the population problem is most acute in industrializing societies, where death rates have dropped dramatically but birthrates have declined hardly at all. There are several reasons for their difficulties. First, until recently most of their leaders were either unaware of, or indifferent to, uncontrolled population growth and its consequences. In some cases, religious or political doctrines (e.g., Catholicism and orthodox Marxism) led leaders to deny that population growth could be a problem. Second, even where there was recognition and concern, there appeared to be no solution: contraceptives were either too expensive or required more education than most people in those countries had. Third, because of the economic value of sons in rural areas and because of the absence of other sources of support in old age, most people resisted efforts to limit the number of their offspring. Finally, until quite recently the development programs sponsored by industrial societies focused almost exclusively on increasing production and ignored the economic implications of population growth. Now all this is changing, and birthrates have begun to decline in a number of Third and Fourth World nations.

Modest reductions in birthrates in the years immediately ahead will not be enough, however. Death rates in these countries are still fairly high (often 20 or more each year per 1,000 population) and improved sanitation and medicine will soon bring them down. Until they reach rock bottom (i.e., about 8 per 1,000), the decline in death rates will simply offset much of the decline in birthrates. Since there appears to be little reason to believe that people in those societies will more rapidly accept either modern contraceptives or small families than people in industrial nations did, some of their governments will almost surely be forced to take a more active part in solving the population problem if they hope to avert famine or other catastrophe.

Until recently, most of these governments have restricted their role to such limited efforts as establishing family planning centers. The next several decades will undoubtedly see these increase, along with state subsidization of contraceptives, abortions, and sterilization. Only time will tell the extent to which these societies will choose, or be forced, to respond to population pressures with such measures as taxes on children or with more extreme, involuntary controls—licensing the right to have a child, for example, or compulsory sterilizations and abortions, or even the use of mass sterility agents administered, perhaps, through public water supplies.

Numbers are not a critical concern only in underdeveloped societies, however. In industrial nations that can easily feed their members, urban problems suggest that humans resemble other animals in their reaction to the stress of crowding.[17] Animal behaviorists have observed for years that, under conditions of crowding, a wide variety of animal populations exhibit abnormal behavior—including suicide, fatal neglect or abuse of their young, gluttony, extreme hostility, withdrawal, and sexual aberrations.[18] When we remember that our own species evolved as members of small bands of hunters and gatherers, perhaps it is not surprising that we have problems adapting to "bands" numbering millions. At any rate, the fact that crowding in human societies results in so many social ills is reason enough for population control.

It is probably premature to ask how far the world's birthrate will eventually fall, but it is interesting to speculate about it. At one point we noted that a new equilibrium of births and deaths might be established somewhere in the neighborhood of 13 to 14 per 1,000 of each per year, which would mean an average life expectancy of seventy to eighty years *in a stable, or*

TABLE 14.4   Rate of growth of world population, 1950–1974

Years	Annual Rate of Growth (in Percentages)
1950–1955	1.77
1955–1960	1.94
1960–1965	2.02
1965–1970	1.96
1970–1973	1.92
1973–1974	1.85

Source: Calculations based on United Nations, *Demographic Yearbook, 1974,* table 1.

nonexpanding, population. Although this seems to be occurring in most of the more advanced industrial societies, it is much less likely to happen in industrializing societies, whose members constitute the majority of the world's population. For the world as a whole, then, the next twenty-five to fifty years will almost certainly see continued rapid growth but at a gradually declining rate—in effect, an extension of the recent trend (see Table 14.4).

Looking further ahead, one can envision a day when societies decide that the great population growth of recent centuries resulted in more people than are really compatible with their values. They might then actually reduce their numbers through very stringent planning of births. This would be a dramatic departure in evolutionary history, but considering the growing concern with the *quality* of human life, it could very well occur—though hardly in this century.*

The population composition of many societies will almost certainly change in the near future. For one thing, the urban populations of industrializing societies will undoubtedly grow much faster than the rural. The age composition of many societies will also change, with a relative increase in the number of middle-aged and elderly people. This is an inevitable consequence of declining birthrates, unless they are offset by drastic reductions in infant mortality or by great increases in adult mortality. Neither of these conditions is anticipated for the more advanced nations, though declines in infant mortality in developing nations could, in many cases, partly offset the effects of declining birthrates. Where the proportion of older people does increase, the effects could be considerable: since youth is generally more favorably disposed toward change than age is, such a shift could act as a brake on the rising rate of social change.

Prospects: Social Structure

Scale of Organization   So far, industrialization has meant larger societies, partly as a result of population growth within existing societies, partly as a result of their enlargement through merger and conquest. These trends have occurred in both industrial and industrializing societies, though conquest has been important only in Africa, where the European powers established the present set of nation-states during the colonial period.

In an increasingly industrial world, the small nation has become an economic and military anachronism. Economically, its home markets are too small to foster the growth of giant enterprises with their economies of scale: militarily, it is incapable of self-defense. As a consequence, multistate

---

*Looking far into the future in one of his science-fiction novels, Fred Hoyle envisions a world in which the human population restricts its numbers to a few million, all of whom live in Mexico. The rest of the earth is left in a natural state and visited only during wilderness vacations.

organizations have begun to form on the regional level, with NATO and the European Economic Community two of the most important to date. Similar organizations would probably be advantageous for most of the societies of Latin America, sub-Saharan Africa, the Middle East, and Southeast Asia, and, should they develop, could well become nuclei for a small number of massive regional super-states in the next century.

By contrast, large-scale empire building of the kind that was so common in the agrarian era seems unlikely in the years ahead. The growth of nationalism in the twentieth century would make control of such an empire very difficult. The most spectacular growth in the size of social organization, of course, would come about through the formation of a single world government; but chances of this happening before 2000 are virtually nil.

Social and Cultural Differentiation Even if political mergers should result in fewer, less dissimilar societies by the year 2000, there would probably be no real decrease in social and cultural differentiation. As machines do more of the work, people are able to devote more of their time and energy to the things they want to do. Because culturally derived interests and needs are virtually limitless, human activities are likely to become even more diversified.

This tendency is already evident in all the more advanced industrial societies. Consider, for example, the need for entertainment: never before have there been so many different forms of it or such a variety of occupations in the field. The same diversity is found in most other fields—sometimes to such an extent that traditional job classifications are rendered obsolete. In a major university, for example, a faculty member often fills a unique niche. When an individual resigns or retires, no one is an exact replacement. Some of the responsibilities are assumed by colleagues, some are discontinued, and the replacement typically takes over part of his or her predecessor's duties and adds others. The old position, in effect, ceases to exist, and a new one is created to fit the new appointee. Although universities are extreme in this respect, many other organizations are moving in the same direction, and this custom-tailoring of occupational roles is likely to become more common in the years ahead.

Opportunities for differentiation and individuality are also growing outside the world of work. In highly productive societies, increased leisure and other resources allow people to develop and express their own distinctive abilities and personalities to an unprecedented degree. This growth in individuality seems almost certain to continue as technological advance provides both greater leisure and higher standards of living. The chief threat to the trend during the next quarter century is likely to come from governments which, because of real or imagined dangers, feel the need to establish more rigorous controls on the behavior of their members.

Social Interaction During the last hundred years, improved systems of transportation and communication have so revolutionized patterns of social interaction that the historical isolation of village populations has been virtually destroyed. It is hard to find the member of an industrial society whose life is still circumscribed by the boundary of his local community; even people who never travel have the world brought to them by the mass media. The same thing is happening in industrializing nations. Better roads and the spread of the mass media are knitting populations together, for the first time, in national networks of communication and interaction. These trends are bound to continue, barring a military or environmental catastrophe.

*Inter*societal interaction, too, has increased fantastically in recent years, largely through the growth of air transportation, which has carried unprecedented numbers of citizens from advanced industrial societies—young people in particular—to other countries. Many industrial and military personnel are stationed abroad; international tourism has become a major industry; and international trade has increased as the new technology has cut the costs of moving goods between nations. There is good reason to expect that these trends not only will continue during the next two decades but will accelerate, for the revolution in social interaction on an international scale is still in an early stage.

Polities Predicting the political future of industrial nations is very risky, largely because their technology, as we have seen, is compatible with a rather wide variety of political systems. The governments of these societies presently range from the highly authoritarian governments of the Soviet Union and East Germany to the fairly democratic governments of the Scandinavian countries. And there is nothing to prevent more extreme types than these from emerging. Such elements of the new technology as computers, data banks, and electronic surveillance equipment could be used to support more authoritarian regimes, just as rising levels of education and increased leisure could foster the growth of more democratic ones.

Despite signs of a very slow drift toward convergence in the political institutions of capitalist and socialist societies, there is little reason to doubt that there will still be considerable political diversity in the year 2000. There are strong forces for continuity in the area of politics, not the least of which is the vested interests of the people in power. There probably will emerge, however, new, intermediate types of government that combine elements of western democracies and socialism. Yugoslav Communism and Swedish Social Democracy are important steps in this direction.* Italian Communism

*Czechoslovakian Communism under Dubcek in 1968 promised to be an even more interesting combination ("Communism with a human face"), but it was tragically crushed by the Soviet invasion—motivated apparently by fear of a system that would become too popular and force changes in their own status quo.

may become another.[19] Its leaders have promised to support a pluralistic, democratic political system. If they come into power and if Italy prospers under their leadership, the Italian system may prove an attractive model for other industrialized societies, and even for some of the more successful industrializing ones.

For most nations that are still industrializing, the prospects for the growth of democracy are poor. If their serious economic difficulties are not somehow alleviated and they cannot substantially improve their standards of living, authoritarian governments of both right and left will almost certainly continue to flourish. This somber prediction could be upset only if industrialized nations took meaningful action to help these developing nations, and prospects of this are dim.

The most urgent political problem that will face human societies during the next quarter century will probably be to avoid nuclear war.[20] The greatest risk may lie in the nuclear capability of one of the lesser powers. There might be a war, for example, between two secondary powers (e.g., Israel and its Arab neighbors, or North and South Korea). Or there might be atomic blackmail by some Third World nation. For example, shortly before Indira Gandhi suspended democratic processes in India, a number of Indian intellectuals were openly discussing a scenario for the future in which the military would seize power and then build a number of cheap nuclear weapons which would be quietly placed on merchant ships and dispatched to major world ports. Indian leaders would then contact the governments of the nations in whose ports the ships were moored, and demand massive financial aid from them as the price for not detonating the hidden nuclear devices.[21]

Unlikely though this may be, it reminds us of the kinds of hazards that await human societies in a divided world in which awesome weapons of destruction are increasingly available at low cost. One would like to believe that the leaders of human societies would be too rational to use nuclear weapons. Recent history tells us, however, that heads of state are not necessarily rational, and that the most irrational are likely to hold power in the most authoritarian political systems, where there are few restraints on their actions (as in the cases of Hitler and Stalin). Thus, we cannot rule out the possibility of a nuclear war, or even a global holocaust, during the next several decades.

The best hope for avoiding such a calamity would undoubtedly be an effective world government. Unfortunately, due in large part to the tremendous social and economic inequalities that have developed among human societies during the last hundred years, this has become extremely difficult to achieve. For if there were a single world state, there would naturally be tremendous pressures from the less affluent majority for a reduction in these inequalities, and the more affluent minority would be reluctant to make the

substantial sacrifices this would require. Per capita income in the United States today, for example, is approximately six times what it is for the world as a whole, which means that Americans would have to cut their standard of living by about 80 per cent to reach the world level. And, since this would be virtually impossible for millions of low-income Americans, the more affluent ones would have to cut theirs even more. Spelling out some of the implications helps us see why prospects for world government in the next few decades are poor.

In the absence of unification, however, the political cleavage between the have and the have-not nations will almost certainly increase. This is likely to be the most important kind of political cleavage in the next quarter century—overshadowing even the differences between socialist and capitalist societies. We have, in fact, already seen it happen. Despite their common adherence to Marxist-Leninist ideology, China and the Soviet Union parted ways when the Chinese charged the Soviets with failing to provide the level of support for economic development that they believed was indicated by socialist principles.

Economies   For many of the world's underdeveloped nations, the best hope for a brighter economic future lies in their control of mineral resources that are essential to industrial nations, but are in short supply. Petroleum is the classic example, but other shortages (e.g., uranium) may well develop. The situation of underdeveloped nations that have no vital resources to bargain with, meanwhile, may well deteriorate, and societies in the Fourth World could easily slide into a situation of complete economic hopelessness unless substantial help were provided by other nations.

For all nations there will be continuing change in economic institutions, change that will reflect past technological innovations as well as those that will occur during the next twenty years. From an evolutionary perspective, the most important trend will probably be an increasing economic interdependence, if not among all societies at least among those above the level of the most disadvantaged. In the thirteen years from 1960 to 1973, an already considerable volume of international trade increased threefold.[22] By the latter date, approximately one-seventh of the world's total production of goods and services was entering into international trade. If present trends continue, most nations will no longer be capable of self-sufficiency by the year 2000, even in an emergency situation of relatively short duration (e.g., six months or a year). Such a prospect may make the affluent nations more receptive to proposals for greater political integration. On the other hand, it may simply encourage them to try harder to reestablish self-sufficiency, especially with respect to such necessities as food and energy.

Growth in international trade will almost certainly increase pressures in capitalist societies for greater governmental intervention in the economy.

When foreign governments and their agents become major participants in vital domestic markets (as when the Soviets became involved in the American grain market), the demand for governmental action cannot be ignored. The increasing economic interdependence of groups and individuals *within* societies, which also seems inevitable, will add to the pressure for greater governmental involvement.

A third probable development will be a continuing shift in the labor force from primary industries located in rural areas to secondary and tertiary industries in urban areas. In the next quarter century, this movement will be concentrated in the industrializing societies of the Third World. Such a massive displacement of people will almost certainly be traumatic, especially in capitalist societies, where there are no assurances of employment and where unemployment and underemployment (i.e., part-time jobs that pay less than a living wage) rates are high. The concentration of large numbers of under- and unemployed people in major urban centers in Third World nations will almost certainly increase the incidence of violence and political unrest. One result may be a number of new socialist revolutions, unless these are averted by military coups.

Unemployment and underemployment are likely to be a continuing problem in the more affluent industrial societies, too. These countries have ample resources that can be used to soften their impact, through such means as unemployment compensation and welfare systems. It remains to be seen, however, whether these solutions will continue to be acceptable to the members of these societies as they come to realize that, side-by-side with unemployment, there are understaffed schools and hospitals, idle factories, and deteriorating cities that could absorb the labor of millions. Politicians and apologists for the present system may find it increasingly difficult to defend present solutions and be forced to come to grips with the fact that unemployment and underemployment in advanced industrial societies are not an inevitable result of their technological advance, but an indication of basic inadequacies of their economic institutions.

Social Stratification All we have said about prospects in the realms of politics and economics makes it abundantly clear that prospects are poor for any reduction of social inequality *at the global level* in the near future, and prospects for the so-called Fourth World nations very dim indeed. Short of pure altruism on the part of more affluent nations, it is difficult to see how these nations can improve their economic situation. By contrast, the more advanced industrial societies seem destined to raise their standards of living still higher, provided they can avoid a nuclear war or a drastic energy shortage.

As a consequence of their democratic and egalitarian ideologies, the members of advanced industrial nations are more sensitive than ever before to inequality and to the possibilities of reducing it—*at least within their own societies.* This has already led to a drastic reduction in economic inequality in socialist societies, and a significant reduction in political inequality in capitalist societies. Looking to the next quarter century, we can expect increasing pressure in socialist societies for greater *political* equality and in capitalist societies for greater *economic* equality. To the extent that these pressures are effective, we will witness the anomaly of greater equality within many societies, but greater inequality among societies as a whole.

Kinship and Marriage The Industrial Revolution probably did more to alter the traditional functions and character of kinship systems than all the innovations of the previous 10,000 years. As a consequence of urbanization, mass public education, birth control technology, and new values and norms, there has been a literal revolution in family life in all the more advanced industrial societies, and it will almost certainly spread to much of the Third World during the next quarter century. While the response of each society will be influenced by its own distinctive cultural traditions, the basic direction of change should be similar to what it has been in Western Europe and North America: smaller families, a decline in the family's role in productive activities, lives that are centered less around the nuclear family and other relatives, changing roles for women, the emergence and growth of youth groups and youth cultures, and rising divorce rates.

Predicting the future of the family in industrialized societies is more difficult. On the one hand, it is possible that the basic trends have already gone about as far as they will go. The birthrate has almost reached the equilibrium point in most of these societies, for example, so there may be little further decline in family size. Similarly, economic production has already been virtually eliminated as a family activity, and children already spend most of their years in school. On the other hand, there are many areas where significant change could still occur. More women could join the labor force; divorce rates could continue to climb; daycare for preschool children could become the norm; and alternative life-styles (e.g., homosexual marriage, communal life, raising children outside of marriage) could become more common.

One of the most disturbing trends to those who see the family as a necessary social institution is the rising divorce rate. In the United States, for example, it increased ninefold between 1890 and 1974.[23] In the latter year there were almost half as many divorces as there were marriages.

Despite this evidence of disappointment in marriages, the institution itself remains extremely popular, and those who divorce commonly marry again. Thus, in the United States in the middle 1970s, 70 per cent of the population eighteen years of age or older were married, and an additional 8 per cent were widows and widowers.[24] This suggests that people continue to need the kind of intimate, comprehensive, and sustained relationships that marriage provides.

Perhaps the most we can predict is that the nuclear family seems certain to survive as an institution, but that it may still experience significant change. The new technology has widened the range of choice in this area as in others. When people marry, they will increasingly do so because they choose to be married rather than single, not because it is an economic or political necessity as in the past. But the needs and values of a society are the ultimate determinants of how its members perceive marriage, and thus they will largely shape future trends in family life.

Prospects: The Higher Goals

Not long ago, Robert Heilbroner, a prominent economist who has long been noted for his insightful analyses of the contemporary scene, wrote a book entitled *An Inquiry into the Human Prospect*. In it, he posed a question which he said is "in the air, more sensed than seen, like the invisible approach of a distant storm." The question: Is there hope for humanity?[25]

As he looks to the future, Heilbroner sees human societies entering an era of what he calls "convulsive change—change forced upon us by external events rather than by conscious choice, by catastrophe rather than by calculation."[26] "Passage through the gantlet ahead," he says, "may be possible only under governments capable of rallying obedience far more effectively than would be possible in a democratic setting. If the issue for mankind is survival, such governments may be unavoidable."[27] In short, the prospects for the higher goals of freedom and happiness are bleak indeed.

Heilbroner bases these unhappy predictions on four assumptions, which, because they are so interrelated, make the chance of finding a solution to our problems much smaller. First, the growth of human population combined with the desire for ever higher standards of living is putting dangerous demands on the environment, and will lead to a breakdown of the ecosystem on which human life depends unless the trend is halted. Some room for growth remains, but far less than most people—or most leaders—realize or are willing to believe. Second, the inequalities among societies created by the growth patterns of the last hundred years have produced dangerous tensions that will not go away unless the more affluent nations are willing to share a substantial portion of their wealth with the less affluent. Third, neither socialism nor capitalism is capable of dealing with these complex and intertwined problems, because both ideologies are predicated on the assumption of unlimited possibilities for economic growth. Finally, Heilbroner points out that our genetic heritage is inadequate for handling the kinds of problems we face today. The same attributes that did so much to propel our species from the Stone Age to the Nuclear Age—our individual-

ism, our self-centeredness, and our expansiveness—could well prove fatal under the new conditions we face. Above all, we need a greater capacity for cooperative action, a greater concern for the needs of future generations, and a greater willingness to deny ourselves, both as individuals and as nations. Genetically, however, we are not programmed that way. Heilbroner concludes his analysis by saying:

> The human prospect is not an irrevocable death sentence. It is not an inevitable doomsday toward which we are headed. . . . The prospect is better viewed as a formidable array of challenges that must be overcome before human survival is assured, before we can move *beyond doomsday.*[28]

But meeting these challenges will mean, in his opinion, substantial sacrifices in terms of human freedom and happiness.

Because of the tremendous advances of the last two hundred years, most of us find it hard to take such a pessimistic forecast seriously. The culture of every modern industrial society is saturated with a belief in the *inevitability* of progress—in terms of the higher goals as well as of technology. Americans, in particular, are indoctrinated in this belief from infancy on.

The study of human societies and their evolution forces us, however, to share Heilbroner's concern for the future, even if we do not entirely share his pessimism. Trends in population growth and in economic development clearly spell trouble, and when we add to the picture an anarchic world polity and a capitalistic world economy marked by gross inequality, the prognosis becomes alarming. Were human societies doomed to continue as they have in the past, their evolutionary course shaped primarily by technological advance, the only sensible prediction would be disaster.

As we have seen, however, the process of evolution itself evolves: as new conditions are established, new forces come into play and new possibilities emerge. This has happened many times in the past. It happened when our remote hominid ancestors developed the genetic capacity to use symbols and build cultures. It happened again when people mastered the techniques of plant cultivation and animal domestication. And it has happened yet again as a consequence of the continuing Industrial Revolution.

Thanks to this most recent period of human history, we now have, in addition to many new problems, new possibilities. For one thing, our store of information about ourselves, our societies, and our environment enables us to look into the future, as Heilbroner has done, and see—while there is still time to act—what will happen if we continue on our present course. This same store of information also furnishes us with the technology that is required to begin to *alter* that course: technology to halt population growth, to recycle materials, to produce protein substitutes, and much more—including the technology required to alert people fully to the dangers ahead.

But foresight and technology can help solve the problem only if they are used properly. And this societies will not do—unless their members, particularly their leaders, recognize that humanity has reached a peculiar point in its evolutionary journey. For technological advance has produced a situation in which some societies have a range of options wider than those of societies of the past, or of most societies today—and yet, if those advanced societies do not make wise choices *now*, that same technology will surely reduce the range of options available to them in the *future*, perhaps drastically so.

Many examples could be used to illustrate this truth, but two will suffice. To begin, the most advanced societies can, at this point, *choose* to offer Third and Fourth World nations irresistible economic incentives to achieve zero population growth quickly; or, they can wait and face that problem when a worldwide food shortage, or perhaps nuclear blackmail by a desperate nation, forces them to respond under conditions not of their own choosing—and with far greater sacrifice than would have been required had they acted sooner. Similarly, advanced nations can, at the present time, still *choose* to design programs to govern the development of alternative energy sources and control the use of the environment, doing it out of concern for their own welfare and that of future generations; or, they can put off making plans until they discover that their options are dwindling and are increasingly dictated by sheer necessity.

Heilbroner is no doubt correct in stating that the future of human societies would be far more secure if humans, like social insects, were genetically programmed for greater cooperation and altruism. But to keep things in perspective, we should remember that traits unique to our species—especially our capacity for symbol use—have, throughout history, enabled humans to *compensate* for many genetic traits that other species have and we do not. Up to this point in sociocultural evolution, most of this compensating has been done technologically: we have concentrated on the kind of information that enables us to take the resources of the environment and reshape and consume them for the satisfaction of our needs and our desires. *But there is nothing to say that technology must continue to be the dominant force shaping the course of human development.* Because culture is more than technology, we can also organize, motivate, and inspire.

Great suffering, loss of freedom, and extinction may not be inevitable for human societies after all. We probably have the resources needed to alter our course.

But we also have the option not to use them.

NOTES

Chapter 1

1. Kingsley Davis, *Human Society* (New York: Macmillan, 1949), p. 27. See also Alfred E. Emerson, "Human Cultural Evolution and Its Relation to Organic Evolution of Insect Societies," in Herbert Barringer et al. (eds.), *Social Change in Developing Areas: A Reinterpretation of Evolutionary Theory* (Cambridge, Mass.: Schenkman, 1965), pp. 50–51.
2. Edward O. Wilson, *Sociobiology: The New Synthesis* (Cambridge, Mass.: Belknap, 1975), part III.
3. Ibid., p. 595.
4. George Gaylord Simpson, *The Meaning of Evolution* (New Haven, Conn.: Yale, 1951), pp. 283–284. Quoted by permission of Yale University Press.
5. This paragraph is based on Paul B. Weisz, *The Science of Biology*, 3d ed. (New York: McGraw-Hill, 1967), chap. 2.
6. Ibid., p. 19.
7. Simpson, p. 281.
8. This is a simplified summary of the basic principles of biological evolution as they are presently understood. It is based on Sir Julian Huxley, *Evolution: The Modern Synthesis* (London: G. Allen, 1942); George Gaylord Simpson, *The Major Features of Evolution* (New York: Columbia, 1953); Ernst Mayr, *Animal Species and Evolution* (Cambridge, Mass.: Harvard, 1963); Sol Tax (ed.), *Evolution after Darwin: The University of Chicago Centennial* (Chicago: University of Chicago Press, 1960), vols. I and III; Weisz, op. cit.; G. G. Simpson and Anne Roe (eds.), *Behavior and Evolution* (New Haven: Yale, 1958); John Maynard Smith, *The Theory of Evolution* (Baltimore: Penguin, 1958); and Helena Curtis, *Biology* (New York: Worth, 1968).
9. Curtis, p. 718.
10. From *This Simian World*, by Clarence Day. Copyright 1920 by Clarence Day, Jr., and

renewed 1948 by Mrs. Clarence Day. Reprinted by permission of Alfred A. Knopf, Inc.

11. Sherwood L. Washburn and David A. Hamburg, "The Implications of Primate Research," in Irven DeVore (ed.), *Primate Behavior: Field Studies of Monkeys and Apes* (New York: Holt, 1965), p. 613.

12. Ibid.

13. W. H. Thorpe, *Learning and Instinct in Animals*, 2d ed. (Cambridge, Mass.: Harvard, 1963).

14. Wilson, pp. 151–152.

15. Ibid., p. 456.

16. Mary-Claire King and A. C. Wilson, "Evolution at Two Levels in Humans and Chimpanzees," *Science*, 188 (Apr. 11, 1975), p. 115.

17. Much of our contemporary appreciation of the importance of symbols in human life stems from Leslie White's challenging essay, "The Symbol: The Origin and Basis of Human Behavior," *Philosophy of Science*, 7 (1940), pp. 451–463.

18. Milton Singer, "Culture," in *International Encyclopedia of the Social Sciences* (New York: Macmillan and Free Press, 1968), vol. 3, p. 540.

19. This paragraph is based on Wilson, pp. 176–185.

20. Karl von Frisch, *Bees: Their Vision, Chemical Senses, and Language* (Ithaca, N.Y.: Cornell, 1950); or "Dialects in the Language of Bees," *Scientific American* (August 1962), pp. 3–7.

21. J. S. Weiner, *The Natural History of Man* (Garden City, N.Y.: Doubleday Anchor, 1973), p. 85.

22. John E. Pfeiffer, *The Emergence of Man*, 2d ed. (New York: Harper & Row, 1972), p. 450, citing Jane van Lawick-Goodall as authority.

23. Leslie White, *The Science of Culture* (New York: Grove, 1949), pp. 37–39.

24. Robert Lord, *Comparative Linguistics*, 2d ed. (London: English Universities Press, 1974), pp. 288–289.

25. John Locke, *An Essay Concerning Human Understanding* (New York: Dover, 1959, first published 1690).

26. Reinhold Niebuhr, *The Nature and Destiny of Man* (New York: Scribner's Sons, 1943), vol. I; Robert Heilbroner, *An Inquiry into the Human Prospect* (New York: Norton, 1974), chap. 4; and Jan Szczepański, *Polish Society* (New York: Random House, 1970), p. 100 and chap. 9.

27. Theodosius Dobzhansky, *Mankind Evolving* (New York: Bantam, 1962), pp. 224–225.

28. Pfeiffer, pp. 425 and 430.

29. René A. Spitz, "Hospitalism," *The Psychoanalytic Study of the Child*, 1 (1945), pp. 53–72, and "Hospitalism: A Follow-up Report," ibid., 2 (1946), pp. 113–117.

30. Pfeiffer, pp. 429–430.

31. Stephen Jay Gould, "Human Babies as Embryos," *Natural History*, 85 (February 1976), p. 22ff.

32. Weisz, p. 819; Curtis, pp. 595–596.

33. Noam Chomsky, *Syntactic Structures* (The Hague: Mouton, 1957), and *Cartesian Linguistics* (New York: Harper & Row, 1966).

34. Pfeiffer, chap. 19.

35. Weisz, p. 819.

36. Dobzhansky, p. 354.

37. Thorstein Veblen provided the classic statement of this principle in his volume, *The Theory of the Leisure Class* (New York: Macmillan, 1899).

38. A. H. Maslow, *Motivation and Personality* (New York: Harper & Row, 1954), especially chap. 5. See also Wilson, p. 143.

39. William Graham Sumner, *Folkways* (New York: Mentor, 1960, first published 1906), p. 32.

40. For a good, brief summary of these developments, see Marvin Harris, *The Rise of Anthropological Theory* (New York: Crowell, 1968), chap. 2.

41. For a good review of the early history of social research, see Bernard Lecuyer and Anthony R. Oberschall, "Sociology: The Early History of Social Research," in *International Encyclopedia of the Social Sciences*, vol. 15, pp. 36–53.

42. See, for example, M. N. Rutkevitch, W. Wesolowski, et al. (eds.), *Transformation of the Social Structure of the U.S.S.R. and Poland* (Moscow and Warsaw: Institute of Sociological Research, Soviet Academy of Sciences and Institute of Philosophy and Sociology, Polish Academy of Sciences, 1974); Eugen Pusić (ed.), *Participation and Self-Management* (Zagreb: First International Sociological Conference on Participa-

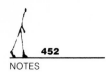

tion and Self-Management, 1972); Murray Yanowitch and Wesley Fisher (eds.), *Social Stratification and Mobility in the U.S.S.R.* (White Plains, N.Y.: International Arts and Sciences Press, 1973); or Szczepański, op. cit.

43. For a pioneering statement of the newer ecological-evolutionary approach, see O. D. Duncan, "Social Organization and the Ecosystem," in R. E. L. Faris (ed.), *Handbook of Modern Sociology* (Chicago: Rand McNally, 1964), pp. 39–45.

44. The revival of interest in ecological-evolutionary theory is even more pronounced in archaeology and anthropology than in sociology. See the work of Grahame Clark, Stuart Piggott, Robert Adams, Robert Braidwood, Leslie White, Julian Steward, Elman Service, Marshall Sahlins, Robert Carneiro, and Marvin Harris, among others.

Chapter 2

1. Anatol Rapoport, "Systems Analysis: General Systems Theory," *International Encyclopedia of the Social Sciences* (New York: Macmillan and Free Press, 1968), vol. 15, p. 454.
2. From "The Mistress of Vision."
3. See, for example, David F. Aberle et al., "The Functional Prerequisites of a Society," *Ethics*, 60 (1950), pp. 100–111; or Talcott Parsons, *The Social System* (Glencoe, Ill.: Free Press, 1951), pp. 26–36.
4. Edward O. Wilson, *Sociobiology: The New Synthesis* (Cambridge, Mass.: Belknap, 1975), p. 510.
5. John E. Pfeiffer, *The Emergence of Man*, 2d ed. (New York: Harper & Row, 1973), pp. 296 and 330.
6. J. S. Weiner, *The Natural History of Man* (Garden City, N.Y.: Doubleday Anchor, 1973), p. 170.
7. Marvin Harris, *Culture, People, Nature*, 2d ed. (New York: Crowell, 1975), p. 98.
8. Ibid., p. 97.
9. Theodosius Dobzhansky, *Mankind Evolving* (New York: Bantam, 1962), p. 280.
10. Harris, p. 96.
11. For brief but fascinating discussions of the relation between human physique and climate, see Dobzhansky, p. 287ff.; Weiner, p. 160ff.; and Adam Hoebel, *Anthropology: The Study of Man*, 3d ed. (New York: McGraw-Hill, 1966), p. 214ff.
12. Weiner, p. 153.
13. Ibid., p. 167.
14. Hoebel, p. 215.
15. Dobzhansky, p. 158ff.
16. Harris, p. 107.
17. Maurice Whittinghill, *Human Genetics* (New York: Reinhold, 1965), fig. 27.2, p. 403.
18. Paul R. Ehrlich and Richard W. Holm, *The Process of Evolution* (New York: McGraw-Hill, 1963), fig. 11.1, p. 253.
19. R. C. Lewontin, "The Apportionment of Human Diversity," *Evolutionary Biology*, 6 (1972), pp. 396–397.
20. Wilson, p. 550.
21. Fred Blumenthal, "The Man in the Middle of the Peace Talks," *Washington Post*, July 14, 1968.
22. Helena Curtis, *Biology* (New York: Worth, 1968), p. 159.
23. Hoebel, p. 35.
24. Karl G. Heider, *The Dugum Dani: A Papuan Culture in the Highlands of West New Guinea* (New York: Wenner-Gren Foundation, 1970), pp. 32–33.
25. Hoebel, p. 35.
26. Robert Lord, *Comparative Linguistics*, 2d ed. (London: English Universities Press, 1974), p. 316. For other interesting examples of changes in the meanings of words, see Charlton Laird, *The Miracle of Language* (Greenwich, Conn.: Premier Books, 1953), p. 54ff.
27. Edward Sapir, *Selected Writings in Language, Culture, and Personality*, David Mandelbaum (ed.) (Berkeley: University of California Press, 1949), p. 162.
28. See, for example, Dell Hymes, "Linguistics: The Field," *International Encyclopedia of the Social Sciences*, vol. 9. p. 22.
29. V. Gordon Childe, *Man Makes Himself* (New York: Mentor, 1951), p. 144ff.

30. This view of ideology borrows from Talcott Parsons' thesis that the prime function of religion is making sense out of the totality of human experience. If the term "religion" is defined to include nontheistic faiths (as we do in this volume), religion and ideology become almost indistinguishable. See Parsons, *The Structure of Social Action* (New York: Free Press, 1968), vol. II, pp. 566–567, 667–668, and 717.
31. See, for example, Robert S. Merrill, "Technology: The Study of Technology," *International Encyclopedia of the Social Sciences*, vol. 15, p. 576.
32. Ralph Turner, "Role: Sociological Analysis," ibid., vol. 13, pp. 552–557.
33. For a more extended discussion of classes, see Gerhard Lenski, *Power and Privilege: A Theory of Social Stratification* (New York: McGraw-Hill, 1966), pp. 73–82.
34. See Reinhard Bendix and Seymour M. Lipset (eds.), *Class, Status, and Power* (New York: Free Press, 1966), pp. 47–72.
35. René Dubos, *So Human an Animal* (New York: Scribner's Sons, 1968), p. 28.
36. Ibid., p. 242. Quoted by permission.
37. Ibid., p. 28. Quoted by permission.

Chapter 3

1. 35,000 B.P. (Before the Present) is the generally accepted date for the emergence of our own species, *Homo sapiens sapiens.* So far as can be judged from existing evidence, only minor genetic changes have occurred since that date.
2. Alfred E. Emerson, "Species: Biology," *Encyclopaedia Britannica*, vol. 29, p. 1149.
3. This paragraph is based on Theodosius Dobzhansky, *Mankind Evolving* (New York: Bantam, 1962), chap. 2; Paul Weisz, *The Science of Biology*, 3d ed. (New York: McGraw-Hill, 1967), chap. 20; and Helena Curtis, *Biology* (New York: Worth, 1968), sec. 3, part II.
4. Dobzhansky, p. 29.
5. Ibid., p. 175.
6. Curtis, p. 422.
7. Comment by Sir Julian Huxley in panel discussion on "The Evolution of Life," in Sol Tax and Charles Callender (eds.), *Evolution after Darwin* (Chicago: University of Chicago Press, 1960), vol. III, p. 112.
8. See, for example, the definition of culture as "a body of nongenetic information transmitted from generation to generation," in Paul Ehrlich and Richard Holm, *The Process of Evolution* (New York: McGraw-Hill, 1963), p. 320.
9. *New York Times* News Service wire report, Nov. 28, 1975.
10. See, for example, Loren Eiseley, *Darwin's Century: Evolution and the Men Who Discovered It* (Garden City, N.Y.: Doubleday Anchor, 1961).
11. Marvin Harris, *Culture, People, Nature*, 2d ed. (New York: Crowell, 1975), pp. 197–198.
12. J. S. Weiner, *The Natural History of Man* (Garden City, N.Y.: Doubleday Anchor, 1973), p. 177, table 8.
13. James K. Feibleman, *The Institutions of Society* (London: G. Allen, 1956), p. 52.
14. For a discussion of a number of interesting examples, including those here, see A. L. Kroeber, *Anthropology* (New York: Harcourt, Brace, 1948), pp. 353–355. For more recent examples, see Howard A. Rush, "Right Time and Place: Many Medical Discoveries Found to Result from Series of Accidents," *New York Times*, June 8, 1969.
15. For an early discussion of this point, see William F. Ogburn, *Social Change* (New York: Viking, 1922), chap. 6.
16. Ogburn mentioned this factor briefly in his study, but did not stress it (ibid., 1950 ed., p. 110).
17. Ralph Linton, *The Study of Man* (New York: Appleton-Century, 1936), pp. 326–327. Reprinted by permission of Prentice-Hall, Inc.
18. Basil Davidson with F. K. Buah, *A History of West Africa* (Garden City, N.Y.: Doubleday Anchor, 1966), pp. 8–9.
19. Ogburn, 1950 ed., p. 107.
20. See Table 5.2, page 126 below.
21. See E. Power Biggs, "Dr. Schweitzer's Intuition Confirmed," *Saturday Review*, Aug. 31, 1968, pp. 41–43, for a fascinating discussion of the technological foundation of Bach's compositions.
22. Marshall Sahlins, "Evolution: Specific and General," in Marshall Sahlins and Elman

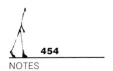
Service (eds.), *Evolution and Culture* (Ann Arbor: University of Michigan Press, 1960).

23. A. L. Kroeber, *Anthropology* (New York: Harcourt, Brace, 1948), p. 375.

24. John Nef, *The Conquest of the Material World* (Chicago: University of Chicago Press, 1964), p. 8.

Chapter 4

1. See Marvin Harris, *The Rise of Anthropological Theory* (New York: Thomas Crowell, 1968), chap. 2; and Robert Nisbet, *Social Change and History* (New York: Oxford, 1969), chap. 4.

2. This method of classification is an expansion and modification of one developed earlier by Walter Goldschmidt in *Man's Way: A Preface to the Understanding of Human Society* (New York: Holt, 1959), chap. 6, and also reflects the influence of V. Gordon Childe, *Man Makes Himself* (New York: Mentor, 1951). For an earlier, and somewhat less satisfactory, version of the present classification, see Gerhard Lenski, *Power and Privilege: A Theory of Social Stratification* (New York: McGraw-Hill, 1966), pp. 91–93.

3. In Africa south of the Sahara, most societies have long manufactured iron tools and weapons but have had a horticultural base. This has been because of the diffusion of the techniques of ironmaking without a corresponding diffusion of the plow and agriculture. For purposes of analysis, these societies are classified as advanced horticultural, since they fail to meet the minimal criterion for agrarian societies (i.e., the presence of the plow).

4. See Jacquetta Hawkes, *Prehistory* (New York: Mentor, 1965), chap. 6, for a good summary of archaeological finds relating to fishing. See also Grahame Clark and Stuart Piggott, *Prehistoric Societies* (New York: Knopf, 1965), chap. 7.

5. Robert Braidwood, "The Earliest Village Communities of Southwestern Asia Reconsidered"; and Karl Butzer, "Agricultural Origins in the Near East as a Geographical Problem," in Stuart Struever (ed.), *Prehistoric Agriculture* (Garden City, N.Y.: Natural History Press, 1971), pp. 222 and 249.

6. James Mellaart, *Earliest Civilizations in the Near East* (London: Thames and Hudson, 1965), p. 105.

7. See, for example, Leslie Aitchison, *A History of Metals* (London: MacDonald and Evans, 1960), vol. 1, p. 41.

8. E. Cecil Curwen and Gudmund Hatt, *Plough and Pasture: The Early History of Farming* (New York: Collier Books, 1961), p. 64.

9. Aitchison, pp. 102 and 111–113.

10. Mellaart, p. 20.

11. William H. McNeill, *The Rise of the West: A History of the Human Community* (New York: Mentor, 1965), p. 150.

12. These data are also available in a book by Murdock entitled *Ethnographic Atlas* (Pittsburgh: Pittsburgh University Press, 1967).

13. See the appendix on pp. 503–507 of the first edition of *Human Societies* for details on the classification of societies. When Murdock's data were insufficient for classification purposes, we returned to the original monographs.

14. Specifically, the codes on industrial societies were often based on the study of a single community that could in no sense be regarded as representative of the society.

15. This particular code was not reported in the Ethnographic Atlas in *Ethnology* but in an earlier paper of Murdock's entitled "World Ethnographic Sample," *American Anthropologist*, 59 (1957), pp. 644–687. This paper provided data on a sample of 565 societies and offered a more limited range of information. The computations reported in the tables in this chapter are our own.

16. Of the hunting and gathering societies 14 per cent were classified as fully migratory, 61 per cent as seminomadic, and 15 per cent as semisedentary.

17. This way of classifying religious beliefs is based on work by G. E. Swanson in *The Birth of the Gods: The Origin of Primitive Beliefs* (Ann Arbor: University of Michigan Press, 1960), chap. 3.

18. Leslie White was the leading proponent of this point of view for many years. See, for example, his stimulating but extreme essay, "Energy and the Evolution of Culture," in *The Science of Culture* (New York: Grove Press, 1949), pp. 363–393.

19. Talcott Parsons is one of many who have consistently minimized the role of technology in the process of social change. Though not as extreme as some in his views, he has been very influential. See *Societies: Evolutionary and Comparative Perspectives* (Englewood Cliffs, N.J.: Prentice-Hall, 1966), especially pp. 113–114, for his views.

Chapter 5

1. For an example of the use of the term "analogous peoples," see Grahame Clark and Stuart Piggott, *Prehistoric Societies* (New York: Knopf, 1965), p. 133. On the value of inferences from ethnography, see Frank Hole and Robert Heizer, *An Introduction to Prehistoric Archeology* (New York: Holt, 1965), especially pp. 211–214 and chap. 16; or Grahame Clark, *Archaeology and Society: Reconstructing the Historic Past*, 3d ed. (London: Methuen, 1957), pp. 172–174. In several instances, contemporary hunters and gatherers have provided explanations for previously unexplained archaeological findings. See, for example, John E. Pfeiffer, *The Emergence of Man*, 2d ed. (New York: Harper & Row, 1972), chap. 15.
2. Clark, pp. 172–173. Quoted by permission of Methuen & Co., Ltd.
3. Pfeiffer, p. 12, and J. S. Weiner, *The Natural History of Man* (Garden City, N.Y.: Doubleday Anchor, 1973), pp. 3–4.
4. Pfeiffer, p. 62ff.
5. Weiner, p. 50ff.
6. Ibid., chap. 2, especially pp. 63–101.
7. Pfeiffer, p. 120.
8. Ibid., p. 144.
9. Jacquetta Hawkes, *Prehistory, UNESCO History of Mankind*, vol. 1, part 1 (New York: Mentor, 1965), p. 172. See also Clark and Piggott, p. 45, or Grahame Clark, *The Stone Age Hunters* (London: Thames and Hudson, 1967), p. 25.
10. Pfeiffer, chap. 6.
11. Ibid., chap. 7, and William Laughlin, "Hunting: An Integrating Biobehavior System and its Evolutionary Importance," in Richard Lee and Irven DeVore (eds.), *Man the Hunter* (Chicago: Aldine, 1968).
12. H. V. Vallois, "The Social Life of Early Man: The Evidence of Skeletons," in Sherwood Washburn (ed.), *Social Life of Early Man* (Chicago: Aldine, 1961), pp. 214–235.
13. Pfeiffer, p. 189ff.
14. Ibid., p. 144.
15. S. A. Semenov, *Prehistoric Technology*, trans. M. W. Thompson (New York: Barnes & Noble, 1964), pp. 202–203.
16. E. Adamson Hoebel, *Anthropology*, 3d ed. (New York: McGraw-Hill, 1966), pp. 176–177, and Hawkes, pp. 212–213.
17. This and the following statements concerning the bow and arrow are based on Semenov, pp. 202–204.
18. Hawkes, p. 212.
19. J. G. D. Clark, *Prehistoric Europe: The Economic Basis* (London: Methuen, 1952), pp. 132–133.
20. Hawkes, pp. 184–188, and Pfeiffer, p. 240.
21. Peter Ucko and Andreé Rosenfeld, *Palaeolithic Cave Art* (New York: McGraw-Hill, 1967), or Grahame Clark, *The Stone Age Hunters*, chap. 4.
22. Clark and Piggott, pp. 93–95.
23. Hawkes, pp. 293–294, including fig. 35b.
24. For good reviews of recent work on hunters and gatherers, see Lee and DeVore, op. cit.; Carleton S. Coon, *The Hunting Peoples* (Boston: Little, Brown, 1971); and Elman Service, *The Hunters* (Englewood Cliffs, N.J.: Prentice-Hall, 1966).
25. This figure is based on Elkin's estimate that there were approximately 300,000 aborigines in Australia at the time of the first white settlement. This estimate was divided by 60, a very generous estimate for the average size of these societies. See A. P. Elkin, *The Australian Aborigines*, 3d ed. (Sydney: Angus and Robertson, 1954), p. 10.
26. See Martin Baumhoff, *Ecological Determinants of Aboriginal California Populations*,

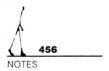
University of California *Publications in American Archaeology and Ethnology*, 49 (Berkeley, 1963), especially pp. 227 and 231. See also Elkin, op. cit., and his estimate of an aboriginal population of 300,000 prior to white settlement. Since Australia contains nearly 3 million square miles, this means an average density of only 1 person per 10 square miles. In Alaska, there was only 1 per 25 square miles at the time of its purchase by the United States (Hawkes, p. 183).

27. See Table 4.2 (page 97 above); Joseph Birdsell, "Some Predictions for the Pleistocene Based on Equilibrium Systems among Recent Hunter-Gatherers," in Lee and DeVore, p. 235; or Gerhard Lenski and Jean Lenski, *Human Societies*, 2d ed. (New York: McGraw-Hill, 1974), pp. 134–135.

28. See, for example, John Garvan, *The Negritos of the Philippines* (Vienna: Ferdinand Berger, 1964), p. 27; or Edwin Loeb, *Sumatra: Its History and People* (Vienna: Institut für Volkerkunde, 1935), p. 283, on the Kubu.

29. Only one of the 15 nonnomadic hunting and gathering societies in Murdock's sample depended on hunting and gathering for as much as three-quarters of its subsistence, whereas more than half of the 136 nomadic hunting and gathering societies were in this category. The one exception among the nonnomadic societies (the Nomlaki) was located in the Sacramento Valley of northern California, a territory as favorable for a hunting and gathering people as any in the world (see Baumhoff, pp. 205–231).

30. Colin Turnbull, "The Mbuti Pygmies of the Congo," in James Gibbs (ed.), *Peoples of Africa* (New York: Holt, 1965), pp. 286–287.

31. James Woodburn, "Ecology, Nomadic Movement and the Composition of the Local Group among Hunters and Gatherers: An East African Example and Its Implications," in Peter J. Ucko, Ruth Tringham, and G. W. Dimbleby (eds.), *Man, Settlement and Urbanism* (London: Duckworth, 1972), p. 201ff.

32. Richard B. Lee, "Work Effort, Group Structure and Land-Use in Contemporary Hunter-Gatherers," in Ucko et al., pp. 181–184.

33. Garvan, p. 29.

34. Lorna Marshall, "The !Kung Bushmen of the Kalahari Desert," in Gibbs, pp. 257–258. Quoted by permission of Holt, Rinehart and Winston, Inc. See also Charles Hose and William McDougall, *The Pagan Tribes of Borneo* (London: Macmillan, 1912), pp. 190–191; Allan Holmberg, *Nomads of the Long Bow: The Siriono of Eastern Bolivia*, Smithsonian Institution, Institute of Social Anthropology, 10 (Washington, 1950), p. 11; or Loeb, p. 300.

35. See, for example, Walter Goldschmidt, *Nomlaki Ethnography*, University of California *Publications in American Archaeology and Ethnology*, 42 (Berkeley, 1951), pp. 333–335 and 417–428.

36. See, for example, Loeb, p. 294, or Holmberg, pp. 30 and 91.

37. Turnbull, pp. 287 and 297; Frederick McCarthy and Margaret McArthur, "The Food Quest and the Time Factor in Aboriginal Economic Life," in Charles Mountford (ed.), *Records of the American-Australian Expedition to Arnhem Land* (Melbourne: Melbourne University Press, 1960), pp. 190–191; Kenneth MacLeish, "The Tasadays: Stone Age Cavemen of Mandanao," *National Geographic*, 142 (August 1972), pp. 243–245; Richard B. Lee, "What Hunters Do for a Living, or How to Make Out on Scarce Resources," in Lee and DeVore, pp. 36–37.

38. See Service, p. 13, and Marshall Sahlins, "Notes on the Original Affluent Society," in Lee and DeVore, pp. 85–89.

39. Goldschmidt, p. 417. See also Asen Balicki, "The Netsilik Eskimos: Adaptive Responses," and the comments of Lorna Marshall and Colin Turnbull, in Lee and DeVore, pp. 78–82, 94, and 341, for challenges to the recent effort to portray life in hunting and gathering societies as idyllic and trouble-free.

40. See, for example, Lee, p. 40.

41. Coon, *The Hunting Peoples*, p. 176.

42. In the sample of hunting and gathering societies in the Ethnographic Atlas, hunting was entirely a male activity in 97 per cent of the cases and predominantly a male activity in the rest. On the other hand, gathering was wholly or largely a female activity in 91 per cent of the societies and predominantly a male activity in only 2 per cent (in the remainder the activity was shared by both sexes).

43. Of the hunting and gathering societies in the Ethnographic Atlas, 57 per cent defined this as a male responsibility, 25 per cent as a female, and 18 per cent regarded it as appropriate to both sexes.

44. I. Schapera, *Government and Politics in Tribal Societies* (London: Watts, 1956), p. 93. See also Holmberg's description of the Siriono headman or chief quoted on p. 176, and Hose and McDougall, p. 190, on the Punan shaman.

45. Other specialists, much less common, may include part-time workers in certain arts and crafts and occasionally an assistant to the headman. Such individuals are most likely to be found in settled communities that depend less on hunting and gathering or in those with especially favorable environments. See, for example, Goldschmidt, pp. 331–332, and Elkin, p. 254ff.

46. See, for example, Turnbull, pp. 287–288; Ivor Evans, *The Negritos of Malaya* (London: Cambridge, 1937), pp. 57 and 112–113; Garvan, p. 66; or Hose and McDougall, p. 191. Turnbull warns, however, that many scholars exaggerate the dependence of the Pygmies on the neighboring horticultural villagers. He maintains that they turn to the villagers only for luxuries and diversion. See *Wayward Servants: The Two Worlds of the African Pygmies* (Garden City, N.Y.: Natural History Press, 1965), pp. 33–37.

47. A. R. Radcliffe-Brown, "The Social Organization of Australian Tribes," *Oceania*, 1 (1930), pp. 44–46.

48. Elkin, p. 56 (Doubleday Anchor edition); emphasis added.

49. Service, *The Hunters*, p. 32ff. For some exceptions, see Turnbull, *Wayward Servants*, pp. 109–112.

50. See, for example, Elkin, p. 50, and Evans, p. 254.

51. See, for example, Garvan, p. 82.

52. Service, p. 42.

53. Coon, *The Hunting Peoples*, p. 192; Laughlin, "Hunting," pp. 318–320; Julian Steward, "Causal Factors and Processes in the Evolution of Pre-farming Societies," in Lee and DeVore, pp. 332–333; and Elman Service, *Primitive Social Organization: An Evolutionary Perspective* (New York: Random House, 1962), chap. 3, especially p. 61.

54. Service, *Primitive Social Organization*, p. 49.

55. See, for example, Elkin, pp. 134–137.

56. Occasionally there might be a second official. See, for example, Kaj Birket-Smith, *The Eskimos*, rev. ed. (London: Methuen, 1959), p. 145; Goldschmidt, pp. 324–325; and Frank Speck, *Penobscot Man* (Philadelphia: University of Pennsylvania Press, 1940), pp. 239–240.

57. Holmberg, pp. 59–60. Quoted by permission of the Smithsonian Institution Press. Following an older usage, Holmberg refers to the leaders of Siriono bands as "chiefs." In current usage, such persons are usually referred to as "headmen," and the term "chief" is reserved for the leaders of tribes or other multicommunity societies. For this reason, the term "headman" has been substituted.

58. See, for example, John Cooper, "The Ona," in Julian Steward (ed.), *Handbook of South American Indians*, Smithsonian Institution, Bureau of American Ethnology, Bulletin 143 (Washington, 1946), vol. 1, p. 117; A. R. Radcliffe-Brown, *The Andaman Islanders* (Glencoe, Ill.: Free Press, 1948), p. 47; Hose and McDougall, p. 182, on the Punan of Borneo; Speck, p. 239, on the Penobscot of Maine; Schapera, *The Khoisan Peoples*, p. 151; and Roland Dixon, "The Northern Maidu," in Carleton S. Coon (ed.), *A Reader in General Anthropology* (New York: Holt, 1948), p. 272.

59. Baldwin Spencer and F. J. Gillen, *The Arunta: A Study of a Stone Age People* (London: Macmillan, 1927), vol. 1, p. 10.

60. Schapera, *Government and Politics*, p. 117. Quoted by permission of C. A. Watts & Co., Ltd. See also A. H. Gayton, *Yokuts-Mono Chiefs and Shamans,* University of California *Publications in American Archaeology and Ethnology*, 24 (Berkeley, 1930), pp. 374–376.

61. See, for example, Colin Turnbull, *Wayward Servants*, chaps. 11 and 12, or *The Forest People* (New York: Simon & Schuster, 1961), on the Mbuti Pygmies. As he indicates, the office of headman is sometimes found among these people, but it has been more or less forced on them by the Bantu villagers and is of little significance except in their contacts with these villagers.

62. See, for example, Schapera, *Government and Politics*, p. 193, or Turnbull, *Wayward Servants*, pp. 100–109.

63. See John Honigmann, *The Kaska Indians: An Ethnographic Reconstruction*, Yale University *Publications in Anthropology*, 51 (1954), pp. 90–92 and 96–97; Radcliffe-Brown, *The Andaman Islanders* pp. 48–52; Schapera, *The Khoisan Peoples of South Africa* (London: Routledge, 1930), pp. 151–155; and Hose and McDougall, p. 182.

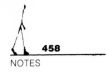

64. Schapera, *The Khoisan Peoples*, p. 152.

65. Radcliffe-Brown, *The Andaman Islanders*, p. 50.

66. Ibid., p. 51, and Schapera, *The Khoisan Peoples*, p. 152.

67. See, for example, Goldschmidt, pp. 330–341.

68. See, for example, Evans, p. 21; Marshall, "!Kung Bushmen," p. 248; or Radcliffe-Brown, p. 29. For an exception, see Birket-Smith, pp. 145–146. For intermediate cases, see Honigmann, pp. 84, 88, and 96; Elkin, p. 45; and H. Ling Roth, *The Aborigines of Tasmania* (London: Kegan Paul, Trench, Trubner, 1890), p. 71.

69. Sometimes certain trees become the private property of an individual who stakes a special claim to them, but this is uncommon and the number of trees involved is generally small. See, for example, Radcliffe-Brown, *The Andaman Islanders*, p. 41, or Goldschmidt, p. 333.

70. See, for example, McCarthy and McArthur, "Aboriginal Economic Life," pp. 179–180; Schapera, *The Khoisan Peoples*, pp. 100–101; Radcliffe-Brown, *The Andaman Islanders*, p. 43; Hose and McDougall, p. 187; or Speck, p. 47.

71. Radcliffe-Brown, *The Andaman Islanders*, pp. 44–48.

72. See, for example, Goldschmidt, pp. 324–326.

73. Among the sample of hunting and gathering societies in the Ethnographic Atlas, 54 per cent had provision for the hereditary transmission of the office, usually to a son of the previous headman.

74. This definition is based on Hoebel, *Anthropology*, p. 572, and Elkin, *The Australian Aborigines*, p. 25.

75. Examples are provided by the Punan of Borneo (Hose and McDougall, p. 183) or the Mbuti Pygmies of Africa (Turnbull, *Wayward Servants*, pp. 100–109).

76. Schapera, *The Khoisan Peoples*, p. 76. Quoted by permission of Routledge & Kegan Paul, Ltd.

77. See, for example, Goldschmidt, p. 324.

78. For a more detailed discussion of this point as it applies to the religion of the Australian aborigines, see W. E. H. Stanner, "Religion, Totemism and Symbolism," in Ronald Berndt and Catherine Berndt (eds.), *Aboriginal Man in Australia: Essays in Honour of Emeritus Professor A. P. Elkin* (Sydney: Angus and Robertson, 1965), pp. 207–237.

79. In part, the diversity of religious beliefs and practices is the result of cultural diffusion from more advanced societies. Apparently the diffusion of religious ideas occurs more easily than other types of diffusion (e.g., the diffusion of complex structural systems). See, for example, Loeb's comments on the religious ideas of various hunting and gathering peoples on Sumatra (*Sumatra*, pp. 216–217, 286–289, etc.). See also Hose and McDougall, p. 186.

80. See, for example, W. E. H. Stanner's comments on this as it applies to the Australian aborigines, in "The Dreaming," in William Lessa and Evon Vogt (eds.), *Reader in Comparative Religion*, 2d ed. (New York: Harper & Row, 1965). See also Evans, chaps. 14–18 and 24; Garvan, chap. 14; Turnbull, *The Forest People*; and others.

81. William D. Davis, *Societal Complexity and the Sources of Primitive Man's Conception of the Supernatural* (unpublished Ph.D. dissertation, University of North Carolina, Chapel Hill, 1971), chap. 5. Davis reports such beliefs in all but one of the eleven hunting and gathering societies he studied.

82. See especially Stanner, "Religion, Totemism and Symbolism," pp. 215–216, or "The Dreaming," p. 159, where Stanner refers to the Australian aboriginal concept of "the eternal dream time," which he suggests may best be translated as "everywhen." See also Turnbull, *The Forest People*, especially chaps. 4 and 8.

83. See Service, *The Hunters*, p. 70.

84. For descriptions of shamans and their practices, see Evans, chaps. 19–20; Coon, *The Hunting Peoples*, chap. 16; Honigmann, pp. 104–108; Schapera, *The Khoisan Peoples*, pp. 195–201; Radcliffe-Brown, *The Andaman Islanders*, pp. 175–179; Elkin, chap. 11; or Gayton, pp. 392–398.

85. See, for example, Dixon, p. 282.

86. Ibid., p. 272.

87. Jacob Baegert, S.J., *Account of the Aboriginal Inhabitants of the California Peninsula*, in Coon, *A Reader in General Anthropology*, p. 79. See also Radcliffe-Brown, *The Andaman Islanders*, p. 177.

88. Turnbull, *The Forest People*, p. 130. Copyright, 1961 by Colin M. Turnbull. By permission of Simon & Schuster, Inc.

89. See, for example, Elkin, chap. 7; Marshall, "!Kung Bushmen," pp. 264–267; Turnbull, "The Mbuti Pygmies," pp. 306–307; or Coon, *The Hunting Peoples*, chap. 14.

90. Herbert Barry III, Irving L. Child, and Margaret K. Bacon, "Relation of Child Training to Subsistence Economy," *American Anthropologist*, 61 (1959), p. 263.

91. Some of the best evidence of religious motivation comes from Australia (see Elkin, pp. 191–192 or 232–234). For an example of art employed as an instrument of sympathetic magic, see Evans, p. 130ff.

92. Turnbull, "The Mbuti Pygmies," pp. 308–312, *The Forest People*, chap. 4, and *Wayward Servants*, pp. 259–267.

93. See, for example, Hose and McDougall, p. 192, and Speck, p. 270ff.

94. Turnbull, *The Forest People*, p. 135.

95. Birket-Smith, p. 44; compare with Table 11.1, p. 302, which shows the rates for industrial societies.

96. Schapera, *The Khoisan Peoples*, p. 116. Some more recent research on the Bushmen indicates greater intervals between births, but these findings have not yet received the careful scrutiny they merit. See N. Howell, in R. B. Lee and Irven DeVore (eds.), *Kalahari Hunter-Gatherers* (Cambridge, Mass., Harvard, 1975).

97. Evans, p. 16.

98. Hose and McDougall, p. 183.

99. Evans, op. cit., and Don Dumond, "The Limitations of Human Population: A Natural History," *Science*, 187 (Feb. 28, 1975), p. 714.

100. One survey revealed that infanticide was practiced in twelve out of fifteen hunting and gathering societies, and thirteen of them also practiced abortion. See John Whiting, "Effects of Climate on Certain Cultural Practices," in Ward Goodenough (ed.), *Explorations in Cultural Anthropology: Essays in Honor of George Peter Murdock* (New York: McGraw-Hill, 1964). The tabulations are our own and are based on table 9, pp. 528–533.

101. Dumond, p. 715.

102. Holmberg, *Nomads of the Long Bow*, p. 85. A more general survey concluded that "individuals who live as long as fifty years are rare" in hunting and gathering societies (cited by Service, *Primitive Social Organization*, p. 80).

103. Lee, "What Hunters Do for a Living," p. 36; and Frederick Dunn, "Epidemiological Factors: Health and Disease in Hunter-Gatherers," in Lee and DeVore, pp. 221–228, or Howell, op. cit.

104. For similar comparisons, see Grahame Clark, *The Stone Age Hunters*, op. cit., and Pfeiffer, op. cit.

105. See, for example, Clark and Piggott, *Prehistoric Societies*, p. 130ff., or Hole and Heizer, *Introduction to Prehistoric Archeology*, pp. 225–226.

106. Orlando Lizama, "Death of Woman Marked Tribe's End: First Seen By Magellan," *Washington Post*, Aug. 17, 1975, p. F3.

107. Pfeiffer, p. 349, and Dumond, p. 717.

108. Marshall, p. 273.

109. Nina Bari Kolata, "!Kung Hunters-Gatherers: Feminism, Diet, and Birth Control," *Science*, 185 (Sept. 13, 1974), p. 932.

Chapter 6

1. Jack Harlan, "The Plants and Animals That Nourish Man," *Scientific American*, 235 (September 1976), pp. 89–97; Jack Harlan, *Crops and Man* (Madison, Wis.: American Society of Agronomy, 1975); or Stuart Streuver (ed.), *Prehistoric Agriculture* (Garden City, N.Y.: Natural History Press, 1971), parts II and IV.

2. V. Gordon Childe, *What Happened in History*, rev. ed. (Baltimore: Penguin, 1964), pp. 65–66.

3. See, for example, Robert Braidwood and Bruce Howe, "Southwestern Asia beyond the Lands of the Mediterranean Littoral," in Robert Braidwood and Gordon Willey (eds.), *Courses toward Urban Life: Archeological Considerations of Some Cultural Alternatives* (Chicago: Aldine, 1962), pp. 137, 152–153, and 346; or James Mellaart, *Earliest Civilizations of the Near East* (London: Thames and Hudson, 1965), pp. 12, 32–38, 47–50, and 81.

4. The technique is so named because it measures the amount of radioactive carbon

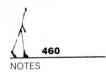

remaining in dead material. For a good description of the technique, see Frank Hole and Robert Heizer, *An Introduction to Prehistoric Archeology* (New York: Holt, 1965), pp. 145–150.

5. Braidwood and Howe, p. 140; Mellaart, chaps. 3ff.; V. Gordon Childe, "The New Stone Age," in Harry Shapiro (ed.), *Man, Culture, and Society* (New York: Oxford Galaxy, 1960), p. 103; E. Cecil Curwen and Gudmund Hatt, *Plough and Pasture: The Early History of Farming* (New York: Collier Books, 1961), p. 33.

6. See Braidwood and Willey, op. cit.; or Robert Braidwood, "Domestication: The Food-producing Revolution," in *International Encyclopedia of the Social Sciences* (New York: Macmillan and Free Press, 1968), vol. 4, pp. 245–247.

7. Jacquetta Hawkes, *Prehistory, UNESCO History of Mankind*, vol. 1, part 1 (New York: Mentor, 1965), pp. 442–452; Mellaart, p. 42; Childe, "The New Stone Age," p. 107.

8. Childe, "The New Stone Age," pp. 100–101.

9. See, for example, B. H. Farmer, "Agriculture: Comparative Technology," in *International Encyclopedia of the Social Sciences*, vol. 1, pp. 204–205; or Curwen and Hatt, p. 68 and chap. 16.

10. Childe, *What Happened in History*, pp. 64–65.

11. Mellaart, pp. 50–51, or Jean Perrot, "Palestine-Syria-Cilicia," in Braidwood and Willey, pp. 156–157.

12. Hawkes, pp. 384–395; Childe, "The New Stone Age," pp. 104–105; or Perrot, pp. 154–155.

13. Hawkes, pp. 395–401, and Mellaart, pp. 40–42.

14. Mellaart, p. 47.

15. Childe, "The New Stone Age," p. 105. Elsewhere Childe speaks of twenty-five to thirty-five households as "a not uncommon number" in central Europe and southern Russia. See *What Happened in History*, p. 66.

16. Mellaart, p. 36, or Hawkes, p. 310.

17. Mellaart, pp. 81–101.

18. See, for example, Childe, "The New Stone Age," p. 106, or *What Happened in History*, pp. 67–68. See also Braidwood and Howe, p. 138.

19. Mellaart, p. 36. See also p. 84 for his views on Çatal Hüyük.

20. Childe, "The New Stone Age," p. 106.

21. Mellaart, pp. 43–44.

22. See Childe, *What Happened in History*, p. 67.

23. Childe, "The New Stone Age," p. 106, and *What Happened in History*, p. 67.

24. For a good review of these developments, see Hawkes, pp. 401–410 and 414–417; or V. Gordon Childe, *Man Makes Himself* (New York: Mentor, 1953), pp. 76–80.

25. Childe, "The New Stone Age," p. 107, or *What Happened in History*, p. 74.

26. Childe, "The New Stone Age," p. 107.

27. See, for example, H. D. Sankalia, *Prehistory and Protohistory in India and Pakistan* (Bombay: Bombay University Press, 1962), pp. 152–155; or Sir Mortimer Wheeler, *Early India and Pakistan* (London: Thames and Hudson, 1959), p. 80ff.

28. For the ethnographic evidence, see Table 4.2, p. 97.

29. On the absence of weaving in Britain, see Hawkes, p. 326.

30. Ibid.

31. See Kwang-chih Chang, *The Archaeology of Ancient China* (New Haven, Conn.: Yale, 1963), pp. 130–131. See also Curwen and Hatt, pp. 16–18, on truths contained in ancient traditions.

32. The quotations in this paragraph are all from Chang, pp. 131–133, and are used by permission of the Yale University Press.

33. Mellaart, pp. 130–131, and V. Gordon Childe, *New Light on the Most Ancient East* (London: Routledge, 1952), p. 118ff.

34. Childe, *New Light*, p. 115, and Hawkes, p. 425.

35. Childe, *New Light*, p. 115.

36. Mellaart, p. 130.

37. Ibid., p. 105.

38. R. J. Forbes, *Studies in Ancient Technology* (Leiden, Netherlands: Brill, 1964), vol. 9, p. 30, or Leslie Aitchison, *A History of Metals* (London: MacDonald and Evans, 1960), vol. 1, p. 21.

39. Aitchison, p. 40.

40. Ibid., or Forbes, vol. 8, p. 26.

41. Childe, *Man Makes Himself*, p. 99.

42. V. Gordon Childe, *The Bronze Age* (London: Cambridge, 1930), p. 11.
43. See, for example, Childe, *New Light*, p. 116. There is still some uncertainty about this point.
44. William Watson, *The Chinese Exhibition* (a guide to the exhibition of archaeological finds of the People's Republic, exhibited in Toronto, 1974), p. 14.
45. Some bronze seems to have been manufactured accidentally a few centuries earlier as a result of using copper derived from ores containing tin, but the deliberate and conscious alloying of metals did not begin until after 3000 B.C. See Forbes, vol. 9, pp. 151–152. Recent research by scholars at the University of Pennsylvania suggests that the invention of bronze may have occurred in Thailand prior to 3600 B.C., which would explain why bronze was an integral part of advanced horticultural societies in China, but not in the Middle East.
46. William Watson, *China: Before the Han Dynasty* (New York: Praeger, 1961), p. 57.
47. Te-k'un Cheng, *Archaeology in China: Shang China* (Cambridge, England: Heffer, 1960), pp. 206–207.
48. Shang kings, for example, mounted "many military expeditions with an army of between 3,000 and 5,000 men." Ibid., p. 210, and Cho-yun Hsu, *Ancient China in Transition* (Stanford, Calif.: Stanford, 1965), p. 67.
49. See footnote 44 above.
50. Cheng, pp. 200–206.
51. Ibid., pp. 200–215 and 248. For a more detailed picture of the system of stratification in the Chou era, see Hsu, op. cit. In reading this book one must keep in mind that the Chan Kuo period, the "period of the warring states," is included, and by then, north-central China seems to have reached the agrarian level of development.
52. Watson, *China: Before the Han Dynasty*, p. 141, and Chang, p. 195ff.
53. Aitchison, p. 97.
54. Hsu, pp. 3–7 and chap. 4.
55. Chang, p. 150.
56. Watson, *China: Before the Han Dynasty*, p. 106. See also Hsu, p. 15ff., on the interrelations between religion and politics in Chou China.
57. Chang, pp. 150 and 159.
58. Ibid., p. 171.
59. Marvin Harris, *Culture, People, Nature*, 2d ed. (New York: Crowell, 1975), p. 208.
60. For a recent survey of these developments, see Harris, pp. 212–228; for an extended survey of the three most highly developed cultures of the New World, the Aztecs, Mayas, and Incas, see Victor von Hagen, *The Ancient Sun Kingdoms of the Americas* (Cleveland: World, 1961).
61. Marvin Harris, *The Rise of Anthropological Theory* (New York: Crowell, 1968), p. 4.
62. A careful comparison of societies in the two eras suggests that modern simple horticulturalists may be a bit less advanced than their prehistoric predecessors. For example, more than a third of those in Murdock's sample did not make pottery and more than half did not engage in weaving, both common practices in simple horticultural societies of prehistoric times.
63. Only 10 per cent of the hunting and gathering societies in the Ethnographic Atlas sample maintained fairly permanent settlements, and virtually all these relied on either fishing or horticulture as a secondary source of subsistence. By contrast, 87 per cent of the simple horticultural societies maintained such settlements.
64. A number of simple horticultural groups have built structures 50 or more feet long. See Gunnar Landtman, *The Kiwai Papuans of British New Guinea* (London: Macmillan, 1927), p. 5, or Gerhard Lenski, *Power and Privilege* (New York: McGraw-Hill, 1966), p. 121.
65. Lenski, pp. 124–125.
66. Ibid., p. 122.
67. See, for example, Steward and Faron's statement (op. cit., p. 300) with reference to villagers who occupied most of the northern half of South America that "kinship was the basis of society throughout most of this area." Many similar statements could be cited.
68. See E. Adamson Hoebel, *Anthropology*, 3d ed. (New York: McGraw-Hill, 1966), pp. 374–376, for a good brief summary of these functions.
69. These figures are based on data in Dean Shiels, "Toward a Unified Theory of Ancestor Worship," *Social Forces*, 54 (December 1975), appendix, part B.
70. For similar findings based on Murdock's earlier sample of 565 societies, see David

Aberle, "Matrilineal Descent in Cross-cultural Perspective," in David Schneider and Kathleen Gough (eds.), *Matrilineal Kinship* (Berkeley: University of California Press, 1961), table 17.4, p. 677.

71. Aberle reached a similar conclusion (op. cit., p. 725). He states that "in general, matriliny is associated with horticulture, in the absence of major activities carried on and coordinated by males. . . ."

72. Multicommunity societies constitute only 2 per cent of all pure hunting and gathering societies (i.e., those in which fishing and horticulture are not important secondary sources of subsistence) but comprise 23 per cent of all simple horticultural societies.

73. Lenski, pp. 119–120.

74. For an early statement of this process, see Lewis Henry Morgan, *Ancient Society* (Cambridge, Mass.: Belknap Press, 1965, first published 1877), p. 109ff.

75. This dual role seems to have been quite common in South America. See Julian Steward and Louis Faron, *Native Peoples of South America* (New York: McGraw-Hill, 1959), p. 301, on the Indians of eastern Brazil and the Amazon Basin; or Julian Steward, "The Tribes of the Montaña and Bolivian East Andes," in Julian Steward (ed.), *Handbook of South American Indians*, Smithsonian Institution, Bureau of American Ethnology, Bulletin 143 (Washington, 1948), vol. III, p. 528. For a slightly different pattern in North America, see Irving Goldman, "The Zuni Indians of New Mexico," in Margaret Mead (ed.), *Cooperation and Competition among Primitive Peoples*, rev. ed. (Boston: Beacon Press, 1961), p. 313.

76. Robert Lowie, "Social and Political Organization," in Steward, *Handbook*, vol. V, p. 345. For examples of this, see Steward, *Handbook*, vol. III, pp. 85, 355, 419, and 478. See also Steward and Faron, p. 244.

77. See, for example, Alfred Métraux, *Native Tribes of Eastern Bolivia and Western Matto Grosso*, Smithsonian Institution, Bureau of American Ethnology, Bulletin 134 (Washington, 1942), p. 39, on the Araona; or Leopold Pospisil, "Kaupauku Papuan Political Structure," in F. Ray (ed.), *Systems of Political Control and Bureaucracy in Human Societies, Proceedings of the 1958 Meetings of the American Ethnological Society* (Seattle), p. 18.

78. For a more detailed discussion of these bases of status, see Lenski, pp. 126–131.

79. See Steward and Faron, pp. 302–303, on the former, and pp. 213–214, 243, and 248–249, on the latter.

80. Data provided by Leo Simmons, *The Role of the Aged in Primitive Society* (New Haven, Conn.: Yale, 1945), show that scalp taking or headhunting was a frequent practice in only one of five hunting and gathering societies but in thirteen of fourteen horticultural societies.

81. Lest this idea appear utterly fanciful, it should be noted that in recent years experimental psychologists have trained various kinds of animals to do specific things and then have ground up their brains and injected the resulting chemical extracts into untrained animals, with the effect that the untrained animals displayed the learned pattern of behavior, indicating a chemical transfer of learning. See Fred Warshofsky, *The Control of Life* (New York: Viking, 1969), pp. 165–167.

82. Alfred Métraux, "Warfare-Cannibalism-Trophies," in Steward, *Handbook*, vol. V, pp. 400–401. Quoted by permission of the Bureau of American Ethnology.

83. Sonia Cole, *The Prehistory of East Africa* (New York: Mentor, 1965), p. 299.

84. Of the simple horticultural societies, 15 per cent had hereditary systems of stratification, compared to 47 per cent of the advanced horticultural societies. None of the simple societies had complex systems of stratification (i.e., three or more classes apart from slaves), compared with 7 per cent of the advanced.

85. Meyer Fortes, in Meyer Fortes and E. E. Pritchard (eds.), *African Political Systems* (London: Oxford, 1940), p. 5.

86. In one study of twenty-two African horticultural societies, a correlation of .67 (Kendall's tau) was found between level of political development and level of social inequality (see Lenski, p. 163). See also Basil Davidson with F. K. Buah, *A History of West Africa: To the Nineteenth Century* (Garden City, N.Y.: Doubleday Anchor, 1966), p. 174.

87. See Lucy Mair, *Primitive Government* (Baltimore, Penguin, 1962), especially chap. 4. The discussion that follows is based largely on her work. See also Lenski, chaps. 6 and 7; Morton Fried, *The Evolution of Political Society* (New York: Random House, 1967); and Elman Service, *Origins of the State and Civilization: The Process of Cultural Evolution* (New York: Norton, 1975).

88. Estimated from the map in Davidson, p. 68.

89. I. Schapera, *Government and Politics in Tribal Societies* (London: Watts, 1956), p. 169. See also the Swazi proverb that "nobles are the chief's murderers."

90. See, for example, Davidson, chap. 14.

91. See, for example, George Peter Murdock, *Africa: Its Peoples and Their Culture History* (New York: McGraw-Hill, 1959), p. 37.

92. See, for example, P. C. Lloyd, "The Yoruba of Nigeria," in James Gibbs (ed.), *Peoples of Africa* (New York: Holt, 1965), pp. 554–556.

93. For an example of multicommunity society, see P. R. T. Gurdon, *The Khasis* (London: Macmillan, 1914). This author reports that these people were divided into fifteen small states averaging 15,000 in population and controlling about 400 square miles apiece (pp. 1 and 66).

94. Lenski, pp. 160–162. See also Davidson, pp. 76–77.

Chapter 7

1. V. Gordon Childe, *What Happened in History* (Baltimore: Penguin, 1964), p. 77.

2. Ibid., chap. 4.

3. This paragraph and the one that follows are based on B. H. Farmer, "Agriculture: Comparative Technology," in *International Encyclopedia of the Social Sciences* (New York: Macmillan and Free Press, 1968), vol. 1, pp. 204–205.

4. See Gudmund Hatt, "Farming of Non-European Peoples," in E. Cecil Curwen and Gudmund Hatt, *Plough and Pasture: The Early History of Farming* (New York: Collier Books, 1961), pp. 217–218.

5. Childe, p. 89.

6. V. Gordon Childe, *Man Makes Himself* (New York: Mentor, 1951), p. 100.

7. Farmer, p. 205.

8. See Childe, *Man Makes Himself*, p. 100. In recent years, some have argued that horticulture is more efficient than agriculture in the tropics and that horticultural societies should not be considered less advanced than agricultural. Though there are some areas where horticulture is more efficient, these are rare (a 1957 study by the Food and Agriculture Organization of the United Nations showed that only 7 per cent of the world's population were using horticultural techniques, and often only because of ignorance of the alternative). Furthermore, horticultural societies clearly have not achieved the efficiency in other areas of technology or the complexity of social structure and ideology that agrarian societies have. Though we know of no single paper that provides a comprehensive, balanced analysis of this problem, we recommend R. F. Watters's excellent paper, "The Nature of Shifting Cultivation: A Review of Recent Research," *Pacific Viewpoint*, 1 (1960), pp. 59–99, especially pp. 77–95.

9. E. Cecil Curwen, "Prehistoric Farming of Europe and the Near East," in Curwen and Hatt, pp. 64–65; or C. W. Bishop, "The Origin and Early Diffusion of the Traction Plow," *Antiquity*, 10 (1936), p. 261.

10. Some scholars have argued that Egypt had no cities at this time. See, for example, John A. Wilson, "Civilization without Cities," in Carl Kraeling and Robert Adams (eds.), *City Invincible: A Symposium on Urbanization and Cultural Development in the Ancient Near East* (Chicago: University of Chicago Press, 1960), pp. 124–136; or William McNeill, *The Rise of the West: A History of the Human Community* (New York: Mentor, 1963), pp. 87–88. Although there were surely differences between Egyptian and Mesopotamian cities, it seems to be semantic gamesmanship to deny the existence of Egypt's cities. Several commentators on Wilson's paper made just this point (see Kraeling and Adams, pp. 136–162). Especially telling was the comment of one Mesopotamian specialist, who noted that when the Assyrians came to Egypt, they spoke of "hundreds of cities" (Kraeling and Adams, p. 140). See also Tertius Chandler and Gerald Fox, *3000 Years of Urban Growth* (New York: Academic Press, 1974), p. 362.

11. Samuel Noah Kramer, *The Sumerians* (Chicago: University of Chicago Press, 1963), p. 123.

12. Childe, *Man Makes Himself*, pp. 143–144.

13. See, for example, Sir Leonard Woolley, *The Beginnings of Civilization*, UNESCO

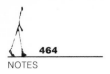

History of Mankind, vol. I, part 2 (New York: Mentor, 1965), pp. 116, 119, 198, 449ff.

14. Sir Leonard Woolley, *Prehistory* (New York: Harper & Row, 1963), vol. 1, part 2, p. 127. Reprinted by permission.

15. Margaret Murray, *The Splendour That Was Egypt* (London: Sidgwick & Jackson, 1949), p. 174.

16. On Mesopotamia, see Woolley, *Beginnings*, p. 356, or A. Leo Oppenheim, *Ancient Mesopotamia: Portrait of a Dead Civilization* (Chicago: University of Chicago Press, 1964), pp. 84–85. On Egypt, see Ralph Turner, *The Great Cultural Traditions: The Foundations of Civilization* (New York: McGraw-Hill, 1941), vol. 1, p. 187; or George Steindorff and Keith Seele, *When Egypt Ruled the East*, rev. ed. (Chicago: Phoenix Books, 1963), p. 83.

17. Robert Adams, "Factors Influencing the Rise of Civilization in the Alluvium: Illustrated by Mesopotamia," in Kraeling and Adams, p. 33.

18. See, for example, Kramer, pp. 88–89; Woolley, p. 125; or Kingsley Davis, "The Origin and Growth of World Urbanism," *American Journal of Sociology*, 60 (1955), p. 431. See also Oppenheim, p. 140, who, though declining to estimate size, reports Nineveh to have been larger than Ur (generally thought to have been over 100,000) and Uruk nearly as large, or Mason Hammond, *The City in the Ancient World* (Cambridge, Mass.: Harvard, 1972).

19. Woolley, *Beginnings*, p. 185ff., or Steindorff and Seele, pp. 89–90.

20. Woolley, ibid., p. 188. Later armies were even larger.

21. Turner, p. 312.

22. McNeill, p. 68; Turner, pp. 310–311; Steindorff and Seele, chap. 9; Pierre Montet, *Everyday Life in Egypt: In the Days of Rameses the Great*, trans. A. R. Maxwell-Hyslop and Margaret Drower (London: E. Arnold, 1958), chap. 10; Oppenheim, pp. 70ff., 230ff., and 276–277.

23. Oppenheim, p. 276. As one writer reports, "Sumerian bureaucracy has left us a staggering number of texts; we are unable to venture a guess as to how many tablets beyond the far more than 100,000 now in museums may be buried in southern Mesopotamia."

24. Childe, *Man Makes Himself*, pp. 148–149, or Childe, *What Happened in History*, p. 144.

25. See especially Kramer, p. 231, or Samuel Noah Kramer, *It Happened at Sumer* (Garden City, N.Y.: Doubleday, 1959), p. 3.

26. See Turner, p. 263, or Childe, *What Happened in History*, p. 118.

27. Childe, *What Happened in History*, pp. 118–119.

28. See Turner's excellent treatment of this topic, pp. 317–323.

29. Adolf Erman, *Life in Ancient Egypt*, trans. H. M. Tirard (London: Macmillan, 1894), p. 128.

30. Childe, *Man Makes Himself*, p. 180, quoted by permission of C. A. Watts & Co., Ltd. See also McNeill, p. 53, or Childe, *What Happened in History*, p. 183ff.

31. *Man Makes Himself*, p. 181. Elsewhere, Childe adds a third innovation (or a fifth to the total list), the invention of glass in Egypt. See *What Happened in History*, p. 183.

32. See Childe, *Man Makes Himself*, chap. 9, for a classic discussion of this subject. The analysis that follows is heavily indebted to Childe's provocative discussion but varies in some details and emphases.

33. See Childe, *What Happened in History*, p. 184.

34. For a classic statement of this principle, see Gaetano Mosca, *The Ruling Class*, translated by Hannah Kahn (New York: McGraw-Hill, 1939), p. 53.

35. For a good summary of the early history of iron, see Leslie Aitchison, *A History of Metals* (London: MacDonald and Evans, 1960), vol. 1, pp. 97–110. The discussion that follows is based largely on Aitchison.

36. Ibid., p. 113.

37. See, for example, Charles Singer's comparison of the level of technology in the ancient empires of Egypt and Mesopotamia prior to 1000 B.C. and later in Greece and Rome, in "Epilogue: East and West in Retrospect," in Charles Singer (ed.), *A History of Technology* (Oxford: Clarendon Press, 1956), vol. II, pp. 754–755.

39. See, for example, Turner, map on p. 232.

40. Jerome Blum, *Lord and Peasant in Russia from the Ninth to the Nineteenth Century* (Princeton, N.J.: Princeton University Press, 1961), p. 278. One might object that much of the Russian empire was sparsely settled, but the same was true of the Egyptian empire.

41. See, for example, the reference maps in T. W. Wallbank et al., *Civilization*, 5th ed. (Chicago: Scott, Foresman, 1965), vol. I, pp. 658–671.

42. This estimate was based on the known boundaries of these societies and on the fact that the Roman Empire, which was much larger and contained a much smaller percentage of uninhabitable land, had a maximum population of only about 70 million. See *The Cambridge Ancient History* (London: Cambridge, 1939), vol. XII, pp. 267–268. It is also noteworthy that in Roman times Egypt had a population of only 6 to 7 million. Even if allowance is made for the greater size of the Egyptian empire in the days of Egypt's independence, it is difficult to imagine a total population much in excess of 15 million. See Charles Issawi, *Egypt in Revolution: An Economic Analysis* (New York: Oxford, 1963), p. 20.

43. Chung-li Chang, *The Chinese Gentry: Studies on Their Role in Nineteenth-Century Chinese Society* (Seattle: University of Washington Press, 1955), p. 102.

44. On India, see Kingsley Davis, *The Population of India and Pakistan* (Princeton, N.J.: Princeton University Press, 1951), pp. 24–25; on Rome, see *The Cambridge Ancient History*, pp. 267–268; on Russia, see Blum, p. 278.

45. See, for example, Tertius Chandler and Gerald Fox, *3000 Years of Urban Growth* (New York: Academic Press, 1974).

46. Turner, p. 911.

47. F. R. Cowell, *Cicero and the Roman Republic* (London: Penguin, 1956), p. 79. Quoted by permission of Penguin Books.

48. See, for example, Blum, pp. 126 and 394–395, on Russia; or Ralph Linton, *The Tree of Culture* (New York: Vintage Books, 1959), p. 231, on China.

49. S. B. Clough and C. W. Cole, *Economic History of Europe* (Boston: Heath, 1941), p. 25.

50. Ibid. See also Blum, pp. 16 and 126.

51. Gerhard Lenski, *Power and Privilege: A Theory of Social Stratification* (New York: McGraw-Hill, 1966), pp. 197–198.

52. For the effect of war on the forms of government, see Herbert Spencer, *The Principles of Sociology* (New York: Appleton, 1897), vol. II, part 5, chap. 17; Pitirim Sorokin, *Social and Cultural Dynamics* (New York: Bedminster Press, 1962), vol. III, pp. 196–198; or Stanislaw Andrzejewski, *Military Organization and Society* (London: Routledge, 1954), pp. 92–95.

53. These figures were calculated from A. E. R. Boak, *A History of Roman Imperial Civilization* (Garden City, N.Y.: Doubleday Anchor, 1959), using Mattingly's list of emperors, pp. 351–355.

54. For figures on several other societies, see Lenski, p. 235.

55. Wolfram Eberhard, *Conquerors and Rulers: Social Forces in Medieval China* (Leiden, Netherlands: Brill, 1952), p. 52; and Blum, p. 558.

56. For an interesting popular account of the former, see Philip Lindsay and Reg Groves, *The Peasants' Revolt, 1381* (London: Hutchinson, n.d.).

57. Sorokin, vol. III, chap. 10, especially p. 352.

58. See, among others, Lenski, pp. 210–242 and 266–284, for more detailed documentation.

59. Robert K. Douglas, *Society in China* (London: Innes, 1894), p. 104.

60. See Max Weber, *The Theory of Social and Economic Organization*, trans. A. M. Henderson and Talcott Parsons (New York: Free Press, 1947), pp. 341–348; and Max Weber, *Wirtschaft und Gesellschaft*, 2d ed. (Tübingen: Mohr, 1925), vol. II, pp. 679–723.

61. Mattingly, p. 137. See also Turner, vol. II., p. 620, or Michael Rostovtzeff, *The Social and Economic History of the Roman Empire*, rev. ed. (Oxford: Clarendon Press, 1957), p. 54.

62. Hans Rosenberg, *Bureaucracy, Aristocracy, and Autocracy: The Prussian Experience 1660–1815* (Cambridge, Mass.: Harvard, 1958), pp. 5–6. Quoted by permission of Harvard University Press.

63. Chung-li Chang, *The Income of the Chinese Gentry* (Seattle: University of Washington Press, 1962), Summary Remarks, supplement 2, and chap. 1.

64. On the king's income, see Sir James H. Ramsey, *A History of the Revenues of the Kings of England: 1066–1399* (Oxford: Clarendon Press, 1925), vol. I, pp. 227 and 261. For the income of the nobility, see Sidney Painter, *Studies in the History of the English Feudal Barony* (Baltimore: Johns Hopkins, 1943), pp. 170–171. For the income of field hands, see H. S. Bennett, *Life on the English Manor: A Study of Peasant Conditions, 1150–1400* (London: Cambridge, 1960), p. 121.

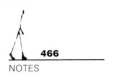

65. Lenski, pp. 219 and 228.
66. See, for example, Albert Lybyer, *The Government of the Ottoman Empire in the Time of Suleiman the Magnificent* (Cambridge, Mass.: Harvard, 1913); or W. H. Moreland, *The Agrarian System of Moslem India* (Allahabad, India: Central Book Depot, n.d.).
67. F. Pelsaert, *Jahangir's India*, trans. W. H. Moreland and P. Geyl and quoted by B. B. Misra, *The Indian Middle Classes* (London: Oxford, 1961), p. 47. Quoted by permission of W. Heffer & Sons, Ltd.
68. Lybyer, pp. 47–58 and 115–117.
69. See, for example, James Westfall Thompson's statement that "the medieval state was a loose agglomeration of territories with rights of property and sovereignty everywhere shading into one another," in *Economic and Social History of the Middle Ages* (New York: Appleton-Century-Crofts, 1928), p. 699. See also Marc Bloch, *Feudal Society*, trans. L. A. Manyon (Chicago: University of Chicago Press, 1962), especially chaps. 14–24; Blum, chap. 2; or Sidney Painter, *The Rise of the Feudal Monarchies* (Ithaca, N.Y.: Cornell, 1951), and *Studies in the History of the English Feudal Barony*, op. cit.
70. For a more detailed discussion of the factors influencing this balance, see Lenski, pp. 234–240.
71. See, for example, Karl Wittfogel, *Oriental Despotism: A Comparative Study of Total Power* (New Haven, Conn.: Yale, 1957), p. 79ff.; Alan Simpson, *The Wealth of the Gentry, 1540–1660* (London: Cambridge, 1961), pp. 107–108; Blum, pp. 82 and 378; Misra, pp. 44 and 50; and Jean Hippolyte Mariéjol, *The Spain of Ferdinand and Isabella*, trans. Benjamin Keen (New Brunswick, N.J.: Rutgers, 1961), pp. 276–277.
72. See, for example, Painter, *The Rise of the Feudal Monarchies*, pp. 127–129.
73. Moreland, pp. 92–100.
74. For examples of the application of the policy of "divide and rule," see Mariéjol, p. 264ff., or Rosenberg, p. 152ff.
75. Robert Heilbroner, *The Making of Economic Society* (Englewood Cliffs, N.J.: Prentice-Hall, 1962), p. 27. See also H. R. Trevor-Roper, "The Gentry 1540–1640," *The Economic History Review Supplements*, no. 1 (n.d.); or Bloch, who wrote of "that age when true wealth consisted in being the master" (p. 192).
76. Heilbroner, pp. 9–44.
77. A. H. M. Jones, *The Later Roman Empire 284–602: A Social, Economic and Administrative Survey* (Oxford: Blackwell, 1964), vol. I, p. 465.
78. See page 196 above on peasant revolts. See also G. G. Coulton, *The Medieval Village* (London: Cambridge, 1926), chaps. 11 and 24–25.
79. Blum, pp. 369–370.
80. Ibid., pp. 356–357.
81. Sjoberg, *The Preindustrial City*, p. 215.
82. See, for example, Chang, *Income of the Chinese Gentry*, pp. 37–51.
83. For a survey of these obligations, see Lenski, pp. 267–270.
84. Ibid., p. 228.
85. See, for example, Blum, p. 232, or Moreland, p. 207.
86. Sansom, *A History of Japan*, vol. III, p. 29.
87. Bennett, p. 236.
88. Ibid., pp. 232–236.
89. See, for example, Moreland, p. 147, on India; or Blum, pp. 163, 266–268, 309–310, and 552ff., on Russia.
90. Douglas, p. 354.
91. Blum, pp. 424 and 428, on Russia; and Gunnar Myrdal, *An American Dilemma* (New York: McGraw-Hill, 1964), p. 931, on the American South.
92. Literally, the right of the first, wedding, night. See Coulton, pp. 80 and 464–469; Blum, pp. 426–427; G. M. Carstairs, "A Village in Rajasthan," in M. N. Srnivas (ed.), *India's Villages* (Calcutta: West Bengal Government Press, 1955), pp. 37–38.
93. Bennett, p. 196; Coulton, pp. 190–191, 248–250, and 437–440.
94. G. G. Coulton, *Medieval Panorama* (New York: Meridian Books, 1955), p. 77, or Thompson, p. 708.
95. William Stubbs, *The Constitutional History of England* (Oxford: Clarendon Press, 1891), vol. I, p. 454n., Wolfram Eberhard, *A History of China*, 2d ed. (Berkeley: University of California Press, 1960), p. 32; and Yosoburo Takekoshi, *The Economic Aspects of the History of the Civilization of Japan* (New York: Macmillan, 1930), vol. I, pp. 60–63.

96. See Boak, *A History of Rome*, p. 127, or Cowell, *Cicero and the Roman Republic*, p. 64. For an example of the application of Cato's principle in medieval Europe, see Bennett, p. 283.

97. See, for example, Bloch, p. 337, or George Homans, *English Villagers of the 13th Century* (Cambridge, Mass.: Harvard, 1942), p. 229.

98. See, for example, Morton Fried, *The Fabric of Chinese Society: Study of the Social Life of a Chinese County Seat* (New York: Praeger, 1953), pp. 104–105; Moreland, pp. 168 and 207; and Bennett, pp. 100–101, 112–113, and 131ff.

99. See, for example, the franklins in thirteenth-century England (Homans, pp. 248–250).

100. May McKisack, *The Fourteenth Century* (Oxford: Clarendon Press, 1959), pp. 331–340; Lindsay and Groves, pp. 30, 34, and 63; Charles Langlois, "History," in Arthur Tilley (ed.), *Medieval France* (London: Cambridge, 1922), pp. 150–151; and Paul Murray Kendall, *The Yorkist Age* (Garden City, N.Y.: Doubleday, 1962), p. 171ff.

101. Sjoberg, p. 83; Lynn White, *Medieval Technology and Social Change* (Oxford: Clarendon Press, 1962), p. 39; Henri Pirenne, *Economic and Social History of Medieval Europe* (New York: Harvest Books, n.d., first published 1933), p. 58; J. C. Russell, *British Medieval Population* (Albuquerque: University of New Mexico Press, 1948), p. 305; Blum, pp. 268 and 281.

102. See Sjoberg, pp. 108–116, or Samuel G. Stoney, *Plantations of the Carolina Low Country* (Charleston: Carolina Art Association, 1938), p. 36.

103. Kendall, p. 157.

104. Carcopino, *Daily Life in Ancient Rome*, p. 70.

105. Ibid.

106. See, for example, Sjoberg, p. 183ff. For an interesting example of the persistence of this pattern into the latter part of nineteenth-century England, see W. Somerset Maugham, *Cakes and Ale* (New York: Pocket Books, 1944), p. 29.

107. On acquisition by marriage, see Elinor Barber, *The Bourgeoisie in 18th Century France* (Princeton, N.J.: Princeton University Press, 1955), p. 89, or Sansom, vol. III, pp. 128–129. On confiscation, see Misra, pp. 25–27; Takekoshi, vol. II, p. 251ff.; Kendall, p. 181; or Ramsay, vol. I, p. 58.

108. John Lossing Buck, *Secretariat Paper No. 1, Tenth Conference of the Institute of Pacific Relations* (Stratford on Avon, 1947), reprinted in Irwin T. Sanders et al., *Societies around the World* (New York: Dryden Press, 1953), p. 65.

109. Clough and Cole, *Economic History of Europe*, p. 445.

110. See, for example, John Nef, *The Conquest of the Material World* (Chicago: University of Chicago Press, 1964), p. 69.

111. Cowell, p. 80. See also William Woodruff, *Impact of Western Man: A Study of Europe's Role in the World Economy* (New York: St. Martin's, 1966), p. 254.

112. Sylvia Thrupp, *The Merchant Class of Medieval London* (Ann Arbor: Ann Arbor Paperbacks, University of Michigan Press, 1962), p. 9.

113. See, for example, Nef, p. 78.

114. Sidney Gamble, *Peking: A Social Survey* (New York: Doran, 1921), pp. 183–185.

115. Thrupp, pp. 19, 30, etc.

116. Ibid., pp. 23 and 29–31; James Westfall Thompson, *Economic and Social History of Europe in the Later Middle Ages, 1300–1530* (New York: Century, 1931), p. 398.

117. Gamble, p. 283.

118. In Asia many were sold into prostitution by their parents. See Gamble, p. 253. Many more, in every part of the world, were ignorant country girls seeking work in the city who were trapped by hired procurers, while still others were driven to prostitution by unemployment and lack of funds. See M. Dorothy George, *London Life in the XVIIIth Century* (London: Kegan Paul, Trench, Trubner, 1925), pp. 112–113.

119. See, for example, Frederick Nussbaum, *A History of the Economic Institutions of Modern Europe* (New York: Crofts, 1933); or Frank Aydelotte, *Elizabethan Rogues and Vagabonds* (Oxford: Clarendon Press, 1913), p. 4.

120. Eberhard, *History of China*, pp. 108 and 274; and Chang, *The Chinese Gentry*, p. 102.

121. Taeuber, *The Population of Japan*, pp. 20 and 41; Russell, p. 235; and D. V. Glass and D. E. C. Eversley, *Population in History* (Chicago: Aldine, 1965), p. 240, on England.

122. Warren Thompson and David Lewis, *Population Problems*, 5th ed. (New York: McGraw-Hill, 1965), p. 386; O. Andrew Collver, *Birth Rates in Latin America: New Estimates of Historical Trends and Fluctuations* (Berkeley, Calif.: Institute of International Studies, 1965), pp. 26–30; Glass and Eversley, pp. 467, 532, 555, and 614. One of the lowest rates for an agrarian society prior to the twentieth century was for

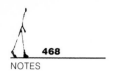
eighteenth-century Sweden, and it was nearly 36 per 1,000 (Glass and Eversley, p. 532).

123. See, for example, Horace Miner, *St. Denis: A French-Canadian Parish* (Chicago: Phoenix Books, The University of Chicago Press, 1963), p. 65; Berger, p. 116; Coulton, *The Medieval Village*, p. 322; Manning Nash, *The Golden Road to Modernity: Village Life in Contemporary Burma* (New York: Wiley, 1965), pp. 265–266.

124. See, for example, John Noss, *Man's Religions*, rev. ed. (New York: Macmillan, 1956), pp. 227, 304ff., and 420–421; and Miner, pp. 65–66.

125. Miner, p. 170.

126. Harrison Brown, *The Challenge of Man's Future* (New York: Viking Compass, 1956), p. 75.

127. H. Hollingsworth, "A Demographic Study of the British Ducal Families," in Glass and Eversley, tables 2 and 5, pp. 358 and 360.

128. Brown, p. 75.

129. Warren Thompson, *Population Problems*, 3d ed. (New York: McGraw-Hill, 1942), p. 73.

130. M. C. Buer, *Health, Wealth, and Population in the Early Days of the Industrial Revolution, 1760–1815* (London: Routledge, 1926), pp. 77–78. Quoted by permission of Routledge & Kegan Paul, Ltd.

131. D. E. C. Eversley, "Population, Economy, and Society," in Glass and Eversley, p. 52.

132. Warren Thompson, p. 58. See also Brown, p. 32.

133. K. F. Helleiner, "The Vital Revolution Reconsidered," in Glass and Eversely, p. 79.

134. See Kenneth Scott Latourette, *A History of Christianity* (New York: Harper, 1953), pp. 15–16.

135. See Robert Bellah, "Religious Evolution," *American Sociological Review*, 29 (1964), pp. 367–368.

136. See, for example, Lenski, pp. 7–9. See also Kendall, p. 232ff.

137. Lenski, pp. 257–258.

138. Ibid., pp. 262–266, gives a more detailed treatment of this aspect of religion.

139. James Thompson, *Economic and Social History of the Middle Ages*, p. 684.

140. See, for example, Carlo Levi, *Christ Stopped at Eboli* (New York: Farrar, Straus, 1947), chaps. 11ff., for a good description of the role of magic in one agrarian community. On fatalism, see, for example, Edward Banfield, *The Moral Basis of a Backward Society* (New York: Free Press, 1967), pp. 36–37, 41, and 107ff.

141. Sjoberg, *The Preindustrial City*, p. 146ff.

142. Ibid., p. 155.

143. Ibid., p. 163ff.; Henry Orenstein, *Gaon: Conflict and Cohesion in an Indian Village* (Princeton, N.J.: Princeton University Press, 1965), pp. 53–57; Kendall, *The Yorkist Age*, chaps. 11 and 12; L. F. Salzman, *English Life in the Middle Ages* (London: Oxford University Press, 1927), pp. 254–256.

144. Bennett, p. 260. Quoted by permission.

145. Ibid. For other descriptions of the uses of leisure in agrarian societies, see Margaret Wade Labarge, *A Baronial Household of the Thirteenth Century* (New York: Barnes & Noble, 1966), chap. 10; Bennett, *Life on the English Manor*, chap. 10; or Coulton, *Medieval Panorama*, chaps. 8 and 44.

146. F. R. Cowell, *Everyday Life in Ancient Rome* (New York: G. P. Putnam's Sons, 1961), p. 173.

147. See, for example, H. van Werveke, "The Rise of the Towns," in *The Cambridge Economic History of Europe* (London: Cambridge, 1963), vol. 3, pp. 34–37; L. Halphen, "Industry and Commerce," in Tilley, pp. 190–192; or Pirenne, *Economic and Social History of Medieval Europe*, pp. 187–206.

148. See, for example, Frederick Jackson Turner, *The Frontier in American History* (New York: Holt, 1920); or James G. Leyburn, *Frontier Folkways* (New Haven, Conn.: Yale, 1936).

Chapter 8

1. According to Murdock's Ethnographic Atlas, the Manus of New Guinea come as close to full dependence on fishing as any people in the world. See *Ethnology*, vol. 6, no. 2 (April 1967), pp. 170–230. Yet, as Margaret Mead indicates in her report, these people

also depend heavily for their subsistence on garden products that they obtain through trade from neighboring peoples and to a lesser degree on pigs that they raise and obtain through trade. See Margaret Mead, *Growing Up in New Guinea* (New York: Mentor, 1953, first published 1930), especially pp. 173–174.

2. For an earlier discussion of this point, see Gordon Hewes's excellent paper, "The Rubric 'Fishing and Fisheries,'" *American Anthropologist*, 50 (1948), pp. 241–242.

3. See Table 4.2, p. 97.

4. For a good illustration of this, see Philip Drucker's excellent description of the Indians of the Pacific Northwest, in *Cultures of the North Pacific Coast* (San Francisco: Chandler, 1965).

5. The averages are hunting and gathering, 40; fishing, 60; simple horticultural, 95.

6. The percentages for permanent settlements are hunting and gathering, 10; fishing, 49; simple horticultural, 87.

7. The percentages are hunting and gathering, 10; fishing, 23; simple horticultural, 21.

8. Unless, perhaps, some evolved into maritime societies. To date, however, there is no real evidence that this ever happened. Maritime societies seem to have evolved out of advanced horticultural or agrarian societies.

9. See Hewes, pp. 240–241.

10. For an interesting account of one such group, see Wilmond Menard, "The Sea Gypsies of China," *Natural History*, 64 (January 1965), pp. 13–21.

11. See, for example, Lawrence Krader, "Pastoralism," in *International Encyclopedia of the Social Sciences* (New York: Macmillan and Free Press, 1968), vol. II, pp. 456–457; or Carleton Coon, "The Nomads," in Sydney Fisher (ed.), *Social Forces in the Middle East* (Ithaca, N.Y.: Cornell, 1955), pp. 23–42.

12. John L. Myres, "Nomadism," *Journal of the Royal Anthropological Institute*, 71 (1941), p. 20.

13. Krader reports that the average density of population in Mongolia was less than 1 per square mile, and among the Tuareg of Africa it was even lower (op. cit., pp. 458–459).

14. The percentages of single-community societies were 90, 78, 77, and 13, respectively, in Murdock's Ethnographic Atlas sample.

15. Found in 62 per cent of these societies as against 3 to 37 per cent of the rest.

16. As shown in Table 4.5, p. 101, class stratification, by Murdock's definition, is present in 51 per cent of these societies.

17. This requirement is found in 93 per cent of these societies, compared to 37 to 86 per cent of other types.

18. This requirement occurs in 97 per cent of herding societies, compared to only 49 to 79 per cent of other types.

19. Among the rest, it is most common in advanced horticultural societies, but even there it occurs in only 16 per cent of the cases; in the other types, the frequency ranges from 2 to 10 per cent.

20. See William McNeill, *The Rise of the West: A History of the Human Community* (New York: Mentor, 1965), p. 126ff.; or Ralph Turner, *The Great Cultural Traditions* (New York: McGraw-Hill, 1941), p. 259.

21. For a good discussion of this important subject, see McNeill, p. 256ff.

22. Ibid., p. 111.

23. On the less familiar Carthaginian empire, see Donald Harden, *The Phoenicians* (New York: Praeger, 1963), chaps. 5 and 6.

24. Compare, for example, the status of merchants and the rate of innovation for Europe during the sixteenth, seventeenth, and eighteenth centuries with the situation in India. Both were higher in Europe. Although this could have been coincidence, the evidence suggests a causal link.

Chapter 9

1. See especially the lectures of Arnold Toynbee (uncle of the recent historian), delivered at Oxford in 1880–1881 and recently republished under the title *The Industrial Revolution* (Boston: Beacon Press, 1956). Though not the first to use the term, Toynbee did much to give it currency in scholarly circles.

2. See, for example, Robert Heilbroner, *The Making of Economic Society* (Englewood Cliffs, N.J.: Prentice-Hall, 1962), pp. 101–102.

3. See, for example, John Nef, *The Conquest of the Material World* (Chicago: University of Chicago Press, 1965), especially part 2.

4. If such refinements and improvements were included, it would be hard to avoid dating the start of the Industrial Revolution ten to fifteen thousand years ago, since technological progress of some kind, however slow, has been virtually continuous since then. One cannot use the criteria stated in the text above to date the *end* of the Industrial Revolution, since many societies have already reached the point where there is virtually no room for increase in the proportion of the population dependent on industrial activity or in the percentage of the gross national product obtained from this source, yet the revolution in the techniques and tools of production is obviously continuing. The only standard we might use to mark the end of the Industrial Revolution would be a drastic slowing in the rate of technological innovation.

5. See especially Phyllis Deane and W. A. Cole, *British Economic Growth 1688–1959: Trends and Structure* (London: Cambridge, 1962), chap. 2.

6. Paul Mantoux, *The Industrial Revolution in the Eighteenth Century*, rev. ed. (London: Cape, 1961), pp. 243–244.

7. Ibid., p. 312.

8. Earlier in the century, Thomas Savery and Thomas Newcomen invented the atmospheric engine, which laid the foundation for Watt's work. Its only practical use, however, was to pump water out of mines.

9. Deane and Cole, p. 212.

10. For 1788, see Clive Day, *Economic Development in Europe* (New York: Macmillan, 1942), p. 134; for 1840, see Deane and Cole, p. 225.

11. Deane and Cole, pp. 55 and 216.

12. W. S. Woytinsky and E. S. Woytinsky, *World Population and Production: Trends and Outlook* (New York: Twentieth Century Fund, 1953), p. 1147.

13. Ibid., tables 30 and 37.

14. U.S. Bureau of the Census, *Historical Statistics of the United States, Colonial Times to 1957*, p. 139.

15. J. H. Clapham, *An Economic History of Modern Britain*, 2d ed. (London: Cambridge, 1930), vol. I, pp. 391–392.

16. S. B. Clough and C. W. Cole, *Economic History of Europe* (Boston: Heath, 1941), pp. 594–595.

17. Ibid., pp. 535–537.

18. Deane and Cole, p. 225.

19. Ibid., p. 216.

20. Clough and Cole, p. 538.

21. Calculated from Woytinsky and Woytinsky, p. 1003.

22. Ibid., p. 1164.

23. This figure is an estimate based on Clough and Cole's report of French production in 1902 (p. 773) and Woytinsky and Woytinsky's report of American production in 1900 and 1902 (p. 1168).

24. Woytinsky and Woytinsky, pp. 1165–1166, including fig. 328.

25. Ibid., p. 966.

26. The 1900 figure is estimated from information provided by Woytinsky and Woytinsky, pp. 897–900; the 1940 figure is from fig. 257, p. 897.

27. J. Frederic Dewhurst and Associates, *America's Needs and Resources* (New York: Twentieth Century Fund, 1955), p. 317; and U.S. Bureau of the Census, *Statistical Abstract of the United States, 1963*, p. 516.

28. Woytinsky and Woytinsky, p. 1171.

29. *Statistical Abstract, 1963*, p. 586, and *Statistical Abstract, 1975*, p. 592.

30. Calculated from United Nations, *Statistical Yearbook, 1970*, p. 458.

31. The 1938 figure is calculated from J. Frederic Dewhurst and Associates, *Europe's Needs and Resources: Trends and Prospects in Eighteen Countries* (New York: Twentieth Century Fund, 1961), p. 627; the 1969 figure is from *Statistical Abstract, 1975*, p. 835.

32. The figure for the late 1930s is based on Woytinsky and Woytinsky's statement about output in the United States and other countries in that period (p. 1201); the 1969 figure is from United Nations, *Statistical Yearbook, 1970*, p. 287, but translated into short tons.

33. *Newsweek*, Feb. 23, 1976, pp. 73–74.

34. Pretrial brief of the IBM Corporation in the case of United States of America vs. IBM, U.S. District Court, Southern District of New York, Jan. 15, 1975, pp. 148–149.

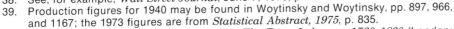

35. *Newsweek*, op. cit.

36. United Nations, *Statistical Yearbook, 1965*, p. 353.

37. *Statistical Abstract, 1975*, table 904, and *World Almanac, 1976*, p. 96.

38. See, for example, *Wall Street Journal*, June 7, 1976, p. 1.

39. Production figures for 1940 may be found in Woytinsky and Woytinsky, pp. 897, 966, and 1167; the 1973 figures are from *Statistical Abstract, 1975*, p. 835.

40. J. L. Hammond and Barbara Hammond, *The Town Labourer: 1760–1830* (London: Guild Books, 1949, first published 1917), vol. I, chap. 3.

41. Ibid., chaps. 2 and 6–9; or J. T. Ward (ed.), *The Factory System* (New York: Barnes & Noble, 1970), vols. I and II.

42. Hammond and Hammond, vol. I, pp. 32–33.

43. Compare and contrast the work of Hammond and Hammond, op. cit., or Eric Hobsbawm, "The British Standard of Living, 1790–1850," *Economic History Review*, 2d ser., 10 (1957), pp. 46–61, with Thomas Ashton, "The Standard of Life of the Workers in England, 1790–1830," *Journal of Economic History*, 9 (1949), supplement, pp. 19–38, reprinted in Friedrich Hayek (ed.), *Capitalism and the Historians* (Chicago: University of Chicago Press, 1954).

44. James M. Wells, "The History of Printing," *Encyclopaedia Britannica*, vol. 18, p. 541.

45. Ibid., pp. 541–542.

46. Clough and Cole, pp. 314–315.

47. Ibid., pp. 127–128.

48. R. H. Tawney, *Religion and the Rise of Capitalism* (New York: Mentor, 1947), p. 117.

49. See Immanuel Wallerstein, *The Modern World-System* (New York: Academic Press, 1974), especially chap. 2.

50. R. H. Tawney, *Religion and the Rise of Capitalism* (New York: Mentor, 1947), p. 257.

51. For the basic statements of Weber's views, see *The Protestant Ethic and the Spirit of Capitalism*, trans. Talcott Parsons (New York: Scribner, 1958); *The Sociology of Religion*, trans. Ephraim Fischoff (Boston: Beacon Press, 1963); and *From Max Weber: Essays in Sociology*, trans. H. H. Gerth and C. W. Mills (New York: Oxford, 1946), pp. 302–322. For a good summary of his views, see Reinhard Bendix, *Max Weber: An Intellectual Portrait* (Garden City, N.Y.: Doubleday, 1960), chaps. 3–8.

52. For an introduction to the critics, see Robert W. Green (ed.), *Protestantism and Capitalism: The Weber Thesis and Its Critics* (Boston: Heath, 1959). This volume gives brief excerpts from a number of the leading critics and provides a useful bibliography on pp. 115–116.

53. Tawney, pp. 92–93. Quoted by permission of Harcourt, Brace & World, Inc.

54. Ibid., p. 192.

55. U.S. Department of Commerce, *Long-Term Economic Growth: 1860–1965* (1966), p. 198; and *Statistical Abstract, 1975*, p. 546.

56. *Statistical Abstract of the U.S., 1975*, tables 907–909.

57. United Nations, Department of Economic and Social Affairs, *The Determinants and Consequences of Population Trends: New Summary of Findings*, Population Studies, No. 50 (New York: United Nations, 1973), p. 89.

58. Joan Huber, "The Future of Parenthood: Implications of Declining Fertility," unpublished paper, p. 9.

Chapter 10

1. This definition of "work" is based on J. Frederic Dewhurst and Associates, *America's Needs and Resources* (New York: Twentieth Century Fund, 1955), pp. 905–906.

2. For 1850, see ibid., p. 1116; by the early 1960s the figure had apparently dropped below 1 per cent according to reports on the increase in the newer energy sources. See, for example, U.S. Bureau of the Census, *Statistical Abstract of the United States, 1963*, table 716, and compare with Dewhurst and Associates, tables 25.3 and 25.4.

3. U.S. Bureau of the Census, *Historical Statistics of the United States: Colonial Times to 1957*, ser. S 1-14 (1960); and U.S. Bureau of the Census, *Statistical Abstract of the United States, 1975*, p. 529. The figure for 1850 has been adjusted to include the horsepower capacity of the human population, which we judge to have been approximately 1 million horsepower.

4. The 1750 figure is from Woytinsky and Woytinsky, p. 1100; the 1970 figure is from United Nations, *Statistical Yearbook, 1971*, tables 121 and 122, and is converted to short tons.

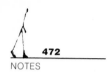
5. The 1820 figure is from W. S. Woytinsky and E. S. Woytinsky, *World Population and Production: Trends and Outlook* (New York: Twentieth Century Fund, 1953), p. 1101; the 1970 figure is from *The World Almanac, 1976*, p. 109.

6. Production figures are from *The World Almanac, 1976*, p. 108. Per capita calculations are our own.

7. The 1871 figure is estimated from data provided in *Historical Statistics of the United States*, ser. F 1-5 and 6-9. It was assumed that the ratio of national income to gross national product was the same in 1869–1873 as in 1897–1901. The 1974 figure is from *The World Almanac*, p. 88.

8. These figures are our own calculations. The British figure is based on data presented by Phyllis Deane and W. A. Cole, *British Economic Growth, 1688–1959* (London: Cambridge, 1962), tables 72 and 90; the Swedish on data presented by Woytinsky and Woytinsky, p. 387, with adjustments for the changing values of the dollar, pound, and krone.

9. These figures are based on those in Woytinsky and Woytinsky, pp. 389–390, and are multiplied by 3.44 to take account of the effects of inflation between 1938 and 1974.

10. John Grauman, "Population Growth," in *International Encyclopedia of the Social Sciences* (New York: Macmillan and Free Press, 1968), vol. 12, p. 379, and *Statistical Abstract of the U.S., 1975*, p. 836. The United States has grown even more rapidly, but that is less relevant to the present problem, since the American population never came close to reaching its agrarian potential.

11. Robert Heilbroner, *The Worldly Philosophers*, rev. ed. (New York: Time Books, 1961), chap 3; and Jacob Viner, "Adam Smith," in *International Encyclopedia of the Social Sciences*, vol. 14, pp. 322–329.

12. Heilbroner, p. 47.

13. See, for example, Heilbroner, chap. 6; or Isaiah Berlin, *Karl Marx: His Life and Environment* (New York: Oxford University Press, 1963).

14. From Lewis Feuer (ed.), *Marx and Engels: Basic Writings on Politics and Philosophy* (Garden City, N.Y.: Doubleday, 1959), pp. 168–169. Copyright, 1959 by Lewis S. Feuer. Reprinted by permission of Lewis S. Feuer.

15. See Evgeny Evtushenko, *A Precocious Autobiography* (New York: Dutton, 1963), p. 42; and Svetlana Alliluyeva, *Twenty Letters to a Friend*, trans. P. J. McMillan (New York: Harper & Row, 1967).

16. Maurice Duverger, *Political Parties: Their Organization and Activity in the Modern State*, trans. Barbara North and Robert North (London: Methuen, 1959), pp. 118–119. Quoted by permission of Methuen & Company, Ltd.

17. Hans Kohn, "Nationalism," *International Encyclopedia of the Social Sciences*, vol. 11, pp. 63–70.

18. Robert Bellah, "Civil Religion in America," *Daedalus*, 96 (Winter), pp. 1–21. See also Will Herberg, *Protestant-Catholic-Jew* (Garden City, N.Y.: Doubleday, 1955).

19. John Grauman, "Population Growth," *International Encyclopedia of the Social Sciences* (New York: Macmillan & Free Press, 1968), vol. 12, p. 379.

20. See United Nations, *Demographic Yearbook, 1970*.

21. Warren Thompson and David Lewis, *Population Problems*, 5th ed. (New York: McGraw-Hill, 1965), pp. 383–385; and Don Dumond, "The Limitation of Human Population: A Natural History," *Science*, 187 (Feb. 28, 1975), p. 718.

22. United Nations, *Demographic Yearbook, 1974*, table 1.

23. Occasionally, however, there were long-run declines. For example, Egypt is estimated to have had a population of 6 to 7 million in Roman times but only 2.5 million in 1798. See Charles Issawi, *Egypt in Revolution: An Economic Analysis* (New York: Oxford University Press, 1963), p. 20.

24. *The World Almanac, 1976*, pp. 682–684.

25. U.S. Department of Labor, *Dictionary of Occupational Titles*, new edition, as reported by Sylvia Porter, Feb. 18, 1977.

26. The percentage of physicians in general practice in the United States dropped from 48 to 15 per cent between 1950 and 1970. See U.S. Bureau of the Census, *Statistical Abstract of the United States, 1968*, table 86, and *Statistical Abstract, 1972*, table 95.

27. *The World Almanac, 1976*, pp. 473–486.

28. *Statistical Abstract, 1975*, tables 952, 969, 976, 993, and 995.

29. *Statistical Abstract, 1975*, tables 851 and 846.

Chapter 11

1. For example, in the 1967 parliamentary elections, Hungarians were permitted to choose between rival candidates for the first time since the Communist seizure of power. According to press reports, there were lively contests in many cases. Similar steps had been taken previously in Poland, and in the Soviet Union some popular participation is now permitted at the nomination stage. See John Reshetar, *The Soviet Polity* (New York: Dodd, Mead, 1971), pp. 218–225. It should also be noted that in 1971 or 1972, East Germany allowed members of its parliament to vote according to their consciences on the issue of abortion, with the result that there was a divided vote for the first time.

2. See, for example, Henry Ehrmann, *Organized Business in France* (Princeton, N.J.: Princeton University Press, 1957), p. 224ff.; V. O. Key, Jr., *Politics, Parties, and Pressure Groups*, 3d ed. (New York: Thomas Y. Crowell, 1952), especially chap. 18; or Drew Pearson and Jack Anderson, *The Case against Congress* (New York: Simon & Schuster, 1968), especially parts II and IV.

3. In Sweden, for example, property restrictions on the franchise were not finally eliminated until after World War I. See Dankwort Rustow, *The Politics of Compromise: A Study of Parties and Cabinet Government in Sweden* (Princeton, N.J.: Princeton University Press, 1955), pp. 84–85.

4. See, for example, *The Conquest of Granada*, by the seventeenth-century poet John Dryden, in which he wrote:

   > I am as free as Nature first made man,
   > Ere the base laws of servitude began,
   > When wild in woods the noble savage ran.
   > (Part 1, act 1, scene 1)

5. Many recent studies have documented the relationship between high rates of literacy and education on the one hand and democratic government on the other. See, for example, Daniel Lerner, *The Passing of Traditional Society: Modernizing the Middle East* (New York: Free Press, 1958), especially pp. 63–64 and 86–89; or S. M. Lipset, *Political Man* (Garden City, N.Y.: Doubleday, 1960), pp. 53–58.

6. On the relationship between democracy and the development of the mass media, see Lerner, op. cit., and Lipset, pp. 51–52.

7. See, for example, Kurt Shell, *The Transformation of Austrian Socialism* (New York: University Publishers, 1962), especially chaps. 6 and 7; Rustow, chap. 8; or Albert Parry, *The New Class Divided: Science and Technology vs. Communism* (New York: Macmillan, 1966), chap. 7. See also footnote 1 above. For evidence of a counter-trend in Sweden, see Leif Lewin, *Planhushallnings debatten* (Stockholm: Almqvst S. Wicksell, 1967).

8. Ivo Feierabend and Rosalind Feierabend, "Aggressive Behaviors within Polities, 1948–1962: A Cross-national Study," *Journal of Conflict Resolution*, 10 (1966), table 3. The measure used is Yule's Q. Results of this study suggest that rates of political instability are greatest in societies making the transition from agrarian to industrial, though results were not statistically significant. See the term "correlation" in the Glossary for an explanation of the meaning of the coefficient .965.

9. The figures shown in Table 11.3 are based on our own calculations, using the following sources: Robert Alford, *Party and Society* (Chicago: Rand McNally, 1963) pp. 136, 202–203, 234–235, and 274–275; Richard Rose (ed.), *Electoral Behavior: A Comparative Handbook* (New York: Free Press, 1974), pp. 147, 294, 334, and 398; Hannu Uusitalo, "Class Structure and Party Choice: A Scandinavian Comparison," Research Report No. 10 (1975), Research Group for Comparative Sociology, University of Helsinki, p. 21; Roy Pierce, *French Politics and Political Institutions* (New York: Harper & Row, 1968), table 10; Richard Rose, "Class and Party Divisions: Britain as a Test Case," *Sociology*, 2 (1968), pp. 129–162; Erik Allardt and Yrjö Littunen (eds.), *Cleavages, Ideologies and Party Systems: Contributions to Comparative Political Sociology*, in series entitled *Transactions of the Westermarck Society* (Helsinki: The Academic Bookstore, 1964), vol. 10, pp. 102 and 212; S. M. Lipset, *Political Man* (Garden City, N.Y.: Doubleday, 1960), pp. 225 and 227; Morris Janowitz, "Social Stratification and Mobility in West Germany," *American Journal of Sociology*, 64 (1958), p. 22; and *Gallup Political Index*, Report No. 17 (October 1966), p. 15 and inside back cover.

10. See, for example, Lipset, chaps. 2 and 4.
11. U.S. Bureau of the Census, *Statistical Abstract of the United States, 1975*, table 402; and U.S. Bureau of the Census, *Historical Statistics of the United States: Colonial Times to 1957*, ser. Y 241–50 (1960). Similar trends are reported in other countries. In France, for example, civil servants increased from 3.7 per cent of the labor force in 1866 to 16.7 per cent in 1962. See Jacques Lecaillon, "Changes in the Distribution of Income in the French Economy," in Jean Marchal and Bernard Ducros (eds.), *The Distribution of National Income* (London: Macmillan, 1968), pp. 45 and 47.
12. U.S. Bureau of the Census, *Statistical Abstract of the United States, 1972*, table 674; and *Historical Statistics of the United States*, ser. Y 205-22.
13. On the social origins of federal officials, see W. L. Warner et al., *The American Federal Executive* (New Haven, Conn.: Yale, 1963), table 33B.
14. See, for example, Edward Banfield and James Wilson, *City Politics* (Cambridge, Mass.: Harvard and M.I.T., 1963), chap. 13 and conclusion.
15. *Encyclopaedia Britannica*, 23, pp. 716 and 800.
16. *Washington Post*, Nov. 9, 1976, p. 1.
17. *The World Almanac, 1976*, p. 208. The figures cited refer to Standard Metropolitan Statistical Areas.
18. S. B. Clough and C. W. Cole, *Economic History of Europe* (Boston: Heath, 1941), p. 48; or G. G. Coulton, *Medieval Panorama* (New York: Meridian Books, 1955, first published 1938), p. 282ff.
19. Associated Press wire-service story in *Raleigh News and Observer*, Aug. 7, 1972, p. 27.
20. See, for example, Daniel Chirot, "Sociology in Romania: Review of Recent Works," *Social Forces*, 51 (1972), pp. 100–101.
21. *Wall Street Journal*, Aug. 17, 1976, p. 1, and Apr. 7, 1977, p. 1.
22. Robert Heilbroner, *The Making of Economic Society* (Englewood Cliffs, N.J.: Prentice-Hall, 1962), p. 9. Quoted by permission of Prentice-Hall, Inc.
23. See, for example, Karl Polanyi's statement that "previously to our own time no economy has ever existed that, even in principle, was controlled by markets. . . . Though the institution of the market was fairly common since the later Stone Age, its role was no more than incidental to economic life." From *The Great Transformation: The Political and Economic Origins of Our Time* (Boston: Beacon Press, 1957), p. 43. Maritime societies may have been an exception to this assertion, but unfortunately we lack the data to test the possibility.
24. Heilbroner, pp. 42–44 and 64–65.
25. Clough and Cole, pp. 693–698.
26. G. Warren Nutter, "Industrial Concentration," in *International Encyclopedia of the Social Sciences* (New York: Macmillan and Free Press, 1968), vol. 7, p. 221. Senator Philip Hart of Michigan introduced a new antitrust bill in the U.S. Senate in 1972 that used the "four companies–50 percent of sales" criterion as one of three indicators of "monopoly power." See the *Washington Post*, July 23, 1972, p. A-8.
27. Ben Bagdikian, "Why Newspapers Keep Dying," *Washington Post*, July 23, 1972, p. B-5.
28. John Kenneth Galbraith, *The New Industrial State* (New York: Signet, 1968), pp. 38–39.
29. Peter C. Dooley, "The Interlocking Directorates," *American Economic Review*, 59 (1969), pp. 314–323.
30. See, for example, Donald M. Nelson, *Arsenal of Democracy* (New York: Harcourt, Brace, 1946), or Albert Speer, *Inside the Third Reich* (New York: Avon, 1970), parts II and III.
31. See, for example, Alec Nove, *The Soviet Economy*, rev. ed. (New York: Praeger, 1966), especially chap. 9; Harry G. Shaffer, *The Communist World: Marxist and Non-Marxist Views* (New York: Appleton Century Crofts, 1967), p. 226ff.; or Erik de Mauny, *Russian Prospect* (New York: Atheneum, 1970), chap. 4.
32. Jan Szczepański, *Polish Society* (New York: Random House, 1970), p. 125. Quoted by permission.
33. Joseph Alsop, "Matter of Fact," *Washington Post*, Jan. 13, 1964.
34. Many Soviet scholars feel that American social scientists try to blur the differences. For a good statement of their view, see Alex Simirenko (ed.), *Soviet Sociology: Historical Antecedents and Current Appraisals* (Chicago: Quadrangle, 1966), pp. 327–339.
35. See, for example, Marchal and Ducros, pp. xiii–xiv and 274.

36. See, for example, Clough and Cole, *Economic History of Europe*, p. 148ff. See also Edward S. Mason, "Corporation," in *International Encyclopedia of the Social Sciences*, vol. 3, pp. 396–403.

37. Calculations based on *Statistical Abstract of the U.S., 1975*, table 803.

38. *Moody's Public Utility Manual, 1975*, p. 1102; and *World Almanac, 1976*, p. 84.

39. See A. A. Berle, Jr., and Gardner Means, *The Modern Corporation and Private Property* (New York: Macmillan, 1932), especially book 1; or Robert A. Gordon, *Business Leadership in the Large Corporation* (Berkeley: University of California Press, 1961), on American corporations. For the trend in Europe, see P. Sargant Florence, *Ownership, Control, and Success of Large Companies: An Analysis of English Industrial Structure and Policy, 1936–1951* (London: Street and Maxwell, 1961); or David Granick, *The European Executive* (Garden City, N.Y.: Doubleday Anchor, 1964).

40. E. S. Mason (ed.), *The Corporation and Modern Society* (Cambridge, Mass.: Harvard, 1959), p. 4.

41. For a classic statement of the problem, see Robert Michels, *Political Parties: A Sociological Study of the Oligarchical Tendencies of Modern Democracy*, trans. Eden Paul and Cedar Paul (New York: Dover, 1959, first published in 1915). Michels's study is of special interest because he focused on the Socialist parties of Western Europe, which had an intense commitment to democratic principles; yet, as he demonstrates, even they could not avoid the development of an administrative oligarchy in their own organizations.

42. See, for example, Emily Clark Brown, *Soviet Trade Unions and Labor Relations* (Cambridge, Mass.: Harvard, 1966); or Roy Medvedev, *Let History Judge: The Origins and Consequences of Stalinism*, trans. Colleen Taylor, David Joravsky and Georges Haupt (eds.) (New York: Knopf, 1971), p. 534.

43. J. Frederic Dewhurst et al., *Europe's Needs and Resources: Trends and Prospects in Eighteen Countries* (New York: Twentieth Century Fund, 1961), p. 754. See also Marquis W. Childs, *Sweden: The Middle Way*, rev. ed. (New Haven, Conn.: Yale, 1947).

44. Nove, pp. 41–45. See also Robert C. Stuart, *The Collective Farm in Soviet Agriculture* (Lexington, Mass.: Lexington Books, 1972).

45. Philip Raup, "Some Consequences of Data Deficiencies in Soviet Agriculture," in Vladimir Treml and John Hardt (eds.), *Soviet Economic Statistics* (Durham, N.C.: Duke, 1972), p. 265.

46. See, for example, Eugen Pusić (ed.), *Participation and Self-Management* (Zagreb: First International Sociological Conference on Participation and Self-Management, 1972), 5 vols.

47. For an excellent description and analysis of trends in American agriculture, see Edward Higbee, *Farms and Farmers in an Urban Age* (New York: Twentieth Century Fund, 1963). For a similar volume on Europe, see P. Lamartine Yates, *Food, Land and Manpower in Western Europe* (London: Macmillan, 1960).

48. Nove, pp. 28–29.

49. This and the following statements are based on Dewhurst et al., *Europe's Needs and Resources*, pp. 436–440.

Chapter 12

1. On the lower classes in Soviet society, see Andrei Amalrik, *Involuntary Journey to Siberia*, trans. Manya Harari and Max Hayward (New York: Harcourt Brace Jovanovich, 1970), chaps. 5ff. On the more favored classes, see Roy Medvedev, *Let History Judge: The Origins and Consequences of Stalinism*, trans. Colleen Taylor, David Joravsky and Georges Haupt (eds.) (New York: Knopf, 1971), pp. 540–541; or Jan Szczepański, *Polish Society* (New York: Random House, 1970), pp. 94–95.

2. Medvedev, p. 540.

3. Personal communication by informed East European authorities.

4. See Szczepański, pp. 95 and 137–138.

5. Ibid., pp. 113–124.

6. One recent report indicates that one-third of the equity capital of the United States' publicly owned companies is owned by employee pension funds. See Peter F. Drucker, "American Business's New Owners," *Wall Street Journal*, May 27, 1976.

7. Herbert E. Alexander, *Financing the 1972 Election* (Lexington, Mass.: Lexington Books, 1976), p. 77.

8. Philip M. Stern, "Tax Preferences to Cost Treasury $91.8 Billion in Fiscal '76," *Washington Post*, Feb. 4, 1975, p. A-13.

9. See Benjamin Bradlee, *Conversations with the President* (New York: Norton, 1975), p. 218.

10. On Canada, see John Porter, *The Vertical Mosaic: An Analysis of Social Class and Power in Canada* (Toronto: University of Toronto Press, 1965), part II, especially chaps. 7–9 and 12–13; on France, see Henry Ehrmann, *Organized Business in France*, (Princeton, N.J.: Princeton University Press, 1957), chap. 5; on Britain, see Bernard Nossiter, "Cozy Conflicts of Interest in Britain," *Washington Post*, Nov. 25, 1975, p. A-15; on Japan, see the many accounts of the scandals involving former Prime Minister Tanaka.

11. See, also, John David Stephens, "The Consequences of Social Structural Change for Development of Socialism in Sweden," unpublished Ph.D. dissertation, Yale University, 1976.

12. Several East European nations even have more than one political party, but as a leading Polish sociologist explains, political decision making is all carried out within the Communist Party's Politburo (Szczepański, p. 54).

13. Milovan Djilas, *The New Class: An Analysis of the Communist System* (New York: Praeger, 1959), especially pp. 37–39. For a more recent treatment of the subject by a Soviet author and Party member, see Medvedev, op. cit. Although Medvedev focuses on the Stalin era, and refrains from using the term "new class," the situation he describes is strikingly similar to Djilas's description, and it is clear that he regards the problem as a continuing one.

14. Estimates of the number of *apparatchiki* range from 100,000 to 250,000. See Merle Fainsod, *How Russia Is Ruled*, 2d ed. (Cambridge, Mass.: Harvard, 1963), pp. 206–207; Jerry Hough, "The Party Apparatchiki," in H. Gordon Skilling and Franklyn Griffiths (eds.), *Interest Groups in Soviet Politics* (Princeton, N.J.: Princeton University Press, 1971), p. 49; and John Reshetar, *The Soviet Polity* (New York: Dodd Mead, 1971), p. 170. With spouses and children, the group might total 750,000 at most, or 0.33 per cent of the population. For Poland, the comparable figures are 7,800 *apparatchiki* and perhaps 30,000 members of the immediate families, or 0.1 per cent of the total population. See Jerzy Wiatr and A. Przeworski, "Control without Opposition," in J. Wiatr (ed.), *Studies of the Polish Political System* (Wroclaw: Ossolineum, 1967), p. 148.

15. See, for example, Amalrik, op. cit.; Medvedev. op cit.; Zhores Medvedev and Roy Medvedev, *A Question of Madness* (New York: Knopf, 1971); or Alexander Solzhenitsyn, *The Gulag Archipelago* (New York: Harper & Row, 1974).

16. Peter Rossi and Alex Inkeles, "Multidimensional Ratings of Occupations," *Sociometry*, 20 (1957), p. 247. The role of *apparatchik* was most dangerous in the 1930s, when 110 of the 139 members of the Party's Central Committee were arrested in a five-year period from 1934 to 1939, with most eventually being executed. Lower echelons of Party functionaries were equally vulnerable. See Medvedev, chap. 6.

17. David Granick, *The Red Executive* (Garden City, N.Y.: Doubleday Anchor, 1961), pp. 22–23.

18. Nicolas DeWitt, *Education and Professional Employment in the U.S.S.R.* (Washington: National Science Foundation, 1961), pp. 536–537.

19. See Reshetar, table on p. 171.

20. *New York Times*, June 10, 1964, p. 25.

21. See, for example, Sen. Russell Long's comments on the hearings on the unethical conduct of Sen. Thomas Dodd. He stated that at least half of the senators who were on the committee investigating Dodd could not stand a similar investigation. For an earlier study of the use of political power for private gain, see Harold Zink, *City Bosses in the United States* (Durham, N.C.: Duke, 1930), pp. 37–38.

22. See, for example, Maurice Duverger, *Political Parties*, trans. Barbara North and Robert North (London: Methuen, 1959), p. 114; or Angus Campbell et al., *The American Voter* (New York: Wiley, 1960), pp. 90–93.

23. *Statistical Abstract of the U.S., 1975*, table 727.

24. See, for example, Alexander Matejko, "From Peasant into Worker in Poland," *International Review of Sociology*, 3 (1971), pp. 27–75.

25. *Statistical Abstract, 1975*, table 200.

26. See, for example, R. Barry Farrell, *Political Leadership in Eastern Europe* (Chicago: Aldine, 1970), table 5/1.

27. For a popular account of the role of the educational elite in Soviet society and its intrusion into politics, see Albert Parry, *The New Class Divided* (New York: Macmillan, 1966), and Skillings and Griffiths, chap. 7.

28. *Statistical Abstract, 1975*, table 639.

29. Members of minority groups usually adopt the dominant group's prestige evaluations for groups other than their own. Sometimes they even adopt its evaluation of their own group. See, for example, Emory Bogardus, *Social Distance* (Yellow Springs, Ohio: Antioch, 1959), pp. 26–29.

30. See, for example, Everett C. Hughes, *French Canada in Transition* (Chicago: University of Chicago Press, 1943), especially chap. 7. See also Porter, *The Vertical Mosaic*, chap. 3.

31. In elections held in November 1976, the Parti Quebécois, which advocates political independence for Quebec, received 41 per cent of the vote in the province, though public opinion polls showed that some who supported the party were not in favor of independence. See *New York Times,* Nov. 21, 1976, Week in Review, p. 2.

32. Calculated from Donald Matthews, *U.S. Senators and Their World* (Chapel Hill: University of North Carolina Press, 1960), fig. 1.

33. W. Lloyd Warner and James Abeggien, *Occupational Mobility in American Business and Industry, 1928–1952* (Minneapolis: University of Minnesota Press, 1955), p. 30; and Mabel Newcomer, *The Big Business Executive* (New York: Columbia, 1955), p. 112.

34. Calculated from Morris Janowitz, *The Professional Soldier* (New York: Free Press, 1960), p. 63; and Robert Lampman, *The Share of Top Wealth-Holders in National Wealth: 1922–1956* (Princeton, N.J.: Princeton University Press, 1962), tables 48 and 49.

35. Hough, table 1.

36. Lampman, p. 96. This study shows that among the rich, women now own about 40 per cent of the wealth.

37. William J. Goode, *World Revolution and Family Patterns* (New York: Free Press, 1963), p. 55.

38. International Labour Office, *Yearbook of Labour Statistics, 1971*, p. 43.

39. U.S. Bureau of the Census, *Historical Statistics of the United States: Colonial Times to 1957* (Washington, 1960), p. 71.

40. Calculations based on *Statistical Abstract, 1975*, tables 558 and 559.

41. U.S. Bureau of the Census, *Current Population Reports*, ser. P-60, no. 101 (January 1976), table 53.

42. Though much has been made of the fact that women constitute three-quarters of the doctors in the Soviet Union, this occupation is not especially lucrative there, and the leading physicians continue to be men. The same seems to be true in most other fields. See, for example, Lotta Lennon, "Women in the U.S.S.R.," *Problems of Communism*, 20 (July–August 1971).

43. For a good summary of much of this, see Harold M. Hodges, *Social Stratification: Class in America* (Cambridge, Mass.: Schenkman, 1964), especially chaps. 6–11.

44. *Statistical Abstract, 1975*, table 82. The difference was 9.6 years in 1920.

45. See, for example, A. B. Hollingshead, *Elmtown's Youth* (New York: Wiley, 1949); St. Clair Drake and Horace Cayton, *Black Metropolis* (New York: Harcourt, Brace & World, 1945); Elliot Liebow, *Tally's Corner* (Boston: Little, Brown, 1967).

46. Calculated from U.S. Bureau of the Census, *Current Population Reports*, ser. P-23, no. 11 (May 1964), table 1.

47. A few surveys indicate an excess of downward mobility, but there is reason to believe that these results sometimes are owing to the failure to ensure that respondents report the father's occupation when he was *their* age. This is important, because mobility also occurs within careers, and here, too, upward mobility is more common than downward.

48. Gerhard Lenski, *Power and Privilege: A Theory of Social Stratification* (New York: McGraw-Hill, 1966), p. 228.

49. On the United States, see Edwin Sutherland, *White Collar Crime* (New York: Holt, 1949); on the Soviet Union, see Amalrik, op. cit., or Medvedev and Medevdev, op cit.

50. Lenski, pp. 308–313.

51. See ibid., pp. 313–318, for a more thorough discussion of this subject.

52. L. J. Zimmerman, *Poor Lands, Rich Lands: The Widening Gap* (New York: Random House, 1965), table 2.8, p. 38.

53. U.S. Bureau of the Census, *Historical Statistics of the United States: Colonial Times to 1970* (Washington, 1975), p. 53.

54. This is our own calculation based on 603 hunting and gathering, horticultural, fishing, and herding societies in Murdock's sample of 915 societies (see p. 96). We have omitted 104 hybrid societies, most of which are preliterate. If these were included, the figure would rise to 15 per cent.

55. George Gilder, "In Defense of Monogamy," *Commentary* (November 1974).

56. In this section, we have drawn heavily on suggestions provided by Joan Huber and on two of her papers, "Toward a Socio-Technological Theory of the Women's Movement," *Social Problems*, 23 (April 1976), and "The Future of Parenthood: Implications of Declining Fertility," unpublished.

57. Virginia Woolf, *A Room of One's Own* (New York: Harbinger, n.d., first published 1929), pp. 48–50.

58. *Statistical Abstract, 1975*, p. 51.

59. Hugh Carter and Paul Glick, *Marriage and Divorce*, rev. ed. (Cambridge, Mass., Harvard, 1976).

60. Calculated from Thompson and Lewis, p. 374; J. Bourgeois-Pichat, "The General Development of the Population of France Since the Eighteenth Century," in D. V. Glass and D. E. C. Eversley (eds.), *Population in History* (Chicago: Aldine, 1965), p. 498; and W. S. Woytinsky and E. S. Woytinsky, *World Population and Production: Trends and Outlook* (New York: Twentieth Century Fund, 1953), p. 181.

61. Calculated from *Statistical Abstract, 1975*, p. 60; or *World Almanac, 1976*, p. 963.

62. *Statistical Abstract, 1975*, p. 115.

63. See, for example, Randall Collins, "Functional and Conflict Theories of Educational Stratification," *American Sociological Review*, 36 (1971), pp. 1002-1019.

64. See, for example, the experience of Andrei Sinyavsky, Yuri Daniel, General Pyotr Grigorenko, Andrei Amalrik, Yuri Galanskov, or Zhores Medvedev. On the other hand, authorities have failed to move against such dissidents as Roy Medvedev and Andrei Sakharov, and merely exiled others such as Alexander Solzhenitsyn.

65. See, for example, Charles Erasmus' moving account of Juan, a Mexican peasant brought to the United States, and his profound unhappiness when compelled to return, in *Man Takes Control: Cultural Development and American Aid* (Indianapolis: Bobbs-Merrill, 1961), pp. 3–8.

Chapter 13

1. These figures are medians. The calculations are based on United Nations, *Yearbook of National Accounts Statistics, 1969*, table 3, and Food and Agriculture Organization of the United Nations, *Production Yearbook, 1970*, table 5. Here, as elsewhere in this chapter, we have ignored the new microstates such as Kuwait, Gabon, and Mauritania.

2. United Nations, *Yearbook of National Account Statistics, 1974*, vol. 3, table 1B.

3. For the period 1938–1961, see United Nations, Department of Social and Economic Affairs, *The Growth of World Industry, 1938–1961: International Analyses and Tables* (New York: 1965), table 4; for the years 1960–1973, see United Nations, *Statistical Yearbook, 1974*, table 4.

4. The figures in this paragraph have all been corrected for inflation and thus are stated as changes in *real* income. The data on income change are from United Nations, *Statistical Yearbook, 1974*, table 188; the correction for inflation is based on data in U.S. Bureau of the Census, *Statistical Abstract of the United States, 1975*, table 678 (retail price index).

5. Manfred Halpern, *The Politics of Social Change in the Middle East and North Africa* (Princeton, N.J.: Princeton University Press, 1963), p. 80.

6. Ibid.

7. See Glossary for an explanation of correlation coefficients. The study cited was Bruce Russett et al., *World Handbook of Political and Social Indicators* (New Haven, Conn.: Yale, 1964), p. 277, and was based on data from fifty-five nations.

8. *New York Times*, June 9, 1976, p. 4.

9. Olga Tellis, "India Proposes Sterilization," *Washington Post*, Mar. 31, 1976, p. A-1.

10. *Washington Post*, May 31, 1976, p. A-22.

11. Dan Morgan, "2.6 Million Sterilized by India in One Year," *Washington Post*, June 16, p. A-3.

12. June Shaplen and Robert Shaplen, "Taking on the Tide," *New York Times Magazine*, Aug. 29, 1976, p. 62.

13. *Statistical Abstract, 1975*, p. 839.

14. Dwight Perkins, "Looking inside China: An Economic Reappraisal," *Problems of Communism*, 22 (May-June 1973), pp. 5 and 10.

15. Jay Mathews, "China Expected to Keep Oil Riches for Itself," *Washington Post*, May 27, 1976, p. A-18.

16. See, for example, A. H. Hanson, *The Process of Planning: A Study of India's Five-Year Plans, 1950–1964* (London: Oxford University Press, 1966), part II, especially chap. 8; Peter Franck, "Economic Planners," in Sydney Fisher (ed.), *Social Forces in the Middle East* (Ithaca, N.Y.: Cornell, 1955), pp. 137–161; Louis Walinsky, *Economic Development in Burma, 1951–1960* (New York: Twentieth Century Fund, 1962), part V, especially chap. 29; or Lennox A. Mills, *Southeast Asia* (Minneapolis: University of Minnesota Press, 1964), chap. 11.

17. Halpern, p. 244.

18. See, for example, David Apter, *The Politics of Modernization* (Chicago: University of Chicago Press, 1965); or S. M. Lipset, *The First New Nation* (New York: Basic Books, 1963), p. 11. For other references on the subject, see the footnotes to the article by Charles Moskos and Wendell Bell, "Emerging Nations and Ideologies of American Social Scientists," *The American Sociologist*, 2 (1967), pp. 67–71. Moskos and Bell challenge the view cited above, but although their article serves as a valuable criticism of deterministic tendencies in some of their opponents (i.e., tendencies to deny that the liberal democratic model can *ever* be made to work in industrializing societies), their basic argument is not convincing.

19. International Labour Office, *Yearbook of Labour Statistics, 1971*, table 2A; and Food and Agriculture Organization of the United Nations, *Production Yearbook, 1970*, table 5.

20. See, for example, Myron Weiner, *Party Building in a New Nation: The Indian National Congress* (Chicago: University of Chicago Press, 1967).

21. Neil Smelser and S. M. Lipset (eds.), *Social Structure and Mobility in Economic Development* (Chicago: Aldine, 1966), p. 29ff. Statistics cited in this paragraph are from the same source.

22. See the Glossary for an explanation of correlation coefficients. The study cited is Russett et al., *Political and Social Indicators*, p. 277.

23. Smelser and Lipset, p. 37, and Jan Szczepański, *Polish Society* (New York: Random House, 1970), table 15, p. 115.

24. Smelser and Lipset, p. 37.

25. Halpern, p. 122.

26. See, for example, Ivan Vallier, "Religious Elites: Differentiations and Developments in Roman Catholicism," in S. M. Lipset and Aldo Solari, *Elites in Latin America* (New York: Oxford University Press, 1967), pp. 190–232; or William V. D'Antonio and Frederick B. Pike (eds.), *Religion, Revolution, and Reform* (New York: Praeger, 1964).

27. For Latin America, see Robert E. Scott, "Political Elites and Political Modernization: The Crisis of Transition," in Lipset and Solari, p. 133.

28. See, for example, F. G. Bailey, *Tribe, Caste, and Nation* (Manchester, England: Manchester University Press, 1960), on the assimilation of the hill tribes in India.

29. Calculations are based on United Nations, *Demographic Yearbook, 1970*, table 9. The figures provided here are medians for eleven industrializing societies and thirty-three industrializing agrarian societies.

30. Calculations are based on gross national product data in Russett et al., table 43, and area data are from *Statistical Abstract, 1966*, table 1287, and *The World Almanac, 1952*, p. 289ff.

31. See, for example, Gwendolen Carter (ed.), *African One-Party States* (Ithaca, N.Y.: Cornell, 1962), pp. 371ff. and 461ff; Guy Hunter, *The New Societies of Africa* (New York: Oxford University Press, 1964), chap. 9, especially p. 223ff.; International Bank for Reconstruction and Development, *The Economic Development of Uganda* (Baltimore: Johns Hopkins, 1962), pp. 23–24; or Ken Post, *The New States of West Africa* (Baltimore: Penguin, 1964), chap. 6.

32. Calculations based on Russett et al., table 64. The figures are based on fifty-five industrializing agrarian and sixteen industrializing horticultural societies. Another indicator of literacy is the rate of newspaper circulation. This, too, varies greatly by societal type.

33. Russett et al., table 65, provides data on the average annual increase in the rate of literacy for forty-three countries since about 1920. The median increase is 0.7 per cent per year; only nine of the forty-three countries had a rate in excess of 1 per cent.

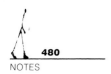
34. Based on Inter-African Labour Institute, *The Human Factors of Productivity in Africa*, as summarized in William H. Lewis (ed.), *French-speaking Africa: The Search for Identity* (New York: Walker, 1965), p. 168. Many of these propositions were supported in papers presented to a recent conference on competing demands for labor in traditional African societies, cosponsored by the Joint Committee on African Studies of the Social Science Research Council, the American Council of Learned Societies, and the Agricultural Development Council. See William O. Jones, "Labor and Leisure in Traditional African Societies," *Social Science Research Council Items*, 22 (March 1968), pp. 1–6.

35. See, for example, J. L. Hammond and Barbara Hammond, *The Town Labourer, 1760–1832* (London: Guild Books, 1949, first published 1917), especially chap. 2.

36. On the latter, see, for example, J. A. K. Leslie's fascinating study, *A Survey of Dar es Salaam* (New York: Oxford University Press, 1963).

37. Hunter, p. 85.

38. Ibid., p. 94.

39. See, for example, Aristide Zolberg, *One-Party Government in the Ivory Coast* (Princeton, N.J.: Princeton University Press, 1964), pp. 202ff. and 286ff.; Hunter, pp. 286–298; or Lucy Mair, *New Nations* (Chicago: University of Chicago Press, 1963), pp. 114–122.

40. See, for example, Brian Weinstein, *Gabon: Nation-building on the Ogooue* (Cambridge, Mass.: M.I.T., 1966).

41. See Leslie, p. 32, or Merran Fraenkel, *Tribe and Class in Monrovia* (London: Oxford University Press, 1964), especially chap. 3.

42. See Apter, *The Politics of Modernization*, pp. 130 and 328–330, or Hunter, p. 289.

43. Mair, p. 122ff.

44. From *The New Societies of Africa*, pp. 286–287, by Guy Hunter, published by Oxford University Press under the auspices of the Institute of Race Relations. By permission of the Oxford University Press.

45. Ibid., p. 288.

46. Ibid., p. 289. See also Daniel Bell, "Socialism," *International Encyclopedia of the Social Sciences* (New York: Macmillan and Free Press, 1968), vol. 14, pp. 528–529.

47. Figures based on *Statesman's Yearbook, 1971–1972.*

48. The figure for Dar es Salaam is from Leslie, p. 210, and that for Tanzania from Russett et al., tables 74 and 75.

49. Fraenkel, p. 154, and Russett et al., tables 74 and 75.

50. From *A Survey of Dar es Salaam*, p. 211, by J. A. K. Leslie, published by Oxford University Press, 1963. By permission of the Oxford University Press.

51. Ibid., pp. 210–211.

52. Fraenkel, pp. 158 and 162.

53. Hunter, p. 74, provides numerous examples.

54. Carter, pp. 433–434. Copyright, 1962 by Cornell University. Used by permission of Cornell University Press.

55. See, for example, Vittorio Lanternari, *The Religions of the Oppressed: A Study of Modern Messianic Cults*, trans. Lisa Sergio (New York: Knopf, 1963), chap. 1, or Mair, p. 171ff.

56. The same has been true of Sékou Touré's Democratic Party in Guinea. See, for example, Apter, p. 299, note 36.

57. Ibid., chap. 8.

58. L. A. Fallers (ed.), *The King's Men: Leadership and Status in Buganda on the Eve of Independence* (New York: Oxford University Press, 1964), p. 99.

59. From *A Survey of Dar es Salaam*, pp. 27–29, by J. A. K. Leslie, published by Oxford University Press. By permission of the Oxford University Press.

60. Ibid., pp. 60–61, or Fraenkel, p. 127ff.

61. Hana Umlauf, "Endangered: Our Daily Bread," *World Almanac, 1976*, p. 129. A more recent report of the World Food Council predicts a grain deficit of 85 million tons in industrializing societies in 1985—"about double the deficit in 1974, a year when the world came close to running out of food." See Dan Morgan, "Politics Seen Provoking Global Food Disaster by 1985," *Washington Post*, June 16, 1976, p. A-2.

Chapter 14

1. From a statement by Karl Deutsch, as quoted in *Yale Alumni Magazine*, May 1967, p. 15.

2. See, for example, Jacques Ellul, *The Technological Society*, trans. John Wilkinson (New York: Vintage, 1967).

3. See, for example, Colin Turnbull, *The Forest People* (New York: Simon & Schuster, 1961); John Garvan, *The Negritos of the Philippines* (Vienna: Ferdinand Berger, 1964); or Kenneth MacLeish, "The Tasadays: Stone Age Men of the Philippines," *National Geographic*, 142 (1972), pp. 218–249.

4. Friedrich Engels, *Herr Eugen Duehring's Revolution in Science (Anti-Duehring)* (New York: International Publishers, 1939, first published 1878), quoted by D. G. Brennan in "Weaponry," in Foreign Policy Association (ed.), *Toward the Year 2018* (New York: Cowles, 1968), p. 2.

5. From *The Challenge of Man's Future*, by Harrison Brown, pp. 222–223. Copyright, 1954 by Harrison Brown. Reprinted by permission of The Viking Press, Inc.

6. See Alvin Toffler, *Future Shock* (New York: Random House, 1970).

7. *New York Times*, Jan. 15, 1967.

8. Herman Kahn and Anthony Wiener, *The Year 2000: A Framework for Speculation on the Next Thirty-three Years* (New York: Macmillan, 1967), p. 98.

9. *Newsweek*, Feb. 23, 1976, pp. 73–74.

10. "Oil and Gas Resources: Academy Calls USGS Math 'Misleading,'" *Science*, 187 (Feb. 28, 1975), p. 725.

11. Stuart Chase, *The Most Probable Future* (New York: Harper & Row, 1968), pp. 13 and 67. Our figure is adjusted to cover the half century from 1922 to 1972 instead of Chase's 1915–1965 and to take account of the growth of population.

12. Willard Gaylin, "The Frankenstein Myth Becomes Reality," *New York Times Magazine*, Mar. 5, 1972, p. 12ff.

13. See, for example, Leon Kass, "The New Biology: What Price Relieving Man's Estate?" *Science*, 174 (1971), pp. 779–788; for a contrasting view, see Bernard Davis, "Prospects for Genetic Intervention in Man," *Science* (1970), pp. 1279–1283.

14. Bernhard Rensch, "The Laws of Evolution," in Sol Tax (ed.), *Evolution after Darwin: The Evolution of Life* (Chicago: University of Chicago Press, 1960), vol. I, pp. 112–113.

15. Immanuel Wallerstein, *The Modern World System* (New York: Academic Press, 1974), especially chap. 7. As Wallerstein notes, even socialist societies, such as the U.S.S.R., are participants in this capitalist world economy.

16. *Newsweek,* Dec. 6, 1976, p. 58.

17. See, for example, Stanley Milgram, "The Experience of Living in Cities," *Science*, 167 (1970), pp. 1461–1468.

18. See, for example, John B. Calhoun, "Population Density and Social Pathology," *Scientific American*, 206 (1962), pp. 139–148.

19. See Robert Kaiser, "Rome and Moscow: An Interview with Wolfgang Leonhard," *Washington Post*, May 30, 1976, p. B-5.

20. See, for example, Robert Heilbroner, *An Inquiry into the Human Prospect* (New York: Norton, 1974), or Kenneth Boulding, *The Meaning of the Twentieth Century: The Great Transition* (New York: Harper Colophon, 1964), chap. 4.

21. Personal communication.

22. *Statistical Abstract, 1975*, p. 835, with 33 per cent correction in the volume of 1973 trade to take account of the decline in the value of the dollar.

23. *World Almanac, 1976*, p. 960.

24. *Statistical Abstract, 1975*, table 46.

25. Robert Heilbroner, p. 13.

26. Ibid., p. 132.

27. Ibid., p. 110.

28. Ibid., p. 138.

GLOSSARY

These definitions are not necessarily the only meanings of these words. Rather, they are the meanings used in this book and generally conform to standard sociological usage.

Adaptation The process of adjusting to, or changing, environmental conditions; hence, broadly, problem solving.

Agrarian era The period in history when there were no societies technologically more advanced than agrarian societies (about 3000 B.C. to 1800 A.D.).

Agrarian society A society in which agriculture is the primary means of subsistence. *Advanced* agrarian societies have iron tools and weapons; *simple* agrarian societies do not.

Agriculture The cultivation of fields using the plow.

Alteration An innovation that involves a change in the form of some element of culture but does not involve either new information or a new combination of existing information.

Anthropoid A member of the suborder of primates that includes humans, great apes, and monkeys.

Apparatchik A political functionary in the U.S.S.R. or other East European society; a member of the Party or state apparatus.

Archaeology The study of cultures of the past through their physical remains.

Artisan A craftsman. The term is usually applied to craftsmen in agrarian or maritime societies.

Ascribed role A role which is assigned an individual (e.g., age, sex, race, kinship position) and which the individual normally finds difficult or impossible to discard or alter.

Association A formally organized secondary group that performs some relatively specialized function or set of functions.

Autocracy Rule by one person (compare with *Democracy*, *Oligarchy*, and *Theocracy*).

Autogenous Self-generated; caused by internal forces.

Autonomous Free from outside political control.

Average See *Mean, arithmetic.*

Band A nomadic community at the hunting and gathering level.

Behavior Any response by an organism to internal or external stimuli.

Biological evolution The process of change and development that occurs in living species as a consequence of changes in genetic information.

Biophysical environment The biological and physical components of the environment.

Biotic Pertaining to life and living things.

Bureaucracy (1) The administrative component of a government or other association; (2) a system of administration characterized by a highly formalized division of labor, a hierarchical system of authority, and action oriented to a complex and formalized system of rules.

Capital goods The goods in a society that are devoted to the production of more goods (e.g., factories, machinery, tools, etc.).

Capitalism An economic system in which the means of production are privately owned and the basic problems of production and distribution are settled by means of the market system, with minimal governmental regulation or control (see *Market economy*).

Caste A hereditary class with minimal opportunities for mobility for its members.

Civilization An advanced sociocultural system. The term is usually reserved for the cultures of societies with writing and urban communities.

Clan A kin group whose members claim descent from a common ancestor.

Class (1) An aggregation or group of people whose *overall* status is similar; (2) an aggregation or group of people who are in a similar position with respect to some specific resource that affects their access to power, privilege, or prestige.

Clique A primary group organized around ties of friendship.

Command economy An economy in which the basic questions of production and distribution are decided by political authorities (contrast with *Market economy*).

Communication The exchange of information by means of signals or symbols.

Community A secondary group that is informally organized and whose members are united by a common place of residence or by a common subculture (see *Geographical community* and *Cultural community*).

Continuity The persistence of cultural elements in a society.

Cooperation Interaction by two or more individuals for mutual benefit.

Correlation A measure of the degree of association between two variables. Correlation coefficients range from .0, when there is absolutely no relationship between the variables, to ±1.0, when there is a perfect relationship (i.e., one value is a perfect function of the other).

Cultural community A community whose members are united by ties of a common cultural tradition (e.g., a racial or ethnic group).

Culture A society's symbol systems and the information they convey.

Democracy A type of political system in which sovereignty is vested in the people (contrast with *Autocracy*, *Oligarchy*, and *Theocracy*).

Demography The study of populations, their size, composition, and change.

Determinism The belief that a specific set of identifiable factors is sufficient to explain completely a given phenomenon.

Development The consequences of an increase in useful information for the various components of a system.

Diffusion An innovation that involves cultural elements acquired from another society.

Discovery An innovation that results from a society's acquisition of new cultural information by means other than diffusion.

DNA Deoxyribonucleic acid; a chemical molecule that embodies genetic information.

Ecological-evolutionary theory Theory concerning (1) the relationships within and among human societies, (2) between societies and their biophysical environments, and (3) the processes of sociocultural change and development.

Ecology The science of the interrelationships of living things to each other and to their environments.

Economic surplus Production that exceeds what is needed to keep the producers of essential goods and services alive and productive.

Energy The capacity for performing work.

Environment Everything external to an entity

(organism, population, society, etc.) that affects it, or is affected by it, in any way.

Era A period of time during which a particular type of society is the most advanced in existence (e.g., the agrarian era).

Ethnography The description of contemporary sociocultural systems.

Ethology The study of animal behavior.

Evolution In general, a process of long-term, pervasive change. In the case of biological and sociocultural evolution, a process of gradual change and development that occurs as a consequence of changing stores of information (see *Biological evolution* and *Sociocultural evolution*).

Extended family A group of near relatives (e.g., cousins, aunts, uncles) who live in close proximity to one another and often engage in common activities. More inclusive than the nuclear family, less inclusive than the kin group or clan.

Extinction The disappearance of elements from a sociocultural system; the elimination of human societies themselves.

Family A primary group organized around ties of kinship; a major institutional system in every society (see also *Nuclear family* and *Extended family*).

Feedback The reversion of part of the effects of a given process to its source, modifying or reinforcing it (i.e., A influences B, thereby causing B to exert an influence back on A).

Fishing society A society in which fishing, or fishing and gathering, is the chief mode of subsistence.

Fixed costs Costs of production that remain more or less constant regardless of the number of units produced (contrast with *Variable costs*).

Fourth World Those underdeveloped nations of the contemporary world with very low per capita gross national products and poor prospects for improvement (compare with *Third World*).

Freedom The availability of alternative courses of action.

Function (1) A characteristic activity of a person, a thing, or an institution; (2) a consequence of, or purpose served by, that activity; (3) a relationship in which changes in the magnitude of one variable are associated in a definite and determined way with changes in the magnitude of another variable.

Functional requisites Conditions that must be met if a society is to survive.

Fundamental innovation An invention or discovery that either (1) opens the way for many other innovations or (2) alters the conditions of human life so that many other changes become either possible or necessary.

Gathering Collecting wild fruits and vegetables.

Gene The basic unit of heredity, conveyer of genetic information.

Gene pool The genes of all the members of a population considered collectively.

General evolution The evolutionary experience of human societies as a whole (contrast with *Specific evolution*).

Genetic constants Genetic attributes that are the same in every population of a species.

Genetic variables Genetic attributes that vary among the populations of a species.

Geographical community A community whose members are united primarily by ties of spatial proximity.

Governing class A largely hereditary class from which the political leaders of a society are recruited.

Gross domestic product Gross national product minus net income from other nations.

Gross national product The monetary value of the goods and services produced by a nation during a specific period (usually a year).

Group An aggregation whose members (1) act together to satisfy common, or complementary, needs; (2) have common norms; and (3) have a sense of common identity. The term is applicable to a society, an intersocietal unit, or an intrasocietal unit.

Guild A mutual aid association of merchants and artisans in the same trade (found in agrarian and maritime societies).

Headman The leader of a local community, usually in a preliterate society; one who leads rather than rules.

Herding society A society in which herding is the primary means of subsistence. *Advanced* herding societies are differentiated from *simple* by the use of horses or camels for transportation.

Hominid A member of the genus *Homo*, which includes our own species as well as an undetermined number of humanlike species that preceded us and are now extinct.

Homo sapiens sapiens Genetically modern humans.

Horticultural era The period in history when there were no societies technologically more advanced than horticultural societies (about 7000 to 3000 B.C.).

Horticultural society A society in which horticulture is the primary means of subsistence. *Advanced* horticultural societies are differentiated from *simple* by the manufacture of metal tools and weapons.

Horticulture The cultivation of small gardens using the hoe or digging stick as the chief tool. Horticulture is differentiated from agriculture by the absence of the plow.

Human evolution The total evolutionary experience of our species, both biological and cultural.

Hunting and gathering era The period in history when there were no societies more advanced than hunting and gathering (to about 7000 B.C.).

Hunting and gathering society A society in which hunting and gathering are the primary means of subsistence.

Hybrid society A society that relies about equally on two or more of the basic modes of subsistence.

Ideology Cultural information used to interpret human experience and order societal life. An ideology consists of a system of beliefs and related norms and values.

Industrial era The period in history when industrial societies have been dominant (from about 1800 A.D. to the present).

Industrialization Increasing reliance on the newer inanimate sources of energy in production, and the technological and economic consequences of this (compare with *Modernization*).

Industrial Revolution The revolution in technology that began in England in the eighteenth century, has since spread to most of the world, and is still continuing.

Industrial society A society that derives most of its wealth and income from productive activities dependent on the newer energy sources (i.e., coal, petroleum, natural gas, hydroelectric power, nuclear power). A society that consumes a minimum of 2,000 to 2,500 kilograms of coal equivalent per person per year.

Information Experience as impressed on a memory system.

Innovation The introduction of new cultural elements into a society (see *Diffusion, Discovery,* and *Invention*).

Institution A system of social relationships and cultural elements that develops in a society in response to some set of basic and persistent needs.

Intelligentsia Well-educated persons; the upper part of the nonmanual class in East European societies (occasionally used to refer to the entire nonmanual class).

Intersocietal selection The process whereby some human societies survive while others become extinct.

Intrasocietal selection The process whereby some cultural elements within a society survive while others vanish.

Invention An innovation that results from a useful new combination of information already possessed by a society.

Language A system of symbols.

Laws Norms sanctioned by the state or government.

Learning The process by which an individual organism acquires, through experience, information with the potential for modifying its behavior.

Legitimate That which is morally or legally justified by the norms or laws of a group.

Legitimize To make legitimate; to provide an ideological or legal justification for a practice that might otherwise be regarded as objectionable.

Macrosociology The branch of sociology that studies large social systems, especially total human societies.

Maritime society A society in which overseas commercial activity is the primary means of subsistence.

Market economy An economy in which the basic problems of production and distribution are settled by the forces of supply and demand (see *Capitalism*, and contrast with *Command economy*).

Mass media Communications media developed in industrial and industrializing societies to reach the masses (especially TV, radio, newspapers, magazines, and movies).

Mean, arithmetic The value that results when the sum of a set of items is divided by the number of items; sometimes referred to as the *average*.

Median The middle number in a series of numbers arranged in order from highest to lowest.

Microsociology The branch of sociology that studies individuals and small social units, such as families and associations.

Mobility, vertical See *Vertical mobility*.

Modernization All the long-term social and political changes that are associated with industrialization (compare with *Industrialization*).

Monopoly A commodity market with only a single seller.

Nation A society in which the administrative, legislative, and judicial functions of government are wholly or largely in the hands of full-time officials.

Nationalism An ideology that emphasizes the importance of the nation-state.

Natural selection The spontaneous process whereby some genes and sets of genes in a population become more common while others become less common or extinct.

Neophilia Love of the new, of change, or of novelty.

Nomad A member of a group that has no permanent settlement and moves about periodically (usually in a well-defined territory) to obtain food and other necessities.

Normative Of, or pertaining to, norms; having a moral and/or legal character.

Norms Definitions of acceptable and unacceptable behaviors for the members of a society in their various roles; norms may be formal (e.g., laws) or informal (e.g., customs).

Nuclear family A man, his wife or wives, and their unmarried children living with them.

Oligarchy The rule of the few (contrast with *Autocracy*, *Democracy*, and *Theocracy*).

Oligopoly A commodity market dominated by a few sellers.

Organism A living entity.

Peasant An agricultural worker in an agrarian society.

Per capita income National income divided by population. (This measure is somewhat misleading as a measure of the standard of living of the average person, since a small number of people with very large incomes can pull the average far above the median.)

Polity The political system of a group, especially of a society.

Population (1) Organisms of the same species that tend to interbreed because of their geographical proximity; (2) the members of a society, or a subgroup within a society, considered collectively.

Priest A religious functionary believed to have supernatural powers bestowed on him by an organized religious group; one who mediates between God, or a god, and humans (contrast with *Shaman*).

Primary group A small group in which face-to-face relations of at least a fairly intimate and personal nature are maintained (see *Family* and *Clique*).

Primary industries Industries that produce or extract raw materials (especially farming and mining).

Primates The order of mammals that includes the prosimians (e.g., tarsiers and lemurs) and the anthropoids (e.g., monkeys, great apes, and humans).

Primitive Having limited sociocultural development.

Process A series of related events with an identifiable outcome.

Race A breeding population in which certain traits occur with a frequency that is appreciably different from other breeding populations.

Regression The consequences of the loss of useful information by a society.

Religion The basic ideological beliefs of a group of people and the practices associated with those beliefs. The term can refer to nontheistic ideologies, such as communism and humanism, but is more often applied to ideologies that involve supernatural explanations.

Retainer An individual who owes service to a person or household of high status (usually found in horticultural and agrarian societies).

Revolution Change that is unusually sudden, rapid, or far-reaching.

Role A position that can be filled by an individual and that has distinctive norms attached to it. The term may also be used to refer to the part a group, institution, or other social unit plays in the life of a society.

Sanction (1) A reward or punishment; (2) to reward or punish.

Science A systemic body of cumulative, verifiable knowledge.

Secondary group Any group that is larger and more impersonal than a primary group.

Secondary industries Industries that process raw materials and turn out finished products.

Selection See *Natural selection, Intersocietal selection,* and *Intrasocietal selection.*

Serf A peasant farmer who is bound to the land and subject to the owner of the land.

Shaman A person believed to enjoy special powers because of a distinctive relationship he or she has established with the spirit world; a medicine man. Not to be equated with *Priest.*

Signal An information conveyer whose meaning is determined genetically (contrast *Symbol*).

Social Pertaining to the interactions among the members of societies.

Social controls Mechanisms that order societal life by controlling and regulating people's actions and relationships.

Social environment Other societies with which a group has contact.

Social institution See *Institution.*

Socialism An economic system in which there is little or no private ownership of the means of production (see *Capitalism*).

Socialist society A society in which there is little or no private ownership of the means of production (not applied to a society where a Socialist Party is in power if this condition is not met).

Socialization The process through which individuals become functional members of their society.

Social movement A loose-knit group that seeks to change the social order.

Social organization See *Social structure.*

Social structure A network of relationships among the members of a society or group.

Society An autonomous group of individuals belonging to the same species and organized in a cooperative manner.

Sociocultural Contraction of *social* and *cultural.*

Sociocultural evolution The process of change and development in human societies that results from growth in their store of cultural information.

Sociocultural system A system composed of a human population, its social structure, culture, and material products.

Sociology The branch of modern science that specializes in the study of human societies.

Specific evolution The evolutionary experience of a single society or a particular set of societies (contrast with *General evolution*).

Stasis The condition of a society that neither develops nor regresses.

Status The relative rank of a person, role, or group, according to culturally defined standards.

Stratification Class or status differentiation within a population; hence, inequality.

Structural-functional theory Theory concerning the internal structures of societies, and the functions of their various parts.

Structure The arrangement of the parts of an entity.

Subculture The distinctive culture of a subgroup within a society.

Subsistence The basic necessities of life; also, the process by which they are obtained.

Surplus See *Economic surplus.*

Symbol An information conveyer whose meaning is determined by those who use it (contrast with *Signal*).

System An entity made up of interrelated parts.

Systemic Having the attributes of a system.

Technology Cultural information about the utilization of the material resources of the environment to satisfy human needs and desires.

Tertiary industries Industries that perform services (e.g., retail trade, government).

Theocracy A society ruled by a priesthood in the name of some deity or by a ruler believed to be divine.

Theory A set of assumptions and principles that has developed in a field of inquiry and that serves as a framework for further inquiry.

Third World In general, the underdeveloped nations of the contemporary world. Sometimes used to refer only to those whose per capita gross national products are relatively high or rising (contrast with *Fourth World*).

Tribe A preliterate group whose members speak a common language or dialect, possess a common culture that distinguishes them from other peoples, and know themselves, or are known, by a distinctive name.

Unilinear theory of evolution A theory which assumes that all societies follow exactly the same path of evolutionary development.

Urban community A community whose inhabitants are wholly or largely freed from the necessity of producing their own food, fibers, and other raw materials.

Values Generalized moral beliefs to which the members of a group subscribe.

Variable Any property that is capable of varying in degree.

Variable costs Costs of production that tend to vary in proportion to the number of units produced (contrast with *Fixed costs*).

Vertical mobility Change of status, either upward or downward.

Working class Members of modern industrial societies who belong to families headed by manual workers.

PICTURE CREDITS

1.2 Rodger, Magnum Photos, Inc.

1.3 Photograph by Baron Hugo Van Lawick, copyright © National Geographic Society.

1.4 Rogers, Monkmeyer Press Photo Service.

1.5 From J. R. Napier, *Nature*, vol. 196, pp. 409–411.

2.1 From Paul Ehrlich and Richard Holm, *The Process of Evolution*, copyright © McGraw-Hill Book Company.

2.3 Courtesy of Department of Antiquities, Ashmolean Museum, Oxford.

2.4 Henri Cartier-Bresson, Magnum Photos, Inc.

3.4 Courtesy of Richard Lenski.

3.5 Ed Fisher, by permission of the artist and The Saturday Review.

3.8 Courtesy of The Bettmann Archives, Inc.

4.2 By permission of Laurence K. Marshall, Peabody Museum, Harvard University.

4.3 United Nations.

5.1 From Grahame Clark, *The Stone Age Hunters*, copyright © 1967 by Thames and Hudson Ltd., London. By permission of the publisher and the British Museum (Natural History).

5.3 From *Prehistoric Societies*, by John G. Clark and Stuart Piggott, copyright © 1965 by Grahame Clark and Stuart Piggott. Reprinted by permission of Alfred A. Knopf, Inc.

5.4 From Hugo Obermaier, *Fossil Man in Spain*, copyright © 1925 by Yale University Press (plate XIV).

5.5 Courtesy of Joffre Coe.

5.6 With permission from *Paleolithic Cave Art*, copyright © Peter J. Ucko and Andreé Rosenfeld, 1967, McGraw-Hill Book Company.

5.7 By permission of the Smithsonian Office of Anthropology, Bureau of American Ethnology Collection.

5.8 By permission of Laurence K. Marshall, Peabody Museum, Harvard University.

5.9 By permission of Laurence K. Marshall, Peabody Museum, Harvard University.

5.10 By permission of Laurence K. Marshall, Peabody Museum, Harvard University.

5.11 From Grahame Clark. *The Stone Age Hunters*, copyright © 1967 by Thames and Hudson Ltd., London. By permission of the publisher.

5.12 Photograph by Richard Gould, courtesy of The American Museum of Natural History.

5.13 Col. Charles W. Furlong.

6.1 From Seton Lloyd and Fuad Safar, "Tell Hassuna," *Journal of Near Eastern Studies* (vol. 4, fig. 36). By permission of the University of Chicago Press.

6.2 Courtesy of Dr. James Mellaart, Institute of Archaeology, University of London.

6.3 From J. Mellaart, *Earliest Civilizations of the Near East*, copyright © 1966 by Thames and Hudson Ltd., London. By permission of the publisher.

6.4 From W. Watson, *Early Civilization in China*, copyright © 1970 by McGraw-Hill Book Company, New York. By permission of the publisher.

6.5 Burri, Magnum Photos, Inc.

6.6 Courtesy of The University Museum, University of Pennsylvania, Philadelphia.

6.7 By permission of Smithsonian Office of Anthropology.

6.8 Courtesy of The American Museum of Natural History.

6.9 By permission of Napoleon Chagnon, *Yanamamo: The Fierce People*, copyright © 1968 by Holt, Rinehart & Winston, New York.

6.10 By permission of Napoleon Chagnon (see his volume *Yanamamo: The Fierce People* for further details), copyright ©1968 by Holt, Rinehart & Winston, New York.

6.11 Courtesy of The American Museum of Natural History.

6.12 United Nations.

6.13 United Nations.

6.14 Courtesy of The American Museum of Natural History.

6.15 From Jacques Maquet, *Africanity, the Cultural Unity of Black Africa* (Oxford University Press, 1972) p. 112.

6.16 Reprinted with permission of the publisher from *The Ancient Maya*, 3/e, by Sylvanus G. Morley, revised by George W. Brainerd (Stanford: Stanford University Press, 1956) plate 28, e, p. 187.

7.1 Courtesy of The Metropolitan Museum of Art.

7.2 Evans, Three Lion Photos, Inc.

7.3 Courtesy of The Metropolitan Museum of Art.

7.4 Courtesy of The Metropolitan Museum of Art. Museum Excavations, 1919–1920; Rogers Fund, supplemented by contribution of Edward S. Harkness.

7.6 United Nations.

7.7 Courtesy of Exxon Corporation.

7.8 Courtesy of Exxon Corporation.

7.9 Courtesy of Exxon Corporation.

7.10 J. Allan Cash, Rapho Guillemette Pictures.

7.11 Courtesy of The Metropolitan Museum of Art, Bashford Dean Memorial Collection, 1929.

7.12 Courtesy of The Metropolitan Museum of Art, Rogers Fund, 1904.

7.14 United Nations.

7.15 United Nations.

7.16 United Nations.

7.17 From F. R. Cowell, *Everyday Life in Ancient Rome*, G. P. Putnam's Sons, copyright © 1961. By permission of B. T. Batsford Ltd., London.

7.18 From Fritz Rorig, *The Medieval Town*, copyright © by Propylaen Verlag. Reprinted by permission of the University of California Press.

7.19 United Nations.

7.21 Courtesy of Exxon Corporation.

7.22 United Nations.

7.23 Courtesy of Exxon Corporation.

7.24 Courtesy of Rhotographie Giraudon, 9 rue des Beaux Arts, Paris 6, France.

7.25 Courtesy of the Kunsthistorisches Museum, Vienna.

7.26 From F. R. Cowell, *Everyday Life in Ancient Rome*, G. P. Putnam's Sons, copyright © 1961. By permission of B. T. Batsford Ltd., London.

8.1 United Nations.

8.2 P. F. Mele, Photo Researchers, Inc.

8.3 Courtesy of Exxon Corporation.

8.4 By permission of Institut Français d'Archéologie, Beirut, Lebanon.

AUTHOR INDEX

SUBJECT INDEX

Page numbers in **boldface** indicate the most basic references. Cross references to a particular subject "*under basic societal types*" refer to Agrarian societies; Horticultural societies; Hunting and gathering societies; Industrial societies; Industrializing agrarian societies; Industrializing horticultural societies.

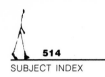